BUSINESS OPPORTUNITIES IN THE FAR EAST

THE COMPLETE REFERENCE GUIDE TO PRACTICES AND PROCEDURES

BUSINESS OPPORTUNITIES IN THE FAR EAST
THE COMPLETE REFERENCE GUIDE TO PRACTICES AND PROCEDURES

Edited by
Lawrence Chimerine
Robert F. Cushman
Charles F. Jacey, Jr.
Kazuo Matsumoto

| Coopers
| &Lybrand

Dow Jones-Irwin
Homewood, Illinois 60430

© RICHARD D. IRWIN, INC., 1990

Dow Jones-Irwin is a trademark of Dow Jones & Company, Inc.

Project editor: Ethel Shiell
Production manager: Diane Palmer
Compositor: TCSystems, Inc.
Typeface: 11/13 Times Roman
Printer: The Maple-Vail Book Manufacturing Group

Library of Congress Cataloging-in-Publication Data

Doing business in the Far East / Lawrence Chimerine . . . [et al.].
    p.   cm.
    ISBN 1-55623-197-0
    1. United States—Commerce—East Asia. 2. East Asia—Commerce—
United States. 3. East Asia—Economic conditions. 4. East Asia—
Politics and government. I. Chimerine, Lawrence.
  HF3126.5.D65 1990
  330.95′0428—dc20   89–23542
                                       CIP

Printed in the United States of America

1 2 3 4 5 6 7 8 9 0 MP 7 6 5 4 3 2 1 0

FOREWORD

THE POLITICAL ENVIRONMENT IN THE FAR EAST:
GO WEST, YOUNG MAN—TO THE EAST

William E. Colby is counsel to the law firm of Donovan Leisure Newton & Irvine, resident in its Washington, D.C., office. He is particularly concerned with its international and East Asian practice, serving clients both in legal matters and in consulting on developments and relationships between the United States and Asia.

Mr. Colby was a career officer in the Central Intelligence Agency, serving in Sweden, Italy, and Vietnam and as chief of the Far East Division. He was director of Central Intelligence from 1973 to 1976. He has written a book, *Honorable Men,* describing his career in the CIA.

In addition to his intelligence career, Mr. Colby was ambassador and deputy to the commander, U.S. Military Assistance Command Vietnam, from 1968 to 1971, directing U.S. government support to the rural pacification program of the government of South Vietnam. In the fall of 1989, he will publish a second book, on the Vietnam War.

The "Pacific Century"—the 21st—is only a decade away. For business leaders, this is a short time to prepare themselves and their businesses to meet new challenges and opportunities, assemble the necessary staffs and expertise, and establish the relationships that will enable them to profit from a new situation and survive new forms of competition. The first requirement is to understand this environment, so as to formulate the strategies and tactics for our businesses to cope with it—and to take advantage of it.

The last half century has seen a transformation of the Asian scene. Colonial dependencies of European and American overlords now stand independent politically and economically and contest for dominance with their former rulers. Regions that formerly provided materials and labor for developed centers now produce high technology and offer major markets. Huge national and private reserves of capital now seek investment in other regions and even support America's consuming appetite. A wise business leader recognizes these changes and adapts to them, so his business may flourish in a new environment.

East Asia has mounted an economic staircase in the past half century. In 1945, it lay in ruins at the end of World War II, and the departing colonial powers left little in the way of capital investment to the new nations that struggled to be born and to survive. The first level of economic effort was basic, subsistence agriculture, raw commodities, and labor-intensive products. The first step up the staircase was taken in the 1950s by Japan, which revived the capital-intensive structure it had created before the war, in its drive for modernism and military power after the Meiji Restoration in the 1860s.

By the 1960s, Japan was ready to take the next step up the staircase, to the so-called knowledge-intensive economy of electronics and other high-tech products. During that period, Korea and Taiwan took the first step up the staircase, creating a capital-intensive industrial economy of steel, shipbuilding, and other major products. The rest of the Asian countries remained at the bottom, barely changed from their prewar economies.

During the 1970s, Japan took the next step, to a services-dominated economy, stressing banking, insurance, and communications, while Korea and Taiwan entered the knowledge-intensive industries. Significantly, capital-intensive investment began to appear in volume in Southeast Asia, in Thailand, Malaysia, and the Philippines, while Indonesia and Burma remained essentially where they had begun. China and Indochina missed this process because they were consumed with war and cultural revolution. Hong Kong and Singapore were special cases because of their small size, but they shared the shift to capital-intensive, knowledge-intensive, and service economies with the others in the region, albeit not in such a methodical fashion.

In the 1980s, after a bit of delay, Japan took the next step, to the development of its domestic economy to provide more leisure, infrastructure, and benefits for its people. Behind it, the rest of Asia took another step up, Taiwan and Korea beginning to develop the services sector, while the more vigorous nations in Southeast Asia moved to the knowledge-intensive level. And, finally, Indonesia began to develop capital-intensive industries, although Burma persisted in remaining behind its self-imposed wall of isolation.

This process will continue in the 1990s, with Korea and Taiwan moving to domestic development assisted by the new democratic governments that have come to power there, in response to pressure from the newly awakened and activated populations of those two nations. Similarly, Thailand, Malaysia, and the Philippines will see the rise of service industries, and Indonesia will move to the knowledge-intensive sectors. Because the process is so clearly under way, some of the governments involved will take steps to accelerate the moves and particularly to begin the process of domestic development for the benefit of newly stimulated populations.

Where will Japan go next? It will certainly move to the stage of active involvement in stimulating development in the countries further down the staircase, as it has already started to do with its large overseas investments and contributions to multilateral and bilateral aid programs. It will also become a more confident and assertive spokesman for the region in world economic deliberations, such as the G-7 meetings of the world developed economic powers, the World Bank, and the International Monetary Fund. It will not establish the Greater East Asia Co-Prosperity Sphere, its World War II goal, in a nonmilitary format, because Japan has discovered it encounters a better reception by seeking cooperation than by seeking domination.

This dynamic development led by the democratic nations of East Asia will put pressure upon the state economies—China, the Soviet Union, North Korea, and Indochina—to open their economies and even their societies so they might share in the progress. They will do so in varying degrees, however, and haltingly, held back by the entrenched bureaucratic classes whose powers and perquisites will have to be reduced to let the breath of freedom, both economic and political, clean out the musty and stagnant societies they have become.

But is this benign prospect not vulnerable to a renewal of the wars and conflicts that have characterized so much of the history of Asia over the past century? Conflicts and contests between some of the nations that neighbor each other in the region will certainly occur, but it is unlikely that any major upheaval will reverse the growth of the region as a whole. Japan appears to be fully convinced that its future lies in growth, and its important role as a world economic power will provide it more satisfaction than any local conquest could. China, long the center-piece of Asia, has a full challenge in caring for the 50 percent increase in its own population over the coming half century, which will raise its total from 1.1 billion today to 1.5 billion. It is even settling its relation-ships with the Soviet Union as it has with the United States and Japan. Even the tangled national relationships in Southeast Asia are turning toward cooperation in the Association of Southeast Asian Nations (ASEAN). And the success of ASEAN has even generated emulation, as the nations of South Asia seek, under Indian leadership, to repeat ASEAN's success through their own South Asian Association for Regional Cooperation (SAARC).

But will the flourishing of East Asia be at the expense of the West, and bring ruinous competition and economic stagnation to Europe and North America? The answer is a clear no, as these two areas are already moving to improve their competitive positions through Europe's elimination of its internal barriers after 1992 and the Free Trade Agreement between Canada and the United States. Those two areas can contribute to a net increase of trade for all three economic regions by steering away from narrow protectionist policies and welcoming the greater exchange of trade that dynamic growth in all three areas can provide for each other.

The three regions can also cooperate to assist the rise of comparable major trading regions in South Asia and Latin America, both of which have the populations and the resources that could make them grow to almost equal partners in a growing world trading system. If the Communist world can develop the flexibility to participate in this process, it will benefit commensurately; if it cannot, it will be left on the margins as it has been for so many years. If the Middle East can overcome its ethnic and religious inhibitions to dealing as partners with the world, it can also benefit. And even the tragic situation of Africa might be assisted by a world conscience to develop decent levels of economic and social action there.

Within this broad scope, East Asia will play a leading role, so the question need no longer be asked about the region: Far from where? The businessperson, American, Canadian, European, or Asian, must identify clearly where in this process is the nation and the sector in which they wish to work and plan ahead for the shifts in emphasis the oncoming stages will present. They must be sensitive to the cultural changes these shifts will require and be patient in realizing that they cannot happen overnight, however much they may be in the interest of the nation and people involved. Corruption has not been eliminated from the advanced nations of Europe and America, and it will not be eliminated soon from the societies of Asia. But adherence to the laws and regulations will not only set a good example, but it also can be good business in the long term.

This is the purpose of this book, to show where each of these nations has come from, where its culture and its rules and regulations are today, and where it is headed. The wise businessperson can use this material as a base upon which they can construct business plans and contribute to the development of the region along lines that will be best for it, and for them.

William E. Colby

FOREWORD

THE ECONOMIC ENVIRONMENT IN THE FAR EAST:
ASIA AS A WORLD PACESETTER

James C. Abegglen is chief executive officer of Asia Advisory Service, Inc., and is a professor and director of the Graduate School, Faculty of Comparative Culture, Sophia University.

Dr. Abegglen received his doctorate from the University of Chicago and, after postdoctoral study at Harvard University, taught at the University of Chicago and Massachusetts Institute of Technology. He first was in Japan in 1945, after service with the 3rd Marines. He returned in 1955 to study Japanese industrial organization, the first research into modern Japanese corporations by a Western specialist. Dr. Abegglen has spent more than half of the following years in Japan as executive, consultant, and professor. He is, according to *Newsweek,* one of "America's 25 top Asia hands."

Author and co-author of 10 books and many articles, Dr. Abegglen's most recent book, *Kaisha, The Japanese Corporation,* has been published in seven languages. He writes a monthly economic commentary for *Tokyo Business Today.* He serves on the Board of Directors of Learning Technologies Ltd. and NCR Japan Ltd. and on the Council of the International House of Japan.

The economic growth advantage of East and Southeast Asia over the rest of the world, a fact of the past two decades, is now widening. The center of world manufacturing, and increasingly that of finance, is shifting from the North Atlantic to the Western Pacific. The map of the world's wealth and power is becoming very different from the map most of us were educated by. The implications, both economic and political, are difficult to make out. At the least, these great changes signal the end of the two or three centuries of Western dominance in world affairs and will continue to produce acute trade and political tensions as long-standing national positions are destabilized.

The driving force in this economic transformation of East Asia has been the historically unprecedented rate of growth of the Japanese economy to its present great size, with per capita output now well above U.S. and German levels. Not only a major manufacturing center, Japan is also now a major source of advanced technology and the major source to the world of new capital. Until now, no Asian nation played these roles. The principle investor in Asia, Japan is now also the dominant supplier of economic and technical aid to the entire area, the major supplier of capital goods, components, and industrial products, and it shares with the United States the role of major market for Asia's output. Comprising 85 percent of the economic activity of all of East and Southeast Asia combined, including the People's Republic of China (PRC), Japan will, for the foreseeable future, remain Asia's dominant economy while Japan's economic dynamism will help pull the area forward in its economic growth.

The Asian advantage in growth rates is remarkable and widening. In the 1970s, the developing economies of the Western Pacific (Asia less Japan) grew nearly twice as rapidly in real terms as did the total world economy. World growth from 1971 to 1975 was 3.4 percent real annually, while Asian growth (less Japan) was 6.3 percent. In each of the next five years, 1976–1980, annual world growth was 3.8 percent while that of East Asia was 6.8 percent. However, in the 1981–1987 period, the growth difference grew even greater. The Western Pacific developing economies grew 2.7 times as rapidly as did the world economy.

Projections of these differences in growth rates, at fairly conservative compounding rates, make for some interesting outcomes. If the 10 countries of East and Southeast Asia—Japan, the People's Republic of China, South Korea, Taiwan, Hong Kong, and ASEAN[1]—grow at just under 5 percent per annum until the year 2000, their combined gross national product (GNP) will be, in 1987 prices and exchange rates, $5,308 billion. If the EC 12[2] grow at 2.6 percent annually to the year 2000—a rate consistent with their historical pattern and the rate gener-

---

[1]The Association of Southeast Asian Nations (ASEAN) includes: Brunei, Indonesia, Malaysia, the Philippines, Singapore, and Thailand.

[2]The European Communities (EC) includes: Belgium, Denmark, France, West Germany, Greece, Ireland, Italy, Luxembourg, the Netherlands, Portugal, Spain, and the United Kingdom.

ally expected in Japanese projections—their combined GNP would be $5,940 billion, or about the same size as East and Southeast Asia combined. Per capita output in East Asia would be much lower, but the area's total economic activity would be about that of the expanded EC at that time. If the economies of the United States and Canada grow at 2.8 percent real per annum over the period, their historical growth rate, the East Asia 10 will be about three quarters the economic size of North America by the turn of the century.

The probability of this rate of economic growth in East and Southeast Asia seems reasonably high. It assumes growth at a lower rate than has been the case over the past 15 years—a period of considerable economic uproar worldwide. Further, these growth rates do not include any additional impetus that might arise from the entry of Vietnam into economic participation in the area, an end to Burma's long isolation, or a resolution of the economically counterproductive confrontation between the two Koreas. The probability of improved economic performance in the area is increased by recent startling changes in economic relations in the area. These include such 1988 and 1989 events as the following:

- Japan now trades more with the Asian 8 (excluding the PRC with which Japan is the major trader) than Japan does with the United States.
- PRC–Taiwan trade is increasing rapidly.
- South Korea is opening diplomatic relations with countries of Eastern Europe, and South Korea and the Soviet Union are exchanging trade missions.
- South Korea and Taiwan are now capital exporters, investing in the PRC and in Thailand as well as in other Asian countries. Northeast Asia is now an economic powerhouse.
- The Soviet Union is making specific proposals for increased trade with Japan, and major Japanese investments in the Soviet Union are being negotiated.

These and similar moves toward increased economic interaction in the area will further stimulate growth.

The more favorable patterns of economic interaction within the area are reinforced by the easing that began in 1987 and 1988 of the acute political tension points in East Asia. Most of this easing has been a consequence of Soviet initiatives, as the Soviet leadership has redeclared its intent to be an Asian major player. The Kampuchea impasse is ending as settlement discussions gain credibility. South Korea and

North Korea continue to probe the possibility of substantially increased interaction. The first PRC–Soviet summit since the 1950s is being held. Japan and the Soviets have the issue of the northern territories on their discussion agenda for the first time after a 40-year stalemate.

These political developments can, if sustained, have major economic impact because they greatly increase the possibility of economic entry into the area of South Vietnam and North Korea, two resource-rich, potentially economically powerful nations. Increased Soviet involvement would allow a further diversification of markets and of raw material sources for the area as well. A major economic vulnerability of the area is the dependence of many of its economies on the United States as market, leaving them at the mercy of U.S. demand. The vulnerability of the area to an economic downturn in the United States remains very real. South Korea, for example, exports nearly 40 percent of its GNP, and about 40 percent of those exports are to the United States—a dependency on that market of more than 15 percent of GNP. However, this is changing. The share of Asian NIC exports to the United States is down from a 1986 peak of 38 percent to an estimated 31 percent in 1988. Given a little more time, with fast-increasing intra-area trade, the vulnerability will become more manageable.

There is increased discussion throughout the area of the possibility of, and potential need for, an Asian, yen-denominated trading bloc. There are very real concerns about Europe 1992 as protectionist and exclusionary. There is some concern too about the U.S.–Canada Free Trade Agreement as exclusionist and also about its entirely bilateral character. Blocs would not be to Asia's advantage, and there are not now any advocates of blocs. An Asian trading bloc will not emerge by Asian choice but as a possible reaction of the nations of the area to increased protectionism against Asian goods by the nations of the West. Whether bloc or not, international corporations would do well to reassess their present position in and their long-range plans for East and Southeast Asia in the light of all of the rapid changes now under way in the area.

Of special significance to corporate planners—as well as to national strategists—is the fact that, by the turn of the century, Japan is expected still to comprise a full 80 percent of the total economy of East and Southeast Asia, down only slightly from its present predominance. Any strategy for Asia must have first an explicit strategy for Japan, which will continue as the source of capital, technology, and aid for the area and will be the major market for the area's products.

James C. Abegglen

FOREWORD

THE EXPORT ENVIRONMENT IN THE FAR EAST:
BUILDING A BETTER RELATIONSHIP THROUGH EXPORTS

Joan M. McEntee was appointed Commerce deputy under secretary for international trade in May 1988. Ms. McEntee was formerly the Commerce deputy assistant secretary for trade development. Before joining the Commerce Department, Ms. McEntee's other positions have included assistant to the vice president and chief counsel and staff director for the Senate Committee on Governmental Affairs. Ms. McEntee has a bachelor's degree from Marymount College and M.A. and J.D. degrees from American University.

For over a decade, the United States has had more trade with East Asia and the Pacific than with any other region of the world. This area accounted for nearly 36 percent of U.S. two-way trade—$241 billion—in 1987.[1] This trade will continue to grow in importance for the foreseeable future.

U.S. trade with East Asia has contributed to stability and progress in the region by providing needed investment, employment, technology, and access to the U.S. market. At the same time, this trade has resulted in a record high U.S. trade deficit that could undermine the relationship between the United States and East Asia. Increased U.S. exports is one way to help ensure the expansion of better relations.

The opinions in this article are those of the author alone and do not necessarily reflect the opinions of any department or agency of the U.S. government.

[1] U.S. Department of Commerce, International Trade Administration, Office of the Pacific Basin.

East Asia holds abundant and diverse export opportunities for aggressive American companies willing to take advantage of them. In 1987, the United States exported goods worth $68 billion to East Asia, an increase of 13 percent over 1986 shipments. This export market continued to expand rapidly during the first 10 months of 1988, up nearly 43 percent from the same period in 1987.[2]

In the past, many U.S. companies that dealt with Asia focused on imports rather than exports. Companies sought to cut production costs by locating lower-cost sourcing or to generate funds through arrangements such as licensing agreements. If they exported, it was often as an afterthought to sell excess production or in response to an inquiry from an overseas distributor.

Recent developments in the economic climate in East Asia, including exchange rate changes and maturing economies that can absorb U.S. goods, make exporting profitable. There are many export opportunities; albeit with special hurdles of language, culture, and geography. For example, few Americans are fluent in Asian languages or familiar with Asian history, and time differences complicate prompt coordination.

U.S. companies need to take advantage of East Asian markets by making exporting a permanent part of their business plans. The U.S. Department of Commerce, through the International Trade Administration, works with the private sector and with state governments to provide export assistance and information.

The Commerce Department's mission includes establishing trade expansion as a major national priority, opening foreign markets, and providing information and services to U.S. exporters. It does this by combining export promotion with trade policy and industry analysis.

The Commerce Department has many export promotion services available to companies seeking business anywhere in the world. These programs form the backbone of the U.S. effort in East Asia. A company can obtain counseling and information on available programs by contacting a Commerce trade specialist at the U.S. and Foreign Commercial Service's 47 U.S. district offices or at its headquarters in Washington.[3] U.S. company representatives overseas can contact U.S. and

---

[2]Ibid.

[3]Further information on specific programs is available by writing the Office of Director General, U.S. and Foreign Commercial Service, International Trade Administration, U.S. Department of Commerce, 14th Street and Constitution Avenue, N.W., Washington, D.C. 20230 or by calling 202-377-3181.

Foreign Commercial Service officers located at 127 posts in 66 countries. These officers also can arrange appropriate appointments with potential trading partners and government officials and can provide valuable information on local economic trends.

These export promotion services include market surveys—general and tailored for individual companies; the agent/distributor service—a personalized search for qualified foreign representatives for U.S. companies; trade missions; trade fairs; world traders data reports—made-to-order background checks on potential trading partners; one-on-one counseling sessions—over 100,000 every year; and many more.

In addition to general export promotion services, the Commerce Department has designed specific initiatives to help U.S. exporters in East Asia. These initiatives change as markets develop and the needs of U.S. exporters change. U.S. companies can take advantage of these and future export promotion initiatives to increase their business in this region.

JAPAN

Japan is the largest market for U.S. exports in Asia. U.S. exports to Japan reached $34,348.4 million during the first 11 months of 1988, up 36 percent compared to the same period in 1987.[4]

The Commerce Department's export promotion efforts for Japan are comprehensive. Commerce has extensive counseling services available in Japan and in the United States. Commerce's U.S. Export Development Office in Tokyo runs a strong program of trade shows and trade missions for a variety of industries. Health care and computer software are examples of industries that have taken advantage of these programs.

The Commerce Department also has specific programs aimed at particular industries. Most of these programs combine government-to-government negotiations with export promotion activities. The combination of bilateral negotiations and export promotion provide the greatest potential benefits for U.S. companies.

For example, after conclusion of the major projects agreement on construction in May 1988, the Commerce Department began a followup program that includes quarterly government monitoring meetings and

---

[4]U.S. Department of Commerce, *U.S. Merchandise Trade: November 1988, FT900 (88-10)* (Washington, D.C.: Bureau of the Census, January 18, 1989).

an extensive outreach program to industry to provide counseling and to distribute information on new projects. There are similar programs for other industrial sectors including automotive parts, supercomputers, medical equipment/pharmaceuticals, and consumer goods.

KOREA/TAIWAN

In late 1988, the Commerce Department launched a broad-ranging export promotion program that focuses on expanding U.S. exports to Korea and Taiwan. This program will serve as a model for future export promotion programs directed toward other industrializing countries in East Asia.

This program includes items such as a series of "Doing Business in Korea and Taiwan" seminars; government/industry working groups to discuss trade and investment issues; development of a data base of U.S. firms and organizations to disseminate market analyses and information on trade opportunities and policy changes; and U.S. trade missions and "Buy American" missions to the United States. As part of this program, the Commerce Department began an initiative in December 1988 called "Export Now Korea" by hosting a Korean machinery purchasing mission. The initiative is designed to increase the awareness of U.S. exporters of trade opportunities in Korea.

PEOPLE'S REPUBLIC OF CHINA

U.S. exports to the People's Republic of China reached $4,482.5 million in the first 11 months of 1988, a 45 percent increase over the same period in 1987.[5] Exports are expected to continue to increase despite continuing problems such as a nonconvertible currency.

The Commerce Department has played an important role in normalizing commercial and financial relations with China and is still looked to by Chinese officials to provide advice and support. The department will continue to develop cooperative programs with key industrial ministries to open doors for U.S. exporters. The Commerce Department has decided to concentrate its export promotion efforts on

---

[5]Ibid.

projects related to China's new strategy for the development of its coastal regions. These projects should generate strong import demand in China for raw and semifinished materials, capital equipment, and technical and managerial services.

SOUTHEAST ASIA

The Southeast Asian region—Thailand, Indonesia, Singapore, Malaysia, Hong Kong, and the Philippines—has been growing dramatically. These nations, taken together, are the United States' seventh-largest trading partner. U.S. exports are beginning to take off, especially to the faster-growing countries in this area.

The Commerce Department's export promotion efforts have increased in its focus on Southeast Asia. In September 1988, Commerce Secretary William Verity visited Indonesia, Singapore, and Thailand, underscoring the region's growing opportunities for U.S. exporters.

The Commerce Department also is working on a regional basis to promote products and sectors of special interest to the Southeast Asian nations. For example, in November 1988, the Commerce Department, the Indonesian government, and U.S. industry jointly sponsored a conference on telecommunications. The conference included a day of presentations by Southeast Asian government officials on their needs and programs and a day of technical presentations by U.S. companies and U.S. government officials.

The programs listed above represent just a few of the Commerce Department's export promotion programs in East Asia. U.S. export promotion programs directed toward East Asia seek to point out opportunities, ensure market access, provide assistance, and educate U.S. companies. U.S. businesspeople should be aware of these programs and use them to enhance their marketing efforts.

The government, however, cannot make sales. Sales can only be accomplished by private companies aggressively seeking long-term exports to East Asia. The expansion of U.S. exports will help build a better relationship between the United States and East Asia.

Joan M. McEntee

PREFACE

COOPERS & LYBRAND EDITION

We are pleased to present this special Coopers & Lybrand edition of *Business Opportunities in the Far East*.

We believe this is an important publication. It recognizes the fact that business now competes globally and that American business executives need to know more about the Far East to determine how it fits into their global competitive strategy. Our aim is to provide insight into the cultural, political, legal, and financial environments of the four major Asian markets.

Coopers & Lybrand professionals who contributed to this book based their knowledge on firsthand experience. Many are citizens or residents of the countries they describe. They represent our Member Firms in Japan (Chuo Shinko Audit Corporation); Korea (Samil Accounting Corporation); Taiwan (Coopers & Lybrand/Prosperity United Firm); China (Coopers & Lybrand PRC). The others are U.S. professionals who have had extensive business dealings in the Far East. They are an important part of our international network in 104 countries through more than 600 offices, with over 61,000 partners and staff worldwide.

We gratefully acknowledge the efforts of the Coopers & Lybrand authors and our contributing friends. We also recognize the contributions of Tom Lumsden, Carter Fletcher, Deanna Casiano, and Michele Sommer in organizing and editing this publication. We trust that *Business Opportunities in the Far East* will be a useful guide to global-minded executives.

Charles F. Jacey, Jr.

PREFACE

The integration of the world economy continues at a speed far greater than even the most optimistic prognosticators forecast several years ago. Furthermore, enormous improvements in worldwide communications, development of new highly mobile production techniques, major scientific and technological breakthroughs, and mobility of capital are likely to result in a continuation and even an acceleration of the process in the years ahead. It is fast reaching the point where virtually every business (not just the very large companies) in almost every country is being affected by the globalization of the world economy and must make business decisions and plans accordingly. For many businesses, these plans must now take into account increasing and more varied foreign competition, as well as the direct and indirect effects of currency movements and other factors on pricing flexibility and potential profitability. While international forces have hurt many U.S. businesses that were not adequately prepared for intense foreign competition, they have also opened major new opportunities for these and other companies. In our view, the best of these opportunities are in the Far East.

This book was written primarily to assist American, European, and Canadian companies to take better advantage of the opportunities occurring in the Far East as well as to help them compete more effectively in U.S. markets. Doing business with the Far East can be a great source of growth and improve profitability for many U.S. companies in the future for the following reasons: (1) The population in the Pacific Basin is extremely large (especially in China) and is growing very rapidly. (2) It is by far the fastest-growing region in the world, with industrialization and the resulting upgrading in living standards occurring at a very rapid rate (a process that is likely to continue for many years). (3) Because of high saving rates, the Pacific Basin is an excellent source of capital. (4) Low-cost labor and high quality standards make many Far Eastern countries an excellent area for sourcing.

This book will help U.S. companies take advantage of these and other attributes of the Far East in order to: (1) find new markets for their products, either by direct export or by joint ventures with local businesses; (2) use the savings that are currently being generated in Japan, Taiwan, and so on to fund future growth; (3) locate joint-venture opportunities in the areas of product development, marketing, and so forth with suitable partners in the Far East; (4) cut production costs by locating lower cost sourcing in the Far East; and (5) better understand the business practices of their Far Eastern competitors here in the United States. This volume will also help U.S. businesspeople decide which type of business relationship with a Far Eastern company might make the most sense and how to achieve it; how to most effectively market their products in each country; and how to take best advantage of the opportunities that exist within these countries.

To achieve these objectives, the editors have brought together many prominent professionals, including bankers, lawyers, accountants, business executives, and economists who are intimately familiar with the Far East countries covered in this volume. The chapters they author will provide detailed information, organized in a manner that provides maximum value to businesspeople on the economies and culture of Japan, Taiwan, South Korea, and China as well as a detailed outline of business practices, regulations, tax laws, and other relevant aspects of these economies.

We believe *Business Opportunities in the Far East* will be the definitive volume in this area, and anyone seeking to do business in Japan, Taiwan, South Korea, and China or with a company based in any of those countries, or anyone who will be competing with products produced in any one or all of those countries will find the information contained in this volume to be the most explicit, accurate, and most relevant of any available.

Lawrence Chimerine
Bala Cynwyd, Pennsylvania
Robert F. Cushman
Philadelphia, Pennsylvania
Charles F. Jacey, Jr.
New York, New York
Kazuo Matsumoto
Tokyo, Japan

ABOUT THE EDITORS

Lawrence Chimerine, until recently, was chairman and chief economist of The WEFA Group. He is now senior economic advisor to WEFA. Dr. Chimerine is president of the Monetary Policy Forum; chairman of the Economic Planning Council; member of the Board of Advisors for the International Management and Development Institute; and he is a member of the Economic Planning Board of the Department of Commerce.

Dr. Chimerine was the chairman and chief economist of Chase Econometrics before its merger with Wharton. Before joining Chase Econometrics, he was the manager of U.S. Economic Research and Forecasting for the IBM Corporation. He is frequently called upon to testify on key economic issues before several congressional committees, including the House and Senate Budget Committees and the Joint Economic Committee, and is an advisor to numerous government agencies. He holds a B.S. in mathematics from Brooklyn College and a Ph.D. in economics from Brown University.

Robert F. Cushman is a partner in the national law firm of Pepper, Hamilton & Scheetz and is a recognized specialist and lecturer on all phases of real estate and construction law. He serves as legal counsel to numerous trade associations, including the American Construction Owners Association, as well as major construction, development, and bonding companies.

Mr. Cushman is the co-editor of *A Guide for the Foreign Investor, Handbook for Raising Capital, The Handbook of Joint Venturing,* and *High Tech Real Estate,* all published by Dow Jones-Irwin, as well as many other handbooks and guides in the insurance, real estate, and construction fields.

Mr. Cushman, who is a member of the Bar of the Commonwealth of Pennsylvania and who is admitted to practice before the Supreme Court of the United States and the United States Claims Court, has served as executive vice president and general counsel to the Construction Industry Foundation. He is a founding member of the American College of Construction Lawyers.

Charles F. Jacey, Jr., is a vice chairman of Coopers & Lybrand, an international firm of accountants and consultants. He presently is responsible for its international operations. In addition, Mr. Jacey is a member of the firm's Executive Committee.

Mr. Jacey is actively involved in a senior capacity with several important international accounts.

During his career with Coopers & Lybrand, which has spanned 30 years, he was the regional managing partner of the New York Metro Region, and has had responsibility for other line and staff areas.

Mr. Jacey is a member of the American Institute of Certified Public Accountants and the New York State Society of Certified Public Accountants. He has served as chairman of the National Retail Merchants Association Committee responsible for revising the Retail Accounting Manual.

He is a member of the Board of Directors and vice president and treasurer of the Police Athletic League (PAL) in Manhattan. He is also a member of the Board of Trustees of Pace University, serving on its University Relations and Budget, Finance, and Facilities Planning Committees.

Kazuo Matsumoto is president of Sanwa Research Institute Corp., an affiliate of the Sanwa Bank, Japan. He was formerly a well-known banker as executive vice president of Sanwa Bank where he was involved in corporate banking and strategic planning.

ABOUT THE AUTHORS

Norris L. H. Chang is a founding partner of Prosperity United Firm CPAs in Taiwan, a member firm of Coopers & Lybrand (International). He is the director and secretary general of the R.O.C. Taxpayer Foundation. Mr. Chang is a former vice chairman of R.O.C. CPA Association's Tax Committee. He has consulted extensively with a number of major Taiwanese companies on tax planning and real estate tax accounting.

David C. Cheng is an attorney practicing corporate law in Taipei and is now partner of CHENG & CHENG Law Offices in Taipei and CHENG & Associates Law Offices in the United States. Mr. Cheng holds a master's degree in law and diplomacy from the Fletcher School and a doctor of law degree from the University of Wisconsin.

Mr. Cheng authored a wide range of articles covering the spectrums of law, trade, and negotiation. He also holds the title of associate professor of law since 1980.

His present interests in legal practice are mergers and acquisitions, outward and inward investments, negotiation and business planning, and trade disputes generally as well as representation of foreign entities in Taiwan.

Fredrick F. Chien earned a Ph.D. degree in international relations from Yale University in 1962. He was appointed minister of state and chairman of the Council for Economic Planning and Development of the Executive Yuan in July 1988. Before his latest appointment, he was representative of the Coordination Council for North American Affairs (CCNAA) for five years and made great contributions to mutual understanding and friendship between the Chinese and American people after the severance of diplomatic relations between the two countries in January 1979.

Among the other important positions he has held are director general of the Government Information Office and administrative vice minister and political vice minister of the Ministry of Foreign Affairs. As chairman of the CEPD, he presides over that body's important functions, which include economic planning, policy coordination, and economic research and project evaluation.

Sung Ho Cho is currently executive director of the Korea Trade Promotion Center in New York, an overseas office of the Korean government's trade promotion agency known as KOTRA. A graduate of Seoul National University, Mr. Cho began his career with KOTRA in 1964 and has served with distinction in the San Francisco, Seattle, and Toronto branch offices. Mr. Cho has also served as the director of the Exhibition, Overseas Research, and Trade Promotion Departments in KOTRA's headquarters office in Seoul. Over the past two years, he has worked closely with U.S. federal, state, and local officials to educate U.S. firms about the export and import market opportunities in Korea. Mr. Cho has been decorated with the Korean Order of Industrial Service Merit, Tin Metal.

Marsha A. Cohan is an associate at the international law firm of Skadden, Arps, Slate, Meagher & Flom specializing in international business and financial transactions. Before joining the firm, she practiced law first with a major New York law firm and then with the Overseas Private Investment Corporation. She has a master's degree in East Asian Studies from Harvard University and received her law degree from Harvard Law School. She studied Chinese law for a year at Beijing University and has lectured on Chinese law at various conferences and law schools in the United States. She speaks fluent Mandarin and has some knowledge of Cantonese.

Richard A. Eastman is a cum laude graduate of Harvard College and the Harvard Law School, admitted to the Bar in California and New York, and since 1987, as a foreign law counselor in Japan. He has practiced international commercial and investment law for most of his career and has advised on joint ventures in Japan, Indonesia, Malaysia, Singapore, and the People's Republic of China, among other countries. He speaks Japanese. He joined McKenna & Co., an English law firm, in 1983 and now heads the Tokyo office of the firm, opened in 1987.

George Fields is chairman of ASI Market Research, a leading firm in its field in Japan. He is the author of seven books in Japanese and English, including *From Bonsai to Levi's* (New American Library) and *Gucci on the Ginza* (Kondansha International, 1989), and a regular columnist for the *Japan Times, Tokyo Business Today,* and several Japanese magazines.

Katherine Hope Francis is senior counsel to Bechtel Enterprises Company where she is involved primarily in project development and international transactions including privatization projects and the negotiation of joint ventures, joint stock companies, and project financing arrangements. She was the Phillip C. Jessup Fellow of the American Society of International Law in 1975 and holds a juris doctor degree from the University of Oregon School of Law (1975) and a bachelor of arts degree from Mills College (1972). She is a member of the California Bar and serves on the Executive Committee of the International Law Section and on the Steering Committee of the ABA Forum on the Construction Industry. Ms. Francis gratefully acknowledges the assistance of Mary Enright, Esq., in the preparation of this article.

Robert H. Garb, a graduate of the University of Michigan Law School, is a senior counsel–special projects at Bechtel, an international engineering and construction firm. During his 20-year career at Bechtel Corporation, his practice has been principally in the international side of Bechtel's business. He has assisted in the establishment of Bechtel operations in Brazil, Egypt, Iran, the People's Republic of China, and Nigeria. He has held several overseas field assignments with Bechtel in Australia and Papua, New Guinea. In making his contribution to this book, he would like to gratefully acknowledge the assistance he received from Connie Gale, Ernie Lam, Michael Selvin, Bill Stevenson, Sy Taubenblatt, and Dorothy Wilson.

Joseph P. Griffin is a partner in Morgan, Lewis & Bockius and is resident in that firm's Washington, D.C., office. He is former chairman of the American Bar Association's Section of International Law and Practice (1987–88) and a member of the Secretary of State's Advisory Committee on Private International Law. He is a member of panels of arbitrators of the American Arbitration Association and the Euro-Arab Arbitration System. Mr. Griffin has edited four books and has published more than 50 law journal articles on international business topics, 8 of which have been translated into Japanese. The primary emphasis of his practice is international business and trade regulation issues, including counseling firms, governments, and trade associations. He has substantial experience in transnational arbitration and litigation.

Raymond V. Haley received a B.A. degree in liberal arts from Syracuse University and an M.A. degree in oriental studies from the University of Arizona. He studied Chinese language at the Mandarin Daily Language Center in Taipei, Taiwan, for 18 months before returning to the United States and receiving a master of international management degree from the American Graduate School of International Management.

In 1985, Mr. Haley joined HongkongBank China Services Ltd., a subsidiary of the Hongkong and Shanghai Banking Corporation in Hong Kong, to work with the bank's clients in China. In April 1987, he was appointed vice president–China Desk in New York, which is responsible for the development and service of China-related business with North American clients. Prior to joining HongkongBank, Mr. Haley was engaged in corporate banking activities in New York and Hong Kong with Marine Midland Bank.

Soon Young Hong joined Korea's foreign service in 1962 after graduating from the College of Law, Seoul National University. Since then, he has assumed a variety of domestic and overseas posts in the Ministry of Foreign Affairs, including director of the North American Division, director-general of the African Affairs Bureau, and ambassador to Pakistan. He also served as secretary for political affairs at the Office of the President (1983–84). Currently, as assistant foreign minister for economic affairs, he is in charge of Korea's overall trade and economic relations with foreign  countries. He acquainted himself with the United States while he served at the Korean Embassy in Washington, D.C., from 1971 to 1974 and Korea's Permanent Mission to the United Nations in New York from 1977 to 1980.

Jamie P. Horsley is a partner in the New York-based international law firm of Paul, Weiss, Rifkind, Wharton & Garrison and specializes in assisting clients in business transactions with the People's Republic of China. A Mandarin-speaking graduate of the Harvard Law School, Ms. Horsley established the firm's presence in Beijing in the autumn of 1981 and resided there until 1984. Before her move to Hong Kong in September 1986, she spent time in the firm's New York and Washington, D.C., offices. Ms. Horsley is the author of many articles on various aspects of Chinese law.

May C. Huang is the resident manager of Coopers & Lybrand Beijing and previously was with Coopers & Lybrand Los Angeles. Before joining C&L, Ms. Huang was an associate professor of law at National Chung Hsing University in Taipei and was also a legal affairs commentator of the China Television and a special columnist for Taipei's *China Daily* for several years. Ms. Huang's current professional focus is to provide tax advice to foreign enterprises doing business in China. Ms. Huang also served the American Chamber of Commerce PRC as governor and treasurer for 1988 and 1989.

Chu Kyu Kim is a Director and Deputy President of the Commercial Bank of Korea, Ltd. He became the bank's deputy president in April 1988 and was elected director in February 1983. Formerly Mr. Kim was director and executive vice president with responsibility for the international banking.

Mr. Kim was born December 15, 1932 in Seoul. He graduated from Seoul National University in 1957 with a bachelor of arts degree. Upon graduation he joined the Commercial Bank of Korea, Ltd. in April 1957.

In 1978 he was assigned to the bank's Los Angeles agency to serve as general manager. Upon completing his assignment in 1980, he was then transferred to the New York agency to hold the position of general manager. In 1982 he returned to Seoul and joined the International Department as general manager.

Mr. Kim and his wife live in Seoul with their three children.

Jin Ouk Kim became a member of the Foreign Capital Inducement Deliberation Committee from 1982 to 1988. He graduated from the Law Department of the Law College, Seoul National University, and obtained a master's degree from the Graduate School of the University of Michigan. He has served as a judge of the Seoul Civil District Court and Seoul Criminal District Court and as a practicing attorney-at-law, has represented many corporate clients including American Express, Chrysler Corporation, Union Carbide Corp., and General Electric.

Yong Kyun Kim is a partner of Samil Accounting Corporation, a member firm of Coopers & Lybrand (International). Mr. Kim is a graduate of Seoul National University and a member of the Korean Institute of CPAs (KICPA). Before joining Samil Accounting Corporation, he spent over six years in the tax area in private industry. His training has also included U.S. taxation while in Coopers & Lybrand's San Francisco office in 1981. Mr. Kim is a member of the Tax Adjustment Supervisory Committee of the KICPA and a contributing lecturer at various seminars, including the  seminar on foreign investment in Korea sponsored by the Belgium government in November 1985 and the International Transfer Pricing seminar hosted by Samil Accounting Corporation in February 1986. In addition, he is a member of Coopers & Lybrand's, Asia Tax Group.

R. Hyukdal Kwon, a general practice partner resident in Coopers & Lybrand's New York office, is the firm's Korea liaison partner, responsible for services to Korean clients and for coordination with offices in the United States and Korea. He has been with C&L's New York office since February 1969, except for 1974 to 1978 when he worked in the firm's Tokyo office.

Mr. Kwon is fluent in Korean and Japanese. He graduated from Yonsei University in Seoul, Korea, and worked for the Economic Planning Board of the Republic of Korea from 1960 to 1964. Mr. Kwon also studied accounting at Southern Illinois University and received his master of science degree in 1966.

Mr. Kwon is a CPA in New York and a member of the American Institute of CPAs, the New York State Society of CPAs, and the Bank Administration Institute. He is very active in the New York Korean community.

Sue-Jean Lee, as manager of the China Desk in the Washington, D.C., office of Coopers & Lybrand, oversees China-related activities including client and public-sector projects. Before joining Coopers & Lybrand, Ms. Lee was manager of the U.S.-China Business Council's Investment Advisory Program where she provided briefings on the China business environment to member companies and assisted them in developing market entry strategies. A graduate of Princeton University, Ms. Lee's previous experience also includes internal cost analysis work for the Chase Manhattan Bank, N.A.

David J. W. Liu is a graduate of National Chung Hsing University in Taipei. He passed the most competitive bar examination in Taiwan 12 years ago. He is now a member of Tsai & Tsai law offices. He has significant experience in trade disputes and litigation, and he has tried some 500 cases. His major interests include labor and investment-related disputes.

Steven Lu is a senior consultant of the Strategic Management Group of the Toronto office of Coopers & Lybrand and was resident manager of the Shanghai office of Coopers & Lybrand for 1988 and 1989. As a business economist, he specializes in strategic planning, market studies, and economic forecasting. While in China, Mr. Lu had added responsibilities to provide the firm's international clients with business and financial advice, local tax consulting, and market research.

Daniel S. Maher is managing partner of Chuo Coopers & Lybrand Consulting Co., Ltd. As the leader of management consulting services practice for the firm, he is responsible for technology transfer of methodology, tools, and techniques from the United States to Japan and is consulting partner for all foreign capitalized Japanese clients. He developed a nationally recognized information systems consulting organization specializing in telecommunications, manufacturing, financial services, health care, government, and utilities industries. He is a member of the American Institute of  CPAs, the Institute for Management Consulting, and the American Chamber of Commerce in Japan.

Shin Matsumi is a senior staff researcher at Sanwa Research Institute Corp., Japan. After working for Sanwa Bank for 16 years, he joined the institute in 1986, where he specializes in problems relating to companies that work on international strategy. He authored Sanwa Bank's publications *Doing Business in Taiwan* and *Doing Business in Singapore*.

Keizo Ohashi is general manager of Sanwa Research Institute Corp., Japan, in charge of international business development. He began his career with Sanwa Bank. He has had extensive experiences in various areas of banking. He has served as a Sanwa Bank officer for 12 years in four different cities of the United States. He is a sought-after speaker at seminars. He graduated from Hitotsubashi University with a B.A. in finance.

Emily Ou is manager of the China Desk in the New York office of Coopers & Lybrand. From 1982 to 1986, Ms. Ou was C&L's registered representative in Shanghai where she assisted clients in identifying appropriate business partners, provided advice on structuring investment projects and commercial transactions, and represented them in contract negotiations. Ms. Ou also organized and coordinated the seminars and training courses C&L cosponsored with Chinese organizations such as the Ministry of Finance, the State Audit Agency, and the China International Economic Consultants.

Ranjan Pal, as part of Business International's global forecasting unit, is in constant touch with world economic developments. He gathers information from analysts and economists worldwide, employing the latest forecasting techniques in his analysis. Mr. Pal oversees the preparation of five-year political and economic forecasts covering 14 countries in the Asia/Pacific region. In addition to drawing up scenarios for the countries concerned, he contributes to all facets of the company's work with a forward-looking element, including client research, publications, and conferences.

Mr. Pal has worked for Wharton Econometric Forecasting Associates (The WEFA Group) in the United States, where he served as director of operations of their Asia Group. He managed the production of quarterly forecast reports, presented regional overviews at client conferences, and provided extensive client support through regional and country economic analysis. Mr. Pal regularly contributed to the firm's *Asia Economic Outlook* and *World Economic Outlook* with regional overviews and country pieces on the Philippines, Indonesia, and South Korea. He also provided articles for the monthly *Foreign Exchange Rate Outlook*.

Mr. Pal was previously employed by the World Bank in Washington, D.C., where he participated in research projects which involved sectoral modeling work for a number of Asian economies. He also wrote reports on trade policies intended to guide the Bank staff in structural adjustment lending to less developed countries.

Mr. Pal received his B.A. and M.A. in economics at Delhi University, India, and an M.P.A. from the Woodrow Wilson School of Public and International Affairs, Princeton University where he specialized in applied economic analysis.

Jaime Quizon is the director of international consulting services at The WEFA Group. Before that he was the director of the Far East service at Chase Econometrics. Dr. Quizon had also previously worked at the World Bank and the Economic Growth Center at Yale University. His work has led to several published papers and a forthcoming book.

Masaki Shiratori is a graduate of Tokyo University and has served as chief, Special Affairs Office; counsellor, Research and Planning Department; director, Overseas Investment Division, International Finance Bureau, all of the Ministry of Finance. He has served as director-general, Ohsaka Customs, Ministry of Finance, and deputy commissioner for International Affairs before becoming senior deputy director-general, International Finance Bureau, Ministry of Finance. He is now executive director for Japan in the World Bank.

Zhang Shou has been vice chairman of the State Planning Commission of the People's Republic of China since 1982. He is also president of the State Economic Information Center, director of the Board of Data for Development International Association, and a consultant for the State Natural Science Foundation of China. He previously taught in the engineering physics and naval architecture departments at Shanghai Jiao Tong University and was a senior vice president there from 1976 to 1982.

James Steinberg is an associate in the international law firm of Pepper, Hamilton & Scheetz. He graduated from the Wharton School of the University of Pennsylvania in 1983 (B.S. in economics) and from Villanova University School of Law in 1986. As a member of the *Villanova Law Review,* he served as a case and comment editor and authored a note on antitrust law titled: "The Long Awaited Death Knell of the Intra-enterprise Doctrine," 30 *Villanova Law Review* 521 (1985). He is a member of the Philadelphia, Pennsylvania, and American Bar Associations (including the Section of International Law and Practice).

Taesik Suh is a graduate of Seoul National University and has a Ph.D. in business administration from the Graduate School of Kyung-Gi University. He has been a member of the Korean Institute of CPAs (KICPA) since 1962 and founded Samil Accounting Corporation in 1971, which became a member firm of Coopers & Lybrand (International) in 1973. Dr. Suh has been the chairman and managing partner of Samil Accounting Corporation since 1974. He has participated extensively in Coopers & Lybrand professional training courses in the United States and has acquired work experience from several U.S. offices of Coopers & Lybrand as well.

Dr. Suh taught auditing at Seoul National University during the 1981–82 and 1987–88 academic years. He was chairman of the Audit Research Committee of the Korean Institute of Certified Public Accountants from 1981 to 1987. He was also a member of the Board of CPA Examiners (1979–89).

In 1989 Dr. Suh was elected president of the Confederation of Asian and Pacific Accountants and he became a member of the Board of Directors of Coopers & Lybrand (International).

Henry X. H. Sun is a vice president at Sun Intertech Corp., a Canadian company based in Burnaby, B.C., Canada. Mr. Sun has an MBA degree from Pennsylvania State University and is working on his Ph.D. dissertation on International Marketing. Before he came to the United States in 1985, Mr. Sun had studied for a master's degree in international business at the Graduate School of the Chinese Academy of Social Science, one of the top graduate schools in China, and had worked in various government positions at the central level in Beijing. With his academic and practical expe-  rience in both China and North America, Mr. Sun can promote international exchanges between the two sides.

Takeshi Suzuki is a senior consultant at Sanwa Research Institute Corp., Japan. He is versed in international finance, especially country risk of East European countries. He was a manager at Sanwa Bank Düsseldorf Br. in West Germany. A graduate of Keio University, he received his M.A. in economics from his alma mater.

Akira Tai is a senior consultant at Sanwa Research Institute Corp., Japan. He is primarily engaged in research and consulting as an expert on Asia, mainly Thailand. His vast knowledge of Thailand supported by his fluency in Thai is very well known. Mr. Tai was formerly a Sanwa Bank officer in Bangkok. He received a B.A. degree in Thai studies from Osaka University of Foreign Studies.

Makoto Taketomi is a senior staff researcher at Sanwa Research Institute Corp., Japan. He stayed overseas for more than seven years as a Sanwa Bank representative, and is versed in the investment climate of Asia. He currently gives numerous Sanwa Bank clients the necessary advice to make informed business judgments. A graduate of Keio University (B.A. in economics), he speaks at various meetings of international businessmen.

Bruce L. Townsend is a partner of Coopers & Lybrand, and director of their International Manufacturing Program, which is responsible for assisting international member firms in developing manufacturing consulting practices. He regularly speaks at forums on the need for an international strategy for manufacturing excellence, as well as technical subjects such as productivity, material requirements planning, and just-in-time.

Mr. Townsend has over 18 years of experience with a major international computer manufacturer and was in charge of manufacturing process marketing for an international division of that company.

He has conducted numerous briefing and planning sessions for manufacturing companies. His international experience enables him to provide a global perspective to those multinational companies implementing manufacturing systems on a worldwide basis.

Francis K. Vita recently took a leave of absence from the World Bank Group to pursue several international business ventures. He has held managerial positions in IFC and the World Bank's Treasury complex, including the position of deputy director of the World Bank Tokyo office from 1984 to 1986. Previous experience in international investments and financing has been extensive, involving both private sector and World Bank project activities. Mr. Vita was educated in economics and finance at Harvard University, University of Pittsburgh, and Georgetown University. He is married, has four children, and lives in Bethesda, Maryland.

Hajime Wada is a senior staff researcher at Sanwa Research Institute Corp., Japan. He primarily advises enterprises that work on international strategy. He joined Sanwa Bank in 1967 and was assigned to Sanwa's affiliates in the state of California and Indonesia, and worked as an international banker. He authored Sanwa Bank's publication *Doing Business in Indonesia*.

Marina Wong is a partner in the Hong Kong office of Coopers & Lybrand where she is responsible for the Corporate Services Division and the China Desk. Ms. Wong maintains an in-depth knowledge of P.R.C. legislation and economic development. She is an authority on Chinese taxation laws, accounting principles, and joint venture arrangements, and she has established a close working relationship with the accounting and taxation authorities in China.

Ms. Wong has extensive experience in providing accounting services and taxation and business advice to both Hong Kong and foreign investors in China. In addition, her specific project experience includes directing the organization of accounting procedures and systems for several joint ventures in China.

Dean A. Yoost is a partner of Coopers & Lybrand, in Los Angeles. He has earned master's degrees from the University of Minnesota and Mankato State University. He joined the Los Angeles office of Coopers & Lybrand in 1974. He moved to the Minneapolis office in 1976 and became a tax partner in 1983. From 1985 to 1989, he served as the partner-in-charge of the Tax Consulting group of Chuo Coopers & Lybrand in Tokyo. He also serves a key regional role for the firm as the director of U.S. Services, Asia-Pacific. He is a U.S. representative in Coopers & Lybrand's Asiatax

group, which is comprised of tax partners in C&L's Asia-Pacific offices.

Mr. Yoost is a frequent speaker for the World Trade Institute, Tax Executive's Institute, American Chamber of Commerce, and other professional groups. He has authored and co-authored articles on international tax matters published in the United States: *International Tax Journal (1983)*, U.S. *Tax*

Management International Journal (1986), and the Japan *International Journal (1988).* He has had significant dealings with many international clients, including Ford Motor Company, 3M Company, Atlantic Richfield Co., American Insurance Group, Goldman Sachs, Mazda Corporation, and Sanyo Electric.

Victor Young is Coopers & Lybrand's U.S. technical advisor and partner resident in Taiwan in charge of international operations. His practice includes advice on inbound and outbound investments. He is a former chairman and president of The Asian Business League of San Francisco and has consulted extensively with clients and Asian businesses in the San Francisco Bay Area. He is a frequent instructor for Coopers & Lybrand's audit and business advisory training programs.

Hee Yol Yu, a graduate of Seoul National University, entered the Ministry of Science and Technology in 1970. Since then, he has assumed a variety of posts in the MOST, including director of the Information Industry Division and the Technology Transfer Division, and director-general of the Technology Policy Division.

He is currently director-general of the Policy Planning Division. He also represented Korea at Korea-U.S. consultative talks concerning technology cooperating issues, and participated in international conferences on technology transfer, foreign direct investment, and other related areas.

He has written many articles of science and technology policy, including "Dynamics of Technological Leadership," "Technology Transfer Policy in Korea," and "Foreign Direct Investment and Joint Ventures in Korea."

CONTENTS

PART 3
KOREA

PART 1

PROBLEMS AND OPPORTUNITIES

CHAPTER 1

BUSINESS IN THE FAR EAST: AN OVERVIEW RESHAPING POLITICAL AND CORPORATE DECISION MAKING

Francis K. Vita

INTRODUCTION

ORIGINS AND ELEMENTS OF THE U.S. TRADE DEFICIT

   Abdications of Manufacturing: The National Nonpolicy

A NEW CAPITALIST STRUCTURE

   Paths to the Present

   Economic Strength Is Production-Based

   A Tenuous Comeback

THE NEW INDUSTRIAL STRUCTURE

THE FAR EAST OPPORTUNITY: A CORPORATE STRATEGY

THE DOLLAR FALLACY

   The Background

   Practical Effects

FOCUS: ELEMENTS OF COMPETITIVENESS

   Banks for U.S. Exporters

UNDERSTANDING JAPANESE PRIORITIES

IDENTIFYING THE RIGHT MARKETS AND PRODUCTS

   U.S. Inc. Clearinghouse Approach

THE COMING "GLOBAL" CENTURY
ASSESSING THE ASIAN COMPETITORS
RECOGNIZING PROTOCOL AND CONVENTIONS
UNDERSTANDING THE GAME
SOME WORKING GUIDELINES

INTRODUCTION

The flow of books and articles about Japan and the Far East has reached staggering proportions. Perhaps with some justification, concern about Japanese economic preponderance in the United States and to a lesser extent Europe and Canada has become an obsession. We cannot hope to cover in this chapter the variety of issues involved in the formation of a new system of global relationships; nor can an introductory chapter expect to evaluate the massive flow of theories and advice being offered to governments and businesses regarding the Asian challenge. However, strategic points of economics and trade policy can bear directly on a businessperson's ability to sell, invest, or in other ways successfully transact business in Asia or at home with Asians. To understand the underlying realities is to take a giant step in being able to structure and consummate the right deal.

The following pages may appear to dwell excessively on the past. However, the goal is to extract the relevant lessons from prior failures in order to avoid repeating previous errors. I shall first examine some real effects of the rather disorganized and unfocused, albeit benevolent, efforts of the U.S. government to improve the trading environment for U.S. exporters and overseas investors. Second, the chapter will explore the practical impact on U.S. business of recent policies, and third, in the light of the formidable range of handicaps and disincentives confronting U.S. business in particular, some advice will be offered to those conducting business in the Far East, particularly Japan.

Many of the arguments will be posed in the context of manufacturing because that sector offers such a stark example of trade and economic mismanagement by U.S. officials and corporations. The irony is that, although seriously debilitated by events of the past decade, manufacturing is now being touted as the main vehicle for bringing about the recovery of U.S. trade. The discussions that follow are often equally applicable to service industries or partially processed primary products.

ORIGINS AND ELEMENTS OF
THE U.S. TRADE DEFICIT

The common view of the factors underlying the U.S. deficit has been that the Japanese, Koreans, Taiwanese, and so on, have worked for less, have leveraged off of U.S. and European product ideas, and have exploited the truly free U.S. markets while severely restricting the flow of North American and European imports. Asians have effectively denied Western competitors access to their own dynamic Asian markets. All of these assertions are correct. (With minor exceptions—the Hong Kong market is as open as that of the United States.) Yet, as a general proposition, the scenario falls far short of reality. To provide a more balanced view, it is equally true that the Western nations, and particularly the United States, responded to the competitive challenge with a mixture of inaction, incompetence, and national self-delusion. Only in the past few years have U.S. policy makers and businesses begun to fully accept the facts that North American and European consumers have known for the past decade—increasing numbers of products coming from East Asia are more reliable and of superior quality than those produced at home. The irony is that the United States, as the bastion of free enterprise, was unwilling or unable to heed the clear and unmistakable messages being sent by its own market.

Abdication of Manufacturing: The National Nonpolicy

Over the past decade, the United States, in particular, has relinquished entire segments or subsectors of its industries. An important part of its manufacturing base was abandoned to Japanese competitors without any real understanding of what was occurring. There was no concerted effort to develop a competitive stance through, say, a comprehensive industrial strategy, to identify for renewal those subsectors of strategic national importance, or even to provide targeted fiscal incentives to help those industries under siege to reinvest, re-equip, and upgrade worker skills. U.S. industries and businesses were and remain "lone rangers," each competing on its own against new and overwhelming odds. Japanese and now Koreans entered the U.S. market in the form of technologically advanced corporate alliances, combining manufacturing firms, trading companies (*sogo shosha*), and financial institutions.[1] In turn, these groupings receive well-focused and broad-based support from the respective government ministries that ranges from thinly disguised grants for research and development (R&D) to an array of fiscal measures fostering exports. The consequences for the United States and other erstwhile competitors have been serious but not irreversible.

A NEW CAPITALIST STRUCTURE

A major, and as yet unfulfilled, task of the United States has been to redefine its response to the free market process in global terms. The rest of the world, and particularly the Europeans and Canadians, has learned that the game is won through industrial and trade strategies. Capitalism is not a blindly held ideology, but a dynamic system of interaction. The lesson in international terms is that countries and trading blocs are now the competitors, not individual businesses and corporations. To hold stubbornly to the notion that everyone plays by the same international rules (GATT agreements notwithstanding) and that the export drive must be left to individual companies to pursue is not a free market response but a formula for unequivocal failure in world trade. The United States must develop a system compatible with its fundamental economic philosophy while allowing it to adjust to meet global economic realities and challenges. The United States has found that effecting such adjustments has been particularly arduous.

Paths to the Present

By the early 1980s, the U.S. political establishment and a sizable part of the corporate community were finding ways of justifying the "hollowing out" of manufacturing. A number of books with lofty titles, such as *Megatrends,* sought to exploit the misguided trend, seizing on the notion that the United States was somehow embarking on a "postindustrial era." It became fashionable to condone the abandonment of large segments of industrial capacity to the Asian competitors. Instead, it was argued, the United States could gain dominance in so-called service industries, led by high technology. The United States was supposed to be moving from an industrial to an information society.[2]

Congress and the White House both accepted the idea of abandoning entire manufacturing subsectors to overseas competitors. The profound economic malaise that resulted was painfully reflected in the emergence of the "Rust Belt," once America's great industrial heartland. This process was viewed in the United States as the inevitable price of a free economy. In fact, it was the absence of clear policy initiatives, as well as corporate confusion, and lack of foresight of public leaders and corporate management that led to the erosion of a large segment of America's industrial base.

Economic Strength Is Production-Based

The argument followed that investment was supposed to flow to the new so-called sunrise industries and away from the dirty smokestacks. Unfortunately, only a few initially grasped that technology is neutral. It could be as effectively introduced into the United States as it was in Japan, Korea, or Taiwan, given the proper incentives to reallocate capital resources to long-term productive uses. Nothing could be done to improve America's position until introduction of a comprehensive industrial strategy involving the appropriate commitments of labor and management, fiscal incentives to encourage R&D, as well as "patient" or long-term capital for investments in automation and high technology. However, the U.S. tax code rewards short-term, high-yielding nonproductive investments and penalizes long-term capital commitments. As a result, despite recent signs of recovery, U.S. manufacturing remains a long way from regaining its former preponderance and will continue to slip behind in many areas so long as policies (and national mentality) continue to foster the economics of instant gratification, an abdication of responsibility to investors, workers, and consumers.

The "postindustrial" philosophy proved to be as destructive as it was self-deluding. The irony now is that those service industries, such as finance, insurance securities, and real estate, in which the United States *was* to have achieved its dominant role have become controlled by Asian corporations, particularly the Japanese, through the wealth derived from manufacturing. Economic development and technological evolution are, and always have been, manufacturing based. History is full of cases of powerful trading or military powers that failed to sustain their respective world positions because they did not convert their accumulated wealth to productive capacity.[3]

For a time, and perhaps still, the United States disregarded the fundamental role played by production in the cycle of creating new ideas, generating new wealth, enhancing human skills, and, most of all, spinning off an efficient and meaningful service sector. Simply put, services do not function in isolation. The service sector is an adjunct to production and the generation of goods, and the connection between the two is both direct and immediate. The emerging postindustrial mentality is reflected in many forms, one of which is subtly illustrated when one of America's proudest corporations, U.S. Steel, redesigns its name to become USX. The symbolic significance of this minor event to America's industrial decline is inescapable. Webster defines X as "an unknown quantity" or "an arbitrarily chosen value from the domain of a variable," or "to cancel or obliterate. . . ."

A Tenuous Comeback

At the beginning of 1989, U.S. manufacturing appeared to be making a visible, if uneven, recovery, providing the main source of the economy's strength and export growth. But the merchandise trade deficit remained in the final months of 1988 between $10 billion and $13 billion. In many cases, the current recovery by U.S. manufacturers was made possible by new equipment and machinery that can *now* only be purchased abroad. The machine tool industry, once the backbone of America's inventiveness and industrial diversity, now ranks a weak fourth behind Japan, West Germany, and the U.S.S.R.

Not only was domestic capacity dismantled or permitted to wear down through continuous disinvestment, but also the skilled or even trainable labor simply no longer exists in the United States. While politicians and educators continue to emphasize ways of increasing the number of bachelor of arts degrees in sociology, art history, or political science, most technical apprentice programs in the United States have long since disappeared, and companies go begging for candidates to fill high-paying technical and engineering jobs, usually resorting to importing skills or transferring operations overseas.[4] Meanwhile, few, if any, well-focused incentives have been devised to help business and industry shoulder the heavy burden of training for the future manufacturing sector. The Japanese and Europeans have focused on maintaining skills through technical training and apprenticeship programs. Their respective educational systems, while being far from perfect, have strengthened their competitive edge vis-à-vis the United States.

THE NEW INDUSTRIAL STRUCTURE

High technology has reinvented the factory no less for Americans than for Asians; and that is what the "Megatrendies" and "postindustrialists" ignored or perhaps never understood. The importance of direct labor costs diminishes as automation and robotics increase productivity and quality. Cost accounting may only now be coming to terms with the strategy that has worked so well for the Japanese. It is no longer sufficient to focus solely on recovering technological investments and plant automation on the basis of the short-run conventional return on investment calculation. The U.S. corporate investor needs to develop a model for understanding and dealing with the deadly implications of losses due to static output, variable quality, and lost markets *if* the investments in design, automation, new technologies, and training *do not* take place.

The U.S. tax code should reward those investors willing to commit to the long-term view. Business (U.S. and foreign) planning to invest domestically *should* be lobbying through associations, elected officials, and the White House for appropriate tax incentives favoring R&D, product design for exports, long-term capital investments, comprehensive training, engineering scholarships, and technical apprenticeship programs.

By contrast, Japanese companies of all sizes receive a range of incentives including 10 to 20 percent tax breaks for investing in automation and new technologies. For example, to stimulate the use of robotics in smaller factories, the Japanese government in 1980 financed Japan's robot equipment makers to establish Japan Robot Lease Company and then provided annual low-interest loans of $12 million. By 1985, the leasing company was generating revenues of $30 million and was placing 200 robots and ancillary facilities per year with companies employing 30 to 75 workers.[5]

THE FAR EAST OPPORTUNITY:
A CORPORATE STRATEGY

If incentives and appropriate policies could work so well in the United States, why should companies bother investing abroad, particularly if so much can be achieved at home? The answer is that one market does not substitute for the other if corporate and business investors are to gain the full advantages of opportunities offered through coherent global strategies. Substantive reasons for doing business and investing in the Far East revolve around capturing new markets in a changing global economy. It is only through a market presence and a familiarity with local tastes and preferences that a company can ensure a long-term competitive advantage and permanent place in a foreign country. If the quality-conscious markets of the Far East can be penetrated, a variety of other world market segments can be captured with relative ease.

Direct export opportunities are becoming increasingly rare, if not unattainable. Asian companies, in particular, learned early to consolidate their respective positions domestically, while they simultaneously captured large portions of the U.S. and other foreign markets.

The lesson is clear. The most effective way for firms to enter and expand in foreign markets is through creation of product linkages between domestic and foreign production. The future will be dominated by companies with well-developed and integrated cross-border operations.

A strong market presence abroad reinforces the corporate position at home and vice versa. Partial exceptions might be farm products and other primary products. However, services such as construction, consulting, and engineering are now as dependent on global opportunities as they are on consolidating secure and long-term linkages to manufacturing activities (both domestic and overseas). In fact, the doors of most countries are completely or partially closed to products and services from companies solely in the business of exporting. The exceptions are cases where goods and services are provided under the umbrella of a program or project loan from a multilateral lending institution (World Bank and regional development banks) or other types of specific investments. Given the dynamism of the Pacific Rim economies and the enormous inroads already made by Asian companies in North America and Europe, the Far East should be the logical setting for overseas expansion by North Americans and Europeans.

Another strategic reason to operate in the Far East is to gain greater access to the technologies and methods essential to achieve improved product quality. Just as North America and Europe have excelled in the generation of original and creative ideas, innovative product designs, organizational systems, and communications technology, Asians have developed superior systems for product-quality management, production processes, design enhancement, production and inventory controls, worker education and training, and, most of all, market planning and development.

Stereotyping never substitutes for reality, but the fact remains that U.S. and European companies can learn a great deal from operating in an Asian environment. Just as Asians have never hesitated for a moment to learn from Americans and Europeans, we should be practical enough to learn from Asians. The companies that survive in the 1990s and beyond will be those best able to operate globally and, in particular, to successfully arbitrage the opportunities between the Far East, North America, and Europe. To be successful in this process, product quality and other lessons mastered by the Asians will have to become an integral and primary focus of U.S. corporate strategy.

THE DOLLAR FALLACY

The Background

Beginning in 1985, with help from central banks of the major industrialized nations, the United States forced a reevaluation of its currency against those of its competitors. This action was to initiate the use of the exchange rate as the *focus* of U.S. trade policy. The yen rose in value from ¥240 = U.S.$1 in mid-1985 to ¥135 by the end of 1987 and about ¥125 by the end of 1988. The U.S. trade deficit with the East Asian countries was $79.8 billion in 1985 and $105.3 billion in 1987.[6] In 1987, European-manufactured exports to Japan increased by 27 percent; exports of manufactured goods from South East Asia rose 57.3 percent, but U.S.-manufactured exports to Japan rose a fractional 0.1 percent despite the weakened dollar. Of the $15.7 billion in consumer goods imported by Japan in 1987, only $2 billion came from the United States.

Meanwhile, despite the strong yen, Japan exported $66 billion in merchandise to the United States in 1987. Conversely, a strong yen provided global bargains for Japanese business. In 1986, Japanese new investment and business ventures in Asia outpaced U.S. corporate competitors by 50 percent. More than 1,400 Japanese companies launched new industrial plants and facilities for textile, steel, automotive, and electronics manufacturing. The Japanese used the massive U.S. dollar exchange rate adjustment as an opportunity to expand their industrial base, consolidate financial and corporate power worldwide, and fine-tune their already efficient export industries.

Manipulating the U.S. dollar exchange rate to stimulate exports has not been a constructive policy for improving the U.S. trade deficit over the long term. In effect, devaluing the dollar subsidizes outmoded technologies and old industries and does nothing to remedy the effects of over a decade of disinvestment in manufacturing. It is the worst kind of quick fix, in that it provides a false sense of achievement. The theory is simple: if one reduces the price of a product far enough it can be sold regardless of quality. But despite the recent rise in U.S. manufacturing exports, many U.S. goods are still perceived as being inferior to those of Japan and Europe. Few if any economic initiatives have so appropriately reflected the prevailing short-term and narrow horizon of U.S. trade officials and manufacturers as the decision to use exchange rates as the key mechanism in correcting U.S. trade imbalances.

Clearly an exchange rate movement provides the easiest and most immediately visible method of stimulating exports. However, in actively and consistently pursuing such a tactic over a two-year period, in the absence of structural adjustment incentives and fiscal actions to remedy the underlying economic causes, the United States bears the burden of a generally failed trade policy. Artificially depressing the dollar will be shown to have had a fundamentally adverse impact on the U.S. economy over the long term while resulting in only marginal and short-term gains in U.S. trade performance.

The U.S. balance of trade can begin to move permanently in a positive direction only when government and industry recognize that product quality and all of the other underlying preconditions to selling goods abroad constitute the driving forces behind a successful and competitive performance. The conventional wisdom has been that the U.S. trade deficit can be solved, to a large extent, by a weaker U.S. currency. This misguided reasoning, which continues to be put forward by many of America's influential economists as well as many in the White House, is hopelessly parochial and simplistic.

Practical Effects

First, the exchange rate argument ignored the impact that consistently higher quality foreign goods have had on U.S. buying habits. Americans and consumers in other industrial markets have simply become far more sensitive to quality.

Second, it ignores the economic structure of America's major Asian and European competitors. To a large degree, Japanese and German producers have thrived on their currencies remaining strong. The already-efficient Japanese and German companies use their own hard currencies to introduce financial discipline and encourage further economic efficiencies in their own manufacturing operations.

Third, it ignores the powerful perception prevalent throughout the rest of the world that a weak, unstable U.S. currency is indicative of a deteriorating and vulnerable underlying economy. This factor is generally discounted by economists because the consequences are hard to quantify. However, a weakened dollar can ultimately effect the willingness to invest in U.S. stocks, and it can have an impact on the ability of the United States to negotiate trade deals from a position of strength.

Fourth, it ignores the fact that Japan, Korea, and Taiwan are major net importers of raw materials and other inputs to service their manufacturing export sectors. Since the U.S. dollar is the currency of trade, enormous underlying cost advantages accrue to Japan's already dynamic and efficient manufacturing export sector. Korea and Taiwan simplify the strategy. They link their respective currencies to the U.S. dollar, thus receiving the benefits of downward dollar adjustments without paying the price.

Still, Americans cannot understand why prices for Japanese products have failed to increase significantly. The enormous export surplus being generated by the sale of Japanese goods in the United States is, of course, in U.S. dollars. It can be argued that Japan having developed a dollar-based export sector (in which both inputs and outputs are denominated in dollars), while importing relatively little dollar-based finished products, has ultimately benefited from, if not neutralized, U.S. exchange rate policies of the past years. Whatever marginal and temporary cost advantages U.S. domestic manufacturers might enjoy as a result of the depreciating dollar, empirical evidence has demonstrated that benefits are short lived and quickly eroded as most U.S. producers take the opportunity to raise their prices in line with imports, thereby stimulating domestic inflationary pressures.

In a very real sense, the United States can in part thank Japanese manufacturers (which have been able to hold to relatively minor price hikes, obviously through self-interest) for the moderate inflationary tendencies through 1988. Far from correcting trade imbalances, U.S. exchange rate policy has permitted Japanese companies to outbid U.S. rivals in corporate and real estate acquisitions in the U.S. market, giving Japanese companies a dominant position in transacting and consummating financial and business ventures in the rest of East Asia. This, in turn, has led to the erosion of U.S. influence in multinational institutions and global economic policy. Finally, the vast proportion of the $73 billion in foreign bonds held by Japanese in 1987 was in U.S. government and corporate debt, raising speculation that it might not be long before Japanese exercise direct veto power over U.S. policies, which a few observers conclude might be an improvement.

The most disheartening aspect of the exchange rate policy is that, even in the face of overwhelming evidence that currency manipulation is no longer an effective instrument for improving the U.S. trade deficit, influential economists continue to argue in favor of further reductions in the U.S. dollar.[7]

It is time to face facts: quality sells products. Quality consciousness, always acute in Japan, has reached global proportions. Japanese will not purchase goods they consider to be inferior even if the yen appreciates to ¥1 = $1. Confirms Kenichi Ohmae of McKensey & Company, "If you want to sell, you have to improve products, not shift exchange rates."[8] What he could also have added was that the United States has nearly reached its capacity in being able to turn out more manufactured exports, even if further currency realignments could conceivably make a difference at this point.

Meanwhile, the U.S. productive base, still weak from years of disinvestment and abandonment, could not expand to meet additional demand in the near future even if capital spending continued at 1988 levels. In some industries, factories are running at more than 90 percent capacity. In mid 1989, capacity utilization averaged almost 85 percent for all U.S. industry. That is near the point at which shortages appear and prices shoot up.[9] Ironically, the United States could have achieved virtually the same short-term trade effects through far more moderate exchange rate realignment. A reasonable level of decline could have permitted those truly competitive U.S. producers, such as Caterpillar, sufficient price advantage without throwing the currency into a tailspin and offering up the United States at bargain basement rates.

FOCUS: ELEMENTS OF COMPETITIVENESS

Banks for U.S. Exporters

Many aspiring U.S. exporters continue to lack a fundamental mercantile mentality as well as most of the related characteristics needed to enter and succeed in export markets. Underlying and accentuating that problem is that small- and medium-sized U.S. export companies have been unable to gain access to first-rate global banking networks.[10] Large multinational corporations can rely on finding international banking services. Yet even with increasing reliance on small- and medium-size firms to act as the engine of the U.S. export drive, the vital financial institutional links required to service this group are woefully lacking. Part of the problem is that laws such as the McFadden Act still restrict banks from establishing branches outside their home states. While some liberalization is occurring and more banks are establishing Edge Act Corporations, the system falls far short of satisfying the enormous range of requirements of U.S. exporters. Simply put, in addition to operating under fiscal disincentives and contradictory economic policies, U.S. businesspeople struggle under the weight of a fragmented and unresponsive financial system unable to provide the aggressive support needed to compete internationally.

Large multinational corporations can introduce products into the global markets through overseas subsidiaries, usually with no positive impact for the U.S. trade position. Conversely, the small- and medium-size manufacturers have few, if any, ways to move their innovative and unique products into foreign markets. Despite some deregulation, a coherent merchant banking system has yet to emerge, no less the concept of a national banking marketplace. The Europeans, and now the Canadians, have developed "universal" banking that places all services under one roof, while the Japanese have trading companies and bank-driven alliances that provide a full "umbrella" to support exporting corporations. The United States must develop its own institutional apparatus in the form of a comprehensive, *nationally based* merchant banking network that provides short- and long-term finance, countertrade operations, advisory services, currency trading, and other trade-supporting activities.

In 1987, about 60 of the 14,000 U.S. banks had international branches, beyond the Caribbean shell branches. However, only a handful of those 60 offer complete and global banking facilities, in contrast to the Japanese, Europeans, and Canadians whose services extend from a small local business to major international operations.

UNDERSTANDING JAPANESE PRIORITIES

Japan is represented by two distinctly different economies that operate in separate orbits but complement each other and are mutually reinforcing. The economy we see is the export economy—capital intensive, efficient, and at the cutting edge of turning out new and improved products. It is a model of how to apply and benefit from new technology. Its momentum and dynamism drive the world trade system.

The second, the domestic economy, is highly traditional. It is this economy that preoccupies Japanese policy makers and influences all of their trade positions. The internal economy absorbs most of the new labor entering the work force. It is cumbersome, multilayered, and aimed at full employment. It is perhaps the most inefficient and economically expensive internal system of any of the industrial nations. But its goal is *social stability* and servicing (and indirectly subsidizing) the export economy. The domestic economy maintains an expensive agricultural sector and an enormous network of inefficient small businesses and industries, the underlying rationale of which is the preservation of traditional values and socioeconomic well-being.

This dual export-domestic system, unquantifiable in Western economic terms or by methods of cost accounting, serves the Japanese well. It is a system for which the vast majority of Japanese are willing to pay. Thus, as every other industrial nation has undergone fundamental and wrenching changes in social structure and institutions, Japan has remained relatively calm and unaltered in a turbulent world. The greatest perceived threat to this relative internal serenity has been U.S. pressures for Japan to open its inefficient and tradition-bound internal markets. Thus far, Japan has successfully resisted the enormous political and psychological onslaught launched both by the United States and Europe. In the back of every negotiator's mind must be an understanding of Japanese priorities, fears, and profound sense of resolve that nothing must disturb the nation's internal balance.

U.S. negotiators have been locked in debate with the Japanese about opening the Japanese market—an absolutely essential and reasonable objective. However, U.S. representatives obviously do not understand the Japanese economy or Japanese socioeconomic priorities. As a result, their efforts have often been misguided, and those U.S. products targeted for Japanese importation have been ill-defined, while other significant opportunities have gone unnoticed. In those few cases where the Japanese have failed to thwart U.S. trade objectives, thus providing an opening for making substantial inroads in the Japanese domestic market, the United States has often mishandled or failed to take advantage of the opportunities.

Take the case of opening major Japanese public works projects to U.S. construction companies. The U.S. construction industry is competitive in terms of operational cost efficiency, building material standards, and systems management vis-à-vis its domestic Japanese counterparts. Thus, here was an area of clear U.S. opportunity. Yet during the prolonged but ultimately successful negotiating period, U.S. authorities made no efforts to ensure that U.S. companies would be ready to aggressively pursue major Japanese contracts when the door was open.

There was virtually no meaningful coordinating structure between U.S. government and industry. There was no effort to prime U.S. contractors to move into action at the proper moment. Let us illustrate what might have occurred: (*a*) translations of complex Japanese bidding procedures could have been furnished well in advance to U.S. trade associations; (*b*) representative trade associations and groups of construction company officers could have participated in the final round of negotiations to identify immediate strategies; (*c*) the Commerce Department in conjunction with industry associations could have provided, for cost-covering fees, literature on project requirements and lists of potential Japanese joint venture partners; (*d*) U.S. Export-Import Bank and OPIC should have been in a position to lead and otherwise mobilize U.S. financial institutions to provide immediate financial support to U.S. construction companies; (*e*) temporary support units staffed by industry representatives should have been established in the U.S. Embassy in Tokyo and outlying consulates to guide companies in bidding or otherwise establishing local business contacts. These are only a few practical proposals. However, neither serious thought nor any form of practical effort was devoted to help overcome the basic international inexperience of most U.S. contractors.

There was simply no understanding of the actual steps to be taken to begin transforming the nonmercantile approach of the U.S. construction industry to an aggressive international trading mentality. As a result of the absence of such a support system, the endeavors of the U.S. trade negotiators resulted more in opening the Japanese market largely to Korean and Taiwanese contractors, rather than to U.S. contractors.

IDENTIFYING THE RIGHT MARKETS
AND PRODUCTS

The long-standing argument that East Asians, and particularly Japanese, will never buy U.S.-manufactured products is not altogether correct. It is true that U.S. goods have come to be perceived as poorer in quality than similar Japanese or European items, but there remains well-established and ingrained longing for things American, particularly among the Japanese youth. Despite an enormous nationalistic and emotional attachment to buying Japanese, most Japanese derive no great pleasure from seeing U.S. products compare unfavorably with goods from other places. First, the Japanese will and can pay handsomely for quality and prestige.

Second, even when a U.S. product is competitive, U.S. producers make little distinction between those and other items that might not meet the exacting Japanese standards.

U.S. Inc. Clearinghouse Approach

To further complicate the picture, all exportable U.S. goods, competitive or not, are likely to run into severe resistance at Japanese customs in the form of a variety of nontariff barriers as well as convoluted internal wholesale market mechanisms and the inevitable barrier of buyer prejudice. One possible solution that could follow on the heels of a successful market opening would be establishment of the previously mentioned system supported jointly by the government and trade associations. The focal point of the system would be expanded commerce and trade offices in each U.S. embassy and consulate that would become the clearinghouses for *identifying* a variety of competitive products and focusing on opening the Japanese market system.

Specific information related to Japanese standards, design preferences, and packaging could be provided manufacturers of potentially competitive products, such as outdoor clothing (an L. L. Bean fad among Japanese youth is waiting to happen); bathroom and kitchen hardware; plumbing materials; work boots, shoes,[11] and sneakers; men's underwear, shirts, and some men's upscale clothing (Brooks Bros. style appeals to businessmen); construction and farm machinery (Caterpillar and Westinghouse, two companies that quite properly benefit from exchange rate adjustments). In service industries, construction, software systems, financial engineering services, engineering, and consulting are all areas in which U.S. companies can develop healthy market niches in the Far East.

THE COMING "GLOBAL" CENTURY

The United States has emerged as much an Asian-Pacific nation as an Atlantic nation. As such, it must aspire to becoming the center rather than being peripheral to the new order of economic relationships. However, to recapture the initiative and continue in a central economic role, U.S. business must operate in a different mode and learn to function in terms of global markets. The most recent "megatrend" to emerge suggests that world economic power is shifting to the Far East and that the next century will be the "Asian era."[12] The most realistic outcome, however, is likely to be a far more *integrated world economy* with East Asian nations performing as *equal* partners in the economic and political system. In effect, the Japanese have taken a critical step toward this global process in committing a large segment of their resources to investments in the U.S. economy and to the lesser extent Canada. By the next decade, Canada will have absorbed a sizable portion of Hong Kong's wealth because of aggressive and clear-minded Canadian government policies.

However, to speak of an Asian ascendancy is to ignore the realities. How durable is the "Asian economic miracle" without a vital U.S. market? The real issue is whether the United States will reconstitute its productive base so a fundamentally strong and self-sustaining economy develops over the long term to replace the increasingly hollow economic shell held together by imported machinery and parts. The North American consumer fueled the so-called Asian miracle, and Asian economic performance will *continue* to depend on the U.S. market. That market can afford to import goods only if it possesses the capacity to produce and sell goods. Although the Asians will become increasingly important as world consumers, they cannot replace America's role in the foreseeable future. Even China, now seeking to develop its own domestic and export industries, is at least a half century away from being able to absorb, or pay for, a fraction of the massive imports now sustained by the United States.

Furthermore, the driving force of innovation and original ideas will continue to flow from North America and Europe because of the nature of their graduate educational systems and cultural disposition. Albeit, an increasing proportion of that creative energy will be generated by the hundreds of thousands of Asian students, researchers, professors, and businesspeople studying and working in North America and Europe. A positive consequence of the new Asian equality is that Asian influence can undoubtedly act to challenge and revitalize Western work habits, productivity, and instincts for quality, just as the West has had much to contribute to the economic development of the Far East.

To diverge for a moment, two minor events in the global economic arena offer constructive lessons about the relative styles of the competing nations. First, the U.S. Census Bureau Center for International Research published in 1988 a "Report on Consumer Trends in China," available for $500. Almost 800 Japanese companies willingly paid the money, while fewer than 100 U.S. companies were prepared to pay the relatively small amount to obtain this basic market tool. Japanese companies were lining up to buy the report before publication. A well-developed Japanese business intelligence system, obviously in conjunction with a well-coordinated network of government and business information-gathering activities, pointed out the source and Japanese companies responded. U.S. companies either did not know of the report or simply failed to grasp its merits and refused to pay the $500. Either way, the U.S. companies lose.

Second, in 1987, Taiwan targeted New York state for a market operation seeking to match joint venture and other investment opportunities in Taiwan with New York-based companies. Over 2,000 companies were sent questionnaires soliciting U.S. corporate investment preferences; 15 companies responded. If this story is any indication of the U.S. business drive to find overseas markets, it is no surprise to learn that, in 1986, Japanese investment in new business ventures in Asia outpaced U.S. investment by 50 percent; 1,400 Japanese firms initiated new plants and facilities for textiles, steel, auto parts, electronics, and other forms of production.[13]

A stable economic future can evolve only if the international trade process is determined by the dynamic of interaction between Asia, North America, and Europe, each contributing its respective pool of talents. Ironically, the "bridge" as well as what is perceived as the weakest link in this global economic chain is the United States. The coming decade will show whether the United States can organize to regain the competitive edge in manufacturing and fully revitalize its industrial capability. If so, the process will entail a fundamental revision in the way the United States operates. It means an industrial policy and a coherent set of fiscal strategies that foster, encourage, and reward productive decisions and actions by U.S. manufacturers and exporters of goods and services.

ASSESSING THE ASIAN COMPETITORS

Official U.S. efforts to open Asian markets, while often fragmented, misdirected, or politicized, have generally been motivated by best intentions. Most of those involved in negotiations with the Japanese and others have been highly competent and dedicated to achieving their objectives. The real problems have occurred in U.S. internal political pressures that have determined the selection of these objectives. Furthermore, as indicated, the lack of knowledge about the motivation and goals of Japanese and other Asian counterparts have sent the talks and results down the wrong path. North American and European governments and corporate negotiators have been handicapped by not having a firm grasp of the driving forces behind the positions taken by their Asian counterparts. Let us explore some of the determinants of Japanese strategies and objectives.

The Japanese have carefully orchestrated the image they present to the world. It is a daunting picture of corporate power and finely tuned competitiveness. That view is soundly supported by superbly finished products and the appearance of unbreakable unity. Similarly, there is the myth of the humane, efficient Japanese corporation. However, it is not so simple. Despite their homogeneity, a factor that Japanese, Chinese, and Koreans generally view as giving them an advantage, neither the Japanese society nor any other East Asian societies can be characterized as "monolithic." Japanese, for example, are as varied in disposition, temperament, and abilities as any other people. However, tradition and conventions, reinforced by centuries of isolation, are powerful forces that are reemphasized at every level of education and social interaction.

Underneath the uniformity lies a nation of individuals, many of whom never truly adapt and a larger-than-expected proportion in various states of silent rebellion. Great numbers of Japanese have opted to work for foreign firms (Europeans being preferred over "less reliable" U.S. companies). Most of those Japanese who would probably function effectively in overtly competitive Western business environments have not yet surfaced, and no one has yet determined how to identify the mass of buried talent in Japan. Japanese corporations put forward their highly valued "best" staff for negotiations, advanced training, and so on. Generally, many of the qualities that make a Japanese successful in a U.S. or European firm are not greatly valued in the Japanese corporate structure. What most Japanese do have in common, and what provides the unique Japanese atmosphere of conformity and compliance, is the overriding *respect* for the social conventions even when there is no agreement as to their value and usefulness. This respect takes many subtle forms that the foreigner doing business or negotiating with the Japanese would be well advised to recognize.

The Japanese corporation provides a rigid, uncompromising system that rewards obedience, selflessness, and subtle forms of competitiveness. This process has its drawback; many of those demonstrating the flashing brilliance so highly prized in a Western company might be considered potentially uncooperative and undesirable as team players.

Thus, many of the brightest and potentially innovative are left behind or buried in the system. Conversely, in terms of human talent, Japanese businesses will often point out that although sometimes lacking the originality and inventiveness prevalent in Western societies, the Japanese have avoided the burdens of the undereducated and unskilled classes. The bottom-up Japanese corporate decision-making process is painful and ponderous by Western standards, but the Japanese are fond of saying that the Japanese "average" is the "best average person" in the world.

RECOGNIZING PROTOCOL AND CONVENTIONS

Foreign businesspeople must know at exactly what point in the corporate system they should intervene when initiating business contacts or advancing the completion of a particular transaction. Entering a proposal at too high a level might result in few decisions and far longer than necessary lead periods. Too low an entry might leave the proposal unrecognized and permanently floundering. Start first by seeking advice from any previous contacts in the organization to which the proposal is being submitted. Never attempt a direct phone call, visit, or letter without going through channels. If the foreign businessperson has not yet established any contacts, request a bank, advisor, or consultant to identify a relatively senior officer in the company. After appropriate introductions, that individual will almost certainly place the foreigner on the right path in his corporate system. There is very little risk that the initial corporate helper will try to "grab" business for his own group or will mislead the foreigner away from potential internal rivals. He will receive his recognition through his demonstration of cooperation as a team player.

Japanese are often appalled by what they correctly perceive as wasteful and misdirected internal competition, or a willful lack of cooperation within U.S. organizations. What Americans often view as healthy competition or creative tension, the Japanese have been able to turn to their own advantage. When Japanese witness or even sense internal rivalries among the staff of a potential U.S. corporate partner or client, one of two responses are likely: the Japanese counterpart will almost immediately opt out of the deal, or the Japanese will remain but will earmark the U.S. company for eventual takeover or dissolution. Japanese interpret lack of loyalty and integrity on the part of U.S. staff as being the source of fundamental corporate weakness.

UNDERSTANDING THE GAME

North Americans and Europeans tend to confuse the concept of *compromise*, which is largely alien to the Japanese, with the idea of *consensus*. Japanese compete fiercely among themselves, striving for complete dominance in any endeavor. Japanese manufacturing corporations will exert merciless control over their thousands of subcontractors (*Shitauke*), dictating terms and conditions that U.S. parts producers would find intolerable. The largest Japanese corporations will not hold more than a half day's inventory of inputs while demanding exact performance in delivery schedules from subcontractors. Similarly, banks, trading companies, and manufacturers cut and slash their compatriot rivals for a fractional percentage point gain in market share. It is therefore no great wonder that North American and European competitors have lost the first round of economic battles during the 1980s.

The strategy for Japanese success was direct and uncomplicated. Initially, Japanese happily took the back seat in the global economy, while borrowing, generating internal savings, and continually striving to improve on product design in carefully targeted areas of manufacturing. Next, they moved cautiously but quickly into the markets with *fully tested* products. The international consumer was not burdened with half-proven goods or expected to test the new product lines for defects. Then, the Japanese outmarketed and undersold their foreign rivals, even when it meant operating at a loss for a decade. Corporations and financial institutions patiently absorbed years of unprofitable operations in order to ensure their permanent market predominance.

The next round will determine whether the Japanese and Europeans combine to dominate the economic system or whether the North Americans will recapture their economic and trade positions. As indicated, competing successfully in Asia (or against Asians) will require a combination of supporting fiscal and economic measures, totally revised corporate strategies, and the infusion of a new mercantile spirit.

SOME WORKING GUIDELINES

For most companies seeking to sell or produce in Asia, whether establishing linkages with production at home or straightforward expansion, the joint venture represents the best mechanism. Recent literature provides valuable facts about forming alliances with Asians.[14] A major strategic goal in Asia is to move up to "value-added scale." North Americans have tended not to understand their own vulnerability to stumbling into partnerships with firms whose ultimate goals involve usurping their partner's basic industrial mission. The rules of survival are basically unchanged.

1. The joint venture must be founded on mutually beneficial and agreed objectives.

2. There must be parallel interests between the Japanese and foreign partners.

3. There must be a sharing of Asian as well as other markets.

4. A thorough investigation of the potential partners and their corporate strategy must be implemented *before* any agreement as the precondition to avoid being "swallowed up." Asians are no different from other people; there are unscrupulous as well as honest businesspeople waiting to form partnerships.

5. To achieve objectives, Asian companies are fully prepared to outwait their foreign counterparts. The sooner this tactic is understood, the easier a negotiation or any type of working relationship will become. Whether the situation relates to negotiations or other business dealings, the time expended in the waiting process can be expensive, so one must be prepared to pay the price but never to display anxieties or anger. Impatience and frustration on the part of Westerners usually signal Japanese negotiators that they have won.

6. The down-up group consensus is a particular Japanese method of decision making. The process consists of painstaking analysis at every stage. Although an informal leader emerges at each level of examination, the group takes responsibility for the final recommendations. The senior officer of a company never takes part in the *details* of a decision; he or she is merely the informed spokesperson who accepts final responsibility for the decision and outcome. Details and intricacies of a transaction should rarely be discussed with a chief executive officer or chief financial officer, and then only under prearranged circumstances.

7. Any form of confrontation will usually destroy a deal. Hostility entails a loss of face on both sides. Calmness and control are essential ingredients to gaining respect among Asians.

8. Asians, particularly Japanese, require considerable time to develop a sense of comfort with foreigners. However, once achieved, solid friendships can evolve. The surest way to set back a relationship is through familiarity. In Japan, do not attempt to use first names; a handshake is a concession to Western manners.

9. To Japanese, in particular, conventions and traditions are as legally binding as formal contracts; thus, the preference of the Japanese to do business and to be with each other. A contractual negotiation between foreigners and Japanese will always be an excruciating, time-consuming, and convoluted experience with layers of false starts and finishes. However, it is virtually certain that the foreign businessperson will have a lasting contract after the negotiating exercise has been completed.

ENDNOTES

[1] Japanese *Keiretsu* and Korean *chaebol* or general trading companies.

[2] John Naisbitt, *Megatrends* (New York: Warner Books, 1982), pp. 249–50.

[3] Contrast the fates of Portugal and Spain of the 16th and 17th centuries to England and France. The U.S.S.R. provides a modern day example of a country that failed to channel resources into a broad range of productive activities.

[4] "America's Toolmaking Gap," *Newsweek*, October 17, 1988.

[5] "High Tech to the Rescue," *Business Week,* June 16, 1986.

[6] U.S. Department of Commerce Statistics: U.S. Export Development Office, 1987.

[7] C. F. Bergsten, "Attacking Deficits," *Fortune,* January 2, 1989.

[8] *The New York Times,* November 28, 1988.

[9] Data Resources Inc., *U.S. Economy,* December 1988 and January 1989.

[10] Robert Heller, "U.S. Exporters Need Global Banking," *Business Week,* June 8, 1987.

[11] Leather products are particularly politically sensitive. Leather workers in and around Osaka form an underclass or "untouchable" whose status dates back to the middle ages when their ancestors worked in the slaughterhouses, an unseemly occupation in Buddhist Japan. The government seeks to guarantee employment security of the modern day descendants in order to stave off social unrest among them.

[12] J. Kotkin and Y. Kishimoto, *The Third Century* (New York: Crown Publishers, 1988).

[13] *Far East Economic Review*, September 4, 1987.

[14] Kotkin and Kishimoto, *The Third Century;* D. Burstein, *Yen!* (New York: Simon & Schuster, 1988).

CHAPTER 2

AMERICAN INCENTIVES FOR DOING BUSINESS IN THE FAR EAST

Katherine Hope Francis
Robert H. Garb
Joseph P. Griffin

INTRODUCTION

THE GATEWAY AGENCY—THE COMMERCE DEPARTMENT

FINANCING ASSISTANCE—EXIMBANK

INSURANCE ASSISTANCE—FCIA AND OPIC

FINANCING ASSISTANCE—OPIC

FINANCING ASSISTANCE—AGENCY FOR INTERNATIONAL DEVELOPMENT

OTHER ASSISTANCE—AID AND OPIC

FINANCING ASSISTANCE—TRADE DEVELOPMENT PROGRAM

DOMESTIC LEGISLATION, INTERNATIONAL TREATIES AND TRADE AGREEMENTS, AND OTHER U.S. GOVERNMENT NONFINANCING-RELATED INCENTIVES

    1. Incentives Arising from the Export Trading Company Act of 1982

    2. Customs Benefits under the Tariff Act of 1930 and the Foreign Trade Zone Act of 1934

3. Incentives Arising from Treaties and Trade
   Agreements between the U.S. and Countries in the
   Far East

CONCLUSION

INTRODUCTION

For the United States, it is no longer business as usual in its Far East marketing efforts. Each of the countries in the Far East is playing by its own rules—rules dictated by its history, culture, and resources—and not necessarily by free market forces (price, quality, and services). When competing with countries like Japan and Korea, the United States cannot afford to ignore the extent these governments support their commercial enterprises in international trade. The Export-Import Bank of the U.S. (Eximbank) Trade and Aid/Mixed Credits Study recently surveyed some 17 industries and 50 countries and concluded that $1 billion of U.S. exports are lost annually as a result of mixed credits offered by competitive foreign governments (probably far more than this figure is lost if you factor in followup sales).[1]

Japan is the world's largest donor of nonmilitary foreign aid, and such aid is frequently tied to the purchase of Japanese goods and services. Japan gives more assistance than the United States to such important Far East countries as China and the Philippines.[2] The concern is that foreign aid will buy Japan political and economic advantage over the United States.

While this chapter analyzes the assistance provided for American business in the Far East by various U.S. government agencies such as Eximbank, the Overseas Private Investment Corporation (OPIC), the U.S. Agency for International Development (AID), and the Trade Development Program of the Department of State (TDP) as well as U.S. legislation, international treaties, and trade agreements and describes numerous success stories resulting from this partnership between the public and private sectors, this subject has to be placed in the proper perspective. The Organization for Economic Cooperation and Development (OECD) countries (other than the United States) have outspent the United States 20 to 1 in their incentive and support programs.[3] Recently, Eximbank's credit programs have been subject to a disproportionately large cut in the federal budget from $5.4 billion in fiscal year 1981 to $695 million in fiscal year 1989.[4]

During the 1980s, the United States has been unsuccessful in negotiating away mixed credits. OECD countries other than the United States view their aid budget as a way to benefit their own economies while helping less-developed economies. The United States still looks at providing aid from a humanitarian point of view. The United States has to start playing by the rules that everybody else does, because the United States will not persuade these countries to change their rules.

This chapter reveals that the U.S. government's assistance to U.S. businesspeople desiring to do business in the Far East is fragmented across various agencies operating under the auspices of different government departments. The authors believe some version of the legislation currently before Congress needs to be adopted to consolidate the fragmented efforts of Eximbank, OPIC, AID, components of the Departments of Commerce and State, and the U.S. Trade Representative into a single Department of International Trade and Industry.[5] This reform should give international trade a higher public profile and more clout, so it can compete more effectively for policy support.

The extent to which other governments support their exporters should be an important factor in determining our international trade policy. The U.S. government has to stop providing assistance to developing countries with little regard for its effect on the U.S. economy. Development assistance needs to be redesigned to provide immediate mutual economic gains to both the United States and the recipient economy.

THE GATEWAY AGENCY—
THE COMMERCE DEPARTMENT

Because there is no consolidated cabinet-level department of international trade and industry, the first stop a U.S. company should make to learn about U.S. government services and incentives for an exporter to the Far East is the nearest Commerce Department's International Trade Administration's (ITA) district or branch offices. There are 48 ITA district offices and 19 branch offices in cities throughout the United States. Each district office can give information about:

- Trade and investment opportunities in the Far East.
- Sources of U.S. government financial assistance for exports to the Far East.

- Information on U.S. export licensing to the country involved and the Far East nation's import requirements.
- Export documentation requirements.[6]

The Commerce Department gathers this information on-site through the commercial officers of the U.S. and Foreign Commercial Service (US & FCS), a part of ITA. The US & FCS offices scattered throughout the Far East also provide assistance in making appointments with key buyers and government officials; identifying and qualifying direct leads for potential buyers, agents, joint venture partners, and licensees; business counseling and market counseling; and representing U.S. companies victimized by trade barriers.[7]

One of the specific services currently offered at the US & FCS overseas posts located in Indonesia, the Philippines, and Singapore is a Comparison Shopping Service. The Comparison Shopping Service (CSS) consists of a customized market survey on a U.S. firm's specific product in each of these countries. CSS provides the firm with concise answers to critical questions on its product's overall marketability, names of competitors, comparative prices, customary entry, distribution, promotion practices, competitiveness, and trade barriers. Each CSS covers a single product in a single-country market.[8]

The US & FCS is committed to increasing the number of U.S. firms, particularly small- and medium-sized firms, involved in international trade.

The Success Stories: Japan

Using Japan as an example, the following are some of the success stories where the Department of Commerce services provided assistance to a U.S. company making its initial entry into the Japanese market.

F. Norman Clark founded the Roaring Camp & Big Trees Narrow Gauge Railroad about 80 miles south of San Francisco. The 1880 steam-powered train carries tourists on a six-mile trip through the redwood forest to the beach at Santa Cruz, California. For many years, Mr. Clark found it difficult to attract enough tourists to stay in business. In 1973, Mr. Clark consulted the Commerce Department's U.S. Travel and Tourism Administration, which promotes tourism to this country. The following year the agency arranged for a dozen major Japanese tour operators to ride the train and have a barbecue dinner around a potbellied stove. They were sold on the adventure! Only five months later, one of Japan's largest tour wholesalers started to operate group tours to Roaring Camp and within three years most major Japanese tour operators began bringing Japanese by the thousands for the ride.[9]

In 1986, a small manufacturer of precision parts for mechanical pens and pencils subscribed to the US & FSC Export Mailing List Service (available through ITA's district offices) in an effort to locate foreign manufacturers of writing instruments. After its initial mailing, the manufacturer established contact with a Japanese firm resulting in an order worth $3,000. Since then the firm's initial business with Japan has grown dramatically, achieving sales close to $300,000 in 1987.[10]

As part of an overall Commerce Department trade strategy of increasing exports to Japan, the US & FSC has laid out a series of trade promotion initiatives. These initiatives are designed to promote awareness and knowledge of this market potential and to capitalize on specific improvements in market access expected from ongoing trade policy negotiations. The strategy includes:

- Aggressive pursuit of trade opportunities, particularly those tied to major project activity.
- The removal of trade barriers in key industry sectors.
- A busy schedule of trade events including Japanese buying missions to the United States and U.S. participation in major trade shows in Japan.
- Close cooperation with state governments and industry associations to help support and carry out the program.[11]

FINANCING ASSISTANCE—EXIMBANK

One of the important services the US & FCS provides is to counsel U.S. businesses seeking financing for their exports. In this regard, US & FCS has a particularly close relationship with Eximbank. ITA's district offices have worked with Eximbank on a cooperative basis for many years. As a part of its business counseling services, US & FCS trade specialists have been providing guidance to U.S. firms on the relevance of Eximbank programs to specific transactions; assisting U.S. firms with application requirements; and providing counsel on Eximbank procedures.

Eximbank is the export credit agency of the U.S. government. Eximbank seeks to create markets for U.S. goods internationally as well as to sustain U.S. jobs. Eximbank offers direct loans to foreign buyers for large projects and equipment sales that usually require long-term financing and mandates that the goods and services must be of U.S. origin. A typical direct credit financial package includes 15 percent of the value of the export contract as a down payment and an Eximbank loan of up to 85 percent, up from the traditional 45 percent or 50 percent. Generally, the bank will not provide long-term lines of credit to developed or wealthy countries.

Eximbank also guarantees loans made by cooperating commercial banks in the United States and overseas to U.S. exporters and to foreign buyers of U.S. products and services. Through a private insurance association, the Foreign Credit Insurance Association (FCIA), Eximbank provides insurance to U.S. exporters, enabling them to extend credit to their overseas buyers. Eximbank's Working Capital Guarantee Program supports loans to United States exporters for export-related marketing or production activities. In 1987, an estimated $9.3 billion in U.S. exports was assisted by Eximbank.[12]

The Export-Import Bank Act Amendment of 1986 extended Eximbank's charter for six years, through September 30, 1992. One important feature was establishment of a tied aid credit fund (War Chest) to combat unfair foreign competition. Since 1986, this War Chest has been used several times to provide financing to U.S. exporters in sales to Far East nations to combat competitor countries' use of foreign aid funds for commercial purposes.[13]

In 1987, after Eximbank identified Indonesia and Thailand as two countries where U.S. high-technology export sales had been lost because of foreign government-to-government concessionary financing arrangements, Eximbank extended two highly concessionary lines of credit of $100 million each to finance high-technology U.S. exports to these countries. Both of these facilities were competitive with tied aid credit financing available in these markets from other governments, including the Japanese Overseas Economic Cooperation Fund and European mixed credits.[14]

In medium- and long-term credits (i.e., credits involving repayment terms of 5 to 10 years after the goods have been shipped or the project completed), Eximbank has been successful to a large degree in matching foreign governments' support of credits.[15]

The Success Stories: China

Eximbank actively supports U.S. exports to China and offers China interest rates and repayment terms that are the most favorable allowed under OECD's arrangement on official export credits—currently an 8.3 percent interest rate and up to a 10-year repayment term. For such services, Eximbank fees are comparable to fees charged by official export financing agencies of other OECD countries.[16]

At the present time, Eximbank and the Bank of China have an operating agreement that provides for the Bank of China to serve as obligor or guarantor for Eximbank long-term financing (loan commitment calling for repayment terms longer than seven years). If the purchasing party in China wishes to use the Bank of China facility with Eximbank, the purchaser should contact the Second Credit Department of the Bank of China Head Office in Beijing.[17] Eximbank may also lend or guarantee long-term credits to an intermediary to finance U.S. exports.

In two instances relating to projects undertaken by the U.S.-based international engineering and construction firm Bechtel, the financing was provided to an intermediary rather than to the Bank of China. In the spring of 1986, Bechtel found that Eximbank financing was essential in securing an important assignment in China; the design, procurement, and construction of a proposed 500-kilovolt, 97-kilometer transmission line project in Guangdong Province. As part of its request for proposal, the client, Guangdong General Power Company (GGPC), specified the need to arrange for 100 percent U.S. dollar financing for the project and a loan grace period running until six months after project completion. GGPC also required that the above-mentioned OECD consensus rates apply to the loan. After discussions with several possible arranging banks, Bechtel secured Citicorp-Hong Kong as its financial advisor. Eximbank showed its responsiveness by providing the loan to Citicorp as the intermediary for 85 percent of the costs of Bechtel's services. The loan fully met all of GGPC's requirements as noted above.

In November 1987, Eximbank again showed its flexibility in response to a Chinese client's demanding financing requirements. In this case, the project involved Bechtel providing quality assurance services over an eight-year period to the Guangdong Nuclear Power Joint Venture Company (GNPJVC), approximately a $3 billion construction project associated with the Daya Bay Nuclear Power Plant. In this case, Eximbank provided a direct loan to GNPJVC to cover 85 percent of the costs of Bechtel's services. The terms of the facility loan included the repayment of principal over 14 years.

INSURANCE ASSISTANCE—FCIA AND OPIC

Two U.S. government-related agencies provide insurance for export transactions to the Far East—the Foreign Credit Insurance Association (FCIA) and OPIC. FCIA is an association of leading insurance companies operating in conjunction with and as agent of Eximbank. It offers insurance policies protecting U.S. exporters against the risk of nonpayment by foreign debtors. OPIC is a federally chartered corporation that provides political risk insurance. Specifically, OPIC provides the following types of coverage to U.S. companies:

- Expropriation.
- Damage due to revolution, insurrection, and civil strife or political violence.
- Risks of currency inconvertibility.
- Loss sustained when a government client fails to settle a dispute in accordance with the provisions of the underlying contract.[18]

The FCIA protection against the risk of nonpayment gives a U.S. exporter fundamental protection on what many would affirm is the riskiest part of a firm's asset portfolio, foreign receivables. The FCIA coverage protects against certain political and commercial risks. Depending on the FCIA policy, either the U.S. exporter or a bank may be the policyholder. Commercial risks insured by FCIA's policies may result from economic deteriorations in the buyer's market area, fluctuations in demand, unanticipated competition, technological changes, or natural disasters such as floods and earthquakes. The political risks include revolution and insurrection, revocation of one's license, or expropriation of one's assets.

FCIA offers U.S. exporters policies tailored to their needs. The short-term single-buyer policy enables U.S. exporters to cover single or multiple shipments to one buyer under a sales contract. Multibuyer export policies are written to enable a U.S. exporter to extend credit terms for products on short-term sales, usually up to 180 days. Companies just beginning to export, or with limited export volume, can take advantage of FCIA's new-to-export policy. The new-to-export policy offers enhanced commercial risk protection for the first two years of a policy's life that includes 95 percent commercial coverage and political coverage for receivables and no deductibles. To be eligible for the new-to-export policy, companies must not have had direct FCIA coverage for two years preceding the date of application and must have a sales history showing average annual export credit sales together with affiliates during the preceding two fiscal years not exceeding $750,000 (exclusive of sales made on terms of confirmed irrevocable letters of credit or cash in advance).[19]

Having FCIA export credit insurance produces additional benefits to a U.S. exporter besides nonpayment protection. It enables the exporter to use receivables as security for financing. Because the exporter is protected against nonpayment, it is often able to arrange more attractive financing. Consequently, the exporter is then able to offer its overseas clients more attractive credit terms than would be available without that protection.[20] For U.S. banks desiring to finance exports in difficult markets, effective backing of the U.S. government through FCIA insurance on foreign receivables allows them to leverage their limited legal lending capacity. U.S. banks commonly accept the FCIA-insured portion of a loan as exempt from their internal limitations on assumption of foreign risks.[21]

OPIC's insurance has three distinct advantages over that offered by private insurers: the amount of coverage per project, the length of policy terms, and the premium rates charged. For example, OPIC provides up to $150 million of coverage per project with country exposure limitations of about $300 million.[22] On the other hand, the American International Group, a private political risk insurer, generally writes up to approximately $35 million worth of coverage per country, and Lloyd's of London syndicates up to $50 or $60 million per project.[23] OPIC's insurance contracts usually cover up to a 20-year commitment, depending on the type of investment, along with an annual option to continue, reduce, or terminate coverage. In contrast to OPIC's long-term policies, the private insurers' policies ordinarily have a maximum duration of three years. In addition, OPIC's annual premium rates are generally lower than those charged in the commercial market.[24]

Since OPIC's insurance is operative only with respect to projects registered with OPIC before an irrevocable commitment is made to the foreign client, the exporter should make sure all projects intended for coverage are registered with OPIC as soon as possible. Registration can be accomplished by simply notifying the OPIC officer of the projects intended to be covered.

In fiscal year 1988, OPIC had an insurance volume of $2.1 billion.[25] In fiscal year 1988, OPIC insured a record 156 projects in 49 developing countries.[26]

Despite the advantages noted above, OPIC does operate under program constraints not found in the commercial market. OPIC can insure only "new investments" in a lesser developed country (LDC). New investments include the expansion or modernization of existing plants, equipment, or additional working capital. A number of other statutory limitations are imposed on OPIC's insurance authority. For example, before assisting a U.S. exporter's investment, OPIC must consider (1) the effect of the investment on the U.S. balance of payments and employment; (2) the human rights record of the host country; and (3) the impact of the investment on the host country's environment.[27]

In most cases, an insured's claim under OPIC insurance does not mature until the foreign government's challenged action has continued for a year. During such period, the insured must take all reasonable measures to prevent or contest the governmental action. This includes redress through the host country's judicial system.[28]

The typical FCIA and OPIC coverages require the policyholder to retain a portion of the risk, commonly referred to by the insurers as *retention*. Such retention requirement is normally 5 or 10 percent of the insured transaction. The retention amount helps assure that the policyholder maintains an interest in the transaction and participation in subsequent recovery efforts.

The Success Stories: Taiwan

In 1979, Bechtel formed a joint company known as Pacific Engineers and Constructors Ltd. (PECL) with the Taiwanese government-sponsored engineering firm Sinotech. The purpose of the joint company was to perform power projects for the Taiwan Power Company and other potential clients both within and without Taiwan. As a 60 percent owner of the joint company, Bechtel considered it important to have OPIC insurance behind its investment. Bechtel elected to put in place only the OPIC insurance for foreign exchange inconvertibility, rather than also include coverage for expropriation or war risks. As an engineering company, PECL would have few physical assets to be expropriated or damaged in the event of a war or insurrection. Bechtel's main asset in the joint company was its investment and the appreciation on its investment. Bechtel has maintained such OPIC insurance of its investment. Every six months, PECL's financial situation is examined and a decision is made as to how much inconvertibility insurance is to be placed on a current basis and how much is to be left on a standby basis to cover subsequent appreciation of Bechtel's investment.

FINANCING ASSISTANCE—OPIC

OPIC provides direct loans, loan guarantees, and equity financing to U.S. investors in Third World countries. Currently, OPIC's equity financing is limited to a few select countries as well as the guarantee of equity investments, the acceptance of convertible debentures (which cannot be converted to equity while held by OPIC), and the acceptance of equity acquired as a result of claims, bad debt restructuring, or foreclosures.[29]

During fiscal year 1987, OPIC's above-mentioned finance programs as applied to the Far East were available in China, Taiwan, Indonesia, the Philippines, Thailand, and Korea.[30] At the close of fiscal 1988, OPIC's financing portfolio, including authorized commitments not yet disbursed, amounted to $814.4 million. In fiscal year 1988, 15 percent of OPIC's finance portfolio was allocated to the Far East.[31]

OPIC is self-sustaining, receiving no congressional appropriations. Sixty-two percent of the 102 projects OPIC assisted in fiscal year 1987 were located in the least-developed countries (i.e., countries with per capita incomes of $896 or less in 1983 dollars). Sixty-one projects, or 37 percent, were located in the middle-income developing countries, having per capita incomes of more than $896 but less than $3,887. The two remaining projects (approximately 1 percent) were located in countries with per capita incomes of $3,887 or more.[32]

The Success Stories: Indonesia

In 1988, OPIC provided a guarantee of the loan for the construction of the P. T. Gunung Salak geothermal project in Indonesia undertaken by the U.S.-based firm Union Geothermal, Inc., a division of UNOCAL. The project will supply electricity from geothermal resources on the Indonesian island of Java and will help meet much of the island's energy demand. The reduced need for petroleum to generate electricity will permit Indonesia to realize substantial foreign earnings.[33]

FINANCING ASSISTANCE—AGENCY FOR INTERNATIONAL DEVELOPMENT

AID, which falls under the International Development Cooperation Agency (IDCA),[34] administers most of the foreign economic assistance programs for the federal government. AID assists U.S. exporters to compete in the sales of goods or services supplied to Far East countries through its loans and grants. AID finances capital and technical assistance and training for infrastructure and basic human needs programs.

AID has played a key role in the economic development of most of the countries comprising the Far East. As the economies of these countries have changed, AID's programs have also changed. They have evolved from direct transfers of capital and food to activities designed to help those countries manage their own resources, especially through the introduction of new approaches to promoting economic growth and development. In addition to serving the foreign policy objectives of the United States, such as maintaining democracy in the Philippines, AID's objective in the region is to ensure that economic growth can be strengthened and sustained.[35]

Generally, an AID-financed project commences by AID issuing a project identification document (PID), which identifies a proposed development project where the host country asks for AID's financial assistance or where a project is developed in collaboration with the host country. Once a PID is approved by AID, the next step is the preparation by AID of a project paper (PP), which provides the detailed project appraisal and all the specifics on how a project will be implemented, including work scope, schedule, budget, and justification. The PP identifies possible American suppliers and/or contractors that can provide equipment and services for the project AID will finance.

If the host government concurs with the project, it will enter into a project agreement, under which the host country enters into contracts for equipment and services or, as agreed with the host country, AID might be permitted to enter into direct contracts with suppliers. If AID enters into the contract directly with the U.S. suppliers/contractors, the commercial terms of contract will generally be based on the Federal Acquisition Regulations.[36]

OTHER ASSISTANCE—AID AND OPIC

One important nonfinancing incentive provided by AID and OPIC has been to sponsor conferences and missions to promote U.S. exports to developing countries. Besides the real business spinoffs that result from these missions and conferences, these events provide the U.S. exporters with detailed knowledge on the economic situations and prospects of each of the country or countries involved.

In August 1988, AID created a new position called the assistant to the administrator for international trade and investment promotion and charged the assistant with the following tasks:

- To establish a single, fully coordinated effort within the agency to work with U.S. businesses to increase U.S. exports and direct investments in developing countries.
- To develop a strong working relationship with the U.S. business community to share information about developing countries.

The objective in establishing this new position was to develop information and service products that make sense to U.S. businesspeople wishing to transact business abroad.[37]

The Success Stories: The Philippines

In 1988, the Philippines were in dire financial straits and recognized that despite high energy needs to support a surging economy, the country could not continue to build enough public-sector power plants. The government began to focus its interest on how to provide incentives to the private sector to build power plants. The Philippine government and industry representatives were interested in knowing what procedures were needed to put private-sector power plants into place. These representatives wanted to have access to the views and experiences of key U.S. practitioners of private power. It was recognized that, of all the nations in the world, the United States is probably the most experienced in building private-sector power plants. It was on this basis that a Manila seminar on private power generation was formulated by USAID's Office of Energy and put together in two months.

The seminar was held in Manila on October 5–6, 1988. The theme of the seminar was "Private Power Generation through Build-Operator-Transfer (BOT)." The following sponsored the seminar:

USAID Office of Energy.

USAID Manila Mission.

Office of Energy Affairs of the Government of the Philippines.

Philippines Chamber of Commerce and Industry.

As a direct result of the seminar, three key Filipino legislators strongly endorsed private power and promised to work for Philippine legislation encouraging private investments in power generation. Also, the following business spinoffs occurred:

- Hopewell Holdings Limited of Hong Kong, which was represented at the seminar, signed a contract to purchase three used Westinghouse 501 gas turbines from the Milwaukee firm of Zaferos Power Systems to provide 200 megawatts of generation capacity to the Luzon utility system on a BOT basis. The total U.S. content of equipment and services for Hopewell's project is estimated to be about $25 million out of a total project cost of $35 to $40 million.

- The North Carolina firm Cogentrix was represented by its local affiliate, Cogentrix Philippines, Inc. It is now negotiating to build, own, and operate a 220-megawatt cogeneration power plant in Luzon. The project is estimated to cost $323 million using major equipment from General Electric, Foster Wheeler, and Detroit Stoker. Negotiations are under way to sell the electricity produced to the National Power Corporation of the Philippines and process steam to the Caltex refinery.
- San Miguel Corporation, a Philippine conglomerate in beer, food, packaging, and other diversified interests that has very energy-intensive operations, has been looking to build its own power plants to serve two clusters of industrial plants, one north of Manila and one south of Manila, with an aggregate capacity of about 20 megawatts and 400,000 lbs. per hour of process steam. Technical assistance is being provided by the Office of Energy of AID to San Miguel to evaluate and select innovative power technologies for these sites. Since one of the sites is in a rice growing area, a power plant using indigenous rice husks is being recommended. This effort has enabled the U.S. firm Agrilectric Power, Inc., to offer its rice husk power technology to San Miguel. Agrilectric's marketing effort has been partially funded by the Trade and Development Program. This is a case in which the synergistic cooperation of two U.S. agencies has proved to be effective in creating a business opportunity for a U.S. firm.[38]

FINANCING ASSISTANCE—TRADE DEVELOPMENT PROGRAM

Trade Development Program (TDP) was established July 1, 1980, as part of the IDCA. The Omnibus Trade and Competitiveness Act of 1988 made TDP an independent agency within IDCA. TDP has the following two missions:

- To assist in the economic development of friendly developing and middle-income countries.
- To promote the export of U.S. goods and services to those countries.

TDP accomplishes these missions by financing preinvestment feasibility studies and other studies prepared by U.S. private-sector firms for projects that are important to the development of the recipient countries and that also represent significant export opportunities. The Trade Development and Enhancement Act of 1983 also places primary responsibility on TDP for information relating to trade development and export promotion.[39]

Essentially, TDP serves as a catalyst to open markets to U.S. firms and to encourage U.S. private-sector involvement in LDC infrastructure development. It does this by undertaking the following activities:

- Funding of feasibility studies that increase the likelihood that U.S. goods and services will be procured for the implementation of projects in those countries.
- Sponsorship of technology symposia.
- Funding of reverse trade missions (where foreign officials visit the United States).

Since its inception in 1980, TDP has financed the planning of 520 projects in 91 countries. By enabling U.S. firms to gain an early foothold in projects that promise substantial short- and long-term markets for U.S. goods and services, TDP-financed feasibility studies and other project planning services have led to over $1 billion in direct exports from the United States.[40] In addition, significant indirect benefits result from TDP's programs. U.S. companies that participate in TDP-funded studies are in a good position to win additional business because of their presence in the country, official contacts made, and confidence engendered with local authorities.

One of the important TDP programs is its Investor Assistance Program (IAP). This program is designed to encourage U.S. private-sector investment in overseas projects that involve U.S. equity and exports. IAP has been available to U.S. businesses since July 1, 1988. At the outset, the U.S. investor must finance the entire study. Once the study is complete, TDP will reimburse the investor for up to 50 percent of the cost of the study. The financing is provided on the basis of a four-year, no-interest loan the investor repays to the U.S. government. Before TDP will provide assistance, financing for the project must be arranged. The U.S. investor must plan to maintain a significant equity position in the project, and the project must have a substantial U.S. export potential.

Because of the strength of the economy of the Far East, since 1981, TDP has generally devoted at least 50 percent of its annual program budget to this region. As of March 1988, approximately $723 million of actual U.S. exports resulted from 39 projects linked to TDP involvement in this region. This does not include another estimated $3.4 billion in the next 5 to 10 years and $1.7 billion in 10 to 20 years. The TDP program in the Far East has enabled U.S. firms to develop new markets in countries that have tremendous untapped export potential.[41]

From fiscal year 1981 through 1988, China has far and away received the largest amount of TDP funds, $22.6 million, representing a total of 73 projects. The following Far East countries rank after China:

Country	TDP Funds Received	Number of TDP Projects
Thailand	$9,626,118	32 projects
Philippines	$5,519,572	32 projects
Indonesia	$5,038,648	19 projects[42]

TDP funding has helped U.S. industry penetrate the Chinese market. For fiscal year 1988, TDP obligated 29 percent of its commitment dollars to China and 38 percent to the rest of the Far East.[43] TDP focused on some newly emerging markets in China and the rest of the Far East, such as pollution control and hazardous waste disposal.

The Success Stories: Thailand and Singapore

In 1981, TDP funded a $120,000 feasibility study of a transmission system to integrate the proposed generation expansion at the Mae Moh site into the existing Electricity Generating Authority of Thailand's (EGAT) Electrical Transmission Network. Lemco Engineers, based in Missouri, completed the study and won the first five phases of the design and implementation contract. Approximately $34.5 million in U.S. goods and services have been procured through Lemco since the original study. Lemco's participation in the project has resulted in Lemco's involvement in several other projects in Thailand.[44]

In 1983, TDP provided a $50,000 grant to Singapore Polytechnic to conduct a study on the implementation of computer-aided design and computer-aided manufacturing systems. As a result of the grant, which assisted in staff visits to U.S. computer users and vendors, visits to Singapore Polytechnic by U.S. consultants, and staff training with U.S. private-sector and U.S. educational institutions, Singapore Polytechnic purchased $17 million worth of U.S. goods and services.[45]

In 1988, TDP funded a $43,000 reverse trade mission to the United States for a Thai delegation of telecommunications officials to visit the "Super Comm '88 Convention" in Georgia and tour several U.S. suppliers and manufacturers of telecommunications goods and services. As an immediate result of this mission, Motorola sold $2 million in trunking network equipment. Trade relations were strengthened, and future sales are expected in the short term.[46]

DOMESTIC LEGISLATION, INTERNATIONAL TREATIES AND TRADE AGREEMENTS, AND OTHER U.S. GOVERNMENT NONFINANCING-RELATED INCENTIVES

1. Incentives Arising from the Export Trading Company Act of 1982

The United States Congress in October 1982 enacted the Export Trading Company Act to "encourage exports by facilitating the formation and operation of export trading companies, export trade associations, and the expansion of export trade services generally."[47] The Export Trading Company Act provides incentives for exporting by allowing small- and medium-sized businesses to work together through export trading companies (ETCs) without risking any substantial antitrust liability.[48] The act also permits banking institutions to invest in export trading companies.[49]

By definition, an ETC can be formed by an individual or a corporation established under U.S. law. An ETC may operate either to export U.S. goods and services or to facilitate such exports by providing export trade services such as "consulting, international market research, advertising, marketing, insurance, product research and design, legal assistance, transportation, . . . , warehousing, foreign exchange, financing, and taking title to goods, when provided in order to facilitate the export of goods or services produced in the United States."[50]

Under the act, several small enterprises may form an ETC to serve as the exporting department for these enterprises, and an antitrust violation will occur only when such an ETC's activity has a "direct, substantial and reasonably feasible (anticompetitive) effect . . . on export trade or export commerce with foreign nations, of a person engaged in such trade or commerce in the United States."[51]

In addition, ETCs or any entity engaged in exporting may obtain a "certificate of review" from the Secretary of Commerce to protect itself from potential antitrust actions.[52] This is because, under the act, the U.S. Attorney General cannot file an antitrust action against the certificate holder unless the conduct "threatens clear and irreparable harm to the United States." Conduct within the scope of the certificate is presumed to be legal. The act further provides that private antitrust plaintiffs may not claim treble damages, but only injunctive relief and actual damages for a certificate holder's failure to comply with the conditions set forth in the certificate.

Finally, an unsuccessful complainant in an antitrust action against a certificate holder is required to compensate the certificate holder for the costs of defending the lawsuit.[53]

The Success Stories: Arrangement of Export Trading Company

Bellsonics, Inc., is an export trading company in El Toro, California, that provides export services to manufacturers of semiconductor test equipment and microwave equipment. Since 1983, Bellsonics has doubled the combined exports for its customers. Bellsonics will take over a firm's export operations, handle a firm's exports only to countries that pose special difficulties, or set up an export operation for turnover to the firm after a year or two.[54]

Ashford International, Inc., is an international trading company in Atlanta, Georgia, that buys high-tech computer peripherals and then exports them to some 45 countries. Ashford's sales team researches each product before making a recommendation to a foreign buyer, making sure it meets all the buyer's technical and compatibility requirements. Many U.S. manufacturers are attracted to Ashford because it relieves them of customs and licensing paperwork. From 1985 to 1988, Ashford expanded from a 5-employee firm with reported annual sales of $1 million to a 30-employee firm with U.S. and German offices and reported sales of $10 million.[55]

2. Customs Benefits under the Tariff Act of 1930 and the Foreign Trade Zone Act of 1934

There are two major customs benefits available to U.S. exporters exporting goods to the Far East. These benefits are:

a. Drawback of Customs Duties under the Tariff Act of 1930

U.S. manufacturers that import components or materials used for assembling or processing before re-export may obtain "drawback" refunds of 99 percent of the customs duties paid on the import components or materials by filing a proposal with the Commissioner of U.S. Customs Service Regional Office or with the Drawback and Bonds Branch, Customs Service Headquarters.[56]

Exporters claiming drawback refunds must establish, however, that the merchandise on which the drawback is being claimed have been re-exported within five years after importation of the components or materials.[57]

b. Exemption of Duties and Excise Tax under the Foreign Trade Zones Act of 1934

U.S. manufacturers engaged in importation of dutiable materials and components that will be processed or assembled for re-export to the Far East are also eligible for customs benefits of U.S. foreign trade zones.[58] These customs benefits include: (1) exemption of customs duties and federal excise tax on imported merchandise (unless the imported merchandise or the final product, instead of being re-exported, are transported out of the foreign trade zone and thereby enter into the U.S. customs jurisdiction), and (2) waiver of quota restrictions imposed on certain imported merchandise.[59]

3. Incentives Arising from Treaties and Trade Agreements between the U.S. and Countries in the Far East

A number of international treaties and bilateral and multilateral trade agreements to which the United States and countries in the Far East are contracting parties provide incentives for U.S. exports to the Far East. These incentives include:

a. National Treatment and Most-Favored-Nation Treatment

The United States has entered into treaties and trade agreements with countries in the Far East, including Japan,[60] the Republic of Korea (Korea),[61] the Republic of China on Taiwan (Taiwan),[62] China,[63] the Philippines,[64] and Thailand.[65] The primary purpose of the agreements is to provide the citizens and corporate entities of the contracting parties with the privileges accorded by either party to its own nationals (i.e., the "national treatment") or to those of the most favored trading partners (i.e., the "most-favored-nation treatment").

These treaties and trade agreements generally provide U.S. citizens and corporations with national treatment and most-favored-nation treatment with respect to entry and sojourn; travel and communication; access to courts of justice and administrative tribunals and agencies; settlement by arbitration of controversies with local individuals and entities; real and personal property rights; establishing branch offices or local corporations, or acquiring and controlling existing corporate entities; protection of patents, trademarks, and industrial property; taxation; remittances and transfers of funds; customs duties and charges; restriction on importation; prompt and impartial review of administrative action relating to customs matters; and so on.

b. Tariff Concessions and Other Incentives under GATT

The United States and a handful of Far East countries, including Indonesia, Japan, Korea, the Philippines, Singapore, and Thailand, are signatories to the General Agreement on Tariffs and Trade (GATT) under which the contracting parties are obliged to extend to one another various preference treatments. China is contemplating GATT membership. The following are some of the principal GATT treatments of interest to exporters to the Far East:

(i) Tariff Concession. Each contracting party must levy on merchandise from other contracting parties no more than the tariff contained in the negotiated schedule for that party.[66]

Taiwan is not a signatory to GATT. However, the United States and Taiwan reached an agreement in October 1979, by exchange of letters between the American Institute in Taiwan (AIT) and the Coordination Council for North American Affairs (CCNAA), under which the United States is obliged to apply its tariff schedules concluded in the Tokyo Round of the GATT negotiations to exports from Taiwan in exchange for Taiwan's tariff concessions to U.S. exports. The agreement also sets forth the two governments' mutual understanding that certain nontariff GATT obligations and benefits concerning subsidies and countervailing measures, customs valuation, licensing, government procurement, technical barriers to trade, and commercial counterfeiting will be mutually observed by the two parties.

(ii) National Treatment of Imports. GATT requires each contracting party to accord merchandise imported from other contracting parties the same treatment as goods of local origin with respect to domestic administrative regulations and taxes.[67]

(iii) Prohibition of Quantitative Restrictions.   Each contracting party may not impose quantitative restrictions (i.e., quotas) on the importation of merchandise from other contracting parties.[68]

(iv) Prohibition of State Trading and Monopolies.   GATT also prohibits contracting parties from creating a state enterprise with a monopoly over certain products.[69]

(v) Fair and Uniform Customs System.   Customs formalities and administration can create nontariff barriers to foreign exports. GATT requires the contracting parties to administer a fair and uniform customs system.[70]

c. Protection of Patent, Copyright, and Other Industrial Property

(i) The Convention for Protection of Industrial Property.   The United States, China, Indonesia, Japan, Korea, and the Philippines are contracting parties to the Stockholm Convention for the Protection of Industrial Property. A primary obligation under this convention is that each contracting country shall extend to citizens and corporations of another contracting party national treatment with respect to protection of industrial property such as patents, utility models, industrial designs, trademarks, service marks, and trade names.[71]

(ii) Universal Copyright Convention.   The United States, Japan, and Korea are also contracting parties to the Paris Universal Copyright Convention.[72] Under Article II of this convention, contracting states are obliged to accord national treatment to works of nationals of another contracting state first published in that state. Such treatment applies to literary, scientific, and artistic works, including writings, musical, dramatic and cinematographic works, and paintings, engravings, and sculpture.[73]

(iii) Patent Cooperation Treaty.   The United States, Japan, and Korea are signatories to the Patent Cooperation Treaty of 1970.[74] This treaty simplified and unified the process of seeking patent protection in the contracting states. Korea and the United States have each agreed to protect the patent rights recognized by the national law of the other.[75]

(iv) Berne Convention.   On January 1, 1989, the United States joined the Berne Convention for the Protection of Literacy and Artistic Works, to which Japan is also a signatory. The Berne Convention provides national treatment of copyright protection for every production in the literary, scientific, and artistic domain, such as books; dramatic or dramatico-musical works; choreographic works and entertainment in dumb show; musical compositions with or without words; cinematographic works; works of drawing, painting, architecture, sculpture, engraving, and lithography; photographic works; works of applied art; illustrations, maps, plans, sketches, and three-dimensional works relative to geography, topography, architecture, or science.[76]

The protection of the Berne Convention generally applies to (1) authors who are citizens or residents of one of the contracting nations for their work, whether published or not; and (2) authors who are not citizens of one of the contracting nations for their work first published in one of those contracting nations.[77]

Although Taiwan is not a contracting party to the above conventions and treaty, a U.S. exporter's copyright, patent, and other industrial property rights and privileges are, to the extent feasible, protected by Article IX of the U.S.-China (Taiwan) Treaty of Friendship, Commerce, and Navigation of 1946, which accords the citizens and corporations of both countries reciprocal protection "in the exclusive use of inventions, trademarks and trade names." In addition, Taiwan has in 1985 and 1987 amended its Copyright Law and Patent Law, respectively, to accord, subject to the principle of reciprocity, national treatment to foreign copyright and patent applicants.[78]

The United States and Indonesia have signed a copyright agreement, effective August 1, 1989, that provides for mutual protection of copyrights. Also, the United States and Singapore, by Letter Agreement dated April 27, 1987, and by Presidential Proclamation of May 16, 1987, have agreed to provide for mutual protection of copyrights.

It is important for U.S. exporters to understand that, despite the existence of the above conventions, treaties, and foreign domestic laws, discrimination against and infringement of U.S. copyrights and patents are still the primary concerns of many U.S. firms exporting to the Far East. Therefore, it is advisable that potential exporters consult with the U.S. and Foreign Commercial Service of the Commerce Department about intellectual property protection for specific industries in particular countries.[79]

The Success Stories: Copyright Protection in Taiwan

In September 1987, the Motion Picture Association of America, Inc., filed its complaint with the Taipei District Court against a group of Taiwan-R.O.C. citizens for piracy of video programs. This action sought copyright protection under Taiwan's new Copyright Law, which became effective July 12, 1985, and the Enforcement Rules and Procedural Manual published and implemented in June 1986.

The defendants contended that works completed before July 1975 must be registered to enjoy protection since copyright protection for these works were governed by the old copyright law that required registration as a condition for copyright protection. In overruling this contention, the Taiwan High Court held that:

> Based on the FCN [Friendship, Commerce, and Navigation] Treaty between the R.O.C. and the U.S.A., works by U.S. copyright owners are entitled to the same protection as works by R.O.C. nationals. Based on the ruling by the Ministry of Interior, (75) Tai Nei Tse number 378062 dated March 6, 1986, U.S. authors enjoy copyright protection upon completion of works. Article 17 of the Copyright Law, which requires registration for works by foreigners, are not applicable to U.S. authors. Consequently, this court holds that the works at issue are protected by the R.O.C. Copyright Law upon completion.[80]

However, victory in battling pirates and copycats does not come cheaply. After four years of quashing cut-rate knockoffs, Apple Computer, Inc., assisted by a former narcotics agent and a battery of attorneys, has finally clamped down on the Taiwanese manufacturers of imitation Apple II computers. The "drug-bust" techniques deployed by Apple even included setting up a dummy computer distributing firm to bait ripoff manufacturers and hiring local citizens to make purchases of counterfeit machines.[81]

Frequently, U.S. exporters holding copyrights or patents on their products find themselves battling not just foreign pirates and copycats, but also the entire legal framework of a foreign country. In Japan, for example, U.S. critics of Japan's patent system have charged that Japanese companies patent their own ideas of possible application for U.S. inventions, making it impossible for the original U.S. inventor to profit from his or her patent. For instance, Fusion System Corp., a small advanced technology firm that holds a patent for its microwave lamp, has learned about Japan's patent system the hard way. Mitsubishi Electronic Corp. bought a Fusion lamp, made a slightly altered version, and filed over 200 peripheral patents on that altered version.[82]

However, it seems possible that an intellectual property right dispute can sometimes be resolved by negotiation. Energy Conversion Devices, Inc., of Troy, Michigan, solved its disputes in 1983 with Matsushita Electronic Industrial, Inc., over an erasable optical memory product and believes its negotiation can serve as "a model of what could be done if one could set aside the animosities."[83]

Sometimes, innovative thinking and good business instinct can be as effective as legal and diplomatic approaches in solving disputes over intellectual property rights. For example, while the Motion Picture Export Association of America is filing its second formal complaint with the U.S. Trade Representative against South Korea for the latter's failure to protect U.S. copyright, MCA Inc., parent of Universal Pictures, has pursued an innovative approach by offering the local film industry financing for new theaters in return for the local filmmaker's support in combatting unlicensed copying and pressing for stricter copyright enforcement.[84]

d. Recognition and Enforcement of Foreign Arbitral Awards

Because the U.S., Japan, and Korea are contracting parties to the New York Convention on the Recognition and Enforcement of Foreign Arbitral Awards,[85] an arbitral award obtained in the United States or another contracting nation to the New York Convention against a Japanese or Korean buyer will be recognized and enforceable in the respective country.

Taiwan, although not a signatory to the New York Convention, is generally required by its domestic statute to recognize and hold enforceable, subject to the principle of reciprocity, an arbitral award validly obtained under the laws of the United States.[86]

e. Market Access

From 1986 to 1989, the United States, through the U.S. Trade Representative, has successfully negotiated with Japan, Korea, and Taiwan, respectively, for the liberalization of markets in those countries for various U.S. goods and services.[87] For an up-to-date regional review of major efforts to open foreign markets see the "Annual Report of the President of the United States on the Trade Agreements Program," which may be obtained through the Office of the U.S. Trade Representative in Washington, D.C. The following are some typical examples of such U.S. efforts to gain access to markets in the Far East:

(i) Japan.   In 1986, the U.S. and Japanese governments concluded a bilateral agreement that provides the U.S. semiconductor industry with

access to the Japanese market. In July 1988, the two governments entered into a settlement agreement, under which Japan will phase out by 1992 its quotas on U.S. imports of fresh oranges and orange juice. Also in 1988, Japan increased U.S. firms' access to the Japanese government construction market and to Japanese science and technology research establishments.

(ii) Korea.   On August 26, 1986, the U.S. and Korea entered into the Agreement on Access of U.S. Firms to Korea's Insurance Market, allowing establishment of U.S. branch offices in insurance business in Korea. On March 18, 1988, the U.S. and Korean governments further reached an agreement regarding opening the life insurance market to U.S. companies by allowing joint ventures. On May 27, 1988, the two governments reached an agreement concerning open and nondiscriminatory access for U.S. cigarettes to the Korean market. Finally, on January 18, 1989, the two governments entered into the Agreement Concerning U.S. Wine Imports to Korea.

(iii) Taiwan.   Like Korea, Taiwan in 1988 opened its market to U.S. insurance companies, wine, beer, tobacco products, and turkey meat parts. To mitigate its trade imbalance with the United States, Taiwan also sends out its "Buy American Promotion Mission" each year to the United States to purchase U.S. products.[88]

(iv) ASEAN.   The Association of Southeast Asian Nations (ASEAN), which includes Indonesia, Malaysia, the Philippines, Singapore, and Thailand, and the United States are studying options for future strengthening of their mutual economic relationship through liberalizing goods and services trade and increasing investment and technology transfer.[89]

(v) China.   In 1988, the U.S. and Chinese governments concluded an agreement on maritime transport to foster efficient, competitive shipping services in the bilateral trade and the growth of economic ties between the two countries.[90]

CONCLUSION

This chapter in its outline of recent trade agreements, in its description of success stories relating to recently created export trading companies and international trading companies, and in its listings of what U.S. government services are available to an exporter to the Far East presents an upbeat picture of the numerous avenues of U.S. legislation and U.S. government's assistance to American business firms seeking opportunities in the Far East. However, as indicated in the introduction, this topic should be looked at in the broader context of how much greater overall assistance is being provided by other OECD countries to their exporters. The United States only recently has begun to realize how closely we are tied to the global economy. The Japanese, for example, recognized this international linkage long ago and are far ahead of the United States in adapting to a global economy by providing significant support and incentives to Japanese firms.

The Japanese market adjusts rapidly to international economic shocks, moves into upscale products, and copes with the emergence of new competitors. Earlier in this chapter, reference was made to U.S. critics of Japan's patent system who have charged that it fosters the filing of slightly altered versions of U.S. inventions, making it impossible for original U.S. inventors to profit in Japan from their inventions. Focusing on this issue of the fairness of a Japanese economic policy like its patent procedures misses the point. The fact is that Japan, Korea, Singapore, and Taiwan have aggressively adapted policies to respond to changing international circumstances; Japanese government procedures like the one that allows for the filing of peripheral patent applications on U.S. and other foreign countries' inventions merely reflect this policy.

The United States has a long way to go to become a modern trading state. The concept and the benefits to be derived from becoming a trading state have been evident for centuries. The United Kingdom was a preeminent trading state in the 19th century, and, before it, the Netherlands and Venice were premier traders. Japan is an example of the modern trading state. In the current era, the reach of the trading state has increased immeasurably. The Industrial Revolution broke the historical links between territory and power. Technology and the rise of multinational corporations extended the scope of the trading states beyond anything previously known.

With the adoption of concepts such as export trading companies and international trading companies, one may opine that the United States is beginning to put into place institutions to successfully compete at the international level.

In order to measure how well the United States is doing within its current institutional framework, we should compare the track record of U.S. export trading companies and international trading companies with their Japanese counterparts. In 1982, Sears formed Sears World Trade to help lead U.S. firms into the international arena. Its activities centered on North America, Europe, and Asia.[91] Sears World Trade is now disbanded. By comparison, Japan's first general trading company, Mitsui, was founded in 1876. By 1986, Mitsui had 210 offices in 89 countries. In 1984, Mitsui had revenues of ¥14,900 billion or $64 billion (at the then prevailing exchange rate of $1/¥235).[92]

To succeed, the United States must do a better job and design its institutions to adapt to the shifts in the global economy, such as by the implementation of the suggestion made at the beginning of this chapter to consolidate the fragmented efforts of Eximbank, OPIC, AID, and the U.S. Trade Representative into a single Department of International Trade and Industry (similar to Japan's Ministry of International Trade and Industry). In current times of rapid change, the ability of a government and private industry to institute in partnership continued and aggressive economic adjustments must be an overriding priority. Those industrialized countries like Japan, Korea, Singapore, and Taiwan that make continued and aggressive adjustments will do well; those that cling to the structures of the past will be left behind.

ENDNOTES

[1] Presentation by James Cruse, vice president for policy, Export-Import Bank of the United States, at Coalition for Employment for Exports, Inc., Winter Seminar, February 22, 1989, Washington, D.C. (hereinafter cited as CEE Winter Seminar).

[2] Douglas Waller et al., "The Cop and the Benefactor," *Newsweek,* February 6, 1989, p. 36.

[3] The OECD was founded in 1960. The group is made up of what is considered to be the developed capitalist world. Its membership consists of Australia, Belgium, Canada, Denmark, Finland, France, the Federal Republic of Germany, Greece, Iceland, Ireland, Italy, Japan, Luxembourg, the Netherlands, New Zealand, Portugal, Spain, Sweden, Switzerland, Turkey, the United Kingdom, and the United States. The OECD Convention commits its members to strive for "the expansion of world trade on a multilateral, nondiscriminatory basis." As a means toward this goal, the members agree "to pursue their efforts to reduce or abolish obstacles to the exchange of goods and services." See CEE Winter Seminar, note 1.

[4] Letter dated February 21, 1989, from the major U.S. trade-related organizations in the United States, including the Aerospace Industries Association,

American Consulting Engineers Council, and the American League for Exports and Security Assistance to the Hon. Jim Sasser, chairman of U.S. Senate Budget Committee.

[5] H.R. 1274, 101st Cong., 1st Sess. (1989), introduced by Representative Watkins (D-Okla.) on March 2, 1989, calls for, among other things, establishment of a new Department of International Trade and Industry within the U.S. government.

[6] "Roadmap to Export Services," *Business America,* March 28, 1988, p. 6 (hereinafter cited as "Roadmap to Export Services").

[7] Ibid., p. 7.

[8] U.S. & Foreign Commercial Service, "A Report to U.S. Business," consisting of 19 unpaginated pages, February 22, 1988 (hereinafter cited as U.S. & Foreign Commercial Service).

[9] See "Roadmap to Export Services."

[10] See U.S. & Foreign Commercial Service.

[11] Ibid.

[12] Thomas Graham, "Sources of Export Financing," *Georgia Journal of International and Comparative Law,* Fall 1984, p. 456.

[13] Export-Import Bank of the United States, *1987 Annual Report* (hereinafter cited as *Eximbank Annual Report*), p. 1.

[14] Ibid., p. 7.

[15] John A. Bohn, Jr., "Eximbank's Role in International Banking and Finance: Loans, Rescheduling and Development," *The International Lawyer,* Summer 1986, p. 831.

[16] Export-Import Bank of the United States, "Eximbank Procedures for China," for information only letter dated January 16, 1989.

[17] Ibid.

[18] Alan C. Brennglass, *The Overseas Private Investment Corporation* (New York: Praeger Publishers, 1983), p. 121.

[19] Foreign Credit Insurance Association, "Your Competitive Edge in Selling Overseas," May 1988, p. 4.

[20] Ibid., p. 3.

[21] Robert Chapman, "The High Utility of FCIA Insurance to Banks in Financing Trade," *Hastings International and Comparative Law Review,* Spring 1986, p. 443.

[22] See Brennglass.

[23] Deborah K. Burand, "Civil Strife Coverage of Overseas Investment: The Emerging Role of OPIC," *Federation of Insurance Counsel Quarterly,* Fall 1983, p. 394.

[24] Ibid.

[25] Overseas Private Investment Corporation, *1988 Annual Report*, p. 5 (hereinafter cited as *OPIC Annual Report*).

[26] Ibid., p. 13.

[27] See Burand, p. 395.

[28] See Brennglass, p. 226.

[29] Overseas Private Investment Corporation, *FY1987 Development Report*, p. 23 (hereinafter cited as *OPIC Development Report*).

[30] Ibid., p. 29.

[31] See *OPIC Annual Report*, p. 12.

[32] See *OPIC Development Report*, p. 8.

[33] Ibid., p. 10.

[34] The International Development Cooperation Agency (IDCA) was established by Reorganization Plan Number 2 of 1979. It is a focal point within the U.S. government for economic matters affecting the U.S. relationship with developing countries. IDCA's mission is to ensure that developmental goals are considered by the executive branch of the federal government when planning policies on trade, financial and monetary affairs, technology, and other economic issues affecting developing countries. It also has policy and budgetary responsibility for U.S. participation in multilateral development organizations and various bilateral development assistance programs. According to the *U.S. Governmental Manual*, the director of IDCA "serves as the principal international advisor to the president and to the secretary of state, subject to guidance concerning the foreign policy of the United States from the secretary of state." The IDCA director also serves as chairman of the Board of Directors of the Overseas Private Investment Corporation.

[35] Agency for International Development, Congressional Presentation Fiscal Year 1990, p. 41.

[36] The Federal Acquisition Regulations (FAR) are the primary procurement policies and procedures used by all U.S. executive agencies in their procurement of goods and services. The FAR can be found in Chapter 1 of Title 48, CFR.

[37] Agency for International Development Notice dated August 1, 1988, from Alan Woods, administrator.

[38] Trip Report dated November 22, 1988, by United States Agency for International Development Conventional Energy Technical Assistance Project, E. Y. Lam, team leader.

[39] United States Trade and Development Program, Congressional Presentation Fiscal Year 1990, p. 1.

[40] Ibid., p. 2.

[41] Ibid., p. 16.

[42] Ibid., p. 13.

[43] Ibid., p. 12.

[44] Ibid., p. 21.

[45] Ibid., p. 20.

[46] Ibid.

[47] H.R. Rep. No. 924, 97th Cong., 2nd Sess. 3, reprinted in *1982 U.S. Code Cong. & Admin. News* 2501.

[48] See R. Arthur, *U.S. Government Export Incentives for Small Business*, 22 Int'l Law, 791, 803 (1988).

[49] The Export Trading Company Act amends the Bank Holding Company Act of 1956 by permitting bank holding companies to invest up to 5 percent of their consolidated capital surplus in one or more ETCs. See 12 U.S.C. Secs. 1841–1850 (1982). The Omnibus Trade and Competitiveness Act of 1988 amended the Export Trading Company Act by inserting a new provision setting forth the standards for qualifying as an ETC. See Aug. 23, 1988, Pub. L. 100–418, Title III, Sec. 3402, 102 Stat. 1107.

[50] Export Trade Company Act Sec. 103(a) (4), 15 U.S.C. Sec. 4002(4) (1982).

[51] Export Trading Company Act Sec. 401, amending Section 7 of the Sherman Act, 15 U.S.C. Sec. 6a (1982).

[52] As of February 1989, the U.S. Commerce Department has issued some 100 certificates covering approximately 4,200 U.S. firms and individuals. See 6 Int'l Trade Rep. (BNA) 245 (Feb. 22, 1989).

[53] 15 U.S.C. Sec. 4016 (1982).

[54] "Exporting Pays Off," *Business America,* March 28, 1988, p. 35.

[55] "Exporting Pays Off," *Business America,* March 14, 1988, p. 11.

[56] 19 U.S.C. Sec. 1313(a) (1984); 19 C.F.R. Sec. 191.21, 191.23 (1988).

[57] 19 U.S.C. Sec. 1313(i) (1984).

[58] See 19 U.S.C. Sec. 81a–81u (1984).

[59] See Department of Commerce, *A Basic Guide to Exporting,* 55 (1986).

[60] U.S.-Japan Treaty of Friendship, Commerce, and Navigation, Protocol and Exchange of Notes of August 29, 1953. Signed at Tokyo, April 2, 1953; entered into force October 10, 1953. 4 UST 2063; TIAS 2863; 206 UNTS 143.

[61] U.S.-Korea Treaty of Friendship, Commerce, and Navigation, with Protocol. Signed at Seoul, November 28, 1956; entered into force November 7, 1957. 8 UST 2217; TIAS 3947; 302 UNTS 281.

[62] U.S.-China (Taiwan) Treaty of Friendship, Commerce, and Navigation with Accompanying Protocol. Signed at Nanking, November 4, 1946; entered into force November 30, 1948. 63 Stat. 1299; TIAS 1871; 6 Bevans 761; 25 UNTS 69. It should be noted that although the United States in July 1979 recognized the government of the People's Republic of China as the sole legal government of China, the U.S. Congress enacted the Taiwan Relations Act, 22 U.S.C. Secs.

3301 *et seq.,* which mandates that all agreements concluded with the Taiwan authority before January 1, 1979, will remain effective and will be administered on a nongovernmental basis by the American Institute in Taiwan (the AIT), a U.S. nonprofit-seeking organization, and its counterpart, the Coordination Council for North American Affairs (the CCNAA). See 22 U.S.C. Sec. 3303.

[63] U.S.-China Agreement on Trade Relations. Signed at Beijing July 7, 1979; entered into force February 1, 1980. 31 UST 4651; TIAS 9630.

[64] U.S.-Philippines Agreement Concerning Trade and Related Matters, Annexes and Exchange of Notes revising the Agreement of July 4, 1946. Signed at Washington, D.C., September 6, 1955; entered into force September 6, 1955. 6 UST 3030; TIAS 3349; 238 UNTS 109.

[65] U.S.-Thailand Treaty of Amity and Economic Relations with Exchanges of Notes. Signed at Bangkok, May 29, 1966; entered into force June 8, 1968. 19 UST 5843; TIAS 6540; 652 UNTS 253.

[66] GATT, Article II (1, 7).

[67] GATT, Article III.

[68] GATT, Article XI.

[69] GATT, Article XVII. This prohibition is subject to the exception of government procurement for its own use.

[70] GATT, Article VII (valuation of imported merchandise), Article VIII (customs fees and formalities), Article IX (country of origin marking), and Article X (publication of trade regulations).

[71] Convention revising the Paris Convention of March 20, 1988, as revised, for the Protection of Industrial Property. Done at Stockholm, July 4, 1967. 21 UST 1583; 24 UST 2140; TIAS 6923, 7727.

[72] Universal Copyright Convention, as revised, with two protocols annexed thereto. Done at Paris, July 24, 1971; entered into force July 10, 1974. 25 UST 1341; TIAS 7868.

[73] Ibid., Article 1.

[74] Patent Cooperation Treaty, with regulations. Done at Washington, D.C., June 19, 1970; entered into force January 24, 1978. 28 UST 7645; TIAS 8733.

[75] U.S.-Korea Agreement Relating to the Reciprocal Granting and Protection of the Right of Priority of Patents. Exchange of notes at Seoul, October 30, 1978. 30 UST 2183; TIAS 9324.

[76] Article 2 of the Berne Convention for the Protection of Literary and Artistic Works of September 9, 1986, completed at Paris on May 4, 1896, revised at Berlin on November 13, 1908; completed at Berne on March 20, 1914; and revised at Rome on June 2, 1928; at Brussels on June 26, 1948; at Stockholm on July 14, 1967; and at Paris on July 24, 1971, and amended in 1979.

[77] Ibid., at Article 4.

[78] See Article 17, Copyright Law (1985) and Article 14, Patent Law (1987) of the People's Republic of China.

[79] For information concerning the 48 Commerce Department district offices, contact:

U.S. & Foreign Commercial Service
International Trade Administration
Department of Commerce
14th and Constitution Avenue, Room 3804
Washington, D.C. 20230
(202) 377-5777

[80] *Lee and Li Bulletin* (Taipei: Lee & Li, Attorneys-at-Law, September 1987).

[81] "U.S. Companies Curb Pirating of Some Items but by No Means All," *The Wall Street Journal*, March 16, 1989, p. A1.

[82] *The Reuter Library Report*, June 30, 1988.

[83] J. Dunphy, S. Dryden, E. Kean, and S. Ushio, 143 *Chemical Bank* 26, July 27, 1988.

[84] "Entertainment Industry Adds Anti-Piracy Tricks," *The New York Times*, November 21, 1988, p. 8.

[85] Convention on the Recognition and Enforcement of Foreign Arbitral Awards. Done at New York, June 10, 1958; entered into force June 7, 1959. 21 UST 2517; TIAS 6997; 330 UNTS 3.

[86] See Sections 30–32, Statute of Commercial Arbitration of the Republic of China.

[87] Because most of these trade negotiations are concluded by exchange of unpublished letters between the governments, potential exporters should contact the Commerce Department district offices for up-to-date information concerning access to a particular market in the Far East. See note 79.

[88] For further information concerning the "Buy American Promotion Mission," contact:

Economic Division
Coordination Council for North American Affairs
4301 Connecticut Avenue, N.W., Suite 420
Washington, D.C. 20008
(202) 686-6400

[89] *Annual Report of the President of the United States on the Trade Agreements Program*, 1988.

[90] A copy of the U.S.-China maritime agreement may be obtained from the U.S. Trade Representatives Office, Washington, D.C.

[91] "Sears Trade Unit Shifts Focus," *The New York Times*, December 2, 1988, p. D1.

[92] "Japan's Trading Giants Look to Year 2000," *The Wall Street Journal*, March 31, 1986, p. 23.

CHAPTER 3

PROBLEMS AND CONCERNS IN DOING BUSINESS IN THE FAR EAST

Robert F. Cushman
James M. Steinberg

While the U.S. government has provided economic incentives and engaged in other efforts to stimulate its export economy, several aspects of U.S. law can inadvertently trap businesses trying to compete on an equal footing in foreign nations. This chapter will discuss some of the U.S. legal restrictions, limitations, and other factors U.S. businesspeople should keep in mind when doing business abroad. These range from laws and regulations by which the U.S. government has attempted to regulate overseas conduct to the impact of international transactions on U.S. laws. Most of the items we discuss are not endemic to the Far East, but apply when doing business with others located in any foreign jurisdiction. Beyond the scope of this chapter, however, are the more specialized areas of U.S. tax treatment in the context of foreign business relations and securities laws applicability to foreign transactions involving securities.

IMPROPER PAYMENTS

Bribes, kickbacks, payoffs, extortion payments, political contributions, facilitating or grease payments, and other improper payments have been an accepted international custom and integral part of doing business in many countries, especially those still in the developing stage, since at least the 1600s.[1] Although such accommodation payments are considered a normal fact of life in most countries, the United States has long condemned such practices as being morally and ethically repugnant and an improper use of corporate funds. The United States has attempted to limit these practices through general application of various laws that were not specifically intended to combat such activities, such as in the tax and antitrust areas. Use of such laws has been only mildly effective in deterring improper foreign payments, in part because such laws were applied to domestic activity rather than conduct occurring abroad.[2] In 1977, however, in the wake of the Watergate scandal and the revelation by many multinational corporations of the widespread use of improper foreign payments, Congress enacted the Foreign Corrupt Practices Act (FCPA),[3] aimed at eliminating such type of activity.[4]

Foreign Corrupt Practices Act

The FCPA operates through two basic mechanisms, an antibribery provision aimed directly at prohibited improper payments and an accounting and record-keeping provision aimed at preventing use of "off-the-books" devices frequently employed to hide improper payments.

Antibribery Provisions

The antibribery sections essentially prohibit all U.S. concerns,[5] and their directors, officers, employees, agents, and stockholders acting on their behalf, from offering, giving, paying, or promising to give anything of value (or authorizing anyone to do any of the foregoing) corruptly to any "foreign official" for the purpose of obtaining or retaining business for itself or others.[6] In this context, Congress has included as a "foreign official"[7] all officers, employees, and representatives of foreign governments and their agencies and departments; all foreign political parties and their officials; all candidates for foreign political office; and any other person where it is known[8] that such person will in any manner make available to any of the foregoing "foreign officials" all or a part of such "thing of value."

Recognizing that certain practices should not be outlawed, Congress has not prohibited facilitating, or grease, payments to foreign officials for the purpose of expediting or securing the performance of routine governmental actions. Thus, for example, the FCPA was not designed to reach small gratuity payments to customs officials to expedite shipment of products through customs or to operators to ensure placement of transatlantic calls to secure required permits.[9] As the FCPA applies only in the context of foreign officials, Congress also has not sought to prohibit "private" foreign corruption.

Finally, payments or gifts not directly related to "obtaining or retaining" business are not proscribed.[10] For example, if a U.S. concern in the middle of performing a substantial contract with a foreign government were to give a high-ranking foreign official a solid gold replica of the contract product suitable for office display, there probably would be no FCPA violation (unless the purpose of the gift was to influence future business decisions). It should be noted, however, if any of the permitted payments described here are not properly recorded, then companies subject to the accounting provisions described in the next section may, nevertheless, be in violation of the FCPA. Furthermore, other laws used to combat corrupt payments before enactment of the FCPA may also be violated by such payment practices.

In addition to certain allowed activities discussed above, the FCPA provides two explicit defenses to conduct that otherwise technically would violate the FCPA. First, the payment to a foreign official was lawful under local *written* law or regulation.[11] Second, the payment was a reasonable and bona fide payment or expenditure (such as travel or lodging) incurred by a foreign official directly in relation to the promotion, demonstration, or explanation of a product or service or the execution or performance of a contract.[12]

Companies doing business abroad need to be aware of the FCPA because of the potential penalties and the potentially broad reach of the statute. Under the FCPA, there is apparently no *deminimus* exception for small violations. Even an offer of a $1 gift to a foreign diplomat to retain business would be a technical violation. Furthermore, no payment need actually be made; an offer or promise is prohibited.

One of the major criticisms of the FCPA is the hasty fashion in which it was passed by Congress and the resulting ambiguity that has led to confusion as to its potential reach.[13] Too many terms are not adequately defined. For example, although the term *foreign official* plainly includes political statesmen and representatives of foreign governments, it is less clear whether it would also reach officers and employees of nationalized industries.[14] This problem is of special concern in the Far East because of the high level of government participation with and control over industries. Similarly, what is the dividing line between routine and non-routine governmental actions? What determines whether a payment was made corruptly? Generally, extortion payments are not proscribed, but any payment or gift intended as a bribe is, irrespective of whether it achieves its purpose.[15]

Also, the FCPA has broad reach because of its inclusion of agents and employees, an area that should be of special concern for U.S. companies operating in the Far East. Because of the language and cultural differences, it is often necessary or advantageous for U.S. companies to retain intermediaries through which to deal with foreign governments. Also, U.S. companies often find it advantageous to establish offices in the Far East that employ Far Eastern citizens. In either case, such individuals having been raised in a culture where influence payments may be a way of life, it may be difficult for the U.S. company to control the actions of its agents and employees. Yet, FCPA liability can ensue for actions of employees and agents that exceed the scope of their authority or even are contrary to express instruction.[16] A U.S. company can take certain measures, however, to minimize the potential for such liability, including setting up foreign subsidiary corporations (rather than branch offices or divisions) and setting forth company policies that prohibit such payments.[17] Also, before engaging any agents, U.S. companies should require them to represent that they in no way are related to or connected with any foreign official and to specifically undertake not to share their fees with any foreign official and not to violate the FCPA in any other fashion. Further, payment of fees should be made directly to the agents, and should not exceed a reasonable amount given the nature of the services rendered.[18]

As mentioned, the other reason U.S. companies should not dismiss lightly the FCPA is because of the stiff penalties that may be imposed for violations. Upon conviction, U.S. companies face a potential fine of up to $2 million for each violation.[19] Stockholders acting on a U.S. concern's behalf and its directors and officers who are convicted of having willfully violated the FCPA may be fined up to $100,000 and/or imprisoned for up to five years.[20] Agents and employees who are convicted of having willfully carried out the activities that constituted the FCPA violation and who are subject to U.S. jurisdiction face a similar potential fine and period of incarceration.[21] Also, civil penalties of up to $10,000 may be imposed even if there is not enough evidence to result in a criminal conviction.[22] Finally, the FCPA forbids U.S. companies from directly or indirectly paying for any such fines on behalf of its stockholders, directors, employees, or agents, and therefore, any indemnification undertakings will be unenforceable.[23]

Accounting Provisions
Section 102 of the FCPA imposes on issuers (SEC reporting companies) regulated under the Securities Exchange Act of 1934 (the 1934 Act) the general obligation to keep accurate books and records in reasonable detail and the duty to establish accounting controls sufficient to prevent the use of "off-the-book" slush funds and other devices used to disguise illegal payments.[24] This Section also requires SEC reporting companies to periodically verify the accuracy of the books and records by inventorying assets and to take appropriate action to correct any resulting discrepancies.[25] This Section does not prohibit illegal payments, but it is violated where such payments are not reflected in the SEC reporting company's books. Most of the critical focus on the FCPA to date has been on the accounting provisions, and there is, therefore, much scholarly commentary regarding its scope, interpretation, and application.[26] Even if the SEC reporting company becomes involved in improper payments that are not prohibited under the antibribery provisions of the FCPA, the company might be in violation of Section 102 if such payments are not accurately reflected in its books and records.[27]

Enforcement

One of the more unusual features of the FCPA is its dual enforcement. The Securities and Exchange Commission (SEC) is responsible for civil enforcement of the accounting and antibribery violations by SEC reporting companies and for bringing criminal violations by SEC reporting companies to the attention of the Department of Justice (DOJ). The DOJ is charged with responsibility for the criminal enforcement of all violations of the FCPA and for civil enforcement of violations by all non-SEC reporting companies.[28] To avoid potential violations, companies may seek DOJ review of a specific proposed arrangement before its implementation. A U.S. company that intends to do business in the Far East may wish to avail itself of this review process before entering into questionable relationships.[29]

The enactment of the FCPA has been credited with the curtailment of foreign illegal payments.[30] The United States and Sweden are the only countries, however, to have enacted legislation aimed directly at affecting the conduct of their businesses in other countries.[31] Thus, the FCPA has been criticized for damaging the ability of U.S. concerns to compete on an equal footing in countries where bribes are an accepted means of doing business. It is interesting to note, however, that relatively few enforcement actions of public record have been brought under the antibribery provisions of the FCPA since its enactment.[32]

Other Bases of Liability

Because the Congressional House Conference expressly rejected a Senate proposal that would have made the FCPA the sole basis of criminal liability for proscribed acts,[33] it is necessary to be aware that other statutes may be violated by the payment of foreign bribes and might serve as an independent basis for criminal prosecution or liability. Unlike the FCPA, which reaches conduct occurring principally abroad (so long as the U.S. jurisdictional basis exists), violations of these other statues will exist only where there is action within the United States that constitutes the crime. The major applicable statutes are:

• Mail Fraud Act—prohibits use of the U.S. mails in connection with any scheme to defraud; potential penalty is $1,000 fine and/or five years in prison.[34]
• Wire Fraud Act—prohibits use of the wire, television, or radio in connection with any scheme to defraud; potential penalty is $1,000 fine and/or five years in prison.[35]

• False Statements Act—violation for any person to knowingly and willfully falsify, conceal, or cover up a material fact or make or use false representations or statements in writing in any matter involving a U.S. department or agency; potential penalty is $10,000 fine and/or five years in prison.[36]

• False Claims Act—violation for any person to knowingly present to the U.S. government a false or fraudulent claim for payment or approval; potential civil penalty of $5,000 to $10,000, plus three times the amount of damages the government sustains.[37]

• Section 162(c) of the Internal Revenue Code—prohibits tax deduction for bribes and kickbacks to governmental officials or any other person if such payments are illegal (under the FCPA or otherwise).[38]

• Various antitrust laws—including Section 1 of the Sherman Act, making it unlawful to conspire in restraint of trade or commerce with foreign nations (discussed more fully later in this chapter), and the Robinson-Patman Act, making it unlawful for any person engaged in commerce to make or receive payments as commissions or allowances, except for reasonable compensation for services rendered in connection with the sale or purchase of goods.[39]

• Racketeer Influenced and Corrupt Organizations Act (RICO)—makes it unlawful for any person to engage in a "pattern of racketeering activity," or to use income derived from that pattern of activity to acquire an interest in an enterprise engaged in interstate or foreign commerce, or to conduct the affairs of the enterprise through a pattern of racketeering activity; potential criminal penalty is a fine and/or twenty years in prison and forfeiture of any interest acquired in violation of RICO; potential civil damages include recovery by private plaintiffs of treble damages, plus attorney's fees.[40]

Of these, and in light of the prior chapter on U.S. incentives, the False Claims Act and False Statements Act may have the broadest reach over companies doing business in the Far East that receive some U.S. financial support (in the form of subsidies or low-interest loans) because many filings are required in connection with such incentive programs, some of which may include information on foreign payments and commissions. For example, the U.S. Department of Agriculture has a Bonus Incentive Commodity Exports Program (BICEP) providing subsidies to eligible exporters of qualifying commodities to help them compete with non-U.S. exporters receiving similar subsidies from their governments. In connection with the subsidy, the exporter may not provide any secret commissions or rebates to the purchaser or its agent and must certify it has not done so in the application with the Department of Agriculture. Thus, payment of a bribe to a foreign official in connection with a BICEP-subsidized sales order could constitute a violation of both the False Claims Act and the False Statements Act.

SOVEREIGN IMMUNITY AND ACT OF STATE DOCTRINES

Because so much business with Far Eastern countries is apt to be directly with foreign governments or their agencies, state trade associations, or nationalized or state-controlled companies, it is important for U.S. businesspeople to be aware that there may be limits on their ability to enforce contracts and other dealings with such entities in U.S. courts.[41] This section will discuss the historical underpinnings for such limitations and why they have left us in a state of uncertainty. This section also will recommend steps the U.S. businessperson can take to minimize the attendant risks in the enforceability of such contracts.

Sovereign Immunity

Although theoretically limited by international law, which governs the relations between sovereigns, as a practical matter, each country has the ability to determine the extraterritorial reach of its own laws. Nevertheless, in international law, the rule developed that a foreign state cannot be made subject to the jurisdiction of any court without its express written consent. This rule came to be known as the *doctrine of sovereign immunity*. Even though based on public policy considerations of comity, the rule prevented U.S. courts from asserting jurisdiction over any cause of action involving a foreign sovereign, whether of a public or private nature.[42] Thus, U.S. concerns with disputes with foreign sovereigns with which they were doing business generally were not able to bring suit in U.S. courts and needed to resort to the courts of the foreign sovereign.

Because sovereign states have become much more directly and heavily involved in commercial activity since the inception of the rule, the modern doctrine has been held to be inapplicable to commercial activity of the sovereign, thereby permitting courts jurisdiction over such activity. The U.S. Congress codified this restrictive approach to the doctrine in 1976 in enacting the Foreign Sovereign Immunity Act (FSIA).[43] The commercial character of activity is to be determined by reference to the nature of the course of conduct of the parties, or to the nature of the particular transaction or act, rather than to the activity's purpose.[44] The test focuses on whether the activity in question is of a private or public nature. Under the FSIA, the commercial activity must, at a minimum, have a direct effect in the United States in order for a foreign state to be subject to suit in American courts based on such activity.[45]

Act of State Doctrine

Sovereign immunity deals principally with U.S. courts' jurisdiction over foreign states and requires the naming of a foreign sovereign as a defendant before it will be available. A judicially crafted rule known as the *act of state doctrine* developed as a corollary to sovereign immunity, although it has since taken on a life of its own. The act of state rule precludes a U.S. court from inquiring into the validity or legality of acts of a foreign sovereign done within its own borders.[46] Thus, the rule has been used as a defense, by both foreign sovereigns and private defendants, once U.S. jurisdiction is determined to exist.

The *act of state doctrine* has not received clear or uniform treatment by U.S. courts, which have developed a number of applications and exceptions in an attempt to ameliorate its often harsh results.[47] For example, in 1976 a plurality of the Supreme Court created a commercial activities exception (similar to the restrictive sovereign immunity approach).[48] This exception has not gained wide acceptance in the lower courts, which have applied other tests, including a balancing test that focuses on the distinction between the public and private nature of the conduct, and a case-by-case approach.[49] This state of confusion has permitted U.S. private defendants to use the act of state doctrine as a shield against their own alleged wrongdoing (i.e., where they motivated the sovereign's acts or benefited by them), thereby diluting the effectiveness of the federal antitrust and securities laws, the FSIA, and the FCPA.[50]

Ramifications on Contracting in the Far East

Because of the inherent conflict between the sovereign immunity and act of state doctrines and the U.S. courts' failure in all instances to distinguish between them analytically, it has become difficult to predict whether U.S. jurisdiction will be available to resolve disputes involving

U.S. businesspeople trading or otherwise doing business with foreign states.[51] Being unclear as to the applicable law can influence the performance of contracts and liabilities of parties for breach of contract, thereby disrupting the stability of commercial transactions.

U.S. businesspeople ought to consider several provisions in contracting with foreign governments and controlled industries to minimize the potential impact of these doctrines. In order to preserve the ability to litigate disputes in the United States, use of a the contract should contain a U.S. choice of jurisdiction clause, combined with an express waiver of sovereign immunity.

Even with the existence of such a clause, for a variety of reasons a lawsuit might nevertheless be instituted initially in another jurisdiction. The conflict of rules laws of the forum usually will control in determining which jurisdiction's governing law will apply to the contract. Because most jurisdictions' conflict of rules laws are not codified and are ill-defined, where the contract is silent it is very difficult to predict which country's substantive laws will control in determining the rights of the parties. This will depend on where suit is ultimately brought. Thus, the contract should also contain a U.S. governing law clause to attempt some predictability as to the application of the doctrines.*

A different and perhaps better solution, which usually avoids the impact of these doctrines, is to agree upon use of commercial arbitration to resolve disputes. Arbitration clauses in agreements are frequently, although not always, upheld by courts in most jurisdictions.[52] Arbitration is a speedy, fair, and relatively inexpensive process by which parties to the dispute pick third parties, who are usually experts, to render a decision. The four fundamental matters to be provided for in anticipation of arbitration are the form of arbitration (i.e., ad hoc or under an already existing institution),[53] the place where it will occur, the procedure to be followed, and the substantive law to be applied.

By contract, the parties can agree that the arbitration can be located anywhere throughout the world and may be governed under rules of their choosing. Arbitration proceedings (both as to the nature of the dispute and specific facts and documents), unlike court proceedings, are confidential. Another advantage is that arbitration panels generally are more neutral than are courts in any given country. Also, public or state-owned

---

*Of course, this discussion assumes that the foreign contracting party will agree to the choice of jurisdiction and governing law clauses, which often may not be the case.

entities that might otherwise claim immunity from the jurisdiction of national courts are usually willing to submit to arbitration disputes relating to business transactions with private parties from other countries.

The other major advantage of arbitration is that, although courts do not generally enforce the judgments of courts located in other jurisdictions, many will honor and enforce the results of arbitration because their countries have ratified or adhered to the major international arbitration conventions, which provide rules for the enforcement of foreign arbitration awards.[54] The United States, Japan, Korea, the People's Republic of China, the Philippines, and Thailand are parties to the New York Convention on the Recognition and Enforcement of Foreign Arbitral Awards 1958, pursuant to which each shall recognize arbitration awards decided in member countries.[55]

ANTITRUST LAWS

The U.S. antitrust laws were enacted in response to the increasing use of trusts to form business combinations and were intended to preserve competition in the marketplace and thereby ensure the continuance of the free enterprise system. Application of the antitrust laws to interstate commerce is well-understood and developed. Their application to foreign commerce, although dating back to the infancy of the antitrust laws, is less developed, and the number of decided cases in this area remains relatively small.

Important Antitrust Laws

At the outset, it is important to mention the major U.S. antitrust laws applicable to foreign commerce. The purpose of this discussion is not to provide an exhaustive analysis, which is beyond the scope of this chapter and better left to separate treatise on the subject matter,[56] but to alert the U.S. businessperson to their existence and general applicability. Also, the development of these laws has occurred primarily in the context of purely domestic situations, but for the most part should apply equally to foreign commerce situations.

Sherman Act
The Sherman Antitrust Act (the Sherman Act) is the preeminent U.S. antitrust statute. Enacted in 1890, it provides in Section 1 that "[e]very

contract, combination in the form of trust or otherwise, or conspiracy, in restraint of trade or commerce among the several States, or with foreign nations, is hereby declared to be illegal. . . ."[57] Section 2 of the Sherman Act makes it a crime to "monopolize, or attempt to monopolize, or combine or conspire with any other person or persons, to monopolize any part of the trade or commerce among the several States, or with foreign nations. . . ."[58] The Sherman Act's major purpose was to preserve and promote unfettered competition in the marketplace. It rests on the premises that free competition will result in the most efficient and best allocation of the country's resources, the highest quality and the lowest prices, while at the same time preserving our democratic, political, and social institutions.[59]

Violations of either Sections 1 or 2 constitute a felony and may result in a maximum fine of $1 million for corporations and $100,000 for any other person.[60] The DOJ through its Antitrust Division has exclusive jurisdiction in the enforcement of the Sherman Act. In addition, civil awards to private plaintiffs injured in business by violation of any antitrust laws are automatically trebled.[61] Recoveries in the millions of dollars by private plaintiffs are not uncommon.

A Section 1 violation requires two or more actors acting in concert to restrain trade.[62] No specific intent is required so long as the natural and probable consequences of the acts would restrain trade. The Supreme Court has adopted a "rule of reason" that holds that only unreasonable or undue (rather than all) restraints of trade are prohibited under Section 1.[63] This generally requires a case-by-case analysis. However, several types of restraints aimed at raising, depressing, fixing, pegging, or stabilizing prices are held by the courts to be unreasonable per se (irrespective of the reasonableness of any aspect of the actual actions), including horizontal price fixing,[64] group boycotts,[65] divisions of market territories,[66] agreements to limit production or control supply,[67] allocation of customers,[68] division of fields of production,[69] and use of patent-tying clauses.[70] Although the amount of commerce affected generally is immaterial under Section 1 in the domestic context, where extraterritorial conduct is concerned the courts generally have required the existence of a substantial amount of U.S. domestic or U.S. foreign commerce.[71]

A Section 2 violation exists when one or more companies or persons possesses monopoly power (i.e., the power to fix prices or exclude competitors), coupled with the intent and purpose to exercise or maintain this power.[72] Section 2 is principally concerned, however, with unilateral behavior that seeks unwarranted control over a particular market. Thus, monopoly power obtained as a consequence of superior product, business acumen, or historical accident is not proscribed. Critical to the monopolization case is the relevant geographic and product market, as a sufficiently expansive definition of either generally will avoid liability.[73]

Clayton Act
The Clayton Act contains several pertinent provisions. Section 2 of the Clayton Act (which is Section 1 of the Robinson-Patman Act) condemns price discrimination in the sale of goods within the United States.[74] Section 3 of the Clayton Act, in general, makes it unlawful to sell or lease goods for use or resale in the United States, on condition that the vendee or lessee will not deal in goods of a competitor, where the effect may be to substantially lessen competition or to tend to create a monopoly in any line of commerce.[75] Section 7 prohibits mergers and acquisitions where the effect may be to substantially lessen competition, or to tend to create a monopoly in the industry.[76] The DOJ and Federal Trade Commission (FTC) bear responsibility for enforcing the Clayton Act.

Federal Trade Commission Act
The Federal Trade Commission Act (FTCA) empowers the FTC, with certain exceptions, to prevent persons and corporations from using "unfair methods of competition in or affecting commerce and unfair or deceptive acts or practices in commerce."[77] The FTCA has been held to regulate acts contrary to the antitrust laws, as well as acts not rising to the level of an antitrust violation.[78] Thus, the FTC effectively has concurrent jurisdiction with the DOJ with respect to acts illegal under the antitrust laws. The FTCA has explicitly been extended to cover unfair practices used in export trade against competitors engaged in export trade, even though the acts constituting the unfair method of competition occurred outside of the territorial jurisdiction of the United States.[79]

Import Related Antitrust Laws
The Wilson Tariff Act declares as illegal and void any combination, conspiracy, or agreement between two or more persons, at least one of whom is engaged in importing into the United States any article from a foreign country, that is intended to operate in restraint of lawful trade or to increase the market price of any imported articles or of any manufacturing process that includes such imported articles.[80] Also, under Sec-

tion 337(a) of the Tariff Act of 1930, as amended, it is illegal in importing articles into the United States or selling imported articles within the United States to use unfair methods of competition or unfair acts that would have the effect or tendency to destroy, substantially injure, or prevent the establishment of domestic industry that is efficiently and economically operated.[81] The International Trade Commission is charged with enforcing this act.

U.S. Jurisdiction in the Foreign Trade Area

As noted, the Sherman Act, Clayton Act, and FTCA by their express terms reach activities affecting U.S. foreign trade. Foreign commerce antitrust cases to date have involved various international commercial activities, such as licensing of technology, acquisitions, and joint ventures and have focused primarily on the U.S. import and export effect from those activities.[82] It is clear that these and the other applicable antitrust laws govern U.S.-based conduct of U.S. entities. The courts have also generally had no difficulty asserting jurisdiction over foreign subsidiaries of U.S. companies (concerning their activity with a direct U.S. effect), treating the subsidiaries as extensions of their parents.[83] Jurisdiction will also lie against foreign citizens or corporations operating in the United States.[84] It has remained the subject of jurisprudential interpretation, however, to determine whether and to what extent the antitrust laws reach conduct of U.S. and non-U.S. entities occurring wholly outside of the United States.[85]

The basic rule, known as the *objective territorial principle*, provides that U.S. jurisdiction will lie for extraterritorial conduct where it can be shown that such conduct has a direct, substantial, and foreseeable effect on U.S. foreign or domestic commerce.[86] The rule has been applied most frequently in the import context, as anticompetitive export activity, by its nature, usually provides the jurisdictional basis.[87] It is generally required that there be both an intent to affect and an actual effect on U.S. commerce.[88] Such intent may be actual (e.g., based on the express terms of an agreement) or inferred from the surrounding circumstances. It should also be noted that the jurisdictional test has become clouded in recent years as some courts have adopted a balancing, or "rule of reason," test that places greater consideration on other nations' interests and on the full relationship between the actors and this country.[89]

Although the jurisdictional approach is neither clearly defined nor uniformly applied, the U.S. businessperson needs to be aware that his or her activity abroad might be subject to U.S. antitrust constraints if it has a substantial effect on U.S. commerce. Conversely, the U.S. antitrust laws probably do not reach conduct of U.S. concerns in other jurisdictions (e.g., price-fixing) so long as the effects are confined solely to other jurisdictions (although such conduct might implicate antitrust laws of those other jurisdictions). Because it may be possible to attribute some U.S. effect to any conduct abroad, U.S. businesses should always proceed with caution when contemplating engaging in any activity that would clearly be a violation of the U.S. antitrust laws if occurring within the United States.

INTELLECTUAL PROPERTY

This section briefly will discuss some of the problems (aside from antitrust concerns) in the intellectual property areas of patents, trademarks, and copyrights that may be implicated in international commercial intercourse. The doctrine of nationality provides that each jurisdiction's protection granted over intellectual property is limited to rights within that jurisdiction.[90] Thus, it is generally necessary for U.S. businesses to file for and secure such protection separately in each jurisdiction in which doing business. Various multilateral treaties do provide limited rights among member nations that permit coordinated filing procedures and reciprocal enforcement relating to intellectual property, and this section will focus on such procedures.

Furthermore, the availability and scope of protection granted upon intellectual property differs among jurisdictions. For example, some countries afford patent protection to inventions not patentable in the United States. Such a discussion is beyond the scope of this chapter as the outcome will depend on the type of property and the country in which protection is sought.

Patents

The U.S. patent laws generally accord priority patent rights to inventors based on the time when they conceived of the invention and first reduced it to practice so long as they file a patent application within one year from such time (irrespective of whether the patent application was filed before a later inventor of the same invention). Under most foreign countries' patents laws, including China and Japan, priority is based on the first inventor to file (irrespective of the date of actual invention). In any case, patent protection usually will not issue for lack of novelty if there exists a prior publication describing or disclosing the invention within a certain period of time prior to the application. Further, the life of U.S. patents is 17 years from the date of grant, without payment of fees, whereas the life of most foreign patents commences from the patent application date and requires payment of an annual fee to continue the patent in effect.

To obtain foreign patents corresponding to the U.S. patent, it is generally necessary to file the application in the foreign jurisdiction within specific time periods from the date of filing in the United States. Conversely, the U.S. patent laws provide that the U.S. application date of an invention for which a foreign application has already been filed shall, if such foreign country provides reciprocal rights, have the same effective date as the foreign application if filed within 12 months of one another.[91] Thus, coordinating the application process can be critical to obtaining worldwide patent protection of inventions.

The Patent Cooperation Treaty (PCT), which the United States, Japan, and Korea have adopted, provides for a coordinated international application process which facilitates the acquisition of parallel patents. Under the PCT, inventors from member countries generally will have a period of up to 20 months from the earliest filing date of a patent application in which to seek patent protection in other member jurisdictions.[92] This is because the PCT provides for an international search report of the prior art (to determine if the invention is patentable), which may take up to 18 months to produce.

Under the Paris Convention for the Protection of Industrial Property, on the other hand, a right of priority in an invention exists for at most 12 months from the date of the earliest filing of a patent application in any member country.[93] Furthermore, under the Paris Convention, member countries will accord the same patent protection to patents belonging to citizens of other member countries as it accords to its own citizens (this right is sometimes referred to as "national treatment" or "assimilation with nationals"). Nearly all sovereign states are members of the Paris Convention.[94]

The major advantage of the PCT over the Paris Convention is the ability to obtain the international search report before incurring various foreign filing fees, the longer filing priority period, and a single application for obtaining a multitude of foreign patents. The PCT and Paris Convention do not supersede one another. Rather, the two may be used in concert to the benefit of United States inventors. Because of the intricate procedures and rules under both vehicles, care must be taken in any coordinated use.

Due to export restrictions, patent applications for inventions made in the United States must be filed in the United States first unless an export license has been obtained from the U.S. Patent & Trademark Office (PTO). Further, without such an export license or appropriate export agency authority, parallel applications generally may not be filed in foreign countries until six months after the U.S. filing date.[95] Failure to obtain an effective export license could result in a loss of patent rights in the United States.[96]

Trademarks

In the United States, trademark protection is provided to the first user of a mark, irrespective of trademark registration, although federal registration provides certain benefits. In most other countries, the first registrant of a mark enjoys exclusive rights to that mark, irrespective of first use. Thus, a company planning to engage in substantial international commerce under a trademark or service mark should consider registering that mark in foreign countries in order to avoid usurpation of the mark. In either case, however, registration generally is desirable.

There are essentially two types of foreign trademark registration protection: national and multinational. National refers to separate filing within each country to obtain trademark protection under the laws of that country. Contrary to the United States, most foreign countries do not require actual use of the mark in the country before filing an application to register the mark.[97] Multinational refers to treaties that provide that filing in one country accords trademark protection under the national laws of other designated member countries. A variation of multinational requires separate filing in each country, but certain rights may extend from the first filing. For example, under the Paris Convention, where an application for trademark protection is filed in a member country within six months of filing within another member country, both applications will be entitled to the earlier filing date for purposes of determining priority against other users or filers.

Copyrights

Prior to joining the Berne Convention in 1989, the United States required certain formalities on works of authorship for copyright protection, including use of a notice with the name of the copyright owner, the year of first publication, and the word *copyright*. Copyright notice currently is optional under U.S. law, rather than mandatory for protection. Some countries, however, continue to require a specific form of copyright notice or other formalities for protection, and it is advisable to examine each country's requisites individually.

The United States currently is a member of two international copyright agreements, the Berne Convention and the Universal Copyright Convention (UCC). Japan, the Philippines, and Thailand have also ratified the Berne Convention, and Japan, the Philippines, and Korea have also ratified the UCC.

Significant international copyright protection is available to Americans under the UCC. In order to obtain protection under the UCC each work must contain an appropriate copyright notice with the name of the copyright owner and year of first publication, and, unlike the United States' former requirement to use the word *copyright*, such work must display the symbol ©.

Under the UCC, member nations will accord the same level of copyright protection to nationals of other members as it provides to its own nationals. It is clearly advantageous to provide the notice under the UCC to ensure such protection. Use of such notice will excuse failure to comply with any other formalities a country might otherwise require as a matter of domestic law. For example, a foreign country requiring publication as a prerequisite for protection could refuse to accord copyright protection to an American work published in the United States without the UCC form of notice. Thus, to be safe, copyrighted works should contain both the U.S. and UCC forms of notice.

The protections accorded under the Berne Convention are not subject to any formalities. The Berne Convention was originally established in 1886 and has since undergone numerous amendments. Adherents may have ratified different versions and therefore may be subject to different rules and levels of protection.

The nature of foreign copyright protection is similar to that of the United States in most instances. Copyright protection includes the right of reproduction, adaptation, distribution, and performance, although such protection may differ in scope from country to country. Generally, however, there is no corresponding right in other countries of the U.S. right of display, i.e., the right to publicly show a copy of the protected work, or of the U.S. right to copyright sound recordings.

U.S. Protection of Patents and Trademarks

Sections 337 and 526 of the Tariff Act of 1930 may enable U.S. patent, trademark, and copyright owners to exclude importation of products infringing on their patents, trademarks, and copyrights.[98] This would be true even where the importer may have a license under a parallel foreign patent, trademark, or copyright.

The U.S. International Trade Commission (ITC) has original and nationwide exclusive jurisdiction to issue orders excluding imports and to issue cease and desist orders to prevent the sale of articles already imported. It may do so only where it finds both use of an unfair method of competition by such import and an effect or tendency to destroy or substantially injure an efficiently operated domestic industry, prevent the establishment of one, or restrain or monopolize U.S. trade. Patent, trademark, and copyright infringements are deemed to constitute unfair methods of competition.

Whether a U.S. domestic corporation's foreign subsidiary may be considered part of the domestic industry, and therefore subject to protection under Section 337, will depend in large part on the value added to a product within the United States. An infringer, however, will never be considered as part of the domestic industry in determining whether the injury component under Section 337 exists. A U.S. company that has licensed a foreign company under its foreign patents but has retained its U.S. patent rights generally may invoke Section 337 to exclude the foreign licensee's products from import into the United States (commonly known as *grey market goods*).[99] Such remedies apply only prospectively, however, and do not include monetary damages. Also, U.S. businesses should be aware that they can avail themselves of the ITC's authority to render advisory opinions on contemplated activities that might violate the Tariff Act.[100]

EXPORT CONTROLS

The export of goods and technical data (including technology, know-how, and trade secrets) from the United States generally requires some form of license from the U.S. Department of Commerce's Office of Export Administration (OEA) pursuant to the Export Administration Act of 1979 (EAA).[101] The EAA authorizes the president of the United States to "prohibit or curtail the exportation of any goods, technology, or other information subject to the jurisdiction of the United States or exported by any person subject to the jurisdiction of the United States, to the extent necessary to further significantly the foreign policy of the United States," or for reasons of national security or short supply of scarce goods.[102]

Under the Export Administration Regulations promulgated under the EAA, the OEA has issued a Commodity Control List that lists by category all commodities and the countries to which each may be exported only upon the issuance of a validated license.[103] U.S. exports are generally prohibited until (1) a general license covering the item to be exported has been established (available usually if the export is of low value, of technical data in the public domain, or of goods in transit from one foreign country to another) or (2) unless a specific exporter has obtained a specific authorization, or individual validation, license (also available is a multiple or special validated license to cover several types of goods for specific projects, end-users, or marketing campaigns).[104] Obtaining a validated license under the EAA is often both expensive and time consuming. Further, because technological data may exist in oral form, U.S. businesspeople negotiating abroad without an export license need to be careful not to disclose too much during preliminary negotiations, thereby inadvertently violating the EAA.

Such export controls have been imposed abroad on three types of activity: (1) prohibition on re-export of goods and technology without prior U.S. consent;[105] (2) prohibition on export of items produced by foreign companies if previously exported U.S. technology was employed in the production process;[106] and (3) prohibition on persons subject to U.S. jurisdiction. The rationale underlying the first two types of activity is that goods and technology originating in whole or in part in the United States should remain subject to U.S. jurisdiction and control throughout the entire production and distribution cycle. Re-export controls are therefore justified as being a condition of the original export authorization and are deemed to extend to goods manufactured abroad using technology exported from the United States. The third category has been interpreted broadly to apply to (1) all citizens and residents of the United States, wheresoever located; (2) all persons actually within the United States; (3) all corporations organized under the laws of the United States or any state; and (4) all partnerships, associations, corporations, or other organizations, wheresoever organized or doing business, which are owned or controlled by any of the "persons" identified in (1), (2), or (3).[107] Thus, the re-export activity of a domestic corporation's subsidiaries and controlled joint ventures generally will be subject to the EAA's provisions.

The Omnibus Trade and Competitiveness Act of 1988 has reduced some of the validated license and re-export authorization requirements. Of these, some of the more important are as follows: Validated licenses for direct exports will no longer be necessary on national security grounds to any COCOM country (NATO countries, less Iceland, plus Japan) or Section 5(k) country (i.e., countries that have agreed with the United States to maintain appropriate export controls of their own—the only Far Eastern country currently included is Singapore) on products in a category exportable to the People's Republic of China solely on the basis of notification to COCOM. Also, now exempted from licensing requirements are (1) goods and technology currently on the list for "notice only" to COCOM countries (unless COCOM reasserts its right to maintain the notification requirement), and (2) most medical instruments and equipment.

In the re-export area, national security controls may no longer be placed on goods and technology (excluding supercomputers, some nuclear items, devices to intercept communications, and shipments to blacklisted persons) exported to a COCOM or Section 5(k) country. Also, with respect to U.S. goods incorporated into other products abroad (excluding supercomputers), no re-export controls based on national security may be imposed where (1) the U.S. goods are less than 25 percent of the total value of the new product, or (2) when re-export of the U.S. goods to a Soviet bloc country would require only notification to COCOM. It should be noted, however, that because these exemptions apply only to national security-based controls, they do not apply to controls based on foreign policy or scarce supply.

Violators of the EAA may be subject to civil or criminal sanctions. The civil sanctions include fines of up to $100,000 for each violation involving national security controls (and $10,000 otherwise), suspension or revocation of exporting privileges, prohibition on importation of goods and technical data for those having violated the national security provisions, and confiscation of unauthorized shipments. Criminal sanctions include fines against corporations up to the greater of five times the value of the export or $1 million and, for individuals, fines of up to $250,000 or imprisonment up to 10 years, or both.[108]

EQUAL EMPLOYMENT OPPORTUNITY ABROAD

Title VII of the Civil Rights Act of 1964, which governs the employment of U.S. citizens by U.S. companies, prohibits employment practices that discriminate among U.S. citizens on the basis of race, religion, sex, and national origin.[109] The types of discriminatory practices addressed include the decision to hire (or not to hire) and to fire an employee; the compensation, terms, conditions, and privileges of employment; and any attempt to limit, segregate, or classify an employee in such a way as would deprive or tend to deprive him or her of individual employment opportunities or otherwise hurt his or her status.[110]

U.S. businesses with foreign operations need to be aware that, although not completely resolved by the courts, there is a strong likelihood that Title VII restricts such foreign operation's employment practices involving U.S. citizens.[111] This might create operating difficulties in countries in which discriminatory practices are customary, encouraged, or even required. In many counties in the Far East, for example, foreign customers may prefer to deal with male business representatives. Such preferences would not justify a domestic employer under Title VII from refusing to hire women for that position.[112]

Domestic employers have asserted three arguments as to why Title VII does not reach their employment practices abroad. First, simply that the statute was not intended to reach foreign operations.[113] Second, even if Title VII does apply, its statutory exceptions exempt discrimination required by a foreign country.[114] Third, even if such exceptions are inapplicable, conflict between Title VII and foreign law require deference to the foreign law, thereby excusing noncompliance with Title VII.[115]

The few courts to have addressed Title VII extraterritoriality all have agreed that the statutory language, legislative history, and U.S. administrative interpretation support extraterritorial application.[116] They disagree, however, on whether discriminatory practices abroad may be justified.

Title VII permits discrimination when a bona fide occupational qualification (BFOQ) is reasonably necessary to the normal operation of that particular business.[117] The defense may be based only on religion, sex, or national origin, not on race.[118] The scope of the BFOQ defense is very narrow, having been interpreted as available only when substantially all of the persons of the specified class are unable to perform the job.[119] In one instance, a court rejected an assertion by an employer of the BFOQ defense in the context of foreign customer preferences.[120] In another instance, the court permitted the BFOQ defense where there was concern for employee safety in the host country because of a host country law that required the employer to act in a discriminatory fashion.[121]

Even if the BFOQ defense is rejected or otherwise unavailable, the foreign compulsion defense may be successful to avoid Title VII liability.

That defense, which is corollary to the act of state doctrine discussed earlier in this chapter, essentially provides that acts of a business that are *compelled* by the laws of the foreign country should be considered as acts of the foreign sovereign itself and, hence, sheltered from violations of U.S. laws.[122] This argument has never been tested in the courts in the Title VII context.

Faced with this potential conflict between Title VII and business practices in the Far East, U.S. companies frequently have several choices. They may hire U.S. citizens in violation of Title VII and risk the penalties. They may comply with Title VII and either seek an exemption from the host country as to the application of its laws[123] or act in violation of those laws. It is always possible, however, that instead of an exemption, the host country may revoke the privilege of such a violator to doing business within its jurisdiction, nationalize the foreign operation, or take less drastic measures. Alternatively, the U.S. concern could hire nationals of the foreign country, thereby complying with the foreign country's laws and avoiding application of Title VII (although even this process would have to be tailored to avoid Title VII violations in the hiring process).

IMMIGRATION LAW ASPECTS

Although easily overlooked at first blush, U.S. immigration laws are another concern for those doing business in the Far East. Frequently, when doing business through subsidiaries, branch offices, or joint ventures, the U.S. concern is likely to want to transfer foreign personnel to its operations in the United States.

This can be complicated because of different requirements for the nonimmigrant visa categories, which are not necessarily mutually exclusive and for which ownership structural changes may be required. The tax needs of the client and the sponsoring company may have an impact on strategy, as will the transferee's credentials and personal situation. Also, tradeoffs may exist between immediate visa eligibility and permanent residence status. Finally, several types of visas require a long lead time to prepare and obtain and sufficient forethought should be given to avoid any timing constraints. Thus, a proper business plan should consider anticipated immigration goals and their implications.

Four primary categories of nonimmigrant visas exist. Each has its advantages in terms of limitations on duration of stay, ability to obtain permanent resident status, speed of issuance, and the likelihood of approval on the merits. These categories, in their commonly known forms, are as follows:

1. B-1   Temporary Visitor for Business, key points:

- Admission for a maximum of one year (in increments of six months).
- Individual must be coming on a temporary basis to conduct business, usually for the overseas employer.
- No salary or other remuneration may be paid in the United States (except for expense reimbursement) and the individual may not be employed in the United States.
- Individual must maintain a foreign residence and intend to remain in U.S. temporarily.

2. H-1   Distinguished Merit and Ability, key points:

- Admission for a maximum initial period of three years, with possible extension for two years.
- Temporary employment by U.S. company of foreign national (although position may be permanent).
- Employee must maintain a foreign residence and intend to remain in U.S. temporarily.
- Employee must qualify as "distinguished merit and ability" (i.e., professionals and persons of sufficient renown).
- Application made in United States with Immigration and Naturalization Service (INS).

3. L-1   Intracompany Transferee, key points:

- Available only to a U.S. company with an overseas parent, subsidiary, affiliate, or branch office.
- Admission for a maximum initial period of three years, with possible extension for two years.
- Temporary employment by U.S. company of foreign national (although position may be permanent).
- Employee need not maintain a foreign residence.
- Employee must (1) have been employed abroad in an executive or managerial position or a position involving specialized knowledge; and (2) have been employed for at least one year on a full-time basis with the overseas company.
- U.S. company and overseas company must be "qualifying" in

that they must continue to do business both in the United States and abroad during the entire period of stay of the alien employee.
- Special problems with a new U.S. office.
- Application made with INS.

4. E   Treaty Trader/Investor, key points:

- Treaty of commerce and navigation between United States and foreign country must exist.
- Available to employees or investors, each of whom must be a citizen of the treaty country.
- Majority ownership of investing or trading company must be held by nationals of treaty country.
- Alien must intend to stay in United States temporarily, but need not maintain a foreign residence.
- Admission for an initial period of one year, with possibility for indefinite extensions.
- Application made with U.S. consulate in treaty country.

5. E-1   Treaty Trader:

- Must exist "substantial" trade of goods or services (dependent upon the volume, number of transactions, and continued course of trade) between U.S. company and treaty country; 51 percent of U.S. company's trade must be with the treaty country.
- Employee must perform executive or supervisory duties, or serve in a minor capacity but have qualifications making the services essential to the efficient operation of the U.S. company.

6. E-2   Treaty Investor:

- Treaty country investor must have made, or be in the process of making, a substantial "at risk" (greater than $100,000) investment in a business in the United States.
- Visa available to a key employee or a 51 percent investor.

CONCLUSION

There are many legal, as well as cultural and economic, facets to doing business in the Far East that are particular to each specific country that will be discussed in other chapters of this book. This chapter has attempted to acquaint the U.S. businessperson in general terms with certain U.S. laws, rules, and regulations that are easy to overlook when entering the competitive and culturally different Far Eastern environment, but nevertheless may be inadvertently violated through activities of U.S. businesses or their foreign subsidiaries. These laws are implicated primarily during the course of the ongoing operations, and U.S. businesses should take preventative measures to ensure compliance with their requirements.

It is important to be sensitive to these laws because of the potentially stiff penalties and fines applicable to U.S. corporations and individuals. Furthermore, foreign incorporation does not always insulate the domestic corporation, nor prevent the U.S. laws from reaching the foreign conduct of the foreign subsidiary. Even though we are entering a period where the country realizes it must coordinate and emphasize its export economy, as evidenced by recent amendments to many of these laws and other incentive-related and protectionist-based programs, they remain alive and a part of the fabric of the risks of international business transactions.

Finally, this chapter has also attempted to describe some of the jurisdictional limitations of U.S. laws that may limit the ability of U.S. businesspeople to obtain redress in a hospitable environment of disputes with Far Easterners and of immigration constraints that might affect plans. Both of these generally may be avoided if dealt with in advance during the planning stages.

ENDNOTES

[1] See Note, "The Antibribery Provisions of the Federal Corrupt Practices Act of 1977: Are they really as valuable as they think they are?" 10 *Delaware Journal of Corporate Law* 71, 72 (1985).

[2] G. Greanias and D. Windsor, *The Foreign Corrupt Practices Act—Anatomy of a Statute* (Lexington, Mass.: Lexington Books, 1982), pp. 12–13. The purpose underlying such statutes was related to a larger scheme of government regulation and control with little or no extraterritorial coverage. Provisions of such statutes were used to combat foreign corrupt payments because no other tools were available. As discussed later in the text, enactment of the FCPA does not render such statutes inapplicable to foreign corrupt payments, and thus they need also be considered by exporting or multinational businesses.

[3] 15 U.S.C. Sections 78m(b), (d)(1), (g)-(h), 78dd-1 to 2, 78ff (a), (c) (1982), as amended by Section 5003 of the Foreign Corrupt Practices Act Amendments

of 1988 (contained in the Omnibus Trade and Competitiveness Act of 1988, P.L. 100-418 [H.R. 4848] (102 Stat. 1107, 3806), Part I, Subtitle A, Title V) (hereinafter referred to as the FCPA 1988 Amendments).

[4] See R. von Mehren, "Introduction to the Foreign Corrupt Practices Act of 1977—Law, Procedures and Practices," in *10th Annual Institute on Securities Regulation* (Practicing Law Institute, New York, N.Y., 1979), p. 67, ed. A. Fleischer, Jr., M. Lipton, and R. Stevenson, Jr. Some of the more sensational public disclosures included payment of more than $1.25 million by United Brands Company to decrease Honduras tax on bananas, $2 million by Lockheed Corporation to secure sales of its planes to Japan, and $3 million by Gulf Oil Corporation to create a favorable operating climate in Korea. For a table showing a more complete listing of such payments, see Greanias and Windsor, pp. 20–23.

[5] The antibribery portion of the FCPA is contained in two separate but parallel sections.

Section 103 of the FCPA applies to any "issuer which has a class of securities registered pursuant to section 12 . . . or is required to file reports under section 15(d)" of the Securities Exchange Act of 1934. These are commonly referred to as SEC reporting companies. Section 103 was implemented by adding a new Section 30A and by amending Section 32 of the 1934 Act.

Section 104 of the FCPA applies to all "domestic concerns" (except SEC reporting companies), defined to include individuals who are citizens, nationals, or residents of the United States and entities organized or having their principal place of business in the United States. Excluded from this broad definition are foreign subsidiaries of U.S. domestic concerns. The legislative history makes clear, however, that the U.S. domestic concern will be in violation of the FCPA for an illegal payment by its foreign subsidiary unless it acted *wholly* without the knowledge or approval of its parent. See Conference Report, No. 95-834, to accompany S. 305, 95th Cong., 1st Sess., 14 (1977) (hereinafter referred to as 1977 Conference Report).

[6] Federal jurisdiction will exist so long as there has been some use of the U.S. mails or other means of interstate commerce in furtherance of the improper payment. See generally Section 30A of the 1934 Act, Section 104 of the FCPA. Although this suggests that no jurisdiction will lie where the activity relating to the improper payment originates and is consummated within the foreign country, as a practical matter, so long as the U.S. concern has some knowledge or should have some knowledge (i.e., it cannot avoid the FCPA by "looking the other way"), there will always exist some direct or indirect use of the jurisdictional means that will subject the U.S. concern to the FCPA.

[7] The term *foreign official* is defined more narrowly in Sections 30A(f)(1) of the 1934 Act and 104(h)(2) of the FCPA, but is used in this chapter to include all categories of persons to whom it is improper under the FCPA to make or offer illegal payments.

[8] The "knowledge" issue arises most frequently where U.S. concerns retain foreign agents. The standard by which a U.S. concern will be deemed to have "knowledge" under the FCPA is unclear, especially since it was changed by the FCPA 1988 Amendments. Although it is a mixed objective and subjective test, a U.S. concern cannot avoid liability by deliberately avoiding learning of the truth. Knowledge may be inferred where there is high probability of the existence of a fact (such as an improper payment) and where the U.S. concern is unable to establish that it had an honest belief to the contrary. See Section 30A(f)(2) of the 1934 Act, Section 104(h)(3) of the FCPA. See also, House Conference Report 576, 100th Cong., 2nd Sess., pp. 919–21 (April 20, 1988) (hereinafter referred to as Conference Report).

[9] See Sections 30A(b), (f)(3) of the 1934 Act, Sections 104(b), h(4) of the FCPA. Routine governmental actions include ordinary and common actions of government officials in obtaining permits, licenses, and other documents to qualify a person to do business in the foreign jurisdiction, processing governmental papers such as visas and work orders, scheduling inspections associated with contract performance, and loading and unloading cargo and similar activities.

[10] The legislative history seems to confine offending payments to those made to influence the direction of business or the enactment of legislation or regulations aimed directly for the benefit of a particular proponent of business. See Senate Report 114, 95th Cong., 1st Sess., 10, 17 (May 2, 1977) (hereinafter referred to as Senate Report). It is unclear, however, whether the FCPA reaches improper payments in connection with the implementation of contracts. It also can be said the legislature did not intend the FCPA to prohibit lobbying or similar activities with government officials. See Conference Report, pp. 918–19.

[11] Section 30A(c)(1) of the 1934 Act, Section 104(c)(1) of the FCPA.

[12] Section 30A(c)(2) of the 1934 Act, Section 104(c)(2) of the FCPA.

[13] See L. Longobardi, "Reviewing the Situation: What Is to Be Done with the Foreign Corrupt Practice Act," *Vanderbilt Journal of Transnational Law* 20 (1987), p. 442. The recent FCPA 1988 Amendments were enacted, in part, in response to such criticism in an attempt to clarify the application of the FCPA.

[14] See *10th Annual Institute on Securities Regulation*, p. 74.

[15] "The word *corruptly* connotes an evil motive or purpose, an intent to wrongfully influence the recipient. It does not require that the act be fully consummated or succeed in producing the desired outcome." Report of the Senate Committee on Banking, Housing and Urban Affairs to accompany S. 305, 95th Cong., 1st Sess., p. 10 (1977). See also Senate Report, pp. 10–11.

[16] See J. Best, *Review of Securities Regulation* II, no. 3 (Feb. 13, 1978), pp. 6–7 (reprinted with permission in *SEC Enforcement and White Collar Crime* II) (New York, N.Y.: Law Journal Seminars-Press Inc., 1979). The legislative history does suggest, however, that the FCPA was not intended to establish

vicarious liability for U.S. concerns where a faraway agent had "run amok" and was not acting pursuant to corporate order.

Also, the conference rejected a House-passed provision to the recent FCPA 1988 Amendments that would have denied vicarious liability for corporations if their employees had disobeyed diligently enforced policies and procedures. See Conference Report, pp. 922–23.

[17] J. Best, p. 5. Although, it should be noted that any U.S. concern making improper payments directly or indirectly through a wholly owned subsidiary will itself be liable under the FCPA (citing 1977 Conference Report, p. 14). The U.S. concern probably will not be liable, however, where it has no knowledge (and has not closed its eyes) of such improper payments by foreign nationals acting on behalf of its foreign subsidiary. See Senate Report, p. 11. See also notes 6 and 8.

[18] See L. Longobardi, pp. 465–73, which discusses several DOJ no-action grants.

[19] Section 32(c)(1) of the 1934 Act, Section 104(g)(1) of the FCPA.

[20] Section 32(c)(2) of the 1934 Act, Section 104(g)(2) of the FCPA.

[21] Ibid.

[22] The civil penalty may be imposed on the U.S. concern and also independently on any director, officer, employee, agent, or stockholder acting on its behalf who has willfully violated the FCPA. See Sections 32(c)(1)(B), (2)(C) of the 1934 Act, Sections 104(g)(1)(B), (2)(C) of the FCPA.

[23] Section 32(c)(3) of the 1934 Act, Section 104(g)(3) of the FCPA.

[24] Section 13(b)(2)(A) of the 1934 Act. A valid defense would be that a certain control measure was not implemented because it was unjustifiable under a cost-benefit analysis. See Section 13(b)(7) of the 1934 Act; Conference Report, p. 917.

[25] Section 13(b)(2)(B) of the 1934 Act. Its primary purpose is to ensure as much as possible that material irregularities or errors in financial reports be prevented, or detected and corrected, within a timely fashion by company employees in the normal course of performing assigned functions.

Excluded from the accounting provisions are SEC reporting companies acting in cooperation with the head of any federal department or agency responsible for matters involving national security if such act is done upon specific, written directive of such head issued under presidential authority. Section 13(b)(3) of the 1934 Act.

[26] See, e.g., S. Perkins, "Bibliography on the Federal Corrupt Practice Act of 1977," *Western State University Law Review* 14 (1987), p. 491. For a good discussion, see "A Guideline to the New Section 13(b)(2) Accounting Requirement of the Securities Exchange Act of 1934," *The Business Lawyer* (November 1978).

[27] Although actions of officers and agents of foreign subsidiaries might not be attributed to an SEC reporting company under the antibribery provisions of the FCPA, an SEC reporting company generally is required to cause its domestic and foreign subsidiaries that it controls, or is able to control, to comply with the internal accounting controls provision, especially if the subsidiaries' results are material to the SEC reporting company. Pursuant to the FCPA 1988 Amendments, new Section 13(b)(6) of the 1934 Act requires an issuer to "proceed in good faith to use its influence, to the extent reasonable under the circumstances," to cause any subsidiaries of which it owns 50 percent or less to comply with the internal accounting control provisions.

[28] Section 104(d) of the FCPA.

[29] 28 C.F.R. Section 50.18 (1978). The U.S. concern must submit all relevant information and material to the proposed transaction. A senior official of the concern with operational responsibility must verify all such information. The DOJ endeavors to respond to each request within 30 days. The DOJ will not include in its review any conduct that violates the accounting provisions of the FCPA. Further, the SEC will not be bound by any determinations of the DOJ (see Section 50.18(1)) and does not render its own prior review of a proposed transaction. See Securities Exchange Act Release No. 14478 (February 16, 1978). Thus, issuers with a no-action grant issued by the DOJ nevertheless face some risk that the SEC will reach a different conclusion. Since the inception of the DOJ review procedure through 1987, only 18 companies had submitted review requests. See L. Longobardi, p. 465.

Section 104(e), as added by the FCPA 1988 Amendments, requires the DOJ to issue guidelines within six months of its enactment describing specific types of conduct associated with export sales arrangements and business contacts that will comply with the FCPA and general precautionary procedures U.S. concerns may follow. As of the date of this writing, such guidelines were still forthcoming.

[30] See R. Witherspoon, "Multinational Corporations—Governmental Regulation of Business Ethics Under the FCPA of 1977: An Analysis," *Dickinson Law Review* 87 (1982–83), p. 531.

[31] See G. Greanias and D. Windsor, p. 96.

[32] See L. Longobardi, pp. 476–78. There have been approximately 10 reported actions since 1979. This number does not include violators who have settled their cases before the commencement of enforcement proceedings. The reasons for little enforcement are probably because of the difficulty of detection and of compelling discovery on foreign soil, because of the lack of cooperation of foreign officials, and because of understaffing of the DOJ and SEC in this area.

[33] See Conference Report, p. 917.

[34] 18 U.S.C. Section 1341 (1982).

[35] 18 U.S.C. Section 1343 (1982).

[36] 18 U.S.C. Section 1001 (1982).

[37] 31 U.S.C. Sections 3729–31 (1982). This is the U.S. government's chief civil fraud statute with respect to instances of government defrauding.

[38] Internal Revenue Code Section 162(c)(1)-(2) (1986), as amended.

[39] See 15 U.S.C. Section (1982) (Sherman Act); 15 U.S.C. Section 13(c) (1982) (Robinson-Patman Act). Although the most effective deterrent before enactment of the FCPA, the Robinson-Patman Act has been of limited utility because it does not provide for criminal sanctions. Since a conspiracy under the Sherman Act requires two or more conspirators, it has been of limited use. See R. Witherspoon, p. 540.

[40] 18 U.S.C. Sections 1961–68 (1988).

[41] Enforcement of contracts with foreign sovereigns by courts located in such sovereign's jurisdiction is a matter of the local law of the particular sovereign. As a practical matter, it is unlikely that such courts will make a determination adverse to their sovereign.

[42] See *Guaranty Trust Co.* v. *United States*, 304 U.S. 126, 134 (1938). The rationale was that the U.S. Constitution gave the political branches of government plenary power over foreign affairs and thus only the political branches could expand or restrict the jurisdictional immunity of sovereign states. See Note, "Adjudicating Acts of State in Suits Against Foreign Sovereigns: A Political Question Analysis," *Fordham Law Review* 51 (1982–83), pp. 722, 726–734.

[43] 28 U.S.C. Sections 1330, 1332(a)(2)-(4), 1391(f), 1441(d), 1602-1611 (1982). Foreign states also are not immune to U.S. jurisdiction if so provided in international agreements to which the United States is a party. 28 U.S.C. Section 1604 (1982).

[44] 28 U.S.C. Section 1603(d) (1982). The fact that a public purpose underlies such commercial act is irrelevant. For example, price fixing by OPEC was considered a commercial activity under FSIA rather than a political decision on how to allocate the sovereign's natural resources. *IAM* v. *OPEC*, 649 F.2d 1354, 1357-62 (9th Cir. 1981), *cert. denied*, 454 U.S. 1163 (1982). Congress' principal purpose in enacting the FSIA was to place determination of the existence of sovereign immunity with the judicial rather than executive branch of government. See H.R. Rep. No. 1487, 94th Cong., 2nd Sess. 16, reprinted in *1976 U.S. Code Cong. and Ad. News* 6615. The goal was to depoliticize the grant of immunity by permitting the judiciary to apply a more objective, and thus predictable, set of criteria.

[45] 28 U.S.C. Section 1605(a)(2) (1982).

[46] See, e.g., *Alfred Dunhill of London, Inc.*, v. *Republic of Cuba*, 425 U.S. 682, 697 (1976) (plurality opinion); *Banco Nacional de Cuba* v. *Sabbatino*, 376 U.S. 398, 401 (1964); *Underhill* v. *Hernandez*, 168 U.S. 250, 252 (1897) (dictum).

This doctrine also represents a judicial reluctance to interfere with the conduct of foreign affairs, reasoning that such relations are best left to diplomatic resolution. It is not constitutionally compelled, but is based on the constitutional underpinnings of separation of powers principles. However, the Supreme Court expressly rejected a court-evolved rule, known as the *Bernstein Exception*, that the act of state defense is unavailable where the U.S. State Department renders an opinion that adjudication will not hinder American foreign policy. See *National City Bank* v. *Banco Nacional de Cuba*, 406 U.S. 759 (1972) (plurality opinion). U.S. courts therefore can, to a degree, affect foreign relations.

This does not mean that all acts that in some way involve a foreign sovereign are shielded. As the Supreme Court noted, "The less important the implications of an issue are for our foreign relations, the weaker the justification [for application of the act of state doctrine and] for exclusivity in the political branches." *Banco Nacional de Cuba* v. *Sabbatino*, 376 U.S. 398, 409 (1964). See also *United States* v. *Sisal Sales Corp.*, 274 U.S. 268 (1927). It is a manifestation of judicial abstention.

[47] The doctrine has never been fully analyzed or detailed by any single court. See M. Bazyler, "Abolishing the Act of State Doctrine," *University of Pennsylvania Law Review* 134 (1985–86), p. 325.

[48] *Alfred Dunhill of London, Inc.* v. *Republic of Cuba*, 425 U.S. 682, 697 (1976) (plurality opinion).

[49] See, e.g., *Mannington Mills, Inc.* v. *Congoleum Corp.*, 595 F.2d 1287, 1294 (3d Cir. 1979); *Industrial Inv. Dev. Corp.* v. *Mitsui & Co., Ltd.*, 594 F.2d 48, 53 (5th Cir. 1979); *Timberlane Lumber Co.* v. *Bank of America, N.T. & S.A.*, 549 F.2d 597, 606-09 (9th Cir. 1976); *Hunt* v. *Mobil Oil Corp.*, 550 F.2d 68, 73 (2d Cir.), *cert. denied*, 434 U.S. 984 (1977).

[50] See, e.g., *Clayco Petroleum Corp.* v. *Occidental Petroleum Corp.*, 712 F.2d 404 (9th Cir. 1983) (dismissing under act of state a suit by Clayco against Occidental alleging secret payments to a relative of a ruler of Umm Al Qaywayn to secure offshore oil concession were anticompetitive and in violation of the U.S. antitrust laws; reasoning that the act of state doctrine precludes judicial scrutiny of the motivation for foreign sovereign acts so as not to implicate foreign relations), *cert. denied*, 464 U.S. 1040 (1984); *Compania De Gas De Nuevo Laredo, S.A.* v. *Entex, Inc.*, 686 F.2d 322, 325–27 (5th Cir. 1982) (dismissing action by Mexican purchaser of natural gas from a Texas supplier that claimed a conspiracy between the Texas supplier and Mexican government had resulted in the government's seizure of the purchaser's assets; reasoning that resolution would require determining the legality of the government's actions), *cert. denied*, 460 U.S. 1041 (1983); *Hunt* v. *Mobil Oil Corp.*, 550 F.2d 68, 72 (2nd Cir.) (independent oil producer, whose assets in Libya were expropriated, charged seven other oil producers with conspiracy to bring about such result; the court did not want to inquire into the expropriation decision), *cert. denied*, 454 U.S. 1163 (1983); *Interamerican Refining Corp.* v. *Texaco Maracaibo, Inc.*,

307 F.Supp. 1291, 1298 (D. Del. 1970) (private party's refusal to sell Venezuelan crude oil to other private party held not to be an illegal restraint of trade because the Venezuelan government had imposed a boycott preventing such sales).

[51] In particular, the Supreme Court has been unable to agree on the scope of the act of state doctrine, the role of the executive branch in its application by courts, or on the status of various exceptions to the doctrine. See M. Bazyler, p. 344. Although a large number of the cases have involved foreign state expropriation of private industry located within its borders, the principles apply equally to normal contractual relations.

Further, because of foreign government's involvement generally in many aspects of international transactions, it is plausible that even those transactions between private parties may be rendered nonjusticiable in the United States by the act of state doctrine (which, unlike sovereign immunity, does not require that a foreign sovereign be a party to the case).

[52] For example, U.S. courts enforcing arbitration awards determined in other countries have found an implied waiver of sovereign immunity where the contract contemplates arbitration in a jurisdiction other than the sovereign's. See, e.g., *Libyan American Oil Co.* v. *Socialist People's Libyan Arab Jamahirya*, 482 F.Supp. 1175, 1178 (D.D.C. 1980); *Ipitrade International, S.A.* v. *Federal Republic of Nigeria*, 465 F.Supp. 824, 826-27 (D.D.C. 1978).

[53] The major arbitration institutions, which have their own set of rules and the administrative capacity to conduct the proceedings, include the International Chamber of Commerce (ICC), London Court of Arbitration, American Arbitration Association, and the Arbitration Institute of the Stockholm Chamber of Commerce. China has an arbitration tribunal known as the Chinese Foreign Trade Arbitration Commission.

In ad hoc arbitration, on the other hand, the parties establish the manner in which the tribunal shall be constituted and the procedures to be followed. Although the rules ultimately chosen may be the domestic arbitration rules of a specific country or of a specific institution, a widely accepted set of rules is the Arbitration Rules for Ad Hoc Arbitration (known as the *Uncitral Arbitration Rules*), adopted in 1976 by the United Nations Commission on International Trade Law. The advantage of the Uncitral Arbitration Rules is their flexibility in considering the differences in procedural approach between common and civil law jurisdictions, in Eastern and Western cultures, in industrial and developing nations, and in different economic systems.

[54] The validity and effect of the arbitration agreement are generally decided and interpreted in accordance with the law of the place of arbitration, as are the nationality of the award and the circumstances under which the award may be challenged in the local courts. See H. Bagner, *International Trade Law and Practice* (London, England: Euromoney Publications, 1983), chap. 15. The legal basis for enforcing arbitration awards is found in the domestic laws of the country in which enforcement is sought.

[55] The New York Convention has been adopted by over 60 countries, including the major trading nations from the East and West. It should also be noted that all of the countries mentioned in the text, except for Japan and Thailand, have declared in adopting the New York Convention that it will apply only to differences arising out of legal relationships, whether contracted or not, which are considered as commercial under those nations' respective laws.

[56] See generally, W. Fugate, *Foreign Commerce and the Antitrust Laws* (Boston: Little, Brown, 1982).

[57] 15 U.S.C. Section 1 (1982).

[58] 15 U.S.C. Section 2 (1982).

[59] *Northern Pacific Ry.* v. *U.S.*, 356 U.S. 1, 4-5 (1958). It should be noted that the "antitrust laws . . . were enacted for the protection of *competition*, not *competitors.*" *Brown Shoe Co.* v. *United States*, 370 U.S. 294, 320 (1962).

[60] 15 U.S.C. Sections 1, 2 (1982). See also Antitrust Procedure and Penalties Act, Pub. L. 93-528, Section 3, 88 Stat. 1704 (1974) (increasing maximum fine from $50,000).

The U.S. Sentencing Commission recommended imposition of short prison sentences coupled with large fines. See Trade Reg. Rep. (CCH) No. 806 at 1-2 (April 27, 1987). Although enacted into law, these guidelines have been challenged in and criticized by the courts and may not survive. See W. Fugate, p. 4.

[61] 15 U.S.C. Section 15 (1982). The U.S. government may recover only actual damages without trebling. Ibid., Section 15a. A foreign government's remedy also is limited to recovery of actual, rather than trebled, damages. See Foreign Sovereign Antitrust Recoveries Act, Pub. L. No. 97-393, 96 Stat. 1963 (1982), 15 U.S.C. Sections 15(b) and 15(c) (1982). Excepted from this "actual damage" limitation are injuries to a "truly commercial enterprise" of a foreign states, including a state-owned corporation, provided it waives any sovereign immunity claims in connection with any claims brought against it in the same cause of action. See H.R. Rep. No. 97-476, 97th Cong., 2nd Sess. 14, reprinted in [1982] *U.S. Code Cong. & Ad. News* 4, pp. 3495, 3508.

[62] See Note, "The Long Awaited Death Knell of the Intra-enterprise Doctrine," *Villaroue Law Review* 30 (1985), pp. 521, 523. In determining what constitutes a plurality of actors for Section 1 purposes, the courts generally have held that, as a matter of law, officers, employees, divisions, branch offices, and wholly owned subsidiaries are to be deemed one actor and therefore are legally incapable of conspiring among themselves. *Copperweld Corp.* v. *Independence Tube Corp.*, 104 S. Ct. 2731 (1984). It remains as unresolved whether a corporation is legally capable of conspiring with a less than wholly owned subsidiary.

[63] *Standard Oil Co. (N.J.)* v. *U.S.*, 221 U.S. 1 (1911). See also *Continental T.V. Inc.* v. *GTE Sylvania, Inc.*, 433 U.S. 36 (1977) (vertical restraints).

[64] See, e.g., *United States* v. *Trenton Potteries Co.*, 273 U.S. 392 (1927); *United States* v. *Socony-Vacuum Oil Co., Inc.*, 310 U.S. 150 (1940); *Keifer-*

Stewart Co. v. *Joseph E. Seagram & Sons, Inc.,* 340 U.S. 211 (1951); *United States* v. *McKesson & Robbins, Inc.,* 351 U.S. 305 (1956); *Arizona* v. *Maricopa Cty. Med. Socy.,* 457 U.S. 332 (1982).

[65] See, e.g., *United States* v. *General Motors Corp.,* 384 U.S. 127 (1966); *Keifer-Stewart Co.* v. *Joseph E. Seagram & Sons, Inc.,* 340 U.S. 211 (1951); *Associated Press* v. *United States,* 326 U.S. 1 (1945).

[66] See, e.g., *United States* v. *Addyston Pipe & Steel Co.,* 85 F. 271 (5th Cir. 1898), *aff'd.,* 175 U.S. 211 (1899); *U.S.* v. *Aluminum Co. of Am.,* 148 F.2d 416 (2nd Cir. 1945).

[67] See, e.g., *Mandeville Island Farms, Inc.* v. *American Crystal Sugar Co.,* 334 U.S. 219 (1948); *United States* v. *Sacony-Vacuum Oil Co., Inc.,* 310 U.S. 150 (1940); *Standard Oil Co. (Ind.)* v. *United States,* 283 U.S. 163 (1931).

[68] See, e.g., *Timken Roller Bearing Co.* v. *United States,* 341 U.S. 593 (1951); *Johnson* v. *J. Schlitz Brewing Co.,* 33 F.Supp. 176 (E.D. Tenn. 1940), *aff'd,* 123 F.2d 1016 (6th Cir. 1941).

[69] See, e.g., *Hartford-Empire Co.* v. *United States,* 323 U.S. 386, *on rehearing,* 324 U.S. 570 (1945).

[70] See, e.g., *Mercoid Corp.* v. *Mid-Continent Inv. Co.,* 320 U.S. 661 (1944).

[71] See notes 86–88 and accompanying text.

[72] *American Tobacco Co.* v. *United States,* 328 U.S. 781 (1946). Thus, actual exclusion of competitors need not be shown. Ibid.

[73] Although never fixed definitively by any court, the Supreme Court has suggested at various times that monopoly power exists above 87 percent (and perhaps even above 75) of the relevant market. See, e.g., *U.S.* v. *Grinnel Corp.,* 384 U.S. 563 (1966); *U.S.* v. *E. I. du Pont de Nemours & Co.,* 351 U.S. 377 (1956).

[74] 15 U.S.C. Section 13(a) (1982).

[75] 15 U.S.C. Section 14 (1982).

[76] 15 U.S.C. Section 18 (1982).

[77] 15 U.S.C. Sections 41 *et seq.* (1982).

[78] See, e.g., *Federal Trade Commission* v. *Brown Shoe Co.,* 384 U.S. 316 (1966) (2nd largest U.S. shoe manufacturer engaged in unfair trade practice in giving special benefits to dealers that concentrated on its shoes and did not handle shoes of competitors); *Federal Trade Commission* v. *Texas Inc.,* 393 U.S. 223 (1968) (invalidating an agreement providing Texaco with a 10 percent commission in exchange for promoting in its service stations sale of B.F. Goodrich's tires, batteries, and accessories).

[79] See Webb-Pomerene Act, 15 U.S.C. Section 64 (1982).

[80] 15 U.S.C. Section 8 (1982).

[81] 19 U.S.C. Section 1337 (1982).

[82] See W. Fugate, p. 44. Exceptions to the antitrust laws exist for certain export activities. The Webb-Pomerene Export Trade Act (Webb Act) excepts from the Sherman Act, with certain limitations, associations of U.S. companies for the sole purpose of joint exportation of goods and the export related activity of such associations. 15 U.S.C. Sections 61-65 (1982). Such associations' activities are not excluded from the Sherman Act if they restrain trade within the United States or artificially or intentionally enhance or depress prices within the United States of the class of goods being exported or restrain trade of any domestic exporter or association. Also, such associations may not combine with foreign cartels or agree to form foreign factories in lieu of exporting. In order to qualify, these export associations are required to register with the FTC and to provide full disclosure regarding their activities.

Title III of the Export Trading Company Act of 1982 provides a similar export trading company exemption (through issuance of an export trade certificate of review) from the antitrust law. 12 U.S.C. Sections 372, 635 A-4, 1841, 1843 (1982); 15 U.S.C. Sections 1, 6a 15, 26, 45, 4001-4021; 30 U.S.C. Section 181 (1982). Unlike the Webb Act, however, the exemption is also available to single companies and to companies that export solely services.

[83] See, e.g. *United States* v. *American Tobacco Co.*, 221 U.S. 106 (1911); *United States* v. *Imperial Chem. Indus. Ltd.*, 100 F.Supp. 504 (S.D.N.Y. 1951), *opinion on relief*, 105 F. Supp. 215 (S.D.N.Y. 1952).

[84] *United States* v. *Pacific & Artic Ry. & Nav. Co.*, 228 U.S. 87 (1913).

[85] As noted, the Webb Act expressly extended coverage of the FTCA to such conduct. See note 79 and accompanying text.

[86] See, e.g., *Continental Ore Co.* v. *Union Carbide and Carbide Co.*, 370 U.S. 69 (1962); *Timken Roller Bearing Co.* v. *United States*, 341 U.S. 593 (1962); *United States* v. *National Lead Co.*, 332 U.S. 319 (1947); *U.S. Sisal Sales Corp.*, 274 U.S. 268 (1927); *Thomsen* v. *Cayser*, 243 U.S. 66 (1917); *Pacific & Arctic Ry & Nav. Co.*, 228 U.S. 87 (1913); *United States* v. *American Tobacco Co.*, 221 U.S. 106 (1911). See also *American Banana Co.* v. *United Fruit Co.*, 213 U.S. 347 (1909) (U.S. laws do not have any application in foreign territory absent an effect upon U.S. foreign commerce).

The Foreign Trade Antitrust Improvements Act of 1982 (FTAIA) amended the Sherman Act to provide essentially that restraints on export trade violate the act only if they have a direct, substantial, and reasonably foreseeable effect on commerce within the United States or on a domestic firm competing for foreign trade. 15 U.S.C. Section 45 (1982). See also Comments of Congressman Rodino, H.R. Comm. on the Judiciary, H.R. Rep. No. 97-686, 97th Cong. 2nd Sess. 7-8, reprinted in *Antitrust and Trade Reg. Rep.* (BNA) No. 1076 (August 5, 1982), p. 308.

In *Papst Motoren GmbH & Co. KG* v. *Kanematsu Goshu (U.S.A.), Inc.*, a patent infringement counterclaim charged that a Japanese company, STC, infringed certain patents by selling the products in question to K-G Japan for resale to defendant K-G USA, which in turn resold in the United States 629 F. Supp. 864 (S.D.N.Y. 1986). The court dismissed the counterclaim under the FTAIA reasoning that the effect of the alleged antitrust activities (the sale by STC to K-G Japan) occurred solely in Japan and thus there lacked any material anticompetitive effect in the United States. Ibid.

[87] As discussed in note 82, however, the Webb Act exempts the activity of certain export associations from the Sherman Act, including price fixing, and thus such instances of violations relating to exports occur less frequently.

[88] See, e.g., *United States* v. *Aluminum Co. of Am.*, 148 F.2d 416, 443-444 (2nd Cir. 1945) (agreement among non-U.S. aluminum producers acting as a cartel to control, among other things, the import of aluminum into the United States was held to be in violation of the Sherman Act). Under the domestic application of the antitrust laws, on the other hand, it is not generally required that there exist any actual antitrust effect; violations will exist as long as the requisite intent is present.

[89] See, e.g., *Timerlane Lumber Co.* v. *Bank of Am., N.T. & S.A.*, 549 F.2d 597, 613 (9th Cir. 1976) (applying a tripartite jurisdictional rule of reason test: *some* actual or intended effect on American foreign commerce; a sufficiently large burden or restraint presenting a cognizable injury to the plaintiff; and examination of the links to the United States to see if sufficiently strong, vis-à-vis those of other nations, to justify assertion of extraterritorial authority), *reaffirmed on remand*, 574 F.Supp. 1453 (N.D. Cal. 1983), *aff'd*, 749 F.2d 1378 (9th Cir. 1984), *cert. denied*, 472 U.S. 1032 (1985); *Mannington Mills, Inc.* v. *Congoleum Corp.*, 595 F.2d 1287, 1297-98 (3rd Cir. 1979) (utilizing a list of 10 factors for consideration in the balance of the interests). But see *Mitsui & Co., Ltd.* v. *Industrial Inv. Dev. Corp.*, 671 F.2d 876 (5th Cir. 1982) (disagreeing that the *Timberline* balance test was a subject matter jurisdiction test), *cert. granted and judgment vacated*, 460 U.S. 1007 (1983), *on remand*, 704 F.2d 785 (5th Cir. 1983), *cert. denied*, 464 U.S. 961 (1983); *National Bank of Canada* v. *Interbank Card Association and Bank of Montreal*, 666 F.2d 6 (2nd Cir. 1981) (suggesting that application of the *Timberline* test might unwarrantedly lead to an assertion of jurisdiction where the effect on U.S. foreign commerce is minimal and, thus, there must be a likelihood of an anticompetitive effect on U.S. interested or foreign commerce).

[90] See, e.g., *Filmvideo Releasing Corp.* v. *Hastings*, 668 F.2d 91, 93 (2nd Cir. 1981) (copyrights); *Griffin* v. *Keystone Mushroom Farms, Inc.*, 453 F. Supp. 1283, 1286 (E.D.Pa. 1978) (patents); *Wells Fargo & Co.* v. *Wells Fargo Express Co.*, 358 F. Supp. 1065 (D. Nev. 1973) (trademarks), *vacated* 556 F.2d 406 (9th Cir. 1977).

U.S. citizens might nevertheless be liable under U.S. laws where committing an act of infringement outside of the U.S. that has an adverse effect on intellectual property rights within the United States. For example, a U.S. court enjoined a U.S. citizen from stamping and selling in Mexico watches containing the federally registered trademark of another. *Steele* v. *Bulova Watch Co.,* 334 U.S. 280 (1952).

[91] 19 U.S.C. Section 119 (1984). This rule applies only if the invention has (1) neither been patented nor described in any preprinted publication in any country, nor (2) been publicly used or sold in the United States more than one year before the actual filing date in the United States.

[92] Further, an applicant may defer for up to 30 months from the initial filing date the payment of filing fees and submissions of translations to the patent offices of the member countries selected within the 20-month period.

The filing date of an international application is deemed to be the actual filing date in the patent office of each designated country. Thus, even if a U.S. applicant files for a patent first in a member country, so long as the applicant has filed the international application within one year of that date, a U.S. patent will not be barred if the U.S. Patent & Trademark Office (PTO) receives the international application after the foreign patent has already issued, even though (outside of the PCT) such priority treatment usually will not lie if the foreign patent is issued before submission of the application to the PTO.

[93] It should be noted that this 12-month grace period is distinct from the one-year public use grace period mentioned in the text. Thus, where patent protection is sought in foreign countries having a shorter public use grace period, a patent application actually must be filed in such country before the end of its public use grace period if the invention has been put in public use.

[94] The Paris Convention does not apply to patents relating to botanic plant varieties. Such varieties are covered separately under the International Union for the Protection of New Varieties of Plants (UPOV), to which both the United States and Japan are members. Like the Paris Convention, the UPOV provides national treatment and a right of foreign priority.

[95] See 37 C.F.R. Sections 5.11(b) and (c); 49 Fed. Reg. 13456 (April 4, 1984). Effective February 22, 1983, the filing of a U.S. patent application has automatically included a petition for an export license for the subject matter of the application.

[96] See 35 U.S.C. Section 185 (1982).

[97] Generally, within such countries, actual use must occur within a specified period (typically three to five years) in order to retain the benefits of a registered mark. Under the recently enacted Trademark Law Revision Act of 1988, however, trademark registration filings in the United States will be permitted before actual use so long as there exists a "bona fide intent to use" the mark in commerce for specific goods or services. Actual use must commence within six months thereafter, unless extensions are granted.

[98] 19 U.S.C. Sections 1337, 1526 (1982).

[99] See, e.g., *Lever Brothers Co.* v. *United States*, No. 87-5151, CADC (June 9, 1989) (third-party imports into United States of foreign goods bearing the same trademark as their U.S.-made versions should be barred even if produced by an affiliate of the United States manufacturer).

[100] 50 Fed. Reg. 47127 (November 14, 1985).

[101] 50 U.S.C. Sections 2401-2420 (1982), as amended by the Export Administration Act of 1985 (Pub.L.No. 99-64, 99 Stat. 120 (1985)) and the Omnibus Trade and Competitiveness Act of 1988 (P.L. 100-418, 102 Stat. 1107 (1988)). Several other statutes control concerning certain particular exports, including:

Munitions: The Arms Export Control Act of 1976 was enacted specifically to regulate the export of defense data and goods. See 22 U.S.C. Sections 2751-2796(c) (1982). It is administered by the Department of State Office of Munitions Control. Munitions and classified products and certain technical data are covered. See 15 C.F.R., Part 370, Supplement No. 2, and International Traffic in Arms Regulations, 22 C.F.R. Section 121.01 (1983). Generally, three types of licenses are available—export, in transit, and temporary export.

Narcotics and Dangerous Drugs: Regulated by the Drug Enforcement Administration of the Department of Justice.

Nuclear Equipment and Materials: Subject to the Atomic Energy Act of 1954, and regulated by the Nuclear Regulatory Commission and the Department of Energy.

Other: Financial transactions (see 31 C.F.R. Sections 103.11 et seq., 500.101, et seq., 515.101, et seq., and 520.01, et seq.), watercraft, natural gas and electric energy, tobacco seeds and plants, endangered fish and wildlife, migratory birds, bald and golden eagles, and patent applications. (See 31 C.F.R. Section 370.10(f)-(j).)

[102] 50 U.S.C. Sections 2405(a)(1); 2404(a)(1), 2402(2)(A); 2406(a)(1); 2402(2)(C) (1982).

[103] See *Commerce and Foreign Trade Regulations*, 15 C.F.R. Section 399.1, Supplement. To determine whether the OEA has asserted export jurisdiction over particular goods or technology, it is necessary to consider the nature of the goods or technology (is the item likely subject to national security controls?), the destination (e.g., Libya, where the nature of the export may be irrelevant), and the end-user or end-use (e.g., use in nuclear reactor).

[104] See *Commerce and Foreign Trade Regulations*, 15 C.F.R. Sections 370-372 (1983). A general license is a license established by the U.S. Department of Commerce that permits certain exports. No application is required for its use, nor is any document issued. If not covered by a general license, then the exporter must apply for and be issued an individual validated license, and he or she will be held strictly accountable for its use whether acting as a principal or agent of another. See *Commerce and Foreign Trade Regulations*, 15 C.F.R. Section 372.2 (1983). Stricter requirements exist generally for exports to the

People's Republic of China than to other nations in the Far East discussed in this book.

Certain exceptions from licensing requirements exist for (*a*) certain exports to Canada, (*b*) certain exports for the U.S. Armed Forces, and (*c*) exports regulated by other branches of government (most of which are identified in note 101).

[105] See *Commerce and Foreign Trade Regulations*, 15 C.F.R. Section 374 (1983). The regulations prohibit re-export from the authorized country of ultimate destination, unless specifically authorized in writing by the United States, unless export could have been made directly to such third country under the regulations, or unless another exemption applies. Regulations contain stricter rules for re-exports to the People's Republic of China, which should be consulted in appropriate circumstances. See, e.g., ibid. at Section 374.2(i), (j).

[106] Ibid. at Section 379.8.

[107] See Comment, "Extraterritorial Application of United States Law: The Case of Export Controls," *University of Pennsylvania Law Review* 132 (1983–84), p. 355.

[108] 50 U.S.C. Section 2410(b) (1982).

[109] 42 U.S.C. Sections 2000e to 2000e-17 (1982). Only employers with 15 or more employees for each working day in 20 or more calendar weeks are subject to Title VII. Ibid. at Section 2000e(b). In any event, Title VII does not by its terms apply to the employment of aliens outside of the United States by U.S. employers. Ibid. at Section 2000e-1.

[110] Ibid. at Section 2000e-2(a). Potential remedies include injunctions prohibiting continuance of unlawful employment practices, reinstatement of employees (with possibility of back pay, with interest), hiring of employees, and seniority and transfer adjustments. Ibid. at Section 2000e-5(g),-5(q); *Franks* v. *Bowman Transp. Co.*, 424 U.S. 747 (1976); *Dual* v. *Griffin*, 446 F.Supp. 791, 800 (D.D.C. 1977).

[111] Title VII should apply equally to foreign branches of domestic companies as well as to foreign companies controlled by U.S. persons or entities. U.S. courts have so held in other contexts such as the antitrust laws. See, e.g., *In re Uranium Antitrust Litig.*, 480 F. Supp. 1138, 1144-45 (N.D. Ill. 1979).

[112] See, e.g., *Fernandez* v. *Wynn Oil Co.*, 653 F.2nd 1273, 1276 (9th Cir. 1981) (dicta) (stereotyped impressions of male/female roles and stereotyped customer preferences do not qualify gender as a BFOQ and justify discriminatory practices). The court also noted that the EEOC has held that the need to accommodate racially discriminatory policies of other nations cannot be the basis of a valid BFOQ exception. Ibid. at 1277. See generally, Note, "The Biases of Customers in a Host Country as a Bona Fide Occupational Qualification," *Southern California Law Review* 57 (1983–84), p. 335.

[113] See, e.g., *Bryant* v. *International School Servs.*, 502 F. Supp. 472, 481 (D.N.J. 1980), *rev'd on other grounds*, 675 F.2nd 562 (3rd Cir. 1982). The primary rationale in support of the argument was that Title VII contains no clear, express provision setting forth the extraterritoriality of the act, and to so apply Title VII would be unwarranted given the sensitive nature of international affairs. Ibid., pp. 481–82.

[114] See, e.g., *Abrams* v. *Baylor College of Medicine*, 805 F.2nd 528, 531 (5th Cir. 1986); *Fernandez*, note 112, p. 1275; *Kern* v. *Dynalectron Corp.*, 577 F.Supp. 1196 (N.D. Tex. 1983), *aff'd mem.*, 746 F.2nd 810 (5th Cir. 1984).

[115] See, e.g., *Bryant*, note 113, p. 490.

[116] See Note, "Equal Employment Opportunity for Americans Abroad," *N.Y.U. Law Review* 62 (December 1978), pp. 1288, 1290-91 and accompanying footnotes. In *Bryant*, note 113, p. 482, the court noted that the language of Title VII, by negative inference, evidenced Congress' intent to provide relief to American citizens both inside and outside of the United States.

[117] 42 U.S.C. Section 2000e-2(e)(1) (1982). Title VII also permits discrimination by a religious institution of individuals who are to perform work in connection with its activities. Ibid. at Section 2000e-1.

[118] See *Knight* v. *Nassau County Civil Serv. Comm.*, 649 F.2nd 157, 162 (2nd Cir.), *cert. denied*, 454 U.S. 818 (1981).

[119] See Note, note 116, pp. 1302–03.

[120] See note 112 and accompanying text.

[121] See *Kern*, note 114. In that case, a U.S. helicopter company required all of its pilots flying to Mecca in Saudi Arabia to be Moslem because of a Saudi law that prohibited the entry of non-Moslems into Mecca under penalty of death. The district court reasoned that the existence of the Saudi law made religion a prerequisite for the job. The Fifth Circuit affirmed without opinion.

One commentator has noted that the Supreme Court has rejected the "worker safety" argument in the domestic context and thus asserts that it is inappropriate to accord a different approach in the international arena. See Note, note 116, pp. 1306–08. See also EEOC Dec. No. 85-10, 2 Empl. Prac. Guide (CCH), ¶ 6851 n.2 (July 16, 1985) (rejecting BFOQ defense based on compliance with host country law prohibiting employment of females in positions in which they would have contact with the opposite sex).

See also *Abrams*, note 114, p. 533, suggesting that in order to substantiate a BFOQ defense of non-Jewishness in connection with a hospital rotation program in Saudi Arabia, the defendant would need to prove that the official Saudi position forbade the participation of Jews in the program and that the defendant determined this position before the conduct that was the subject of the Title VII action.

[122] See Note, note 116, p. 1314. In order to be available in the antitrust law context, courts have also required that the penalty for violation of the foreign law be harsh. Ibid., p. 1315.

[123] Past experience has shown that many foreign countries will accommodate the need of U.S. companies to comply with Title VII extraterritoriality. Ibid.

CHAPTER 4

JOINT VENTURING IN THE FAR EAST

Richard A. Eastman

The author of this chapter wishes to thank Wonda Clyatt, John H. Davies, Martin Mendelssohn, and Leung Yee for their assistance in the preparation of this chapter. David Laverty of Lee & Ko, Seoul, Korea, was also an important contributor. Responsibility for errors is my own.

JOINT VENTURING IN JAPAN
      Foreign Investment Background
      Reasons to Joint Venture
      Corporate Joint Ventures
      Unincorporated Joint Ventures
JOINT VENTURING IN THE REPUBLIC OF KOREA
      Foreign Investment Background
      Reasons to Joint Venture
      Corporate Joint Ventures
      Unincorporated Joint Ventures
JOINT VENTURING IN MALAYSIA
      Foreign Investment Background
      Incorporated Joint Ventures
      Unincorporated Joint Ventures
JOINT VENTURING IN THE PHILIPPINES
      Foreign Investment Background
      Reasons to Joint Venture
      Unincorporated Joint Ventures

In this chapter, we focus on joint ventures. The importance of joint ventures as a mode of investment and operating in East Asian countries is shown by the prominence of joint ventures in the chapters on each of the countries of East Asia in this book.

WHAT ARE JOINT VENTURES?

While businesspeople usually know what they mean when they use the expression *joint venture*, a number of different arrangements may go under this name in international business.

   Historically, joint ventures started as "joint adventures" that were specific joint trading ventures of limited purpose and limited duration.[1] Today, the term is still used broadly to describe a cooperative venture of limited scope between two or more otherwise independent enterprises,[2] but a small number of specific forms have evolved that ought to be kept distinct.

   • The incorporated joint venture: A separate company is created in which the venturers become shareholders.

- The "integrated" contractual joint venture: An unincorporated enterprise is undertaken, pursuant to contract, in which the parties invest and whose profits, losses, and risks are shared by the members in specified percentages.
- The "unintegrated" contractual joint venture: A business or enterprise is undertaken, pursuant to contract, jointly by two or more parties, who allocate the responsibilities, risks, and proceeds of the venture among themselves by contract.

Incorporated Joint Ventures

Typically, when Americans or Europeans talk about a joint venture in, say, Japan, they mean a Japanese joint venture company. Incorporated joint ventures are overwhelmingly the most common type of joint venture in such countries as Japan[3] and Korea[4] and are found in all countries of East Asia.[5]

We will address variations on incorporated joint ventures in various East Asian countries, but before doing so, we will discuss the general, commonly shared features of incorporated joint ventures in East Asia. Typically, an incorporated joint venture is, from the legal point of view, a separate company almost always conveying limited liability to its shareholders.

Choice of Corporate Vehicle
Unlike the United States but like Europe, the corporation laws of most East Asian countries afford a menu of types of companies, such as Japan's *kabushiki kaisha* and *yugen kaisha*,[6] some of which may be better suited to joint venturing than others.

Shareholders' Agreement
The so-called joint venture agreement in the case of an incorporated joint venture had better be called what it really is—a shareholders' agreement. The typical East Asian shareholders' agreement is an agreement between the parties to the joint venture that, in effect, attempts to govern their internal relationships as if they were partners while preserving their status as shareholders with limited liability to the outside world.[7]

Matters typically addressed by joint venture company shareholders' agreements are:

Selection of Directors.   As a corporation, the joint venture company will be run by a board of directors. The directors are normally elected by shareholders. In some cases, the ratio of shareholdings and procedures for "cumulative voting" may assure each of the shareholders that they may elect the desired or agreed number of directors from their side. However, if this is not the case, provisions will be required in the agreement specifying the number of directors to be elected by each side. If possible, the provisions should also be in the charter of the company (articles of incorporation) because, as will be seen in specific cases, otherwise the agreement may not be effective as a matter of corporate, as distinct from contract, law. This point will apply to many elements of the joint venture agreement. In the United States, such mechanisms as classes of shares or voting trusts are used in such cases. These are generally not customary in East Asia and may not be available under local law.

Selection of Corporate Managers.   The selection of managing directors, president, and so on will normally be a matter of decision by the board of directors. In corporate joint ventures, the parties will often legislate this matter by their agreement. The validity of such provisions may vary according to the local law and according to what type of corporate form is selected in the given country, and it should not be taken for granted.

Protection of the Minority.   As a corporation, the joint venture company's business policies are, under the corporate laws of most countries, a matter for decision by its directors, in principle at their own discretion. In the joint venture context, care must be taken not impermissibly to restrict directors' discretion under the relevant law. In practice, the directors normally represent their principals. Matters not decided by the directors will be voted on by the shareholders. In either case, if one or more shareholders in the joint venture controls less than 50 percent of the voting rights (or less than half the directors), the shareholder will wish protection against being overruled and oppressed on important decisions. This is usually done by providing in the agreement and if possible in the articles for "super majorities" or unanimity on an agreed list of matters.

Restrictions on Transfer of Shares and Issue of New Shares.   Naturally, all parties to a joint venture wish to be assured that they will not be faced with new, previously unknown partner-shareholders who may not have entered the shareholders' agreement. On the other hand, some forms of corporation in East Asia countries may presume or require the transferability of shares and assume the directors may decide to issue new shares. The shareholders' agreement should deal with these matters. If possible, so should the articles. First, transfers of shares must be controlled. This may be done by contractual restrictions inserted in the articles on transfer, rights of first refusal, "puts" and options to buy among shareholders, and requirements of directors' approval of transfers. Decisions on new issues of shares may be subject to a super majority vote by contract and if possible in the articles. Shareholders should have preemptive rights to purchase a new issue of shares pro rata to their existing holdings.

Dealing with Deadlock; Means of Dissolution.   The premise of the joint venture relationship is unanimity on important matters, and we have mentioned already that each partner-shareholder should have in effect a veto if he or she does not agree with a proposal affecting such important matters. The success of the relationship will then depend on a certain degree of common interest, mutual trust, and good communication. If these are lacking, deadlock on important issues will arise, and one or both sides may wish to escape the joint venture. The shareholders' agreement should therefore provide means of ending the joint venture relationship in case of deadlock or where one party desires (perhaps after a minimum term of years) to get out. Such mechanisms will necessarily entail either (*a*) buy-out or (*b*) liquidation. Buy-out provisions will normally be possible under local law as a matter of contract law, although governmental approvals and restrictions on foreign ownership over specified percentages exist in certain countries and can create serious obstacles to "cleaning up" a troubled joint venture.

Other Important Matters.   The shareholders' agreement will often deal with such matters as:

- Methods of finance, amount of borrowings, and shareholders' guarantee of borrowings.
- Distribution (or re-investment) of profits.
- Dealings with shareholders.

Ancillary Agreements

Joint venture companies frequently will enter contracts with one or more of their shareholders. Classically, the Japanese joint venture, for example, was a vehicle for entry of foreign technology into Japan. On formation, the company would enter a license and or technical assistance agreement with the foreign shareholder. Other possible ancillary agreements might be for supply, sales, trademark licensing, management, and so on.

Contractual Joint Ventures

The subject of unincorporated contractual joint ventures in East Asia (except the People's Republic of China) has been much less explored in legal and business literature, probably because their use was, and still remains, relatively limited, and more interest attached to the corporate type. However, unincorporated joint ventures are quite common in many East Asian countries in such sectors as construction and natural resource extraction. In locally specialized forms, they are quite common through the gamut of business in fields in which foreigners may be active in the People's Republic of China and Indonesia, as discussed below. Unincorporated joint ventures are entirely governed by contract, although the laws of the host country may contain provisions that may affect the relations of the joint venturers. As we have noted above, unincorporated joint ventures are of two fundamental types: those that pool the risks, profits, and losses ("integrated" joint ventures) and those that do not ("unintegrated" joint ventures).

Integrated Contractual Joint Ventures

An integrated but unincorporated joint venture is set up as a separate organization with its own staff, management, property, and books of account. As such, it will be recognizable to businesspeople and lawyers from America, England, and British Commonwealth countries as very like a partnership. International construction joint ventures in East Asia as elsewhere are often documented on a North American model of agreement for construction joint ventures that shares many characteristics of a typical partnership agreement. The main difference from a partnership is that the members at all times intend to limit the joint venture's activities and are free to have other business interests.

In common with the corporate form of joint venture, integrated joint venture agreements must deal with control, often exercised through a committee similar to a board of directors, and management, usually by full-time managers seconded by one or more of the members to posts, the most important of which will be designated in the agreement. The joint venture agreement must deal with contribution of capital, both initially and as required later; the percentage sharing of profit and loss (which need not be the same); dealings of the joint venture with its members (supplies of services, equipment, technology, etc.); default; deadlock; and dissolution. Because each member of the joint venture is liable to the outside world for all debts and liabilities of the joint venture, there must be provision for one or more of the members to take over the enterprise and carry on if one member becomes bankrupt and/or fails without just cause to contribute working capital as required for the carrying on of the joint venture's business.

Unintegrated Contractual Joint Ventures

The most common type of unintegrated, unincorporated joint venture is found in construction and contracting for major projects. A consortium may be formed to undertake construction of the entire project, and the members may then parcel out the work among themselves, in effect subcontracting the work to the members for fixed sums, the total of which represents the contract price. Common expenses will be limited and will typically be borne pro rata to the division of income.

The contractual provisions for a joint venture of this type will differ considerably from those used in the integrated type. Each venturer has the prerogative to control dealings with the client of the joint venture as to matters affecting his or her own scope of work; where a matter affects the affairs of more than one of the members, there must be two parallel negotiations. Control provisions are therefore radically different. Often each of the venturers indemnifies the other(s) as to any consequences of his or her own failure to perform; this feature makes unintegrated joint venturing extremely volatile and risky, and its implications are not always adequately considered in advance.

There are also joint ventures of a mixed type: capital investments, operating expenses, and operating risks may be shared in a fixed ratio, but operating profit and loss is not. Instead, product is divided according to an agreed ratio and sold separately by the parties. To the author's knowledge, joint ventures of this mixed type are typically used in the spheres of resource extraction[8] and rarely, if ever, encountered in East Asia in any other context.

WHY AND WHEN ARE JOINT VENTURES ENTERED?

Parties choose to enter a joint venture for several reasons, and these will vary from country to country and business to business. Historically in East Asia, the majority of countries have restricted foreign investment. This has been the overwhelmingly common reason for joint ventures in Japan, Korea, the People's Republic of China, Indonesia, and several other countries. However, joint ventures are also useful to spread risk; to assemble large sums necessary for investment, for instance, in a new, major project to be financed on a limited recourse basis (BOT contracting); to "incentivize" local employees; to win access to local distribution networks; to get know-how or, conversely, to keep a "piece of" licensed technology; to qualify for investment incentives; and for other reasons. In the sections on particular East Asian countries that follow, we will suggest locally relevant considerations.

Avoidance Devices

In several countries of East Asia, where restrictions on foreign investment are strongest, a variety of devices have been employed to give foreign investors a larger share in control and/or in equity and profit than local government policy would normally countenance. Many of these devices are of questionable legality or efficacy. In the context of the incorporated joint venture they include pledges of shares by the local investor to a third party or the holding of shares by local nationals under a contract in favor of the foreign investor. Another common device is a "cooperation agreement" that effectively creates an unincorporated joint venture, which operates through a locally incorporated and locally owned entity that functions as its nominee for purposes of local trading. Often such arrangements will feature assignments of accounts, escrow bank accounts, and the like to afford some security to the offshore parties to such schemes.

Joint Venturing—Do It Right

In the balance of this chapter, we try to provide an encapsulated legal guide to joint venture practices in certain East Asian countries. We discuss joint venturing in the People's Republic of China, Indonesia, Japan, Korea, Malaysia, and the Philippines. Regrettably, we have had to omit coverage of several important countries including Hong Kong, Singapore, Taiwan, and Thailand.

Before proceeding, however, there are a few points of importance:

• Choose good local lawyers, accountants, and other professionals. Obtain legal advice on the particular country and the particular tax, foreign investment, and other relevant regulations.
• Understand as best you can the country and the people you are dealing with. They do not necessarily think and feel as you do; on the other hand, they are people whose motives, feelings, and goals can and should be understood and respected.
• Keep it as simple as you can.
• By all means enter sound, well-drafted agreements. Remember, however, to inquire into the available remedies if there is a dispute. The practical efficacy of your agreement may not be the same as in your own country.

JOINT VENTURING IN CHINA

Foreign Investment Background

Since the late 1970s, the People's Republic of China (the PRC) has experienced a rapid transformation from Soviet-style central planning to a more market-oriented economy. Before this period, the vast majority of all urban enterprises, from major steel factories to street-corner tailor shops, were state-owned. Practically no foreign investment was allowed.

During the last 10 years, policy has shifted toward decentralization of the economy and encouragement of limited forms of private ownership and foreign investment.[9] The legislative and administrative bodies at the national, provincial, municipal, and other levels have promulgated literally hundreds of laws and regulations related to foreign investment in China, covering organizational structure, taxation, labor management, foreign exchange control, technology transfer, and other aspects.

The PRC so far does not have any general corporations law under which investors, whether foreign or domestic, can organize their business entities.[10] Although the concepts of separate juridical person, limited liability, partnership, mergers and acquisitions, board of directors, and bankruptcy are present, these terms are be viewed in a different light.

The concept of equal treatment between foreign-invested business and domestic business also does not exist in the PRC. Legal treatment for enterprises involving foreign equity investment is distinctly different from that for domestic enterprises. Even for a commercial nexus as fundamental as contract law, there is one Chinese contract law governing foreign-related transactions[11] and a separate Chinese contract law governing strictly domestic transactions.[12] Foreign-invested enterprises are required to pay different rates of taxes and observe other different obligations but are also entitled to certain privileges.

It is possible in certain circumstances to invest in the PRC by way of a wholly foreign-owned enterprise (WFOE) structure without involving any local equity participation.[13] A requirement for a WFOE, as opposed to an equity joint venture or cooperative joint venture, is that all or most of its products must be exported.

Forms of Joint Venture

There are three primary vehicles for foreign equity investment—equity joint venture, cooperative joint venture, and wholly foreign-owned enterprise.

Equity Joint Venture. In the case of a Sino-foreign equity joint venture (EJV), at least one foreign party and one Chinese party, each contributing certain assets as equity capital, form a limited liability company.[14] The assets so contributed may consist of tangible or intangible property such as cash, land, building, equipment, patent, trademark, proprietary technology, and other intellectual properties. The cash value of any in-kind contribution is by agreement of the parties. The total assets contributed by the parties then form the "registered capital" of the EJV. The share of the registered capital contributed by the foreign party or parties may not be less than 25 percent.

The highest management authority for an EJV is its board of directors. The directors are appointed by the parties generally according to their respective proportions in the registered capital. The exact numbers of the directors to be appointed by each party is determined by agreement of the parties as set forth in the joint venture contract and the articles of association. The chairman of the board must, however, be appointed by a Chinese party. The general manager, in charge of the day-to-day management under the board's direction, may be appointed by any party and is usually appointed by a foreign party. Profits and losses of the EJV and the liquidated assets are shared by all parties pro rata to their respective contributions to the registered capital.

To form an EJV, the parties must first submit a feasibility study to be approved by the relevant Chinese government authorities. Thereafter, the parties will execute their joint venture contract, articles of association, and other ancillary documents such as technology transfer agreements to be also approved by the authorities. The EJV is not formed until all the approvals are effected and the business license issued. An EJV must have a term, often 10 to 20 years, although theoretically it may be 50 years or more. The EJV will be dissolved upon expiration unless extended by the parties' agreement with government approval.

After the EJV's formation, any transfer of a party's equity interest is subject to the right of first refusal and agreement of the other party or parties as well as approval by the authorities. Any major amendments to the joint venture contract, articles of association, or other documents, including any changes to the type or scope of business and dissolution, are also subject to approval by the authorities.

An EJV is somewhat like a close corporation except for the limited life and the omnipresent government approval requirements—from its formation to change of ownership, change of business direction, and liquidation.

An EJV may theoretically be set up to engage in any business. But because of the government approval process starting from the feasibility study stage, realistically, foreign companies may invest only in the businesses preferred by the government at the time of application. In addition, foreign investors can theoretically choose any one of the three investment avenues. But, again, in reality they will be guided into one avenue favored by the government.

Partly because of the more detailed laws and regulations governing EJVs and the opportunity to maximize management involvement by the Chinese parties, EJV is the mode of foreign investment preferred by the government. Most of the foreign-invested manufacturing enterprises have apparently been organized under this structure.

Previously, many EJVs were formed by the Chinese party contributing the land-use right plus some cash in Reminbi, the official currency, and the foreign party contributing cash in foreign currency, equipment, and technology to build new facilities. The results in many cases were not satisfactory because of the difficulty for the Chinese party to come up with the money to match the foreign party's contribution in order to achieve the desirable investment ratio, e.g., 50 : 50. A solution of the Chinese party was to artificially boost the value of land-use right, which eventually led to disincentive for the foreign parties to invest.

In most recent years, policy makers have realized that the price for land use must be better controlled in order to induce foreign investment. Consequently, most local governments now impose guidelines on valuation of land. The policy makers have also realized that improving existing facilities can be a lower-cost and more realistic alternative to building new facilities. A number of recent EJVs obtain their equity capital in the following manner: the Chinese partner contributes a substantial portion or all of its existing building and equipment, land, work force, and raw material channels, while the foreign partner contributes cash capital, technology, and export channels. The emphasis is on upgrading and better utilizing existing plants and equipment. The effect is actually like an acquisition of an interest in a going concern by the foreign investor.

Cooperative Joint Venture.   Before the promulgation of the cooperative joint venture (CJV) law in April 1988,[15] Sino-foreign joint ventures in the PRC could be neatly divided into two categories—EJVs that could be considered as "incorporated" joint venture or limited liability companies, and CJVs that could be considered as "unincorporated" joint ventures or partnerships. But the new cooperative joint venture law provides for a CJV to become an independent legal person entailing limited liability, thereby blurring the distinction between EJVs and CJVs. Nevertheless, a CJV remains different from an EJV in a number of other aspects.

CJVs and EJVs are governed under two separate sets of income tax laws and are therefore liable to different rates of income tax, to be discussed further below. In addition, CJVs are not governed by detailed regulations as in the case of EJVs and can therefore be structured more flexibly by agreement of the parties. For example, there is not the minimum 25 percent equity requirement for foreign participation; the chairman of the board of directors need not be appointed by a Chinese party; the profits and looses need not be shared pro rata between the parties.

The formation procedure and other government approval requirements for a CJV are similar to those for an EJV. Although the law fails to specify that the other parties have the right of first refusal in case of any transfer of equity interest by a party, the effect is nearly the same because any such transfer is still subject to agreement by such other parties and approval of the government. In practice, whether for CJVs or EJVs, any transfer of interest to a party other than to the original joint venture partners or an associated company is relatively unusual probably because of the highly personal nature in any Sino-foreign investment cooperation.

Partly because of the flexibility of sharing profit and loss disproportionately, the CJV structure has popularly been adopted in hotel joint ventures. The typical arrangement is for the Chinese partner to contribute land and for the foreign partner to contribute all financing required to build a new hotel. The hotel will then be operated jointly by the two partners, but the actual management is often contracted out to an international hotel management company. Most of the profit derived during the initial period, e.g., 15 years, would belong to the foreign partner; the principal and interest of the financing can be repaid first plus a certain return to the foreign partner. At the end of such period, all interests to the hotel will then revert to the Chinese partner.

The CJV structure has also been used in various other circumstances in which the foreign investment needs to be structured under the guise of joint venture for political or other purposes but would also avoid the limitation imposed by the EJV regulations. For example, a certain foreign soft drink company organized a CJV in the PRC consisting of two elements—a concentrate plant, in effect wholly owned and operated by the foreign partner, next to a bottling plant, in effect wholly owned and operated by the Chinese partner. The two partners jointly form a management committee to coordinate the two plants and to cooperate on marketing and distribution. In so doing, the manufacturing operations can be approved and practiced under a joint venture mode, but the Chinese partner gains little access to the concentrate production process, resulting in better control of the quality, quantity, and trade secret of the concentrate by the foreign partner. This type of flexibility would not be available to an EJV, in which the highest management authority must be the board participated in by the Chinese partner with the right to oversee and control all details of the joint venture operations.

Other Forms of Investment

A popular form of foreign investment in the PRC is the processing arrangement, although this is technically not a form of equity investment. A processing arrangement typically involves a contract under which a foreign party supplies raw materials, equipment, and technology to a Chinese party that provides factory premises and labor to manufacture products specified by the foreign party. The Chinese party receives a fee for the processing from the foreign party, which takes back all the finished products. Although the processing contract is still subject to Chinese government approval, the foreign party is not deemed to have created an "establishment" or legal person in China for tax and registration purposes. The factory premises remain the property, and the labor force remains the employees of the Chinese party, although the foreign party may have exclusive contractual right to use the premises and station management personnel there on a long-term basis.

A major requirement for a processing arrangement is that all products must be exported. For foreign investors who mainly want to utilize the more inexpensive and available labor of the PRC for manufacturing but want to avoid formally entering into a joint venture there, the processing arrangement is ideal for simplicity. This form has been most popular with foreign manufacturers in the labor-intensive industries such as electronics, toys, and textiles. On the other hand, the processing arrangement would not be suitable for those who would like to penetrate the Chinese domestic market.

Certain recent regulations allow foreigners to lease small-scale state-owned enterprises on a short-term basis.[16] After paying the government a leasing fee and signing a lease contract, the lessee can presumably operate the enterprise with autonomy and keep most of the profits. The degree of popularity and the general result of this new type of leasing arrangement remain to be seen.

Foreign Exchange Balance

The PRC's official currency, Reminbi (RMB), is not convertible internationally. A Sino-foreign joint venture may need foreign currency to pay for the import of parts and materials, the compensation of expatriate personnel, and the royalty for trademark and technology. In addition, although the foreign partner's share of the joint venture profit is freely repatriatable (subject to a withholding tax under certain circumstances), in practice it can be remitted only to the extent of foreign exchange available to the joint venture. Achieving foreign exchange (forex) balance thus becomes one of the most common problems confronting Sino-foreign joint ventures, other than those that are export-oriented and the hotels that receive forex payments from their foreign tourist customers.

For the joint ventures that are profitable on paper but face forex balance difficulties because most of their products are sold domestically, there are only a few alternatives—none of them fully satisfactory. The joint venture may sell its products domestically under an "import substitute" scheme to receive payment in forex. But any such scheme is subject to government approval. Even after approval, much arm-twisting by a friendly government agency is needed for the scheme to be effective. A domestic enterprise that has forex on hand to do the shopping would normally prefer to buy overseas instead of paying the same money for locally produced products.

Another alternative is to exchange RMB for forex at a Foreign Exchange Adjustment Center (FEAC). A number of FEACs have been established by the government in various cities as legalized markets for currency swap, originally to stem the rampant black market activities. The rates are set by the FEACs, which float according to supply and demand and are much higher than the official exchange rates. For example, the official exchange rate has been US$1 = RMB ¥ 3.72. But the FEAC rate was 7.1 in November 1988 and 6.5 in March 1989. Furthermore, even at such a higher rate, the availability of forex offer is not assured, and only a limited number of Chinese enterprises with a limited percentage of their forex income can trade at an FEAC.

Sino-foreign joint ventures are also allowed to export products unrelated to their own products to earn forex. But, in reality, practically all exportable Chinese products have had existing export channels, and it is risky for any company to be engaged in trading unfamiliar product lines.

The Chinese government makes it clear that forex balance is a Sino-foreign joint venture's own responsibility. The government has provided forex assistance in only a small number of most extraordinary cases. It has encouraged each joint venture to export, which may also be the most feasible forex solution. But for many joint ventures, either the products are not of internationally competitive standard or any export may upset the foreign partner's existing international market.

A careful analysis of the forex balance question is advisable at the feasibility study stage. A last alternative, which has apparently been taken by some foreign investors with a very long-term view on the PRC, is to keep the RMB profits in China indefinitely.

Other Matters

When applying for establishing a joint venture, whether EJV or CJV, the parties must specify the amounts of registered capital and total investment. As discussed, the registered capital is the sum of the cash and in-kind equity contributions by all parties. The total investment is a theoretical figure signifying the envisioned scale of the enterprise. The total investment figure is used primarily to ascertain the level of government approval authority—a larger figure means higher level of authority. Once the registered capital and total investment are approved, they cannot be altered without further approval. The parties must pay in their respective share of the registered capital within certain time limits specified by the regulations.[17]

Any borrowing in the name of the joint venture is limited to the difference between the total investment and the registered capital. For example, if a joint venture's approved total investment is US$10 million and its approved registered capital is US$8 million, borrowing in the joint venture's name would be limited to US$2 million. If for any reason the joint venture later needs to borrow another US$1 million, then the parties must apply to the government for approval to increase its total investment to US$11 million. There are also limits to the ratio between the amounts of total investment and registered capital to prevent any overleveraging by a joint venture.[18]

Although, subject to the above limit, Sino-foreign joint ventures are free to borrow internationally, foreign lending to strictly domestic companies is highly regulated.[19] A potential lender is well advised to seek evidence of advance government approval for any borrowing from such domestic borrowers. Any lender that wishes to lend to a Sino-foreign joint venture partner using such partner's interest in the joint venture as security should also be aware of the transfer restriction discussed earlier. Because any transfer of any JV interest is subject to government approval, such security may be of doubtful value.

Although only certain major decisions, such as amendment to the articles of association and dissolution of the EJV, statutorily require unanimous board resolution,[20] the parties to any joint venture are free to agree whether any other issues require board decision by simple majority, super majority, or unanimity. In practice, foreign partners often detail in the joint venture contract and articles of association numerous types of decisions as requiring unanimous board approval, which are normally accepted by the Chinese parties and the government approval authorities. The EJV regulations specify that a director may appoint a proxy to attend board meetings. This practice can be applicable to CJVs by agreement of the parties.

A number of Chinese laws and regulations govern and protect the licensing of patent, trademark, and proprietary technology by foreign entities to Chinese enterprises, including Sino-foreign joint ventures.[21] It is common for the foreign partner to license for royalty its intellectual property to a joint venture to which it is a party. A frequent thorny issue is the exportability of the licensed products. The PRC regulations specify that export is not to be unreasonably restrained. Like most other types of contracts, technology transfer licenses require government approval, the standard of which differs from locality to locality. Although the concept of copyright is mentioned in the General Principles of Civil Code,[22] the PRC has not yet promulgated its copyright law. The situation presents a special problem for computer software protection.

Sino-foreign joint venture contracts and related agreements typically contain an arbitration clause specifying as the arbitration forum the Arbitration Commission of the Stockholm Chamber of Commerce or the China International Economic and Trade Arbitration Commission (formerly the Foreign Trade Arbitration Commission) in Beijing. The willingness to arbitrate in Stockholm is a historic anomaly. During the long period of East-West tension, the PRC considered Sweden as almost the only suitably neutral country. Consequently, the Chinese party as a standard practice would agree to a Stockholm arbitration clause if the foreign party to a transaction insisted on arbitration at a third country. Although the open policy of the late 70s has largely dissipated such East-West tension, the Stockholm arbitration clause practice continues as a tradition. Increasing willingness of the parties to accept Hong Kong as the arbitration forum has, however, been seen during the last one or two years.

Land Use

With the amendment of the Constitution in 1988,[23] under which land-use right transfer to private interests on limited terms is legitimated, real property law in the PRC appears to have entered into a new but perhaps confusing era. Previously, almost all urban enterprises were state-owned. State enterprises were simply allocated land for their own use by the government on an indefinite basis. With the advent of Sino-foreign joint ventures, some of these state enterprises participated in the joint ventures using part of their allocated land as capital contribution. The land so contributed can only be used and not be owned by the joint venture—theoretically, the contributed land will revert to the Chinese party at the expiration or termination of the joint venture.

As part of the land-use reform experiment, since late 1987, a number of cities including Shenzhen, Shanghai, and Guangzhou have promulgated "compensatory transfer of land use right" regulations.[24] Subsequently, a number of highly publicized cases were seen in which plots of land in these cities purportedly had been "sold" to various enterprises, including foreign companies, by the respective local governments through either auctions or negotiations. But, in reality, the term *sale* used in the press reports is a misnomer. Foreign investors interested in land investment in the PRC are well advised to pay attention to the following aspects. First, *sale* does not mean transfer of fee simple title. It actually means *lease* or transfer of a leasehold interest normally for up to 50 years, with lump sum rental payment by the "purchaser" at the outset. The ownership of and title to the land remains with the state. Second, land "sold" to date has been undeveloped or semideveloped land in the newly designated industrial zones. Any transfer of the more valuable land in the city centers, which has long been occupied by various state enterprises, would essentially be problematic for ideological and practical reasons. Third, the "purchaser" of the land must enter into a "land-use contract" with the government setting forth the rights, obligations, and limitations regarding land use. Although the land-use right is assignable for consideration, the assignees are bound by the terms of the original land-use contract. The market value of such land would therefore be adversely affected.

Other than contribution of allocated land by a state enterprise to a joint venture and the primary or secondary transfer of a leasehold interest under the above-mentioned experimental scheme, no other legal ways exist to transfer land-use right to foreign interests unless specifically approved by the appropriate government department. Foreign investors should be cautious when approached by any state enterprise or individual regarding any proposed "sale" of land.

Taxation

The basic income tax rate for EJVs is the flat rate of 33 percent.[25] Under normal circumstances, the company is exempt during the first two profitable years, and the rate is reduced by half during the next three years. The basic income tax rates for CJVs and WFOEs are graduated between 30 percent and 50 percent.[26] There is no exemption or reduction under normal circumstances. Despite the flexibility offered by the CJV structure, many foreign investors have chosen the EJV structure because of the lower tax rate and tax holidays as well as the more detailed, certain regulations governing EJVs. There is, however, a plan to consolidate the taxation for all types of foreign-invested enterprises, namely EJV, CJV, and WFOE.[27]

There are further tax concessions for each foreign-invested enterprise designated as a technologically advanced or export-oriented enterprise, whether it is an EJV, CJV, or WFOE.[28]

All domestic and foreign-invested enterprises are liable for Commercial & Industrial Consolidated Tax (CICT), a multiple-layer import/sales tax levied at the import, ex-factory, and retail levels based on the value of the goods or services at the respective level.[29] The rates range from 1.5 percent for gray yarn to 3 percent for construction service to 69 percent for grade A cigarettes. Goods for export are exempt at the ex-factory level.

Equipment, materials, and so forth brought into China by the foreign partner as part of the capital contribution to a joint venture are exempt from import tax and duties. Similarly, the portion of equipment and materials imported to be used by a joint venture or processing arrangement to produce goods for export are exempt from import tax and duties.

JOINT VENTURING IN INDONESIA

Foreign Investment Background

Foreign investment in Indonesia is regulated by the Law Concerning Investment of Foreign Capital, as amended (FCIL).[30] The FCIL applies to all foreign investment made after the act came into force (January 1967) and covers investment in the expansion or modernization of existing enterprises as well as new investment. The FCIL is administered by the Capital Investment Coordinating Board (BKPM), which examines and approves prospective foreign investment.

The broad principles that the BKPM considers when assessing an application for investment are:[31]

1. The foreign capital company (Penanaman Modal Asing or PMA) will carry on business in a field of investment that is "open" to foreign investment.
2. There is a minimum capital investment for the project, which, before the recent deregulation packages, was usually US$1 million.
3. The foreign joint venturer has a program to transfer skills to Indonesians in the shortest possible time with Indonesians taking an increasing role in management and key operational positions. Specific training programs are often required.
4. An Indonesian company or national is to be appointed as the PMA's agent/distributor in Indonesia.
5. Indonesian investors hold at least 20 percent of the equity (reduced in certain cases to 5 percent) and should acquire a 51 percent shareholding within a specified time frame.

In addition to satisfying that BKPM on these points, a substantial amount of additional documentation is required including:

1. The draft/final joint venture agreement and incorporation and financial details of the foreign and Indonesian joint venturers.
2. A description of the planned activities of the PMA including the production process to be used; other information relating to the planned activities including drawings, plant layout, and land needs.
3. The annual production and marketing program including export marketing.
4. The construction schedule (if appropriate).
5. Any agreement(s) relating to the utilization of technology and expertise from abroad.

Despite several efforts over the years to streamline procedures, the approval process still presents a significant disincentive to investment by foreigners. Many foreign enterprises have resorted to alternate modes of operation in Indonesia as a result.

The FCIL provides that an enterprise operated wholly, or for the greater part, in Indonesia as a separate business unit must be a legal entity organized under Indonesian law and have its domicile in Indonesia.

There are significant exceptions to this requirement, and it is possible to avoid some of its strictures.

Indonesian Corporate Law

Companies are regulated by the Indonesian Commercial Code, which was instituted in 1848[32] based on the Dutch law in force at that time. The Indonesian Code has undergone limited change since. This is illustrated by the fact that the formal law that regulates corporations is limited to some 21 articles of the Commercial Code.[33] Only one type of corporate entity with limited lability is recognized. There is no equivalent to the English private company or Dutch B.V.

Limited Liability Company

The *Naamlose Vennotschap*, in Indonesian *Perseroan Terbatas* or PT, is the corporate body provided for under the Commercial Code. The PT offers limited liability as a legal entity separate and distinct from that of its shareholders. The capital of a PT is divided into shares, and the liability is limited to their face value.

The articles of incorporation must be drawn up in the form of a notarial deed. The articles of incorporation include the rights and duties of shareholders, the name of the company, its purposes, total capital, share value, and management.

The PT structure may include not only a board of directors but also a board of supervisors (*komisaris*), which may be given power to approve certain decisions of the directors.

After the articles have been notarized, they must be submitted to the Ministry of Justice for approval.

The company does not achieve legal status as an entity, and the incorporators remain personally liable for the obligations incurred by the company until approval of the notarial deed (the articles) by the Minister of Justice. The directors are deemed liable thereafter until the articles are registered with the relevant district registry office of the *Pengadilan Negeri* (court) and published in the official gazette (*Berita Negara*).

The articles of incorporation of a PMA company are first approved by the BKPM before being notarized.

While the articles of approved PMA companies are normally approved by the Ministry of Justice and gazetted within a reasonable time, other companies often suffer inordinate delays at various stages and an extraordinary proportion of the PT companies encountered in practice do not have limited liability.

Corporate Joint Ventures
Joint venture or shareholders' agreements follow a common pattern for such documents.

Control Devices and Issues in a PMA Company
One device that may be considered by foreigners facing minority share ownership is diversification of the Indonesian ownership to two or more independent groups that, it is hoped, will not act in concert against the foreign partner.

Provisions may be inserted in the joint venture agreement and the articles for the protection of minority shareholders. Classes of shares are permitted, with the power to appoint directors and supervisors.[34]

Irrevocable powers of attorney or voting trusts are *not* feasible devices to change the balance of voting power at the shareholder or board level.[35] However, agreements, such as provisions in the joint venture agreement, as to how shares will be voted are valid and enforceable, and a vote in contravention of such an agreement may not be valid.[36]

Pledge agreements with signed share transfers are also resorted to by foreign investors to give them power to take over a company in time of dispute. While these may have some practical efficacy, their legal strength is dubious because among other things Indonesian law does not recognize rights of private sale of collateral.[37]

Alternates to the PMA Company
Because of the restrictions on foreign investment under the FCIL, including exclusion from certain businesses, high minimum capital requirements, bureaucratic inertia, and other problems, such as discrimination against foreigners in government contracting,[38] many foreign companies enter the Indonesian market in other forms.

Some of these, such as agency arrangements, are not joint ventures, strictly speaking. However, many joint ventures are set up using a variety of structures, always based on doing business in Indonesia through a domestically owned company. Shares in that company may be held by a nominee of the foreign investor. The local company may enter cooperation, technical assistance, and/or management agreements that constitute, in effect, an unincorporated joint venture operating behind the screen of the local entity. Limited liability is often sought to be preserved through use of an offshore joint venture company as the other party to the cooperation and related agreements.

The precise arrangements vary enormously, and it is advisable to seek legal and tax advice in structuring such arrangements.

Unincorporated Joint Ventures

Approved foreign investment must normally be through a PMA company. There are limited exceptions in the areas of mineral extraction and construction funded by foreign loans. Unincorporated joint ventures, usually called joint operations, are found particularly in the construction sphere.

It is thought that the joint operation is a kind of Commercial Code partnership, or *firma*.[39] There is a Civil Code form of partnership, the *Maatschap,* and the Civil Code provisions are applicable by reference to *firma*.[40] Joint operation agreements which the author has seen have followed a pattern common to integrated unincorporated construction joint ventures used in major international construction projects.

JOINT VENTURING IN JAPAN

Foreign Investment Background

For many years, Japanese restrictions on foreign investment were very strict. However, the current restrictions on foreign investment outside a limited number of industries are not onerous, and foreign investment controls as such are no longer a major factor in new joint ventures in Japan.[41]

Reasons to Joint Venture

Research and Development. Research joint ventures between Japanese and foreign companies have become more common, to share technology and spread the risks and burdens of major R&D efforts.[42]

Access to Customers; Local Knowledge; Local Distribution Channels. Foreign companies often find Japan difficult because of language barriers and local custom. Japanese distribution networks are intricate and present formidable barriers to new products. Joint ventures may be used to overcome these factors.[43]

Construction Industry.   In recent years, the Japanese government has become more willing to license foreign companies as construction contractors. Most of those licensed have formed associations with Japanese construction companies. Moreover, they are bidding in joint venture with various Japanese contractors.[44]

Antimonopoly Considerations.   Japan has an antimonopoly law enforced by the Fair Trade Commission (FTC).[45] Joint venture and license agreements should be filed with the FTC,[46] which has developed guidelines relative to anticompetitive licensing practices.[47] Relatively little concern has ever been demonstrated about the potential anticompetitive effects of joint ventures between enterprises in the same business, which in U.S. thinking might be suspect as horizontal restraints.[48]

Corporate Joint Ventures

Japan was at the forefront in the development of corporate joint ventures in the 1950s and 1960s, and extensive literature is available describing relevant Japanese law, typical agreements, and typical agreement clauses.[49]

Forms of Company
Almost all Japanese corporate joint ventures take the form of *kabushiki kaisha* (KK),[50] or company limited by shares, which resembles its model, the German *Aktiengesellschaft*. This is despite the fact that the KK form is not well adapted to closely held companies and creates many legal problems when used for joint ventures.[51]

Better suited is the *yugen kaisha*,[52] analogous to the English private company and originally modeled on the German *Gesellschaft mit beschraenkter Haftung* (GMBH), but this form of company conveys an image of small business to Japanese and consequently is rarely used for joint ventures despite the recommendations of some legal writers.[53] In the past, offshore companies have rarely been used as the vehicle for a Japanese joint venture, although in principle there are probably no longer any good legal reasons for this. Certainly, the Japanese would regard it as odd, so it would run into various difficulties in implementation.

Control Problems and Shareholders' Agreements

As noted, the KK form is not well-suited to joint venturing. Its use raises many legal issues, including the validity and effectiveness of agreements on voting for directors and restrictions on transferability of shares.[54] Directors may not vote by proxy,[55] and shareholders may not make decisions in writing but must meet and vote.[56] Shareholders' agreements should be written with these problems in mind. Moreover, wherever possible, any matter should also be regulated in the articles of incorporation (*teikan*) as well. Any matter covered only in the agreement may be valid between the shareholders but will not prevent corporate actions in violation thereof from being valid.[57] Classes of shares are recognized but apparently seldom used to solve control problems in joint ventures. Super majority provisions are also used, but their efficacy to protect any shareholder who has less than one third of the voting shares is dubious because it appears the articles may *always* be amended by a vote of over two thirds.[58] The discussion of Korean control devices below will also generally apply to Japan.

Contributions in Kind

Contributions of capital to a KK other than in the form of money require court approval.[59] It is therefore customary to pay in money and then for the joint venture company, after it comes into existence, to buy the asset to be contributed.[60]

Restrictions on Transfers

Japanese law expressly allows restrictions on transfer of shares to be imposed by provision in the articles of the company.[61] However, such restriction is limited to the requirement of board approval, and if the board disapproves, the shareholder may request the board name a substitute buyer. The extent to which the shareholders may agree to restrictions different from those recognized by the Commercial Code is subject to differing views. The more common view is that agreements among shareholders or between shareholders and the company would be valid, although they might not bind third parties.[62]

Unincorporated Joint Ventures

Unincorporated joint ventures are in common use among Japanese in the construction industry (*kyodo kigyotai*).[63] Outside of construction, unincorporated ventures are relatively rare. While the typical foreign investor will not wish to use an unincorporated vehicle for doing business in Japan, such a form may be appropriate in some circumstances.

Forms Available

Under Japanese law, partnerships (*nin'ikumiai*) are regulated by the Civil Code Articles 667 et seq. *Nin'ikumiai* are not recognized as juridical persons and are unable to hold title to land or to file lawsuits as such; the members must do so as a group or through a nominee. Likewise, there is no *nin'ikumiai* income tax return; the members include their ratable shares in their own returns. Members of *nin'ikumiai* are jointly and severally liable for debts incurred by any of them for the business.

The Commercial Code, Article 535 et seq., provides for an anonymous partnership (*Tokutei Kumiai*). In this form, one party carries on the business in his or her name and profits are shared. However, the anonymous partner is not liable to third parties; conversely, he or she may have no role in management.

In the author's experience, Japanese tend to expect unincorporated joint ventures between foreigners and Japanese to follow an international and therefore usually a common-law format. With the increase in involvement with foreign enterprises, a greater relevance of joint venture arrangements has appeared. The Japanese are studying the methods of joint venturing with foreign enterprises within Japan.

JOINT VENTURING IN THE REPUBLIC OF KOREA

Foreign Investment Background

The government of the Republic of Korea has historically encouraged foreign investment pursuant to a preferential policy that has viewed foreign capital and technology as necessary for economic development. At the same time, Korea's foreign investment laws have been structured to protect domestic industries and regulate the outflow of foreign currency. The economy continues to thrive and mature, and the trend in Korea is said to be toward a neutral policy that neither actively encourages such investment nor interferes with it. An increasing range of economic sectors have been opened to foreign investment activities. Nonetheless, the Korean government continues to exercise broad discretion in comprehensively regulating foreign investment.

Foreign direct investment in Korea is principally governed by the Foreign Capital Inducement Act[64] (FCIA) and regulations and guidelines issued pursuant thereto. The FCIA stipulates conditions and procedures for foreign investment as well as incentives and guarantees in relation to foreign investment. Foreign investment pursuant to the FCIA is accompanied by foreign exchange approval, which is required for virtually all foreign exchange transactions under the Foreign Exchange Control Act (FECA).[65] Furthermore, technology licensing agreements that involve a repatriation of royalties are subject to review and approval pursuant to the FCIA and FECA.

Reasons to Joint Venture

The incorporated joint venture has been a favored investment vehicle for foreign investors in Korea. Perhaps the principal reason for this has been the Korean government's strong policy preference for the joint venture. From a policy perspective, the joint venture is attractive because it offers both the influx of foreign capital to Korea and the transfer of knowledge from the foreign to the local partner. Thus, the FCIA has favored joint ventures over wholly owned subsidiaries. Foreign investment in some industries has been prohibited unless it is accomplished through a joint venture with a Korean partner (examples include tractor manufacturing, distilling ethyl alcohol, and manufacturing optical fibers, as set forth in Ministry of Finance Guidelines).[66] Furthermore, though a foreign investor in industries open to foreign investment may theoretically acquire up to 100 percent equity in a Korean corporation, in practice, government approval may be difficult to secure for a wholly owned subsidiary.

A second reason for the popularity of joint ventures is the importance many foreign investors have placed on the Korean partner's role in providing guidance in unfamiliar business practices and customs. The importance of this role varies among industries and, for example, may be more important if the investor must rely upon local distribution channels than if the Korean operation will be manufacturing strictly for export.

Corporate Joint Ventures

Available Types of Business Entity. For historical reasons, the law of Korean business organizations is relatively similar to that of Japan. Two types of corporate business entities are recognized under the Korean Commercial Code[67]—the *yuhan hoesa* (closely held limited liability company) and the *chusik hoesa* (joint stock company limited by shares). In practice, virtually all joint ventures in Korea have taken the form of a *chusik hoesa*, a corporate form that limits the liability of shareholders to their stock subscriptions. The *yuhan hoesa*, which also limits the liability of shareholders, though with several exceptions, has its own attractive features but is seldom used, largely because of the prestige Korean investors have attached to the *chusik hoesa* and the connotations of the small, family business associated with the *yuhan hoesa*.[68]

The *yuhan hoesa* may provide greater flexibility in restricting the transfer of shares and is generally easy to establish, but it requires a minimum of 2 shareholders and a maximum of 50. The *chusik hoesa*, on the other hand, has no such limitations in the number of shareholders and offers a greater range of investment devices, such as different forms of common and preferred stock and bonds and debentures.

Control Issues in Korean Joint Ventures. Assuming the foreign investor adopts the popular *chusik hoesa*, parties to a Korean joint venture will almost invariably enter into a joint venture agreement that defines their relationship and is intended to take precedence over the *chusik hoesa*'s articles of incorporation. In drafting the joint venture agreement and articles, the foreign investor must be aware of certain basic requirements and techniques for exercising some measure of control over the decisions of the Korean joint venture company. Article 368 of the Korean Commercial Code generally provides that all share- holders' resolutions must be adopted by a majority of the shareholders present at a shareholders' meeting who represent a majority of the total number of issued shares, except as otherwise provided in the Korean Commercial Code or in the articles of incorporation.

If the foreign investor cannot obtain government approval for a majority interest in a joint venture or otherwise accepts an equal or minority holding, various other control options are open to it.

At the shareholder level, a foreign investor who cannot exercise positive control over a majority of shares may turn to the passive control of holding the minimum number of shares necessary for blocking res- olutions of a meeting of shareholders. Furthermore, a foreign investor with a minority holding should at least consider a special quorum pro- vision that would ensure undisclosed action cannot be taken. Among the devices permitted, the foreign investor may reserve certain decisions to the shareholder and expand upon the Korean Commercial Code's list of decisions that require a "special" resolution of a two-thirds vote, which includes amendments to the articles of incorporation (Article 433), a transfer of a significant part of the company's business (Article 374), removal of a director or internal auditor from office (Articles 385 and 415), reduction of capital (Article 438), or voluntary dissolution (Article 517).

The foreign investor could add, for example, capital expenditures, indebtedness, or guarantees in excess of certain amounts to the items that by law require a "special" resolution. Moreover, if the two-thirds requirement will not ensure the foreign investor a voice, such as if the foreign investor holds less than one third of the shares, decisions that require unanimous consent may be added to the Korean Commercial Code list, which includes exemption of promoters, directors, or auditors from liability or reorganization of the company into a limited partnership. Because Article 433 provides that the articles may be amended by a two-thirds vote, "unanimous consent" provisions in the articles may arguably be amended by a vote of more than two thirds. However, this would constitute a breach of the joint venture agreement.

Control can also be exercised by the foreign investor at the board of directors level. As is true of most Western legal systems, in Korea, a company's board of directors is responsible for the "administration of the affairs of the company" (Article 393). However, day-to-day managerial decisions are made by one or two representative directors who are responsible to the board but are, in practice, very powerful. Absent notice to the contrary, third parties dealing with representative directors are entitled to accept that they have power to bind the company.

Although various methods of exercising control at the board of directors level are permitted, the foreign investor may not appoint a number of directors that exceeds the ratio of shares or equity of the foreign investor. Such power is considered to be an unfair trade practice, according to Article 4(4) of an Economic Planning Board Public Notice that governs unfair trade practices in international agreements, including joint ventures ("EPB Unfair Trade Criteria").[69] Article 4(5) of the EPB Unfair Trade Practice Criteria further provides that it is also an unfair trade practice in the case of a 50 : 50 joint venture if a director appointed by the foreign investor has the right to cast a tie-breaking vote.

Apart from the limitation imposed upon the foreign investor's ability to control the number of directors, special quorum and super majority requirements may be imposed at the board level, requiring, for example, a two-thirds vote or some other percentage that gives the foreign investor's directors veto power over certain important decisions. The Korean Commercial Code would not prevent such requirements.

As pointed out above, in Korea, the control over representative directors, who are particular directors empowered to represent and bind the company, is also important. Because it is common for the Korean partner to appoint the representative director in cases where the parties have roughly equal equity shares, the foreign investor could restrict the representative director by stipulating in the articles of incorporation or the joint venture agreement certain important decisions that must be made by the board. In the alternative, the foreign investor could appoint a second representative director who would jointly represent the company, thereby assuring that all major decisions that bind the company would be jointly taken.

Under Korean law, certain problems may arise in attempting to exercise rights of control, even if they have been agreed to in the joint venture agreement and articles of incorporation. Chief among these is enforcing agreements between joint venture partners to vote in a particular manner. Joint venture agreements typically include provisions directed toward ensuring the selection of each others' nominees for the board of directors or removal or vacancy of a director. In Korea, however, a vote made in violation of a voting agreement is still valid under the Korean Commercial Code, and the violator would be liable only for damages. Voting trusts are seldom utilized in Korea, and their validity has not been clearly established. Likewise, classes of shares have not been used for this purpose. Some joint venture agreements stipulate liquidated damages that are payable in the event of a breach of a voting agreement.

The second common problem in connection with preserving control over a joint venture arises with enforcing restrictions on the transfer of shares. While it was earlier noted that the transfer of shares is statutorily limited for a *yuhan hoesa*, Article 335 of the Korean Commercial Code provides that, for a *chusik hoesa*, "the transfer of shares may not be prohibited or restricted even by the provisions of the articles of incorporation." However, as in the case of voting agreements, in practice, such restrictions are frequently included in joint venture agreements. If the agreement is breached, the transferee would legally acquire the shares and, though no Korean court has yet addressed this point, it is believed damages could be sought from the transferor. It may be best to provide a liquidated damages provision to cover such a possibility.

Government Approval Process. Once the structure of the joint venture has been determined, the joint venture agreement and a business plan, among other documents, must be submitted for government approval pursuant to the FCIA, though it should be noted that approval pursuant to the FECA is theoretically available.

In principle, foreign investment is permitted in all industries except those identified in the "Negative List" as restricted or prohibited and those designated as reserved for small- and medium-size industries. In both cases, foreign investment may be permitted subject to special criteria. As of July 1, 1987, the foreign investment approval process was streamlined for projects with a foreign investment ratio of less than 50 percent, which can now receive expedited approval though the Bank of Korea (BOK) if the total foreign capital to be induced is US$3 million or less, no tax exemptions are sought, and the investment is in a manufacturing project that is not prohibited or restricted. Such an eligible project may be approved within 10 days of filing an application with the BOK. The Korean government plans to expand eligibility for expedited BOK approval to all foreign investments meeting the foregoing criteria irrespective of the amount of foreign capital induced. Most foreign investment projects in the manufacturing as well as in the service sectors will eventually be shifted to a notification system.

All projects ineligible for expedited approval must be submitted to the Ministry of Finance (MOF), a process that is more time-consuming than BOK review and includes the participation of additional concerned ministries that the MOF will consult and that will conduct economic and feasibility studies of the project pursuant to Article 35 of the FCIA. The MOF will also request the Economic Planning Board to review the joint venture agreement to determine compliance with the EPB Unfair Trade Criteria, which, in addition to the restrictions on the nomination of directors previously noted, also prohibits provisions such as those that impose unreasonable restraints on exportation of the joint venture's products and restrictions on the parties from which raw materials can be purchased. (It should be noted that, in practice, even projects that are eligible for the BOK's expedited approval are subject to the EPB Unfair Trade Criteria.) A proposed investment of over US$5 million further requires deliberation by the Foreign Capital Review Committee. Upon review of the opinions of the concerned ministries and the EPB, the MOF will issue its approval.

In doing so, the MOF has broad discretion and may condition approval, for example, on a change in the foreign investment ratio or a change in the business plan.

Unincorporated Joint Ventures

The Korean Commercial Code also provides for the *hapmyung hoesa* (partnership) and the *hapcha hoesa* (limited partnership).[70] These vehicles are each registered as companies, may hold property, and are considered juridical entities. However, a foreign company cannot form a *hapmyung hoesa* or a *hapcha hoesa* as a joint venture and become a member with unlimited liability because Article 173 prevents any company from becoming a member with unlimited liability in another company. Thus, these two vehicles would be limited to use by an individual and not a corporate foreign investor.

The Korean Civil Code also provides for an unincorporated partnership form known as a *johap*,[71] which is not deemed a legal entity. This form is rarely used and is unfamiliar to Korean business. It has not been used by foreign investors.

JOINT VENTURING IN MALAYSIA

Foreign Investment Background

Foreign investment in Malaysia is constrained in a number of ways. At present, any company engaging in "manufacturing activity" with shareholder's funds of M$2.5 million or more and with 75 or more full-time employees must obtain a license from the Ministry of Trade and Industry.[72] Where foreign investment is involved, application should be made to the Malaysian Industrial Development Authority (MIDA). Under current guidelines, if a company is to export 80 percent or more of its product, foreigners may own 100 percent of the equity. If application is made to MIDA by December 31, 1990, 100 percent foreign ownership may be permitted if the company is to export 50 percent or more of its products, or employs 350 or more Malaysians, and the company's products do not compete with existing local products. For companies that will be producing high-technology or high-priority goods for the Malaysian domestic market, up to 51 percent foreign ownership is permitted. Otherwise, foreign ownership is permitted in a range from 30 percent to 79 percent, depending on the proportion of product to be exported, the amount of high-technology input, and a variety of other factors.

Yet another approval, from the Foreign Investment Committee, is required for the acquisition of any assets in the country of a value in excess of M$5 million. Normally such approval will be given only if the investment is made through a joint venture company whose ownership meets applicable guidelines.

Also relevant is the new economic policy that mandates basically that all Malaysia companies should eventually be controlled at least 70 percent by Malaysians and at least 30 percent by "bumiputra" Malaysians, i.e., ethnic Malays or certain other indigenous ethnic groups.

Subject to the above, foreign investment in land is not restricted. However, certain land is reserved for ownership by ethnic Malays only.

Incorporated Joint Ventures

Reasons to Joint Venture
The preeminent reason for entering into a corporate joint venture in Malaysia is to comply with the several laws and policy guidelines requiring that business of any magnitude be carried on in this form.

Forms of Company
Forms of company available are based on English and even more closely on Australian law. They include the public limited company and the private limited company. Other available forms, such as the company limited by guarantee or the company with unlimited liability, are relatively rare. The private company, or *sendirian berhad*, is the best-adapted to joint ventures and is commonly used.

A private company, according to the Malaysian Companies Act:

1. Restricts the right to transfer its shares.
2. Limits the number of its "members" (shareholders) to not more than 50.
3. Prohibits any invitation to the public to subscribe for shares in the company.
4. Prohibits any invitation to the public to deposit money with the company.

Control Mechanisms in Incorporated Joint Ventures
Since Malaysian company law is generally close to that of England and other Commonwealth countries, control mechanisms in private companies are likewise similar. Classes of shares may be used, so a vote on important issues requires a majority vote of both (or all) classes. Like-

wise, each class may elect directors, and decisions of the board may require a vote of directors chosen by shareholders of each class.

Unincorporated Joint Ventures

Use of unincorporated joint ventures between foreign interests and local ones is not uncommon in Malaysia. For instance, a foreign investor may invest through a wholly owned local company but overcome government procurement policies favoring local and especially *bumiputra* investors by bidding for contracts in joint venture or consortium with a local company. In some cases, the arrangement may use subcontracting arrangements while being in substance a joint venture.

Malaysian law is very similar to that of English law in its treatment of unincorporated joint ventures.

JOINT VENTURING IN THE PHILIPPINES

Foreign Investment Background

In the Philippines, the foreign investment regime significantly restricts foreign investment. Joint ventures have proved to be a popular method of market participation.

Filipino law regards a locally incorporated company as a "Philippine" national if 60 percent of the voting equity is Filipino. In general, therefore, up to 40 percent foreign equity investment in the capital stock of a company is permitted without the need for prior approval from the Board of Investments (BOI).[73] For foreign investment exceeding 40 percent, the BOI must satisfy itself before granting approval that the investment is consistent with the Investment Priorities Plan (IPP), the area of investment involved is not yet adequately exploited by Filipino companies and/or nationals, the project would contribute to the sound and balanced development of the Philippine economy on a self-sustaining basis, and the business does not promote monopolies or conflict with the Philippine Constitution. If the BOI is satisfied in relation to these matters, then higher foreign equity participation is possible provided the company does not operate in an area in which there are minimum Filipino ownership requirements (discussed below). Slightly different criteria apply for projects that qualify for incentives.[74]

If foreign participation does not exceed 40 percent, the foreign investor is required to file a report on the foreign investment with the BOI only for record purposes.

In addition to the above general restrictions, there are certain areas in which there can be no foreign participation such as mass media, rural banking, retail trade business, and public works and construction for national defense. There are also higher minimum Filipino ownership requirements for other areas of economic activity such as banking (70 percent of voting stock; 60 percent with president's approval), advertising agencies (70 percent), public works construction (75 percent), and shipping on bays and rivers (75 percent). Further areas are open only to "Philippine" companies (i.e., those with 60 percent or more Filipino ownership). These areas include public utilities, finance companies, coastal shipping, and the disposition, exploitation, development, or use of private and public lands.

Land
Only Filipino citizens or corporations and associations whose capital is at least 60 percent owned by Filipinos may own private land.[75]

Licensing of Know-how/Patents
Although there are laws that relate exclusively to patents and trademarks,[76] foreign licensing agreements, of the type often used in joint venture arrangements, are subject to examination and approval. Foreign licensing, as understood in the Philippines, covers a variety of contractual arrangements. It generally encompasses the situation where a foreign company will make available its patents, trademarks, manufacturing know-how, services (technical, managerial, and marketing), and other assets to a Filipino corporation in return for royalties and other forms of payment.

All such technology-transfer arrangements entered into directly or indirectly with foreign corporations and/or foreign-owned corporations must be registered with the Bureau of Patents, Trademarks and Licenses (BPTL) if the object of the agreement is to:

1. Transfer, assign, or license for use or exploitation patents for inventions, improvements, industrial models, and drawings.
2. License the use of or exploitation of trademarks.
3. Furnish technical know-how and information by plans, diagrams, models, specifications, instruction, and training of personnel.

4. Provide technical consultancy, services, and assistance in any form.

The applicant must prove the agreement is registered with the BPTL when seeking Central Bank authorization to remit royalties, fees, or other transactions under a technology transfer agreement.

In evaluating and approving contracts for registration, the BPTL requires that the appropriateness of and need for the technology or industrial property right be established, the fees and technology payments be reasonable, Philippine law governs the interpretation of the contract, and the term of the contract does not exceed five years.

Loans by Foreigners to Locals

Borrowing from abroad is possible but is subject to minimum criteria as to cost and repayment terms laid down by the Monetary Board.[77] Foreign loans, including loans from parents or associated companies, must be approved and registered with the Central Bank before the remittance of interest and principal can be approved. Loans will be sanctioned only if they meet the repayment terms laid down by the Monetary Board. In general, firms whose products are clearly designed for export and those that are earning foreign exchange are more likely to obtain approval.

Remittance of Dividends, Profits, Royalties, and Interest

Interest.   As noted above, foreign loans require Monetary Board approval before being taken out. Once approved and registered, they can be serviced by the remittance of interest.

Profits and Dividends.   Central Bank approval through the Management of External Debt and Investment Accounts Department (MEDIAD) is required before the remittance (net of taxes) of profits, capital gains, and dividends. Repatriation in full is allowed at the interbank guiding rate prevailing on the date of actual remittance. However, such remittances should not be financed by domestic borrowings.

Royalties.   For Central Bank authorization to remit royalties, fees, or other transactions under a technology transfer arrangement, the applicant must prove the arrangement is registered with the BPTL. Once this criterion has been satisfied, such remittances can be made.

Reasons to Joint Venture

As can be seen from the above, a variety of reasons militate toward joint venturing as a means of participation in the Philippine economy.

Corporate Joint Ventures
In the Philippines, corporations are primarily divided into stock and nonstock corporations.[78] Nonstock corporations are not appropriate vehicles for joint ventures because of various restrictions applicable to such corporations (such as a prohibition on the distribution of dividends). They are generally confined to charitable, religious, and educational bodies.

Stock corporations in the Philippines have a separate and distinct juridical personality from that of the incorporators. Stock corporations are formed for a stated purpose or purposes set out in the articles of incorporation. Only natural persons, not fewer than 5 nor more than 15, and a majority of whom are Philippine residents may form a corporation. The statutory minimum paid up capital of a corporation is P 5,000.

Government Approval Process
If a stock corporation is to be used as a joint venture vehicle in which the non-Philippine joint venturer(s) owns or controls more than 40 percent of the outstanding capital, then it is necessary to obtain written authorization from the Board of Investment (BOI) before doing business or undertaking economic activity in the Philippines. Below 40 percent, BOI approval is generally not necessary, although such investments must be reported to the BOI for its records.

To facilitate the granting of such authorization, the BOI has established a "One-Stop Action Center." This center deals with processing, inquiries, and documentation necessary for foreign investments.

To register with the BOI, it is also necessary to obtain, if applicable, a locational clearance. This clearance is necessary for projects requiring construction of plants, buildings, or other land improvements. This locational clearance is issued by the Housing and Land Use Regulatory Board.

If the proposed area of activity is in an environmentally critical industry, an Environmental Compliance Certificate needs to be obtained from the National Pollution Control Commission. Environmentally critical industries include metal manufacture, petroleum and petrochemicals, smelting, resource extraction, chemicals, textiles, forestry, pulp and paper production, and manufacture.

Once the appropriate BOI approval and certificates have been obtained, the incorporation documents can be lodged with the SEC for processing and issue of the Certificate of Incorporation.

Control Issues

Under Filipino law, a specific type of stock corporation, known as a close corporation, can be used as a joint venture vehicle.[79] As discussed below, some aspects of the close corporation make it an attractive joint venture vehicle. A close corporation is analogous to an English private company.

A close corporation is a corporation whose articles of incorporation shall provide that all of its issued stock shall:

1. Be held by not more than 20 persons.
2. Be subject to restrictions on transfer.
3. Not be listed on any stock exchange or make any public offerings.

These restrictions distinguish a close corporation from other stock corporations. Any corporation may be incorporated as a close corporation except for mining and oil companies, stock exchanges, banks, insurance companies, public utilities, educational institutions, and corporations declared to be vested with public interest.

In addition to the above restrictions, which are applicable to all close corporations, other agreements can be made or features incorporated into the articles of incorporation to make a close corporation an attractive joint venture vehicle. These include:

1. The classification of shares or rights and qualifications for owning or holding same.

2. Great quorum or voting requirements in meetings of stockholders or directors than provided for by the Code of Corporations for stock corporations that are not close corporations.

3. The classification of directors into one or more classes, each of whom may be voted for and elected solely by a particular class of stock. The articles of incorporation may also provide that the business of the corporation shall be managed by the stockholders of the corporation rather than by the board of directors, and that all offices and employees shall be elected or appointed by stockholders instead of by the board of directors.

4. The ability for a pre-incorporation agreement, made by and among stockholders and executed by all stockholders, to survive the incorporation and continue to be valid and binding between and among the stockholders to the extent that the agreement is not inconsistent with the articles of incorporation.

5. A written agreement between two or more stockholders and signed by the parties thereto, to provide that in exercising voting rights, the shares held by them shall be voted as therein provided or as they may agree.

Section 103 of the Code of Corporations further provides that a two-thirds majority is needed to amend the articles of incorporation of a close corporation.

Control Mechanisms in Stock Corporations Generally

Although the above restrictions are applicable to close corporations, there are arrangements that can be adopted in all stock corporations to enhance control by one joint venturer. These arrangements include:

1. Having more than one Filipino partner so as to spread the local ownership and militate against a "head-to-head" clash regarding the operation of the joint venture corporation.

2. Using management contracts. By the use of such a contract, one joint venturer may, notwithstanding a minority interest, exercise effective control over the joint venture vehicle. However, under the Code of Corporations, these management contracts are generally limited to five years, but they may be renewed.

3. Using licensing agreements. As noted above, such agreements are the subject of review by the relevant government agency. Despite this, if the joint venture involves the transfer of technology by the foreign joint venture, then a carefully drawn technology transfer agreement often combined with a management agreement can give a substantial degree of control over the management of the joint venture corporation.

4. Having a voting trust arrangement. Such an arrangement, whereby a stockholder or stockholders confer upon a trustee the voting and other rights of shares, is permissible under Filipino law, but such an arrangement cannot exceed five years. If a voting trust is an integral part of a loan agreement, Filipino law provides that it shall expire on the full payment of the loan.

5. Using a share pledge. This is analogous to a voting trust whereby a loan may carry with it a condition that the lender may have the right to vote at shareholders' meetings.

Unincorporated Joint Ventures

Partnerships

Although partnerships in the Philippines may be informally constituted (i.e., without a written instrument of partnership), such will generally not be the case in a partnership being used as a joint venture vehicle. For every contract of partnership having a capital of P 3,000 or more or that involves property or real rights, the partnership agreement must appear in a public instrument that must be recorded with the SEC.

Partnerships in the Philippines have a juridical personality separate and distinct from that of the partners. In addition, under Filipino income tax law, partnerships, except for general professional partnerships, are treated as corporations. This, combined with the unlimited liability of the investor partners, makes general partnerships less attractive than corporations as joint venture vehicles.

Partnerships may be general or limited. A general partnership is one where all partners are personally liable for the contracts of the partnership once its assets have been exhausted. In a limited partnership, only the general partner or partners need have unlimited liability.

As with corporations, where a proposed investment would result in the partnership having a foreign ownership of more than 40 percent, approval of the BOI should be secured before registering the articles of partnership with the SEC and securing the necessary municipal licenses. The criteria the BOI uses to assess such investment are the same as that applied to a corporation.

Partnerships present similar control problems to corporations, and some of the control devices discussed above can be applicable to partnerships (such as management contracts and licensing agreements). In addition, carefully drawn articles of partnership may contain provisions that can prevent oppression of a minority partner/joint venturer or ensure effective control rests with one of the joint venturers. In addition, when the articles of partnership address such matters as management, contribution of capital, sharing of profits, and dispute resolution, they should be drafted so as to provide for the desired balance of interests of the partners.

In general terms, the partnership provisions of the Filipino Commercial Code address such matters but are applicable only in the absence of specific provision by the partners in the partnership agreement. Thus, there is scope for flexibility by the draftsman of the articles of partnership.

ENDNOTES

[1] See generally Jaeger, "Joint Ventures: Origin, Nature and Development," *American University Law Review* 9 (1960), p. 1 and Jaeger, "Joint Ventures: Membership, Types and Termination," *American University Law Review* 9 (1960), p. 111.

[2] *Black's Law Dictionary* (St. Paul: West Publishing, 1979), p. 751: ("Joint Adventure"), p. 753: ("Joint Venture").

[3] See note 48 below and accompanying text.

[4] See notes 65 and 66 below and accompanying text.

[5] See discussion below relative to joint ventures in Indonesia, Malaysia, People's Republic of China, and the Philippines.

[6] See notes 49–57 and accompanying text.

[7] Henderson, "Contract Problems in U.S.-Japanese Joint Ventures," *Washington Law Review* 39 (1964), pp. 479, 596.

[8] See "Joint Development of Resources Projects—A Comparison," Proceedings of the Regional Energy Law Seminar, Singapore, September 30, 1985, International Bar Association (London, 1986).

[9] This Joint Venture in China portion was written prior to May 1989. Since the removal of Zhao Ziyang from the post of Chinese Communist Party General Secretary in June 1989, there has been indication that the government has moved toward the direction of slowing the economic liberalization.

[10] Compare the provisional regulations of the People's Republic of China on private enterprises promulgated by the State Council on June 25, 1988. These regulations on experimental basis legitimate private enterprises by providing for sole proprietorship, partnership, and limited liability company structures. The regulations are not applicable to state-owned enterprises, which still comprise the vast majority of all enterprises in China. Note that the owners under the limited liability company structure are characterized as "investors" instead of "shareholders."

[11] The Foreign Economic Contract Law of the PRC adopted by the National People's Congress on March 21, 1985.

[12] The Economic Contract Law of the PRC adopted by the National People's Congress, December 13, 1981.

[13] The Law of the PRC Concerning Enterprises with Sole Foreign Investment adopted by the National People's Congress on April 12, 1986.

[14] See the Law of the PRC on Joint Ventures Using Chinese and Foreign Investment (also called the Law of the PRC on Sino-Foreign Equity Joint Ventures) promulgated by the National People's Congress on July 8, 1979.

[15] The Law of the PRC on Sino-Foreign Cooperative Enterprises adopted by the National People's Congress on April 13, 1988.

[16] The PRC Management of Leasing of Small-Scale State Industrial Enterprise Tentative Regulations accepted in principle by the State Council on May 18, 1988.

[17] See Article 4, Certain Regulations on the Subscription of Capital by the Parties to Sino-Foreign Joint Equity Enterprises promulgated jointly by the Ministry of Foreign Economic Relations and Trade and the state Administration for Industry and Commerce on January 1, 1988.

[18] Provisional Regulations of the State Administration for Industry and Commerce on the Ratio between the Registered Capital and Total Investment of Sino-Foreign Joint Equity Enterprises promulgated on March 1, 1987.

[19] Strengthening the Administration of International Commercial Borrowing Circular issued by the State Council on February 14, 1989. See *People's Daily* (Chinese edition), February 15, 1989, p. 2.

[20] Article 36, the Regulations for the Implementation of the Law of the PRC on Joint Ventures using Chinese and Foreign Investment, promulgated by the State Council on September 20, 1983.

[21] See the Regulations on Administration of Technology Import Contracts of the PRC promulgated by the State Council on May 24, 1985; the Trademark Law of the PRC adopted by the National People's Congress on August 23, 1982; the Patent Law of the PRC adopted by the National People's Congress on March 12, 1984.

[22] Article 94, General Principles of Civil Code of the PRC adopted by the National People's Congress on April 12, 1986.

[23] Amendment to Articles 10(iv) and 11 of the Constitution of the PRC, passed by the National People's Congress on April 12, 1988.

[24] See Regulations of the Shenzhen SEZ on Land Management promulgated by the Guangdong Provincial People's Congress on January 3, 1988; Measures of Shanghai Municipality on the Compensatory Transfer of Land Use Rights promulgated by the Shanghai Municipal People's Government on November 29, 1987; Measures of the Guangzhou Economic and Technological Development Zone on the Compensatory Transfer and Assignment of Land Use Rights promulgated by the Guangzhou Municipal People's Government on March 9, 1988.

[25] Article 3, the Income Tax Law of the PRC Concerning Joint Ventures with Chinese and Foreign Investment promulgated by the National People's Congress on September 10, 1980.

[26] Articles 3 and 4, the Foreign Enterprise Income Tax Law of the PRC adopted by the National People's Congress on December 13, 1981.

[27] See Report in *China Daily* dated June 27, 1988, citing Mr. Jin Xin, director of the State Administration for Taxation.

[28] Regulations of the PRC for the Encouragement of Foreign Investment

promulgated by the State Council on October 11, 1986. In addition, the tax rates are lower in certain designated areas such as the Special Economic Zones and the Economic & Technological Development Zones.

[29] Regulations of the Consolidated Industrial and Commercial Tax of the PRC (Draft) adopted in principle by the National People's Congress on September 11, 1958.

[30] Law No. 1 of 1967.

[31] The BKPM annually issues a priority list (Daftar Skala Prioritas or "DSP") so investors will know what sectors are favored, although BKPM has recently begun saying that the absence of a sector from the DSP should not prevent inquiries to BKPM. BKPM also issues a list of sectors closed to investment. It should be noted that BKPM also administers the Domestic Capital Investment Law, No. 6 of 1968 amended by No. 12 of 1970 under which PMDN companies are approved and established. It is also possible for Indonesians to establish companies that are neither PMA nor PMDN; foreign shareholders, however, are permitted only in PMA companies and to enforce this the Ministry of Justice will generally not approve articles of incorporation allowing bearer shares.

[32] The Indonesian Civil and Commercial Codes were promulgated as colonial ordinances of the Dutch East Indies in 1848. The official texts are still in Dutch, although most people use unofficial Indonesian-language translations. The author is not aware of published English translations of the Civil or Commercial Codes.

[33] Indonesian Commercial Code, Articles 36-56.

[34] The Commercial Code itself addresses preferences and voting rights in Articles 49 and 54, respectively. Dutch jurisprudence is generally applied to interpret and augment the code. Practice is dictated by the policies of the Ministry of Justice, which is empowered to approve the articles of incorporation.

[35] While the Commercial Code Article 54 clearly contemplates shareholders' proxies, the legal or practical efficacy of purported irrevocable proxies is highly dubious. At the board level, the Commercial Code Article 44 entrusts management to the directors "with or without supervision by a board of supervisors." It is not thought this can be irrevocably or permanently delegated.

[36] This position appears to be taken by Indonesian jurists based on general legal principles embodied in Civil Code Articles 1320 (requirements for binding agreement) and 1338 (contracts are effectively the law governing the parties and must be carried out in good faith).

[37] Indonesian Civil Code Articles 1154, 1155, and 1156. Decision of the Court of Appeals, Surabaya, March 22, 1951.

[38] In a series of presidential decisions (*kepres*) beginning with Kepres 14 of 1979, the Indonesian government has required governmental procurement (in-

cluding virtually all business in the petroleum and mining sectors) to favor indigenous contractors and products. Those policies are ultimately enforced by an organ directly reporting to the president called *Sekretariat Negara*—the well-known *Sekneg*.

[39] The *firma* is the form of partnership generally used by commercial partnerships such as trading and service enterprises. The *firma* is primarily governed by the provisions of the Commercial Code (Title III, Section 2).

[40] The provisions on *Maatschap* are found in the Indonesian Civil Code, Book III, Title 8. The provisions of the Civil Code are generally applicable to transactions governed by the Commercial Code.

[41] See the discussion of Japanese foreign investment controls in Chapter 1.

[42] See for instance the Japanese Fair Trade Commission "White Paper" on Joint R&D, September 1984. The United States passed legislation to ameliorate antitrust concerns in joint R&D in the same year: National Cooperative Research Act of 1984, P.L. 98-462 (S. 1841), Oct. 11, 1984, codified at 15 USC Secs. 4301-4305.

[43] See discussion in Glazer, in Ballon, ed., *Joint Ventures and Japan* (Tokyo: 1967), pp. 1, 14–15.

[44] For example, "Construction Accord Reached," *Japan Times*, March 31, 1988, p. 1; "Kumagai, Turner Form New Ties," *Asian Wall Street Journal*, June 6, 1988, p. 3; "Austin Licensed to Build in Japan," *Asahi Evening News*, May 20, 1989, p. 4.

[45] Japanese Act Concerning Prohibition of Private Monopoly and Maintenance of Fair Trade (Dokkenkinshiho), Law No. 54 of 1947.

[46] Article 6 of the Antimonopoly Law. This is a requirement of notice within 30 days after the fact.

[47] FTC, Guidelines for the Regulation of Unfair Trade Practices with Respect to Patent and Know-How Licensing Agreements, February 15, 1989. These guidelines supersede earlier ones issued in 1968 covering only international licenses. See Ishikawa, "Antitrust Enforcement by the Japan Fair Trade Commission," *Antitrust* 3, no. 3 (1989), p. 11.

[48] See discussion by Ariga, *Joint Ventures and Japan*, p. 59. While foreign investment was required to be in joint venture form by Japanese government policy, antimonopoly concerns centered on restraints on export, not the effects on potential competition within Japan.

[49] See, e.g., *Joint Ventures and Japan*; Bradshaw, "Joint Ventures in Japan," *Washington Law Review* 38 (1963), p. 58; Swisher, "Use of Shareholder Agreements and Other Control Techniques in Japanese Joint Venture Corporations and Their Validity under Japanese Corporation Law," *International Lawyer* 9 (1975), p. 159; Henderson, "Contract Problems"; Yanagida, "Joint Venture," in *Doing Business in Japan*, ed. Kitagawa (New York: 1982), Part 7.

[50] Japanese Commercial Code, Book 2, Chapter 4.

[51] See Henderson, "Contract Problems," p. 491.

[52] Japanese Private Company Law (Yugengaisha), Law No. 75 of 1938. The Commercial Code also provides for a registered partnership company (*gomei-gaisha*) Book 2, Chapter 2 of the Commercial Code and a limited partnership (*goshigaisha*) Book 2, Chapter 3. Ibid.

[53] See discussion in Henderson, "Contract Problems," pp. 490–91.

[54] See Yanagida, "Joint Venture," Sec. 3.03[5].

[55] See Yanagida, Sec. 3.03[6].

[56] Matsueda and Ihara, "Company Law in General," in *Doing Business in Japan*, ed. Kitagawa Part 7, Sec. 1.06[19].

[57] See Yanagida, Sec. 3.04[1].

[58] Japanese Commercial Code, Article 343.

[59] Japanese Commercial Code, Article 173.

[60] See Eastman, "Tax Aspects of Doing Business in Japan Part II," in *Current Legal Aspects of Doing Business in the Far East*, ed. Alison (Chicago: American Bar Association, 1972).

[61] Commercial Code, Articles 204 through 204-4.

[62] See Swisher, pp. 171–73, and authorities he cites; Yanagida, Sec. 3.03[5](c).

[63] The term commonly used for an incorporated joint venture is *goben-gaisha*. Sometimes *gobenkigyo* is heard as a word encompassing both types. All these terms are colloquial business terminology and do not appear in the Commercial or Civil Codes.

[64] Foreign Capital Inducement Act, Law No. 3691, enacted December 31, 1983, as amended.

[65] Foreign Exchange Control Act, Law No. 933, enacted December 31, 1961, as amended.

[66] Guidelines for Foreign Investment, Ministry of Finance Notification No. 87-21, January 7, 1988, as amended on October 15, 1988, Article 7.

[67] The Commercial Code, Law No. 1000, enacted January 20, 1962, as amended ("Korean Commercial Code").

[68] Korean Commercial Code, Articles 550, 551, 553, and 593.

[69] Economic Planning Board Public Note No. 87-14, "Scope and Criteria of Unfair Trade Practices in International Agreements," September 13, 1987, issued pursuant to Article 23(2) of the Monopoly Control and Fair Trade Act.

[70] Korean Commercial Code Articles 178-267 (*Hapmyung Hoesa*) and 268-287 (*Hapcha Hoesa*). These forms are directly analogous to the Japanese *gomei-gaisha* and *goshigaisha*. See note 51.

[71] Korean Civil Code Articles 703-724.

[72] Industrial Coordination Act, 1975, S. 2. The discussion that follows is believed to be current as of March 1989.

[73] Book II of the Omnibus Investments Code of 1987 (Executive Order No. 226).

[74] Book I of the Omnibus Investments Code of 1987 sets out the requirements and criteria.

[75] The Constitution of the Philippines (Section 14, Article XIV).

[76] For patents, Republic Act 165 of 1947 (with amendments). For trademarks, Republic Act 166 of 1947 (with amendments).

[77] Central Bank Guidelines.

[78] The Filipino law pertaining to corporations is contained in the Code of Corporations.

[79] See Code of Corporations, Sec. 97 et seq.

PART 2

JAPAN

CHAPTER 5

A TRADITIONAL CULTURE IN A MODERN COUNTRY

Keizo Ohashi
Hajime Wada
Akira Tai

LANGUAGE
>   Japanese
>   English

ECONOMY
>   Economic Growth
>   Finance
>   International Balance of Payments
>   Employment
>   Prices
>   Developments in Industry
>   Money Markets

HISTORY

The islands that are today known collectively as Japan were once part of the Asian continent. Since the end of the Ice Age approximately 20,000 years ago, however, Japan has been an island nation, separated from the Korean peninsula and China by the Sea of Japan. Flying distances from Tokyo to Seoul and Tokyo to Shanghai are 869 miles and 1,216 miles, respectively.

Being an island nation has had a profound effect on Japan's development. Although Japan's geographical position placed it within proximity of the older civilizations of China and Korea, Japan was sufficiently isolated from the Asian continent to develop an independent culture, based on the absorption of the Chinese and Korean cultures, and to remain aloof from direct involvement in the political struggles occurring on the continent.

The comparison with England, also an island country, is interesting. Situated close to the European continent, England followed a different course of development from Japan.

Early records reveal that Japan's inhabitation by humans dates back over 10,000 years to the Paleolithic Period. Ancient Chinese documents from the period between 100 to 200 B.C. suggest, however, that Japan's early inhabitants were splintered into more than 100 small autonomous groups. From about the third to fourth centuries A.D., Yamato, or Nara as the area is known today, emerged as a dominant political force. Initially, the Yamato chief was called the *Daio* (*Okimi*), but from the end of the sixth century was referred to as *Tenno*, or Emperor, the title used in modern Japan to refer to the present emperor. The Yamato political structure centered on the Daio and the strong, wealthy tribes surrounding him and his court. This dominant force strove to promote the nation's progress through the skillful introduction of aspects of more advanced cultures. During the fifth century, iron production, architecture, pottery, cultivation of silkworms, civil engineering, and various other skills were introduced by people who emigrated from the Korean peninsula. From the sixth century, Buddhism, Confucianism, Chinese characters, or ideograms, were brought back systematically from China.

At the end of the sixth century, Shotoku Taishi, the regent for the emperor, took various steps to establish the base of Yamato political power. These steps included establishment of the first constitutional laws and emphasized the emperor as the center of the nation's administration and simultaneous promotion of Buddhism. Envoys were sent to China periodically, and achieving equality with the Chinese dynasty of the time was stressed. Students were sent to China with the envoys, and much effort was made to absorb the advanced culture.

Early in the seventh century, the Sui Dynasty was replaced by the T'ang Dynasty in China. Japan, following the lead of the T'ang, developed a system of laws. That is, various laws and regulations necessary for the administration of the nation were enacted, and a political structure was developed from the lowest levels of administration upward. Taxation and military service obligations for citizens and regulations for bureaucrats were clearly defined. A legal system was also inaugurated.

This system, however, was short-lived, beginning its decline in the eighth century in tandem with private land ownership by the aristocracy. It is at this time that the Fujiwara clan, which had close ties to the imperial family through marriage, began its spectacular rise. Real political power would shift from the emperor to the Fujiwara.

Buddhist culture flourished in the capital and among the imperial family and the aristocracy. Then, in the 10th century, the T'ang Dynasty fell in China, while concurrently in Japan the *bushi* (warriors) began their ascendancy to power with the decline in influence of the aristocracy, marking the appearance of a culture uniquely Japanese. In addition to the Chinese ideograms introduced earlier and known in Japan as *kanji, kana* characters were brought into use. Culture began to spread throughout the country—a Japanese culture in which warriors and ordinary citizens were partners.

Thus, at the end of the 12th century, the first *bakufu* (warrior family regime) came into existence, based in Kamakura. The leader of the warrior class was appointed *shogun* (generalissimo) by the emperor. The shogun was the highest-ranked warrior in the nation. Real political power, which had previously been transferred from the emperor to the aristocracy, was completely in the hands of the shogun from that time. Political control by the warrior class was to continue for 700 years, until 1868, when the Tokugawa shogunate finally collapsed.

Japan's first contact with Europeans came in the middle of the 16th century when a Portuguese vessel drifted ashore on Tanegashima, an island south of Kyushu. It is said that guns were introduced to Japan at that time. The Portuguese thereafter came to Japan nearly every year, followed in close succession by the Spanish, Dutch, and English. In addition to foreign trade, the Catholic faith was propagated.

Foreign trade and Christianity greatly affected Japan. Warriors switched from cavalry units to rifle-bearing units. The method of constructing castles was changed. The number of Japanese Christians increased among all classes, and there was an increase in the number of Japanese actively involved in foreign trade. A considerable number of Japanese went abroad, and some settled in Siam (Thailand), the Philippines, and other Southeast Asian countries.

Trade with Spain and Portugal was closely tied to the propagation of the Christian religion. As trade flourished, the number of Japanese converting to Christianity also increased. The government of the time feared a connection between Christianity and the territorial expansionism of Spain and Portugal. Furthermore, the Christian belief that all people are equal before God conflicted with feudal thinking, and thus there was a gradual tendency to suppress Christianity. At the beginning of the 17th century, the government issued an edict prohibiting Christianity in Japan. To thoroughly enforce this edict, relations with foreign nations were prohibited in 1635. Exceptions were made for China, Korea, and Holland, a Protestant country with no interest in propagating Catholicism. This resulted in the so-called closed nation policy.

About 50 years before promulgation of the closed nation policy, the strongman of the time, Hideyoshi, had disarmed all the farmers in Japan and so had ensured peace for about 250 years after the closed nation policy came into existence.

During this period, Japan became remote from technical and cultural developments in Western Europe, though literature and arts unique to Japan continued to flourish.

The center of Japanese culture shifted from Kyoto and Osaka to Edo (now Tokyo). As this era of peace continued, the economic power of the merchants overwhelmed that of the warriors. Education of the common people in reading, writing, use of the abacus, Confucian thinking, and other things by *terakoya* (temple schools) became widespread. Curiosity in all things intellectual emerged as a prevalent characteristic of Japanese society and was undeniably responsible for the rapid modernization of Japan after the collapse of the feudal system.

In 1792, envoys from Russia requested trade relations with Japan. In 1853, Commodore Perry of the United States arrived in Japan and demanded the opening of Japanese ports. The shogunate gave up its closed nation policy and entered into a treaty with the United States, thus reopening Japan. Subsequently, England, Russia, France, Holland, and others all signed similar treaties with Japan.

The resumption of relations with Western Europe, however, contributed to the decline of the Tokugawa shogunate. In 1868, the 700-year dominance of the warriors gave way to a new government centered on Emperor Meiji.

To compensate for the long years of isolation, the new Meiji government developed various policies aimed at developing a wealthier nation with strong military power, increasing production, and modernizing culture.

Political power was transferred from the *shogunate* and *daimyo* (feudal lords) to the central government; a constitution was promulgated; and a state with three independent executive branches was established. A political system modeled after that of the Western European nations was developed. The capital was moved to Tokyo from Kyoto. A national conscription system was developed to modernize the military. A modern education system was brought into being with government-run schools opened throughout the nation, at minimal expense to the public. This reform enabled intelligent children of poor families to receive a higher education, which greatly contributed to the modernization of Japan.

The economy was improved by land reform and the development of modern industries through government-operated industries, such as the predecessor of the present Shin-Nippon Steel Co. Many Europeans and Americans were invited to Japan to teach modern science and technology, a step that made Japan an increasingly powerful nation. After the end of World War I, a multiparty political system was inaugurated.

The world panic of 1929 and Depression that followed seriously affected the Japanese economy, enabling the military to gradually increase its power to the point where it controlled Japan's politics and foreign policy. In 1937, the Sino-Japanese War broke out. Unbridled hostilities caused the fighting to escalate and extended the war beyond the boundaries of Asia when, in 1941, Japan declared war on the United States and Great Britain.

With the defeat and unconditional surrender of Japan in August 1945, World War II came to an end.

Japan's surrender and subsequent occupation were the most trying times in its history. The Allied powers, led by the United States, instituted various policies, including agricultural reform; the promulgation of labor legislation; and the Constitution of Japan, the three key principles of which are sovereignty by the people, a national policy of peace, and respect for human rights. Article 9 of the Constitution, which renounces war, is unique. The Anti-Monopoly Law and the School Education Law, which introduced the present 6-3-3-4 system, were enforced to facilitate the democratization of Japan. The emperor, who was regarded as being divine during the war, became a mere symbol of the state.

Japan was fortunate in that it did not share the fate of Germany, which was split into two countries. The occupation measures were implemented indirectly, through the Japanese government. But this was a period of great confusion in Japan. The collapse of the munitions industry, the increase in the number of unemployed because of the return of soldiers from overseas, combined with a shortage of food and severe inflation brought many difficulties for the people. Strikes became frequent, and a general strike, centered on the civil service, was only narrowly averted.

The difficulties of the immediate postwar period were gradually overcome, and with the San Francisco Peace Treaty of September 1951, Japan was able to reenter international society as a peaceful, democratic nation. A mutual security treaty was entered into with the United States, and cooperation with the United States became the fundamental policy of the government.

Factories that had been destroyed in the war were rebuilt as modern plants with new innovations and techniques from Europe and the United States. The combination of a unique management system, based on consensus, and a superb and diligent work force facilitated the rehabilitation of Japan and offset the country's lack of raw materials.

By making the greatest possible effort to modify and improve technology, develop products that match the needs of customers, and cultivate export markets, Japan has emerged from the ruin of military defeat, escaped virtually unscathed from the two potentially crippling oil crises in the 1970s, and become a world economic power as a peaceful nation.

PEOPLE

Some of the most readily apparent characteristics of Japanese society are the advanced and universal quality of education, loyalty of employees to their company, the excellent health and welfare facilities provided by companies for their employees, and intracompany teamwork. The combination of these elements has helped to make Japan's management structure extremely strong. The following discussion looks at the characteristics of Japanese from the standpoint of business.

Diligence

Several factors contributed to the strong work ethic of Japanese. Because of the high population density and scarcity of natural resources, Japanese have always had to struggle for survival. Confucianism, which spread throughout Japan during the feudal ages, also propounds a strict work ethic. These tendencies were further strengthened after the Meiji Restoration, when the abolition of the feudal class system gave individuals the freedom to advance through ability and personal effort.

Seniority System

Traditionally, in Japanese companies, promotions and salary increases are given at regular intervals based on the length of time an employee has worked there. This system is suited for Japanese society, which places great importance on respect for one's seniors, a high level of education, egalitarianism, and preservation of a group-based system. The company is family for the Japanese salaried worker, and complete loyalty is expected of employees until retirement. In return, employees are assured of promotion and pay increases according to seniority. As a result, employees feel secure and devote themselves to working for the company. In recent times, the increasingly harsh operating environment has prompted numerous companies to abandon this system and adopt an approach that places greater emphasis on individual ability. Nevertheless, seniority-based promotions and wage increases will continue to be the rule instead of the exception in the foreseeable future.

Group Consciousness

At one time, Japanese were primarily farmers who employed wet-paddy cultivation to grow rice. Because this method of cultivation is labor-intensive, farmers relied on collective cultivation to produce sufficient yields. Moreover, because it was necessary to devise systems for the equitable allocation of water for the irrigation of paddies, Japanese developed a strong sense of belonging to the village community. Confucianism instilled a similar sense of belonging in the family unit, and Japan's *samurai* warriors traditionally maintained a strict code of duty and obligation within the feudal clan.

This predisposition toward group consciousness has been culturally transmitted through the generations and is the foundation for the current attitude of salaried workers toward their companies. Because human relations is the cement that binds the workplace together, the cultivation of close ties with coworkers and superiors after normal working hours through drinking and various recreational activities is extremely important.

In large companies, a bottom-up style decision-making process is practiced much more than a top-down style. In the bottom-up style, employees in the lower ranks make a detailed draft of a proposal and, using a special document called a *ringisho*, obtain the approval of management. This process, however, involves extensive advance preparation—called *nemawashi*, literally meaning "binding the roots"—in which anyone even remotely involved with the proposal is personally briefed and their informal compliance obtained. This process usually includes frequent departmental and interdepartmental meetings at which opposing views or problems are brought up and negotiated, and revisions hammered out. Only after a consensus has been reached is the *ringisho* passed around for the heads of departments to register final approval. Because even those in lower ranks understand and participate in the formulation of management policy, there is greater incentive to achieve policy goals.

Education System

The Japanese educational system consists of six years of elementary school, three years of junior high school, three years of high school, four years of college, and various graduate schools. Japanese children enter elementary school at the age of six, and 99.9 percent of these children graduate from junior high school to complete the nine years of compulsory education. Of junior high school graduates, 94.3 percent continue on to high school, and nearly one third of these students advance to college, providing a wide educational base among the population.

Because school records are weighed heavily in determining employment prospects for Japan's top companies and government ministries, there is severe competition for entrance into the best high schools and universities. School entrance exams are extremely difficult, and many students from elementary school on up attend private cram schools after normal school hours. This intense competition is frequently referred to as "examination hell" or "examination war."

GOVERNMENT INFLUENCE

As a free market economy, private enterprise is fully responsible for planning and management of its own activities. However, because of efforts to catch up with Western nations before World War II and to recover from the devastation after the war, Japan's government has historically played a major role in promoting economic welfare. For example, in the prewar period the government operated Yawata Steel—the predecessor of Shin Nippon Steel—and the former Japan National Railways. In the postwar era, it helped to protect domestic industries and to support and strengthen vital export industries. However, as one of the leading economic powers in the world, Japan now champions liberalization of such areas as trade, foreign exchange, finance, and capital and is pursuing the privatization of government-managed enterprises. As a result, government influence in business has gradually declined.

Governmental Expenditures

Although the Japanese government's financial position was at one time sound, the oil shocks of the 1970s necessitated a conversion to deficit financing (see Table 5–1).

Formulation of Economic Plans

Since the immediate postwar period, the Japanese government has exercised loose influence over private enterprises by drawing up economic plans that provide guidance and serve as important reference material.

TABLE 5–1
Government Revenue and Expenditures (1970–1985) (Units: Billion Yen)

Fiscal Year	Revenues	Expenditures	Balance	Expenditures as a Share of GNP
1970	8,112.0	8,187.6	−75.6	11.1%
1975	16,192.9	20,860.8	−4,667.9	14.0%
1980	29,870.4	43,405.0	−13,534.6	17.7%
1985	41,684.6	53,004.5	−11,319.9	16.5%

Source: Bank of Japan statistics.

The current plan, covering 1988 through 1992, targets a real annual economic growth rate of about 3.75 percent for the period (about 4.75 percent in nominal terms). Other well-known economic plans in the past include the National Income-Doubling Plan prepared by the Ikeda cabinet in the 1960s.

Drafting Bills

In contrast to the United States, in Japan the right to draft legal measures is not the exclusive preserve of the legislative body. More bills are submitted by the cabinet than by Diet members, and the rate of passage for bills sponsored by the cabinet are substantially higher than those sponsored by Diet members (see Table 5–2).

Administrative Guidance

Japan's unique process of administrative guidance, led by the Ministry of International Trade and Industry (MITI), has been widely recognized overseas as a major factor contributing to Japan's superb economic

TABLE 5–2
Submission and Passage of Bills in 1986 and 1987

Fiscal Year	Presented by Lower House Members		Presented by Upper House Members		Presented by the Cabinet	
	Submitted	Passed	Submitted	Passed	Submitted	Passed
1986	32	10	14	2	115	97
1987	33	13	8	1	114	85

performance in the postwar era. Administrative guidance can be defined as actions taken to achieve a certain goal. Without a legal or regulatory basis, this process relies on the ability of government agencies to persuade private enterprises through the prudent use of recommendations, requests, incentives, and warnings.

The success of administrative guidance in Japan is probably due to a variety of factors, including the emphasis placed on cooperative relations between the government and private sector, the extraordinary deference given to the wisdom of government officials, wariness of the government's power of approval, and a strong sense of patriotism and national unity among Japan's business leaders and government officials. MITI, for example, has used administrative guidance to implement policies designed to raise the competitiveness of Japanese industries, such as the coordination of capital investment plans in specially designated industries (petrochemicals, synthetic fibers, etc.), production cut recommendations (steel), and promotion of large-scale mergers (autos, steel, etc.). The complexities involved in passing legislation are avoided under administrative guidance, making it highly effective and responsive. However, this process has also generated criticism from foreign countries by propagating the myth of Japan, Inc.

Bank of Japan's "Window Guidance"

The Bank of Japan (BOJ), the central bank of Japan, has a number of methods to adjust financial markets. In addition to such conventional methods as changing the official discount rate, altering deposit reserve ratios, and conducting open market operations, the BOJ exercises direct control over Japanese banks through guidance and persuasion. During the postwar recovery, the BOJ indirectly financed the tremendous corporate demand for funds by providing loans on favorable terms to banks whose financial position was hurt as a result of extending such funds. As a result of such activities, the BOJ has retained a substantial degree of indirect influence over banks.

Interchange of Personnel

There are very few cases of personnel joining the government bureaucracy from private-sector positions. However, the movement of bureaucrats into private-sector positions is more common. In recent years, ex-bureaucrats have also begun to accept positions in prominent foreign-affiliated firms.

GEOGRAPHY AND CLIMATE

Geography

The Japanese archipelago consists of four large islands—Hokkaido, Honshu, Shikoku, and Kyushu—and about 4,000 small islands. The distance from the northernmost Japanese island (45°33′ north latitude), which has been occupied by the Soviet Union since 1945, to the southernmost island (20°25′ north latitude) is 3,800 kilometers. The capital, Tokyo, is on Honshu and is situated at 35°41′ north latitude and 139°46′ east longitude. The total area of Japan is about 378,000 square kilometers (146,000 square miles), roughly one twenty-fifth the size of the United States, or about the same area as the state of Montana. Seventy-one percent of the land is mountainous. Japan has more than 40 active and dormant volcanoes and over 100 extinct volcanoes. Because of constant volcanic activity, Japan is earthquake-prone.

Japan has 12 mountains that are higher than 3,000 meters (9,800 feet), the most famous of which is Mount Fuji (3,776 meters). The many hot springs in all areas of the country are popular with the Japanese both for sight-seeing and for health.

There is little arable land in Japan, with 78 percent of the population living on the few plains. The population is concentrated in urban areas, and land in major cities and their suburbs is expensive. The coast of Japan is rugged, with many peninsulas, capes, and bays. Transportation to the interior is poor in the many areas where mountains are close to the coast.

A warm current flows from the south in both the Pacific Ocean and the Sea of Japan, while a cold current flows south from the Sea of Okhotsk. This makes the sea off the northeast coast of Honshu extremely fertile fishing grounds.

Japan has almost no mineral resources such as petroleum, iron ore, and coal, and it imports 85 percent of its energy resources. Japan's self-sufficiency in food production is as follows: soybeans, 5 percent; wheat, 10 percent; fruit, 80 percent; and rice and vegetables, 95 percent.

The administrative regions of Japan comprise one metropolis (*to*), one area (*do*), two urban prefectures (*fu*), and 43 prefectures (*ken*). Each prefecture is subdivided into counties, cities, towns, and villages (see Figure 5–1).

FIGURE 5–1
Names of Prefectures and Prefectural Capitals

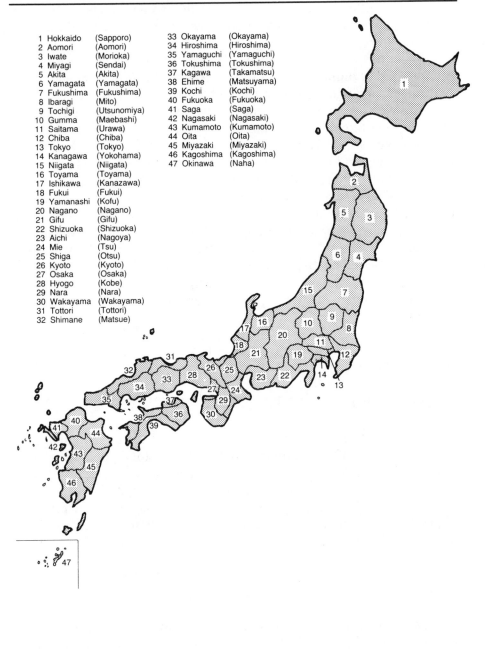

1	Hokkaido	(Sapporo)
2	Aomori	(Aomori)
3	Iwate	(Morioka)
4	Miyagi	(Sendai)
5	Akita	(Akita)
6	Yamagata	(Yamagata)
7	Fukushima	(Fukushima)
8	Ibaragi	(Mito)
9	Tochigi	(Utsunomiya)
10	Gumma	(Maebashi)
11	Saitama	(Urawa)
12	Chiba	(Chiba)
13	Tokyo	(Tokyo)
14	Kanagawa	(Yokohama)
15	Niigata	(Niigata)
16	Toyama	(Toyama)
17	Ishikawa	(Kanazawa)
18	Fukui	(Fukui)
19	Yamanashi	(Kofu)
20	Nagano	(Nagano)
21	Gifu	(Gifu)
22	Shizuoka	(Shizuoka)
23	Aichi	(Nagoya)
24	Mie	(Tsu)
25	Shiga	(Otsu)
26	Kyoto	(Kyoto)
27	Osaka	(Osaka)
28	Hyogo	(Kobe)
29	Nara	(Nara)
30	Wakayama	(Wakayama)
31	Tottori	(Tottori)
32	Shimane	(Matsue)
33	Okayama	(Okayama)
34	Hiroshima	(Hiroshima)
35	Yamaguchi	(Yamaguchi)
36	Tokushima	(Tokushima)
37	Kagawa	(Takamatsu)
38	Ehime	(Matsuyama)
39	Kochi	(Kochi)
40	Fukuoka	(Fukuoka)
41	Saga	(Saga)
42	Nagasaki	(Nagasaki)
43	Kumamoto	(Kumamoto)
44	Oita	(Oita)
45	Miyazaki	(Miyazaki)
46	Kagoshima	(Kagoshima)
47	Okinawa	(Naha)

Climate

Although the Japanese archipelago is in the temperate zone, its varied topography, sea currents, and seasonal winds result in great differences in temperature.

Japan has clearly distinguishable seasons. Spring in Japan is from March to May, summer is from June to August, fall is from September to November, and winter is from December to February.

The weather in spring is fine—flowering trees and plants bud and many flowers bloom. In the summer, the long days are hot and humid, with seasonal winds from the Pacific bringing frequent rain. Fall is cool and refreshing and is the harvest season. The winter is cold in most of Japan and the nights are long. The Japan Sea coast, which is affected by seasonal winds from the Asian continent, has heavy snow. The Pacific Coast, however, is dry with many clear days during the winter. The weather is most favorable in the spring and fall. The rainy season in June and July, the typhoon season in September, and the heavy snow in winter on the Japan Sea side bring landslides, high tides, and other natural disasters, though this heavy precipitation contributes greatly to resources of water. Japan has precipitation well above the international average.

POPULATION

Total Population

According to the government, as of October 1985, the total population of Japan was about 121 million, or roughly half the total population of the United States. Japan accounts for 2.5 percent of the world's total population, ranking seventh behind the People's Republic of China, India, Soviet Union, United States, Indonesia, and Brazil. Of Japan's population, 59.5 million are male and 61.5 million female. There are approximately 38 million households with an average of 3.17 persons each.

Labor Force

In 1986, the working population over 15 years of age was estimated to be 60 million people, which is divided into three broad categories by industry. Of the Japanese labor force, 60.2 percent is male and 39.8 percent female. At 2.8 percent in 1986, the unemployment rate is lower than in the United States but has witnessed a gradual increase over the years.

Category	Examples	Share of Labor
Primary industries	Agriculture, fishing	8%
Secondary industries	Mining, construction, manufacturing	33%
Tertiary industries	Commerce, finance, transportation, communications	58%

Demographics

With a population density of 325 people per square kilometer, Japan is the 16th most densely populated country in the world (this compares with the U.S. figure of 25 people per square kilometer). Among the most densely populated prefectures are Tokyo, Osaka, Kanagawa, Saitama, and Aichi, whereas Hokkaido, Iwate, Akita, Kochi, and Shimane prefectures are rather sparsely populated.

Japan's annual population growth rate of 0.7 percent is far below the 1.7 percent growth rate for the world (average annual growth from 1980 to 1985) and continues to decline. The concentration of population in the Tokyo metropolitan area and prefectural capital cities is steadily increasing.

Average Life Span

According to a 1988 report by the Ministry of Health and Welfare, the average life expectancy of Japanese in 1987 was 75.61 years for males and 81.39 years for females. The combined average gives Japan the highest life expectancy for any country in the world. This is largely due to a decline in the mortality rates for the middle-aged and elderly and a decline in the birthrate. Because of improved health care systems, the Welfare Ministry expects life expectancy to rise even further, making preparations for the "graying" of Japanese society increasingly important.

Expatriates in Japan

In 1986, there were approximately 867,000 non-Japanese living in Japan, or about 0.7 percent of the total population. A large proportion of these people were Koreans and Chinese who immigrated to Japan before

World War II. By nationality, 678,000 of the foreign residents are Korean, 84,000 Chinese, 31,000 American, 19,000 Filipino, and the remaining 55,000 various nationalities. The population of 202,000 non-Japanese residents in Osaka is the highest, followed in descending order by Tokyo, Hyogo, and Aichi. A breakdown of the foreign community by nationality reveals that Osaka is the center of the Korean population, whereas Chinese and Americans are concentrated in the Tokyo area.

LANGUAGE

Japanese

One school of thinking maintains that Japanese is one of the most difficult languages in the world. It is true that three types of written characters are used—46 *hiragana* and 46 *katakana* characters and over 40,000 Chinese characters called *kanji*.

The spoken Japanese language, however, has vowel sounds that are similar to Spanish. The mastery of spoken Japanese is generally not too difficult for foreigners, and the number of foreigners who speak fluent Japanese is increasing.

Interest is increasing in expanding facilities to teach Japanese to foreigners and to train specialized teachers. Conditions in Japan for foreigners studying Japanese are gradually improving.

The characteristics of the Japanese language are described below.

Pronunciation
Numerous words end in vowels. There are also words that are comprised only of vowels.

Also, many words with the same pronunciation have different meanings. It is necessary to either see the Chinese characters of the word or decide on the meaning from the context of the sentence.

Nearly all of the individual words have no accents and raising or lowering intonation is unusual.

Written Language

Hiragana and Katakana. There are 46 characters in each set of modern *kana*.

Kanji.   There are over 40,000 Chinese characters, or *kanji*.

The Ministry of Education has selected 1,945 frequently used *kanji* to be taught in the compulsory education years (six years of elementary school and three years of middle school).

Sentences usually comprise a combination of *hiragana* and *kanji* characters. *Katakana* is commonly used for scientific words and foreign words.

Japanese can be written both vertically and horizontally. Newspapers and novels use vertical writing.

Grammar

Many sentences have no subject, particularly when the subject is first or second person. Frequently, no distinction is made between singular and plural.

There is no distinction as to sex in articles, nouns, and other words.

Sentence Structure.   The object precedes the verb.

The word order does not change in questions. Instead, a final particle is attached to the end of the sentence to indicate it is a question. For example, the statement "This is a book" (*kore wa hon desu*) becomes the question "Is this a book?" (*kore wa hon desu ka*) when *ka* is added.

Adjectives and adverbs precede the noun and verb they qualify.

Usage

In Japan, it is customary to use expressions of respect when addressing a superior or a person older than oneself.

It is necessary to use the correct expression of respect, humbleness, and courtesy according to the situation.

There are differences between words used by men and women.

Standard Japanese and Local Dialects

The Japanese used in Tokyo is regarded as standard Japanese. Each region has its own dialect, and some of these dialects are difficult even for Japanese people to understand.

English

The English language is taught in middle school and high school. Because the English education system in Japan is traditionally centered on reading and writing, many Japanese cannot speak English fluently. Recently, however, greater attention is being given to spoken English, and the number of people who can speak English is increasing.

In first-class hotels, airports, large enterprises, central government offices, and so on, the number of employees who understand English is comparatively high.

There are also a number of English-language newspapers in Japan.

There is an English-language radio station, FEN, for American military personnel and their families in Japan.

The number of bilingual (mainly English) television broadcasts is increasing, and some cable television channels show U.S. news programs. Satellite television is becoming common, and broadcasting in English is likely to increase.

ECONOMY

Economic Growth

The development of the Japanese economy since the end of World War II can generally be divided into the following three stages.

Stage 1 (August 1945–1952)
The American policy to aid Japan, as symbolized by the Dodge Plan, and the outbreak of the Korean War enabled the Japanese economy to recover to its prewar level.

Stage 2 (1953–1973)
While the United States and the developed countries of Europe had an average real economic growth rate of 3 percent to 5 percent during this period, the Japanese economy had a high growth rate of about 10 percent.

The reasons for this were:

1. Worldwide peace was maintained during this period, making sustained growth possible.
2. Japan, which was late to develop, was able to introduce already developed technologies from Europe and the United States.
3. There was an abundant supply of diligent workers in Japan, and the Japanese government directed a policy of economic growth.

Stage 3 (1974–Present)

Low Growth Period after the Oil Shocks.   Although the Japanese economy recovered more rapidly from the two oil shocks than did the economies of the other developed countries, it was often said there was zero growth or low growth during this period. There was a worldwide slowdown in economic development. However, in comparison with the United States and the developed nations of Europe, Japan achieved a better economic performance and thus became the world's top creditor nation.

One of Japan's greatest problems today is how to share its overseas net assets with other countries, while simultaneously changing its heretofore export-oriented economy to a domestic demand-directed economy. (See Table 5–3 for a comparison of the U.S. and Japanese economies.)

TABLE 5–3
Japan-U.S. Economic Comparison

	United States	*Japan*
Land area	9,370,000 sq. kilometers (about 25 times the size of Japan)	380,000 sq. kilometers
Population	243,770,000 (June 1987)	122,090,000 (June 1987)
Total domestic production	$4,488,600 million (1987)	¥344,888,000 million (1977)
Per capita national income	$17,180 (1986)	$16,267 (1986)
Actual economic growth rate	2.9% (1986) 2.9% (1987)	2.4% (1986) 4.2% (1987)
Consumer price increase rate	1.9% (1986) 3.7% (1987)	0.6% (1986) 0.1% (1987)
Unemployment rate	6.9% (1986) 6.1% (1987)	2.8% (1986) 2.8% (1987)
International income and expenditures	(1987)	(1987)
Exports	$249,570 million	$233,435 million
Imports	$409,850 "	$139,401 "
Trade balance	−$160,280 "	$ 94,034 "
Ordinary balance	−$153,964 "	$ 84,474 "
Total balance	−$ 18,461 "	−$ 15,979 "
Foreign currency reserves	$ 48,517 million (Dec. 1986) $ 45,798 " (Dec. 1987)	$ 42,230 million (Dec. 1986) $ 81,479 " (Dec. 1987)

Finance

Until the oil crises, Japan pursued a strictly balanced fiscal policy based on the Occupation Era Dodge Policy. At the time of the oil crises, Japan adopted an aggressive fiscal policy-led economic policy that called for the issuance of national bonds to cover deficits. The accumulated balance of these national bonds has reached a very high figure.

At present, the Japanese government is restructuring its finances by enthusiastically pursuing administrative reform, including rationalization through reduced expenditures, and the privatization of previously public enterprises (NTT, Japan Monopoly Corporation, Japan National Railways, and so on). However, at the end of fiscal 1988, the outstanding balance of national bonds had reached ¥158 trillion (43.2 percent of Japan's GNP), which is very high on a stock basis.

International Balance of Payments

The current account of Japan's international balance of payments moved into surplus in the mid-1960s. There was a deficit in Japan's international balance of payments at the time of the two oil crises, but since then Japan has had a surplus in its balance of payments. This current account surplus has become especially pronounced since 1981 because of increased exports stemming from (1) the gradual decline in the value of the yen, (2) the drop in crude oil prices, and (3) the recovery of the U.S. economy.

Japan recorded its strongest balance of payments performance in fiscal 1986, with a current account surplus of $94.1 billion, due to the effects of the J curve and despite the sudden, rapid appreciation of the yen.

Meanwhile, since 1981, Japan's long-term account of the balance of payments moved into deficit, as the result of direct and portfolio investments in the United States. There has been a massive outflow of capital, with the deficit reaching $168.2 billion in fiscal 1987. Japan has a massive surplus in its current account, but a deficit in its overall balance.

Employment

Until recently, the employment system in Japan was based on three basic principles: lifetime employment, a wage system based on seniority, and labor unions organized at the company level. However, the years of low growth from the time of the two oil crises have led to a reevaluation of these long-accepted principles. Recently, there has been greater emphasis on efficiency and full utilization of human resources, the emergence of midcareer reemployment, and the introduction of wages based on ability.

The promulgation of legislation creating equal wages and working conditions for men and women is likely to further the employment prospects of women, especially homemakers. This legislation prohibits discrimination in type of employment, wages, and labor conditions.

Although the retirement age for most Japanese workers is presently between 55 and 60 years of age, the increase in the life expectancy of the Japanese will inevitably prompt changes in this aspect of the Japanese management system.

Prices

Although prices in Japan rose drastically with the first oil crisis in 1973 to what were considered extremely high prices, timely intervention to control credit by the Bank of Japan at the time of the second oil crisis in 1979 prevented a second round of major price increases.

There has been an average of only 0 percent to 2 percent increase in prices since then, due to the appreciation of the yen and low crude oil prices. However, in urban areas, the rising cost of land has increased the cost of living because of increases in fixed assets taxes, rent payments, and repayments of housing loans.

Developments in Industry

The two oil crises brought a sharp rise in energy costs and greatly affected energy-consuming industries, especially the aluminum industry. Furthermore, the increase in the cost of raw materials structurally depressed the petrochemical industry. Redundant facilities in the iron and steel industries became apparent and necessitated large-scale rationalization measures.

The dramatic appreciation of the yen and increased trade friction from the latter part of 1985 encouraged the automobile and electrical machinery industries to step up overseas production facilities and led to discussions of a "hollowing out" of Japanese industry.

The appreciation of the yen, increased trade friction, and competition from the Asian newly industrialized economies (NIEs) have compelled the Japanese economy to shift from an export-oriented economy to a domestic-demand-oriented economy.

The volume of goods imported into Japan increased by more than 20 percent in the first half of 1988 over the same period of the previous year. Imports from the Asian NIEs rapidly increased because of the improving quality of their products. Close to half the textiles, cameras, and certain other products sold in Japan in 1988 were imported.

Multinational enterprises in the fields of electronics, biotechnology, and fine chemicals, such as IBM, Nestlé, Esso, Coca-Cola, and Johnson and Johnson are making inroads in the Japanese market because of their technological and financial strengths.

Enterprises in the following categories have special potential in Japan in the immediate future:

- Information and communications.
- Biotechnology
- New materials.
- Leisure.
- Housing and urban redevelopment.
- Industries providing goods and services to older people.

Money Markets

The Japanese money markets heretofore have been characterized by:

1. Furnishers of funds have been individuals, while borrowers have been corporate and public enterprises. This pattern is more pronounced than in other nations.
2. Indirect financing through banks has been predominant, while fund-raising through stock issues has been low.
3. As there was greater demand for funds for corporations, rather than for individuals, during the period of high growth, corporations were "overborrowed" and banks in turn relied on loans from the Bank of Japan.

However, after the first issue of equity at market value by a Japanese company in 1969, rather than the customary Japanese method of allocating increases of capital to shareholders at par value, issuing equity at market prices has become common. Therefore, capitalization levels that were low for Japanese companies have rapidly increased.

In 1980, both domestic and international capital transactions were liberalized through amendments to the Foreign Exchange Control Law, so fund-raising by enterprises in the Japanese and overseas capital markets has become much more active. With the increasing national bond debt and the growing sensitivity to interest rates among enterprises and individuals, the desire for further liberalization of money markets has intensified.

CHAPTER 6

EFFECTS OF GLOBALIZATION ON THE JAPANESE MARKET

George Fields

THE CRAZE FOR "KOKUSAIKA"
(INTERNATIONALIZATION)
JAPAN TO SAVE LESS, SPEND MORE, AND
WORK LESS
WORKING AT LEISURE
DEALING WITH THE NEW OPULENCE
RESTRUCTURING FOR THE LONG HAUL
IMPORT OR BUST
LIGHT AT THE END OF THE DISTRIBUTION
TUNNEL
THE DAWN OF GLOBALIZATION

THE CRAZE FOR "KOKUSAIKA" (INTERNATIONALIZATION)

In 1985, *kokusaika* ("internationalization") became a buzzword in Japan and remains a hot topic today. Triggered initially by *endaka* (another buzzword meaning the rising value of yen), the initial focus was on macroeconomic aspects and its effect on the industrial infrastructure.

However, *kokusaika*'s effect turned out to be multidimensional, touching not only industry but also corporate values and even Japanese racial insularity. This chapter will concentrate on internationalization's impact on the consumer and the market culture in the even broader context of globalization.

For the consumer, internationalization means a rational approach to products irrespective of their source. The lack of a strong advocate for the Japanese consumer has been noted by many foreign observers, but consumers in Japan have always displayed a tendency to put the country ahead of their own interests, indirectly assisting market nationalism. Here the first changes have been inorganic (i.e., those forced by the trade issue), but ultimately, organic changes will be effected, via a rise of a more self-centered and hedonistic younger generation that is less concerned with helping others just because they happen to be fellow Japanese.

In light of the events of 1988, the Ministry of International Trade and Industry's (MITI) "White Paper on Trade for 1986" seems prophetic in that it pointed out that if the trade imbalance continues, "not only will it be difficult to deal with individual sources of trade friction, but all the countries of the world will start to feel insecure with the current trading system and it would become impossible to maintain the system of free trade." Somewhat earlier, Prime Minister Nakasone had asked 17 leaders from various sectors to advise him as a nonofficial study group, with Haruo Maekawa, the ex-governor of the Bank of Japan, as leader. (Maekawa died in September 1989 and his name is immortalized with the report.) The team was officially designated "the group to study the restructuring of the economy for international cooperation." MITI's White Paper virtually endorsed much of the Maekawa recommendations and thus internationalization ostensibly became national policy.

Accordingly, it is now widely acknowledged that Japanese survival depends on maintenance of the free trade system and that the Japanese market must become more open. The key concepts in the Maekawa report are "expansion of domestic demand," achieved to a remarkable extent in 1987; "restructuring of industry," evidenced in the enormous increase in direct overseas investments; and "liberalization," with some removal of bureaucratic controls in evidence and relaxation of agricultural imports such as for beef and oranges effected, but the distribution system still looms as a largely untouched major area of contention.

JAPAN TO SAVE LESS, SPEND MORE, AND WORK LESS

The following is an excerpt from a letter to the Japanese-language *Asahi* newspaper in the spring of 1987:

> We are being attacked from overseas because we have earned an annual trade surplus of $50 billion, but the common soldiers of Japan Inc. are gasping under the weight of housing loans and high taxation, crushed by the solitude of job transfers away from families, and hardly able to breath on packed trains. . . . Where did those spectacular sums of money disappear to?

The *Asahi*'s analysis is that most of that surplus went back to the United States as short-term investments (now increasingly long-term); it also helped to sustain the American consumer's high spending habits. The letter sums up the main issues raised on internationalization by the consumer. According to prevailing world opinions, the Japanese should:

- Save less and spend more on themselves, preferably on foreign goods.
- Work less, at least no more than their counterparts in advanced economies.

Symptomatic of the problem in the spring of 1987 was that actions taken on lowering imported costs at the consumer level had been minimal. The fact that the Japanese protective stance toward agriculture is at the expense of the average taxpayer has been well publicized in the local media. Yet, at a consumer meeting in 1987, a vote against the liberalization of rice imports was passed unanimously. Even at the cost of seven times higher than alternate imports, it was felt that Japanese farmers had to be protected. In essence, the consumers agreed it was in the interest of the Japanese to help each other.

Writing from New York, Reona Ezaki, the Nobel laureate physicist, said in the *Yomiuri* newspaper, "[Despite the seeming internationalization of the visible youth in cities such as Tokyo and Osaka] when it comes to food and the cost of imported products, Japanese internationalism declines rapidly. Products are expensive, not only more so than in the United States, but more than in most advanced industrial economies, and are beyond international standards. Whatever the cause, they demonstrate Japanese insularity." Dr. Ezaki also said the majority of Japanese agree to internationalization and liberalization as a general principle, but when it comes to issues that directly affect their self-interest, they take an insular attitude of maintaining the status quo.

While acting on self-interest is not a characteristic unique to the Japanese, willingness to sacrifice one's personal benefit for the sake of other Japanese may be a more intensely nationalistic attitude than that held by consumers in most other cultures. No short-term changes can be expected among the mature segment of the population, although external pressures reported in the media have created a spirit of compromise.

Motherland allegiance aside, the Japanese have always been international in absorbing information from outside. They are leaders in their import of knowledge on world politics, economics, and academic happenings. This is the historical legacy of a small country influenced by the happenings of giants, and the Japanese consumer is probably less insular than most in his concern for what others think of him.

To expand domestic demand, the primary need is to improve housing to bring it closer to the standards of other economically advanced countries. Especially important is creation of housing space proximate to work and development of new residential areas around the metropolis. Unfortunately, the immediate scheme to stimulate domestic demand in this respect has backfired. There have been spectacular developments of urban commercial complexes, but the result has been an extraordinary rise in land prices, pushing affordable housing for the average wage earner farther out from the centers, contradicting the Maekawa report's call for better allocation of the fruits of economic growth to the wage earner.

The Japanese save too much. But they have to in order to pay for the house. If the housing burden is alleviated, more money will be available for furniture, travel, and entertainment. This solution is not in sight. So attention is being given to the other side of demand stimulation, which perhaps can be more easily manipulated, i.e., an increase in leisure time. The Japanese cannot stay in the world community by continuing to be workaholics.

WORKING AT LEISURE

Leisure is new to modern Japan. While younger Japanese are becoming more comfortable with the concept of leisure and its attractive options, those who worked to put the nation back together in the postwar years still show signs of resisting the notion of too much of the "good life."

Such attitudes are inherent in the current rigidities of the system where it is difficult, if not impossible, for an individual worker to demand his or her rightful number of holidays unless the whole group does so.

The media have continued to report that the international perception of the Japanese as workaholics contributes to further trade friction. It is now becoming a kind of "patriotic duty" to "play" more, but the corporate attitude stressing survival through hard work is unable to cope with the situation unless some lead is given from the top. The closure of government services and banks on Saturdays and the granting of, for Japan, extended holidays have begun to have an effect. Still, the incidences of collective shutdown of plants and offices in the summer, since 1986, are still quite small. The government has announced a target of 2,000 working hours a year, down from 2,152 now, through administrative guidance; currently, the corresponding hours are 1,898 in the United States, 1,938 in Britain, and 1,613 in West Germany. What will happen in the long term, when there is a top-down enforcement of holidays?

First, there will be a change in societal values that postulate work as the ultimate virtue. If the government and elite establishments start giving their employees increased time off, it will become the smart thing to enjoy leisure, and there will be a rapid redefining of it. Next, because of the tremendous pressure exerted by the strong yen on small manufacturing concerns (more than 90 percent of manufacturers have fewer than 300 employees, accounting for almost half the manufacturing output), there is official encouragement for a structural shift in employment toward the leisure-related industries. This, too, will result in a heightened awareness of leisure. MITI considers it serious enough to form a project team to examine the shortening of working hours and the concomitant issues of leisure.

The growth in products and services catering to the new leisure needs will continue, but not at the rate optimists expect. The strongest institutional factor that will inhibit the increase in leisure hours in the short term is the preponderance of family-type, small businesses—both in manufacturing and distribution. It is argued that under the present circumstances, in which there is stronger awareness of intercompany rivalries than management/labor conflicts, penalties would have to be imposed by law for noncompliance of shorter working hours. Given the government's deference to business, such a move is highly unlikely. The continued erosion of union strength removes the institutional pressure that was instrumental in shortening working hours in the West. In any event, medium to small businesses are less unionized than larger ones, and they will be the ones to continue to ignore the call.

Most women, yet unbound by corporate restraints, are finding *rejah* (the Japanese pronunciation for the English *leisure,* for which presumably there is no exact Japanese equivalent) to their liking. They are leading the trend, along with those under 30 years old, toward leisure activities. The most radical change in the past 20 years has occurred in the perception of overseas travel, which initially included only a small number of the chosen dispatched to bring back something to the nation, usually technical know-how or cultural wisdom. Now, travel abroad is within the reach of the majority of the population. The strongest utilizers of leisure travel, in the mass sense, have been young women—and the men have simply followed.

Although women take a less rigid view toward leisure, ironically, the increase in working women will inhibit changing the current patterns for leisure travel, clustering in periods that include public holidays. Well over half of married women are working, and their numbers will further increase. Not all will be able to match their leave with that of their husbands. In addition, the relatively short summer holidays for the schools still place an absolute limit on extended travel outside the August school vacation period. For those with school age children, educational reform in this respect will be necessary. While the leisure industry, and especially the travel segment, can look forward to major growth, not too much in the way of off-season activities can be expected for the immediate future.

One of the major objections raised by the Japanese consumer to having more leisure time has been the cost, due to the lack of an adequate domestic infrastructure. Parks and other free facilities are inadequate. A day at Tokyo Disneyland, for example, costs between ¥4,000 and ¥5,000 per person and cannot be a frequent event for the average family. However, on superficial observation, the money is there. In 1988, the average family savings reached an astounding ¥10 million (about $70,000 at the exchange rate of ¥140 to $1). Do they need to save so much, especially since Japan is acquiring U.S.-type consumer credit facilities, albeit there is a long way to go?

Traditionally, the large savings were considered necessary because of the relative lack of government welfare provisions. To the average Japanese, it is inconceivable not to have something put aside. This cultural attitude is not likely to change in the short term until the present-day youths enter the work force to eventually form the majority. They will be the first group to be free of the insecurity that plagues the majority of modern-day Japanese. They will be familiar members of a credit society that will encourage them to hold numerous credit cards and utilize loan facilities.

DEALING WITH THE NEW OPULENCE

Internationally, the mighty yen's effect has been awesome, but domestically, it has spawned a new buzzword—the *Nyuu Ritchi* (new rich). The word carries an impact among the Japanese that is difficult for most outsiders to comprehend. It shakes the relatively recent Japanese faith in a totally middle-class society and even affects the traditionally held virtue of thrift.

Since 1955, the average household's assets have risen 36-fold and outstanding consumer loans by more than 116-fold. In terms of consumer spending power, the strong yen has not translated into correspondingly lower retail prices, although it has removed inflation from the national vocabulary for several years. The new rich are currently loosely defined as those with assets of more than ¥100 million (U.S. $770,000), and 6 percent of households in 1988 are estimated to belong to this privileged category. More than half of them recently joined the ranks with the sudden sharp rise in real estate values in the past three years. Aside, perhaps, from discovering oil deposits in the backyard, few people in the world could hope for a bigger windfall than that realized from the sale of property in a Japanese metropolitan area.

While the size of the group is impressive in a country with a population of 100 million or approximately 30 million households, it is the rate of increase that has fueled the consumption boom. The new rich show a higher percentage of ownership of virtually all the accoutrements of the good life—foreign cars, oil paintings, art objects, and memberships in country clubs. The strong yen has made overseas travel a bargain, not just for the new rich but also for everybody. Perhaps nothing serves as a bigger eye-opener to the Japanese perceptions of their own living standards, especially in terms of housing. The realization that this gap is not about to be narrowed is responsible for a growing appetite for foreign real estate.

History may someday recognize that a momentous shift occurred, not when the economy of Japan began to bring a satisfactory level of middle-class prosperity to the populace, but when the combination of lower interest rates, expanded money supply, and abolition of tax-free savings drove vast amounts of savings into circulation and unleashed a Pandora's box of change.

RESTRUCTURING FOR THE LONG HAUL

Basic export industries such as automobile and electronics have begun, and will continue, to shift a portion of their operations overseas to reduce their export component. An acceleration of diversification into the newly industrialized economies (NIEs) is already occurring in the semiconductor and personal computer industries. It will not be long before finally assembled Japanese automobiles are imported into Japan. The West Germans have been rightly lauded for cornering almost 75 percent of the imported car segment but still account for only about 2 percent of all cars registered. Informal trade barriers in the form of awesome difficulties in establishing a dealer network and a marketing force in the automobile business are likely to persist, insulating the Toyotas and Nissans from severe competition from foreign cars. To varying degrees, this will apply to other finished manufactured durables. So the bulk of the imports for durables will be Japanese brands produced elsewhere—a pattern with which the United States is familiar.

In parallel, those industries that are, or will be, losing their competitive edge (shipping, textile, aluminum refining) will merge or convert to high value-added production. The Japanese market economy has been technology-driven in the modern past, with technologists at the helms of industry for the most part. They have a greater inclination toward long-term investment. Coupled with their awareness of the need to adapt new methods—a skill for which the Japanese are renowned—Japanese corporations that they lead will prove to be more flexible in the global market than their financially and legally driven U.S. counterparts.

Despite this, the trauma of internationalization will be in the ascendancy of the money managers who, on a free market basis, will always prevail in the short term. Conscious of this fact, the opening of the Japanese financial markets will be restrained until government and industrial leaders feel comfortable that short- to medium-term industrial objectives are not being disrupted. The most immediate objective is to restructure Japanese industry while limiting the hardships to small and medium-size enterprises. Under the circumstances, the technologists will continue to prevail over the money people, who are less concerned with long-term restructuring. Because the most disruptive effects of short-term pressure from the global market will come from the freeing of the financial markets, the Japanese government will continue to stall amid the cries of "unfair" from Western companies trying to gain a toehold in this Japanese sector.

Agriculture is not spared from the pressures of restructuring because it is the constant target of the United States on Japanese trade inequities. It is unlikely that Japan can totally liberalize, with an already low self-sufficiency rate for basic staples—4 percent for soybeans, approximately 10 percent for wheat, and an overall 30 percent including rice for comfort in times of national emergencies. There is clearly room for improvement in official pricing policies to place greater emphasis on the natural market mechanism. The Maekawa report believed imports should be expanded on agricultural products that have large price discrepancies with those from overseas, and it seemed to include everything except rice. Industries have had to cope with restructuring and disemployment in the past, so there is no reason farmers should be exempted from the free workings of the market. They, too, will have to face up to tough adjustments, together with the manufacturing sector.

IMPORT OR BUST

Japanese ministries have demonstrated in the past that there are innumerable ways in which to drag their feet when it comes to allowing entry of outsiders into Japan. In recent years, the Ministry of Health was most frequently accused of obstructive bureaucratic practices against free trade. The complaints centered on certification procedures for food and drugs.

These are rapidly undergoing simplification and one of the last bastions of resistance will shift to the financial market, and the Ministry of Finance has replaced MITI for coping with the outside threat to "industrial harmony." MITI officials increasingly see themselves as important lubricants to international business by acting as a liaison between Japanese and foreign business, a far cry from the "notorious MITI," as perceived by foreign businesspeople of yore. The transition is from an authoritarian approver of organization to a server of business through the provision of information.

Acutely conscious that progress in the retail market will be too slow for Western patience, MITI announced in February 1988 a system to facilitate importation of items by medium to small stores. MITI planned to establish in 1989 an International General Distribution Center—a place where trading discussions can occur between overseas exporters, local importers, and medium to small wholesalers and retailers. The center will employ the so-called third-sector formula, with participation from government, self-governing bodies, and corporations. This third sector will construct the building, calling on the trade to establish their offices in it. By pooling resources, it is hoped that the smaller businesses that lacked capital and know-how to make direct overseas contacts will be encouraged toward importing more merchandise.

LIGHT AT THE END OF THE DISTRIBUTION TUNNEL

Far more has to be done to eliminate the perception that Japan is limited in terms of market access. A multipoint action program was announced in 1986, including the lowering or abolition of tariffs on 1,853 items, which was effected with unusual speed. However, the world remains skeptical as to the nontariff barriers, especially that concerning the distribution system.

To the foreign critic, the foremost of these is the Large Retail Establishment Restriction Law. Isao Nakauchi, chairman of Daiei, the largest retail chain in Japan, reported in a speech in late 1988 that his company must wait five to seven years to open a new store, during which time it has to file 73 applications to obtain 26 permits required under the law. This is a classic example of the Japanese emphasis on *wa* (internal harmony), which in this case protects the small stores from the encroachment of the large, so "peace" will be maintained in the shopping streets.

The current law proposes a process of arbitration after a full discussion among three parties—the large store that wishes to open, the incumbent local stores, and the consumer. A committee represented by these three interests theoretically becomes the adjudicating body. Importantly, without local approval, an application cannot even be filed to start the arbitration process. But Nakauchi, who first fought former Prime Minister Nakasone, the then-minister in charge at MITI, on this issue, testified that MITI explained the law in different ways to supermarkets, department stores, and the medium to small stores, so each went away with a separate interpretation that resulted in administrative chaos.

Whether this was deliberate or simply a typical Japanese preference for ambiguity is not clear, but it is a wonder any large stores managed to open. When they did, it was a triumph of patience and money—with a great deal of the latter sometimes suspected of moving into the pockets of the local boss. MITI's stance naturally favored those with the biggest political clout, the conglomeration of small stores.

Regulations beget regulations, and the large store applicant wanders into a bureaucratic wonderland when it starts an approach. Some Japanese commentators are hopeful that all this is going to change because of Prime Minister Takeshita's promise at the Toronto summit of 1988 to reform the Japanese distribution system. Western cynics will recall other Japanese prime ministers who have made promises of one kind or another about the opening of the Japanese market, so it is unlikely any of the summit members jumped up in wild anticipation of a distribution revolution in Japan.

However, all indications are that the wheels are in motion. In a startling—in the domestic context—new twist, another government department, the Economic Planning Agency, has publicly stated the operation of the law was contrary to consumer interests. (It may be ungracious to comment that such an obvious fact needed to be stated.) The agency suggested that those in the adjudicating committee be designated semi-public officials, which will make them subject to audit, a not-so-veiled reference to the possibility of bribes.

Fortunately for the global market, a bandwagon appears to be rolling, with the government's General Affairs Department and the *Keidanren* (Federation of Economic Organizations) also offering advice for reform. However, the enormously fragmented retailing system can't be reformed in one swipe. The average trading population for a Japanese retail store is only 69 compared to the United States' 136, West Germany's 166, and Britain's 240. All that can be expected is an acceleration of the trend already in motion.

For the first time in recorded history, the retail census of 1985 showed a decline in the number of stores from 1.72 million in 1982 to 1.63 million, down 5 percent. The most severe drop was among the mom-and-pop outlets that normally employ no outsiders. There are still 887,000 of them, a formidable number by most Western standards, but nevertheless down 12.3 percent. The latest census of 1988 showed that the decline in the number of small stores was halted, largely due to the domestic boom and the shifting in the nature of the small stores—from the old style "mom-and-pops" to boutiques and 24-hour convenience stores, the latter run by the large chains. Still, the underlying trend will be for a resumption of the reduction in the numbers of small operators. The law cannot prevent the workings of organic factors, i.e., the lack of a willing successor to tend the store when the owner dies, the worsening of geographic conditions, or the acceleration of land prices, which makes it more tempting to sell.

The number of wholesalers has decreased correspondingly to the retailers as shown in the 1985 census and it stabilized in 1988, but there is still approximately one wholesaler to every six retailers. This is possible only because they form vertical delivery points from the large to the small. It has been some time since the argument was advanced that the Japanese distribution system should begin to reduce its mountain of wholesalers more in line with most of the Western economies, giving better direct access to the retailer by the international marketer. Yet, in the 15 years since the first oil shock, total wholesale value has increased by almost five times, exceeding the GNP growth by slightly over four times.

As long as there remains such a proliferation of retailers, the cost of distributing directly from the manufacturer's warehouse will exceed that for using wholesalers. The fragmentation of consumer needs will compensate for further reduction in retailers. Wholesalers can still survive because of their ability to stock small quantities of many items. It was, in fact, the wholesalers who supported the 20 percent per annum growth of the convenience stores—not coming under the restrictions placed on large establishments because of their small square footage—with their "just-in-time" delivery. On the other hand, it is beyond the capabilities of the average wholesaler to cater to the ever-fragmenting demand. There will be an increase in specialized, focused wholesaling.

While the wholesaling industry has demonstrated a toughness for survival, the steady erosion of margins has now accelerated to critical proportions. Just as the export-oriented manufacturing sector is embarking upon a program of direct overseas investment, major wholesalers are now increasingly looking toward overseas procurement—the domain of trading companies until now. They may well be more adept at bringing overseas products to the consumer than the trading companies, whose past performance has been dismal.

Finally, the growth of direct marketing in Japan has increasingly become an attractive alternative to the foreign marketer. Major American players such as Avon and Amway have been successful in their door-to-door operations. Direct mail, in niche marketing, has also been successful, but as a mass marketing device, it is still in its infancy, although some companies have boasted spectacular growth. For example, Cecile, which sells women's underwear through a catalog, much of it from Southeast Asia, expects its current sales level of ¥133.5 billion to grow 2.5-fold in the next three years. However, as opposed to approximately 10 percent of all retail sales in the United States, the scale of mail order in Japan is much smaller, constituting just slightly over 1 percent of all transactions. If anything, catalog marketing has proved at least as challenging as conventional retailing.

THE DAWN OF GLOBALIZATION

The traditionally insular Japanese are being pushed onto the international stage. The ripple effect, set off by the need to stimulate domestic demand in compliance with global realities, is spreading rapidly through the marketplace.

In the consumer market, women, less constrained by institutional rigidities, are acting as a catalyst. With fewer children, a longer life expectancy, better educational opportunities, and the push for employment equities, the modern Japanese woman is closing the gap between herself and women in other economically advanced societies.

The hitherto hierarchical nature of the market is also being disrupted by young consumers, who are less concerned about corporate symbols and more with brands that fit their individual self-image. Together, women and youths are taking to the new concept of leisure—dragging the reluctant male workers along a new path.

Overseas demands for market access are putting pressure on reform, some possible in the short term, others relying on slower organic change. Barriers that remain tend to be due to cultural values rather than deliberate obstructions. While the Japanese market is not going to be a replica of the United States, Europe, or any other area—why should it be—the forces of globalization are creating unprecedented opportunities for the foreign marketer to challenge Japan's vast richness.

CHAPTER 7

BUSINESS ASPECTS OF TRADING WITH JAPAN

Hajime Wada

INITIATIVES TO ATTRACT BUSINESS
    Establishment of a Special Office to Promote Foreign
      Investment
    Investment Promotion Discussion Meetings
    Market Opening Measures
    Establishment of the Office of Trade and Investment
      Ombudsman
    Finance and Insurance
    Reports and Overseas Activities by Government-
      Affiliated Institutions
    Private Activities
COMMUNICATION
    Domestic Telephone Services
    International Telephone Services
    Modular Telephone Services (Automobile Telephones)
    Wireless Signals (Pocket Beepers)
    Comprehensive Digital Communications Network
    Facsimiles
    Telex Machines
    Postal Services
    Courier Services

TRANSPORTATION
Railway Transportation
Roads
Automobile Transportation
Marine Transportation
Airplane Transportation

INITIATIVES TO ATTRACT BUSINESS

As an island country poor in natural resources and food, Japan has used foreign trade as its principal tool to promote national advancement since the Meiji era. An export-oriented economy was seen as particularly important to cover imports, and measures to support expansion of exports—such as preferential financial treatment, export insurance, and sanction of enterprises contributing to exports—were enacted. As a result, Japan is a leading industrial power with a large trade surplus.

In recent years, however, other countries have become increasingly adamant in their demand that Japan further open its markets. In response, serious efforts have been made to remove import barriers and eliminate restrictions related to foreign investment in Japan. With a few notable exceptions, these efforts have helped to make the Japanese markets among the most open in the world.

Some prominent steps recently taken toward this end include:

Establishment of a Special Office to Promote Foreign Investment

The Ministry of International Trade and Industry (MITI) provides various information and consulting services through this office.

Investment Promotion Discussion Meetings

MITI conducts sessions to exchange views with foreign-affiliated enterprises and to examine various aspects of doing business in Japan, such as management policies, expatriate living conditions, and procurement of human resources.

Market Opening Measures

Market opening measures announced in July 1985 have the following concrete goals:

- Lowering and abolishing of customs duties.
- Alleviation of import restrictions.
- Improvement of import inspection procedures.
- Rationalization of the distribution system
- Revision of the import financing system.
- Active promotion of imports.

Establishment of the Office of Trade and Investment Ombudsman

The Economic Planning Agency uses this office to process complaints related to imports and investment.

Finance and Insurance

In the reorganization of import and financial systems promoting investment in Japan, the Japan Development Bank has forwarded a policy that gives preferential treatment to foreign firms investing in Japan and to the Japanese and foreign companies pursuing projects in import activities. This includes bank loans of 5.1 percent and 5.7 percent with a financing ratio of 40 percent (as of September 13, 1988).

Under a loan system for import settlements, the Export-Import Bank of Japan carries out joint financing with private financial institutions for import settlement funds, providing yen-denominated loans at 4.9 percent and 5.1 percent and dollar-denominated loans at 0.125 percent over the six-month U.S. Treasury bill rate.

Import insurance covers the cost of prepaid imports should cargo fail to arrive.

Reports and Overseas Activities by Government-Affiliated Institutions

A broad range of highly informative English-language pamphlets are being published. The Japan External Trade Organization (JETRO), an extragovernmental organization for promotion of trade, has over 78 overseas branches, including 9 in the United States. Local governments in Japan have also been active in cultivating overseas ties and promoting personal, economic, technical, and cultural exchanges through such means as trade fairs and the establishment of sister-city relationships and overseas offices. JETRO and local government offices in the United States are listed below.

Location	Japanese Institution
Atlanta	JETRO
Chicago	JETRO, City of Osaka
Dallas	JETRO, Aichi Pref.
Denver	JETRO
Houston	JETRO
Los Angeles	JETRO, Hokkaido, Tokyo, Kanagawa Pref., Shizuoka Pref., Nagano Pref., Aichi Pref., Hiroshima Pref., Hiroshima City
New York	JETRO, Tokyo, Osaka, Hyogo Pref., Fukui Pref.
San Francisco	JETRO
Seattle	Hyogo Pref.
Puerto Rico	JETRO

Private Activities

Japanese banks (including directly affiliated companies) and trading companies posses extensive worldwide networks and provide numerous services to assist foreign companies entering Japanese markets. There are many factors recommending the use of the services offered by Japanese banks, especially considering their enormous information capacity, the comprehensive strength of related enterprises, and their close connections with client organizations. Through directly affiliated general research institutes, such as Sanwa Research Institute, Japanese banks employ expert staff to provide trade and investment advice; corporate tie-ups, acquisitions, and postacquisition management strategy planning; and a wide spectrum of other services.

COMMUNICATION

Domestic Telephone Services

Telephone services cover all areas of Japan and are efficient and highly reliable. In 1986, the number of telephone numbers in use in Japan was 46.8 million, or 38.4 for every 100 people. The total number of telephone units reached 62.8 million, or 53.0 units per 100 people, compared with 181.9 million units or 71.0 units per 100 people for the United States. In addition to the fact that 98.4 percent of all Japanese households possess a phone, there are 6.8 public telephones per 1,000 people. There are six communications companies in Japan, with Nippon Telegraph and Telephone Corp. (NTT), the former government monopoly that has undergone privatization since 1985, far and away the largest.

Company Name	Service Coverage
NTT (Nippon Telegraph and Telephone Corp.)	National
Japan Telecom Co., Ltd.	Long distance
Daini Denden Inc.	Long distance
Teleway Japan Corp.	Long distance
Tokyo Telecommunications Network Inc.	Kanto region
Osaka Media Port	Osaka

Compared with NTT charges, telephone call charges for the other companies are about 20 percent less expensive. For example, a weekday afternoon call from Tokyo to Osaka costs ¥400 for the first three minutes through NTT, but only ¥300 through three other carriers. A call within an area code, however, is only ¥10 for three minutes, making local calls a bargain compared to medium- and long-distance calls.

International Telephone Services

International telephone services are politically neutral in the sense that they link the entire world, making communications possible even between nations for which no formal diplomatic relations exist. Japan's international telephone companies are an integral part of these services, and the three principal international telephone companies in Japan are Kokusai Denshin Denwa Co., Ltd. (KDD); Nihon Kokusai Tsushin; and International Digital Communications.

There are two basic types of international telephone service: direct dialing and operator-assisted. Table 7–1 shows KDD's charges for international direct dialing and operator-assisted calls.

Modular Telephone Services (Automobile Telephones)

As of September 1987, there were about 59,000 modular phone contracts in Japan, compared to roughly 350,000 in the United States. This represents a diffusion rate of 0.05 percent of the total population (0.15 percent in the United States) and 0.15 percent of all automobiles (0.22 percent in the United States). NTT, Nippon Ido Tsushin, and Teleway Japan Corporation provide modular phone services throughout Japan. At the time of installation, fees include a security deposit of ¥200,000, a contract fee of ¥800, a distribution and installment fee of ¥80,000, and monthly basic charges of ¥19,050 for rental of modular units. Call charges are ¥10 for every 6.5 seconds within 160 kilometers and for every 4.5 seconds outside of this range.

Wireless Signals (Pocket Beepers)

Twenty-two Japanese companies provide signaling services, including NTT, and approximately 3.1 million of these devices were in use as of June 1988. Wireless signaling services are limited to the local contracted area, and monthly leasing charges run from ¥2,300 to ¥3,200 per unit, with security deposits of ¥14,000 to ¥24,000.

Comprehensive Digital Communications Network

In April 1988, NTT introduced the integrated service digital network (ISDN), which uses a fiber optic cable to simultaneously transmit sound, pictures, data, and other electronic media. Monthly fees for use of an ISDN line are ¥5,400 for office use and ¥4,600 for household use. ISDN call charges are the same as for conventional telephone calls. Nevertheless, the high price of current ISDN machines, the incompatibility between different brands of ISDN, and the general lack of support services in this field have limited the popularity of these devices.

TABLE 7-1
KDD's Charges for International Calls as of September 14, 1988 (Units: Yen)

| Area | International Direct Dialing (per 6 seconds) | | | | | | International Operator Assisted | | |
| | Daytime | | Evenings or Holidays | | Late Night | | Base Rate (first 3 minutes) | | |
	First Minute	Each Additional Minute	First Minute	Each Additional Minute	First Minute	Each Additional Minute	Station to Station	Person to Person	Each Additional Minute
Continental United States	45	22	36	18	27	13	1,890	3,150	450
Hawaii	45	22	36	18	27	13	1,890	3,150	450
Guam	45	22	36	18	27	13	1,830	3,050	450

Facsimiles

Facsimile, or fax, machines are widely used in Japan for domestic and international communication. As of September 1987, NTT had roughly 148,000 fax service contracts, and an estimated 1.4 million fax machines were in use in March 1988. Charges for the use of fax machines are the same as those for telephones.

Telex Machines

In recent years, use of telex machines in Japan has declined dramatically because of the increasing popularity of telephones and facsimile machines.

Postal Services

Japan has 23,793 post offices (1987 figure) and 150,380 mailboxes (1986), compared to about 395,000 in the United States. Mail is collected one to five times per day and delivered one to two times per day, or three times in the case of special delivery. Air mail service between Japan and the United States generally takes about one week. Table 7–2 details postage costs.

TABLE 7–2
International Postal Charges (as of October 1, 1988)

Service	Destination	Charge (yen)
Airmail letters (10 g.)	Asia	¥ 80
	North America	100
	Europe	120
Airmail postcards	Asia	70
	North America	70
	Europe	70
Air parcel post (5 kg.)	East Asia	4,850
	North America	9,500
	Europe	10,700

Courier Services

There are 22 companies nationwide that provide international express mail service, 10 of which are foreign affiliates. To send an average-length document from Japan to New York by courier service would take about two to three days and cost approximately ¥2,500.

TRANSPORTATION

Since the beginning of the Meiji era, the government has made great efforts in the construction of railways, with the network of routes steadily expanding. The Japanese railways are world famous for their punctuality and exemplary safety record.

Development of the automobile industry and construction of expressways have made the automobile the predominant means of transportation, both for cargo and passengers.

Airports have been constructed both in major and regional cities, and the development of bus routes and an efficient taxi service have led to a substantial improvement in public transportation.

However, as Japan is a small and mountainous country, roads are inferior both in quantity and quality to those in Europe and the United States. This restricts the possibilities for automobile transportation. Furthermore, in the larger cities, commuter trains are congested in rush hours and costs of transportation (Japan Railways, airline tickets, expressway tolls, and gasoline) are higher than in most other nations. Figures 7–1, 7–2, 7–3, and 7–4 detail usage rates of the various modes of transportation.

Railway Transportation

Including the JR Group (the former Japanese National Railways) and the 15 major railways started as private enterprises, there are over 80 railway enterprises.

Many of these enterprises are engaged in a variety of businesses other than railway transportation, such as buses, taxis, real estate, and retailing. Some even own professional baseball teams.

FIGURE 7–1
Forms of Cargo Transportation (Unit: Percentage of Tons Transported)

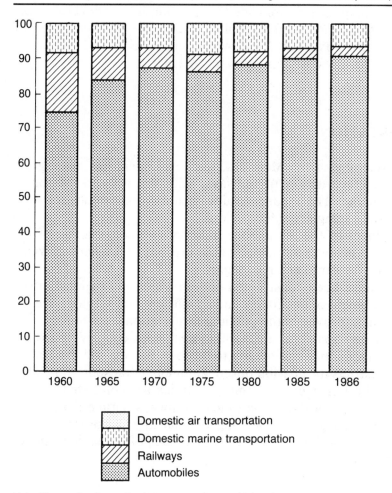

Domestic air transportation
Domestic marine transportation
Railways
Automobiles

Note: Figures for domestic air transportation are below 1 percent.

The Shinkansen (Bullet Train), which is the pride of the JR Group, has extended its lines from Tokyo to Hakata, Niigata, and Morioka. It has a maximum speed of 240 kmh (150 mph). The Shinkansen runs the 552 km (345 miles) between Tokyo and Osaka in three hours, providing convenient main-line passenger transportation.

Subways exist in nine cities. They operate with safety and accuracy on tight schedules and are welcomed by the citizens for their cleanliness and convenience.

FIGURE 7–2
Forms of Cargo Transportation (Unit: Percentage Ton-Kilometers)

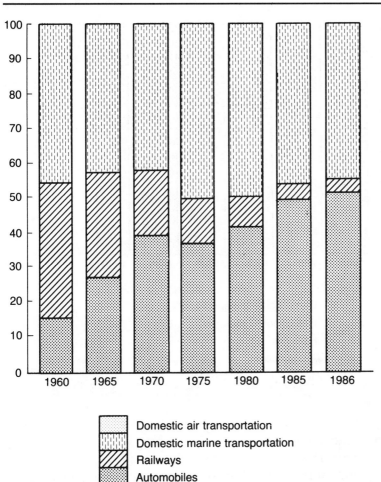

Domestic air transportation
Domestic marine transportation
Railways
Automobiles

Note: Figures for domestic air transportation are below 1 percent.

Roads

The standard of Japanese road conditions, considering the population, the number of vehicles in use, and the absolute volume, is insufficient in comparison with the United States and the major countries in Europe. The construction of better road systems is anticipated.

In comparison with the United States, the major characteristics of Japanese roads are:

FIGURE 7–3
Forms of Passenger Transportation (Unit: Percentage of Passengers)

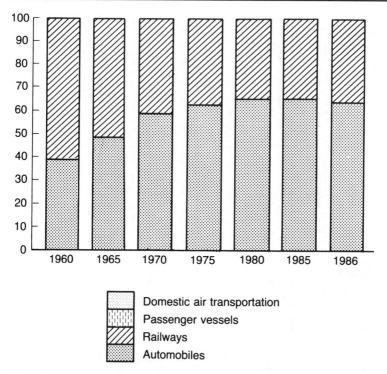

Domestic air transportation
Passenger vessels
Railways
Automobiles

Note: Figures for passenger vessels and domestic air transportation are below 1 percent.

- Fewer traffic lanes.
- Many narrow roads.
- Parking difficulties and traffic congestion in city centers.
- Restrictions on overweight goods and overloaded vehicles.
- Weak foundations.
- Many curved roads.
- Low-ceiling tunnels and low electric cables.
- Permits sometimes required from local governments and police in cases of transporting bulky cargos and in other instances.
- Insufficient number of loop roads.
- Low ratio of paved roads.
- Problems of high-speed highways: limited number/mileage, high tolls, and frequent congestion.
- Driving on the left side.

FIGURE 7–4
Forms of Passenger Transportation (Unit: Percentage of Passenger-Kilometers)

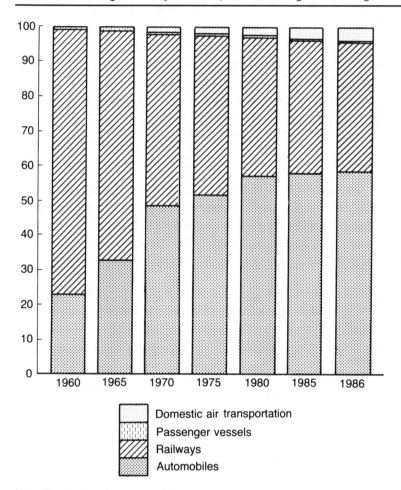

Domestic air transportation
Passenger vessels
Railways
Automobiles

Note: Figures for passenger vessels are 1 percent or below.

Automobile Transportation

Japan, which has become the world's top manufacturing country on a unit basis, ranks second to the United States in the number of automobiles on the road. Japanese automobiles are high quality with good fuel efficiency ratings and a low number of defects. Imports from West Germany, however, have been increasing recently.

For safety and pollution control, cars must be inspected every two to three years. However, because of the high cost to the car user, there is much criticism about the car inspection system.

Automobiles are the main means of transportation of both people and cargo. From the standpoint of passenger transportation, however, the share accounted for by automobiles in Japan is not as great as in Europe or the United States. As described previously, there are still many problems with roads in Japan.

Taxis are safe and clean. A general policy of no tipping and the fact that some taxis accept credit cards also contribute to their convenience, but the fares are higher than in Europe and the United States.

Marine Transportation

In Japan, which is surrounded by oceans and exists on foreign trade, there are about 1,100 harbors, and harbor facilities are highly developed and well-maintained. Japan ranks first in the world in terms of the number of vessels and third, following Liberia and Panama, in terms of gross tonnage. Japanese-related marine cargo makes up about 20 percent of the world's total.

Japanese vessels are highly evaluated for both safety and reliability. However, in recent years, high costs and reduced competitiveness have become problems.

Airplane Transportation

At present, there are 54 airports with departures and landings of scheduled flights in Japan. Of these, 12 are international airports, including Narita (New Tokyo), Haneda (Tokyo), Osaka (Itami), and Fukuoka.

The New Tokyo International Airport handles 66 percent of Japan's international air passengers and 80 percent of international air cargo. It serves as Japan's main air transport gateway. Figures for 1986 show it ranks seventh in the world in the number of international air passengers and first in quantity of cargo handled, surpassing Kennedy Airport in New York. However, it is far from downtown Tokyo, about 65 km (40 miles) and has some inconvenient aspects, such as only one runway. Also, at present, none of the airports in big cities or suburbs permits early-morning or late-night departures or arrivals due to noise problems.

To solve this problem and expand capacity, the Kansai International Airport is being constructed in the southeast part of Osaka Bay on reclaimed land. It will operate 24 hours a day and is scheduled to open in 1993. Also, Narita and Haneda, the two airports in Tokyo, are undergoing expansion.

CHAPTER 8

OPERATING A BUSINESS IN JAPAN

Shin Matsumi
Keizo Ohashi
Daniel S. Maher

LICENSING, ROYALTIES, AND
TECHNOLOGY TRANSFER
Background and History
Role of Government and Universities
Licensing and Royalty Agreements
Intellectual Property Trends
Approach to Technology Transfer
Manufacturing, Location, and Facilities

SETTING UP A FOREIGN OPERATION

Liberalization of Foreign Investment

The Foreign Exchange and Foreign Trade Control Law was broadly
revised in 1980. The approval system for the establishment of foreign
enterprises in Japan and the introduction of technology was changed to a
prior-reporting system.

Movement of Foreign Investment into Japan

Investments in Japan by foreign enterprises have increased in recent
years. Foreign investment in the advanced fields of chemicals, pharmaceuticals, and electronics has been especially strong, as has been the
entry into the commercial sector of enterprises based in the Asian newly
industrialized economies (NIEs). According to the Ministry of Finance,
there have been 27,124 direct foreign investments in Japan, and the total
amount invested reached $8 billion from 1950 through the end of 1987.

Research into the Activities of Foreign Enterprises
The principal findings of the Ministry of International Trade and Industry's (MITI) 1987 "Research on Activities of Foreign Enterprises" are
given below. (The survey covered 2,094 companies, with 894 companies
(42.7 percent) giving valid responses.)

The composition according to industry was: manufacturing industries, 409 companies (45.7 percent), and commerce, 352 companies (39.4
percent). These two categories accounted for most investments. Of the
companies covered, 434 (48.5 percent) were from the United States, 318
(35.6 percent) were from Europe, and 99 (11.1 percent) were from Asia.

As for the ratio of foreign investment, 407 companies (45.5 percent) were wholly owned subsidiaries of foreign enterprises, 208 (23.2 percent) were joint ventures with over 50 percent foreign capital participation, and 279 (31.2 percent) were joint ventures with 50 percent foreign capital investment.

The total sales of these companies in fiscal 1984 amounted to ¥13.6 trillion (the average net sales for a single company was ¥15.2 billion), or 1.4 percent of the sales of all corporations in Japan. In fiscal 1984, the ratio of current profits to total sales was 3.4 percent, which was superior to the 2.1 percent registered by Japanese enterprises. Generally, foreign capital enterprises in Japan have had better business performance than have Japanese enterprises.

As for the reason for entering the Japanese market, an overwhelming 41.7 percent of the foreign enterprises surveyed stated they were "taking advantage of the growth of the Japanese market," while 17.8 percent stated they were "securing a position to advance into the Asian market." Problems encountered by these foreign enterprises included "competition with Japanese companies," "differences in business customs," the "expansion of sales channels," "high corporate taxes," "legal restrictions and government guidance," and the "securing of human resources."

Attitude of Japanese Corporations toward Foreign Capital Enterprises

How do Japanese corporations view foreign capital enterprises? According to MITI's 1987 research study (this survey covered 1,026 companies, with 447 enterprises (43.6 percent) giving valid replies) of the smooth introduction of direct investments into Japan:

1. More than 50 percent of Japanese companies have already established some form of corporate relations with foreign capital enterprises, and 60 percent of these Japanese companies wish to maintain such relationships with foreign enterprises. Sixty percent of Japanese companies have already engaged in some kind of business transaction with foreign capital enterprises.

2. Foreign capital enterprises are highly regarded in terms of management ability, eliciting such comments as "excellent management know-how," "superior financial position," and superior technical development capabilities." However, Japanese corporations have a low evaluation of the foreign capital enterprises in areas that are considered important in the Japanese market, such as service (including aftersales service) carefully tailored to client needs, observance of Japanese business customs, prompt delivery of the specified quantity of goods, and development of products for the Japanese market.

In general, however, Japanese enterprises have a favorable attitude toward foreign capital enterprises.

Methods of Entry and Related Laws and Regulations

A foreign enterprise may enter Japan in three ways—by setting up a representative office; establishing branches, factories, or other business facilities; or setting up a corporation. There are no legal restrictions on the establishment of representative offices, with the exception of foreign banks, securities firms, and insurance companies.

The establishment of branches of all other foreign enterprises, or of Japanese subsidiaries of foreign corporations or joint ventures, are classified as direct domestic investments under the Foreign Exchange Control Law and require prior notification. However, investments that affect national security and maintenance of public order, have a detrimental effect on the Japanese economy, or involve reciprocal agreements with other countries require an investigation. For example, direct foreign investments in agriculture, forestry and fishery industries, mining, oil, hides and leather, and related products are subject to review.

The establishment of a branch or subsidiary must conform to the Commercial Code or the Limited Company Law (*Yugen Gaisha Hoo*). Proper notice must be given and branches and other operations and subsidiaries must be registered. Also, for some types of enterprises, applicable laws require licenses, approvals, notifications, and/or registration. All business activities must conform to the Anti-Monopoly Law. Also, all new companies, after opening their offices, must report their establishment to the tax offices having jurisdiction over their areas.

Procedures for Direct Investment in Japan

Foreign investors who are required to file reports are individuals with nonresident status, foreign corporations and other organizations, and Japanese companies that have dominant ownership by foreign entities (capital that is held by the first two types of investors).

The Scope of Direct Investment in Japan
In addition to the direct investments mentioned above, the Foreign Exchange Control Law stipulates the following acts entail intent to participate in management and are direct domestic investments.

1. Acquisition of an interest share or stocks of a nonpublicly owned corporation. These are considered to be direct domestic investments, regardless of the acquisition ratio.
2. The transfer to foreign investors of nonpublicly owned stocks that were acquired by investors before becoming nonresidents.
3. Acquisition (by a single foreign investor or closely related group of investors) of 10 percent or more of publicly owned stocks (listed stocks and stocks traded over the counter) of a Japanese company.
4. A substantial change in the business activities of a company in which a foreign shareholder owns more than one third of the total stock (the total of their stock ownership ratios in case of more than one foreign investor) and approves such change.
5. Establishment of branches, factories, and other business facilities, and changes in the type of business or objectives of the business.
6. Loans to Japanese legal entities when the loan period exceeds one year, but is less than five years, and exceeds ¥200 million, and loans that are for over five years and exceed ¥100 million.
7. Acquisition of privately placed bonds.
8. Acquisition of an interest in corporations established under special status.

Procedures for Investment in Japan

Direct investment in Japan is, in principle, free, and prior reporting is all that is necessary. Under this prior-reporting system, the foreign investor must submit a report through the Bank of Japan (in a prescribed format) to the Minister of Finance and the minister with jurisdiction over the type of business three months before the day the direct investment is to be made in Japan (see Figure 8–1). Furthermore, if the foreign investor is a nonresident corporation or other entity, the report must be submitted by an agent who is a resident of Japan.

The direct investor cannot in principle act until 30 days have passed from the date the report is received. In actual practice, however, investment can usually begin immediately except for business in the following areas: agriculture, forestry and fishery industries, the oil industry, the mining industry, hides and leather manufacturing, and industries that affect the national safety (areas where Japan is withholding full liberalization under the OECD code of liberalization of capital). For those industries, investment may begin two weeks after the report is received by the authorities.

FIGURE 8–1
Reporting Procedure for Direct Investments in Japan

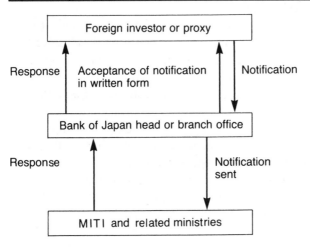

Source: JETRO.

In restricted business where an investigation is necessary, the inspection is conducted by MITI and other ministries and agencies according to the Foreign Exchange Control Law.

In the case of the acquisition of an enterprise, with certain exceptions (refer to "Acquisition of Japanese Enterprises" later in this chapter), there are no restrictions as long as a proper report is made. However, even though acquisitions among Japanese companies are gradually increasing, it is not yet a general practice. The Securities Exchange Law addresses takeovers through the acquisition of publicly traded shares as a means of acquiring enterprises.

FORM OF BUSINESS

Establishment of Representative Offices

In cases where a foreign investor wishes to establish a representative office in Japan, the investor is free to do so with no obligations under either the Foreign Exchange Control Law or Japanese commercial and tax codes regarding gaining of approval, reporting, registration, and issuing of annual reports. However, a foreign corporation engaged in banking, insurance, or securities must procure the necessary approvals and permits for setting up a representative office under the enterprise laws applicable to these industries.

Establishment of Branches

Under the Foreign Exchange Control Law, a foreign corporation that wishes to establish a branch office in Japan must submit a report through the Bank of Japan to the Minister of Finance and the minister who has jurisdiction over the industry concerned three months before the establishment. Also, when establishing a branch under the Commercial Code, it is necessary to register an agent with resident status in Japan and a place of business with the local branch of the Legal Affairs Bureau of the Ministry of Justice. Branches established by foreign corporations must be registered within three weeks after establishment and announced publicly. It is also necessary to register the laws applicable for establishment of the company and the name and address of the representative in Japan. Appropriate notification and application must also be made to the tax office.

Establishment of Domestic Corporations

Types of Companies
In Japan, three types of companies are defined under the Commercial Code: joint stock (*kabushiki gaisha*), limited partnership (*gooshi gaisha*), and unlimited partnership (*goomei gaisha*). A fourth type of company (*yugen gaisha*), or limited company, falls under the Limited Company Law. When a foreign investor establishes a subsidiary company or joint venture company, it usually takes the form of a *kabushiki gaisha,* or what corresponds to a corporation in the United States.

Establishment of Corporations

Outline of Establishment Procedures. If the establishment of a company has followed procedures pursuant to the provisions of the Commercial Code, it acquires corporate status, and unless it is a special type of industry, approval by administrative authorities is not necessary. When establishing a corporation, promoter establishment or subscription establishment procedures must be taken (see Figure 8–2). In other

206

FIGURE 8–2
Comparison of Procedures for Subscription and Promoter Establishment

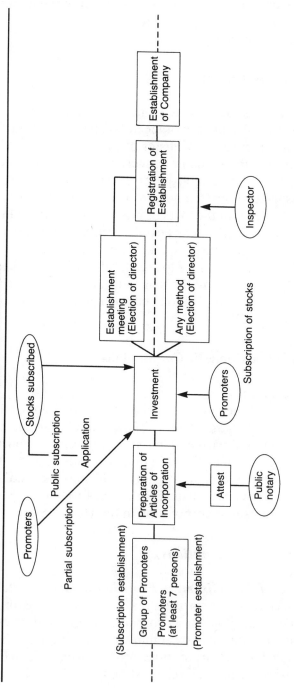

words, one of two procedures is followed. In the first (promoter establishment), the total number of stocks issued at the time of the company's establishment are taken up solely by the promoters. In the other, stocks other than those taken up by the promoters are offered for subscription. This is referred to as subscription establishment. In the former case, an inspector appointed by the court must investigate. This investigation is usually not required under a subscription establishment. Therefore, the subscription establishment of a company is more common.

Selection of Promoters. Establishment of a corporation requires seven or more promoters, and these promoters must acquire a minimum of one share of the company. There are, however, no restrictions as to the status (individual or a corporation) or the location of the promoter. In cases where a foreign investor establishes a domestic corporation, seven Japanese residents can acquire a small number of the shares and, after the establishment of the company, transfer their shares back to the foreign investor.

Preparation of Articles of Incorporation. The promoters must prepare the articles of incorporation and place their signatures or official seals on it. The articles of incorporation must then receive notarization by a public notary. Three types of articles are included in such articles: mandatory, effective, and optional.

Decision on Items Related to Stock Issuance. After the articles of incorporation have been notarized, the promoters must unanimously decide, with regard to the issuance of stocks, the following:

- The type and number of stocks to be issued at the time of establishment and the issuance price of those stocks.
- In cases where stocks with no par value are to be issued, the amount of the issue price that will not be included in the paid-in capital.

The company can issue par-value or no-par-value stocks and can issue both. With regard to par-value stocks, the amount of value must be equal for all shares, and the issuance price cannot be below par value. At the time of establishment of the company, however, the par value of one share must be over ¥50,000 or more.

Par-value stocks issued after the establishment do not have price restrictions. As long as the net assets of the company exceed ¥50,000 per share, shares may be broken down into units of ¥50,000 or less.

Types of stocks that may be issued, besides common stock, are preferred stocks, subordinated stocks, nonvoting stocks, and redeemable stocks.

Underwriting of Stocks by Promoters. When the issuance price of stocks issued at the time of establishment is decided, each promoter must then acquire the minimum of one stock. This must be clearly stated in the Stock Underwriting Certificate as the price of the stock.

Subscription of Stocks. Subscription of stocks will be carried out by the Stock Application prepared by the promoters. The promoters shall allocate the stocks on application from subscribers and require payment equal to the subscribed amount into a certified bank account at the same time as the application is accepted. The bank holds the payment until the last day of the subscription period.

Inaugural General Meeting. After the investment of initial capital has been completed, the promoters will hold an inaugural general meeting where they will report to the stockholders the establishment of the company and the stockholders will elect a minimum of three persons as directors and a minimum of one person as auditor. The directors and auditor(s) elected are required to examine the procedures taken to set up the company and then report their findings at the inaugural general meeting. Thus, the operation of the company will pass into the hands of the stockholders from the promoters. The directors elected at the meeting will immediately hold a meeting to elect a representative director(s).

Registration of Establishment. Within two weeks following completion of the inaugural general meeting, the company must file an application to register its establishment and its corporate seal with the local branch of the Legal Affairs Bureau of the Ministry of Justice. The company is established only after the registration of establishment is made. At the time of the registration, registration permit tax of 0.7 percent of paid-in capital (or a minimum of ¥150,000) must be paid. The completion of the registration process takes at least one month, including the prior-reporting procedures required under the Foreign Exchange Control Law. In addition to the foregoing, notifications based on tax laws in connection with the establishment of the company must be submitted to the tax office. Also, notification with regard to employment of workers is required by the Labor Standards Inspection Office. With regard to the commencement of a business after obtaining special approval from government ministries, reports must be submitted to the government office having jurisdiction over that particular business.

Permanent Functions of the Company

The necessary permanent functions or organizations of the corporation are the stockholders' general meetings and meetings of the board of directors, representative directors, and auditors.

Stockholders' General Meetings. These meetings consist of regular general meetings held following the end of each accounting period and of extraordinary general meetings held from time to time. The regular general meeting must be held once a year and within three months after the end of the company's accounting period. Extraordinary meetings are held when necessary. These meetings are called by the representative director(s) pursuant to a resolution at the board of directors meeting. If the chairman of the general meeting is not specified in the articles of incorporation, he or she is usually chosen at the beginning of the meeting. Minority stockholders, under certain conditions, have the right to call for a general meeting and submit proposals for the agenda. The stockholders' general meeting conducts discussions and makes decisions on items listed on the agenda. This agenda is sent to stockholders, along with a notice calling for the meeting, at least two weeks before the day of the meeting. Each stockholder exercises his or her own voting rights on two types of resolutions: ordinary and special.

Ordinary resolutions require attendance of stockholders owning more than a half of the total number of issued stocks (a quorum) and are resolved by votes of a majority of stockholders attending.

Special resolutions for very important matters, which include mergers, changes in the articles of incorporation, and reductions in capital, require attendance of stockholders holding more than half of the total number of issued stocks (a quorum) and are resolved by votes of two thirds or more of the stockholders attending.

Directors and Meetings of the Directors. The board of directors is composed of directors (minimum of three persons appointed for two-year terms) elected at the stockholders' general meeting. The board makes decisions regarding the execution of the business of the company and also supervises the execution of the directors' work. At least one director is appointed representative director. Representative directors represent the company outside and are also responsible for overseeing the execution of the company's business. Execution of routine and less important matters may be delegated to representative directors or directors. The execution of important business matters, however, is the exclusive right of the board of directors.

Auditors.   Although auditors are elected at the stockholders' general meeting (for large firms, at least two persons must be elected, and for smaller companies, at least one person), they cannot also assume a position as a director, manager, or employee of the company or its subsidiary companies. The term of appointment is stated as "through the end of the ordinary general meeting of the final accounting term ending within two years following appointment." In the case of large companies, the auditor is responsible for a careful examination of the operations of the company as well as the accounts. Also for large companies, an independent, external audit is required. But for smaller companies, the auditor is responsible only for the accounts.

LABOR, IMMIGRATION, AND COMPENSATION

Recent Labor Market Conditions

Employment Conditions.   In 1987, the labor force totaled 60,840,000, an increase of 640,000 over the previous year. The number of those employed was 59,110,000 (35,510,000 males and 23,600,000 females), a 1 percent increase over the previous year. A breakdown by industry shows agriculture and forestry with 4,460,000 persons and other industries with 54,650,000. The order of ranking by number of employees for fields other than agriculture and forestry is (1) wholesale and retail, financing, insurance, and real estate, (2) manufacturing, (3) services, and (4) construction. The average annual number of unemployed in 1987 increased to 1,730,000 persons, 60,000 higher than in the previous year. The rate of unemployment, 2.8 percent, was the same as in 1986, the highest rate recorded so far. Table 8–1 and Figure 8–3 detail Japan's unemployment picture.

Labor Market Trends.   Employment in tertiary industries has advanced, with the service industry showing the greatest expansion. According to types of workers, the number of white-collar workers has

TABLE 8–1
Trends in Japan's Employable Population (Unit: Million Persons)

	15 Years or Older	Employable Population	Working Population	Fully Unemployed	Rate of Unemployment (percent)	Nonemployable Population	Employable in Total Population (percent)
1984	93.5	59.3	57.7	1.6	2.7%	33.7	63.4%
1985	94.7	59.6	58.1	1.6	2.6	34.5	63.0
1986	95.9	60.2	58.5	1.7	2.8	35.1	62.8
1987	97.2	60.8	59.1	1.7	2.8	35.8	62.6

Source: Management Coordination Agency, Annual Survey of Employment.

FIGURE 8–3

Comparison of Unemployment Rates of Japan, Europe, and the United States

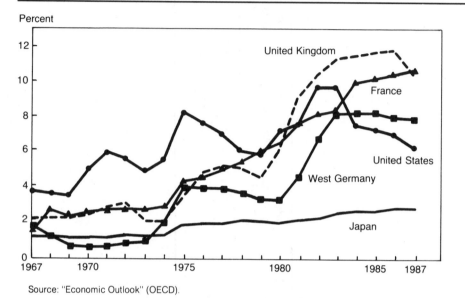

Percent

Source: "Economic Outlook" (OECD).

risen, and the structure of those employed by age shows an increase in the number of older persons among those employed. Since 1975, the labor force has shown a rise of 1 to 1.2 percent, or an increase of 600,000 persons each year. Although this increase is steady, the number of older workers and females workers has advanced more rapidly in recent years. Since 1965, however, the unemployment rate has been moving upward because of decreased labor demands and structural changes in the labor market, owing to the lower rate of economic growth. The lifetime employment wage scale is unique to Japan, and the disparity of wages between male workers of different ages is quite apparent under this system. Due to the restraint in public works and other factors, employment in local areas has been sluggish and, although a corrective tendency to increase employment exists, there are still wide gaps in employment among local areas.

Labor and Employer Relations

Labor Laws and Regulations. There are three fundamental labor laws for labor relations in Japan: the Trade Union Law, the Labor

Standards Law, and the Labor Relations Adjustment Law. These laws provide only general guidance for labor relations. The actual provisions for labor and the employer are those practices established between employers and labor within the enterprise itself, court judgments regarding labor laws, and notifications issued by labor administration organizations. Among practices established by labor and employers in Japan, attention must be given to the lifetime employment system, the wage-by-seniority system, and the organization of unions at the company level, which are quite different from labor and employer relations in Europe and the United States. There are important differences based on Japanese-style management.

Lifetime Employment.   The lifetime employment system is said to be a representative example of Japanese management practices; it refers to a system where an employee is hired by a company for his or her lifetime, i.e., until retirement, which is now between the ages of 55 and 60. The system, together with the retirement age system and wage-by-seniority system, is one of the key features of labor relations in Japan. Despite the lifetime nature of the system, an employee can quit the company before he or she reaches retirement age, but the company cannot easily discharge an employee. The advantage of the lifetime employment system is the stability of employment and income it provides. This promotes loyalty toward the enterprise and smoother technological innovation. However, the inflexibility of employment and the stifling of personal self-development are major problems. The wage-by-seniority system means wages and position rise according to how many years one serves the company. The general thinking, however, is to compensate the employee over his or her full employment career.

Hiring.   The majority of Japanese enterprises hire new graduates in April, owing in great part to the Japanese school year, which runs from April until March of the following year. Since lifetime employment is common in Japan, the number of persons who change jobs after entering a company is very low. Recently, however, it has become more common for companies to hire a qualified person for a job requiring special qualifications in midcareer. Also, it has been common for most female employees to quit the company when they get married, but this practice has been changing in recent years. Employment tests for new employment candidates are generally administered in the fall before hiring. Recruitment is carried out through schools and by advertisements in newspapers or personnel recruitment magazines. Foreign companies, however, usually make use of personnel consultants to recruit management-level personnel.

Labor Unions and Labor Relations. The predominant characteristic of Japanese labor unions is that they are organized by company and thus differ from the labor unions in Europe and the United States, which are organized by skill and industry. A union by company is comprised from workers of that company; it has its own rules and is independent in its operations. Various unions have come together to organize a federation of unions by industry.

As of June 1987, there were about 73,100 labor unions and approximately 12,270,000 union members (accounting for 27.6 percent of the employed work force) in Japan.

The posture of labor unions in Japan is realistic since unions are contained within the company. This is understood by both employers and unions; if union demands are just and fair, every effort will be made to approve them to the extent the company's situation allows. In addition, the unions, under the lifetime employment system, trust the company and thus there is a strong tendency to make demands upon full consideration of the employer's situation. Although the company and the union are opposed to each other on the distribution of profit, both unions and management weigh the prosperity of the company. This is an important characteristic of labor relations in Japan.

Labor Conditions

Wages and Fringe Benefits. In 1987, at companies with over 30 employees, the average monthly wage was ¥251,298 per employee. If two yearly bonuses are included, the average amount becomes ¥335,944. The average initial monthly wage for a new university graduate for clerical office work was ¥148,200. Each spring, labor negotiations to raise wages begin and uniform demands are made by industry. One feature of wages in Japan is the large disparity in wages between large companies and small- and medium-size companies. Although the system of wages based on seniority is still fundamental, job ability is gradually becoming more important. Also, in recent years, the demand for female part-time workers is steadily rising. Almost all wages are paid on a monthly basis, and the majority of companies pay their employees between the 20th and the 25th of each month. Increasingly the most popular form of wage payment is the transfer of wages into employee bank accounts. In 1987, the wages per actual working hour for labor in manufacturing industries were as follows:

Average Hourly Wages in Manufacturing

	Japan	U.S.	U.K.	West Germany	France
Labor costs in yen converted at end-1987 rate	¥1,374	¥1,330	¥1,028	¥1,740	¥1,179
Index of labor costs (Japan=100)	100	97	76	128	87
Foreign exchange rate at the end of 1987	—	¥122	¥228.36	¥77.07	¥2.73

Note: The yen-dollar rate is the Tokyo closing rate for 1987. Rates for the pound, mark, and franc are New York closing rates

Sources: Japan Ministry of Labor, Monthly Survey of Labor Statistics; IMF, International Financial Statistics; and data of respective nations.

In addition to the foregoing, Japanese companies usually establish company dining facilities, company housing, and other health and welfare facilities. Also, a retirement allowance is equivalent, on the average, to about 35 to 40 months of the employee's monthly salary at the time of retirement.

Labor Hours.   The Labor Standards Law, enacted in 1947, set the workday at eight hours and the workweek at 48 hours, with one day off a week. It also stipulated the number of vacation days with pay annually at between 6 and 20 days, determined by the number of years of service in the company. However, in the revised Labor Standards Law, enforced from April 1988, the labor hours for one week are now 40 hours (although as an interim measure, they have been reduced only to 46 hours), and vacation days with pay are now 10 to 20 days. In addition, many companies have New Year's vacation and holidays to commemorate establishment of the company.

Even though Japan's yearly actual working hours are being reduced each year, by international standards, they are still quite long. In 1987, total average monthly labor hours were 175.9 hours, or a 0.4 percent increase over the previous year. As of 1986, the yearly total labor hours for Japan were 2,150 hours; the United States, 1,924 hours; the United Kingdom, 1,938 hours; West Germany, 1,655 hours; and France, 1,643 hours. The reason for this difference is that observance of two holidays per week is not very common in Japan and that many Japanese workers do not use their paid vacation days. Beginning in February 1989, all financial institutions were closed on Saturdays as well as Sundays.

Health and Welfare Expenditures.　For legal, health, and welfare expenditures, the following must be borne in part or in total by the company.

- Health insurance covers payment of necessary medical treatment for injury or illness outside of business, death, or birth.
- Welfare pension insurance provides a pension to an employee after he or she retires. The pension is payable to those participating in the system for 20 years or more when they reach 60.
- Unemployment insurance is paid when the employee becomes unemployed and is intended to contribute to stability of workers' incomes. Sixty to eighty percent of former monthly wages are paid for between 3 and 10 months.
- Employee accident compensation insurance is paid for death, illness, and injury caused by accidents that occur on the job.

Foreigners are treated in the same manner as the Japanese, and in cases where the required conditions are met, they are required to participate in these programs.

Other welfare expenditures that are not required by law do exist, such as provisions for company housing, dormitories, company loan and interest subsidy systems to assist employees in buying their own homes, expenditures for food and leisure, and for other activities. Also, savings promotion systems have become more common in recent years.

Foreigners in Japan

Entry into Japan and Attaining of Residence Status.　According to the "Statistics on Resident Foreigners" by the Ministry of Justice, as of 1986 year-end, there were 867,237 registered resident foreigners (a 3.1 percent increase over the previous year); 7,148 persons (an increase of 20.3 percent) whose purpose was "long-term commercial business" (managers of foreign corporations); and 6,242 persons "employed" (employees of Japanese companies) (a 107.8 percent increase over the previous year).

Foreigners who wish to enter Japan must, in principle, obtain a passport from their native country, then receive a visa that corresponds to their reasons for entry by applying to an overseas Japanese embassy or consulate. Foreigners who want to reside in Japan receive a landing permit from the entry examiner and are assigned a specified status of residence. This status means the foreigner may carry out certain activities during his or her period of residency. There are six statuses for a foreign resident wishing to engage in business or other activities and earn remuneration. These statuses are stated under the Immigration Control and Refugee Recognition Law, Article 4, Paragraph 1, and are as follows: Item 5, Commercial; Item 7, Teaching; Item 9, Entertainment; Item 12, Providing of skills and techniques; Item 13, Skilled laborer; and Item 16-3, Other employment.

The determined period of residency is up to three years, depending on the status of the resident foreigner, and renewals are possible. Also, foreign residents are required to register themselves as foreigners at the city, town, or village office where they reside within a certain period of time after their residency begins.

Employment of Foreigners in Japan.   In Japan, with the exception of the residence provisions concerning work permits described above, there are no restrictions on the employment of foreigners. However, employment of foreigners, when compared to the employment of Japanese, is in some cases comparatively more expensive. Companies that employ foreigners have, in general, less than five foreigners, with the average between one and three.

The most common forms of employment are part-time employees and contracted employees whose contract period is one year. In the case of a regular employee, wages and status are, in principle, the same as for Japanese employees. About half of part-time employees and contracted employees are paid on an annual salary basis and half on a monthly salary system.

Although the amount of payment depends on individual negotiations, when looked at on an annual income basis, the wages are higher than for Japanese of the same age and same position.

To cope with the high cost of Japanese housing, when viewed on an international basis, many companies will give preferential treatment to

TABLE 8–2
International Comparison of Retail Prices

Commodity	Quantity	Tokyo (¥)	New York Converted Price (¥)	New York Price Comparison (Tokyo=100)	Hamburg Converted Price (¥)	Hamburg Price Comparison (Tokyo=100)
Bread	1 kg.	371	293	79	351	95
Beef	100 g.	354	141	40	183	52
Pork	100 g.	146	96	66	127	87
Chicken	100 g.	104	61	59	43	41
Eggs	1 kg.	254	180	71	345	136
Sausage	100 g.	141	133	94	127	90
Cabbage	1 kg.	226	106	47	79	35
Onions	1 kg.	144	104	72	159	110
Bananas	1 kg.	229	106	46	200	87
Sugar	1 kg.	257	158	61	156	61
Edible oil	700 g	341	279	82	298	87
Suits (winter)	1	51,300	40,144	78	25,670	50
Shirts (long sleeve)	1	3,865	3,590	93	2,166	56
Underwear	1	385	517	134	744	193
Skirts (winter)	1	8,810	12,149	138	14,046	159
Color television	1	125,600	62,615	50	122,150	97
Men's shoes	1 pair	9,186	10,472	114	8,291	90
Detergents	1 box (2.65 kg.)	879	723	82	779	89
Color film	1 (24 exposures)	535	364	68	513	96
Gasoline	1 liter	125	38	30	69	55
Telephone calls (local)	1	10	13	130	17	170
Haircuts	1	2,755	1,816	66	2,358	86
Permanent wave	1	5,750	7,646	133	6,657	116
Dry cleaning (for suit)	1	881	966	110	1,271	144

Commodity	Quantity	Tokyo (¥)	London		Paris	
			Converted Price (¥)	Price Comparison (Tokyo=100)	Converted Price (¥)	Price Comparison (Tokyo=100)
Bread	1 kg.	371	238	64	282	76
Beef	100 g.	354	252	71	190	54
Pork	100 g.	146	95	65	104	71
Chicken	100 g.	104	56	54	83	80
Eggs	1 kg.	254	330	130	339	133
Sausage	100 g.	141	131	93	88	62
Cabbage	1 kg.	226	204	90	158	70
Onions	1 kg.	144	231	160	158	110
Bananas	1 kg.	229	299	131	329	144
Sugar	1 kg.	257	148	58	153	60
Edible oil	700 g	341	352	103	202	59
Suits (winter)	1	51,300	35,792	70	59,044	115
Shirts (long sleeve)	1	3,865	2,956	76	10,978	284
Underwear	1	385	568	148	913	237
Skirts (winter)	1	8,810	9,734	110	15,752	179
Color television	1	125,600	114,555	91	108,733	87
Mens' shoes	1 pair	9,186	8,386	91	9,107	99
Detergents	1 box (2.65 kg.)	879	705	80	939	107
Color film	1 (24 exposures)	535	580	108	591	110
Gasoline	1 liter	125	83	66	101	81

TABLE 8–2 *(concluded)*

Commodity	Quantity	Tokyo (¥)	London Converted Price (¥)	London Price Comparison (Tokyo=100)	Paris Converted Price (¥)	Paris Price Comparison (Tokyo=100)
Telephone calls (local)	1	10	20	200	16	160
Haircuts	1	2,755	1,521	55	3,068	111
Permanent wave	1	5,750	8,462	147	7,753	135
Dry cleaning (for suit)	1	881	831	94	1,426	162

Notes: 1. The research on food items was conducted in October 1987 and on other items in January 1988.
2. The yen exchange rate is based on the rates of each country at the time of research.
3. Price comparison is based on Tokyo=100.
4. Quality and specifications are not uniform. As the number of samples is restricted, a strict comparison cannot be made.

Sources: For retail prices in Tokyo, "Retail Research Study" by the General Affairs Agency, Statistics Bureau; for other cities, retail price research in the world's principal cities (Japan External Trade Organization, case studies of supermarkets in related cities). For other items, Economic Planning Agency assigned research (by Japan External Trade Organization).

foreigners over their Japanese counterparts. Some companies also give temporary home leave and pay the employee's expenses to return home.

In addition, most companies provide social insurance (including medical and pension insurance) and labor-related insurance (unemployment and accident compensation) for foreign employees.

Living in Japan.   The cost of living is high for foreigners living in Japan. The monthly rent (within Tokyo) for a condominium for foreigners was an average of ¥20,000 per 3.3 square meters (one *tsubo*) in 1986.

There are many department stores and supermarkets throughout Japan, and it is easy to obtain anything one desires. Also, food is easily obtained whether one is living in the city or the country. Japan's medical system is maintained at a first-class world level and, if the foreigner is a member of the social insurance system, medical care can be obtained at low cost.

International schools can also be found in Japan. There were, as of 1987, 24 international schools throughout the country (1 in Sapporo, 10 in Tokyo, 3 in Yokohama, 1 in Nagoya, 1 in Kyoto, 5 in Kobe, 1 in Hiroshima, 1 in Fukuoka, and 1 in Okinawa).

Table 8–2 compares the cost of living in Japan to other countries. The table is based on the ''Price Report for 1988'' prepared by Japan's Economic Planning Agency.

ACQUISITION OF JAPANESE ENTERPRISES

The Environment for Acquisitions in Japan

There is a great difference in the definition of enterprises between Japan and the United States and Europe. In Japan, corporations are considered to be collections of people, rather than assets. There is a school of thought in Japan that the acquisition of an enterprise is tantamount to ''the selling and buying of people.'' Moreover, the lifetime employment system creates close ties between management and employees. Therefore, many people still regard corporate acquisitions as evil. Most of the corporations listed on the Japanese stock exchanges have made great efforts to ensure that much of their stock is held by closely related trade partners, employees, and financial institutions.

For these reasons, corporate acquisitions, with a few exceptions, have not become accepted in Japan, as they are in the United States and Europe.

However, foreign attorneys have been permitted to practice law in Japan, under certain restrictions, since April 1987. In addition, with the diversification of financing, it is now possible to obtain ample funds for use in acquiring enterprises.

A difficult environment resulting from the appreciation of the yen and pressure from ASEAN have made the restructuring of Japanese corporations inevitable. As the younger generation has assumed positions of responsibility, thinking about companies has begun to change. More emphasis is being placed on ability in personnel, people are being hired away in mid-career, and the lifetime employment system has begun to crumble.

Though most acquisitions of companies, including those carried out by Orient Lease, Misawa Homes, Toyo Sash, and others, have been rescue operations, corporations with aggressive expansionist policies have begun to appear.

Case Histories of Acquisitions of Enterprises in Japan

Acquisitions among Japanese Corporations

In the prewar era, there were acquisitions to further the wartime economy and to recover from the Great Depression.

In the postwar years, there were some major corporate mergers to facilitate greater international competition. Yawata Steel and Fuji Steel formed Shin-Nippon Steel; the Dai-ichi Bank and the Kangyo Bank merged to form the Dia-ichi Kangyo Bank; and Osaka Shosen and Mitsui Shipping merged into Shosen Mitsui. Other acquisitions included the takeover of Yashica by Kyocera, Sord by Toshiba, and Osawa Shokai by the Seibu Saison Group. These, together with the acquisition of the Heiwa Sogo Bank by the Sumitomo Bank, may be classified as rescue mergers.

The acquisition of a depressed enterprise generates the least opposition in Japan, and it is expected that this will be the most common type of corporate takeover in Japan in the future.

Acquisition of Japanese Enterprises by Foreign Corporations

Only a few takeovers of Japanese corporations by foreign firms have occurred and are described below.

These takeovers include the acquisition of Sagami Denki by Siemens of West Germany; Japan Marantz by Philips of the Netherlands; and the plant of Toko by Motorola of the United States, which began as a joint venture with Motorola.

In the pharmaceutical and chemical industries, the major foreign acquisitions include the acquisition of Banyu Pharmaceutical by Merck of the United States and of Funai Pharmaceutical by Dow Chemical of the United States.

In the automobile industry, Isuzu Motors and Suzuki Motor Co. were partially acquired by General Motors, Corp. while Mazda was also partially acquired by Ford Motor Co.

All of these takeovers were of a friendly nature. Furthermore, 100 percent acquisitions are rare, with most takeovers concentrating on purchasing a portion of capital and participation in management.

Many foreign corporations have formed joint ventures with Japanese companies, including Tohoku Semiconductors (Motorola and Toshiba), Toyo Petrolight (Toyo Ink and Petrolight), and Yokogawa-Hewlett-Packard (Yokogawa and Hewlett-Packard). Further information on existing joint ventures is available in *Foreign Affiliated Companies in Japan—a Comprehensive Directory* (published annually by Toyo Keizai Shinpo).

How Can a Japanese Corporation Be Acquired?

Making Full Use of a Good Advisor
The use of expert advice in this area is as important in Japan as it is in the United States and Europe. When acquiring an enterprise in a foreign nation, the services of a top-quality advisor are essential.

The services of accountants, lawyers, and other experts should be sought, as should be the advice of banks and related companies, securities companies, and trading companies. Relations between banks and their customers are much closer in Japan than in other countries; therefore, the advice that banks can offer is valuable and should be used for the development of business in general.

Cases Where Acquisition Is Not Very Difficult

Corporations in Depressed Industries. Some industries are in a depressed condition due to the appreciation of the yen and other factors. In Japan, such an acquisition is the least likely to cause friction, especially if the company is a subsidiary of a large corporation.

Enterprises that Have High Ratios of Overseas CB/Warrant Issues. In cases where the holders of these debentures are not tightly controlled by the company that issued the bonds, or the underwriter, it is possible to acquire stocks in such companies by aiming at this blind spot and then converting the bonds into stocks.

However, when such bonds are converted into stocks, the restrictions specified in the Foreign Exchange Law are likely to be enforced.

Companies that Have Not Been Successful in Creating a Group of Stable Stockholders. It is fairly easy to acquire stocks of companies with a relatively low ratio of stable shareholders or of companies that do not number first-class financial institutions and prestigious corporations belonging to the Japanese establishment among the top 10 shareholders. It is also possible to acquire stocks from an investment group (corporate raider).

Acquisitions Made Possible by Corporate Restructuring. Parent companies may also sell subsidiaries that are profitable. Subsidiaries that are, from a future perspective, not strong or are far removed from the parent corporation's main field of business may be disposed of when the time is right.

Venture Enterprises. There are often bottlenecks in capital and human resources in venture enterprises that limit the growth of the corporation. There have been instances of entrepreneurs selling their companies after the difficulties attendant with setting up the business in the startup have been overcome and it is generating profits.

In the future, the number of tie-ups and mergers supported by venture capital and with participation of foreign corporations may increase.

Company Founders with Difficulty in Finding a Successor. Some founders of companies have no children or have children with no interest in the business. In such cases, it is possible the founder will sell the company.

Points Requiring the Most Attention
In Japan, it is essential that the party attempting a corporate takeover maintain a low profile. Maintaining a low profile is necessary for achiev-

ing a smooth transition and gaining the cooperation of the company that is acquired.

It is rumored that one corporate takeover fell through when, at the cocktail party held the night before the final purchase contract was to be signed, a speech made by the acquiring party offended the sensitivities of the chief executive officer of the company being acquired.

Restrictions on Acquisitions

There are numerous restrictions on corporate takeovers under the Anti-Monopoly Law, the Securities Transactions Law, and the Foreign Exchange Law (Foreign Exchange and Foreign Trade Control Law).

Restrictions under the Foreign Exchange Law
When a foreign investor acquires 10 percent or more of the total stock of a company listed on the Japanese stock exchanges or registered for over-the-counter stock trading, a notification must be filed, through the Bank of Japan, with the Ministry of Finance and the ministry with jurisdiction over the company whose shares are to be invested in. Although the stock investment cannot, in principle, be made for 30 days, this waiting period can be shortened. In special cases were a lengthy investigation is required, the waiting period can be extended to five months. Furthermore, in the case of unlisted companies, all stock acquisitions by foreign parties, regardless of the percentage of stock acquired, must be reported to the above authorities.

Although investments in Japanese securities by foreign parties are being liberalized, restrictions can be placed on the investments when they endanger national security, endanger the safety of the general public, very seriously damage business operations of companies in the same field in Japan, or hamper the smooth functioning of the Japanese economy.

Procedures for Mergers

Although a foreign corporation cannot legally merge with a Japanese corporation, such a merger is permissible through a subsidiary in Japan. The procedures is as follows:

1. Passing resolution by the board of directors approving the merger.

2. Drawing up of the merger memorandum.
3. Signing of a merger contract.
4. Making available financial statements.
5. Executing demand rights to acquire stocks of shareholders not agreeing to the merger.
6. Approving the merger contract by a special resolution of the stockholders' general meeting.
7. Filing the merger notification with the Fair Trade Commission.
8. Dealing with any objections by creditors to the merger.
9. Holding a stockholders' general meeting to report on the merger.
10. Registering the merger.

Convenient and Simpler Substitutes for a Merger

Transfer of Business
Under this method, the stockholders and part of the liabilities of the company acquired do not have to be taken over. However, the transfer of a major portion of the business requires the approval at a general meeting of the stockholders of the company acquired. There may also be problems when stockholders opposed to the transfer of business demand that their shares be purchased. In addition, proper notification must also be made to the Fair Trade Commission.

Transfer of Assets
There are a number of interesting possibilities in this area because of the high value of real estate in Japan. Resolutions of the stockholders and notification to the Fair Trade Commission are not necessary.

Takeover Bids

There have only been two cases of tender offer of companies in Japan—the acquisition of Jidosha Kiki Co., Ltd., by Bendix Co. and of Okinawa Electric Power Distribution and Chuo Electric Power Distribution by Okinawa Electric Power. Both of these acquisitions resulted from special circumstances and were conducted in a extremely friendly manner.

It is not likely there will be many tender offers in Japan because the Japanese joint-stock company system is based on stable shareholders and these conflict with the business atmosphere in Japan. The steps necessary for public tender offers are as follows:

- The acquirer files a tender notice with the Ministry of Finance. Items to be covered in the notice are: period during which shares are to be acquired, price, objective, amount of funds, acquirer, outline of company to be acquired, and so on.
- The tender offer notification becomes effective 10 days after it is filed.
- Actual acquisition of stock commences after the notification becomes effective and after public notice has been given.

The acquisition period takes 20 to 30 days under uniform purchase conditions.

The price may not be lowered after it becomes effective. Any increase in price after the purchase becomes effective must be applicable to all the parts.

LICENSING, ROYALTIES, AND TECHNOLOGY TRANSFER

Background and History

In general, Japan is extremely receptive to technology transfer through licensing, direct investment, and joint ventures. The Japanese government aggressively supports development of technology. Japan is poor in natural resources and requires extensive imports to fuel its growing economy. The Japanese economy has overcome many recent shocks. The oil price increase of the 1970s, the U.S. grain embargo, and increasing competition from the newly industrialized countries in electronics, textiles, steel, shipbuilding, and construction have had a profound effect on the Japanese psyche. Another adverse factor overcome by the Japanese economy is the rapid rise in the value of the yen, called *endaka*. In the 1970s, the yen floated with other currencies in a range of over 300 yen to the U.S. dollar. By December 1989, the exchange rate varied between 130 and 145 yen to the dollar.

After the destruction of the war, Japan was desperate for technology transfer. Initially, this demand was met by transferring technical expertise from the Western world, primarily the United States. For years, Japan had the reputation of being able to copy ideas and transform those ideas into more innovative, adaptive, low-cost products. This form of technology transfer was effective to meet the demands of Japan in the 1950s and 1960s.

As the Japanese economy became more successful, the technology transferred became increasingly more sophisticated. Gone were the days when Japanese business visitors were seen photographing U.S. and European plants. Japan had developed its own strong, competitive production capacity supported by such unique concepts as just-in-time delivery, total quality control, zero inventory, and Kanban.

Technology transfer shifted from basic production processes to engineering and technological concepts. A fundamental shift occurred in the 1970s when Japan became more interested in basic technology than in the process of using the technology. Nowhere was this more evident than in the area of computer technology.

Most of the original basic research and development of computer technology was conducted in the United States. Innovators such as Texas Instruments, Fairchild, IBM, and Intel had developed basic patents on processes necessary to compete in the electronics industry. The manufacturing processes were generally known; the only barrier to becoming a competitor was access to the patents. More and more, the means of Japanese companies to transfer technology was through licensing technology and providing for royalty payments to patent holders. The recent acceptance of a licensing and royalty agreement among IBM, Fujitsu, and Hitachi covering operating systems software is just one highly visible case. In many cases, these basic technologies were modified and improved—generally by simplifying the manufacturing process or the basic product design. Today cross-licensing agreements are common with such large companies as Hewlett-Packard and Yokogawa Electric and Fuji and Xerox.

With the success of the Japanese economy, increased wealth and leisure time was now available in the general population. As a whole, Japanese are very discriminating buyers. Japanese people are concerned with quality and are willing to pay a high price for quality merchandise. International products with top reputations for quality are highly regarded in Japan. High-quality brand names have great value with Japanese buyers. Gucci bags, Burberry coats, Remy Martin brandy, and so on all possess high consumer loyalty.

In many cases, these brands have high consumer acceptance but require an existing Japanese network to distribute the product in Japan. Licensed distributors able to handle product positioning, distribution, advertising, and other market functions are necessary to make the product successful. In other cases, licensed manufacturers are used to manufacture a product that carries the product or brand logo or name. To protect product or brand image and to limit offpricing, discounting, and so forth, most foreign companies require exclusive licensing from the manufacturer, trading company, or other distributor.

Japan in the 1980s has had an extensive hollowing out of traditional manufacturing industries, particularly agriculture, electronics, ship-building, and textiles. Instead of accepting the loss of jobs and related negative economic impact, Japanese *Kaishas* (corporations) have increased investment, reduced costs, and increased the technology of their products. Seiko-Epson moved from watches to personal computers and computer peripherals. Nihon Steel moved into factory automation. These transitions often required extensive technology transfer. In other cases, manufacturing was moved offshore to countries including Thailand and the People's Republic of China.

Japan has met the challenge by focusing on value-added manufacturing. To achieve this objective, Japan has relied heavily on technology and R&D. Research and development expenditures are 40 percent higher for Japanese companies than for their American counterparts. Japanese corporations pay little, if any, dividends. They rely on reinvestment of internally generated capital to expand into new facilities or new markets.

Role of Government and Universities

The Japanese university system and government help technology transfer as well. Certain key strategic technologies such as fifth-generation software development are jointly sponsored by MITI and industry or trade groups. The Sigma Project (a project for developing fifth-generation computer programming techniques that leapfrog current technology) is one such example of such cooperative approaches. Leading university professors, government leaders, and industry groups are jointly sponsoring the costs and benefits of the efforts. As products or technologies are developed, licenses will be granted to the participants. In the Japanese government's view, the marketplace will determine the ultimate victor in usage of the technologies developed. This proactive stance of government and academia is markedly different from the laissez-faire stance of most Western economies.

Licensing and Royalty Agreements

Licensing and royalty agreements should be approached very carefully and cautiously in Japan. Selecting the proper company to license technology and/or to support a brand name is critical to success. In some cases, the Japanese partner is more interested in obtaining technology or expertise that can be used to further its own objectives instead of the interests of the foreign partner. In other cases, after a decision is made to select a licensee in Japan, the licensee may not aggressively market or support the product. Care should be exercised with any license agreement so the company or brand name is not damaged to an extent to limit its potential in the market.

Licensing basic technology has similar problems. In the case of patentable technology, the Japanese system is often criticized. The characteristics of the Japanese patent system are frequently cited by other countries as nontariff barriers to competing in Japan. The criticism is threefold. First, the Japanese patent system often requires three to five years or longer to obtain a patent compared to two to three years in the United States. During this time, "patent pending" protection is not as extensive as in the Western world. Second, patents are allowed for "minor" innovations of current technology, including improvements to technology for which patents are pending. Third, patents are awarded for first application for the item, not the first one to discover or design the item. These significant differences from most Western countries cause Japanese companies to file extensive numbers of patent requests and to focus on patents that can be quickly transferred into marketable products. Extensive cross-licensing of patents is often seen, even between competing companies.

Many companies seeking to enter the large Japanese domestic market often see licensing technology as a quick way to selling their product in Japan. However, in most cases, product rollout requires more than one year, and profits often are not recognized until the third to fifth year. There are four major reasons for delay in a product's market entry.

1. *Searching for a suitable partner to distribute the product.* Searching for a suitable joint venture partner requires careful selection and negotiation on both sides. Generally a minimum of three to six months is required to select, negotiate, and close a joint venture for licensing a product. If the item to be licensed is a process for manufacturing, a prototype test period may be required before acceptance.

2. *Training the Japanese partner's staff in the product and customer support issues.* Once the partner is selected, the Japanese staff responsible for the product must be trained, generally by the foreign company's staff, on the product functions and features along with any unique customer service and support requirements. Transfers of experienced staff from the home office to Japan generally suffer from language and cultural barriers and are not always effective.

3. *Translating and localizing the product.* In some cases, products may be covered by a series of safety and regulatory rules that may require product certification, testing, and/or approval of regulatory bodies. In some cases, the product may have to be physically modified or re-engineered. Product support materials including operating manuals, marketing materials, and so on must be translated and, in some cases, localized for cultural differences.

4. *Obtaining distribution/retailer acceptance.* Even after the first three steps are completed, there is often significant resistance to the product from the distributors or retailers. In Japan, space in shops is very limited, and there may not be adequate shelf space to carry the new item without eliminating other competing items. Given a choice, many retailers are hesitant to change brands.

Failure to adequately address these four key points can delay a product's entry into the market for years.

Intellectual Property Trends

In the Western and Japanese press, there has been significant criticism of Japan for violations of intellectual property rights. Through such techniques as reverse engineering, companies have been able to re-create products (particularly microcircuits) without paying licensing or copyright fees. This problem is not adequately covered under international business conventions and laws.

Recently, however, Japan has addressed the intellectual property issue. Japan's Council for Science and Technology, an administrative advisory body focused on science, has promulgated six targets for Japan in science and technology. These include:

1. Stable supply and conservation of resources.
2. An enhanced living environment with environmental safety improvements.
3. Improved health through hygiene and enhanced medical care.
4. Leading-edge and basic fundamental science and technology.
5. Technology capability that contributes to international goodwill and international competition.
6. Advancement in basic science.

Japan has joined the leaders of the world in technological innovation in such diverse areas as ceramics, rare earth magnetics, electronics, and computer dynamic random access memory (DRAMs). Japan is quickly becoming a world-class innovator. New developments in space exploration and magnetically levitated trains are world class in success and investment. In all these areas, the trilateral cooperation of government, academia, and industry are the benchmark to which the rest of the world aspires.

This is not to say there are not basic flaws in the system. One basic criticism of Japan is the relatively small role Japanese universities play in basic research. Japan produces about 15 percent of the world GNP but has produced only seven Nobel prize winners, five of the prizes were for the physical sciences. University promotion for bright postdoctoral students is slow, and the paternal seniority system forces many successful academics to leave Japan to do basic research and teach in American universities.

Approach to Technology Transfer

Given the focus on technology and brand licensing and the difficulty of entering the Japanese market, foreign firms wishing to do business in Japan will have to increasingly focus on licensing and royalty agreements.

Great care should be taken to avoid mistakes in the technology transfer process. A market survey should be conducted to evaluate the potential marketplace for the product, technology, or service. As a general rule, caution should be exercised in selecting a Japanese partner to assist in the survey. The best situation is an already existing relationship with a Japanese firm that can be expanded to cover the new products, technology, or service.

In the case where no prior relationship exists, the foreign company should select an independent market research or consulting firm to do a basic feasibility study before committing to any marketing approach. If a company that would be involved as a licensee or joint venture partner is used to do the research on market entry strategy, strong confidentiality and nondisclosure agreements should be negotiated. Legal counsel is readily available and should be consulted before any major market commitment is made.

Even after the long searches and plans, nontariff barriers can create obstacles. A November 1988 issue of the *ACCJ Journal,* published by the American Chamber of Commerce in Japan, included an article on Japan's nontariff barriers written by Todd Thurwacher, a former U.S. Embassy (Japan) commercial officer. The author cites several cases of unusual barriers. In one case, the Japanese consumer product safety commission decided to establish unique new ski-equipment safety standards, rejecting European/American standards because of Japan's "unique" snow. When questioned on what made the snow unique, the reply noted "unique Japanese geothermal activity (in other words, mineral rich hot springs, etc.)." This reply ignored the fact that snow in Japan comes primarily from evaporated ocean water, not hot springs. Other problems cited included the traditional Japanese business habit of *Keiretsu*, a normal Japanese business tendency to take business to affiliated Japanese suppliers, even if it means developing a new product.

Agencies are available to help foreign companies, including the Chamber of Commerce. In Japan, the American, British, and Canadian Chambers of Commerce are very active in promoting their members' products. The foreign embassies generally have commercial service departments attached to the embassy staff. Finally, there is the Japanese Office of the Trade Ombudsman (OTO). Generally, these groups are most effective when the country of the entering firm is prepared to support a company's complaint with a General Agreement on Trade and Tariff (GATT) action or other trade pressure.

Manufacturing, Location, and Facilities

Most companies entering Japan do so through joint ventures and/or licensing agreements. However, as sales grow and volumes strain overseas capacity, manufacturing in Japan becomes a potential option. This major decision requires careful consideration.

By any measure, Japan is a world-class manufacturing country. Workers in Japan are hard-working, and their productivity and output per worker is on a par with the best U.S. or European workers. Labor union and management relations are excellent by Western standards, and the Japanese government is generally supportive of business. In these respects, the general business climate for manufacturing in Japan is very favorable.

On the negative side is the overwhelming cost of land, raw materials, and facilities. Much has been written of the cost of land in Tokyo. However, recently, major production areas such as Osaka, Kyoto, Nagoya, and Fukuoka have had annual land price increases of 25 percent or more. This ever-spiraling land cost makes purchase or lease of facilities prohibitive for many manufacturers, especially those that require processing and/or storing bulky or voluminous products.

On a similar note, the cost of raw materials and utilities is very high. Most of Japan's electricity is generated by nuclear or hydroelectric means and is expensive by Western standards. All oil is imported and is very expensive. Most raw materials must also be imported. Water shortages are common in many areas, so extensive recovery systems are often required to conserve water used in the manufacturing process.

Japan is a seismically active country. As a result, buildings must meet strict fire and earthquake standards to protect workers from injury. This significantly increases the cost of constructing a manufacturing facility.

Finally, developing a labor force is critical to a successful operation. Many large Japanese manufacturers provide extensive benefits to workers, including company-owned or subsidized housing. The typical Japanese worker does not change jobs often and is very suspicious of Western companies. In Japan, foreign employers often have a negative image, sometimes earned, that *gaijin* (foreign) companies are not as dedicated to employees as Japanese companies. In Japan, most companies develop a "social contract" between the worker and the company. The company agrees to provide lifetime employment in exchange for worker loyalty to the company. Such cradle-to-grave employment practices make recruiting quality, experienced workers very difficult for most newly established foreign companies. This can be overcome when the foreign company becomes affiliated with one of the major Japanese companies as a joint venture partner.

In summary, setting up a new company to manufacture products in Japan is a very difficult process and requires considerable analysis and planning.

CHAPTER 9

LIBERALIZATION AND INTERNATIONALIZATION OF JAPANESE FINANCIAL MARKETS

Masaki Shiratori

INTRODUCTION

Today, Japan is the largest creditor country in the world. Total bank deposits in Japan at the end of 1987 amounted to $1,968 billion, far larger than the $329 billion in the United Kingdom and almost equal to the $2,009 billion in the United States. The Tokyo Stock Exchange is now the world's largest with the outstanding values of $2,726 billion in stocks and $1,014 billion in bonds at the end of 1987. The corresponding figures in New York were $2,132 billion and $1,599 billion, respectively. The Tokyo foreign exchange market is also as big as New York. The daily volume of transactions was $48 billion in Japan in March 1986, slightly below $50 billion in the United States.

Japanese financial markets have expanded rapidly in recent years, reflecting extensive liberalization and internationalization efforts by the Japanese government. The Japanese Finance Ministry has been vigorously promoting liberalization and internationalization under the recognition that they contribute to development of the national economy through greater efficiency of financial activities and optimum resource allocation.

Japanese financial liberalization has been advanced with internationalization of the Japanese yen. Internationalization of the yen means an increased usage and holding of the yen in international transactions. The yen has been increasingly used and held in recent years. The ratio of yen-denominated exports to total Japanese exports is now about 35 percent, while that of yen-dominated imports is approximately 10 percent. The Japanese yen is more widely used in capital transactions. In the primary market for international bonds, for example, yen-denominated bonds accounted for 15 percent of the total issues in 1987, next to 35 percent of U.S. dollar issues. Euroyen bond issues are particularly active. The Japanese yen is now the third reserve currency at about 7 percent of world foreign exchange reserves at the end of 1986, behind the dollar (67 percent) and the DM (15 percent).

In sharp contrast to the general unwillingness on the part of major European countries, which fear the loss of freedom of action in domestic monetary policy, the Japanese government encourages internationalization of the yen. Because international financial markets are inseparably related to domestic markets, Japanese financial liberalization will be facilitated by internationalization of the yen. Internationalization of the yen is the result of natural evolution. For the currency of a country to be used as an international currency, it is necessary for that currency to be stable, for the financial markets of the country to be well-organized, and for various obstacles to be removed. This is what the Japanese Finance Ministry has been endeavoring to do in recent years.

Liberalization and internationalization of Japanese financial markets will respond to the increasing needs at home for diversified and sophisticated financial products. They will also give foreigners enlarged fund-raising and portfolio management opportunities. For foreign financial institutions doing business in Japan, they will mean a larger, more competitive and more open market with an increased potential for profits.

BACKGROUND TO LIBERALIZATION
AND INTERNATIONALIZATION

The household savings ratio in Japan has traditionally been quite high. These household savings have been deposited at banks and post offices at low controlled interest rates. Banks and post offices in turn have financed private companies and public corporations, respectively. Overall, about 90 percent of funds were raised on the money market, and only about 10 percent on the capital market.

The basic structure of the current Japanese financial system was formulated after World War II against these backgrounds.

One of the characteristics of the Japanese financial system is the separation of various types of business among financial institutions:

First, short- and long-term finances are separated. Commercial banks specialize in short-term finance with funds raised by deposits. Long-term finance is carried out by long-term credit banks and trust banks. These banks raise funds by issuing debentures and loan and money trusts, respectively.

Second, trust business is separated from banking business. Only specially licensed banks can engage in trust business.

Third, like in the United States, banks are not allowed to undertake securities business, and securities companies are not allowed to engage in banking business.

Interest rates in Japan have been controlled. The regulation of leading rates, however, is quite loose. Only short-term lending rates are regulated. Moreover, legally controlled interest rates are fixed at relatively high levels. Banks are free to determine actually applied interest rates of their own within this range. In practice, however, there is a standard interest rate called ''short-term prime rate,'' which is fixed at a certain margin above the official discount rate. Long-term lending rates are not regulated and are decided by long-term credit banks at their own discretion. In practice, however, there is a standard interest rate called ''long-term prime rate,'' which is customarily fixed at a certain percentage above the coupon rate on five-year bank debentures.

Ceilings are rigidly paced on deposit rates. Bank deposit rates used to be fixed at relatively low levels so as to reduce financial costs of borrowers.

The official discount rate is the rate set by the Bank of Japan for funds supplied to the banking system. Controlling the supply of such funds used to be a key mechanism in the operation of the monetary policy. This mechanism worked efficiently because banks depended heavily on the Bank of Japan for the supply of credit. Also, tight foreign exchange control had been used to reinforce the mechanism. Households were prevented from seeking higher interest rates abroad. Likewise, Japanese corporations were not able to escape domestic credit restraint by borrowing abroad.

The Japanese financial system came under increasing pressure following the first oil shock of 1973 and the resulting shift of the Japanese economy from high growth to moderate growth. The investment ratio fell sharply. The corporate sector's need for borrowed funds was reduced. Bond and stock issues increased, while borrowings from banks decreased. Corporate portfolio management has also become active with funds going into instruments with market interest rates. Household behavior has also become more cost and benefit conscious on financial transactions. Thus, the share of bank deposits decreased, while those of stocks, bonds, investment trusts, and so on increased. As a result of these changes, the net surplus of private domestic savings has been increasing.

The counterpart of it is the growing government deficit as well as the large capital export to the rest of the world. Long-term government bonds had not been issued until 1965, and large issues started in 1975 to stimulate the Japanese economy. The government has thus become the biggest borrower of funds. The outstanding balance of government bonds will amount to ¥162 trillion at the end of March 1990. As large issues of government bonds continue, the primary and secondary bond markets have naturally developed and expanded. Today, government bonds, including short-term bonds, account for some 40 percent of total new issues and 95 percent of total value of dealings in the secondary market. The expansion of the secondary market for government bonds has stimulated liberalization of Japanese financial markets.

The emergence of Japan as a net capital exporter is another promoter of financial liberalization. Since the latter part of the 1960s, Japan's current account tended to show a persistent surplus, with the interruptions of two oil shocks. Foreign exchange controls have been successively liberalized to facilitate international capital flows. The overall revision of the Foreign Exchange Control Law in December 1980 is particularly important. Until then, external transactions had been banned in principle and had been freed only as an exception to the rule. The new Foreign Exchange Control Law reversed the rule. External transactions are now free in principle, while controls are limited to the minimum. As Japanese financial markets have become better integrated with those abroad, various domestic financial regulations have inevitably been relaxed.

Financial transactions have become more sophisticated and diversified in recent years as a result of rapid technological innovations, in particular computerization of banking. These technological innovations have undermined the effectiveness of regulations.

LIBERALIZATION IN DOMESTIC MARKETS

Liberalization of Short-Term Financial Markets

Japanese short-term financial markets consist of interbank markets and open markets.

The open markets, where nonfinancial institutions can participate, have developed only recently as a result of the emergence of a large secondary market in government bonds. The first open market was the *Gensaki* market, which developed during the 1970s. This is the market where long-term bonds are traded with a repurchase agreement at a specified short-term future. In May 1979, banks were permitted to issue negotiable certificates of deposits (CDs). Several new open markets have emerged and developed since—money market certificates (MMCs) in March 1985, banker's acceptances (BAs) in June 1985, large denomination time deposits in October 1985, treasury bills (TBs) in February 1986, and commercial papers (CPs) in November 1987.

Short-term government bonds are particularly important in the open markets. Government short-term securities had been issue well before the TB market opened in early 1986, but these financing bills (FBs) had been, and are, issued for treasury's daily cash management purposes. The need for refinancing large-scale government debt called for diversification of the range of government debt instruments. Accordingly, the Ministry of Finance started issuing TBs from February 1986. Since TBs have high credibility and uniformity, they are desired both by the Bank of

Japan for market operation purposes and by investors, particularly foreign investors, as one of the most important short-term assets. The Ministry of Finance decided to double the amount of TBs to be issued in fiscal year 1989 to about ¥4 trillion. Diversification of maturity, currently six months, is also under consideration. Three-month TBs will be issued this fiscal year.

Liberalization measures have been taken also in the interbank markets, i.e., the call and bill discount markets. The call market was established in 1902 for very short-term fund transactions between financial institutions. The bill discount market was established in 1971 to facilitate transactions of one month or longer. The Bank of Japan uses this market for its market operation.

In parallel with deregulations in other fields, several liberalization measures have been taken in these markets in recent years. Among these measures is the implementation of a wider variety of money transactions such as the introduction of uncollateralized call money in July 1985. Direct transaction between financial institutions is now allowed. Formerly, transactions had to be carried out via six money market dealers. The Bank of Japan introduced a "new monetary adjustment mechanism," effective November 1988. With the introduction of the shorter-term discount bills (one to three weeks), the Bank of Japan is going to conduct its market operations only against these instruments. The discount rates for the longer-term bills will be freely decided by market forces. Thus, there will be increasing arbitrage between the interbank market and the open market.

The short-term financial markets have expanded fourfold in the past three years to the equivalent of about 35 percent of GNP at the end of June 1988.

Liberalization of Interest Rates

The rapid development of bond and money markets has led to gradual changes in the Japanese interest rate structure. Market-determined interest rates now co-exist with regulated rates.

As for lending rates, the short-term prime rate has come under increasing pressure for change. With the rapid increase of nonregulated interest rate commodities in the total funds raised by banks, the short-term prime rate tends to diverge from actual funding costs. Today, over 50 percent of funds are raised in the free markets by city banks. Accordingly, commercial banks decided to introduce a new system, effective

January 1989, under which the rate is set at the level of average funding costs plus an appropriate margin.

Deposit interest rates are also deregulated. However, sudden liberalization could result in disorder in the financial system and a loss of protection for depositors. Accordingly, deregulation has been proceeding gradually, starting from large deposits. The first step toward the liberalization was the introduction of CDs in May 1979. In the spring of 1985, MMCs were introduced, and in October 1985, interest rates on large denomination time deposits were liberalized. The minimum lots of these commodities have been progressively reduced, while the maturities have been diversified.

Liberalization of interest rates on small deposits is also under consideration. Here, however, the postal savings problem arises. Postal savings in Japan have shown a marked increase in recent years and now account for one third of all household deposits. The rapid expansion of postal savings is largely because of special privileges given to them, such as exemptions from tax, deposit insurance, and reserve requirements. Thus, postal savings could offer such advantageous commodities as time deposits with fixed interest rates at a compound basis, the rates being unchanged for 10 years. Private financial institutions are unable to offer such deposits. It is therefore essential to establish a level playing field between commercial banking and the postal savings system. After tough negotiations between the Ministry of Finance and the Ministry of Posts and Telecommunications, small lot MMCs were introduced in the spring of 1989.

INTERNATIONAL LIBERALIZATION

Liberalization of International Capital Transactions

Both inward and outward capital flows have been increasing rapidly. The Japanese long-term capital account has been recording net outflows since 1975. The size of the net outflow was particularly large in the late 1980s; it amounted to $130 billion in 1988.

The use of the yen in the Euro market had been prohibited. This policy was changed in 1984 when the Japanese Finance Ministry started to encourage internationalization of the yen. Thus, Japanese residents were allowed to issue Euroyen bonds in April 1984, and nonresidents were also authorized to do so in December 1984. Foreign banks and overseas branches of Japanese banks were allowed to issue Euroyen CDs in December 1984. Overseas branches of Japanese banks have been authorized to lend short-term Euroyen to nonresidents since June 1983. Likewise, overseas branches of Japanese banks as well as foreign banks have been allowed to make short-term Euroyen lendings to residents since June 1984. Medium- and long-term Euroyen loans by overseas branches of Japanese banks to nonresidents was liberalized in April 1985. The Ministry of Finance liberalized these loans to Japanese residents in May 1989.

Furthermore, together with the establishment of the domestic CP market, issue of Euroyen CPs by qualified nonresidents was liberalized, effective November 1987. They were also allowed to issue yen-denominated CPs on the domestic market in January 1988. With the progressive relaxation of eligibility, qualification standards, number and size of issues, and so on, the use of the yen in the Euro markets expanded rapidly in the past few years.

Access of Foreign Financial Institutions to Japanese Markets

In response to the globalization of economic activities, Japanese banks and securities firms have made active access to the world financial centers. Foreign banks and securities firms are also actively setting up in Japan. There are now 119 branches, 9 subsidiaries, and 125 representative offices of foreign banks in Japan, while foreign securities firms have set up 50 branches and 132 representative offices. A particularly difficult problem was the treatment of universal banking institutions in the context of the strict separation of banking from securities business in Japan. The Ministry of Finance introduced the so-called 50 percent rule, under which a license is given to foreign securities companies affiliated with universal banks only when the ownership by the parent banks is 50 percent or less. Such treatment is not given to Japanese financial institutions. Since the introduction of the 50 percent rule in December 1985, 26 foreign securities firms, including 8 American firms, have been licensed.

The membership of the Tokyo Stock Exchange was opened to foreign companies in February 1986. The TSE now has 22 foreign members, or 20 percent of the total membership, which is much higher than in New York.

Trust banking licenses had been given to only seven trust banks, one city bank, and two regional banks, all Japanese. In October 1985, nine foreign banks were allowed to set up trust banking subsidiaries in Japan.

Foreign financial institutions have eagerly sought access to the primary market of government bonds. The most important government bond issue in Japan is the 10-year bond issue, which accounts for over 80 percent of the total government bond issues. While most other maturities are sold and priced through auctions, 10-year bonds had been issued through a syndicate. In response to the strong request for larger shares by foreign financial institutions, an auction system was introduced for 20 percent of the issue amount in November 1987. A further major change in the procedures was announced in September 1988. First, 40 percent of new issues will be sold by auction starting in April 1989. Competition will be introduced to decide the acquisition price. Second, for the portion to be sold through a syndicate, the foreign share was increased from 2.52 percent to 7.96 percent, effective October 1988. Third, four foreign firms will be allowed to co-manage the syndicate, starting from April 1989. As a result of this major change, any foreign financial institution will now be able to get access to as much of the 10-year Japanese government bonds as it wants.

Establishment of Japan Offshore Market and Financial Futures Market

The Japan Offshore Market (JOM) was established in December 1986. This market was modeled on New York's International Banking Facility (IBF). It is insulated from domestic markets; fund-raising and portfolio management are to be undertaken outside Japan. A number of special measures have been enacted. Transactions in the JOM are exempt from interest rate restrictions, deposit insurance, and reserve requirements. They are also exempt from the withholding tax on interest earned by nonresidents. There are now 189 banks, including 73 foreign banks, participating in the JOM. The JOM has expanded rapidly; total assets reached $414 billion at the end of 1988.

With the rapid advance of financial liberalization come increasing needs for hedging various risks associated with volatile movements in stock and bond prices, interest rates, and foreign exchange rates. Accordingly, the Ministry of Finance has set up two financial futures markets, a market that deals with securities products and one for banking products. Stock index futures trading started in September 1988 on the Tokyo and the Osaka Stock Exchanges. Futures trading of currencies and deposit interest rates started in June 1989 at the newly established Tokyo International Futures Exchange. In the meantime, Japanese financial institutions have been allowed to engage in financial futures transactions on the futures markets abroad on their own accounts. Japanese residents other than financial institutions will be also able to participate in financial futures transactions in overseas markets in the near future.

CONCLUSION

The Japanese Ministry of Finance has committed to promoting liberalization and internationalization of Japanese financial markets and has made substantial progress in this direction in the past few years. Japan will make further efforts by deregulating some remaining restrictions in areas such as seasoning rules that restrict sales of Euroyen CDs, CPs, and bonds to Japanese residents for certain periods after issuance, issuance abroad of CPs by residents, and so forth.

Several problems must be reviewed in a medium- and long-term perspective. The Japanese financial system has a long history and can not resort to drastic measures if it wants to maintain a sound credit system. One such problem is the institutional segmentation of financial business. The Ministry of Finance is studying the problems of the distinction between short- and long-term financing as well as the distinction between trust banks and other banks. The separation of banking and securities business is another difficult problem. Securities companies vehemently oppose allowing banks to launch securities business on the grounds that it would put the banks in too strong a position vis-à-vis Japanese industry. Thus, for example, overseas subsidiaries of Japanese banks are prohibited from lead underwriting bond flotation by Japanese companies abroad. The Ministry of Finance is now reviewing this distinction, respecting each industry's inherent fields of business and considering changes in domestic and international situations.

Another important problem is the activation of the Tokyo capital market, in particular, the bond market. Japanese corporate bond issues in overseas markets amount to a little below half of the total issues now, because it is easier, faster, and cheaper to bring a yen bond issue to overseas markets. The Ministry of Finance has taken several measures to activate the Tokyo bond market. For example, the qualification standard for the issuance of uncollateralized bonds was relaxed in February

1986, a rating system was introduced in July 1986, the "proposal method" (open-bid issuing method) was introduced in April 1986, disclosure procedures for public offering were simplified, and the shelf registration system was introduced in October 1988. Nevertheless, a further study is needed with respect to quantitative limitation, trustee system, diversification of commodities, registration procedure, and so forth.

Liberalization and internationalization of financial markets expand business opportunities for financial institutions on the one hand, but at the same time increase various risks with respect to credit, foreign exchange rate, interest rate, price, liquidity, etc. Efficient asset and liability management is all the more required for financial institutions. Furthermore, the enhanced risks endanger not only local financial system but also the world financial system. Accordingly, it is necessary for authorities of major world financial centers to cooperate in their supervision over their financial institutions as well as to harmonize their rules and regulations. Such efforts resulted in the agreement on the international standards for capital adequacy of banks engaging in international transactions in June 1988 at the Basle Supervisors' Committee. The Japanese Finance Ministry has already issued the required guidelines to Japanese banks.

APPENDIX

RECENT MAJOR LIBERALIZATION MEASURES OF JAPANESE FINANCIAL MARKETS

I. Liberalization of interests on deposits
   1. Removal of interest rate ceilings on large denomination time deposits: Progressively liberalized since October 1985. As of the end of 1988, there are no interest rate ceilings on large denomination time deposits of over ¥30 million with the maturity of between one month and two years. The minimum denomination is scheduled to be lowered to ¥20 million in the spring of 1989 and further to ¥10 million in the fall of the same year.

2. Introduction and deregulation of deposit instruments with market determined interest rates: Money market certificates were introduced in March 1985 and have been progressively liberalized since. As of the end of 1988, MMCs are allowed for a minimum denomination of ¥10 million with maturity of between one month and two years.

   Small lot MMCs were introduced for a minimum amount of ¥3 million in the spring of 1989 for maturities of six months and one year, and in the fall of the same year for the maturities of three months, two years, and three years. The minimum denomination is expected to be lowered further by taking into consideration depositors' needs and its effects on financial institutions.

3. Relaxation of guidelines: Certificates of deposit (CDs) were introduced in May 1979. Guidelines on CDs have been progressively liberalized. As of the end of 1988, the minimum lot is ¥50 million and the maturity between two weeks and two years.

II. Developments in short-term financial markets

1. Establishment of a yen-denominated banker's acceptance (BA) market: A yen-denominated banker's acceptance market was established in June 1985. As a result of progressive liberalization, current minimum denomination is ¥50 million with the maturity of one year and less.

2. Issuance of short-term government debts: Treasury bills (TBs) were first issued in February 1986. As of the end of 1988, the minimum maturity is six months and the minimum denomination is ¥50 million.

3. Establishment of a domestic commercial paper (CP) market: A domestic commercial paper market was established in November 1987 with the minimum trading lot of ¥100 million and the maturity of between one month and six months. The maturity range was widened to between two weeks and nine months in December 1988.

4. Improvement and expansion of an interbank money market: Uncollateralized call money transactions were authorized in July 1985. Two new transactions were introduced effective November 1988—shorter than one month discount bill and longer than one month uncollateralized call money.

III. Promotion and expansion of financial futures and options markets

1. Liberalization of resident's participation in financial futures and options transactions abroad: Effective 1987, financial institutions were permitted to participate in financial futures and options transactions with nonresidents on their own accounts. They were further au-

thorized to participate in cash options transactions abroad on their own accounts, effective March 1988.

Participation of Japanese residents other than financial institutions will be liberalized in the near future.

2. Promotion and expansion of domestic financial futures and options markets: A government bond futures market was established in October 1985.

Packaged stock futures trading started on the Osaka Stock Exchange in June 1987. Trading of stock index futures started on the Tokyo Stock Exchange and the Osaka Stock Exchange in September 1988.

Futures and options tradings in deposit interest rates and currencies were introduced in June 1989 at the newly established Tokyo International Financial Futures Exchange.

IV. Establishment of Japan Offshore Market (JOM) in December 1986

V. Improvement of capital markets

1. Vitalization of corporate bond primary markets: With respect to uncollateralized bonds, qualification standard for issuance was relaxed in February 1987, and a rating system was introduced in July 1987.

With respect to collateralized bonds, qualification standard for issuance was relaxed in June 1987, and a rating system was introduced in November 1987.

The "proposal method" (open-bid issuing method of particular corporate bonds) was introduced in April 1987. Private placement of corporate bonds was liberalized in June 1987.

2. Improvement of disclosure procedure: Disclosure procedures were simplified, including the introduction of shelf registration system, in October 1988.

VI. Liberalization of business activities of financial institutions

1. Brokerage and dealing of public bonds by banks: Banks were allowed to sell newly issued public bonds, effective April 1983. They were permitted to deal with already-issued public bonds, effective June 1984; 216 banks are licensed as of the end of 1988.

2. Abolition of real demand rule and swap limitations: The real demand rule in foreign exchange transactions was abolished in April 1984. The limits on oversold spot foreign exchange positions were removed in June 1984.

VII. Access of foreign financial institutions to Japanese financial markets

1. Membership on the Tokyo Stock Exchange: Six foreign companies were granted membership to the Tokyo Stock Exchange in Feb-

ruary 1986. A further 16 foreign companies were admitted in May 1988.

2. Participation of foreign banks in trust banking business: Nine foreign banks were licensed to start trust banking businesses in October 1985.

3. Enhanced access to government bond primary market by foreign financial institutions: Effective April 1984, 35 foreign banks and 36 foreign securities companies were admitted to the underwriting syndicate. Their underwriting share was increased in October 1987.

   Effective April 1989, four foreign securities companies were selected as co-managers of the syndicate. Also effective April 1989, 40 percent of 10-year government bonds were to be auctioned.

4. Access to Japan by foreign securities companies: 46 foreign securities companies were licensed as of the end of 1988.

   The so-called 50 percent rule was introduced in December 1985. Under this rule, foreign universal banks are allowed to set up in Japan through their affiliated securities companies established abroad, on the condition that the shares of the parent banks in the affiliated companies are less than 50 percent; 23 foreign universal banks have been licensed as of 1988.

VIII. Development of Euroyen markets

1. Euroyen bond issue by nonresidents: Nonresident private companies were allowed to issue Euroyen bonds in December 1984. Subsequently, guidelines on Euroyen bond issues by nonresidents have been progressively eased, including relaxation of qualification standards, expansion of the scope of eligible rating agencies, and removal of the restrictions on the number and size of issues.

2. Euroyen bond issue by residents: Guidelines on Euroyen bond issues by residents have been progressively eased since April 1984 when qualification standards were introduced.

3. Lead and co-lead management of Euroyen bond issue: Restrictions on the lead and co-lead management of Euroyen bond issues were removed in December 1984. Foreign companies are now free to become lead and co-lead managers.

4. Euroyen CD issue: Euroyen CD issues were liberalized in December 1984. Minimum maturity is now two years.

5. Euroyen lending: Short-term Euroyen lendings were liberalized to nonresidents in June 1983 and to residents in June 1984. Euroyen lendings with a maturity of over one year were liberalized to nonresidents in April 1985, and to residents in May 1989.

6. Euroyen CP issue by nonresidents: Nonresidents were allowed to issue Euroyen CPs in November 1987. Nonresidents were allowed to issue CPs in Japan in Japanese yen effective January 1988 and in foreign currencies effective December 1988.

CHAPTER 10

FINANCIAL AND TAX CONSIDERATIONS

Takeshi Suzuki
Dean A. Yoost

CORPORATE INCOME TAX
> General Corporate Tax Concepts
> Filing Requirements
> Tax Accounting Procedures for Income
> Tax Credits

INTERNATIONAL TAX PLANNING
> Taxation of Various Business Forms
> Transfer Pricing
> Tax Sparing
> Tax Treaties

PERSONAL TAXATION
> General Tax Concepts
> Expatriate Taxation

TAXES OTHER THAN INCOME TAX

THE INSURANCE INDUSTRY

INTERPRETING JAPANESE FINANCIAL
STATEMENTS
> General Analysis
> Accounting Principles

ATTRACTING CAPITAL SOURCES

Until the end of the 1970s, corporate Japan relied on borrowing from financial institutions for the great majority of its fund-raising needs. In the 1980s, however, corporations have increasingly raised capital directly from the securities markets through such means as bond issues. In addition, important developments led to substantial diversification in the issuing markets. New share issuing procedures became more varied, and, in the bond market, new types of bonds were introduced, the range of maturities widened, and major advances were made in subscription procedures. Figures for external fund-raising by companies capitalized at ¥1 billion or more are revealing. In 1975, such companies raised 25 percent of such external funds through the securities markets. In 1985, this had grown to 63 percent. In recent years, the proportion of funds raised in oversees markets through foreign currency-denominated issues has expanded. The value of funds raised through such overseas bond issues, for example, has exceeded that raised in the domestic bond market.

This shift occurred as Japan entered a period of low growth following the oil crises of the 1970s. This curtailed corporate demand for funds to support capital investment and encouraged extensive efforts among companies to improve profits and their financial positions through increasing their net worth positions. In addition, Japanese corporations become active fund-raisers in foreign currencies, as exports and overseas investment grew, to counter exchange rate risks associated with increasing levels of foreign currency-denominated assets, and as the yen strengthened.

This section will deal essentially with long-term fund-raising in the securities market.

Raising Funds in the Securities Market

New Equity Issues

Issuing System. The principal means of increasing paid-in capital through the issue of shares is through public offerings at market price. While both listed and unlisted companies are free to raise capital through allotments to shareholders and third-party offerings, raising capital through public offerings is restricted to listed companies and some companies registered on the over-the-counter market. Rules designed to protect investors require companies raising capital through public offerings to do so through a securities company. The securities company is responsible for ensuring that issuing companies conform to strict eligibility criteria and that they meet rules regarding passing on profits to shareholders subsequent to the issue. Other forms of equity issues to increase capital are gratis share offerings and stock dividends. These are used to adjust a company's capital structure and to redistribute profits to shareholders.

Listing Shares. For new shares to be listed on Japan's stock exchanges, the following requirements laid down by the exchanges must be met. The TSE (Tokyo Stock Exchange) criteria for listing a foreign company's shares are:

1. The relevant stock must already be listed on a securities exchange recognized by the TSE in the company's home country.
2. Minimum requirements regarding the number of shares to be listed are:

- If the stock is to be traded in units of 1,000 shares, 20 million shares.
- If the stock is to be traded in units of 100 shares, 2 million shares.
- If the stock is to be traded in units of 50 shares, 1 million shares.
- If the stock is to be traded in units of 10 shares, 200 thousand shares.

3. The company must have been incorporated at least five years previously.
4. The stock must have good liquidity in the home securities market.
5. There must be 1,000 or more stockholders in Japan.
6. On the last day of the immediately preceding business year, the company's capital stock must be at least ¥10 billion.
7. Pretax profits must be ¥2 billion or more for each of the preceding three business years.
8. Dividends must have been paid for each of the preceding three business years, and the company must be expected to be able to pay dividends continuously after listing.
9. There must be no irregularities in the financial records for the previous three years. In principle, the financial statements for the immediately preceding term must be approved without qualification by the auditors.
10. There must be no restriction of transfer of shares (except where approved by the TSE).
11. The form of the share certificates must conform to criteria laid down by the TSE.
12. The institution designated to process share transactions and the bank entrusted with the distribution of dividend payments must either be specified by the company or it must show it has obtained the consent of such institutions to act for it in these capacities.

Shares—The Secondary Market.   The secondary market for shares comprises the stock and over-the-counter markets. In 1987, the average daily trading value on all domestic exchanges totaled ¥1,081 billion, of which the TSE held the lion's share of 85 percent, followed by the OSE (Osaka Securities Exchange) with 12 percent. At the end of 1987, 1,912 companies were listed on all exchanges in Japan, of which 1,532, or 80 percent, were listed on the TSE.

Equity trading on each exchange is confined to member securities companies of the respective exchange. Clients buy and sell shares on the exchanges through securities companies that act as brokers on their behalf.

Stock trading on the exchanges is conducted under the market-convergence system, under which orders to buy and sell are contracted on a competitive basis among all orders in the market.

Trading hours on the TSE are normally from 9 A.M. to 11 A.M. (morning session) and 1 P.M. to 3 P.M. (afternoon session) Monday to Friday. Settlement is normally made on the third working day following the contract date.

Japan's OTC market is still relatively small, with only 193 registered companies and average daily trading volume of about 1.5 million shares. Recently, however, the market has become more active as the fund-raising needs of medium- and small-sized businesses have increased.

The Bond Issuing Market

The bond market attracts capital from a wide range of sources, from individual investors to financial institutions to institutional investors. Its high liquidity makes it a valuable and stable vehicle through which companies can raise funds on favorable terms to meet their long-term capital needs. The Commerical Code stipulates that bonds can be issued only by corporations and must, in principal, be secured. This reflects the overriding priority of Japan's bond market, which is to safeguard investors.

To ensure effective investor protection, bond issuing is subject not only to various provisions of the Commerical Code, the Mortgage Debentures Trust Law, the Law for Registration of Bonds and Debentures, the Securities and Exchange Law, and other legal provisions, but also to the Bond Issuing Standards. These set out specific eligibility criteria relating to size and financial structure of the issuing company. Bond Issuing Standards are discussed later in this chapter.

Because of low interest rates, Japanese corporate fund-raising has tended to focus increasingly on the bond market, at the expense of the equity market. In fiscal 1986, new equity issues represented a mere 7 percent—¥475 billion—of total capital raised by Japanese companies in domestic and overseas securities markets. Bonds, on the other hand, accounted for an overwhelming share—convertible bonds representing

42.5 percent, and bonds with warrants, 22.6 percent. Issues of such equity-linked bonds have grown at a much faster rate than those of straight bonds, a trend that has been encouraged by the advantageous terms on which convertible and warrant bonds can be issued and by the positive effect they have on a company's net worth when converted to equity. We have, nevertheless, chosen here to set out the procedures for issuing straight bonds because they are broadly representative of the bond market as a whole.

Issuing System.   Most bonds are currently issued through underwriting syndicates. Under this system, a trustee company (or commissioned bank) is selected, and the management of the issue is handled by the underwriters. If the issue is undersubscribed, the underwriters are required to take up the remainder of the issue. Where bonds are issued through private placement, the trustee company or a third party can contract with the issuing company to underwrite the entire issue.

Issuing Procedures.   Before bonds are issued, the company must select a trustee and lead manager, set the terms of the issue, and determine collateral.

The trustee and lead manager (underwriter) advise the company on a range of issues including its eligibility to issue bonds and the employment of funds. Eligibility criteria for public offerings of straight bonds are set out in Table 10–1.

The issue amount, coupon (interest rate), price, maturity, and other terms are set, according to the issuing company's credit standing, by those involved in the flotation, with the trustee company playing a central role.

In Japan, bonds must, in principal, be secured. This is to ensure effective investor protection. Rights of bondholders to payment, in case of default, is customarily treated as taking precedence over those of other creditors.

Securities Companies

Securities companies undertaking securities business in Japan must obtain licenses from the Minister of Finance, after which they come under the supervisory direction of the Ministry of Finance. The securities business is regulated by the provisions of the Securities and Exchange Law.

TABLE 10-1
Eligibility Criteria for Public Offerings of Straight Bonds

Minimum Net Assets (¥billion)	Minimum Net Worth Ratio (%)	Minimum Net Asset Ratio (times)	Minimum Ratio of Operating Profits to Total Capital Employed (%)	Minimum Interest Coverage (times)	Dividends per Share
10	10	1.2	5	1.0	Minimum of ¥3 for each of the last 3 years, or at least ¥4 in the immediately preceding year.
6	12	1.5	6	1.2	Minimum of ¥4 for each of the last 3 years, or at least ¥5 in the immediately preceding year.
3	30	3.0	8	3.0	Minimum of ¥5 for each of the last 3 years.

At the end of 1986, there were 243 securities companies in Japan, including 22 foreign companies and 6 *Saitori* members that act as brokers' brokers within the exchanges. Of the total, 67 were active in all four major areas of securities business—dealing, brokerage, underwriting, and selling. Securities companies capitalized at ￥3 billion or more are known as integrated securities companies and are allowed to act as lead managers of underwriting syndicates while concurrently engaging in other securities business. The Big Four, Nomura, Daiwa, Nikko, and Yamaichi, have a dominant presence in the market. In a recent year, they held a combined 48 percent share of equity trading volume, 63 percent of bond trading volume, and 69 percent of the value of securities underwritten by all Japanese securities houses.

Bond and equity markets have both experienced a stunning increase in trading volumes since 1983, as Japan's investible funds have swelled, corporate and individual investors have sought higher returns, and liberalization has transformed the markets. Consequently, assets and revenues of securities companies have increased dramatically. In the future, though, the environment is likely to become more difficult. As the market continues to undergo diversification and internationalization, securities companies will need to meet such challenges as increasing competition from financial institutions and liberalization of commissions.

Other Means of Raising Capital

In addition to bank lending and the securities markets, other options are open to companies seeking to raise capital. These include factoring—for short-term working capital—and leasing (in Japan this is most commonly finance leasing), which can be an effective source of equipment funds. Factoring and leasing are discussed in another section. Here we shall briefly outline a different source of corporate fund-raising, the recently established domestic commercial paper market.

Since November 1987, it has been possible to issue commercial paper in the Japanese domestic market. The right to issue commercial paper is restricted to listed companies eligible to issue unsecured straight bonds and to companies eligible to issue secured straight bonds. In principle, a backup credit line from a financial institution is necessary, but this is optional for companies of exceptionally high standing. The minimum issue amount is set at ￥100 million and maturity is limited to between one and six months. Such commercial paper is sold through securities companies to institutional investors and corporations at a discount to its face value. As yet, this market is still relatively small, but the amount of outstanding commercial paper is increasing rapidly.

TRADE FINANCING AND PROTECTION

Japan, being poor in natural resources, has since the Meiji era made it national policy to base its economy on foreign trade. Provisions have been made for all types of foreign trade financing and foreign trade insurance. Table 10–2 details foreign trade financing.

TABLE 10–2
Foreign Trade Financing

Item			Comments
Export Financing	Short-term	Export advances	After export contract is concluded, financing is required for production and delivery to port of the export products. The limit of the advance is 80%–90% of the contract value (or L/C amount).
		Purchase of export drafts	The banks will purchase the draft after the shipment is loaded, to enable exporters to recover their costs.
	Medium-to long-term	Joint financing with the Export-Import Bank of Japan	For the export of equipment and parts, yen-based funds are provided to finance procurement, production, or extended payment for the exports. In principle, finance is provided jointly with private banks. Interest is based on the long-term prime rate, and the term of the financing is generally up to five years.
		Guarantees	Indirect support for financing, not involving direct loans. Bid bonds, performance bonds, guarantees for return of advance payments, and other types of guarantees are available.

TABLE 10–2
(concluded)

Item			Comments
Import Financing	Short-term	Acceptances	Financing based on fixed-period documentary drafts drawn on usance L/C. The bank issuing the L/C carries out discount financing in international financial markets until settlement is made on the due date of the draft.
		Foreign exchange bank usance (domestic loans)	The foreign exchange bank in Japan dealing with the importer settles with overseas exporters using its own foreign currency funds and lends foreign currency funds to the importer. A grace period is given on the settlement due date.
		Refinancing	Financing of settlement funds for import drafts payable on sight. Refinance drafts with fixed periods are issued by the importer and the bank issuing the L/C procures funds from the bill discounting market (BA market).
		Yen loan funds for import draft settlements ("jump" financing)	For parties importing goods on at-sight conditions, instead of providing import usance, banks will provide yen funds for import settlements.
	Medium- to long-term	Joint financing with the Export-Import Bank of Japan	The Export-Import Bank of Japan will finance to importer or users together with private banks for the import of goods regarded as very important (natural resources, airplanes, etc.) and other items, such as equipment, parts, and fittings.

Foreign Trade Financing and Protection

In foreign trade transactions, there are many types of risks that are not covered by ordinary privately-operated insurance companies. Some of the more typical risks include:

1. Credit risk: Bankruptcy of the buyer or risk of not being able to collect invoices due to deterioration of the business environment; risk of failure of goods to arrive on time because of nonexecution of the contract by the exporter even though advance payment has been made by the Japanese importer; and the inability to recover the advance payment.

2. Emergency risk: Risk of foreign exchange restrictions in the importing country; import restrictions or nonexecution of the contract due to major problems such as wars, overthrow of governments, and so on.

3. Foreign exchange risk: Risk due to changes in foreign exchange rates.

In order to protect companies in Japan engaged in foreign trade from these risks and to promote the sound development of trade transactions, the Japanese government and regional governments have established various types of risk insurance. For example, export bill insurance (applicable when an authorized foreign exchange bank purchases the foreign trade bill) is provided by the Ministry of International Trade and Industry for 82.5 percent of the face value amount of these bills and the insurance provided by the regional governments covers 15 percent.

Domestic Trade Financing and Protection

Japanese Business Customs

With the exception of some cash sales (including sales with credit cards) conducted by retailers and restaurants, there are numerous cases where the buyer is provided with the goods or services on credit, resulting in the creation of credit sales claims. These sales are often collected later in cash but, in many cases, through promissory notes having maturities of one to four months. There are also instances of payment through a combination of cash and promissory notes.

The method of promissory note payments began after the end of World War II, when companies, to compensate for the lack of capital, issued promissory notes as a form of payment instead of cash. According to current practice, the notes are held until the due date at which time the cash value is collected. As a result of this practice, the total period required for collection of receivables often ranges up to six months, which is very long by U.S. standards.

Financing of Accounts Receivable by Banks

Many financial institutions provide finance for operating funds based on accounts receivable. In Japan especially, there are many instances of financing through the discounting of notes based on commercial transactions.

The discounting of notes in Japan is carried out mainly by banks, with recourse should the payee go bankrupt. If this happens, the bank can demand that the party that bought the notes for discounting buy them back. For this reason, it is important to keep close watch on the credit standing of one's customers.

Factoring

Factoring services that buy receivables without recourse and guarantee collection are also available in Japan. The large banks have factoring companies in their groups. Sanwa Factor, established by the Sanwa Group, was a tie-up with the First National Bank of Boston and was the first company in Japan to enter into the factoring business. Commissions for factoring are, in general, 2 percent to 3 percent of the receivables.

To give one example of factoring services unique to Japan; in Japan, there are many cases where the seller does not want the buyer to know that the accounts receivable have been sold to a factoring company. If it becomes known that a factoring company is involved in the sale, it may be construed as meaning the seller has doubts as to the financial condition of the buyer. In other words, the seller does not want to "hurt the buyer's feelings." To prevent this from occurring, payment of the receivables is guaranteed. This means the promissory note received by the seller from the buyer is copied and the copy is sent to the factoring company. The factoring company will then issue the seller a document of guarantee. The actual promissory note from the buyer is held by the seller until it is presented to the buyer on the due date. Therefore, the buyer does not know that the factoring company is involved.

Leasing

Payments for the sale of machinery and equipment are sometimes spread over a number of years. In order to avoid credit risks, a leasing company may be used as a financial intermediary. The facilities and machinery are sold to the leasing company and it is responsible for collection of payments from the user. In other words, the credit risk is passed on to the leasing company.

Although Japan's leasing industry is still young (the first leasing company was established in 1963), it has developed rapidly. In fiscal 1986, the amount of new leasing contracts concluded was ¥4,757 billion, or seven times the amount 10 years ago and double that of 5 years ago. There are currently 23 major leasing companies, many of which belong to groups headed by banks and other financial institutions, general trading companies, and large manufacturing companies. Competition among these companies is intense. The large leasing companies are placing more emphasis on international transactions and are setting up operations abroad. At present, these companies have a total of 112 overseas locations in 17 countries.

Financing under Guarantees Provided by Credit Guarantee Corporations

Because many companies have limited collateral, credit guarantee corporations have been established to provide guarantees for borrowings from financial institutions. To promote imports, a special guarantee limit, in addition to regular loan guarantees, of ¥8 million to ¥10 million per debtor has been established for loans for import settlements.

BANKING AND LOCAL FINANCING

Japan's Financial System

Characteristics

Since World War II, Japanese private financial institutions have been operating under strict restrictions consisting of laws and administrative guidance. Typical of these restrictions have been the separation of long-term and short-term financing, of trust business from banking business, and of banking and securities businesses. Through these restrictions, the banking industry has been orderly and the industry has steadfastly remained sound and stable. Since the end of World War II, there has not been a single case of bankruptcy.

However, in recent years, because of changes in the structure of the financial services industry and a growing trend toward internationalization, the tempo of finance liberalization has quickened and restrictions on private financial institutions are being lifted gradually. In short, commercial banks, which once concentrated on short-term financing, have moved into long-term financing, and the businesses of banks and securities houses have become more similar. With the conversion of *sogo*, or mutual banks, into commercial banks, the entrance into Japan of a substantial number of foreign banks and securities companies, and the increase in the variety of financial products, competition among financial institutions is expected to intensify.

Structure of the Financial System

Japanese financial institutions are under the supervision and guidance of the Ministry of Finance and the Bank of Japan (see Figure 10–1). As of fiscal 1986, 244 banking institutions, including commercial banks, long-term credit banks, trust banks, *sogo* (mutual) banks, and foreign banks, had funds amounting to ¥540.8 trillion, a ¥367.4 trillion balance in loans outstanding, and 452,000 employees. (Note: 52 of the 69 *sogo* banks became local banks in February 1, 1989.)

Commerical banks have the largest volume of funds and play an important role within Japan's financing system. These consist of city banks (12), one specialized foreign exchange bank, local banks (64), and foreign banks (77). (Table 10–3 lists U.S. banks in Japan.) The six largest city banks have each formed their own group of customers, including large companies from virtually all major industries.

Financial institutions for long-term credit (three long-term credit banks and seven trust banks) once played an important role in supplying funds for plant and equipment investment. In recent years, they have been placing more weight on real estate activities, securities-related operations, and international banking activities and have become competitors of the commercial banks.

Bank Borrowing by Corporations

Loans, discounting of promissory notes, guarantees, consumer finance, and public system financing are the types of bank borrowing found in Japan. Foreign companies wishing to borrow can do so under the same conditions as for Japanese companies. (Foreign trade financing has been explained in a previous section of this book.)

FIGURE 10–1

Financial Institutions in Japan (as of December 31, 1987)

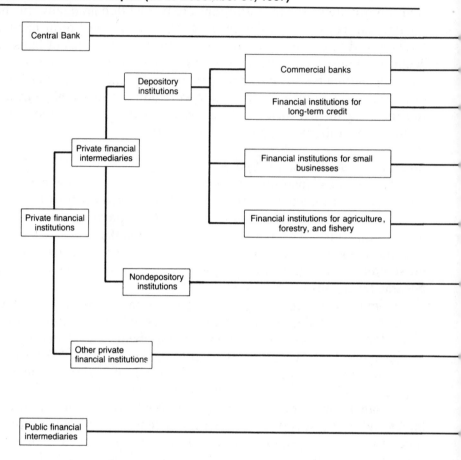

[1] Foreign affiliated trust banks excluded.
[2] Foreign insurance companies excluded.
[3] Foreign securities companies excluded.
[4] Foreign exchange specialized brokers excluded.
[5] 52 of the 69 mutual banks became local banks as of February 1, 1989.
Source: The Bank of Japan.

The Bank of Japan

City banks
Specialized foreign exchange bank (1)
Local banks (64)
Foreign banks (77)

Long-term credit banks (3)
Trust banks (7) [1]

Mutual banks (69)
The National Federation of Credit Associations
    Credit associations (456)
The National Federation of Credit Cooperatives
    Credit cooperatives (448)
The National Federation of Labor Credit Associations
    Labor credit associations (47)
The Central Bank for Commercial and Industrial Cooperatives

The Central Bank for Agriculture and Forestry
    Federations of credit agricultural cooperatives (47)
        Agricultural cooperatives (4,286)
    Federations of credit fishery cooperatives (35)
        Fishery cooperatives (1,753)

Securities investment trustor companies (11)
Life insurance companies (23) [2]
Nonlife insurance companies (23) [2]
Various mutual aids (48)
Housing loan companies (8)
Consumer credit institutions
Venture capitals
Securities finance corporations (3)

Securities companies (212) [3]
Money market dealers (6) [4]

Postal Savings Special Account (post offices)
Trust Fund Bureau, Postal Insurance Fund
  and Industrial Investment Special Account
The Export-Import Bank of Japan
The Overseas Economic Cooperation Fund
The People's Finance Corporation
The Small Business Finance Corporation
The Small Business Credit Insurance Corporation
The Environmental Sanitation Business Finance Corporation
The Agricultural, Forestry, and Fishery Finance Corporation
The Housing Loan Corporation
The Public Enterprise Finance Corporation
The Hokkaido and Tohoku Development Corporation
The Okinawa Development Finance Corporation
Government-affiliated finance institutions (13)

TABLE 10–3
U.S. Banks in Japan

Branches	Representative Offices	Trust and Banking Companies
Bank of America National Trust & Savings Association	First City Bancorp. of Texas	Morgan Guaranty International Finance
Citibank N.A.	Harris Trust and Savings Bank	Bankers Trust
Continental Illinois National Bank & Trust Company of Chicago	California First Bank	Chase Manhattan Bank N.A.
Morgan Guaranty Trust Company of New York	The Philadelphia National Bank	Citibank N.A.
Manufacturers Hanover Trust Co.	First Hawaiian Bank	Manufacturers Hanover International Finance
Wells Fargo Bank N.A.	Brown Brothers Harriman & Co.	Chemical International Finance
Security Pacific National Bank	Seattle First National Bank	
Chemical Bank	Bank One, Milwaukee, N.A.	
First Interstate Bank of California	Bank of Guam	
The First National Bank of Chicago	American Express Bank Ltd.	
Bankers Trust Co.		
Irving Trust Co.		
National Bank of Detroit		
Mellon Bank N.A.		
The First National Bank of Boston		
Bank of California N.A.		
Bank of Hawaii		
Republic National Bank of New York		

Loans

Loans on Notes.   With the company as the paying party and the bank as the receiving party, a promissory note is given to the bank and funds are borrowed. This is the most common form of note loan borrowing. The period of the note is, in principle, three months or less and interest is prepaid. Loans on notes are used mainly for short-term operating funds and fiscal year-end working funds.

Loans Based on Agreements.   For this type of loan, the borrowing party provides the bank with a document describing the amount of the loan, period of payment, interest, and other terms. The period of borrowing is generally over one year. Interest is paid on specified dates, and repayment is made in either one payment at the term or in partial payments. Security for the loan is provided by giving collateral or supplying a guarantor, but in some cases, loans may also be made on the credit standing of the borrower alone. Loans based on agreements are used primarily for financing capital investment and for long-term operating funds.

Current Account Overdrafts.   For overdrafts, interest is short-term and is usually paid after three months. Term limits of the loan can be fixed or open. In general, interest for the overdrawing of current accounts is high, and this type of borrowing is used only by top-ranking Japanese and foreign companies.

Discounting of Promissory and Other Notes
This refers to financing through the discounting of promissory notes, notes accepted by banks, and discounting of trade documentary drafts by banks.

Guarantees and Other Arrangements
Other types of finance-related arrangements include bank guarantees, loans secured by securities, and loans by government financial institutions for which private banks act as agents.

Consumer Finance
Consumer finance is available not only for purchases of durable goods by individuals but also for the financing of real estate, housing, and businesses.

Public System Financing
The government has established system financing under special laws for specific industries and for small and medium-size companies; these systems make it possible to raise long-term funds at low interest rates. (But the size of individual loans may be small.)

Interest on Bank Borrowings

Interest on borrowings is decided by negotiations between borrowers and lenders and depends upon such considerations as the type of financial institution, credit standing of the borrowing party, form of financing (whether or not collateral is given), and prevailing financial conditions.

Generally, short-term loan rates are based on the short-term prime rate (which, at the end of November 1988, was 3.375 percent), which is applicable to the discounting of notes and loans to corporations with high credit ratings and moves in line with the official discount rate (which was 2.5 percent as of the end of November 1988). The prime rate for long-term loans was 5.7 percent at the end of November 1988. An important recent development has been the shift to spread lending, where banks add a specified margin above the cost of funds raised from market sources. Rates on spread loans vary along with changes in CD and other market rates.

Documents Necessary for Borrowings

Banks usually require a bank transaction contract, registration of authorized signatures, and the application for the borrowing, including a description of contents of the proposed project, financing program, manufacturing and sales plans, and other information. If the borrower is a foreign company, balance sheets, statements of income, and the annual report of the parent company for the past three years are required.

COPING WITH EXCHANGE RATE FLUCTUATIONS

Outline of the Tokyo Foreign Exchange Market

Against the background of the Japanese economy's internationalization and the relaxation of foreign exchange controls, the Tokyo foreign exchange market has developed at a rapid pace in recent years. In 1986, market turnover reached $2.5 trillion, 50 times its size in 1973, when the floating exchange rate regime was adopted. As transaction rules have moved closer to international norms, the Tokyo foreign exchange market has, both in name and reality, come to rank alongside New York and London as one of the world's three largest markets.

Special Features
Compared with the New York and London markets, the Tokyo market has the following special characteristics (data as of March 1986).

Currency Trading. Although dollar-yen trading still occupies a large share of total transactions, fund-raising by Japanese enterprises in

European financial markets has risen recently, bringing increased dealing in European currencies.

Futures Trading. Futures and swap transactions account for 60 percent of turnover, a high level compared with New York (35 percent) and London (26 percent). This high percentage is the result of high volume of forward contracts for export and import transactions and increased swap transactions in connection with fund-raising, investing, and arbitrage transactions.

Transactions on Behalf of Customers. This trading occupies 33 percent of turnover, a high level compared with those of New York and London, both at 11 percent of turnover. This is because of the importance of foreign trade transactions in Japan's economic structure, which gives rise to a large volume of transactions in foreign currencies.

Market Structure

Market Participants. Authorized foreign exchange banks, eight foreign exchange brokers, and the Bank of Japan are the participants. In addition, foreign banks and other enterprises operate in the market indirectly.

Trading Hours. Trading hours are from 9 A.M. to 12 P.M. and 1:30 P.M. to 3:30 P.M. However, since 1987, Tokyo banks have engaged in 24-hour trading through brokers.

Delivery Day of Spot Deals. Delivery is two business days after the deal.

International Brokering. Japanese brokers are now able to receive and execute trading orders from overseas financial institutions.

Abolition of the Real Demand Principle. In April 1984, the Foreign Exchange Control Law underwent a further revision, eliminating the actual demand principle for foreign exchange trading. Any enterprise may freely book advance orders based upon movements of the exchange market, its independent assessment of the market, and profit objectives. Also, enterprises hedge their advance orders once booked by placing a counter order and rebooking at a later date.

Mechanisms of Market Movements

Factors Influencing Market Movements
Since 1973, when the floating exchange rate system was adopted, movements in the yen-dollar rate have become larger (Figure 10–2). For those Japanese enterprises highly dependent upon exports, market fluctuations are an extremely important management problem. The factors influencing exchange rate movements are:

- Differences in economic growth, inflation rates, and balance of international payments conditions among countries, especially the recent surpluses in Japan's current account.
- Interest rate differentials between Japan and other countries, especially the United States.
- Speculative pressure.
- Policy coordination among the economically advanced countries.

FIGURE 10–2
Trends in the Yen-Dollar Rate (Leading Rate in the Tokyo Forex Market)

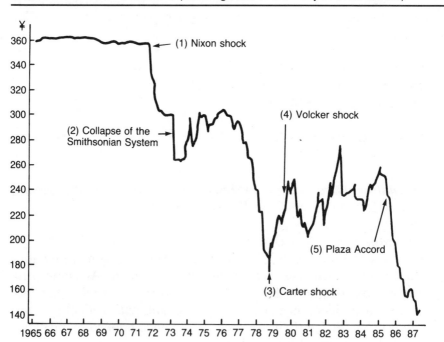

Market Rates and the Customers' Rates

Market Rates.   The foreign exchange market price is determined by buying and selling between banks. Not only do banks execute foreign exchange trades on behalf of their customers, but the banks also engage in forex market dealing operations. The foreign exchange positions of banks are covered on the market. When Japanese exports are active, banks' dollar positions increase and, because this leads to the selling of some of these dollars, a lower dollar (higher yen) market price results.

Customer Rates.   Banks also add a certain margin to the interbank rate to determine rates for their customers. Customers rates consist of spot and futures quotations, each with its own selling and buying rates. In accordance with the risks of each transaction and the prepayment of interest, an officially announced market is set up along the following lines.

Selling market rates:

Telegraphic selling rate (TTS) = Interbank rate + bank's margin
At-sight payment import bill settlement market rate (acceptance rate) = TTS + mailing period prepaid interest
Cash selling market rate (cash selling rate) = TTS + insurance premium + delivery charges + interest

Buying market rates:

Telegraphic buying market rate (TTB) = Interbank rate − bank's margin
At-sight payment bill buying rate (at-sight buying rate) = TTB − mailing period prepaid interest
Usance bill buying rate (with letter of credit) (usance buying rate) = At-sight buying rate − usance period interest
Usance bill buying rate (without letter of credit) = Usance buying rate − risk premium due to lack of letter of credit
Cash buying market rate (cash buying rate) = TTB − insurance premium − delivery charges − interest

The interbank rate of the dollar for these rates is decided on the basis of the daily interbank spot rate at about 10 A.M. plus swap cost for two days. The banks' margin is, at present, determined on the basis of the spot U.S. dollar market rate and is currently ¥1.00 per U.S. dollar. The rates of other currencies are calculated based on the average, officially announced U.S. dollar market rate and rate of that currency against the dollar.

Exchange Risk Hedge Methods

Enterprises use the following risk hedging methods.

- Match or marry. Foreign currency assets and liabilities are combined and offset. To adjust for the time lag between receipt and payment, impact loans and foreign currency deposits are used.
- Forward forex contracts (see below).
- Use of leads and lags.
- Use of an overseas financial subsidiary.
- Change into yen-based transactions.
- Sale of foreign currency receivables.
- Use of leases.
- Exchange rate insurance.

Of the foregoing, the most commonly used method is forward forex contracts. There are two types: fixed-date delivery and optional date delivery (in which the customer can select the execution date). In the latter case, a month is decided on, and contracts can generally be delivered and executed at any time in that month. Booking of futures is done by telephone with banks, fixing the time and rate. Written confirmation of booking is exchanged afterward. At the time of the booking, the bank may require security.

EXCHANGE CONTROLS

Japan's Foreign Exchange and Foreign Trade Control Law governs external transactions such as foreign trade and capital transactions. This law has been revised several times since its passage in 1949. It is referred to below as the Foreign Exchange Law.

Characteristics

At present, external transactions, in principle, are free from restrictions.

Foreign trade transactions are also generally free from restrictions, and procedures for these types of transactions have been simplified.

Capital transactions are usually free from restrictions, except when "emergency situations" are declared, but in some cases, advance notice is required. The term *emergency situations* applies to cases when Japan experiences international payments difficulties and when sharp fluctuations in the yen exchange market occur.

Imports of foreign capital and technology require advance notice.

In principle, foreign exchange transactions must go through one of the 181 (as of April 1988) authorized foreign exchange banks.

Government Agencies with Supervisory Authority

Ministry of Finance is responsible for movements of capital and currency and other conditions related to external transactions, investments from foreign countries. restrictions on imports of foreign technology, and others. It also supervises authorized foreign exchange banks.

The Ministry of International Trade and Industry is responsible for supervision of foreign trade and for transfers of industrial property rights.

The Bank of Japan, by delegation of authority from the Minister of Finance, is responsible for intervention into the foreign exchange market and processing of approvals and notifications.

Restrictions on Capital Transactions

Deposits

A resident of Japan can freely make a foreign currency deposit at any of the authorized foreign exchange banks. In cases where the resident wants to make a deposit overseas, the resident must obtain approval first regardless of whether or not the deposit is to be in yen or in some other currency (Foreign Exchange Law, Article 21).

A nonresident can also freely make a deposit with any of the authorized foreign exchange banks in Japan.

Trusts

A trust that creates a foreign currency claim between residents or between a resident and a nonresident must have the approval of the Ministry of Finance.

Loans and Borrowings

A foreign exchange bank can freely lend foreign currency to a resident. For a loan from a resident to a nonresident, advance notice is required and the loan conditions will be examined by supervising government authorities. A loan by a nonresident to a resident requires only prior notice to the proper authorities.

Offer and Issuance of Securities

For a nonresident to offer or issue securities in Japan, advance notice is necessary and will be examined by the Ministry of Finance (Foreign Exchange Law, Articles 22 & 23). The offer of issuance of yen-denominated securities overseas by a nonresident also requires approval of the Ministry of Finance.

Real Estate

A resident can freely purchase real estate oversees. In cases where a nonresident wishes to purchase real estate in Japan, advance notice is required. However, if the nonresident is making the purchase for personal housing purposes, a notice is not necessary.

Import of Technology into Japan

A contract for the import of technology requires the submission of a notice to the Ministry of Finance and the minister having jurisdiction over the particular matter within three months before the conclusion of the contract. The party submitting the notice then cannot close the contract for 30 days (Foreign Exchange Law, Article 29). For contracts dealing with airplanes, weapons, explosives, and other technologies that may affect the safety of the country, approval may take as long as five months from the date the notice is submitted.

JAPANESE TAX STRUCTURE

The National System

Legislation

The Tax Bureau of the Ministry of Finance drafts tax bills, which are then sent to the House of Representatives in the Diet. Due to the complex and controversial nature of taxes, bills are sent to the Standing Committee for Finance for study. After the study, the bill is voted on by the House of Representatives. Assuming it is passed, it is sent to the House of Councillors. The bill becomes law upon their approval and usually becomes effective on the following April 1.

FIGURE 10–3
National Tax Administration System

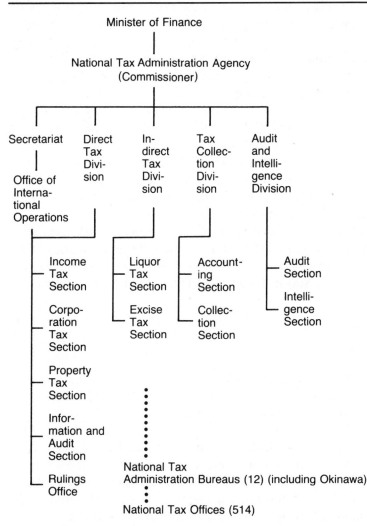

Minister of Finance

National Tax Administration Agency
(Commissioner)

| Secretariat | Direct Tax Division | Indirect Tax Division | Tax Collection Division | Audit and Intelligence Division |

Office of International Operations

- Income Tax Section
- Corporation Tax Section
- Property Tax Section
- Information and Audit Section
- Rulings Office

- Liquor Tax Section
- Excise Tax Section

- Accounting Section
- Collection Section

- Audit Section
- Intelligence Section

National Tax Administration Bureaus (12) (including Okinawa)

National Tax Offices (514)

Administration
The National Tax Administration Agency (NTA) is responsible for the administration of national taxes. The NTA is semi-autonomous but is under the control of the MOF (see Figure 10–3). The NTA is composed of a central office, 12 NTA bureaus, and 514 NTA offices. The National

Tax Tribunal (NTT) resolves taxpayer disputes at the administrative level. The NTT consists of 1 central office and 12 local offices.

To ensure uniform administration of the tax system, the director of the NTA issues directives or ruling instructions. These often result from differences in the tax law interpretations of various NTA bureaus and offices. Although ultimate authority on tax matters lies with the courts, these directives are rarely overruled. Advance rulings regarding specific transactions are generally not made.

When a dispute arises over the amount of tax due, a taxpayer makes a request for reinvestigation with the local NTA office within two months of receiving a notice of determination.

A taxpayer who files a blue return need not request a reinvestigation but may immediately seek a request for reconsideration by the NTT. If a request for reinvestigation is made, an appeal must be made to the NTT within one month of the reinvestigation decision.

If a taxpayer is dissatisfied with an NTT decision, the taxpayer may go to court. An appeal of an NTT decision must be made within three months. There are three judiciary levels. Lower court decisions may be appealed to higher levels, but this process can extend for many years.

The Local System

Legislation
Similar to the powers the Constitution grants the Diet on the national level, the Constitution grants prefectures, cities, towns, and villages the authority to administer taxes under the Local Autonomy Law.

The type of taxes that may be levied and the maximum rates permitted are delineated under another law, the Local Tax Law. Local taxes include prefectural inhabitant and enterprise taxes and municipal inhabitant taxes. Since the local tax law legislates the maximum rates for these taxes (LTL), local tax rates do not vary substantially. Additional taxes may be instituted upon the approval of the Ministry of Autonomy.

Administration
Prefectures and municipalities collect and administer their own taxes. Because local taxes are a function of national corporate taxes, adjustments to national taxes arising from a tax dispute should result in corresponding adjustments to local taxes. Generally, audits are con-

ducted by the NTA, which informs the local administrators of the changes to taxable income that the taxpayer must make.

CORPORATE INCOME TAX

General Corporate Tax Concepts

Rates
The Japanese corporate tax rates are among the highest in the world. Even after the 1988 tax reform, the combined effective corporate tax rate is approximately 51 percent. This rate is the sum of the three taxes paid by a corporate business form in Japan—the national corporate, corporate inhabitant, and corporate enterprise tax—reduced by the deductibility of the corporate enterprise tax for computing the national corporate income and inhabitant tax.

National Corporate Income

	April 1, 1989		April 1, 1990
	Earmarked for Dividends	Balance	All Income
Corporations with paid-in capital greater than 100 million yen	35.0%	40.0%	37.5%
Corporations with paid-in capital less than 100 million and nonjuridical association, etc.			
First 8 million yen of taxable income	26.0%	29.0%	28.0%
Remainder	35.0%	40.0%	37.5%
Cooperation association, etc.	25.0%	27.0%	27.0%

Earmarked dividends have historically been assessed a lower national corporate tax rate in recognition of the double tax characteristic of a corporation. In corporate tax years beginning on or after April 1, 1990, there will no longer be a lower national corporate tax rate for earmarked dividends.

Local Corporate

Inhabitant.   The inhabitant tax is composed of a corporate and a per capita levy.

The corporation levy is based on the amount of national corporate tax owed, before certain deductions such as withholding taxes and foreign tax credits. If a business has offices in different areas, the tax is prorated among the different locales based on the number of employees in each office. If a corporation does not have an office or a place of business in a prefecture or municipality, it is exempt from the corporation levy. The per capita levy depends on the amount of share capital. A ceiling rate is the maximum rate a taxing jurisdiction can assess. Most taxpayers pay the ceiling rate.

Corporate Levy

	Standard Rate	Ceiling Rate
Prefecture	5.0%	6.0%
Municipality	12.3%	14.7%
	17.3%	20.7%

Per Capita Levy

Capital Amount (in yen)	Standard Tax Amount (in yen)	
	More than 50 Persons Engaged in Office in Municipality	50 or Less Persons Engaged in Office in Municipality
10 million or less	130,000	50,000
More than 10 million but not more than 100 million	180,000	150,000
More than 100 million but not more than 1,000 million	500,000	250,000
More than 1,000 million but not more than 5,000 million	2,250,000	900,000
More than 5,000 million	3,750,000	1,150,000

Corporate Enterprise

Taxable Income (in yen)	Standard Rate	Ceiling Rate (110%)
Less than 3.5 million	6%	6.6%
3.5 million–7 million	9%	9.9%
More than 7 million	12%	13.2%

The Tokyo, Osaka, and other large prefectural governments use the maximum tax rates rather than the standard rates depending on the amount of capital stock of a corporation or its annual taxable income. The Tokyo metropolitan government uses 1.05 times the standard tax rates for corporations. The reduced rates of 6 percent and 9 percent are not applicable to corporations with offices in three or more prefectures and share capital of 10 million yen or more. In certain developing areas, a portion of taxable income can be exempted for qualified industries.

Special Tax on Land Sales

There is a special 20 percent additional national tax and 4.14 percent additional inhabitant tax imposed on gains from the sale of land or rights to land held for five years or less. The holding period is determined as of January 1 of the year of sale. Furthermore, if the sold land or land rights have been held less than two years, the rate of the tax will increase to 30 percent for national tax purposes and 6.21 percent for inhabitant tax purposes.

Filing Requirements

The corporate taxpayer's tax year is the accounting year—fiscal or calendar. A 52- or 53-week year is not allowed. (Certain accounts may be closed 10 or fewer days before the year-end, if these accounts are so closed annually.) Consolidated returns are not permitted in Japan.

National Corporate Tax

Interim Return. If a corporation's tax year is longer than six months, an interim return must be filed. The return and tax are due within two months after the six-month period. The tax liability may be established in one of two ways. First, the company may compute its ordinary income for the six-month period and pay the appropriate amount of tax. Second, the company may prorate last year's tax liability over a six-month period and pay this amount.

If the amount due is 100,000 yen or less, an interim return is not necessary. Interim returns also need not be filed during a corporation's first year of business. If a corporation had no tax liability the previous year, an interim return need not be filed.

Final Return.   A corporation is required to file a final return within two months of the end its tax year. The tax due is calculated on the basis of a corporation's financial report, which must be approved by the shareholders. If the shareholders' meeting will not be held before the tax return is due, or there are other problems with the return, a one-month extension may be granted.

The final return must be accompanied by a corporation's balance sheet, profit and loss statement, and other supplementary documents. Any refunds that are due are payable on demand once a final return has been filed.

Blue Return.   A corporation may file a "blue return," if the corporation has secured the approval of a tax office and conforms to certain accounting procedures.

The tax law requires that the following items must be maintained in good order at the head office for seven years:

1. Books of account.
   - Journals.
   - General ledger.
   - Substitute books of account.
2. Financial statements.
   - Balance sheet.
   - Income statement.
   - Other documents relating to fiscal closing.
   - Inventory list.
3. Contracts and other vouchers.
   - Orders, contracts, invoices, receipts, estimates, etc., received from third parties.

- Copies of orders, contracts, invoices, receipts, estimates, etc., prepared by the taxpayer.

The retention period for the books of account begins on the due date of the corporate tax return. The retention period for the other categories commences from the end of the relevant fiscal year.

Despite the record retention requirements, there are many advantages of the blue return over the white (nonblue) return, including:

- Carried-over net losses for accounting periods five years before the current period may be deducted as current expenses.
- Carried-back losses beginning within one year before the current period can qualify the corporation for a tax refund.
- Most accelerated depreciation provisions and reserve deductions apply only to companies filing blue returns.
- The tax office cannot make corrections to the return unless mistakes in the calculation of income are revealed by an audit.
- The tax office must give written reasons for any corrections.
- A corporation filing a blue return may request immediate reconsideration by the NTT without first making a request for reinvestigation at the NTA.

Local Taxes

Inhabitant taxes are paid on the same schedule as national corporate taxes. The two types of inhabitant taxes are prefectural and municipal (in Tokyo, they are combined). Prefectural taxes are payable at the prefectural tax office; municipal taxes are payable at the municipal tax office.

Enterprise taxes are levied on corporate profits. The filing and payment requirements for enterprise taxes are the same as those for national corporate taxes.

Penalties and Interest

Penalties are levied as administrative charges on incorrect tax returns. There are three basic types of penalties. The first is levied on returns that show an incomplete declaration of income. The penalty is 10 percent or 15 percent of the increment due, if the original return was filed in a timely manner. The 10 percent penalty applies if the amount due is below a certain level; the 15 percent penalty applies if it is above that level. The second type of penalty results when a return has not been filed in a timely manner. This tax is 15 or 20 percent depending on the amount due. The third type of penalty tax is levied for fraud. The tax is 35 percent of the increment due if the return was filed in a timely manner and 40 percent if it was not.

Interest on a deficiency or a refund is computed at a 7.3 percent annual rate. If after receiving a notice of the deficiency, the taxpayer delays payment longer than two months, interest is computed at a 14.6 percent rate after the two months.

Statute of Limitations
In nonfraud cases, the tax authorities have three years from the date of filing to challenge a taxpayer's return. In fraud cases, the tax authorities have seven years.

For three years after the date of filing, a taxpayer may amend a return to declare more tax due. For one year after the date of filing, a taxpayer may request a correction for a tax refund.

Tax Accounting Procedures for Income

Installment Sales
Installment sales proceeds are collected in regular installment payments. The criteria for an installment sale are:

1. The payment must be made in three or more installments, either monthly, annually, or otherwise periodically.
2. The period from the date of delivery of the object of the sale or contract to the due date for the last installment must be at least two years.
3. The amount payable by the date of delivery must not exceed two-thirds of the total liability for the sale or contract.

If these three tests are satisfied, installment sales, as well as deferred payment sales and deferred payment contracts, may be recorded on a collection basis. This method must be applied to all installment sales.

Long-Term Contracts
For most construction-type contracts or manufacturing contracts involving either a unique item or an expected production period of over one year, the completed contract or percentage of completion method may be used to record net income. The percentage of completion amount is usually calculated based on a percentage of total estimated costs.

The partial completion rule must be applied when many items of the same or similar type are constructed under one contract but accepted unit by unit, or when a construction contract is divided into several parts and each part of the contract is paid for as the construction is completed. Under this rule, gross income and expenditures attributable to completed and accepted parts are accounted for in the business year they are accepted.

Dividends Received
As a rule, for tax years beginning on or after April 1, 1989, 90 percent of the dividends a Japanese corporate investor receives from another Japanese corporation are deducted from taxable income. For tax years beginning on or after April 1, 1990, the deduction percentage drops to 80 percent. Dividends received by a Japanese corporation that owns 25 percent or more of the Japanese payer continue to be fully deductible from income.

To the extent that dividends received exceed dividends paid, 12.5 percent of the excess is taxable income for tax years beginning between April 1, 1989, and March 31, 1990, inclusive. For tax years beginning after April 1, 1990, no excess will be added back.

Donation Income
When one corporation transfers an asset to another corporation for less than the fair market value, the donee is deemed to recognize donation income based on the fair market value of the transferred asset. This applies regardless of whether the donor and the donee are related parties. Such donation income is taxable to the donee at the regular corporate tax rates.

The donor of the asset is deemed to have sold the property for its fair market value and generates a gain. In addition, the donor incurs a donation expense equal to the deemed gain. The donor's ability to claim a tax deduction for its donation expense is limited to the following formula: 50 percent of (2.5 percent of predonation income + .25 percent of capital and capital reserves).

Deductions

Entertainment Expenses. The deduction of entertainment expenses is limited. Ceiling amounts have been imposed based on a corporation's level of capitalization. For a business entity with more than 50 million yen of capital, entertainment expenses are not deductible. For a business entity with 10 million yen to 50 million yen of capital, the maximum entertainment expense deduction is 3 million yen. For a business entity with less than 10 million yen of capital, the maximum entertainment expense deduction is 4 million yen.

If the disbursement of entertainment funds is at the discretion of the corporate directors and the deductibility of the entertainment expense is not satisfactorily proved, the expenses will be counted as personal income for the directors.

Deferred Assets.   Expenditures that are properly chargeable to a capital account and recoverable by means of amortization over a period longer than one year are called deferred assets.

The amortization of deferred assets is computed by means of the straight-line method. The useful life of the deferred asset is determined by considering the estimated period over which the benefit accruing from the expenditure is enjoyed. To make the accounting procedures simpler, deferred assets of less than 200,000 yen per item may be charged as current expenses.

A corporation may deduct in full the following deferred assets in the business year of their disbursement:

1. Incorporation costs.
2. Interest paid to shareholders before the business becomes profitable.
3. Startup costs.
4. Research costs.
5. Costs for issuing shares or debentures.
6. Bond discounts.

If these items are not deducted in full as expenses in the year of disbursement, they may be deducted in subsequent years.

Incorporation expenses, startup costs, and research costs must be deducted no faster than the book amortization. Book amortization, under the requirements of the Commercial Code, may not last longer than five years.

Intangible Assets.   For book purposes, goodwill must be amortized within five years and may be amortized more rapidly under a straight-line method. For tax purposes, goodwill amortization may not exceed the book rate.

The straight-line tax accounting amortization lives of patents, trademarks, utility model rights, and design rights are 8, 10, 5, and 7 years, respectively.

Bad Debt.   Bad debt deductions may be computed under either the specific writeoff or the bad debt reserve method.

Under the bad debt reserve method, when a corporation credits a certain amount to the bad debt reserve account in a particular business year, the credited amount is deductible within the following limits in computing the income of that business year:

A.   The statutory bad debt percentage of receivables outstanding:

Retail or wholesale business	1.0 percent
Retail installment sales	1.3 percent
Manufacturing	0.8 percent
Financial or insurance business	0.3 percent
Other business	0.6 percent

The ceiling limits may be increased by 16 percent for corporations with capital amounts of 100 million yen or less in business years that begin before April 1, 1990.

B.   The actual average bad debt percentage during prior three years:

$$\frac{\text{Average bad debt loss account during prior 3 years}}{\text{Average accounts receivable outstanding during 3 years}} \times \begin{array}{l}\text{Accounts receivable outstanding}\\\text{at the end of the business year}\end{array}$$

Retirement Allowance Reserve

In addition to contributions made to a qualified retirement plan, a corporation can deduct a reserve for a non-qualified plan. The amount credited to a reserve for retirement costs may be deducted, depending on the applicable circumstances, up to the lowest of the following amounts:

- Up to the increase in the total retirement allowances claimable if all employees remaining at the end of the accounting period had terminated their employment on a voluntary basis, computed according to the retirement allowance policy established by the corporation.

- Up to 6 percent of the salaries, bonuses, and allowances paid in the accounting period if the retirement allowance policy is not based on a labor union agreement. If the company reports to the tax office that it has notified every employee of the retirement allowance regulations, this test is not applied.
- Up to 40 percent of the total retirement allowances claimable by all employees remaining at the end of the accounting period had all employees terminated their employment then on a voluntary basis, less the related allowances claimable by all such employees in the preceding accounting period.

Bonus Reserves.   When a corporation credits a certain amount to a bonus payment reserve account to provide for the payment of bonuses in the future, the credited amount is deductible up to a certain limit in computing the amount of income.

The limit is computed by applying formulas based on whether a corporation does or does not reward a fixed bonus payment amount. The former system uses data based on the prior year's bonus amounts; the latter system uses data based on the current fixed bonus agreements.

Depreciation and Depletion

Unless recorded in the books, depreciation and depletion are not deductible for tax purposes. Estimated useful lives of depreciable assets are prescribed in the tax law and regulations. Unless prior approval of the tax authorities is obtained, these prescribed useful lives must be used. Several methods of depreciation are allowable. The declining balance method is most commonly used. Assets are usually depreciated to 5 percent of cost.

In addition to ordinary depreciation based on the statutory useful lives, additional depreciation ranging from 8 percent to 36 percent (up to 50 percent in Okinawa) is allowed in the first year for designated depreciable assets. Newly constructed residential rental properties have allowances of 30 percent or 50 percent of additional ordinary depreciation for the first five years. Also, assets costing 200,000 yen or less may be immediately expensed.

Inventory Valuation.   For tax and book purposes, inventories may be valued at cost or the lower of cost or market. Essentially, inventory is valued under full absorption principles. For recording inventory flows, the average, FIFO, LIFO, retail price, or specific identification methods are allowed.

Interest.   There are no debt/equity rules under Japanese tax law. Thus, companies may and do leverage themselves highly.

There are minor indirect limits on interest expense. For example, certain allocable interest expense is, in general, allocated against dividend income and, thus, does not generate a tax benefit at the corporation's full effective tax rate.

Interest expense on funds borrowed by corporations for the acquisition of real property after December 30, 1988 (including the right to use land and securities economically equivalent to land) must now be capitalized. The capitalization period begins on the date of acquisition and continues until the land is placed in business use. In calculating interest capitalized, a corporation can use either a deemed annual interest rate of 6 percent or the actual average interest rate of financing for the corporation.

Tax Credits

Foreign Tax Credits

A foreign tax credit is allowed against the corporate national and inhabitant taxes on the income received from abroad by a domestic corporation. Alternatively, a deduction from taxable income may be taken in lieu of the tax credit.

The tax credit is generally limited to the Japanese tax that is allocable to the foreign source income on an overall basis as opposed to a per country or per nature of income basis.

In certain cases, however, foreign tax credits allocable to interest income, may be limited. Three new restrictions have been imposed on the foreign tax credit. First, the total foreign source income is limited to 90 percent of the taxable income of the corporation. Second, if the jurisdiction's tax rate exceeds 50 percent, the amount of tax which exceeds 50 percent will not be creditable. Third, 50 percent of foreign source income that is untaxed in its country of source may be excluded from the calculation of the foreign tax credit limitation. Excess foreign taxes may be carried back or forward for three years.

On dividends received from a first-tier affiliated foreign corporation whose voting shares are 25 percent or more owned by the Japanese corporation (10 percent if the affiliated foreign corporation is an American, Australian, or Brazilian corporation), foreign corporate income taxes paid with respect to the profit out of which dividends are paid are included as foreign taxes paid and as foreign source income.

For enterprise tax purposes, foreign withholding taxes and indirect foreign taxes are treated as deductions from taxable income and deemed dividend income.

On the sale of a first-tier foreign subsidiary, foreign taxes paid on earnings generated while the shares were held will not be deemed foreign taxes paid by the seller. A presale dividend may be appropriate.

Tax Credit for Incremental Research and Development Expenses

If research and development expenses for an accounting period exceed the largest annual research development expenses of any year since 1966, 20 percent of such excess may be credited against the corporate national tax to the extent of 10 percent of the national tax. Further, if a corporation acquires and places in service certain depreciable assets designated by the MOF as facilities for researching and developing fundamental high technologies, the corporation may credit against the corporate national tax the lower of: (1) 20 percent of the increment in R&D expenses plus 7 percent of the acquisition costs described above, or (2) 15 percent of the corporate national tax. If the share capital of the corporation and the parent corporation do not exceed 100 million yen, 6 percent of research and development expenses of the current year may be used in lieu of 20 percent of the increment.

Tax Incentives for Capital Expenditures That Contribute to the Efficient Use of Basic Energy Resources

A corporation that acquires qualifying machinery, equipment, and other depreciable assets may use special depreciation rates based on 30 percent of the assets' acquisition costs (36 percent if assets are imported, 15 percent if assets are mining rights for overseas oil fields) or elect an investment tax credit at 7 percent to 5.25 percent (8.4 percent for imported assets, 3.5 percent if assets are mining rights for overseas oil fields) of the acquisition costs to the extent of 20 percent of corporation tax.

INTERNATIONAL TAX PLANNING

Taxation of Various Business Forms

Different forms of business are taxed in different ways. The form of business is dictated by the level of service and type of activity the Japan office will be required to provide.

Nonpermanent Establishment
Every fixed place of business in Japan is not a permanent establishment (PE). Under Japanese tax law, non-PEs include offices used solely for the following purposes: advertising, promotion, supplying information, marketing, basic research, and other auxiliary functions. Frequently, an income tax treaty with Japan will supersede Japanese tax laws definition of a PE.

An example of a treaty provision overriding Japanese tax law is Article 9 of the U.S.-Japan Income Tax Treaty, which excludes from PE status the following:

1. The use of facilities for the purpose of storage, display, or delivery of goods or merchandise belonging to the resident.
2. The maintenance of a stock of goods or merchandise belonging to the resident for the purpose of storage, display, or delivery.
3. The maintenance of a stock of goods or merchandise belonging to the resident for the purpose of processing by another person.
4. The purchase of goods or merchandise, or the collection of information, for the resident.
5. Advertising, the supply of information, the conduct of scientific research, or similar activities that have a preparatory or auxiliary character, for the resident.

Unregistered Liaison Office
The function of an unregistered liaison office is to act as a liaison between the head office and its Japanese customers. This function is insufficient to constitute a PE. A liaison office may be created by sending an employee to Japan or by employing an existing consultant. No Japanese income tax liability arises because the liaison office is not treated as a PE.

The disadvantage of this business form is its limited scope. The office may not solicit sales or engage in customer negotiations. A treaty, however, may permit a liaison office to operate in Japan as a solicitor or negotiator of sales as long as the contracts are concluded by other personnel outside of Japan.

Dependent Agent
Rather than sending a liaison, companies may rely on a third party to promote their business interests in Japan. Care must be taken because under Japanese tax law, an agent can establish a PE for a foreign corporation through being:

1. A contracting agent.
2. An order filling agent.
3. A negotiating agent.

A contracting agent exercises the authority to conclude contracts for the foreign corporation. A PE is not established if the contract is an isolated incident or if the authority is limited to purchases of goods.

An order filling agent maintains in Japan sufficient goods to meet the normal requirements of the corporation's customers and delivers these goods. A negotiating agent exclusively or principally secures orders, negotiates, or performs other important sales-related acts on behalf of the corporation.

Frequently, a country's income tax treaty with Japan will supersede Japanese tax law on a dependent agent. For example, under the U.S.-Japan treaty, only the activity of a contracting agent constitutes a PE.

Construction Site
Japanese tax law states that construction, installation, assembly, supervision, superintending, or a similar activity carried out over more than 12 months constitutes a PE. Treaties may amend this. For example, the U.S.-Japan treaty extends the period to 24 months, and the U.K.-Japan treaty excludes any reference to "supervision."

Service Branch or Subsidiary
If a greater degree of sales promotion is desired, a service subsidiary or branch of a subsidiary should be established. Under many Japanese income tax treaties, including those with the United States and United Kingdom, service branches or subsidiaries may engage in sales promotion, solicitation, and negotiation services and still be deemed the seller of the product. Of course, the main constraint on a service entity is that it cannot have or habitually exercise authority to conclude contracts that are binding on the parent company.

Service entities may compute their taxable income under the "cost plus 5 percent" method. This method allows the entity to declare its income as a 5 percent markup of its total operating expenses.

Under the cost plus 5 percent method, an increase in costs means an increase in taxable income. Thus, as many expenses as possible should be allocated away from Japan. For example, entertainment and travel expenses involving the parent can be borne by the parent, assuming they have not already been recorded on the books of the service branch.

To adopt the cost plus 5 percent method, the service entity and the beneficiary of the services should enter into a written agreement that states how the services will be rendered and how the fee will be computed.

Full-Service Foreign Branch or Subsidiary
If the head office requires that a full range of business be conducted in Japan, a full-service branch or subsidiary should be established. These entities may conduct unlimited business activities, are classified as PEs, and are subject to Japanese income taxes computed on taxable income.

Differences between Branches and Subsidiaries. The following are the main differences in the Japanese tax treatment of a Japan branch and a Japanese subsidiary:

1. If the parent corporation is domiciled in a country that has a tax treaty with Japan, a Japan branch is taxable only on income attributable to that branch. If the branch is from a nontreaty nation, all Japan source income is taxable. A Japanese subsidiary is taxed on worldwide income.

2. The payment of dividends from the subsidiary to the parent corporation is subject to a withholding tax of 20 percent, unless reduced by tax treaty. Branch profits are not subject to this tax.

3. The parent company can control its flow of profits and foreign tax credits through control of dividend payments by a subsidiary. Branch profits and tax credits for taxes paid accrue from current operations.

4. Japanese tax authorities may attempt to obtain financial records from the foreign parent in order to reallocate branch income and expense.

5. Intercompany transactions between a subsidiary and the foreign parent must meet the arm's length requirement of Japan's intercompany pricing legislation. However, the taxpayer can request that the Japanese tax authorities review the transactions before their occurrence.

6. A subsidiary must be capitalized. Because Japan has no debt/equity requirements, subsidiaries may be capitalized at relatively low levels. Japanese law requires that at least seven shares must be issued and subscribed by seven promoters at the time a subsidiary is established. Each share must be worth at least 50,000 yen. Thus, the minimum capitalization is 350,000 yen. The shares may be transferred to a single shareholder after subscription.

7. The status of a director of a Japanese corporation imposes more Japanese individual tax than the status of a branch manager.

Tax planning is an important factor in strategic planning, but other factors must be considered in selecting a business form. For instance, conducting business through a Japanese subsidiary may convey a more stable commitment to the Japanese markets than a liaison office or a branch.

Transfer Pricing

Because of Japan's relatively high tax rate, companies have attempted to shift their revenues outside of Japan through international intercompany pricing policies. To prevent an erosion of its tax base, Japan enacted transfer pricing legislation. This legislation applies to transactions between a domestic (Japanese) juridical person or a foreign corporation which has a PE in Japan and a foreign-affiliated juridical person. Information on intercompany transfer pricing must be supplied annually to the NTA.

Affiliation

Affiliation exists between two juridical persons if one has a 50 percent or greater ownership in the other or if a "special situation" exists.

50 Percent Test.   If a juridical person owns, directly or indirectly, 50 percent or more of the outstanding shares of another juridical person or has invested half or more of the total capital, a subsidiary situation exists.

If a parent corporation owns 50 percent of two subsidiaries, an affiliation also exists between the brother and sister companies. An affiliation can also exist between a corporation and its "grandchild." The 50 percent test is not a proportional calculation. In Figure 10–4, although Corporation A does not proportionally own 50 percent of Corporation D, the corporations are still deemed to be affiliates.

FIGURE 10–4
50 Percent Rule

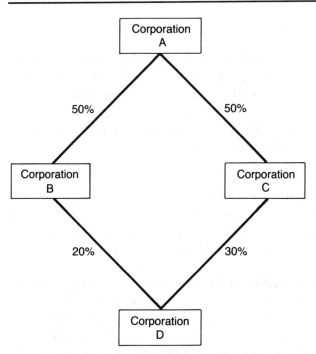

In the case of a partnership, general provisions of the Japanese tax law provide that each partner is deemed to hold proportionately the assets of the partnership. Accordingly, in the case of stock in a corporation, the number of shares deemed held by each partner is proportionate to the partner's ownership in the partnership.

Special Relationships.   Special relationships can be used to show affiliation in cases where the 50 percent requirement does not exist, but the conditions for manipulative pricing do. These include:

1. 50 percent or more of the officers of a company were officers of the other company. Officers include directors and statutory auditors.
2. The representative director is or was an employee or officer of the other company.
3. A certain, as yet unstated, percentage of the company's operating transactions are with the other company.

4. A certain, as yet unstated, percentage of the company's outstanding loans have been borrowed from or guaranteed by the other.

Transactions Covered

The intercompany transfer pricing rules explicitly target only transactions involving the sale or purchase of tangible personal property. However, a vague phrase, ''and other transactions,'' has been included in the law to allow flexible enforcement. These other transactions can be assumed to include all types covered in U.S. regulations, such as rent, royalties, interest, and fees for intercompany services.

Arm's Length Pricing

Arm's length pricing requires that intercompany transactions between two affiliated juridical persons must reflect the price that would be charged to an unrelated company under similar circumstances. Any one of several pricing methods may be used by a corporation.

Comparable Uncontrolled Price Method (CUP). This method determines the price an unaffiliated party would have paid for similar merchandise under similar circumstances. Some leeway is given due to the difficulty of defining similar merchandise and similar circumstances. Consideration is given to variables such as the volume transferred, the location of the market, the desire to penetrate a new market, the value of a brand name, and seasonal sales fluctuations.

Resale Price Method. This method is based on the theory that in specific transactions with unaffiliated parties, an average profit margin exists. Thus, in transactions with affiliated persons, the average profit margin must be applied as income. This average profit margin may be based on industrywide averages or on the profit margins for similar transactions. Leeway is given for adjustments in the similar transactions.

Cost Plus Method. Under this method, price is determined by adding an average markup to the cost of goods sold. The average markup may be determined through the use of industry averages or the markup on similar transactions.

Other Methods. If none of the transfer pricing methods listed above can be practically applied, the taxpayer may use a method of its choice. Currently, no other methods have been clearly defined.

Burden of Proof

In the event of a dispute between the NTA and the taxpayer regarding transfer pricing, the NTA price is assumed to be correct unless the taxpayer can prove otherwise. Placing the burden of proof on the tax-payer makes the transfer pricing laws unique in Japanese tax adminis-tration.

Advance Approval

Because of the time and expense involved with auditing transfer pricing cases, the NTA has devised a system whereby advance approval of pricing techniques may be given. The application for preapproval should be made by the affiliate based in Japan. If the NTA deems the proposal to be reasonable, it will give verbal approval. In clear cases, the NTA will give written approval. If the actual facts presented on the tax return conform with those set forth in the application, the NTA will abide by its verbal approval.

Tax Sparing

To encourage Japanese investment, several countries have concluded treaties with Japan that offer tax incentives. These incentives may take the form of full or partial tax waivers or credits. To retain the benefits of these treaties, companies can claim foreign tax credits on their Japanese income taxes as if the waived taxes were paid.

For example, the income of a Singapore branch of a Japanese com-pany would generally be subject to both Singapore tax (33 percent) and Japanese tax (50 percent) as shown below:

FTC Calculation	
Branch income	100 yen
Japan tax	(50)
FTC for Singapore tax	(33)
Japan tax	17 yen

Income Calculation	
Branch income	100 yen
Singapore tax	(33)
Japan tax	(17)
Net income	50 yen

Under a tax sparing treaty, the tax would be calculated as follows:

FTC Calculation		Income Calculation	
Branch income	100 yen	Branch income	100 yen
Japan tax	(50)	Singapore tax (0%)	(0)
FTC for Singapore tax	(33)	Japan tax	(17)
(not paid)	—	Net income	83 yen
Japan tax	17 yen		

The net income utilizing the tax sparing provision is 83 yen, as opposed to a net income of 50 yen without tax sparing.

Tax Treaties

Dividends and interest paid to domestic and foreign corporations and individuals are subject to withholding tax. The national withholding tax rate on dividends and royalties is 20 percent. The national withholding tax on interest paid on securities is 15 percent and 20 percent on interest paid on loans to a non-Japanese taxpayer.

The nations listed in Table 10–4 have enacted tax treaties with Japan. Companies or individuals domiciled in these countries are subject to the rates shown in the table rather than the rates mentioned above.

PERSONAL TAXATION

General Tax Concepts

National Rates

National Income (All Amounts in Yen)

Over	Not Over	Tax Rate	Amount Deductible
0	3,000,000	10%	—
3,000,000	6,000,000	20	300,000
6,000,000	10,000,000	30	900,000
10,000,000	20,000,000	40	1,900,000
20,000,000		50	3,900,000

TABLE 10–4
Countries with Tax Treaties

Recipient	Dividends	Dividends (substantial holdings)*	Interest	Royalties
Nontreaty	20%	20%	20%	20%
Treaty country:				
Australia	15	15	10	10
Austria	20	10	10	10
Belgium	15	15	15	10
Brazil	12.5	12.5	12.5	12.5/25
Canada	10	10	10	10
China	10	10	10	10
Czechoslovakia	15	10	10	0/10
Denmark	15	10	10	10
Finland	15	10	10	10
France	15	10	10	10
Germany	15	10	10	10
Hungary	10	10	10	0/10
India	20	20	20	20
Indonesia	15	10	10	10
Ireland	15	10	10	10
Italy	15	10	10	10
Korea	12	12	12	12
Malaysia	15	10	10	10
Netherlands	15	10	10	10
New Zealand	15	15	20	20
Norway	15	10	10	10
Pakistan	20	15	0/30	0
Philippines	25	10	10/15	10/25
Poland	10	10	10	0/10
Romania	10	10	10	10/15
Singapore	15	10	15	10
Soviet Union	15	15	10	10
Spain	15	10	10	10
Sri Lanka	20	20	0/20	0/10
Sweden	15	10	10	10
Switzerland	15	10	10	10
Thailand	20/25	15	0/10/20	15
United Arab Republic	15	15	20	15
United Kingdom	15	10	10	10
United States	15	10	10	10
Zambia	0	0	10	10

* Substantial holding rates vary depending on the tax treaty provision; e.g., 10 percent for the United States, 25 percent for the United Kingdom and the Netherlands, and 50 percent for Austria.

Local Tax

Inhabitant Income Tax* (All Amounts in Yen)

Taxable Income		Tax Rate	Amount Deductible
Over	Not Over		
0	1,200,000	5%	—
1,200,000	5,000,000	10	60,000
5,000,000		15	310,000

* In addition, a per capita tax of 3,200 yen is payable.

Special Tax on Real Property Sales

Special rules apply to capital gains from sales of real property other than a principal residence by individuals. Gains are classified as either long-term or short-term for national income tax purposes. This depends on whether the real estate is held for more or less than five years, determined as of January 1 of the year of sale. Long-term gains are generally taxed at a flat rate of 20 percent on amounts up to 40 million yen and 25 percent on amounts above that level for national tax purposes. The local tax rates are 6 percent and 7.5 percent, respectively. Short-term gains are generally taxed at a minimum of 40 percent.

Special Tax on Other Capital Gains

For sales of securities on or after April 1, 1989, a resident or nonpermanent resident taxpayer is subject to income tax on gains derived from the disposition of securities (stocks, convertible bonds, and so on). The gains are not subject to withholding tax but are subject to separate taxation at a flat tax rate of 26 percent (20 percent national and 6 percent local). No withholding taxation is required.

Gains derived from futures transactions and gains derived from the disposition of golf club memberships in the form of securities are not taxed separately but should be aggregated with other income and taxed at the graduated rates.

The following computation rules apply:

1. The net taxable gain is the total gains less the total losses derived from the disposition of securities during the year.

2. A net loss incurred as a result of netting total gains and total losses during the year cannot offset other income. Moreover, the loss cannot be carried forward or back to other years.

3. If a taxpayer held stock more than three years before it was listed on the stock exchange and sells the stock within a year after it was listed, the taxable income is deemed to be 50 percent of the net gain.

4. Taxpayers who received proceeds from the sale of securities must present official documents to securities companies, indicating the name and address of the recipient.

5. A securities company that pays proceeds from the sale of securities to a resident taxpayer or a nonresident taxpayer with a permanent establishment in Japan must issue a certificate of payment.

Rather than being taxed at the 26 percent rate, a taxpayer may elect to be taxed at a flat withholding tax rate of 1 percent of the proceeds derived from the disposition of all listed securities companies operating in Japan. Under this method, the net taxable gain (profit) is deemed to be 5 percent of the sales proceeds of the securities. A tax rate of 20 percent is applied to the deemed gain to provide the flat withholding tax rate of 1 percent of the sales proceeds. No inhabitant tax is imposed.

A taxpayer who elects the flat withholding tax rate must file an application through a securities company before the payment of sales proceeds. The securities company will forward the application to the tax authorities. The securities company will not be required to confirm the name and address of the taxpayer but must file a certificate of payment.

The application will be valid until canceled. Re-election will not be restricted following cancellation. This method may not be elected for margin transactions.

Other Special Categories of Income
Aside from capital gains on property, income is divided into many categories. Certain deductions may be applied only against certain types of income. Other categories of income include: interest income, dividend income, real estate income, business income, employment income, occasional income, forestry income, retirement income, and miscellaneous income. Interest income is only subject to 20 percent withholding tax (15 percent national and 5 percent inhabitant) if the interest is paid in Japan. Taxpayers can elect to have dividend income be subject only to national withholding tax at the rate of 35 percent and thus be excluded from taxable income.

Common Deductions and Allowances
Adjustments to taxable income include deductions as well as personal and dependent allowances. The earned income deduction is calculated as follows:

Salary, Allowance, Etc. (Column 1)		Multiply Column 1 by (Column 2)	Amount Added to the Product of Column 2
Over	Not Over		
0	1,425,000	use 570,000	0
1,425,000	1,650,000	40%	0
1,650,000	3,300,000	30	165,000
3,300,000	6,000,000	20	495,000
6,000,000	10,000,000	10	1,095,000
10,000,000		5	1,595,000

Personal allowances include a basic personal exemption, as well as old age, widow, widower, handicapped, and working student allowances. The availability of these deductions depends on the taxpayer's income.

Dependent deductions may be taken for the spouse and each other dependent, provided the dependent's income is under 350,000 yen. Additional deductions are available for handicapped, elderly, and teenage dependents.

Special allowances for taxpayers with income under 10 million yen, the handicapped, the retired, and homemakers who perform work in the home may also be utilized.

Reporting Requirements

An individual must file on a calendar year basis. The final national income tax return is due by March 15. Many individuals do not file returns because their withholding tax on their salaries satisfies their liability. No extensions are granted. An individual may not carry forward or back a net operating loss unless there has been an election to file a blue form return.

During the taxpayer's first tax year, no estimated taxes need to be filed. After that, national tax estimates must be paid July 31 and November 30. The payments should represent one third of the taxpayer's total liability for the year.

The inhabitant tax return is due March 15, but it is paid in equal installments June 30, August 31, October 31, and January 31. The inhabitant tax is analogous to a property tax, which has a levy day of January 1. If a taxpayer is resident in Japan on January 1, his or her prior year Japanese income is subject to inhabitant tax. Thus, the inhabitant tax based on the income for the year 1988 is paid in 1989 and 1990. Rather than four installments, the tax may be paid entirely June 30. A small discount is given for the lump-sum payment.

Expatriate Taxation

Status
Foreigners have one of three residency statuses under the Japanese tax code. They can be nonresidents, nonpermanent residents, or permanent residents. The determining criterion is length of residence. A nonresident's intended Japanese stay is less than a year. A nonpermanent resident's intended Japanese residence is at least one year but no longer than five years, a permanent resident's residence is more than five years.

A nonresident is taxed at a flat rate of 20 percent on all salary, remuneration, and allowances received while in Japan. However, under some treaties, a nonresident staying in Japan less than 183 days and who is paid by a taxpayer not filing a Japanese tax return is not subject to Japanese tax. A nonpermanent resident is subject to Japan's progressive income tax on all Japan source income, as well as non-Japan source income remitted into Japan. A permanent resident is subject to Japanese tax on his worldwide income.

Taxable Income of an Expatriate
Generally, all types of compensation are viewed as taxable benefits. However, some items are accorded special treatment. For example:

• If the lease is in the employer's name, the employer pays the rent directly to the landlord, and the employee/director pays a lower "economic rent" to the employer, the difference in the rents is not taxable.
• The amount of economic rent is determined by the sublessee's position in the company. If he or she is an employee, the rent is usually only 5 to 10 percent of the actual monthly amount paid. If the sublessee is a director, the rent is 35 percent (if the house is also used for business purposes) or 50 percent (if it is not). If the employer makes a reimbursement to the employee/director for the economic rent, this is a taxable benefit.
• Transportation costs to the home country are generally not taxable. A home leave allowance is taxable.
• If an employer makes a contribution to a school that has an established contribution plan and the school then provides free education to employee children, the benefit is not taxable.

• Reimbursement for moving expenses is not taxable.
• The cost of language lessons for employees, and under certain situations their spouses, is not a taxable benefit.
• The payment of fees resulting from tax advice and preparation is not a taxable benefit.
• The cost of temporary living expenses before moving into a permanent Japanese residence is not a taxable benefit.

The following items will be treated as additions to taxable income: utilities, children's tuition (except as noted above), local inhabitant and national tax reimbursements, and maid service.

Director versus Employee Status

Besides the economic rent calculation, there are areas in which the tax treatment of expatriates depends on whether they are classified as employees or directors of the company. In general, the tax treatment of employees is more favorable. However, Japanese subsidiaries of foreign corporations are required to have at least one director in residence.

All remuneration paid to a director is considered to be Japan source income, regardless of whether the director spends business days outside of Japan or into what country the money is actually paid. This does not apply if the directorship is of a company incorporated abroad. Thus, a director's tax burden can be reduced by being a director of the parent company and an employee of the subsidiary. Employees are taxed on their Japan source income and foreign source income which is paid in or remitted to Japan.

Bonus payments made to directors cannot be deducted from the employer's income. However, if the bonus is paid monthly it can be deducted.

TAXES OTHER THAN INCOME TAX

Payroll Taxes

Health, welfare pension, unemployment, and worker's accident compensation insurance are government sponsored, and generally participation is compulsory for both employers and employees. Except for worker's accident compensation insurance, the premiums are generally paid equally by the employer and employee. The combined monthly health insurance premium approximates 8.3 percent of monthly compensation up to 695,000 yen and remains the same thereafter. The combined monthly welfare pension contribution approximates 11.8 percent and 12.4 percent, for female and male employees respectively, of their monthly compensation up to 470,000 yen. The combined monthly unemployment and worker's accident compensation insurance premium approximates 1.95 percent of monthly compensation, with 1.4 percent borne by the employer and .55 percent borne by the employee.

Sales/Consumption Tax

In general, a sales tax of 3 percent on the value of all goods and services, imported goods, and rentals of property, at all levels, will be imposed. To prevent multiple taxation on the same goods and services, credits may be claimed for taxes already paid. The tax is similar to a value-added tax but requires less reporting than is required under value-added taxes in many other countries.

Structure of the Tax. Almost all domestic sales of goods or services are subject to the tax, as are all imports of foreign goods. The tax is payable by the enterpriser or, in the case of imports, by the person removing the goods from the bonded area. The tax base is the total price, including any other taxes or tariffs, based on book accounts. Until 1992, an additional 3 percent tax will be levied on certain automobiles.

Transfers between related parties either within Japan or between countries are viewed as taxable transactions because related parties are considered separate legal entities.

Application of the Tax. The total of the taxable transactions for the period is multiplied by the tax rate. The amount of taxes already paid "upstream" is then offset against this amount to determine the current liability. These credits must be detailed in a ledger or the actual invoices and receipts must be retained.

The taxable period for the sales tax is the same as the payer's income tax year. A corporation must also file interim returns (and make an interim payment) within two months of the end of the first half of its tax year. The payment may either be the actual amount of tax owed for the period or half of what was owed the previous year. If the interim amount owed is 300,000 yen or less, it may be postponed to year-end.

In the case of importers, the consumption tax is paid directly to the customs agents when goods are received. It may be necessary to file year-end reports to receive tax credits or to make other adjustments. This is a timing disadvantage to importers.

Special Provisions and Exemptions. Small businesses may take advantage of three special tax provisions.

1. If revenue is under 30 million yen in the one-year period ("base year") beginning two years prior to the current tax year and ending one year prior to the current tax year, no tax return need be filed.
2. If current year revenue is between 30 million yen and 60 million yen, a partial tax reduction applies.
3. If revenue is under 500 million yen, in the base year a simplified computation of the tax liability may be utilized. If the taxpayer chooses the simplified computation, this method must be utilized for at least two years.

The following items and transactions are expressly exempt from the consumption tax:

1. Exports, including international transport. Exporters may claim the "upstream tax" credit for previously paid consumption tax on the exports.
2. Sales and rentals of land.
3. Sales of securities.
4. Sales of means of payment, such as promissory notes.
5. Payments of interest on loans, insurance premiums, and so on.
6. Foreign exchange transactions.
7. Tuition, medical services, and certain other welfare services.

Real Property Acquisition Tax
This prefectural tax is levied when real property is acquired or when a building is completed. The tax is not imposed on land acquired through a corporate merger or through an inheritance. The tax is 4 percent of the "assessment value", which is usually substantially less than the purchase price. A special deduction of 10 million yen may be taken from the market value of a newly constructed residential home. Land acquired for residential purposes is also permitted preferential tax treatment.

Fixed Assets Tax
A fixed assets tax must be paid annually by the registered owner as of January 1. The subject property includes land, buildings, or other depreciable assets (except automobiles). The tax rate is 1.4 percent and is imposed on an "assessment value" that is determined every three years by the municipality.

Transaction Taxes

The securities transaction tax is levied on sellers of securities in Japan. The tax is usually withheld at the source—the securities dealer. The tax rates range from .12 percent to .30 percent depending on the type of security traded.

The bourse transaction tax is levied only on brokers' or bourse members' transactions that are settled by the actual transfer of merchandise or by spot transactions of merchandise in the contrary direction. Transaction proceeds are taxed at rates ranging from .001 percent to .01 percent depending on the type of security traded.

The stamp tax applies to certain types of documents including promissory notes, work contracts, and transfers of real estate, businesses, surface rights, and so on. Other taxable documents are listed exhaustively in the Stamp Duty Act. Their tax is usually 200 yen. The tax is paid by affixing and canceling a stamp on the documents. The 1988 tax law abolished the stamp tax on many items.

The registration and license tax is levied on the occasion of an entry in official books concerning property rights, companies, and business and professional licenses.

Inheritance and Gift Taxes

Inheritance tax rates range from 10 percent on amounts under 4 million yen to 70 percent on amounts over 500 million yen. There is a one-time spousal deduction as well as special annual deductions for heirs who are handicapped or under age 20.

Gift taxes also range from 10 percent to 70 percent. A spousal deduction and special handicapped deductions are also available.

THE INSURANCE INDUSTRY

Regulatory Authority

The regulatory authority of the insurance industry is the MOF. The Insurance Business Law of 1939, the Law Concerning Foreign Insurers of 1949, and related regulations govern the form and content of the reports to be submitted to the MOF, the methods of valuing assets and liabilities, and the admissibility of assets for solvency purposes.

Returns to the Regulatory Authority

An insurance company is required to submit various reports on either a monthly or annual basis. In addition, the MOF may require an insurance company to submit reports on matters including accounting, actuarial reporting, and sales.

Authorization Procedures

A license for each class of insurance business (e.g., life, marine, fire, etc.) must be obtained from the MOF before conducting business operations in Japan. The documents required to be submitted include, but are not limited to, a pro forma business plan showing estimated premium income for the first five years of operation, articles of incorporation, and documents showing the method of conducting business in Japan. Authorization to obtain a license may take two years.

Solvency Requirements

Solvency requirements differ for resident and nonresident insurers. A resident insurer must have share capital of at least 30 million yen. A nonresident insurer must make a deposit of 10 million yen or more. In addition, a nonresident company must have been in existence for a minimum of three years in its home country at the date of filing the application and must have had profits at the close of the latest financial year to be eligible to apply to the MOF for authorization.

Non-life insurers must submit monthly business reports to the MOF, submit annual unaudited accounts, and in Japan maintain assets of a value not less than the company's specific insurance reserves.

Financial Statements and Audit Requirements

Japanese insurers that have capital of at least 500 million yen or liabilities of at least 20 billion yen are required to have an audit by an independent accountant of both annual and semiannual financial statements. The independent accountant must be a CPA or an audit corporation licensed under the Certified Public Accountants' Law of Japan.

Taxation

Tax on Specific Funds. A tax on specific funds is levied on insurance companies, trust companies, banks and stock companies conducting approved pension business, employees' welfare pension business, or employees' asset formation business. The 1 percent tax is imposed on the specific funds at the beginning of the business year.

General Insurance. Taxable income of a non-life insurance company is determined by MOF regulations and is subject to the same taxes as other companies. In addition, the enterprise tax paid by insurance companies is based on net taxable premium income during a fiscal period. The standard rate for computing the enterprise tax is 1.5 percent; the maximum rate is 1.65 percent.

Life Insurance. The taxable income of a life insurance company is the greater of the following amounts:

- The current year's surplus, plus or minus certain items.
- Seven percent of the current year's surplus.

Captive Life Insurance Companies
Captive insurance companies do not exist in Japan because insurance is so readily obtainable and because of the time and cost of establishing an insurance company.

Insurance Companies
A foreign corporation entering Japan has insurance needs similar to the insurance requirements of the business in other parts of the world. In general, insurance for operations in Japan is purchased from an insurer operating in Japan.

INTERPRETING JAPANESE FINANCIAL STATEMENTS

General Analysis

An experienced reader of financial statements who views the financial statements of a Japanese company may be startled. Standard ratio analysis and a standard understanding of the hidden value of assets such as real property have no utility in analyzing Japanese financial statements. As discussed previously, Japanese tax accounting is quite similar to that practiced in many parts of the world. Likewise, Japanese financial accounting is similar to that of other parts of the world. Thus, understanding the accounting principles of Japanese financial statements should be relatively simple.

The difficulty, however, is becoming accustomed to the comparative ratios of Japanese companies and to the degree of hidden value in the book value of certain assets. Also, the statement of changes is not a required financial statement.

The current ratio of a Japanese corporation is much lower than the ratio of a comparable non-Japanese corporation. This is because Japanese banks supply a huge amount of short-term credit to Japanese corporations. Banks also lend an enormous amount of longer term credit to corporations. Thus, the debt equity ratio of Japanese corporations is much higher than that of non-Japanese corporations.

Land and perhaps securities will likely be listed on the balance sheet. These amounts are usually extremely undervalued. Both land and securities values have soared in Japan in the last decade.

Also, there will be very little goodwill on the balance sheet, because acquisitions, even among Japanese companies, are infrequent. Moreover, when they occur, any arising goodwill must be amortized within five years and could be amortized immediately.

There will be a large amount of depreciation on the balance sheet because the Japanese financial statements generally employ the same method of depreciation as utilized in tax returns. This means depreciation is recorded much faster for a Japanese corporation than a non-Japanese corporation.

Another example of this rapid expensing policy is the treatment of interest costs during construction. These costs are generally expensed rather than capitalized. These rapid amortization and depreciation policies contribute to the seemingly lower operating margins of the Japanese corporations. Also lowering net income is Japan's high tax rate.

Generally, Japanese financial statements do not contain deferred taxes because Japanese financial and tax accounting are approximately the same. If deferred taxes appear on the financial statements, they represent future taxes to be paid by a consolidated subsidiary.

It is important to make certain the financial statements are consolidated. Under Japanese accounting standards, consolidation is required only for publicly traded companies. Consolidated financial statements are generally issued one month after the parent has separately reported its financial statements. The consolidated financial statements are supplementary material to filings under the Securities and Exchange Law. In the future, consolidated financial data will be required to be reported earlier.

When consolidation occurs, the Japanese consolidation rules are unique and potentially misleading. For instance, subsidiaries constituting up to 10 percent of the assets, revenues, or income of the remaining group members may be excluded from the consolidated financials under the 10 percent rule of materiality. Another example is that a subsidiary can have a year-end three months different from that of the parent. Thus, information can go unreported. Even for domestic operations, interim reporting need only be made on a semiannual, rather than a quarterly, basis.

Accounting Principles

While Japanese accounting principles are generally similar to those of many countries, Japanese accounting principles permit the corporation much more discretion regarding accounting treatment and disclosure.

Balance Sheet

Balance sheet values are listed at their historical cost; there are no markups to fair value. Markups to fair value would occur when a corporation is acquired in a purchase transaction. However, acquisitions are rare, and disclosures ragarding acquisitions need not be made. Likewise, terminology and distinctions like purchase and pooling accounting are not utilized.

Assets and liabilities are divided into current and noncurrent categories. Essentially, current account items are convertible into cash during the next accounting year.

Bad debt reserve accounting is utilized. Often the reserve computed is the same as the maximum reserve allowed for tax purposes, which is based on either a mandated percentage of outstanding sales or three-year historical data.

Inventory is generally stated at cost. Only when the fair market value of the inventory is materially lower than its cost will the inventory be written down. First-in-first-out (FIFO), last-in-first-out (LIFO), average cost, specific identification, and retail methods are all acceptable methods of reporting the flow of inventory costs, if reported on a consistent basis. Given the lower inflation rate in Japan and the low level of inventory, most Japanese companies utilize the FIFO method. When valuing maufacturing inventory, assets are essentially reported under full absorption accounting principles.

Like inventory, marketable and investment securities may be reported under a cost method that need be revalued only if the market value is significantly below cost.

There are no accounting rules regarding the capitalization of leases. Therefore, most leases are recorded as operating leases. The tax law, however, requires certain leases to be capitalized. To enable the Japanese corporation to utilize the full tax deductibility of depreciation and interest expense, the corporation must capitalize the lease for book purposes.

The shareholders' equity section generally contains four accounts: common stock, capital reserve, legal reserve, and retained earnings. At least half of the proceeds of a stock offering must be included in common stock regardless of the par value of the shares. Legal reserve is an amount of earnings set aside under the Commercial Code. Ten percent of all cash dividends must be set aside until this reserve equals 25 percent of the common stock.

In the financial statements of Japanese corporations, there are also no treasury stock accounts. Under the Commercial Code, treasury stock is not permitted. A company's stock is acquired only on two occasions:

1. When the stock is acquired to be canceled.
2. When a business acquisition occurs.

Income Statement

Income and expense are recognized when they are realized and measurable. Extraordinary items are reported separately.

Installment sales reporting is allowed in all industries subject to the requirements listed in the Tax Accounting Procedures Section. Long-term contract reporting is allowed under either the percentage of completion or completed contract methods.

Disclosure

Disclosure is often more limited in Japan than in other countries. For example, only public companies are required to disclose a schedule of their long-term debts. In this schedule, only those debts carrying unusual interest rates need be disclosed.

Another example of the lack of disclosure is that only the amounts of related party transactions need be disclosed. The actual transactions and the related party's relationship need not be disclosed. Also, business segment reporting is not required.

A third example is that no disclosure need be made regarding pension liabilities. There is no requirement of funded pension plans. As stated in the tax accounting procedures section, for tax purposes, a tax deduction may be taken for a retirement allowance reserve. Book deductions often utilize the tax return deduction. Arguably, to the extent that financial accounting reserve accounts are the allowable tax deductions, the financial statements overreport income and underreport liabilities.

Yet, in other respects, disclosure is much more detailed than in other countries. For example, much more detail regarding a company's plant, property, and equipment is disclosed in Japan. This is particularly useful in estimating the value of appreciated real estate.

PART 3

KOREA

CHAPTER 11

KOREA: THE "HERMIT KINGDOM" MEETS THE WORLD

Robert Kwon

HISTORY

A few recurring themes tell the story of Korea from ancient to modern times.

Its location as a peninsula jutting south from China to the northern islands of Japan makes it a strategic bridge, fought for and occupied by armies from Japan, China, Manchuria, Russia, and America. This same proximity to China and Japan has also blended the Koreans' distinct national character into a larger picture in the eyes of the world.

The strength of the Korean people themselves—who today carry on an ancient civilization rooted in Confucian values—has sustained a rich, traditional culture; built ironclad warships and invented movable metal type long before Europeans; and summoned the collective resiliency to surmount long and devastating hardships.

This last point is best illustrated by South Korea's current economic "miracle"—the fruit of a 25-year campaign to rebuild the country after half a century of oppression, poverty, and strife. Since the end of the Korean War, national income has increased 1,200 percent in real terms, South Korea is the noncommunist world's 17th-largest economy and 12th-largest trading nation, and the average citizen is working and well-educated.

Ancient History

Korean legend dates the nation's founding to 2333 B.C. by Tangun, a god-king descended from a heavenly father and a bear totem tribe mother. His descendents are said to have reigned for more than a millennium.

History of the past 2,000 years—when Korea came to be called *Chosun,* or the "Land of the Morning Calm"—starts with the division in 57 B.C. of the peninsula into three kingdoms, Shilla, Koguryo, and Paekche. In 688 A.D., the country was unified under Shilla. This regime lasted until 918 when the kingdom was taken over by the Koryo dynasty (the source of the name *Korea*).

In 1392, General Yi Song Gye, backed by the Chinese, seized power and began a reign that lasted until the Japanese annexed Korea in 1910. During these 500 years, however, Korea was invaded, influenced, and fought over by its larger neighbors. The first major Japanese invasion occurred in 1592 when the Yi monarch refused to allow Japanese warlords to use the peninsula as a conduit in conquering Ming China.

In a devastating period for Korea, the Japanese swept to Seoul armed with Portuguese muskets that easily overpowered Korean bows and arrows. The royal court fled and appealed to China for aid. At the same time, however, Korean Admiral Yi Sun-Sin launched a dazzling series of counterattacks, cutting off Japan's seagoing supply lines with his fierce-looking ironclad *geobukseaon,* or turtle boats. Together with Korean guerrilla actions and Ming reinforcements, the Japanese retreated. But in 1597, they invaded and were repulsed again.

This war followed by a Chinese invasion in 1627 devastated Korea—decimating the population and arable land. The strife also gave rise to isolationism—a period in which the Yi kings sought to close off the nation and protect themselves from future foreign buffeting. Until the late 19th century, Korea came to be known as the Hermit Kingdom.

In 1876, Japan returned with a trade treaty seeking and gaining special privileges. Other nations, including Russia, the United States, Great Britain, and France, followed in pursuit of trade. Rivalry between Japan and Russia soon turned to war, however, with Korea set in the middle as hostilities began off Inchon and Port Arthur in 1904. Although Korea proclaimed neutrality, Japan tightened its grip on the Seoul government. After its victory, Japan annexed Korea in 1910 and closely ruled the country as a colony until 1945.

Korean War to Present

As World War II ended, the United States and Soviet Union agreed at Yalta that Japanese forces in Korea would surrender to the United States south of the 38th parallel and to the Soviets north of the line. Intended only as a temporary partition until talks could reunite the nation, the division became a battle line instead.

In 1950, after continuing communist intransigence in negotiations and pullout of U.S. forces from the south, North Korea—the Democratic People's Republic of Korea under Kim Il Sung—claimed sovereignty over the entire peninsula and invaded the Republic of Korea. In response, the United Nations sent troops led by the United States to assist the Republic, which the United Nations had recognized as Korea's only lawful government, and its first president, prominent nationalist Syngman Rhee.

After three years of fighting, an armistice was signed in 1953 at Panmunjom. Lacking a comprehensive peace agreement, this pact remains in force today, its tenets tensely monitored by forces marshaled on either side of the demilitarized 38th parallel. Reunification talks have been held over the years with little progress.

In the south, Syngman Rhee served as president until 1960 when demonstrations against election irregularities forced him to step down. (Kim Il Sung remains ruler of North Korea.) After Rhee, a democratically chosen but administratively ineffectual government lasted until 1961, when it was overthrown in an army coup led by Maj. Gen. Park Chung Hee.

Although General Park disbanded military rule and instituted civilian government in 1963, he also drafted a new constitution that greatly strengthened the executive branch's powers. Reelected as president three times, he continued to tighten his control until his assassination in 1979.

However, the Park years were also marked by the beginning of Korea's ascent to prosperity. A series of five-year plans engineered by Park's government achieved rapid industrialization, extraordinary economic growth, and modernization.

Maj. Gen. Chun Doo Hwan next seized the government, first declaring martial law and then, in 1980, beginning the Fifth Republic with a new constitution that largely retained the strong executive and indirect presidential elections (for one term only). Chun was elected to a seven-year term as president in 1981.

In the meantime, a booming economy had created an independent and well-educated middle class. Korea's people wanted more of a say in their own government, and when Chun's term approached an end, they demanded that democratic processes pick the next president. Roh Tae Woo, the successor Chun had selected, assented to the popular will and in doing so became the first ruler of modern South Korea to reach power through fully democratic elections, in which he won 36 percent of the vote.

Roh faces a number of challenges. First, Roh must practice democratic rule through compromise with a parliament he does not control and the leaders of Korea's opposition parties, who are asking for an interim test of public confidence in his government. Then, Roh must keep the economy advancing at levels the people have come to expect while responding to increasing calls for more comprehensive social development programs.

Although the sharing of power means less orderliness and efficiency in Korea's society today, it also promises to build a strong and broad base for the nation's continuing economic strength and national security.

PEOPLE

Korea can be described as a country with one tremendous natural resource—a hardworking, intelligent, and cultured people.

Koreans are the descendants of several tribes who migrated into the peninsula from central and northwestern Asia. Some of these people also settled in Manchuria, and Koreans and Manchurians still show physical similarities. However, Koreans are racially and linguistically homogeneous, with no indigenous minorities. They are also independent and distinctive in their culture, language, dress, and cuisine.

Religious life and tradition play a major role in Korea, with a diverse fabric of Shamanism, Buddhism, Confucianism, and Christianity coexisting in harmony.

Shamanism is largely a folk tradition today, but its bells, cymbals, and superstitions remain part of the Korean heritage. Buddhism had been the dominant influence in Korean life before the 14th century. Today, represented by several major sects, it remains the nation's largest religion. Korea's many temples and statues prominently show the continuing Buddhist influence. With the coming of Westerners, Christianity took a significant and growing hold on the nation through many Protestant sects and the Catholic church.

But Confucianism—more a code of behavior than a religion in the strict sense—has been the moral backbone of Korea since the 500-year Chosun dynasty instituted it as the state religion in 1392. Honesty, courtesy, dignity, and consideration, all hallmarks of the Korean people, are primary tenets of Confucianism.

While embracing no supernatural beings (apart from an impersonal idea of heaven), Confucianism sets up an ideal ethical system intended to keep all relationships within the family and the state in harmony. It mandates a strict code of behavior based on subordinations: of the son to the father, of the younger to the elder brother, of the wife to the husband, and of the subject to the throne. It also demands loyalty to friends, reverence for ancestors, and filial piety. Confucianism regards scholarship and aesthetic cultivation as fundamental prerequisites for advancement.

Korea's Confucian heritage keeps the family at the center of daily life despite the pressures of rapid modernization. First birthdays are tremendous occasions of family joy, marking entrance into life, and 60th birthdays are celebrated as time for retirement and completion of a full cycle. Even after death, respect for the extended family continues in accord with ancient Confucian rituals.

Family names are few in Korea. Kim, Lee, and Park are most common among the nation's approximately 300. A woman does not change her name when she marries; in Korean conversation she will be referred to as Park's wife, by her full maiden name of Lee Hye-chong, or by Mrs. Lee. (Although traditional distinctions between the sexes continue, Korean women today are well-educated, employed throughout all professions and industries, and active in political and social movements.)

Confucianism's legacy can also be seen in the priority Koreans place on education: more than 95 percent of all children who complete compulsory primary school go on to middle school, and 90 percent of children move on to high school. Competition to enter college is keen, and many students pursue advanced degrees in Korea and abroad.

Korea also has a rich artistic legacy that remains alive in painting, calligraphy, sculpture, music, and dance. Although much of this derives from the Confucian tradition of mastery in literature and the arts, many examples of the refined Korean aesthetic can be found in pottery and painting dating back thousands of years.

Finally, the tremendous strides of the past few decades have affirmed the value of age-old traditions with modern accomplishments. The Korean people have completed a cycle—transcending oppression and strife with boundless aspiration and energy. Great optimism, patriotism, and confidence are among the most manifest characteristics of modern Koreans.

GOVERNMENT INFLUENCE

Basic Organization

Governmental authority in the Republic of Korea is highly centralized and concentrated in a strong president, whose service is limited to one five-year term. The president is also chairman of the National Security Council.

Legislative power rests with the National Assembly, consisting of 299 members, three quarters of whom are elected by direct popular vote and one fourth by proportional vote. The term of office is four years. Legislators and the president can both introduce bills. The president formulates and submits the annual budget bill for deliberation and approval.

The president has the power to dissolve the National Assembly in consultation with the assembly's chairman and resolution of the executive branch's State Council (or cabinet). The president also has the right to veto legislation and issue emergency measures in case of natural disaster, serious fiscal or economic crisis, and state of war.

Judicial power lies in the hands of the Supreme Court and other courts at various levels. The Supreme Court has the final power to review constitutionality.

Administratively, the Republic is divided into nine provinces and four cities with provincial status (Seoul, Pusan, Daegu, and Inchon). Local governments are directed by the central government. The president appoints principal officials.

Government Economic Influences

Korean industry and commerce are predominantly privately owned and operated, with the free enterprise system guaranteed and generally accepted. However, government influence is considerable throughout the economy.

The government is heavily involved in establishing economic policy objectives and seeing that their implementation moves toward goals of maintaining national security, furthering industrial development, and raising living standards. The government directly influences economic, business, and financial priorities through its control of approvals and licenses as well as through the allocation of labor and credit.

The Economic Planning Board is responsible for developing national economic policies, including the five-year economic and social development plans that have guided the economy since 1962. Over the years, the plans have emphasized:

- Development of import substitution industries and economic infrastructure.
- Light manufacturing industries with high export potential.
- Rural development (through the Saemaul Undong, or new community movement) to modernize and improve living conditions in the countryside.
- A deepened industrial structure and investments in heavy industries.
- Economic stabilization (after worldwide recession caused by oil shocks and high inflation), liberalization of the economy, and improvements in social conditions.
- High-technology industries and social development (see "Economy" section for further discussion).

The Economic Planning Board directs the economy through policies carried out by various ministries. For instance, the Ministry of Finance implements fiscal, financial, and monetary policies. To encourage particular industries, the government uses financial assistance, tax incentives, and protection from foreign competition.

The Bank of Korea is the Republic's central bank. Its Monetary Board formulates and implements the nation's monetary policy and supervises Korea's banking institutions. The Ministry of Finance also works closely with the Monetary Board.

Monetary policy is implemented by influencing the reserve positions of banking institutions, principally through changes in the terms and conditions of rediscounts, open market operations, and changes in reserve requirement ratios. The Bank of Korea may also set or alter maximum interest rates on deposits and loans, and in periods of extreme monetary expansion, it can control the volume and nature of bank credit.

Defense and Welfare

With a belligerent power on its northern border and the threat of war ever present in the Korean consciousness, national defense remains a government priority. The Republic maintains an army of 630,000 people. Six percent of the gross national product is devoted to defense. (North Korea fields an army of 830,000 and spends 20 to 25 percent of its GNP to keep it going.) Two thirds of both North and South forces are deployed within 60 miles of the 38th parallel demilitarized zone.

Between the pressures of economic development and national defense, the government has found it difficult to expand social programs quickly. However, with continuing prosperity and popular demands, social welfare in areas such as pollution control, welfare benefits, public health, and housing programs are becoming a higher government priority.

GEOGRAPHY AND CLIMATE

Korea consists of a mountainous peninsula jutting out from China and touching on the Soviet Union. It is separated from Manchuria by the Yalu River, Mount Paektusan (the Mount of Eternal Snow), and the Tumen River, which also borders Siberia. Two oceans encircle the peninsula—the Yellow Sea on the west and the East China Sea on the east. The latter also bounds Japan lying close by on the southeast.

The peninsula is 622 miles long and 170 miles wide on average—roughly the size of England and Scotland. Some 3,500 islands, only 200 of which are habitable, are scattered along a coastline indented with many bays, inlets, and harbors.

Since 1948, the peninsula has been divided into two parts separated by the demilitarized zone at the 38th parallel. The Republic of Korea is somewhat smaller than North Korea, at 38,276 square miles versus 47,268.

Most of Korea is hilly or mountainous with extinct volcanoes and sandstone and marble mountains that largely stand on a granite foundation. Only about 20 percent of the land lies in plains suitable for cultivation. The South (in addition to twice the population of the North) possesses most of the peninsula's arable land. Korea has a relatively large number of rivers and streams.

The climate of Korea is roughly equivalent to the northeastern seaboard of the United States, except for the rainy summer monsoon characteristic of Asia.

Four distinct seasons define the temperate climate. Summers are hot, humid, and rainy (70 percent of the annual precipitation occurs between June and September) with average July temperatures of 79 degrees Fahrenheit. Winters are long and cold with 23 degrees the average January temperature. Both spring and autumn are short but pleasant and crisp with abundant sunshine. April temperatures average 55 degrees and October, 62 degrees Fahrenheit.

POPULATION

The recent metamorphosis of Korea's population strikingly reflects the economic transformation of the last 30 years, in which the Republic has changed from a rural to a largely urban society, with a quarter of its people living in Seoul.

Although disparities in wealth do exist, Korea has a healthy and expanding middle class, and the fruits of economic gain have been widely distributed, especially compared to other developing countries. Unemployment has fallen from 7.7 percent in 1964 to 3.8 percent in 1986. Enrollment in higher education (now at 28 percent) has produced a large pool of professional and technical workers.

The Republic had a population of 42 million in 1987 (compared with North Korea's approximately 22 million). With 424 South Koreans per square kilometer in 1987, the Republic is among the world's most densely populated countries. Major population centers are in the northwestern Seoul-Inchon area and the southern fertile plains. (Expatriate Koreans live mostly in China, 1.2 million; Japan, 600,000; and the United States, 500,000.)

While the population of Korea increased rapidly after World War II, careful family planning has controlled expansion, cutting the annual growth rate from 2.7 percent in 1960–66 to 1.25 percent in 1980–85. Improved health services have decreased the mortality rate from 13 per 1,000 in 1960 to 6.5 in 1982.

Significantly, the nation's population structure is growing younger. The 1985 census showed that 51 percent of the population was under 25, and the number of people in the economically active age bracket over 15 years old has increased from 21 million in 1975 to 29 million in 1985. The scope of the economically active population has also expanded in pace with the diversifying social structure.

With industrialization, however, rural migration to urban centers has created a disturbing trend in a nation that not long ago was totally agrarian. Since 1971, the 15 million Koreans who lived on farms has been cut in half. By 2000, 77 percent of Koreans are expected to live in cities compared with the 60 percent that currently do so. The government's long-term development plan aims at discouraging heavy urban concentrations and dispersing the population among provincial areas through relocated economic opportunities, balanced land development, the *Saemaul Undong* (new community) movement to aid farmers, and improved nationwide transportation.

LANGUAGE

Like its people, the Korean language derives from the Ural-Altaic family of central and northwestern Asia that includes such tongues as Manchurian and Mongolian. Korean is highly inflected, polysyllabic and atonal with conspicuous euphony smoothing the sound.

Korean bears no linguistic relationship to Chinese. However, much like the Latin and Greek derivations of many European languages, centuries of close contact and adoption of the Confucian culture incorporated many Chinese words. (English is the second language for educated Koreans but is rarely spoken outside cities. Most Koreans over the age of 50 speak Japanese, as taught during the occupation, but the Korean language shows minimal Japanese influences.)

Korean has a regular and simple grammatic structure, with easy-to-read script. This efficiency, which makes Korean more penetrable to foreigners than Japanese or Chinese, originates with a reading and writing system embodied in the *hangul* alphabet. Conceived in 1446 by an enlightened Chosun monarch, King Sejong, *hangul* provided a way to promote popular literacy with a logical, phonetic, and totally national language—as opposed to Chinese, which was then prescribed as the official written language for the educated.

The language is rich in sound and possesses a large vocabulary, with many words for human feelings and sentiments in addition to concrete things. Like Japanese, however, Korean is complicated by the use of honorifics used in accordance with social structure.

Today, written Korean in the Republic involves a mixture of *hangul* and limited number of Chinese characters, called *hanja*. (This dualism has created some scholarly dispute on modernism versus tradition.) The North uses *hangul* exclusively.

ECONOMY

Over the past 25 years, the Republic of Korea's economic growth has been spectacular—perhaps best described as a manmade miracle built on hard work and study, good planning, and a favorable international environment.

In one generation, the nation has advanced from one of the world's poorest to nearly full industrial development, despite the need to maintain a massive military establishment.

Moreover, at postwar partition of the peninsula, North Korea got most of the land's mineral and hydroelectric resources as well as the existing heavy industry built by the Japanese. South Korea inherited a large, unskilled labor pool and most of the peninsula's limited agricultural land. Although both sides suffered from the widespread destruction of the Korean War, an influx of refugees added to the South's burdens. Therefore, when the bisected nation began its two new lives, the South's gross national product lagged far behind the North's.

But the Republic of Korea has dramatically reversed this picture with three tools: constant encouragement to a highly literate, motivated, and hardworking labor force; a continually outward-oriented development policy; and carefully planned yet flexible government intervention in the economy's long-term direction.

Today, the Korean economy is one of the most successful in the world. Over the last quarter century, the nation's annual growth in real gross national product averaged over 8 percent. At the same time, the share of manufacturing in the economy has doubled. Exports and imports have risen from about 24 percent to 82 percent of GNP, making Korea the world's 12th-largest trading nation. Exports have more than doubled as a proportion of GNP from 14.5 percent in 1963–73 to 39.5 percent in 1981–87.

In 1986, Korea recorded its first merchandise trade surplus at $3.5 billion and its first significant current account surplus of $4.6 billion. The country has also pulled in its foreign debt from a high of 52.5 percent gross debt-to-GNP ratio in 1980 to 22 percent in 1988. In fact, the nation was projected to become a net creditor in 1989.

Many factors caused this economic turnaround. But government policies have been at the fulcrum, promoting growth through exports and foreign borrowing. Korea's economic success and political stability have also helped government economists and planners, largely a generation of American-educated technocrats, make bold gambles with respect to the economy. At the same time, the worldwide economic environment has been receptive to open international trading and rapid export growth.

Since the first five-year plan in 1962, the government has controlled the economy through credit rationing, managed exchange rates, strict controls of the financial sector, and a comprehensive industrial policy that the country supports. For instance, the country's *chaebols*—huge industrial holding companies such as Hyundai, Samsung, Daewoo, and Lucky-Goldstar—have moved largely in step with government direction.

While planners aggressively employed protectionist measures to nurture the economy—pampering infant industries, building high tariff barriers, and discouraging imports through bureaucratic walls—they also maintained the foresight to push growth outward through subsidies and tax breaks to export industries. (Only now is Korean demand, like Japan's, growing large enough for the nation to sustain its own economic growth.)

Korean economists also helped control inflation by avoiding big budget deficits. While businesses did go deeply into debt, public-sector restraint sheltered the economy from rises in world interest rates. Therefore, when dollar rates rose in the early 1980s, companies were pressed to cut costs, but no national budget crisis was triggered.

Meanwhile, the continued dedication to hard work of the Korean people remains the turbine at the center of the economy. Koreans have simply been willing to put in the time necessary (in manufacturing, an average 54-hour week versus 46 in Mexico and 41 in America and Japan) to keep productivity high. Manufacturing labor costs per unit of output in South Korea are 11 percent of America's, 14 percent of Japan's, 75 percent of Taiwan's, and 80 percent of Hong Kong's.

The well-educated, disciplined quality of the work force adds to productivity. For instance, 89 percent of the Republic's secondary school-age children are enrolled, a rate 4 percent greater than the developed world in general and over 60 percent higher than South Korea's enrollment 30 years ago.

Aside from brief setbacks and a few miscalculations, Korea's broad plan has worked well over the last three decades, with adjustments engineered as national needs and world conditions dictated.

The export drive of the 1960s provided powerful incentives to labor-intensive manufactured exports. Per capita GNP grew an average 7 percent annually from 1962 to 1971.

In the 1970s, fear of weakened U.S. military backing siphoned government support to heavy industries, which ultimately imbalanced and hampered the economy. Sharp increases in oil and basic commodity prices in 1973 and 1974 impeded the rate of growth. But Korea rebounded rapidly from recession thanks in part to continued reliance on the export-driven policy. The rate of growth in real GNP soared from 7.7 percent in 1974 to 14.1 percent in 1976, and the current account deficit fell from $2 billion to $314 million in the same period.

With increased oil prices and worldwide recession, Korea began the 1980s with a 5.2 percent drop in GNP (its first decrease in two decades), a poor harvest, and unrest after the assassination of President Park. Subsequently, the nation returned to fast growth and price stability through more market-oriented policies, adoption of tight monetary measures and currency devaluation, and lows in dollar and interest rates as well as oil prices. Gross national product increases hit 12.5 percent and 12 percent in 1986 and 1987, and consumer price increases settled into the 3 percent range.

As the 1980s end on notes of increased worldwide protectionism and the nation embarks on its sixth five-year plan, Korea is stressing the value-added content and complexity of its exports, in areas such as high-technology manufacturing especially. Electronics are now overtaking textiles as the country's leading export earner. Scientific and technological research and development spending is targeted to rise to 3 percent of GNP by 1991.

As for future challenges, labor unrest in 1987 won large wage hikes (11.6 percent for the average manufacturing worker and 20 percent for a *chaebol* employee). But Korea's overall productivity equation holds labor costs to a small share of factory prices.

The Republic also faces the challenge of managing a delicate balance among the needs and demands of its two dominant trading partners, the United States and Japan, and its own. America is its number one export market, purchasing 40 percent of Korea's exports in 1986, and its number two source of imports. Japan is its principal supplier of capital and intermediate goods, and it is fast becoming an increasingly important export market where sales rose 55 percent in 1987.

Finally, in keeping with the country's move toward democracy, economic policies are being relaxed through liberalized regulations in the financial sector and increased openings in the import market. And internal programs, such as balanced regional development and expanded social welfare, are receiving more attention. Looking toward the future, a nation where unilateral economic and political decision making ruled for 25 years is thus far showing signs of its ability to compromise with populist voices and adapt its economy to a freer market.

CHAPTER 12

KOREAN MARKETS AND PRODUCTS: THE TIGER COMES OF AGE

N. Ranjan Pal

INTRODUCTION

The successful hosting of the 24th Olympics was the crowning achievement of Korea's drive to achieve recognition on the world stage. The Korean national team topped the Asian medals tally in much the same way the economy has done. 1988 marked the third successive year in which the economy produced double-digit growth, an enviable record by any standard. The phenomenal export boom that has driven the economy is now giving way to a more modest boom in domestic demand as its effects begin to become apparent in a rapidly rising standard of living. The Korean people are beginning to enjoy the fruits of their success as their country prepares to leave the ranks of the developing world. Policy makers are making sweeping decisions that will change the nature of Korea's political and economic links with the rest of the world as never before.

While the Korean success story may have burst upon the world's consciousness only recently, it is the culmination of years of solid economic progress. In the early 1960s, the economy was characterized by low per capita income and a high level of unemployment. The country was densely populated, the natural resource base thin, and 85 percent of output came from agriculture. The situation changed dramatically during the next two decades. Real gross national product (GNP) increased at an annual average rate of 9 percent during 1961–78 and 8.3 percent during 1980–86. Per capita income more than quadrupled in real terms, catapulting Korea into the top rank of developing countries. Perhaps no other country has come so far so fast and with so little.

Economic development was propelled by the growth of exports, which were concentrated initially on labor-intensive manufactured goods. Real exports of goods and services rose 26 percent a year during 1961–78 and 12.4 percent a year during 1980–86, and manufacturing output rose 18 percent and 10 percent. From 1960 to 1986, the share of exports of goods and services in GNP rose from 4 percent to 43 percent, while the share of manufacturing output in GNP rose from 9 percent to 32 percent. By 1986, the country was exporting a large variety of products, ranging from light manufactured goods to heavy machinery, automobiles, ships, and electronic goods. Thus, the strategy of export-led growth has enabled Korea to successfully exploit its comparative advantage and overcome the constraint imposed by the limited size of its domestic market.

The product composition and overseas destinations of exports has changed markedly over the years. The trend has been toward more skill-intensive products with higher technology because Korea's traditional light industries, such as textiles, clothing, and leather goods, face increasing competition from other developing countries and have become the principal targets of protectionist measures in major foreign markets. Exports of iron and steel, automobiles, ships, electronics, industrial machinery, and chemicals now account for almost 60 percent of Korea's total exports. There has also been a shift within the traditional light industries in the direction of more sophisticated, higher-quality products. While the United States and Japan remain Korea's two most important markets, Korea is penetrating new markets in Europe, the Middle East, and Southeast Asia.

The benefits of growth were broadly shared. Income of urban households increased significantly as both employment and real wages rose rapidly. The rate of unemployment fell from 8 percent in the early 1960s to less than 4 percent in 1986. From 1974 to 1985, large gains in productivity in the manufacturing sector made possible real wage increases of about 8 percent a year. Considerable productivity growth in agriculture, together with government policies to support farm incomes, ensured a broadly parallel growth in rural and urban incomes. Within the rural sector, a vast redistribution of land in the late 1940s helped to spread the expansion of agricultural income. The incidence of poverty declined markedly, with the share of the population under the poverty level dropping from about 40 percent in the mid-1960s to 15 percent in the mid-1970s. Korea has also made great progress in meeting basic needs, particularly nutrition, health, and education.

Korea's growth strategy has relied on three key components: labor, investment, and government intervention. The hardworking and well-educated work force, together with high rates of investment, led to rapidly growing labor productivity. Nominal wage restraint plus productivity growth enabled Korea to achieve the enviable combination of increased competitiveness and real wage gains. These two factors were supported by sensible macroeconomic policies and active interventionism. Taxes have risen relative to income, providing noninflationary finance for government expenditures. Fiscal deficits and monetary growth have both been kept under control, and, with the exception of a few years in the late 1970s, the government has maintained competitive exchange rates. Now we examine each of these factors in detail.

LABOR AND WAGES

The Korean work force can be characterized as highly trained, hardworking, and productive with wages that are low by international standards. The Korean workweek, which has increased since the 1970s, is the longest in the world at 54 hours per week. This makes it 35 percent longer than that in industrialized countries and 17 percent longer than that in Mexico. During the several decades of Japanese occupation before World War II, Korean citizens suffered from a poor educational system. Consequently, they placed an enormous value on education in the reconstruction period following independence and the Korean War. The average education level of employed males in the nonagricultural sector was 7.2 years in 1960, 9.3 years in 1970, and 10.3 years in 1980.

Today, enrollment levels in secondary schools and higher education is rapidly approaching the educational standards of industrial countries. Most importantly, Korea has a strikingly low wage by international standards. A comparison of hourly compensation in major industrialized countries and the Asian newly industrialized economies (NIEs) for 1987 shows that Korea had the lowest dollar wage at $1.79 an hour.

All of this would not have happened without the official sanction of the state. Under the government's authoritarian growth-first policy, tough labor laws favoring management were enacted in order to keep wages low and the work force disciplined. Unions were closely controlled by managements in cooperation with government authorities, their membership limited to companywide rather than industrywide participation, and their existence continually threatened by the government's power to dissolve them. Strikes were virtually outlawed, and those that did occur were dealt with swiftly and often harshly. While real wages have risen, they have lagged behind the growth in labor productivity, helping Korea maintain its competitive export base.

Things are changing, however, and rapidly. Presidential candidate Roh Tae-Woo's dramatic call for wide-ranging political reforms at the end of June 1987 was like the breaking of a dam of pentup frustrations and demands. In line with its decision to give more free play to democratic forces, the government announced a new hands-off policy of letting unions and management settle their own problems. Reacting quickly to this change of heart, labor unrest gathered strength, culminating in nationwide strikes that spread like wildfire, affecting all sectors of Korea's industry. In the third quarter of 1987, there were close to 3,200 labor disputes, more than in the previous 10 years, resulting in hundreds of millions of dollars in lost output and exports. The demonstrations covered the broad spectrum of labor issues from the demand for better pay and working conditions to the right to form independent labor unions. The higher wage settlements that were concluded after the strikes pushed up wage rates in manufacturing by an average 19.4 percent in 1987.

Labor trouble came to the surface again in the second quarter of 1988 as unions and companies went through the annual ritual of spring wage negotiations. However, it was on a much smaller scale than in the previous year with an average of 5.6 new strikes a day in the first five months compared with 19.7 a day in the second half of 1987. Also, very few were accompanied by violence, the prevailing attitude on both sides of the bargaining table being one of "let's play by the rules," now that the rules had been changed. Since the right to form independent unions was no longer in question, a major motivation for violent action was eliminated, and the negotiations focused on economic issues of better wages and working conditions.

The unions seem to be learning from past experience and becoming better organized and more disciplined. Union leaders prevented workers from damaging equipment during strikes and warded off infiltration of the labor movement by campus radicals or company provocateurs. The rank and file reciprocated by showing greater faith in their leaders, which has contributed to a greater degree of stability in union leadership. Of the 360 or so strikes in early 1988, more than two thirds had been settled by the end of April. Workers in the major textile, apparel, and footwear companies settled on wage raises of 10 percent to 14 percent. Wage settlements in the automobile, electronics, and shipbuilding industries were 10 percent to 15 percent higher.

The era of cheap Korean labor is over. Now that the labor-management equation is more balanced, workers can be expected to demand and get real wage increases in line with productivity. Labor can also be expected to slacken off somewhat in its work efforts and begin to enjoy the fruits of its labor more in the form of leisure. Thus, it is likely that Korea's competitive edge will narrow and it will begin losing ground, particularly in labor-intensive lines of production, to other producers in the region such as Thailand and China. Nevertheless, the labor force will remain highly skilled and industrious. Matched with a well-developed infrastructure and high rates of investment, this will give Korea an incomparable advantage in developing its modern high-tech sector.

SAVINGS AND INVESTMENT

Rapid economic growth has been accompanied by a considerable increase in the ratio of investment to GNP, which has more than doubled to nearly 34 percent in 25 years. Higher investment has been financed primarily through substantial growth in domestic savings, both in the private and public sectors, but also through foreign borrowing. The increase in the rate of private savings was associated with the development of financial institutions and domestic capital markets. In the public sector, the savings ratio increased substantially in the late 1960s and again in the late 1970s, as the tax to GNP ratio rose in response to changes in the tax system and improvements in tax administration. A liberal credit policy for industry supported economic development, but it resulted in high rates of inflation. The rate of increase of the consumer price index averaged about 14 percent during 1961–78.

With the notable growth of domestic savings, there was less reliance on foreign savings. The share of foreign savings to GNP declined from 7 percent during the first half of the 1960s to 4.5 percent in the second half of the 1970s. Nevertheless, these savings remained an important source of funds, particularly after the first wave of oil price increases, which raised the need for foreign resources. The use of foreign savings has been characterized by heavy reliance on borrowing from commercial sources, with limited resort to concessional sources or to direct foreign investment inflows. The availability of private foreign capital, in turn, has been facilitated by Korea's excellent export performance and its relative political stability. By the end of 1985, Korea's external debt had reached $47.6 billion, fourth-highest in the developing world.

The turning point for the Korean economy came in 1986. Three worldwide economic developments combined to push the current account into surplus. First, interest rates declined from their peaks of 1982–83, and debt service fell sharply. Second, the crash in oil prices saved Korea hundreds of millions of dollars on its oil import bill. Finally, and most importantly, the sharp decline of the dollar and the pegging of the won to the dollar dramatically improved Korea's international competitiveness at the expense of Japan. Thus, what Korean economists referred to as "the blessing of the three lows"—low interest rates, low oil prices, and the low dollar—were responsible for triggering the Korean boom. This has already resulted in three successive years of double digit growth and a cumulative current account surplus of almost $30 billion. Thus, the trend toward narrowing structural deficits on the country's external savings account has been consummated, and a pattern of structural surpluses appears finally to have emerged.

In 1986 and 1987, the mushrooming current account surpluses went into paying off the public external debt. As a result, total debt fell to $35.6 billion by the end of 1987, dropping Korea down the ranks of the large Asian borrowers to third place behind Indonesia and India. More recently, policy makers have been running into difficulties in getting private entities to prepay their external debt. The rising won and high domestic interest rates make it more attractive to hold foreign rather than domestic liabilities. Thus, almost two thirds of the influx of foreign exchange in 1988 had gone into building up reserves. Central bank reserves reached $12.35 billion by year-end 1988, up sharply from $3.58 billion a year earlier. This put policy makers in a bind because the rapid buildup in reserves adds to the money supply and inflationary pressures. However, in a more liberal policy environment, their ability to force private borrowers to follow their directives is more restricted. Thus, we expect that Korea's current account surpluses will continue to run ahead of the repayment of debt, so debt will decline only gradually to $19 billion by 1991.

As regards domestic savings, Korea has been running budget surpluses since 1982. Although the central account was projected to be in balance in 1988, the continued net inflows through the 17 special accounts caused the consolidated surplus to reach 1.68 trillion won (1.3 percent of GDP). The booming economy has continued to bring in above-target tax revenue growth. Revenues rose 19 percent in 1988, well in excess of the 12.7 percent growth originally foreseen. Thus, the continued improvement in the external situation has helped in further strengthening Korea's healthy public savings account. Private savings have also been rising steadily as the robust performance of the economy at the macro level is reflected in growth in personal incomes at the micro level. The overall national savings rate (36 percent in 1987) has now risen to the point where it has outstripped the investment rate (31 percent in 1987). This situation can only be expected to continue, so, increasingly, Korea will have to find mechanisms to channel its savings surplus overseas through direct investment, commercial lending, and foreign aid.

GOVERNMENT POLICY

Korea is a case study of how government intervention can work if it is properly designed and implemented. The government adopted a two-step strategy of import substitution followed by export promotion rather than rely exclusively on one or the other. After the end of the Korean War in 1953, Korea started out with an industrialization strategy based entirely on the import substitution of nondurable consumer goods and intermediate inputs. It used tariff protection and licensing to create a sheltered market for the development of infant industries in textiles and footwear. However, by 1960, Korea had exhausted all possibilities for further rapid growth because of the limited size of the domestic market. This factor and large capital requirements, especially of foreign exchange, precluded the import substitution of machinery and consumer durables industries and their intermediate inputs.

Thus, Korea turned its industries toward producing for world markets through a system of subsidies, credit, and exchange rate policy. The credit system channeled financial resources at subsidized rates to preferred export activities. The tax system provided an exemption from import duties for export content (often amounting to much more than a drawback), favorable tax rates on profits and incomes, and direct cash subsidies. Finally, with the exception of the period 1979–81, government policy avoided an overvalued exchange rate, thus sustaining the profitability of the traded goods sector. Unlike the Latin American experience, Korean policy makers shrewdly took advantage of the base they had created through import substitution to develop an export sector at a later stage rather than place too heavy and too long an emphasis on import substitution.

The pattern of development Korea had followed for its light manufacturing industries was repeated when it decided to develop a base in heavy and chemical industries (HCIs) in 1973. The change in strategy had both political and economic roots. The opening of U.S. relations with China and the fear of a possible withdrawal of American troops prompted the government to seek an industrial base for an independent defense effort. On the economic side, the objective of deepening the industrial structure was seen as a logical response to the rapidly rising Korean wage rate and increased global competition in some of Korea's traditional export industries. At the same time, Japanese penetration of global steel, electronics, and automobile markets provided a model of immediate relevance.

Thus, Korea entered a new phase of industrialization. The government picked an industry to develop, granted it blanket protection from imports, and financed entrepreneurs through subsidies and preferential loans. The targeted industries included iron and steel, machinery, shipbuilding, automobiles, and petrochemicals. Forced private savings were used to mobilize resources and these were then channeled, often at negative real interest rates, into HCI projects. As a result of these policies, the HCI sector expanded rapidly, accounting for 57 percent of value added in manufacturing by 1984. The investments were large enough to exploit the economies of scale needed to make these industries competitive on world markets, and by the late 1970s, having successfully met the objective of import substitution, most of them began to come on-stream as export industries.

The second oil price hike of 1979 highlighted the shortcomings of such an aggressive heavy industrialization drive. The global recession that followed the oil shock created substantial amounts of underutilized capacity in the HCI sector. Also, the policy of focusing almost exclusively on the development of this sector implied that Korea's comparative advantage in light industries was not fully realized. More fundamentally, the HCI program substituted bureaucratic judgment for the test of the market in determining which industries to promote. As a result, in many cases, companies suffered from a lack of experience in selling on international markets resulting in targets not being met, high unit costs, and substantial losses.

The problems of the industrialization drive led to a rapid reorientation of policies. The HCI sector was forcibly restructured in line with its diminished growth prospects, and credit was reallocated toward light industries and small firms. Selective liberalization of imports of intermediate products crucial to the export sector was carried out to keep Korean products competitive on world markets and also to defuse protectionist pressures among Korea's major trading partners. As a result, the import liberalization ratio reached 92 percent in 1986 from 68 percent in 1979, and tariff rates were reduced from 39 percent to 20 percent over the same period.

In the face of continuing trade demands from the United States based on a bilateral trade surplus that began to decline only last year, current economic discussion in Korea revolves around the need to open markets more quickly to foreign goods while minimizing the damage to—and political opposition from—domestic interests. This has opened the door to a debate on the country's cornerstone export-led growth strategy itself. Proponents of a more domestically oriented economy argue that all incentives for exporters should be abolished and the government should not assist in building new export industries. In fact, government intervention has been declining, as is clear from comparing two key emerging industries—cars and electronics—with the shipbuilding and heavy chemicals industries developed in the 1970s.

RECENT DEVELOPMENTS

Domestic Sector

Real GDP grew 11.3 percent in 1988, slightly lower than the previous year's 11.8 percent. This was powered by surging exports, which grew 13 percent in real terms, and brisk investment spending, which rose 11.8

percent. Private consumption spending accelerated to 9.6 percent, a lagged response to the strong growth in the economy in 1986 and 1987. On the supply side, manufacturing output, which accounts for about a third of the total, registered a 13.0 percent expansion despite the widespread work stoppages caused by labor disputes in the third quarter. 1988 marked the third year of the export boom, but growth is increasingly being supplemented by domestic demand. Domestic sales of cars and consumer durables have registered 30 percent to 40 percent growth, causing manufacturers to expand capacity rapidly.

GDP growth will slow to 6.5 percent in 1989 as export growth decelerates due to a stronger won and renewed work stoppages. Export demand from the United States is becoming weaker as Korea sells less and buys more from its biggest trading partner. However, export demand from Japan is surging. Korean exports to Japan are sucked in by a domestic demand-led boom in the Japanese economy. Rapidly growing exports to European markets will also contribute to economic expansion, although protectionism here is a bigger problem than in the United States.

The hallmark of Korea's banking system has been the reliance on quantitative restrictions rather than the price mechanism in determining the allocation of credit. In a truly revolutionary move, the government took the first step toward deregulation in December 1988 by allowing commercial banks to set their own lending rates. Deposit rates, however, will be deregulated in a phased manner over the next 18 months. Previously, all interest rates were set by the Bank of Korea within a band of 10 percent to 11.5 percent annually. With the demand for funds outstripping their supply at these rates as industrialists make plans to add to capacity, lending rates have moved up after decontrol. However, in the longer run, interest rates should settle back down, given that the country's savings rate is now outstripping the investment rate.

One negative side effect of the booming economy has been the resurgence of inflation. In 1988, consumer price inflation reached 7.1 percent, while wholesale price inflation averaged 2.7 percent. By comparison, the CPI rose 3 percent and the WPI rose 0.5 percent in 1987. The government has attached a very high priority to fighting inflation. Through the course of 1988, it cut domestic oil prices, reduced utility rates and excise taxes, and attempted to rein in the growth of the money supply through the issue of monetary stabilization bonds and the raising of the rediscount rate. Over the longer run, inflation should subside as the current account surplus is reduced and the surge in liquidity is controlled by dismantling foreign exchange controls and increasing imports.

External Sector

Korea's phenomenal success in the last few years has been driven by an export surge that produced the country's first significant current account surplus in 1986. The revaluation of the yen against other major OECD currencies has given Korean products a tremendous competitive advantage in world markets. The boom continued unabated in 1988 with preliminary estimates indicating exports reached $59.7 billion, 29 percent higher than in 1987, while imports totaled $48.2 billion, a 25 percent rise. The trade surplus amounted to $11.5 billion, up from $7.7 billion the year before. Buoyed by strong revenue growth in tourism and transportation and reduced interest payments, the current account surplus reached a record $14.2 billion, 44 percent larger than 1987.

Korea's export successes have not been without cost, however. They have exacerbated the imbalances in its trading patterns with its major partners, increasing trade frictions. Based on the tremendous success that low-cost Korean manufacturers have had in penetrating the U.S. consumer market, Korea has run a growing trade surplus against the United States since 1982. The surplus peaked at $9.6 billion in 1987. In relative terms, the United States is Korea's largest single trading partner buying 39 percent of its exports but supplying only 21 percent of its imports in 1987. Korea has come under heavy pressure from the United States to open its markets to American products and services and to revalue the won.

After months of sometimes heated controversy, Korea finally agreed to the opening of its beef market in 1988, increased purchases of agricultural products, and the removal of sales restrictions and tariffs on the imports of U.S. cigarettes. Starting in July 1988, the government also announced an accelerated program of tariff reductions that would take the prevailing average tariff rate of 18.1 percent to 7.1 percent by 1993. While further progress is inevitable on market opening if Korea is to continue to rely on expanding exports to the U.S., the government will be constrained in its ability to move as quickly and decisively as the United States would like because such moves are politically unpopular with the Korean population.

The revaluation of the won against the dollar, which began in July 1986, has also been attacked as another concession to U.S. pressure.

Nevertheless, the government will have to continue to raise the won in an effort to rectify the U.S. trade imbalance. From July 1986 to the end of 1988, the won has been revalued a cumulative 23.7 percent. In 1989, we project it to rise another 9 percent, ending the year at 620 to the dollar. These measures have begun to have some effect on the bilateral trade surplus. For the first time in seven years, the surplus fell by 9 percent in 1988, to $8.7 billion, as imports from the United States jumped 45.7 percent while exports to the United States went up only 16.9 percent.

The growing trade deficit with Japan, which has partly offset the growing surplus with the United States, is likely to turn around even more quickly. The deficit dropped 30.5 percent, to $3.6 billion in 1988. Efforts to sell into the Japanese market are meeting with success as exports rose 46.1 percent. In an ironic twist, the Japanese, who have often been the target of protectionist actions in the past, are now considering such moves to restrict knitwear imports from Korea. At the same time, Korea is diversifying its sourcing for industrial imports away from Japan through a combination of localization and increased purchases from the United States. Thus, imports from Japan increased only 16.2 percent during 1988.

Export growth is expected to decelerate to 10 percent in 1989. The rising won will feed through into higher prices for Korean products and dampen demand in the major U.S. market. However, the potential of the Japanese market where Korea enjoys a huge cost advantage has not been fully tapped. The sourcing of imported machinery, parts, and components will continue to be switched from Japan to the United States and Europe as Korea makes progress toward correcting the imbalances in its trading patterns. Overall imports will register 23 percent growth in 1989, resulting in a trade surplus between $6 billion and $6.5 billion and a current account surplus again in the range of $8–9 billion.

In the face of rapidly mounting reserves, Korea is taking steps to control the infusion of liquidity into the economy by allowing a greater outflow of foreign exchange. Restrictions on overseas purchases of real estate are to be drastically eased, and steps are to be taken to promote direct and portfolio investment overseas by Korean firms. Overseas investment by Korean firms reached $397 million in 1987, more than double the amount recorded the previous year and more than 40 percent of the total invested abroad over the past 20 years. Setting up plants overseas also defuses protectionism, so it seems logical that the pattern of investment by region is weighted toward the United States and Canada and by sector toward manufacturing.

The government has allowed limited portfolio investment to the extent of $330 million by domestic financial institutions in overseas markets. In 1988, the outflow reached only $189 million because the continued appreciation of the won, high domestic real interest rates, and the booming stock market make investment in domestic assets more attractive. The first Korean mutual fund to invest in overseas equities was to be launched late in 1989 with a planned investment of $50 million. The government has also tightened restrictions on the inflow of speculative capital from abroad, which has been going into real estate purchases and driving up land prices.

THE STOCK MARKET

For years, foreign interest has centered around the question of when the Seoul stock market would be opened to overseas investors. However, the current account surpluses Korea began generating three years ago have given policy makers second thoughts about letting an influx of portfolio investment add to the surge in liquidity the economy has been experiencing in recent months. The Ministry of Finance has finally circulated a draft plan that allows for a gradual opening of the stock market, culminating in 1992 when foreigners would be allowed to buy directly into domestic companies.

The plan has four distinct phases. In the first phase in 1989, a third offshore country fund would be established in Tokyo to complement the existing New York-based Korea Fund and the London-based Korea Eurofund. Three more closed-end trust funds totaling about $100 million would be floated, and domestic companies would be given easier access to overseas financing. In the second phase in 1990, restrictions on the use of proceeds from Euro-equity issues would be relaxed, and the Korea Fund and the Korea Euro-fund would be allowed to issue a third tranche each. In 1991 restrictions on the conversion of existing convertible bonds and on the domestic trading of the shares resulting from the conversions would be eliminated. Finally in 1992, direct foreign investment in listed Korean companies up to a limit of 5 percent would be permitted, foreign securities firms would be allowed to upgrade their representative offices to branch offices, and limits on foreign ownership of Korean brokerage houses would be relaxed from 10 percent to 30 percent.

PROSPECTS AND CONCLUSIONS

The Korean economy seems set to grow at between 7 percent and 7.5 percent annually over the next decade. Exports will continue to be the main engine of growth over this period, although their direction and composition will change markedly. Japan is becoming more important as a second engine of export growth in the Pacific region because its domestic boom is drawing in substantial imports of low-tech consumer products from the Asian NIEs. Korea is also eagerly expanding trade ties with the European Economic Community and pursuing trade opportunities with the Communist world, an area that had been largely ignored. The diversification of export markets will put the economy less at risk in the event of a downturn in the U.S. market. Also, the domestic market, while not deep enough to sustain growth on a long-term basis, can be reflated to cushion some of the impact of a drop in external demand. The export successes of the last 10 to 15 years have led to a steady rise in per capita incomes in the NIEs, giving them the capacity to expand domestic demand faster than any other region in the world.

Korea is also being forced to confront the problem of industrial restructuring for its declining industries such as shoes, textiles, and toys. Two factors have made this necessary—the continued rise of the won against the dollar and rising labor costs. Both these factors have negative implications for the competitiveness of Korea's labor-intensive products such as textiles, footwear, and toys, which are facing increasing competition from other developing countries. On the other hand, Korea needs to upgrade and improve its product range in order to stay one step ahead in the export game. In the past, the government had been integrally involved in the business of picking winners and losers. Now it is trying to reduce its interventionist role in industrial development by no longer supporting declining industries and promoting rising industries. However, this is going to be difficult. The declining industries, such as shipbuilding, are ones the government actively pushed in earlier years, so it has to bear some of the responsibility for restructuring. Also, as Korea moves up the ladder of development, higher value-added technology-based industries become more important—and more expensive. A valid argument can be made that the government cannot afford to remain neutral if such emerging industries as aerospace and biotechnology are to develop successfully.

On balance, it is likely the government will continue to encourage, though less overtly than in the past, the development of the high-tech sectors, such as automobiles and electronics, that are beginning to give Korea a new profile on its export markets. An increasingly large proportion of GNP will need to be devoted to research and development in order to ensure Korea's export products remain competitive. The development of small- and medium-sized enterprises, which has been largely neglected in the drive for industrialization, will be emphasized as suppliers of parts and components to the large industrial conglomerates. Rising labor costs are less relevant to the modern high-tech sector because these industries are more capital intensive. Also, larger productivity increases will allow them to absorb the impact of higher wages comfortably. High productivity growth is the result of both a well-developed infrastructure and a pool of highly motivated, well-educated labor that Korean industries can draw on.

The sharp reversal in Korea's fortunes has its planners grappling with a new problem—the problem of plenty, or how to deal with sustained current account surpluses. The surge in liquidity this has led to has caused inflation to rise to its highest level since 1981. The limited measures taken so far to bring the surplus under control—the revaluation of the won, the removal of nontariff barriers, and the reduction of import tariffs—have not had much effect. We project continued current account surpluses, declining only gradually. The fall in external debt will not match these large surpluses until interest rates come down and the won stabilizes against the U.S. dollar. Without drastic measures such as the elimination of all restrictions on capital outflows, reserves will continue their rapid rise and inflation will stay in the 5 percent range.

REFERENCES

[1] Aghelvi, Bijan B., and Jorge Marquez-Ruarte, "A Case of Successful Adjustment: Korea's Experience during 1980–84," *Occasional Paper 39,* International Monetary Fund, August 1985.

[2] Dornbusch, Rudiger, and Yung Chul Park, "Korean Growth Policy," *Brookings Papers on Economic Activity 2* (1987).

[3] *Far Eastern Economic Review,* various issues.

[4] *The Asian Wall Street Journal,* various issues.

CHAPTER 13

SELLING INTO THE KOREAN MARKET

Hee Yol Yu
Soon Young Hong
Sung Ho Cho

A NEW MARKET FOR U.S. PRODUCTS

INTRODUCTION

Korea, now a newly industrializing economy whose balance of payments has shifted from chronic deficits to sustained surpluses, is striving to realize the qualitative development needed to attain the status of an industrially advanced country.

The recent Seoul Olympics substantially boosted Korea's international status. Korea finds itself at a crucial point at which it must respond to new and changing conditions.

The remarkable turnaround in Korea's current account position raised new challenges for Korea, which had previously directed its efforts toward dealing with a weak and precarious external position. Initially, there was some apprehension that the strengthened external position might only be transitory.

However, Korea responded throughout 1988 with a broad range of measures to stem the rise in the current account surplus. Import liberalization and tariff reductions were accelerated, financial incentives for imports were introduced, while those for exports were cut, foreign exchange and investment controls were eased, and the gradual appreciation of the Korean won against the U.S. dollar since mid-1986 was continued.

Despite major and prolonged political disturbances during midyear, the economy continued to improve in 1988, Korea becoming the 10th-largest trading nation in the world with a trade volume of $112.5 billion. Taking advantage of this booming economy, foreign investment missions have rushed to Seoul to do business.

This chapter first covers the current situation of the Korean economy, focusing on the issue of internationalization, followed by business opportunities available in Korea.

ECONOMIC OVERVIEW

For the past quarter century, Korea has continuously enjoyed high economic growth, together with phenomenal expansion of trade volume. Of all the various success factors that have been cited, perhaps the key element has been the favorable combination of a hardworking labor force, innovative entrepreneurs, and appropriate government policies that made possible the successful implementation of an outward-oriented development strategy.

From 1986 to 1988, the Korean economy has recorded an impressive average annual growth rate of 12 percent with relatively stable prices. This outstanding performance is mainly the result of the stabilization efforts that have been pursued since the early 1980s along with the favorable international economic conditions that have emerged since the mid-1980s.

A significant drop in oil prices, a decline in interest rates, and drastic realignment in the exchange rates of the major currencies helped create the supportive environment that has enabled the Korean economy to convert the chronic external deficits of the past into surpluses since 1986. Subsequently, the foreign debt, which amounted to over half of the GNP in 1985, has been rapidly reduced, with Korea projected to become a creditor nation for the first time in 1989.

In 1989, the nation's economic growth rate is likely to slow to 8 percent, compared with 1988's 12.1 percent (see Table 13–1). This does not mean the Korean economy is in a recession, but rather that, as many experts have pointed out, the Korean economy is now on the right track, departing from its previously overheated state.

The Korean government forecasts the GNP for 1989 will total $193 billion, with per capita GNP reaching $4,570. Also, the current account surplus is projected to $9.5 billion, compared with the estimated $13.8 billion in 1988, with the trade surplus falling to $7.5 billion in 1989, from $10.8 billion the previous year.

The jobless rate is seen to rise to 2.8 percent in 1989 from the 2.6 percent in 1988, mainly because of the steady speed of economic growth in 1989 in comparison with 1988's rapid pace.

TABLE 13–1
Macroeconomic Projections for 1989 (Units: $ billion)

Item	1987	1988	1989
GNP	$118.6	$156.1	$193.0
GNP growth rate	12.0%	12.1%	8.0%
Per capita GNP*	$2,861	$3,728	$4,570
Current account	$ 9.9	$13.8	$ 9.5
Trade balance	$ 7.7	$10.8	$ 7.5
Exports	$46.2	$60.7	$69.0
Imports	$38.6	$51.8	$61.5
Outstanding foreign debt	$35.6	$32.0	$28.5
Overseas assets	$13.2	$25.3	$31.5
Net foreign debt	$22.4	$ 6.7	$−3.0
Inflation rate			
Wholesale prices	0.5%	3.0%	3.0%
Consumer prices	3.0%	7.0%	5.0%

* Unit: dollars.

MAJOR ECONOMIC POLICY DIRECTIONS IN KOREA

The Korean government places priority on the following objectives in order to realize the goal of becoming a developed country and to guide social changes by emphasizing balanced growth: (1) market opening and internationalization, (2) promotion of economic autonomy and fairness, and (3) balanced development and improvement of the quality of life.

Market Opening and Internationalization

Considering Korea's stage of economic development and trade volume, an important policy objective for Korea is to maintain harmonious international economic relations.

Even with some difficulties and dangers being exposed, particularly in the fields of agriculture and small and medium industry, the Korean government realizes that internationalization is vital for the continued growth of the economy. Through internationalization, greater competitiveness will be fostered as domestic industries are forced into open competition in the world economy.

Furthermore, internationalization is, to a large extent, an inevitable step for a highly trade-dependent economy like Korea in a world that is becoming increasingly interdependent. In other words, one's export growth can be sustained only when it is supported by increased imports from one's trading partners.

Against this background, Korea has made substantial progress in many fields since embarking on the task of internationalization in the early 1980s.

The opening of domestic markets to imports will be pursued on a broader scale, including manufactured goods, agricultural products, and services. In 1989, 96 percent of all imports into Korea require no prior import licensing, with further liberalization being realized in the next few years up to the level of advanced countries.

In the manufacturing sector, Korea has virtually liberalized all imports, while restrictive measures on imports imposed by various special laws have also been relaxed. In the service sector, markets such as advertising and shipping were recently opened up to foreigners. The government also has a plan to reduce average tariff rates annually, from the 12.7 percent of 1989 to 6.2 percent in 1993.

In addition, the government has made a more favorable environment by enhancing the protection of intellectual property rights.

However, as expected, the greatest difficulty lies in the liberalization of agricultural trade. Liberalization in this area will take more time and needs to be implemented in combination with measures to help farmers maintain their income levels.

To more effectively open domestic markets, the government has recently set up four special task forces on such policy issues as "Import Liberalization of Agricultural Products," "The Protection of Intellectual Property Rights," and "Import Regulation under Special Laws."

A second important feature of internationalization is the recycling abroad of the Korean external surpluses. This will not only contribute to the stabilization of the domestic economy but will also help the stable growth of the world economy by financing the needs of deficit nations. In this context, Korea has already recycled most of its surpluses through repayments of its foreign debt.

Furthermore, the government has recently been promoting overseas investment by Korean firms, as well as expanding its foreign aid through the Economic Development Cooperation Fund (EDCF). The anticipated effects of overseas investment include a more efficient international division of labor, while also facilitating the process of technology transfer, which is vital for smooth industrial adjustment across borders.

Liberalization of foreign exchange and capital markets will also be pursued. As a newly instated IMF Article VIII nation, Korea is undertaking appropriate measures to further liberalize foreign exchange transactions and also to gradually internationalize its currency, the Korean won. In addition, Korea's capital markets are expected to be opened on a broad scale to foreigners in the not-too-distant future.

Last, but not least, internationalization can be achieved through greater policy coordination with other nations. Closer policy coordination between nations with external surpluses and nations with deficits will help relieve the current external imbalance problem of the world economy. Surplus nations should strive for increased domestic consumption, while deficit nations should cut consumption and increase exports by implementing a proper combination of monetary and fiscal policies. A significant reduction in the world's external imbalances will be followed by a decline in protectionism and other unfavorable effects produced by these imbalances.

Korea has been endeavoring to contribute to policy coordination by cutting its current account surpluses, amounting to almost 8 percent of GNP, by opening domestic markets to imports, rapidly appreciating the won, and increasing domestic aggregate demand. It seems much more preferable for the Korean economy, however, to cut its surplus by emphasizing increased imports as opposed to rapid appreciation of the won. Appreciating the won alone would not contribute much to increasing imports and would hurt Korean exports. By following a formula that increases imports while allowing the export sector to remain viable, Korea's external surplus could be significantly reduced without excessively impairing Korean industry.

Promotion of Economic Autonomy and Fairness

The achievement of economic autonomy and fair trade is one of the most important economic policies in Korea. In this effort, the government will introduce tax reforms to alleviate the burden of low-income earners as well as to discourage windfall income through real estate speculation. The government will also liberalize the financial sector in order to establish a competitive framework for financial institutions. At the same time, Korea will continue to support the fair trade system to prevent monopolistic practices as well as to reduce the concentration of economic power.

**Balanced Development and Improvement of the
Quality of Life**

One of the government's primary policy objectives is to promote balanced development between rural and urban areas. To this end, various incentives will be provided for businesses to locate their facilities in rural areas, thereby increasing employment opportunities and nonagrarian income. Korea will also expand educational, medical, communications, and other public facilities in rural areas.

To improve income distribution and the quality of life, a minimum wage law was enacted and a national pension program drawn up. Both became effective in 1988. Also, in 1989, all citizens were covered by a nationwide medical insurance program. Meanwhile, the government will boost its efforts to upgrade living standards for people in low-income brackets.

The Korean Economy in the Future

As a consequence of the aforementioned efforts, we forecast that through 1991, the target year of the plan, the Korean economy will record an average annual growth rate of 9 percent, GNP will reach $240 billion, and per capita income will be $5,500. It is also expected that the trade volume will reach $150 billion in 1991, with Korea maintaining its position as one of the world's 10 biggest traders. In addition, the current account surplus will remain at a level of about $6 billion, staying within 2 to 3 percent of GNP. Meanwhile, foreign debt will continue to decline, while foreign assets will increase such that the latter will exceed the former during 1989.

The income of farmers and laborers is expected to double during this period, exceeding the national average income level and improving income distribution.

As a result, the Korean economy will enter a more structurally sound and mature stage. The Korean government will strive to maintain harmonious relations with its economic partners and assume a responsible role appropriate for its position in the international community.

BUSINESS OPPORTUNITIES IN KOREA

Foreign Direct Investment

Overview
The legal system covering foreign investment in Korea is provided for in the Foreign Capital Inducement Act (FCIA). Based on FCIA, a wide range of policy measures actively induce foreign investment, protect foreign-invested enterprises, and facilitate their smooth operation.

Various incentives and guarantees such as tax benefits and the remittances of dividends and principal are included in these measures. In addition, the adoption of a negative list system and an automatic approval system that indirectly approves potential projects by omissions substantially broadened the range of projects eligible for foreign investment while simplifying the authorization procedures for approval.

At present, of 999 industries in the Korean Standard Industrial Classification, 788 do not appear on this list. In the manufacturing sector, 98 percent of the industries are now open to foreign investment. Also, as part of the ongoing efforts to actively induce foreign investment, the government revised the Presidential Decrees and Working Rules concerning FCIA.

Highlights of the revision include an increase in projects qualifying for automatic approval, delegation of authority to handle automatic approval projects to the governor of the Bank of Korea, and reduction of industries eligible for exemptions.

Guidelines for Foreign Investment

The current Guidelines for Foreign Investment, effective from January 7, 1988, are as follows:

Minimum Foreign Investment Amount. The minimum allowable amount of foreign investment shall be the equivalent of US$100,000. This amount may be reduced to $50,000 when the foreign investor introduces technology and enters into a joint venture agreement with a domestic small- or medium-sized company to form a new small- or medium-sized enterprise. There is no restriction on additional investment.

Approval of Eligible Projects. The Ministry of Finance approves foreign investments in the wholesale and retail sectors that are not prohibited or restricted under the guidelines set forth and consults with the minister concerned when approving investments that fall under the following cases:

1. General wholesale trade:
   - In the case where a business sells foreign brand products.
   - In the case where a business sells imported goods.
2. Retail trade:
   - In the case where a business establishes a single shop, the floor area of which is over 700 square meters, or two or more shops, regardless of the floor area.

The Minister of Finance approves foreign investment in the following areas (as listed in the Korean Standard Industrial Classification), provided a joint venture is formed with an existing company either authorized or licensed for that area of business:

- Construction.
- Nonlife insurance.
- Distilling of ethyl alcohol, or the manufacture of ginseng wine, *soju on cheongju* (traditional Korean liquors).

The Minister of Finance approves foreign investment in the following industrial sectors only for joint ventures with an existing Korean company in the same line of business:

- Manufacture of diesel engines (above 320 horsepower).
- Manufacture of cultivators, tractors, rice planters, binders, combines, and sprayers.

- Manufacture of excavators, loaders, bulldozers, cranes, and motor-graders.
- Manufacture of transformers, circuit breakers, gas-insulated sub-stations (GIS), disconnecting switches of ultra high voltage (above 154 kilovolts), and heavy electric machinery.
- Manufacture of optical fibers, optical fiber-covered wires, and cables.
- Manufacture of motor vehicles.
- Manufacture of electronic switching systems.
- Manufacture of textile fabrics.
- Manufacture of silicon steel, manganese steel, and silicon-manganese alloy steel.
- Bleaching, dyeing, and finishing textiles.
- Manufacture of vegetable oils and fats, and husking and milling cereals.
- Manufacture of beans and similar products.
- Manufacture of starches.

The Minister of Finance approves foreign investment in projects inherent to small- and medium-sized enterprises and small- and medium-sized industry systematized items in accordance with the Small and Medium Industry Adjustment Law and the Small and Medium Industry Systematization Promotion Law.

Foreign Investment Procedures
The procedures required for foreign investment are summarized in Figure 13–1.

Tax Incentives

Korea, as is the case in most countries, treats foreign-invested companies the same as domestic companies. All laws, including those dealing with finance, administration, tax procedures, and employee relations apply equally to all firms in Korea. The many tax benefits and exemptions domestic companies receive are provided to foreign-invested companies as well. These benefits include special depreciation or tax credits for investing in certain key industries, such as machinery and electronics. Or, if the industry is considered a small and medium industry, a number of tax incentives encourage investment, development and innovation of technology, and large export amounts. Again, all these tax

FIGURE 13–1
Flow Chart for Foreign Investment

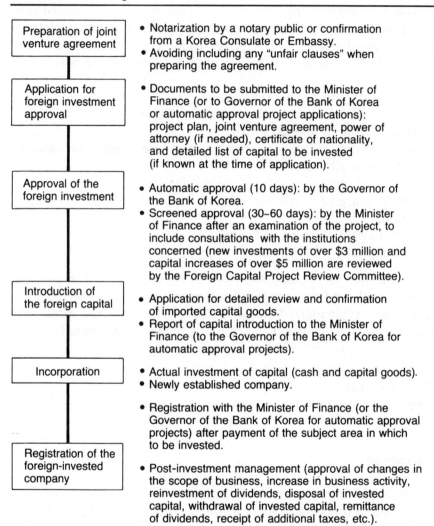

benefits and incentives are available to both foreign-invested and domestic enterprises.

The exempted taxes are the corporation tax, the dividend income tax, the acquisition tax, and the property tax. In the meantime, FCIA stipulates the conditions, one of which must be fulfilled, for projects eligible for tax benefits, as listed in Table 13–2.

TABLE 13–2
Eligibility for Tax Benefits

Projects	Necessary Conditions
Projects accompanied by advanced technology	The project must be accompanied by the relevant technology when the following conditions exist: • Domestic self-development is considered difficult. • It is used in technology-intensive or high-tech industries as announced by MOF. • It is recognized as having remarkable economic or technological benefit by the Minister of Finance after consulting with relevant ministers and the Minister of Science and Technology.
Projects invested in by nonresident Korean nationals	Only in manufacturing industries.
Projects located in Free Export Zones	
Other projects	The project should be small- and medium-sized and should fall under the list of Industries for Preferred Fostering as a Small- and Medium-Sized Enterprise with Tax Exemptable Status.

The Negative List System

The negative list is a revised system of listing all the industries in Korea prohibited or temporarily restricted from foreign investment. This means that of the 999 industries categorized in Korea, only those industries restricted or prohibited are listed, leaving all other industries open to foreign investment. Before this negative list was a positive list system, which listed all those industries open to foreign investment. This change demonstrates the progress made by the government in its continuing efforts to open Korea's industries to foreign investment because it is much easier to list the few industries not open to foreign investment than to list the majority of those that are.

As of December 1988, 788 of these 999 industries, 79 percent of the total, were open to foreign investment. In the case of the manufacturing sector, 509 of the 522 industries, or 98 percent, were already open to foreign investment.

Foreign Investor Ownership and the Repatriation of Capital

There are no restrictions on foreign investor ownership in Korea. The amount of equity owned by the foreign investor is decided by the foreign investor and the Korean partner. Their mutual decision reached on an equity ratio will be respected by the government.

Korea has also eliminated all restrictions on the repatriation of capital and dividends. In the past, foreign investors could withdraw their investment only after two years, and were limited to remitting only 20 percent of that investment per year. These restrictions have been abolished, and the principal and dividends can be withdrawn any time the foreign investor desires.

Foreign Investment Performance

Foreign investment in Korea is booming, as manufacturers hoping to supply fast-growing export industries like automobiles and electronics, as well as those taking advantage of a buoyant domestic economy, are eager to establish their businesses in Korea.

The amount of foreign investment, on an approval basis, increased from $532 million in 1985 to $1.283 billion in 1988. Meanwhile, the number of foreign investment projects increased from 127 to 342 over the same period. 1987 and 1988 broke all records, as foreign-investment approvals edged past the $1 billion mark. Foreign investment in 1987 and 1988 alone accounted for more than 39 percent of all the foreign investment approved between 1962 and 1988. The government calculates that wholly or partially foreign-owned ventures accounted for 5.1 percent of GNP in 1986, compared with 3.5 percent in 1977.

Korea is well on its way to becoming a regional manufacturing power, if foreign investment is any indication. Car parts suppliers, from tire makers to door panel manufacturers, are rapidly establishing footholds in Korea to supply Hyundai, Daewoo, and Kia Motors. General Motors, which has a joint venture with Daewoo, and Ford Motor Co., which has a stake in Kia, are expanding their commitments.

All this investment is good news for companies selling to the domestic market. For example, the U.S. computer manufacturer Wang, which sells on the local market, figured its domestic sales would skyrocket from $2 million in 1987 to $15 million in 1988.

Japan continues to comprise most of the foreign investment—more than half of the total in 1988—accounting for $696 million, up from $494 million in 1987 (see Table 13–3). The Japanese investments are more heavily weighted in the service sector, which made up nearly half of Japan's total last year, because of the large number of Korean-Japanese who invest in Korea's service businesses rather than manufacturing.

European investments are also growing quickly, from $210 million in 1987 to $240 million in 1988, whereas American investments increased to $284 million from $255 million in 1987.

Korea's cheaper labor costs and a highly motivated, well-educated work force are the most obvious attractions for foreign companies. According to a foreign banker familiar with the car industry, in mid-1987, labor costs for U.S. car workers were $26 an hour; for Japanese, $13; and for Koreans, $2.50.

However, investment here differs from classic third world investment in search of little more than cheap assembly labor. Korea has a far superior infrastructure to its archrival Taiwan, according to leading expatriate bankers, businesspeople, and diplomats. In addition, companies investing in Korea can buy steel from one of the world's most efficient producers, while those in Taiwan must rely on imports. Besides Korea's increasingly sophisticated export industries and its growing domestic market for food, beverage, and pharmaceutical manufacturers, it is an increasingly attractive alternative to expensive Japanese production sites.

Also, foreign component supplier firms fit appropriately into the national policy of reducing Korea's reliance on imported technology.

Technology Inducement

Current Policy
The government formerly approved technology license agreements only after reviewing the necessity and extent of the technology and the amount of the royalties paid for it. Currently, however, the applications are considered automatically approved if a supplement for adjustment is not requested by the relevant ministry within 20 days of application. The system has changed from an approval system to a reporting system.

The government also further liberalized technology imports by revising the regulations governing the technology licenses effective July 1, 1988.

In general, the changes affecting technology licenses both reduce the scope of licenses that must be reported to the government for ap-

TABLE 13–3
Foreign Investment in Korea (Unit: Number of Cases/US$thousands)

Country	1962–1982	1983	1984	1985	1986	1987	1988	Total	Percentage
United States									
Cases	275	19	37	43	49	93	104	620	21.9
Amount	591,966	54,135	193,326	108,007	125,128	255,140	284,401	1,612,103	26.9
Japan									
Cases	1,137	37	52	58	109	207	177	1,777	62.9
Amount	1,066,208	168,136	164,870	364,253	137,654	494,394	696,244	3,091,759	51.7
Total									
Cases	1,576	76	108	131	205	373	352	2,821	100.0
Amount	1,055,131	269,424	422,346	532,197	353,740	1,060,212	1,282,732	5,975,782	100.0

* As of the end of 1988, Korea had 1,220 TNCs in operation.

proval and limit the types of licenses eligible for tax exemption. Until the end of June 1988, all technology license agreements with a contract term of one year or longer had to receive government approval. Pursuant to the new regulations, however, only those agreements with a contract term or royalty payment period of more than three years, including renewal terms, and with certain types of royalty payment provisions must be approved by the relevant ministry under the Foreign Capital Inducement Act. In other words, an agreement with a contract term or royalty payment period of three years or less and with a type of royalty payment provision that does not fall under a specific category does not require ministry approval.

The royalty categories that require such approval are: (1) a lump sum royalty payment of more than $100,000; (2) an initial royalty payment of more than $50,000 in combination with any running royalty; (3) a running royalty that exceeds 2 percent of the net sales amount; or (4) a royalty payment that is to be made by any method other than the aforementioned.

Moreover, an agreement with a term of less than one year and a royalty that amounts to less than $100,000 does not even need to be reported to a foreign exchange bank. In such a case, the foreign exchange bank's role is limited to certifying royalty remittances when royalties are paid.

While many foreign licensors will benefit from the reduced role of the Korean government, foreign licensors as a group will find it more difficult to qualify for tax incentives that were once available. Until the end of June 1988, foreign licensors of other than bare trademark licenses and licenses that fell into particular categories enjoyed a five-year exemption of corporate or income tax on their royalties. Now, under the new regulations, only certain highly advanced technologies are eligible for tax exemptions.

In order to qualify as highly advanced, the technology must satisfy the following four requirements listed in the new regulations: (1) the technology must be necessary to the domestic industry, (2) if other technology has already been induced for the manufacture of similar products, the new technology must be induced within four years from the date of acceptance of the reporting of such previous technology; (3) the technology must be such that it would greatly benefit the national economy and greatly contribute to the advancement of the industrial structure to which it relates and to the enhancement of competition; and (4) the technology must be for one of eight enumerated industries, i.e., the

TABLE 13–4

Number of License Agreements and Amount of Royalty Payments

	1962–81	1982	1983	1984	1985	1986	1987	1988	Total
Cases	1,977	308	362	437	454	517	637	618	5,310
Royalties ($ million)	565	116	150	213	295	411	524	676	2,950

machine, electronic, aeronautical, defense, oil refining and fine chemical, biotechnology, new material, or new energy development industries.

The relevant ministry may also require an applicant for tax exemption to submit detailed information regarding its technology, such as text certificates, patent details, and other evidence that reveals how advanced the technology is.

Number of License Agreements and Amount of Royalty Payments

The total number of technologies induced from 1962 through 1988 was 5,310, with the total amount of royalties paid being approximately $2,950 billion (see Table 13–4).

Analysis of Technology Inducement by Country

By the end of 1988, the number of technology inducements from the United States stands at 1,329, with royalty payments of $1,362 million, while the number of inducements from Japan is 2,794, with royalty payments of $923 million (see Table 13–5). The total number of inducements from and the total amount of the royalty payments to the United States and Japan is 4,123 (78 percent of total inducements) and $2,285

TABLE 13–5

Technology Inducements by Country (1962–1988)

Classification	Japan	United States	France	Germany	Others	Total
Number of inducements	2,794	1,329	209	292	686	5,310
Royalties ($ million)	923	1,362	124	112	429	2,950

TABLE 13–6
Technology Inducements per Industry (1962–1988)

	Industry					
	Mechanical	Electricity & Electronic	Petro-chemical	Metallic	Others	Total
Number of technology inducements	1,434	1,169	913	342	1,452	5,310
Percentage	27.0	22.0	17.3	6.4	27.3	100.0

million (78 percent of total royalty payments). The sources of technology inducement are heavily inclined toward these two countries.

It can also be seen from Table 13–5 that despite the number of technology inducements from the United States being smaller than that from Japan, the royalties paid to the United States constitute a larger amount than that paid to Japan. Thus, though such a sweeping statement may cause some contradictions, generally the technology induced from the United States is of a higher level than that from Japan.

Technology Inducements per Industry
According to industry, technology inducements in the mechanical, electricity and electronic, petrochemical, and metallic industries form the mainstream, possessing 73 percent of the total technology inducements in absolute numbers (see Table 13–6).

Additionally, the technology inducements in the above four industries tend to increase year after year, helping the development of industrial technology.

MAJOR POINTS INVOLVING BUSINESSES IN KOREA

Korean Management Culture

Although there may be broad agreement internationally concerning the lexicon of business, the cognitive maps that guide the thought and behavior of those conducting business can vary significantly from one society to another. Following are some characteristics of Korean management culture.

Many American and European managers are working for Korean firms in Korea and elsewhere. Numerous personal contacts with them have revealed they are either frustrated, confused, or delighted in their binational work setting. They often mention the Korean manager's humanistic concern for employees, as represented by fringe benefits, job security, and collective values, as well as being expressed in the company-as-family ideology and consensus decision making.

Korean culture greatly differs from Western culture, and as such, the culture of Korean firms is different from Western firms. With the surge of global interest in Korea's economic success, Koreans are establishing more overseas companies. For instance, Lucky Gold Star has expanded from Alabama to New Jersey, and from Korea to Germany. The Korean style, or culture, of management may confront and then clash with local, American, or European styles of management culture. In this sense, cultural consonance, cultural dissonance, or cultural adjustment will evolve.

Of course, Korean firms can recruit American or European managers and workers who can understand the Korean culture and style. There are many Western managers and workers who are fond of Korean culture and Korean people. These are the best people available. Foreign managers are very important because they greatly contribute to the internationalization or Americanization of Korean firms while involving themselves in close interaction with Korean people at the headquarters. Their attitudes tend to become very delicate and sensitive when "Korean only" meetings exclude Westerners from information and decisions they consider critical.

American managers of Korean firms tend to talk about constraints in terms of cultural differences. *Cultural differences* is an inclusive term frequently used by them as shorthand for explaining their frustrations in communication breakdowns. The concept of the job differs between Korean and Western managers, especially American managers. As such, the title, responsibility, authority, and pay differ in crucial ways. To Western managers, the Korean concept of one's title is somewhat vague, authoritarian, and not pragmatic. The Korean concept of responsibility is also vague and not specific, minimal not maximal, or, "you shape your responsibility because you are the manager." Also, the Korean concept of authority is visible only after you pay your dues to your company—your remarkable contribution to the firm's success. Lastly, the Korean concept of pay is that money is not important. Money is not the most beautiful thing to Koreans—no sensible Korean asks how much they will receive for compensation.

In the United States, a written record of the requirements and rights of a particular job is expected; a job description represents the normal guidelines for orderly and predictable action. Korean firms don't begin with the job description. Rather, they begin with the person. The job description, if any, is simply the formal, basic, or minimum standard work content. American or Western managers are confused at this.

Korean firms ask their managers to create their own environment, delegating their responsibilities. In this way, there is no one-paragraph job description for Korean managers as there is in the United States. By Korean thinking, one paragraph cannot cover the unlimited scope of the manager's duties. No specific job description has brought about Korea's economic success. Even though American and European managers can understand that, they cannot get used to it.

Korean managers view the firm first, while American managers tend to view their own interests over that of the firm's. Therefore, the possibility of clashes exists in a firm in which Koreans and Americans work together. This is especially true when Koreans interpret American behavior as being a self-serving concern. "Avoiding blame" or "getting ahead" is realized at the expense of group unity. In short, Koreans emphasize teamwork much more than Americans do.

The Korean pay system can also be understood from that perspective. Differential pay is present, but most Korean firms and workers prefer flat increases, assuming everybody works equally hard. As this differential pay hurts teamwork and the individual worker's welfare, Korean firms downplay the money. But Americans consider the pay as one of the most important factors, if not *the* most. In a sense, Korean firms positively test the Maslow hierarchy of need theory and the Herzberg motivator theory.

Conducting Successful Business in Korea

For those involved in selling to Korean consumers, problems arise in the areas of marketing and distribution. The distribution channels in Korea are virtually controlled by the conglomerates that constructed them, and they do not provide foreigners with easy access.

For those attempting to establish a presence on Korean soil, the problems become even more complex. The Korean management style is based on a hierarchy extending from the very lowest worker through to the upper reaches of management, and right on into the government. The government works as a third partner in most business dealings. Unless foreigners carefully attend to the government role, they will never attain success.

More often than not, foreign businesspeople try in vain to impose their own style of management and problem solving on Koreans. This distances the newcomers from those they should befriend and also blocks whatever lines of communication might have initially opened. Communication turns out to be the greatest area of conflict in any arrangement between Koreans and foreigners, and it is not just a result of differences in language.

All of our conversations with foreign businesspeople in Korea contained a common thread. First, to do business in Korea, common sense and basic business steps must be followed. There are no free lunches here or anywhere else.

Second, attitude counts. If foreigners are too proud of themselves or if they fail to show respect for those they encounter, they will not succeed. This lesson can be applied throughout the world.

Neither of these messages are great revelations. We were surprised to find that every minor gripe as well as every major conflict on the part of both Koreans and foreigners belonged to one of these points of fundamental advice. By listening to the problems people have generally encountered, we discovered that difficulties could often be avoided through self-control, tolerance, and interest.

This seems easy enough, but in reality it isn't. It is difficult to look in a mirror and judge yourself as others will judge you, and all too simple to color your vision with expectations.

EXPORT OPPORTUNITIES IN KOREA

DYNAMISM OF THE KOREAN ECONOMY

Korea's economy is exploding. From 1986 to 1988, the Korean economy registered growth rates of about 12 percent. Once a quiet and poverty-stricken nation, often described as "the Land of Morning Calm," Korea has transformed itself into a bustling industrial powerhouse. For a quarter of a century from 1962 to 1988, Korea's gross national product expanded from $2.3 billion to $156.1 billion, and per capita GNP soared from $87 to $3,728. Trade volume expanded almost 200-fold in the same period, reaching $112.5 billion in 1988.

Dynamic expansion of the Korean economy has provided participants with both precious opportunities and formidable challenges. Those who faced the challenges and capitalized on the opportunities prospered, but the risk-avoiders were left behind. A poor college boy turned multibillionaire is not uncommon. On the other hand, few of the top 10 companies of the 1940s survived the rapid transition in the following decades.

The fast pace of the transition gives fresh shocks even to the local residents. The rapidly changing Korean economy poses a myriad of problems to foreign businesses. But lucrative business opportunities are there. Fruits of growth are waiting to be exploited and reaped by those who have insights into where the Korean economy stands and in which direction it is moving.

KOREA'S ECONOMY: THE PAST AND THE PRESENT

Korea has undergone in the last 25 years or so what could be described as a shortened version of Britain's industrial revolution. While an overpopulated, resource-poor nation was on a single-minded march toward industrialization and growth, it was unavoidable that the nation made trade-offs among priority areas and became plagued with excesses and tensions.

Through the implementation of a series of five-year economic development plans, Korea has developed a unique mix of free market economy combined with heavy government intervention. The government has maintained majority holdings in all of the major commercial banks and exercised tight control over the inflow of foreign capital. With its quasimonopolistic command over financial resources, the government has implemented various industrial and export incentive systems and concentrated investment in strategic industries. Labor-intensive light industries of the 1960s followed by the heavy and chemical industries of the 1970s were high in the priority of the government.

Such a policy carried mixed blessings. It rapidly drove Korea up the ladder of industrialization but generated many undesirable by-products as well. The ensuing distortion in the allocation of resources had become apparent as the projects involved were getting too large and complicated to be controlled by the bureaucrats. More importantly, pursuit of economies of scale, which were regarded as essential to compete in the world market, led the government to concentrate investment and discourage competition. As a result, giant conglomerates prospered in close collaboration with the bureaucracy.

To finance the import of capital goods necessary for massive industrialization, Korea borrowed heavily from abroad. Short on foreign reserves, the government preached that consumption was a vice and consumption of luxury imports purchased with hard currency was an even more serious sin.

Such a regimented system based primarily on the perseverence and austerity of people could not be of a stable or lasting nature. The system began to display signs of strain in the late 1970s and early 1980s. Persistent inflation and growing rigidities in the economy were the symptoms of the disease.

It was, however, not until 1987–88 when political democratization of the nation was in full gear that the long-overdue problems were brought to the surface. With the sweeping democratic reforms, voices from all strata of society began demanding a more opened, pluralistic system both in political and economic areas. The stake was no longer in the mere size of the pie but in its distribution as well. On the international front, Korea faced a heightened level of expectation from its trading partners for a more opened market, especially in the aftermath of the successful 1988 Olypmics.

It has thus become imperative that the government make a pivotal change in its economic and trade policies. Growth is no longer a miracle medicine that cures all diseases. The government should be poised to fulfill the compound task of achieving social equity without sacrificing efficiency and entrepreneurship. It was in this context that the economic development plans of the past have been replaced by an economic and social development plan, which has become a plan for deplanning.

NEW DIRECTION IN KOREA'S ECONOMIC POLICY

The government's answer to the efficiency objective is the privatization of the economy. To maximize the creativity of the private sector, the government is committed to lifting its interventionist policies of the last two decades. Direct governmental intervention in economic activities will be minimized, thereby revitalizing the role of the market mechanism in the economy and promoting private initiatives. The privatization of government-owned enterprises and the commercial banking system is a clear example of such efforts. Relaxation of arbitrary administrative price controls and stricter enforcement of antimonopoly regulations are other examples of the efforts to introduce freer competition in the domestic marketplace.

Unlike the hands-off policy on general economic activities, the government will step up its role in promoting social and economic welfare. Instead of a Western-style welfare program of giving outright benefits to the less well-to-do, which may have a dampening effect on the vitality of the economy, the government will focus on providing the underprivileged sectors of the society (small businesses, rural sectors, and low-income families) with enhanced access to financial resources and various social services. The government will also allocate more investment in such areas as housing, health care, environment, and education.

Containment of the current account surplus is also high on the agenda of the government. Besides causing trade disputes with the major trading partners, the growing surpluses lead to worries about increased inflationary pressures at home. The government is responding to this problem with a two-tier strategy. The first is to liberalize imports, and the second is to boost domestic consumption.

The growing tendency toward a consumer society now appears irreversible. Expansion of domestic consumption is required not just to reduce the current account surpluses but also to meet the increasing expectations and demands of the consuming public. Expansionary policies are also expected to alleviate Korea's excessive dependency on trade. (Korea's ratio of foreign trade to GNP stands at over 70 percent.) Consensus is building within the government that it is now time to move from the export-led growth of the past to a growth sustained by balanced expansion of domestic and foreign demand.

KOREA'S MARKET-OPENING POLICIES

In addition to liberalization in the domestic market, entry barriers to foreign goods and investment have also been gradually dismantled since the early 1980s. From 1983 to 1988, 1,161 items (under CCCN eight-digit classification) have been switched from import-prohibited to automatically approved status, raising the import liberalization ratio from 74.7 percent to 95.4 percent. As a result, import restrictions on manufactured goods are virtually nonexistent. Contrary to the conventional practices of countries that raise tariff rates when they introduce liberalization measures to cushion the surge of new imports, Korea lowered tariff rates simultaneously with the introduction of liberalization measures. Tariff rates have been reduced from an average of 23.7 percent in 1983 to 18.1 percent in 1988.

Until the early 1980s, foreign direct investment had been subject to a "conditional welcome" policy. Foreigners were allowed to invest only in selected industries detailed in the positive list announced by the government. In 1984, a negative list system was introduced. Under the new system, foreign investors were no longer required to obtain explicit approval of the government unless their projects appeared on the list. Since then, the scope of the list has been significantly reduced, raising the liberalization ratio to 83.6 percent in 1987 from 66 percent four years earlier. By 1988, the manufacturing sector had almost completely been opened to direct foreign investment.

Earlier liberalization efforts were concentrated in the manufacturing sector. As the liberalization of the manufacturing sector nears completion, however, Korea faces far more formidable targets—agriculture and services sectors. These new targets, though small in terms of the number of products or industries involved, touch upon the most sensitive spots of the Korean economy.

Nevertheless, Korea has every reason to move forward with its programs of market liberalization. Surpluses in Korea's balance of payment will alleviate one of the most important constraints on the earlier market opening efforts. Competition from abroad is as important as competition within the domestic market for the optimal allocation of resources and the enhancement of international competitiveness of domestic industries in the longer run. Further, the enhanced qualities prompted by foreign competition will undoubtedly help meet the increasingly sophisticated demands of consumers for higher-quality products and services. The Korean government is prepared to boldly tackle the last hurdle in order to transform its economy into one that is comparable to OECD countries.

Execution of these liberalization programs will require a highly cautious approach on the part of government. The die-hard deficit mentality, so deeply rooted in the mind of the average citizen during the long deficit era, will continue to put enormous pressure on the government. Resistance by interest groups directly affected by the market opening will constitute another major constraint. But much more damaging to the liberalization efforts is the public perception that the market opening measures are being taken to accommodate foreign pressure. Such a perception will induce even the general consumers, who are considered to be the beneficiaries of the open market, to turn against market opening, depriving the government of a major support base for the implementation of liberalization programs.

It is therefore imperative that liberalization measures be taken step by step following a preannounced long-term plan by the government. A system of advance notice of phased liberalization, designed to give domestic producers time to adjust to the new market conditions, has been useful not only in cushioning the impact of liberalization but also in preventing the sensitive public reaction toward a "forced or imposed" liberalization.

As part of such a phased, preannounced liberalization scheme, a five-year tariff reduction plan was announced at the end of 1988, which envisions reduction of the average tariff rate from the current 18.1 percent to 7.1 percent in 1993, a level comparable to that of OECD countries. The government also announced a four-year plan to gradually open Korea's capital market, which will ultimately allow direct purchase of stocks by foreign investors by 1992. It will soon be followed by other major long-term liberalization packages designed to gradually remove residual import restrictions in agricultural products, lift entry barriers in services industries, relax controls on foreign exchange transactions, and streamline import procedures.

CHALLENGES TO U.S. BUSINESS

Such is the future direction of Korea's market opening policies that the United States, with its proven competitiveness in services and agriculture, will undoubtedly be in a superior position to penetrate the Korean market. On top of this, Korea's business cycle makes no secret that it intends to switch the source of imports away from the countries with which Korea runs trade deficits (Japan, most notably) to countries like the United States with which the nation is accumulating trade surpluses. Under the initiative of the private sector known as import diversification scheme, more than 300 products have been identified and listed as targeted items for such diversification.

One of the important items subject to the scheme is factory equipment. The Korean market for factory equipment stands at a multibillion-dollar level and is rapidly growing as factories rush to outfit themselves with new and advanced equipment. However, the "Buy American" experiment in this area has been viewed with skepticism by many factory managers or engineers who have strong reservations about American-made equipment. Their dissatisfaction with American equipment often involves not the quality or technological sophistication of the equipment but the poor service and less-than-expected devotion of the American engineers dispatched to install new equipment in their factories. The source of the problem is not of material but of cultural nature.

Many disputes between Korean and American businesspeople are attributable to their cultural differences. Korean businesspeople, especially of older generations, feel less comfortable when they are working with Americans than with Japanese. One of the reasons behind such discomfort lies in different attitudes toward a written contract. The Americans usually expect that the contract covers all the contingencies to be anticipated and, once the contract is signed, it is observed to its letter regardless of the changed circumstances. The Koreans tend to view the contract merely as a basis of their continuing relations and expect that any future problems be addressed through mutually agreeable renegotiations.

The American obsession with contracts is not the only source of emotional displeasure to Korean businesspeople. Perhaps more hurting to the image of the Americans is their insistence on *their* way of doing business.

Many times, Americans suffered major setbacks because of their disregard of emotional subtleties of the Korean people and their ignorance of Korea's business practices. It was Americans that stood on the front line in demanding market opening, but the market was often exploited by countries other than the United States. In other cases, the Americans were so bogged down in the beachhead they had secured through their fierce landing efforts, that they aroused serious popular resentment. Cases in point are the American cigarette makers and insurance companies whose respective market shares showed no sharp increases even after the market has completely liberalized.

Mastering the cultural and emotional aspects of doing business in Korea must be a complex and time-consuming undertaking for American businesspeople with a markedly different cultural background. Still, such efforts will pay off in the long run. Cultural barriers will linger long after legal or institutional barriers are lifted.

TOWARD INTRAINDUSTRY COOPERATION

No one will deny that there is a wide range of complementarity between the Korean and American economies. In the past, Korea's specialization in labor-intensive, light industries and America's concentration in capital- and technology-intensive industries represented a typical division of labor between the two countries. Today, however, Korea's increasing sophistication in its industrial capacity adds a new dimension to such division of labor.

Intraindustry business coalition is one of the new methods of exploiting this changing pattern of competitiveness. Under a typical arrangement, an American firm supplies a combination of machinery, technology, and raw materials to a Korean partner in a joint venture or on a long-term supply contract basis. The Korean firm assembles the finished products, and the Korean and American companies share the worldwide marketing of their joint products.

The steady increase in two-way flows of investment between Korea and the United States stands witness to the fact that the business communities of the two countries are seeking new and diversified methods of cooperation instead of the mere sales-and-purchase relations of the past.

Such an intraindustry collaboration will find extensive and useful applications in Korea's recent drive to accelerate an economic interchange with the socialist countries. An ideal match could be obtained by combining Korea's skilled labor, medium-level technology, and industrial infrastructure with America's high technology and managerial expertise. In an emerging market like China, America's accumulated experience in the market and Korea's geographic proximity and cultural homogeneity will perfectly supplement each other in a productive and mutually beneficial way.

A GROWING MARKET FOR U.S. PRODUCTS

The driving force behind Korea's phenomenal economic success in the past was a pool of well-educated human resources that supplied energetic and pioneering entrepreneurs, hardworking laborers, and highly devoted bureaucrats to Korea's development process. Contrary to the popular expectation that the pursuit of success and education would be dampened as people grow wealthier, the zeal for education among the

Korean people shows no sign of declining despite the ever-rising standard of living. Moreover, as the generations born in the post-Korean War baby boom enter the labor market, the rate of increase in the labor force is expected to surpass that of population growth in the near future. So long as this engine of growth remains unimpaired, the current frenzy of expansion will continue well into the next century.

On the demand side, a slowdown in exports will be supplemented by an increase in domestic demand, which will play an increasingly important role in the years to come. In 1988, the average nominal wage soared approximately 18 percent, well over the rate of increase in per capita GNP. Because of the rising level of expectation among low-income wage earners, wage hikes at a double-digit rate are expected to continue in the near future. Rapid wage hikes cause a transfer of resources from the savings-prone high-income classes to the consumption-prone low-income families. This will sharply increase domestic consumption at an accelerated pace, and much of the increased spending will be directed at imported products that are priced lower as import barriers are gradually eliminated and the Korean currency grows stronger.

Rapid growth, increasing openness, and expansion of domestic demand will make Korea an increasingly attractive market for U.S. businesses in the future. Korea's increasingly affluent 40 million consumers will be exposed to aggressive foreign traders and investors. A forward-looking and positive marketing strategy is required to make it in this growing market. However, a bullish attitude alone is not sufficient. The strategy will have to be formulated with tact and supported by a thorough understanding of Korea's market, culture, and economic policies.

BUSINESS OPPORTUNITIES IN KOREA

OVERVIEW OF KOREAN ECONOMY

For the last three decades, Korea has achieved rapid economic growth despite scant natural resources, high population density, and the constant presence of a military threat from the North. Korea's real GDP growth has been one of the highest in the world, averaging 8.9 percent from 1962 to 1988. Per capita income has grown from less than $100 at current exchange rates to $3,700 over the same period.

The industrial structure has also changed dramatically. In 1962, agriculture accounted for 37 percent of GDP; manufacturing, 16 percent; and social overhead capital, 47 percent. By 1987, the ratio was reversed, with manufacturing accounting for 35 percent and agriculture only 12 percent.

The growth of Korea's exports has also been striking. The export volume from 1962 to 1988 rose 1,103 times from $55 million to $60.7 billion. There has been a shift in the composition of exports from textiles and processed raw materials to ships, motor vehicles, integrated circuits, and consumer electronics.

It was Korea's persistent commitment to an outward-looking development strategy, generally supported by sound macroeconomic policy and a well-disciplined work force, that has made this economic change possible. The successful performance of the Seoul Olypmic Games and recent contacts with Communist countries also make the future of the Korean economy brighter than ever.

However, this progress has not been achieved without some adverse developments. Since Korea's current account shifted from deficit to surplus in 1986, cumulative external surpluses have asserted monetary and inflationary pressures upon the Korean economy and fueled protectionist sentiment. Korea's current account surplus amounted to $4.6 billion in 1986, $9.8 billion in 1987, and $14.3 billion in 1988.

The increasing U.S. trade deficit with Korea is a major cause of the protectionist pressures directed toward Korea. Since near balance in 1980, the trade deficit of the United States with Korea grew rapidly to $9.6 billion in 1987, though it was reduced to $8.6 billion in 1988. The Korean government understands these new realities and has implemented a broad range of trade and other measures designed to control the size of Korea's external surpluses and increase imports from the United States.

OPEN-DOOR ECONOMIC POLICY

In October 1985, the Korean government announced a full-scale liberalization schedule. Despite the current wave of protectionism in its major trading partners, Korea has opened markets by its own initiative in order to continue to grow and remain competitive in the international trading arena. Korea's first current account surplus in 1986 provided additional momentum for import liberalization and tariff reduction.

Import Liberalization Measures

The liberalization of imports has gathered momentum gradually since 1967 when Korea joined the General Agreement on Tariffs and Trade (GATT) and import policy was changed from a positive to a negative list system.

Under its phased liberalization program, the government lifted controls on 235 items in 1985, 302 items in 1986, and 169 items in 1987, raising the liberalization ratio to 91.5 percent.

In April 1988, 145 items were liberalized for entry into the Korean market ahead of schedule. Those items consisted of 91 machinery products, 17 electric and electronic products, 15 chemical products, 11 miscellaneous goods, and other steel, textile, and primary goods. As a result of these measures, the domestic markets for industrial products such as steel, machinery, metal, electric and electronic products are now completely open.

The Korean government also added 71 items to the import liberalization list in July 1988, raising the import liberalization rate to 94.8 percent based on Harmonized Commodity Description and Coding System 10-digit headings. These items had not been included in any of the previously announced import liberalization schedules. Products included are consumer goods such as avocados, vegetable juice, meat extracts, and protein concentrates.

Some items are still restricted, most of which are agricultural products such as meat, dairy products, vegetables, fruits, and fish, and certain precious metals. A number of products that have been postponed in the import liberalization program will be liberalized by the early 1990s. The liberalization rates will reach 97 percent by that time.

Tariff Reduction

Until the 1970s, Korea imposed relatively high tariffs to protect its infant domestic industries. However, with Korea's emergence as a successful NIE in the 1980s, the government has reduced tariffs to strengthen the international competitiveness of domestic industries.

In the fall of 1983, the Tariff Act was revised and a schedule for reducing tariffs on a year-to-year basis was announced. As a result, the average tariff rates on all products dropped from 23.7 percent in 1983 to 18.1 percent in April 1988. However, in practice, much lower tariff rates were applied in accordance with the concessionary and flexible tariff systems.

Under a new overall tariff reduction plan announced by the government in September 1988, Korea's average tariff rate will be lowered to the level comparable to that of OECD countries during the 1989–93 period. Under this plan, the basic tariff rate imposed upon most imported industrial products will be lowered from 20 percent to 8 percent and that on manufactured goods from 16.9 percent to 6 percent.

Foreign Investment Liberalization

By revising the Foreign Capital Inducement Act in 1985, Korea introduced a negative list system and abolished various restrictions on foreign investment in Korea in order to smooth the transfer of foreign technology and provide greater opportunities for foreign investors.

In October 1985, the government announced new measures on Korea's direct foreign investment policies. The announcement included the opening of 102 additional industries to foreign investment, raising the foreign investment liberalization ratio to 76 percent.

The government lifted restrictions on 40 types of industries in 1986 and 27 in 1987, raising the overall decontrol ratio to 83.6 percent, and the liberalization ratio of the manufacturing sector to 97.7 percent. All types of industries, except for the strategic and public-sector industries, are scheduled to be completely liberalized by 1991.

Investment procedures were simplified by the revision of administrative regulations. The revised regulations reduced the red tape and paperwork faced by foreign investors wishing to obtain licenses.

In early 1988, the government took steps allowing foreign invested firms, in which foreign partners hold less than a 50 percent equity, to conduct foreign trade without limitations on allowable items. However, firms that have more than a 50 percent equity share held by foreigners were selectively allowed to join the trading business, depending on whether or not they own manufacturing facilities. Importers of foreign technologies are no longer required to obtain prior government approval.

Financial Liberalization

Since 1982, Korea has gradually carried out its financial-sector liberalization program. The program has been accelerated since 1986, after Korea recorded its first current account surplus.

In the first phase of liberalization the government divested shares in commercial banks to encourage the private sector to take a more active role in financial management.

The second phase was aimed at easing restrictions on the operations of foreign bank branches in Korea. In 1984, foreign bank branches were allowed to join the Korea Federation of Banks and the Korea Clearing and Credit Reporting Center. The branches were also granted access to the Bank of Korea's rediscount window for export financing. They were permitted to engage in the trust business in 1985, accorded full access to the Bank of Korea's loan facilities on the same footing as domestic banks in 1986, and could open more than one branch in Korea in 1987.

The third phase opened the insurance market to foreign companies in 1985, although the domestic industry was still vulnerable to foreign competition. Under the new policy, two American fire insurance firms were allowed to operate in Korea in 1986 and two American life insurance companies were allowed to do the same—one in 1986 and the other in 1987. In February 1989, five joint venture life insurance companies were permitted to initiate business. Under the revised Insurance Law, the Korean insurance market will soon be opened completely to all foreign insurers.

The last phase of liberalization was the opening of the stock market to foreigners. In 1981, the government announced the opening of Korea's capital market to foreign investors to encourage the inflow of foreign capital with the Korean stock market through the medium of international investment trusts. It is also planned that overall liberalization of foreign direct investment in Korean securities will be completed in the early 1990s. Eventually, foreign corporations will be permitted to list their stocks on the Korean Stock Exchange.

According to a capital market opening schedule finalized in late 1988 by the Ministry of Finance, foreign securities firms will be allowed to establish branch offices or form joint venture stock firms with Korean security firms in the beginning of 1991. Foreign stock investors who hold convertible bonds issued overseas by Korean firms will be permitted to invest in the domestic security market in 1991, while individual foreigners will be allowed to make direct investments in the Korean security market in 1992.

Protection of Intellectual Property Rights

In December 1986, the government revised its intellectual property laws, the Patent Law, Copyright Law, and Trademark Law, and enacted a new Computer Program and Management Law.

Under the revised Patent Act, effective July 1, 1987, patents are protected for 15 years, as opposed to the previous period of 12 years. Patent coverage has been expanded to include protection for chemical and pharmaceutical products in 1987 and microorganisms in 1988.

The Korean government has also made intellectual property protection available for foreign R&D products, despite public outcry that it was still premature to protect the copyright of imports.

The new Copyright Law protects works of individuals for a term of life plus 50 years and of legal entities, such as corporations, for a period of 50 years from the first publication in the country of origin.

The protection of computer programs copyrighted in their countries of origin is guaranteed under the new Computer Law, thereby protecting computer programs according to the same principles as other literary works.

Import Diversification Program

The Korean government has stepped up its efforts to correct Korea's continuing trade deficit with Japan and to smooth out trade imbalances with major trading partners by sponsoring import diversification programs. Since the latter part of 1986, these programs have been targeted primarily to increase imports from the United States.

As part of these efforts, the government has singled out 335 major industrial products that Korean companies can purchase from the United States rather than Japan. These products include processed chemicals, paper, plastics, scientific instruments, both low-tech and high-tech machinery of all kinds, certain vehicles, and consumer items such as golf clubs.

Korean companies' efforts to switch sources of supplies from Japan to the United States have begun to bear fruit. In 1986, the import diversification program resulted in an additional $180 million in new purchases from U.S. suppliers. In 1987, $500 million in products previously purchased from Japan, such as machine tools and drilling equipment, were instead purchased from the United States.

Currency Appreciation

At the request of the United States, Korea has appreciated its currency by 15.8 percent over the last year, altering the exchange rate from 792 won per dollar at the end of 1987 to 684 won per dollar at the end of 1988. This appreciation rate corresponds to the 15 to 19 percent originally proposed by the United States at the beginning of 1988. This rapid currency appreciation has decreased the growth of Korean exports to the United States from 31.9 percent in 1987 to 17.1 percent in 1988. In 1989, the won was expected again to appreciate further reducing Korea's export growth rate.

RECENT TRENDS OF IMPORTS AND FOREIGN INVESTMENT

Imports

As a result of market liberalization and currency appreciation, imports have increased, showing high annual growth rates. In 1986, at the initial stage of market opening, the annual growth rate of imports was only 1.4 percent, totaling $31.5 billion. In 1987, as government measures took effect, imports grew 29.9 percent to more than $41 billion. By 1988, imports had expanded to $51.8 billion, 26.3 percent over the 1987 level.

For decades, Japan and the United States have remained Korea's largest import sources. Japan particularly provided much of the industrial equipment and components Korea needed for its recent industrialization. In 1988, imports from Japan amounted to $16 billion, while those from the United States were $12.7 billion.

Recently, a slight change in this trend has been visible. The growth rate of Korea's imports from the United States has risen sharply for the period 1986–88, while the growth rate of imports from Japan has decreased. In 1986, the import growth rate from the United States was 0.9 percent; in 1987, 33.8 percent; in 1988, 45.7 percent. By contrast the import growth rate from Japan was 43.8 percent in 1986, 25.7 percent in 1987, and 17.0 percent in 1988. This phenomenon may be attributed to the strong yen and weak dollar as well as the conscious diversification of trading partners.

Korea's main imports include machinery, chemicals, and electric/electronic products. From January to November 1988, Korea's imports of machinery—the most important imported items for Korea—amounted to $4.3 billion from Japan and $2.6 billion from the United States. However, the growth rate of imports from the United States reached 72.9 percent (compared with the same period in the preceding year), while that from Japan was only 17.7 percent. The switch from Japanese to American products has also occurred in imports of chemicals and electric/electronic goods.

American exports are apparently recovering competitiveness in the Korean market, though this has not yet been fully realized.

Foreign Investment

The inflow of foreign capital to Korea is increasing as per the government's foreign investment policy. In 1987, total foreign investment amounted to $1,060 million on approval basis, almost three times the $354 million of the preceding year. From January to October 1988, foreign investment reached $1,135 million.

The total amount of foreign investment from 1962 to 1988 (as of the end of October) reached $5,826 million in 2,686 cases on approval basis. By country, Japan topped the list with $3,047 million in 1,737 cases, followed by the United States with $1,560 million in 602 cases, and Hong Kong with $190 million in 53 cases.

The major investment fields, by case, include machinery (467 cases) and the electric/electronic sector (511 cases). The development of the auto industry has produced opportunities for joint ventures in the production of parts and components. Advanced industries have also created great demand for high technologies in the electronics field. The Seoul Olympic Games have made the hotel and tourist sector promising, though these cases are fewer in number (72).

Of total foreign investment, $1,573 million was in the hotel and tourist sector, $951 million in electric and electronic industries, $784 million in the chemical industry, and $497 million in the auto industry.

Investment in the financial sector recorded $256 million in 24 while foreign indirect investment in the stock market amounted to $450 million.

HOW TO APPROACH THE KOREAN MARKET

U.S. exports and investment in the Korean market are increasing rapidly thanks to Korea's open-door policy. This trend is sure to provide even more opportunities for American businesses in the Korean market. In fact, the Korean domestic market has remained nearly untouched because so little attention has been paid to it by domestic businesses, and because its development has often been blocked by government policies and taxes. The recent explosion of demand for automobiles is indicative of the potential of the consumer market.

Promising Fields for Business in Korea

According to a recent survey in Korea, many Korean businesses believe the retail and motor vehicle industries are the most promising fields in Korea.

Retail Industry
The modernization of the distribution network in Korea began in the very early 1980s. Despite the sizable slowdown of economic growth at that time, sales volume in the retail industry surged, thanks to new investment and the introduction of modern management skills by big companies. Moreover, the advent of new specialty and discount stores further accelerated the development of the retail industry.

However, there is much room for improvement. Distribution channels for imported consumer goods are still complicated since several intermediaries may interfere in every step. For example, the longest channel is as follows: importer → exclusive purchasers → brokers → wholesalers → retailers → consumers. Streamlining of such an inefficient distribution system could be facilitated by well-developed American retailers.

Motor Vehicle Industry
Until the mid-1980s, the motor vehicle industry was principally concerned with supplying a small domestic market. After Hyundai's success in Canada in 1984, the Korean motor vehicle industry geared up for an assault on world markets in cooperation with major producers. In 1987, almost 1 million cars and buses were produced, and 543,000 vehicles were exported, up 78 percent from the previous year.

In 1988, the industry produced more than 1 million cars and buses, but exports increased only 3 percent from 1987 due to lack of diversity in model and to sales expansion of Japan's locally manufactured cars in North America. Instead, domestic sales rose as the income of Koreans increased, oil prices stabilized, and cars began to be viewed as necessities. With the increasing demand of the domestic market, the motor vehicle industry was expected to grow by an estimated 15 percent in 1989.

The major problem for the industry lies in component production, particularly serious given recent currency appreciation. Joint venture production of components can be mutually beneficial to both sides. For example, Samsung and Chrysler have invested jointly in component manufacture, with a view toward producing vehicles together in the future.

Production of Industrial Parts and Components

Many parts and components for manufacturing ships, autos, machinery, and even television sets are imported from Japan for reasons such as price, quality, afterservice, and availability of spare parts. However, the appreciation of the Japanese yen is leading Korean manufacturers to search for other sources of supply. The auto industry, for example, has begun joint venture production with American firms.

By its nature, the production of parts and components is well-suited for small- and medium-size businesses. Joint ventures are easier in this field because gigantic investment is not needed. Joint venture production will not only lead to increased exports of U.S. machinery and equipment but will also lessen Korean frustration with U.S. afterservice because the U.S. partner can facilitate the import of spare parts from the United States. The Korean government has also instituted policies that support the production of certain industrial parts and components by small- and medium-size companies.

Other Opportunities

Korea is making efforts to develop high-technology industries such as advanced electronics, computers, semiconductors, airplanes, biochemistry, and nuclear energy. Korean industries are readjusting to these high value-added sectors.

The sports and leisure industries are also promising as national income rises and people concentrate on how to enjoy their lives. The Seoul Olympic Games has added momentum to the development of these industries.

For some time, textile production was considered a fading industry in Korea because of its labor-intensive nature, the strong price competitiveness of Chinese textiles, and the appreciation of the won. However, the Korean textile industry is overcoming these difficulties by developing new materials and making high-quality products. Korean textile products are seldom found at low-priced department stores in the United States. In order to remain competitive, many textile firms are moving their production facilities overseas to Southeast Asia or Caribbean countries for more efficient production and better access to major markets.

Marketing Activities in Korea

Advertising

As in other countries, effective advertising is a prerequisite to successful marketing in Korea. A survey conducted by the Korea Chamber of Commerce and Industry in 1985 showed that 86 percent of those questioned were influenced in their purchasing decision by advertising.

There are four kinds of major advertising media in Korea: three TV networks, four commercial radio networks, six national dailies, and some 50 monthly magazines. According to a 1983 survey, 35 percent of those surveyed preferred drama series in TV programming, 32 percent news, and 16 percent sports. In another survey in 1985, 67 percent of those questioned read newspapers, among them 32 percent read political columns, 24 percent social, and 14 percent sports.

Opening of Branch Office

A variety of Japanese and European firms have opened branch offices in Korea for active marketing promotion as well as the prompt afterservice many Koreans expect. Recently, some of these firms began publishing catalogs, brochures, and other marketing material in the Korean language.

When a nonresident establishes a branch office in Korea, he or she must report to the governor of the Bank of Korea. If the business of the branch office involves the remittance of business profits, he or she must obtain a permit from the governor. When a foreign firm seeks to establish a domestic branch office involving credits, financing, security underwriting or insurance, a permit must be obtained from the Minister of Finance.

Using Korea's Import Promotion Policy

In order to achieve balanced trade with the United States, Korea has dispatched many buying missions to America and has sponsored seminars and a variety of exhibitions such as the U.S. Products Show and the Import Source Diversification Show. At the U.S. Products Show, which took place in Seoul in November 1987 and was organized by KOTRA, some 220 companies from 33 states displayed various items, including metalworking equipment and tools, chemicals, computers, and electronic communication products. The $90 million in sales contracted and under negotiation reveals the prospective opportunities in these market areas.

Direct Contact with Department Stores

Importers of consumer goods in Korea prefer to sell to department stores because they are an easy and quick way to introduce new foreign-brand goods to consumers easily. Since most quality-oriented consumers in the middle and upper income brackets tend to purchase at department stores, contacting department stores directly can be an effective marketing strategy.

Consumer Behavior

The improvement in the standard of living resulting from the nation's economic growth has given rise to consumer demand for quality, diversity, and aesthetic values in their choice of products. Consumers have sometimes shown a high propensity to spend disproportionate to their level of income if a product satisfies their requirements.

Heightened interest in leisure and health is evident among both urban and rural populations. Rapid Westernization of life-style is occurring and will be even more prevalent among the younger generation. Western fashion, music, and even fast-food chains are major influences on urban life. The Korean consumer has shown a strong preference for foreign-made brands, even at higher prices. At the same time, reasonably priced goods of foreign origin remain in stable demand by many purchasers. The Korean market is, therefore, receptive to a wide range of goods of all prices from all sources. Competition among these foreign suppliers is, however, very keen.

A survey conducted by the Korea Chamber of Commerce and Industry in 1986 revealed that 70.7 percent of the population surveyed was satisfied with the quality and price of foreign goods.

According to the same survey, electric home appliances topped the list of most frequently purchased foreign goods with 28.1 percent, followed by cosmetics and beauty supplies with 15.5 percent, and foodstuffs with 15.3 percent.

As imports have increased, however, more complaints have been filed with consumer protection agencies. In a test conducted by the Consumer Protection Board in February 1988, defects in size, quality, or security were detected in imported goods.

Better Understanding of Korean Customs and Mentality

The emotional factor of the Korean mentality is extremely important. Consequently, success or failure of a foreign product in Korea is not always assured by rational calculation.

For example, despite a wonderful price arrangement, U.S. cigarettes have not sold nearly as well as suppliers expected. This phenomenon is indicative of the mentality and outlook of Koreans today. Contrary to U.S. suggestions that restrictions on the sales network and antismoking campaigns have inhibited sales, the poor sales of U.S. cigarettes in Korea are due largely to the Koreans' emotional response to seemingly excessive U.S. pressure for marketing cigarettes in Korea.

The rapid Westernization of life-styles in Korea can, however, have a positive impact on foreign business opportunities in Korea. For instance, Wendy's and McDonald's have received an exciting response in Korea because of their careful consideration of the changes in Korean life-style.

CONCLUSION

The opportunities for success in Korea are endless, provided an American company is willing to dedicate the time, effort, and resources necessary to devise an effective marketing strategy for its product. Special attention must be paid to fostering the personal relationships that are so important to the Korean business arena. Patience and sensitivity to cultural differences can go a very long way. The Korean government has done its part to create an atmosphere for fair competition and is committed to supporting policies that will bring Korea up to the level of the rest of the industrialized world.

CHAPTER 14

TRADING WITH KOREA

Jin Ouk Kim

TRADE REGULATIONS

Imports

Korea gradually began to liberalize imports in 1967 when the nation joined the General Agreement on Tariffs and Trade (GATT) and changed import policy from a positive to a negative list system, specifying prohibited rather than permitted imports. Since then, the government has been increasing the import liberalization rate every year.

Under the ongoing liberalization program, the government included agricultural imports, to be implemented step by step over three years.

This action to satisfy foreign demands for an open policy responds to the worldwide allegations that Korea is no longer a developing country, and therefore it should not take shelter under Article 18 of GATT.

Beginning January 1, 1988, the government adopted the Harmonized Commodity Description and Coding System (HS), created by the Customs Cooperation Council for trade and customs. All items are classified in 21 sections, 1,241 headings, and 4,019 subheadings.

Tariffs

The Korean tariff system generally works on the stated base rates. However, the system is quite flexible for certain items, and the authorities may change the base rates, on due notice, within prescribed limits. New rates are listed on special, frequently revised schedules. Korea has recently been under pressure from advanced countries that demand decreasing customs duty rates and a substantially open market. Because of this, the government decreased customs duty rates January 1, 1989, and announced rates for the 1990–93 period (see Table 14–1). By 1993, customs duty rates are scheduled to be level with OECD countries.

Exports

Foreign trade has played an increasingly important role in Korea's economy, with exports comprising an ever-widening share of the GNP. In 1988, exports accounted for 10.9 percent of Korea's GNP.

TABLE 14–1
Prenotice of Customs Duty Rate (Unit: Percent)

Section	1989	1990	1991	1992	1993
Noncompetitive raw materials	1–2	1–2	1–2	1–2	1–2
Competitive raw materials	5	5	4	4	3
Primary processed goods	10	10	9	9	5
General industrial products	15	13	11	9	8
General consumer goods	15	13	11	9	8
Luxurious consumer goods	20	16	13	11	8

Most exports are automatically approved. There is a restricted list for which individual licenses are required and a prohibited list that primarily includes agricultural products. There is also a list of countries to which exports are forbidden, but restrictions may be relaxed in individual cases.

INCENTIVES

Financial Considerations

Investment Incentives
Two basic types of investment incentives exist: (1) relief from taxes including export duties and (2) liberalized credit and other capital inducements.

Tax.   Exports are exempt from commodity taxes. Customs duties on imported components are refunded when the finished goods are exported. In addition, excess depreciation is allowed on fixed assets used in export operations. Tax allowances are also available for domestic corporations engaged in designated priority activities, as well as companies with foreign participation.

Tax Exemption and Reduction Control Law.   The Tax Exemption and Reduction Control Law (TERCL) is Korea's most important law covering tax incentives. It was enacted to enhance the equity of the tax burden and contribute to the national economic development by regulating tax exemption and reduction matters. The TERCL is frequently amended to reflect changing conditions. (See Figure 14–1 for a summary of the more significant tenets.)

Corporation Tax Law.   To further encourage financial improvement for domestic corporations, a portion of newly paid-in capital is deductible over 36 months for corporate tax purposes. The amount deductible in any one year is 15 percent (18 percent in case of a public company or statutory small- and medium-size company) of the newly paid-in capital. This provision does not apply unless the additional capital investments are made in cash by an individual or foreign corporation.

FIGURE 14–1
Tax Incentives under the TERCL

Criteria for Eligibility	Exemption or Reduction
Newly organized small- and medium-size companies having generally no more than 300 employees (200 in the case of the construction industry), and operating in the manufacturing or mining industries. Company's total assets should not exceed a certain limit that ranges between 8 and 30 billion Korean won, depending on its industry type. In addition, the industry should be classified as technology intensive, or the company should be located in the agricultural or fishery area to qualify for the tax exemption.	Corporation tax is fully exempted for the period of the first taxable year plus three years thereafter and reduced by 50% for the subsequent two years. Registration tax, acquisition tax, and property tax are also reduced.
Small- and medium-size companies defined as companies having generally no more than 300 employees (200 in the case of the construction industry), operating in the manufacturing, mining, construction, transportation, or fishery industries.	A deductible provision for investment up to 15% of the book value of business assets as of the end of the fiscal year. In addition, for the manufacturing and mining industries, special depreciation of 50% (or 100%) of the normal depreciation on machinery and equipment only.
Resident or domestic corporations, including foreign-invested companies, operating in the manufacturing, mining, construction, or engineering services industries who are making expenditures for technology or manpower development.	A deductible provision for technology development up to 1.5% (or 2%) of gross receipts or 20% (or 30%) of net income, whichever is greater. In addition, an investment tax credit of 3% (10% when domestic equipment is purchased) of expenditures for technology or manpower development.
A new company starting a business using new technology.	Either an investment credit of 3% (or 10%) of expenditures for technology development or special depreciation of 30% (or 50%) of the normal depreciation at the taxpayer's option.
Resident or domestic corporation, including foreign-invested companies, earning foreign currency.	The following deductible provisions: • Provision for overseas market development of 1% of foreign receipts or 50% of taxable income. • Provision for overseas market development of 1% of foreign currency receipts. • In addition, special depreciation generally at 30% of normal depreciation.

FIGURE 14–1
(concluded)

Criteria for Eligibility	Exemption or Reduction
Resident or domestic corporations, including foreign-invested companies, investing in facilities for: • Improving productivity. • Energy conservation. • Pollution control. • Prevention of industrial hazards. • Distribution industry. • Mine safety.	Either an investment tax credit of 3% (or 10%) of the amount invested in the enumerated facilities or special depreciation of 30% (or 50%) of the normal depreciation on such facilities, at the taxpayer's option.

Foreign Capital Inducement Law. The Foreign Capital Inducement Law (FCIL) is the primary law governing foreign investment in Korea. Tax incentives previously granted virtually automatically to the approved foreign investments have been largely eliminated and are now available only in very limited situations. In general, FCIL tax incentives will be considered for qualified companies that:

- Require inducement of high technology.
- Are located in a free-export zone.
- Are invested by a Korean living abroad.
- Are approved by the Foreign Capital Inducement Deliberation Committee to receive tax benefits in consideration of diversifying investments or increasing employment, e.g., investment in small- and medium-size companies in designated industries whose foreign ownership is less than 50 percent.

If the company qualifies for FCIL tax incentives, corporate, property, and acquisition taxes may be exempted in proportion to the amount of foreign ownership. Corporate tax withholding on the foreign investor's dividends also may be fully exempted, upon approval of a specific application, for a period of 5 consecutive years to be selected by the applicant within the first 10 years of the company. (The first five years of the company is mandated in the case of acquisition and property taxes.) As an option, a qualified company may apply for approval to deduct special accelerated depreciation in lieu of tax exemptions. This is calculated as normal depreciation multiplied by the percentage of foreign ownership. The total cumulative amount of this special depreciation claimed cannot exceed the amount of foreign investment.

If a foreign-invested company subsequently increases its capital, it must apply for the tax exemption or special accelerated depreciation in the same manner as for the original investment. In this case, the exemption period is five years, starting with the first taxable year after registration of the capital increase.

Upon application, capital in-kind—including both capital equipment and preproduction inventory—to be invested in industries that qualify for the tax exemption under the FCIL may be allowed exemption of customs duty, special excise tax, and value-added tax. Because of the recent liquidity problems in Korea, foreign investment is encouraged to be made in the form of in-kind rather than capital investment.

Foreign Employees of Foreign Entities. Foreign technicians can be exempt from income tax for five years if they have specific education or experience and work for Korean corporations—including foreign-invested companies incorporated in Korea—operating in certain industries, such as manufacturing or construction. This also applies to foreigners working under a technical service agreement as approved by the Technical Service Promotion Law.

Going Public. The government may recommend that financially healthy companies go public under the Capital Market Promotion Law.

Recently, the government announced that recommendations to go public would also be applied to foreign-invested companies that meet requirements of financial health and where the foreign investment was applied for on or after January 1, 1989. If this type of foreign-invested company does not comply with the Ministry of Finance recommendations to go public, it will be subject to sanctions such as loan restrictions.

TRADEMARKS, PATENTS, AND COPYRIGHTS

Patents and Trademarks

Technology and trademarks are protected only when they are registered under the appropriate law concerning industrial property rights, such as the Patent Law and Trademark Law. When registered industrial rights and patents are damaged, compensation can be claimed by filing a suit in court. Chemical and pharmaceutical companies currently can acquire only process patents and product patents.

Korea signed the Paris Convention in 1980 governing the protection of industrial rights. Under the pact, foreign patent holders are given the same protection as local patent holders.

Patents are granted for 15 years and are not renewable except for pharmaceuticals which may be extendable up to five years. Trademarks registered with the Patent Office are protected by law for 10 years and are renewable indefinitely. Trademarks must be used to remain valid. Trademarks not used for one year can be canceled by cancellation trial initiated by an interested party.

Foreigners can register patents and trademarks in their own names. Nonresidents usually work through an agent for an initial search of similar patents or trademarks, registration thereof, as well as monitoring of new registrations.

COMMUNICATIONS

Korea has up-to-date communications, including more than 10 million telephones with direct dialing throughout the country. International telegraph, telephone, and television connections use a communications satellite, telex, facsimile, and data transmission system to link the Republic with more than 160 countries. Waiting time for telephone, telex, and facsimile installation is negligible. The Korea Telecommunications Authority is moving toward a nationwide digital switching and communication system. The nation's telecommunications system is also being upgraded to allow for increasing data communications, including simultaneous voice and data transmissions.

Nine radio networks and four television networks operate in Korea. Six of the radio networks and three of the TV networks are government-owned. The TV networks cover the country through relay stations. The U.S. Army also operates radio and TV stations that transmit throughout the country.

Mail service out of the country is generally reliable and fast. Several international courier services are available for speedier deliveries.

TRANSPORTATION

The government has widely improved and expanded the transportation sector of the economy. Considerable future upgrading is also planned to meet the growing demand created by increased traffic.

The railway network operated by the Korea National Railroad covers 3,930 miles (6,285 kilometers) of track, 26 percent of which is double-tracked and 14 percent electrified. Passenger service is available on all major lines, and freight rates are kept low to benefit low-income and rural people.

The nation's highway infrastructure has expanded as the number of vehicles has skyrocketed. Paved roads connect all population centers of 50,000 or more, and there are several modern expressways. First-class buses link major cities.

Korea's international air connections center at Seoul's Kimpo Airport; other international airports are located at Pusan and Cheju Island. At least five flights daily link Seoul and Tokyo. The principal carriers are Korean Air Lines and Japan Air Lines. There is also daily direct service to the United States, Southeast Asia, the Mideast, and Europe. Within the Republic, Korean Air and the newly established Asiana Air operate daily service.

Korea has 24 first-grade ports, with Pusan, Inchon (both equipped with container terminals), and Kunsan the biggest. In terms of overall tonnage, Korea sails the 15th-largest merchant fleet in the world. New port facilities are planned, particularly in Cholla provinces in anticipation of greater trade with China.

CHAPTER 15

OPERATING A BUSINESS IN KOREA

Taesik Suh
Bruce L. Townsend

SETTING UP A FOREIGN OPERATION

Foreign investment in the Republic of Korea is encouraged, although priority is given to investments consistent with the country's prevailing economic development policies and to those that do not hinder the growth of domestic industry. Although tax incentives for foreign investment have been reduced gradually, foreign-invested enterprises may still receive privileges not extended to domestic investors.

Industries Open to Foreign Investment

Under the current Foreign Capital Inducement Law (FCIL), foreign investment is generally permitted in any industry except those specifically restricted or prohibited on the negative list.
   Restricted industries are those that:

- Receive special support from the government.
- Are large consumers of energy or in which the usage of imported raw materials is substantially greater than the usage of domestic raw materials.
- Cause pollution.
- Are deemed highly extravagant consumer-oriented industries.
- Are involved in farming or fishing.
- Need protection in the startup stage of development.

Prohibited industries comprise:

- Services for the public welfare normally provided by the government or public organizations—water supply and sewage, telegram and telephone, railroad transportation, manufacturing of tobacco and red ginseng, and other industries listed in the implementation guidelines.
- Those hazardous to the public health and environment, as listed in the implementation guidelines.
- Those harmful to the social morality, such as gambling houses.
- Other miscellaneous industries, including newspaper publishing, radio broadcasting, grain planting, and those that may be listed in the implementation guidelines.

Approval of Foreign Investment

Applications for investment under the FCIL are automatically approved by the Bank of Korea without requiring further review by the related ministries if all the following conditions are met:

- The industry is not on the negative list.
- Foreign ownership is less than 50 percent.
- The amount of foreign investment does not exceed US$3 million for a manufacturing industry or $100,000 in the case of other industries.
- The company does not request a tax holiday.

All other investment applications will be subject to individual review by the Ministry of Finance in consultation with other relevant ministers or the Foreign Capital Inducement Deliberation Committee (FCIDC).

Location

Because industrial concentration has saturated certain districts around Seoul and other cities, Korea is diverting new industrial construction to less crowded areas, in some cases even mandating a different province from the one requested. However, authorities have also been flexible when foreign investments are involved, and a foreign-affiliated enterprise generally should be able to work out a satisfactory compromise. An agricultural and industrial corporation may qualify for a tax exemption or reduction and financing support.

Repatriation and Reinvestment of Funds

For investments approved under the FCIL, unlimited remittance of profits is guaranteed at the rate of exchange prevailing at the time of transfer. Similar guarantees apply to repatriation of invested capital, repayment of principal and interest on foreign private loans, and remittance of royalties and fees.

Earnings of the foreign venture may be reinvested upon submission of a report to the MOF. Approval is required if the reinvestment results in foreign ownership exceeding the originally approved ratio or is made in another enterprise.

FORMS OF BUSINESS

The corporate form covers most large industrial enterprises in the Republic of Korea. A few forms predominate.

The Joint Stock Company

Most Korean corporations are known as joint stock companies (*chusik hoesa*). They are the only business organizations permitted to publicly issue shares or debentures. There may be as few as one shareholder, but at least three directors are required. The maximum term for a director is three years, but re-election is permitted. There are no citizenship or residency requirements.

The law recognizes common and preferred shares and permits both the bearer and the registered type. Shares must have a par value of at least W5,000, and common shares must carry voting rights.

Voting at shareholders' meetings is ordinarily by simple majority. For certain specified matters, such as revision of the articles of incorporation, the law prescribes a two-thirds majority. Any shareholder group with a total interest of 5 percent or more of outstanding share capital may call a meeting of shareholders or demand a special audit.

The statutory auditor (*Kamsa*) is elected by shareholders for a two-year term. The auditor's chief duty is to examine the company's overall operations and financial statements (as prepared by, or under the supervision of, the directors) and to report to the shareholders.

Disclosure requirements are minimal. The annual balance sheet must be published in at least one newspaper, but certain companies, including those listed on the Korea Stock Exchange, must have their annual statements audited by an independent CPA firm.

Joint stock companies are required to maintain a reserve equal to 50 percent of the total capital subscribed. This reserve need not be attained at the outset but may be built up by annual contributions equivalent to not less than 10 percent of annual cash dividends.

The first step in organizing a joint stock company is drawing up articles of incorporation and having them signed by at least seven persons. These seven founding members or promoters need not be citizens of the Republic.

The next step is submitting the articles, together with a statement of the amount and form of the contemplated initial equity issue, to a district court. If the court approves the application, the corporation can begin operations after registry, which must occur within two weeks after the first shareholders' meeting.

At least 25 percent of all shares authorized must be subscribed for at incorporation, and the total capitalization must be at least W50 million. After registration, the legal status of the promoters terminates, although any member may remain as a shareholder. Directors are elected at the first general meeting of the corporation.

Within 30 days of registration, domestic corporations must file an establishment report and an application for business registration with the tax office of the district in which the corporate head offices will be located. The report consists of basic information, submitted on a form, together with a certified copy of the register required by the commercial code, a copy of the articles of incorporation, and the opening balance sheet of the company with detailed account balances.

Organizing a *chusik hoesa* with foreign participation—one in which foreign investment is at least US$100,000—requires obtaining the approval of either the MOF or the BOK, depending on the appropriate authority, and complying with the standard formalities associated with domestic enterprise. Applications for approval must be accompanied by a description of the project, a certificate attesting to the nationality of the controlling investors, and, where applicable, a joint venture agreement. Normally the application will be acted upon within 10 to 60 days, depending on the nature of the investment. Within 24 months, the company must register with the MOF or the BOK, declaring completion of the inducement of the foreign capital, including capital in-kind, as set out in the approved application for foreign investment. This registration is a prerequisite to securing the status of the foreign-invested corporation and the granting of any tax benefits.

Branches and Liaison Operations

Establishing a branch of a foreign entity in the Republic of Korea requires registration with a domestic court and with the BOK. Among the issues to consider when planning a branch office in Korea are repatriation of the original investment and future earnings, licensing requirements for particular activities, and foreign exchange controls. Extensive planning can be required. If authorized, the foreign branch must maintain a legal representative with power of attorney in the Republic. Like domestic corporations, foreign branches must file an establishment report with the tax office within 20 days of startup.

A special class of branch is a liaison office, which confines itself to such activities as providing information on local market conditions, maintaining business contacts, or carrying on a buying operation. Because a liaison office does not conduct income-producing activities, it is not subject to the corporate tax and need not file corporate tax returns. However, it is required to report its existence to the BOK.

A liaison office may conduct its activities only for the legal entity of which it is a part. Conduct of activities on behalf of another party, including affiliated companies, forfeits its liaison status and turns it into a taxable branch office.

Other Forms

Other forms of business organization include a combination of limited liability company and partnership (*yuhan hoesa*) and an incorporated unlimited partnership (*hapmyong hoesa*). Neither of these entities is likely to offer any advantage to foreign investors.

LICENSING, ROYALTIES, AND TECHNOLOGY TRANSFER

Licensing

Licensing and technical-assistance agreements are popular ways of entering the Korean market. Agreements must be submitted for approval when the technology is related to the defense industry and when the term of payment or the effective period of the technology inducement agreement exceeds three years and:

- The fixed royalty exceeds US$100,000.
- The down payment exceeds $50,000 or the running royalty exceeds 2 percent of the net sales of the contracted products concerned.
- The payment method is other than above.

In the absence of a request for supplemental information, suitable agreements are automatically accepted by the appropriate minister after

20 days. Agreements outside the above categories must be reviewed by foreign exchange banks.

Royalties

Fully exempt from tax for five years from the date of acceptance are royalties or fees paid for the use of high technology designated by the FCIDC as necessary for the Korean economy but difficult to develop domestically.

However, agreements will not be accepted if they:

- Have a main purpose of selling raw materials, spare parts, or accessories.
- Contain significant unfair provisions, such as limits on exports.
- Are deemed unacceptable by the Minister of Science and Technology because the concerned technology is already developed domestically and is being protected.
- Induce technology barred by other laws.

MANUFACTURING

Thirty years ago, Korea was virtually an industrial vacuum. But an all-out effort, starting with the first five-year plan in 1962, developed a diversified manufacturing capability, including textiles and wearing apparel, chemicals and chemical products, packaged foods and beverages, ships, electronic components, basic articles of steel and nonferrous metals, motor vehicles, and construction materials. In the early 1980s, the manufacturing industry advanced into a new stage stressing technology-intensive sectors, including the electronics, automobile, precision machinery, and computer industries.

Despite rapid growth in production of industrial machinery and equipment, these industries have suffered because the quality of Korean machinery has been lower than imported products. However, for machinery using low and medium technology, Korean products are very competitive in domestic and export markets.

The Korean shipbuilding industry, which held a 25 percent share of the world market in 1988, has been hurt in recent years by a falling demand for ships and the world's overcapacity in shipbuilding. Korean shipbuilders now will focus efforts on producing more special-purpose, technically sophisticated vessels with higher value-added content.

Because Korea has no domestic sources of oil, significant investments are required in power-generating facilities. Korea's energy policy has recently focused on the replacement of petroleum power sources with nuclear and coal energy. Ten nuclear plants should be completed by the early 1990s. In 1986, 44 percent of the nation's electricity output was nuclear-generated. In addition, coal-fired electrical generators are being constructed to replace oil-burning plants.

LOCATION AND FACILITIES

Natural Resources

Korea's tungsten reserves are among the largest in the non-Communist world. In addition, modest deposits exist of iron, zinc, copper, lead, gold, and silver. Much more abundant are the nonmetallic minerals, including kaolin, limestone, pyrophyllite, silica, and talc. Coal supplies are ample but of poor quality and difficult to mine. About one third of the country is forested, with conifers accounting for half of the commercially useful trees. There is a wide variety of marine life in Korean coastal waters, but several species of food fish show signs of depletion.

Production

Agriculture and Fisheries
Approximately 60 percent of Korea's land consists of uncultivated and forested mountain slopes. Residential and industrial sites occupy another 10 percent, leaving only 30 percent available for agriculture. The principal food crop is rice, followed by barley and soybeans. Wheat and corn are also produced but not sufficiently to supply domestic needs. However, improved farming has boosted grain production in recent years. Korea is a world leader in sericulture and other special crops, such as ginseng and tobacco.

While inland and nearby coastal fishing have long played an important part in Korea's economy, deep-sea fishing is catching on quickly. Korea now has 800 vessels harvesting pollack and pike in the North Pacific, octopus and squid off Northwest Africa, and shrimp off Brazil. Coastal fishing, which amounts to nearly half the industry's total production, is dominated by small-scale operations. As nations enforce 200-mile limits, prospects for the industry depend on Korea's success in negotiating fishing rights with other countries.

Mining
Korea's mining activities are generally limited to coal, tungsten, limestone, talc, silica, lead, and zinc. Nearly all production is consumed domestically. Korea has total coal reserves equal to 1.6 billion tons. But because production costs are high, imported coal proves more economical to use.

Marketing

Korean consumer tastes generally reflect modern industrial society. This is shown by the high demand for appliances, labor-saving devices, and leisure equipment. On the other hand, tradition still dictates food preferences.

Media

Over 97 percent of the people of Korea are literate, and the country has more than 20 daily newspapers. Eight of them, all published in Seoul, have a national distribution. Of those, at least four have a circulation of over 500,000. There are also a number of magazines, several of which print more than 100,000 copies. Virtually every Korean household has at least one television set.

Distribution Channels

Retail merchandising in the Republic of Korea is dominated by the one-family shop or booth, often stocked with a variety of goods. Department and chain stores are meeting with growing acceptance, although they are still confined to large cities. Independent distributors are an important factor in the marketing of goods. These merchants may be considered wholesalers, since wholesaling, as commonly understood in Korea, does not preclude direct sales to the public. Manufacturers of large industrial products often prefer to act as their own wholesalers.

LABOR, IMMIGRATION, AND COMPENSATION

Labor

The Republic of Korea's labor force is one of its primary resources, and a full range of labor is in abundant supply. Because of comprehensive educational system, over 97.5 percent of the people are literate. Well-trained, high-quality manpower is available in various fields because of a rapid increase in technical and vocational schools.

However, there is a chronic shortage of executive and supervisory personnel. The competition for qualified managers is intense and has undoubtedly contributed to high employee mobility in the Republic. Many companies consequently overhire to provide a reserve against shrinkage. About 240,000 students graduated from college in 1988, and bilingual graduates are available in most fields. Companies interested in college-trained personnel can contact college administrators for recommendations.

The law does not limit the number of foreign nationals working in the Republic of Korea. After 90 days, however, foreign nationals must have a residence certificate from the immigration authorities.

Compensation

The Ministry of Labor has recently adopted a minimum wage law that provides for a minimum wage of W600 per hour (W690 in 1990)—about W144,000 per month (W165,600 in 1990)—in the manufacturing, mining, and construction industries. Current monthly wage ranges for industrial workers in foreign-owned companies are:

- Unskilled—US$300 to $600.
- Semiskilled—US$400 to $800.
- Skilled—US$550 to $1,100.

Middle-management salaries around Seoul range from about $15,000 to $25,000 annually, and upper-management are compensated at rates comparable to those in the United States and Western Europe.

In general, the highest-paying industries are mining, petroleum, construction, and service. The lowest-paid major industry is textile manufacturing. From 1977 to 1980, salaries for various industrial jobs increased from 20 percent to 30 percent annually, but from 1981 to 1986, salary levels remained relatively constant. Salary levels for women remain about 20 percent below those of men.

In 1986, the U.S. Bureau of Labor Statistics estimated the hourly cost for production workers in Korea to be $1.38 per hour. A less rigorous but more recent study placed the hourly wage rate in Korea at $1.57 per hour (as compared to Singapore at $2.40 and Hong Kong at $1.89). Wages in Korea continue to increase substantially. Real wage rises of approximately 15 to 20 percent per year for Korean workers are expected over the next three to five years.

Benefits

The typical benefits package, including both mandatory and nonmandatory benefits, is:

Mandatory. Employers with five or more employees must establish an employee retirement fund and must provide a medical examination for all employees at the time of hiring and at least once a year thereafter. They must also subscribe to industrial accident compensation insurance through the Ministry of Labor.

Nonmandatory. The law does not address many benefits taken for granted in other countries. Nevertheless, paternalistic conventions with nearly the force of law give most Korean workers benefits. Among the most common nonmandatory benefits are bonuses (ranging from one to six months' salary), free or nominally priced lunches, transportation allowances, and free tuition for special schooling. Several companies provide workers with housing allowances and interest-free loans.

Working conditions

The basic legislation governing working conditions in the Republic of Korea is the Labor Standards Law. This establishes the minimum employable age (at 13), forbids practices such as arbitrary dismissal or dismissal during absence for reasons of health, and lays down rules on working time and on special compensation.

Working Time. An unusual feature of Korean legislation is its elasticity in regard to the definition of workday and workweek.

The workday is limited to eight hours (seven hours for minors under 18 years), and the standard workweek is 48 hours (42 for minors), although it may extend to 60 hours under a labor-management contract. In practice, the workweek generally extends over six days. Further extension of hours requires prior approval of the Ministry of Labor.

Time worked over the standard 48-hour workweek must be paid at 150 percent of the hourly norm. Similar rates apply to night work.

An employee who is exposed to hazardous working conditions may not work more than 6 hours a day or 36 hours a week. By special authorization from the Ministry of Labor, the maximum may be 8 hours and 48 hours, respectively.

Normal work and lunch breaks are required, as well as a paid weekly rest day, normally Sunday. Women with children under the age of one are allowed at least one hour a day for nursing. There are 19 official holidays a year.

Special Compensation.   The right of employees to compensation in the event of dismissal, severance, and disability is explicitly recognized. Employers must give either 30 days' notice or extra severance pay. Employees with more than a year of creditable service are assured at least one month's severance pay for each year employed. Dismissed employees are also entitled to an additional 30 days' pay in lieu of notice.

For on-the-job injuries, the employer must pay medical costs, compensation for permanent disability or disfigurement, and 60 percent of the employee's base salary for the period of absence. If an employee dies, the employer must pay the family the equivalent of the employee's wages for 1,000 days.

Special Leave

Employees who have perfect attendance records over a calendar month are entitled to one day of paid holiday in addition to the 19 official holidays. This allowance is cumulative. For a year of perfect attendance, eight additional paid holidays are granted. For 90 percent attendance during a calendar year, the reward is three days' leave. Women are entitled to one day a month menstruation leave and to a maternity leave of 60 days.

Employee Grievances

A national Labor Dispute Mediation Committee exists for conciliation, mediation, and arbitration of labor grievances.

Only recently have labor unions become a potent force in Korea. Traditionally, the Korean government had actively discouraged, and in some cases suppressed, unions and labor organizing activity. Recent political developments, however, have increased government tolerance of labor activity. The government now attempts to encourage management and labor to resolve their differences together.

Currently, there are over 7,000 company unions. Several industry unions also exist. Knowledgeable observers have estimated that union and union-eligible Korean employees number about 8.6 million out of a total work force of 20 million. Union activity is expected to increase in the future.

The right to strike is effectively denied in certain industries considered important to the national economy, such as most of the defense industries. Collective bargaining is normally allowed in these industries, but if management and labor cannot agree, the government exercises its power to settle disputes.

Bargaining is normally conducted at the plant level with a bargaining unit negotiating on behalf of all workers, whether or not union members. Contracts usually run for two years and are concerned with the basic issue of employee compensation.

The labor laws call for establishing permanent labor/management committees. The committees, consisting of 3 to 10 members from both management and labor, have the power to deal with grievances. The committees do not replace unions, but they preempt most union functions.

Entry and Residence

Foreigners entering the Republic of Korea must have a current passport and an entry visa, obtainable from any Korean consulate, unless they can prove they intend to stay for no more than 15 days. The duration of visas is 90 days and they are not usually renewable. To obtain a long-term entry visa, a company or individual in Korea is required to sponsor the employment of a foreigner by providing a letter to Korean consular officials. (Additional letters of recommendation can be helpful in obtaining approval.)

Once an individual enters Korea on a long-term entry visa, he or she must apply for a residence certificate within 90 days of arrival. The application for a residence certificate must be made at the local District Immigration Office. Holders of a residence certificate who intend to leave and return to Korea must also obtain a re-entry permit. Application to extend an entry visa must be made before it expires and submitted to the District Immigration Office.

A verbal customs declaration is possible if no valuables are being brought into Korea. However, if valuables are being carried in or if the declaration covers unaccompanied baggage, a written declaration form must be presented to Korean customs officials upon arrival at the port of entry. Foreigners entering Korea for a stay of at least two years may import appropriate household items at the time of entry or within six months of arrival. They are subject, however, to customs duties on certain luxury items.

CHAPTER 16

FINANCIAL AND
TAX CONSIDERATIONS

Chu Kyu Kim
Yong Kyun Kim

THE STOCK MARKET

The Korea Stock Exchange, located in Seoul, is privately managed under the jurisdiction of a Securities and Exchange Commission. The sale of securities was a secondary source of capital in Korea until the 1980s. But volumes have been rising rapidly, jumping almost 30-fold between 1975 and 1987.

Since the issuance of overseas convertible bonds (CBs) by Samsung Electronics in 1985, the market has been bullish. This is partially because the Korean government has consistently backed its development. But more importantly, anticipation of capital liberalization has fueled hopes that foreign investors will enhance stock prices, which currently are relatively low on a worldwide scale.

The Korean stock market, with only indirect participation of foreign investors (by way of foreigners' exclusive investment trust funds), has been growing considerably in both volume and quality. Expectations are strong that when the threshold of direct investment rises in 1992 for foreigners, the domestic capital market will grow still further.

As of December 1988, there were nearly 500 companies listed on the market and 7 million investors in securities. The total market value of stocks amounted to W64 trillion (approximately US$90 billion), with the composite stock index of over 900 points. To increase market size and strength and to widen the investment opportunities, some unlisted corporations have been encouraged by authorities to go public if they meet requirements set by the Securities and Exchange Commission. In addition, some listed companies with weak capital structures have been prodded to increase their equity capital. For similar reasons, an employee stock ownership system and a scheme of national stock ownership (starting with the public offering of Pohang Steel & Iron Company) have been introduced and are expected to spread.

BANKING AND CREDIT

Monetary policy in the Republic of Korea is formulated by the Monetary Board and administered by the nation's central bank, the Bank of Korea. The ex officio chairman of the board is the Minister of Finance. The banking system of Korea has been subordinated to the government's direct and indirect controls since the early 1960s when government reorganized the financial system by taking over major ownership of the commercial banks to facilitate financing of Korean economic development programs. Since the early 1980s, however, various measures have been taken for liberalization and promotion of competition in the financial sectors, including banking. The economic policy shifted away from government-led management to the implementation of wide-ranging structural adjustments aimed at promoting greater reliance on the market mechanism and enhancing competition in every sector of the economy.

Major efforts in the 1980s to liberalize the banking sector included a 1982 revision of the General Banking Act and the privatization of four nationwide commercial banks. With the Commercial Bank of Korea in private hands since 1972, this resulted in five leading commercial banks being privately owned.

With respect to bank fund operations, direct credit controls through ceilings on individual banks were replaced by indirect controls through management of bank reserves by the 1982 act. Together with liberalization of interest rates on bank loans (effective December 1988), the banking system is growing increasingly autonomous. Expected reform of the Bank of Korea Act should push in the same direction.

The Banks

The Korean banking system is made up of commercial banks, specialized banks, nonbanking credit institutions, and government-controlled development banks.

The Republic of Korea's commercial banking system includes 7 nationally chartered commercial banks, 10 regional banks, more than 60 branches of foreign banks, and 7 specialized banks including the Korea Exchange Bank. Although the relative importance of commercial banks is declining, they are still an important source of short-term credit.

Other banking institutions include finance companies, insurance companies, and a number of merchant banks. In general, these are nondepository, although the merchant banks and finance companies carry out a kind of depository function through the issuance of promissory notes. The merchant banks engage in a broad range of activities, including discounting promissory notes, underwriting securities, financing leases, and borrowing and relending foreign capital.

Various other banking institutions are government-funded, nondepository institutions that make loans on projects deemed important to the economy. These include:

- The Korean Development Bank, which provides long-term credit to major projects in the areas of public works, transportation, communications, and industry.
- The Export-Import Bank of Korea, which finances all aspects of foreign trade and overseas investment, extending credit to foreign governments, banks, and industrial corporations.
- The Korea Long-Term Credit Bank, which promotes private enterprise through medium- and long-term industrial loans (often on the basis of equity participation), usually in foreign currencies.

Availability of Credit

Short-term credit is available in the form of general loan or promissory notes for terms of one year or less. While the state rates have ranged from about 10 percent to 11.5 percent, beginning December 5, 1988, due to the liberalization of bank loan interest, each bank can determine its own lending rate within a certain specified range. Loans for longer periods are hard to get. The Korean Development Bank and the Korea Long-Term Credit Bank are probably the principal providers of middle-term (one to three years) and long-term credit, but their lending policy is very selective. Renewal of promissory note loans on a continuous basis is common, however.

Borrowing from Foreign Lenders

Because of the characteristically tight credit situation in the Republic of Korea, foreign borrowing assumes a special importance in Korean operations, even if it is under close government control. Borrowing outside the Republic requires the approval of the Minister of Finance or the central bank, which is conditioned on the size, interest rate, terms of repayment, and purpose of the loan. In general, approval is granted only for major development projects or for importation of plant and machinery unavailable domestically. There are no restrictions on borrowing from foreign sources within the Republic (e.g., branches of foreign banks). These lenders, however, generally require a guarantee of repayment by a domestic bank. Further discouraging this type of borrowing is the fact that balances for the disposal of foreign lenders have been chronically unequal to the demand.

FOREIGN EXCHANGE CONTROL

Foreign exchange control in Korea originated with the Foreign Exchange Control Law of 1961. The law, revised several times since passage, is designed to control outflow of foreign exchange and effectively use incoming foreign exchange for economic development, to counterbalance chronic foreign exchange shortages, to maintain international equilibrium in general, and to stabilize the currency.

Foreign exchange control mechanisms mainly consist of fulfillment of transactions based on the official exchange rate, obligation of concentration of foreign exchange, restriction on foreign payment, and restriction on capital transactions.

Generally, all residents in Korea were prohibited from possessing foreign exchange except for the cases set forth in the law or separately approved; to enter a contract that leads to foreign payment; or to make foreign payments. The law also regulates capital transactions such as borrowing from overseas and investments bound overseas.

However, because Korea's trade balance went into the black in 1987 (hitting about US$4 billion that year and approximately US$13 billion in 1988), significant change is expected in foreign exchange control.

Through a number of revisions since 1987, control on foreign payments has eased gradually, and the need to control foreign receipts has been stressed.

- In practice, any resident is now allowed to keep foreign means of payment which was bought from a bank or achieved through transactions to a maximum of US$5,000.
- Overseas investments not exceeding US$2 million are now granted automatic approval as long as certain minimum requirements set by the Bank of Korea are met.
- On the other hand, major restrictions have been imposed on the import and conversion of foreign exchange by both residents and nonresidents in order to curtail the inflow of hot money.

These changes were spurred primarily because a large volume of incoming foreign currency followed optimistic forecasts of the Korean economy. This elevated the won, as well as the Korean stock market, and destabilized the economy.

Many forces now favor repeal of foreign exchange control regulations. Foreign exchange liberalization, the prerequisite to capital liberalization, is commonly expected to be achieved soon.

THE TAX SYSTEM

Two levels of taxation exist in the Republic of Korea: the national and the local. Taxes on income, value-added, and certain categories of consumption are levied at the national level; taxes on real property and residences are levied either by the provinces or the municipalities.

Taxable Entities—Corporations

The law recognizes three categories of corporations: domestic, resident foreign, and nonresident foreign. A domestic corporation is one that is incorporated under the laws of the Republic of Korea, or has its head office in Korea. Domestic corporations are subject to tax on their worldwide income.

A resident foreign corporation is a corporation with a permanent establishment operating, but not incorporated, in the Republic of Korea. Considered as permanent establishments are branches (and sub-branches); sales outlets; warehouses; sites of construction, installation, or assembly, including factories; and mines. Many agent operations constitute permanent establishments, but liaison activities generally do not.

In general, resident foreign corporations are taxed only on their Korean source income and at the same rate as domestic corporations. Even if a parent company sells goods directly to buyers in the Republic, bypassing its own Korean establishment, that establishment will be deemed the seller of the goods and the profit from the sales will be included in its taxable income, unless described otherwise in the tax treaties. The tax authorities look closely at the allocation of costs between resident foreign corporations and their Korean permanent establishments.

Foreign corporations without permanent establishments in the Republic are classified as nonresident foreign corporations and are subject only to withholding tax on their Korean source income.

Parties unsure of how their proposed activities will be classified should seek professional advice.

Determining Taxable Income

Taxable income of corporations is generally determined on an accrual basis. For banks, insurance companies, and other financial institutions, the cash basis is acceptable, although the accrual method is still the norm. The tax treatment of specific items of account is discussed below.

Gains and Losses.   Capital gains or losses of legal entities are treated the same as ordinary income or loss, except gains from the sale of land or buildings are subject to special surtax rates.

Realized exchange gains or losses resulting from actual collection or payment of foreign currency assets and liabilities are recognized currently. Translation gains and losses from short-term foreign currency assets or liabilities are recognized currently, whereas translation gains and losses from long-term foreign currency assets or liabilities, which are due after one year from the fiscal year-end, must be deferred and amortized over the period remaining until their maturity.

Consolidation.   Consolidation of income for tax purposes by a parent company and its subsidiaries is not permitted.

Loss Carryover.   Corporations are not permitted to carry losses backward. They may, however, carry losses forward for five years.

Expenses.
1. Depreciation: The charge is based on cost less salvage value (10 percent of cost) allocated over depreciable life specified by the tax authorities for the particular class of asset. Straight-line or declining-balance methods are acceptable for most depreciable items; most users prefer the latter. Additional depreciation may also be taken for certain classes of assets, such as for machinery and equipment used in mining and manufacturing (for 12 hours or more daily) and in certain industries designated in the Tax Exemption and Reduction Control Law. Depreciable assets costing less than W300,000 may be expensed at the time of purchase.

2. Amortization: Deferred expenses that can either be expensed as incurred or capitalized and amortized over future periods include organization expenses, preoperating expenses, stock and debenture issuing expenses, and research and experimentation costs. Other intangibles are deductible over specified useful lives.

3. Interest payments: Interest is normally deductible on an accrued basis. However, interest on borrowings associated with purchase or self-construction of fixed assets must be capitalized. Interest on borrowings where the identity of the lender is not disclosed (e.g., "curb-market" loans), and interest on borrowings associated with acquisition of equity in other companies are not deductible.

4. Royalty expenses: Royalties are generally deductible when incurred.

5. Bad-debt allowance: Up to 1 percent of total receivables may be deducted for bad debts without regard to actual experience.

6. Provision for severance: Companies that accrue severance benefit reserves under law, union agreements, company policy, and so on may credit to that reserve each year either 10 percent of the total salaries (including bonuses) claimed as expenses or one half of the total severance liability accrued at the end of that year minus any reserve carried over from the previous year, whichever is less. Any excess amount of severance actually paid over the reserve balance may be expensed in the year actually paid. When a company that provides a greater amount of severance benefits than are tax deductible uses an insurance company to fund the excess benefits, the premiums to the insurer are tax deductible within certain limits.

7. Other deductible reserves: Tax-deductible reserves are permitted for a number of purposes including investment by small- and medium-sized companies, losses on exports, and technology development costs.

8. Entertainment expenses: Expenses incurred for business entertainment or through business-related gratuities are deductible as incurred up to a maximum. This maximum, which is computed for a 12-month period, is W6 million plus either 2 percent of paid-in capital, or W100 million, whichever is less, and 0.1 percent (0.2 percent for small- and medium-sized companies) of gross annual revenue. If any portion of the expenses is unsupported and the company has a written guideline on disbursement of confidential expenses, the limit on that portion is computed as 0.05 percent of gross revenue plus either 1 percent of paid-in capital or W50 million, whichever is less. The amount of confidential expenses calculated should be treated as a part of the entertainment expenses, subject to the deduction limitation.

9. Directors' remuneration: Salaries paid to directors for services are fully deductible. The same is true of retirement payments made in accordance with the provisions of the company's articles of incorporation. If they are not provided for in the articles, the payments are deductible to the extent of 10 percent of total directors' salaries for the year, multiplied by the number of their service years. Bonuses paid to directors who are shareholders, partners, or investors are not deductible.

10. Contributions: Charitable contributions to Korean organizations operating in the public interest are deductible up to a predetermined limit. Contributions for war relief, to natural disaster victims, or to the government are deductible in full. In principle, however, a corporation having operating losses carried over from prior taxable years is not permitted to include a charitable contribution in deductible expenses.

11. Taxes: National and local income taxes are not deductible in determining corporate taxable income.

Credit may be given for foreign corporation tax, excess profits tax, or similar taxes paid on foreign income up to the amount of Korean tax applicable to the foreign income. The credit is calculated based on the per country limitation.

12. Nondeductible expenses: Items specifically excluded from allowable expenses include appropriations of retained earnings that have been recorded in the books of account as expense, fines and expenses in connection with delinquent taxes.

Inventories.   Inventories may be valued at cost, market, or the lower of cost or market. A broad range of methods is permissible for determining cost. Among them are specific identification; first-in, first-out; simple average; moving average; last procurement cost; and last-in, first-out. The method selected must be reported to the tax office by the due date for submitting the tax return for the taxable year in which the date of incorporation falls. Similar advance reporting is required when changing from one method to another.

Calculating Taxable Income and Tax Payable
The calculation of taxable income begins with book income, adjusted to conform with the tax regulations. Adjustments to book income are essentially as shown below.

Taxable Entities—Individuals

Resident individuals are subject to Korean taxation on worldwide income, while nonresident individuals must pay on domestic source income. If a foreign individual resides in Korea for one year or more, the individual shall be classified as a resident individual under the domestic tax laws. Where a foreign individual is a resident of both Korea and a foreign country, whether he or she is a Korean resident should be determined in accordance with the provision of the tax treaty concerned. Nonresident individuals are taxed on domestic source dividends, interest, royalty income, and so on, on a withholding basis.

Net profit (loss) after taxes as per books	W ___
Add:	
Corporation, defense, and resident taxes	___
Depreciation charged over tax limit	___
Excess entertainment expenses	___
Charitable donations over tax limit	___
Shareholder bonuses if charged to income	___
Provision for retirement allowances over tax limit	___
Other	___
Deduct:	
Refund of corporation and resident taxes credited to income	___
Other	___
Taxable income	___
Deduct:	
Loss carryover	___
Other, such as income deduction for capital increase	___
Tax base	W ___
Tax computed at appropriate rates (1)	W ___
Deduct:	
Tax exemptions*	___
Foreign tax credit	___
Other tax credits, such as R&D tax credit	___
Net corporation tax	___
Deduct:	
Withholding tax and prepaid interim tax	___
Net corporation tax payable	W ___

$$* (1) \times \frac{\text{Exempt income}}{\text{Tax base}}$$

Korean tax law recognizes four categories of gross income. The broadest is global, which consists of wages and salaries, interest, dividends, profits from real estate, profits from business activities, and miscellaneous receipts (occasional income). The remaining three categories are retirement payments, capital gains, and profits from forestry. Where total personal deductions exceed the global income, the balance may be applied to the next three categories in the above order.

Capital gains and losses on the sale of securities are generally excluded from taxable income of a resident individual, and gains incurred on the sale of land or buildings are subject to capital gains tax.

Individuals are entitled to certain tax credits. In addition, credits on all categories of income are available to Korean residents for taxes paid under the laws of foreign countries, computed on a similar basis as for corporations. Individuals, including both resident foreigners and Koreans, who receive their salary income in foreign currency from a foreign corporation (excluding a permanent establishment in Korea of the foreign corporation), are entitled to a 20 percent credit for such compensation voluntarily declared and subjected to monthly withholding through a taxpayers' association. The credit is given on the condition that the salary payment is not included in the deductible expenses of a permanent establishment in Korea of the foreign corporation paying the salary.

THE TAXES

Income Tax

Corporations are subject essentially to two rates, depending on their net income. Individuals are taxed according to a progressive schedule ranging from 5 percent to 50 percent.

Corporate. Tax rates depend on which of three classifications the corporation falls into. The first classification is a large unlisted corporation, which means a corporation whose capital stock exceeds W5 billion, or whose total shareholders' equity exceeds W10 billion, and is not listed on the stock exchange. A second classification is the not-for-profit organization that engages in certain activities that produce taxable income. All other corporations, including branches of foreign corporations, comprise the third classification (see Table 16–1 for the rates).

On the gain from sale of land or buildings, special surtax rates apply. The rate on property registered with the court upon acquisition is 25 percent and on property never properly registered on acquisition, 40 percent. In computing taxable gain, the difference between the sale price and purchase price is adjusted by an amount calculated as acquisition

TABLE 16–1
Corporate Tax Rate

Income	Large	Not-for-Profit	Other
First W80 million	20%	20%	20%
Balance	33%	27%	30%

cost times period of ownership times average annual inflation rate (measured by wholesale price index).

Foreign corporations having no permanent establishment in Korea are subject to withholding taxes on Korean source income.

Individual.   The taxation of nonresident foreigners having no permanent establishment in Korea is the same as for nonresident corporations without permanent establishments in the Republic.

Defense Tax

The defense tax is a special surtax levied on income tax, other taxes, and the price of imported goods. The tax is levied on corporations and individuals. The defense tax rate is 20 percent of the corporation tax if taxable income does not exceed W500 million and 25 percent of the corporation tax when the taxable income exceeds W500 million.

Resident Tax

Business entities and individuals (including nonresident individuals liable for income tax, corporation tax, or farmland taxes) are subject to a resident tax. The tax is 7.5 percent of the relevant corporation tax, income tax, or farmland tax.

Other Taxes

Value-Added.   The value-added tax (VAT) is computed by applying a fixed rate, currently 10 percent, to sales and by crediting against the value-added tax paid on purchases during the same period. Certain goods and services, such as unprocessed foodstuffs and professional services, are exempted from the VAT. A zero tax rate is applied to exports, services furnished from outside the country, and goods or services earning foreign exchange.

Education Tax.   The revenue of banks and insurance companies is subject to a 0.5 percent education tax. Education tax of 10 percent is applied to liquor and 5 percent to certain interest and dividend income.

Registration Tax.   A person who registers the incorporation of a company or registers ownership of real estate, vehicles, and so on, should pay the registration tax. The tax rate for the registration of an incorporation is 0.4 percent of the value of total shares, while the tax rates for registration of the ownership of an asset extends from 0.3 percent to 5 percent of the value of the asset. If a company is established within certain major cities, the tax rates are increased by five times the normal rate.

Special Consumption.   A national consumption tax is assessed on certain items.

Asset Revaluation.   When assets are revalued upward, the amount added is taxed at 3 percent.

Acquisition.   When real property, motor vehicles, ships, heavy equipment, and mining or fishing rights are acquired, a tax is levied on the asset's declared value. For purchases on deferred terms, the tax is on successive installments. The standard rate is 2 percent, but when the property is to be used in connection with industrial facilities to be constructed in major cities, the rate is 10 percent. A 15 percent rate applies to corporate-owned land not used in business and golf courses, and both ships and motor vehicles of a "high standard."

Property.   A local property tax is assessed annually on buildings, ships, aircraft, and mines at rates between 0.3 percent and 7 percent. A newly built factory located in a major city is assessed at a rate equal to five times the normal rate for a period of five years from the date of initial payment. The tax on mines is W50 per hectare of minelot.

Land.   A person who owns land taxable under the local tax law is subject to the local land tax at progressive rates that range from 0.2% to 5%. The tax base is calculated by adding together all the values of land owned by a taxpayer.

FORMALITIES OF COMPLIANCE

The agency responsible for the collection of national taxes is the National Tax Administration (NTA), an arm of the Ministry of Finance.

Filing Requirements

Returns, both individual and corporate, are filed together with supporting schedules at the tax office of the district in which the taxpayer is
located. Companies in their first two years of operation, companies with
substantial borrowings, and companies receiving certain tax benefits are
required to include with the return a tax reconciliation schedule prepared
by a CPA or an independent tax accountant.

Corporate returns are generally due within 60 to 90 days from the
end of the fiscal year. Extensions may be granted in unusual circumstances, but these are rare and very limited. Revisions are permitted as
long as they affect only the computation of the tax and not the books of
account. Revised returns may be filed within six months of the due date.
Taxes are ordinarily paid when the return is filed.

Corporations whose fiscal periods exceed six months must pay an
interim tax covering this period. The corporation has the option of
paying either half the corporate income tax payable during the preceding
year or the corporate income tax payable on the basis of the actual
operating results for the interim period. The tax becomes due at the end
of the six-month period, but the taxpayer has 30 days in which to pay.
The balance of the tax due for the year, taking into account the interim
prepayment, tax credits, and withheld taxes, is payable within the period
allowed for submission of the return.

PART 4

TAIWAN

CHAPTER 17

TAIWAN: TRADITIONAL VALUES IN A MODERN CULTURE

Jaime B. Quizon

HISTORY

Once connected to the Chinese mainland during the Ice Ages, Taiwan was first populated by aborigines in prehistoric times. It was settled by the Chinese and made a protectorate of the Chinese empire in 1206.

Sixteenth-century Portuguese traders christened the island *Ilha Formosa*, or Beautiful Isle, a name it had been popularly referred to until recently. Taiwan, which means terraced bay, has always been its Chinese name. It is also an appropriate description of the leaf-shaped, mountainous island as tiered rice paddies are found almost everywhere.

Because of its attractive location along the lucrative trade routes to the Far East, southern Taiwan was invaded and settled by the Dutch in 1624. In 1626, the Spaniards occupied the north. The Dutch secured the entire island in 1641 by driving out the Spaniards. This Dutch presence was short-lived. In 1661, the Dutch were overthrown by the Chinese patriot Cheng Cheng-kung (Koxinga), who claimed Taiwan for the Ming Dynasty. In 1684, the island was annexed as a prefecture of the Fukien province, and in 1887, it was finally granted its provincial status under China, which still remains, in principle, to this date.

In the Treaty of Shimonoseki that concluded the first Sino-Japanese war, Taiwan was ceded to the Japanese, who occupied the territory from 1895 to 1945. During this time, Japan wielded full control and considerable influence on the island. Despite the enhancement of the island's economic strength by the establishment of good roads and a rail system, local armed resistance to the Japanese presence never ceased. Taiwan eventually became a staging ground in Japanese operations against Southeast Asia. It took the Japanese defeat in World War II for Taiwan to revert back to Chinese rule in 1945.

The Nationalist KMT (Kuomintang) government took over the island in 1945. When mainland China was overrun by the Communists in 1949, over a million refugees, who are still collectively referred to as mainlanders, arrived in Taiwan. The territory became the provisional seat of the Central Government of the Republic of China under the KMT Party, a position that remains.

While the KMT promises to reoccupy the mainland someday, this is more rhetoric than reality. The reconquest of the mainland by the KMT is hardly possible since the United States, Taiwan's most ardent big-power supporter, has made it clear it would not support any military incursion into the mainland. The reunification of Taiwan under Beijing's loose sovereignty, though still farfetched, is more likely as both Taipei and Beijing share the common ideal of a unified China under a single political rule. How Hong Kong fares in its transition from British to Chinese rule in 1997 is being closely watched. Meanwhile, the KMT government has shown a growing political flexibility in its dealings with the mainland. It has recently allowed elder residents with ties to China to visit their relatives in the mainland and vice versa. During 1988, the government also allowed indirect trade with the mainland through third countries and permitted the local reprinting of nonpolitical literary and academic works published in the mainland.

These recent developments show a softening of Taiwan's long-standing, hard-line policy of having no dealings (no contact, negotiations, or compromise) with the People's Republic of China (PRC). This changing attitude has resulted in an increasingly more pragmatic foreign policy, in part, because of Taiwan's continued diplomatic isolation (it has diplomatic relations with only 23 countries). It has chosen to participate in international events, including the Olympic Games, and to renew its active membership in international bodies such as the Asian Development Bank and the GATT. It had also encouraged trade missions to the Soviet Union and other socialist states and legalized indirect trade with China through third countries.

However, many of these changes reflect the new and emerging political climate in the territory also. In the past, the development of Taiwan's international political stature seriously lagged behind the economy's ascendance in world economic importance. With the rise of a more articulate and vocal middle class and with the decline of emotional ties with the passing away of aging mainlanders, a political transformation favoring democracy and a new openness to the outside world is gathering momentum. This is unavoidable if Taiwan wants to maintain its economic importance in the free world.

GEOGRAPHY AND CLIMATE

Taiwan is a mountainous island in the western Pacific Ocean, some 100 miles southeast of mainland China and separated from it by the Taiwan Strait. Surrounding the island are three other bodies of water, the China Sea, the Pacific Ocean, and the Bashi Channel between southern Taiwan and the northern Philippines. Including other offshore islands (i.e., the Penghu archipelago), Taiwan proper has a total area of nearly 14,000 square miles. Only a fourth of the land, largely in the western coastal plains, is considered arable. Mountains cover nearly two thirds of the island. There are 62 peaks of more than 10,000 feet, the tallest being Yushan, the highest in northeast Asia.

The southern part of the island lies on the Tropic of Cancer. The climate is subtropical in the north but tropical in the south. The temperature averages from a low of 12 degrees Celsius (54 degrees Fahrenheit) in January and February to 95 degrees Fahrenheit in July and August. Pollution, particularly in the main cities, is a pressing problem, especially during the summer.

All the principal cities in the island are well connected by main highways and rail lines. Taipei is the provisional capital city of the Republic of China and is in the north. Kaohsiung, the other principal industrial center, is along the southwest coast. It is connected via Taipei to Keelung, the other international seaport in the north, by a freeway and electrical rail. The east and west coastal belts are also connected by main highways, and the eastern coastal city of Taitung and Taipei are connected by both rail and highway.

POPULATION AND LANGUAGE

Taiwan's population is largely homogeneous. While there are some 260,000 who belong to nine aboriginal tribes, the majority of the nearly 20 million population has ancestors who came from the mainland, either as original settlers from coastal and northern China a number of centuries ago or as refugees from the Communist takeover of the mainland in 1949. It is estimated that nearly four fifths of the present population is Taiwan born.

With economic prosperity has come a remarkable decline in the annual population growth rate, from 2.4 percent in 1970 to 1.1 percent at present. And although Taiwan has one of the densest populations in the world, the economy is self-sufficient in foodstuffs. However, the country must import most of its oil and raw material needs. This is one reason trade remains crucial to the island economy. Taiwan's hardworking and highly motivated people, centered around the extended family, are its most important economic resource. A program of social reform, which includes provisions for adequate health and welfare services and a compulsory nine-year public education system, has built on this economic resource and has transformed Taiwan into an industrial leader in the region. Education is highly valued with 82.3 percent of senior high school graduates enrolled in schools of higher education.

Although Mandarin is the official language, most Taiwanese speak several Chinese dialects from the nearest mainland province of Fukien, notably Hakka and Amoy. However, the written language, which is not phonetic but ideographic, is uniform. Mandarin was introduced as the official language by the ruling Nationalists who took over the island in

1949. Before this, Japanese was the official language. Although Mandarin remains the principal language of instruction in schools, English is taught as a first foreign language from junior middle school (seventh grade).

GOVERNMENT INFLUENCE

A relatively stable political system over nearly four decades has allowed Taiwan to focus on economic development concerns. While the government adheres to a capitalist system, it operates in areas that are considered to be of national strategic importance—banking, shipbuilding, railroads, fertilizers, steel, electricity generation, petroleum refining, alcohol, tobacco, and sugar. Recently, there have been recommendations that the government privatize some of these publicly held firms. However, vested interests have stalled the implementation of most privatization plans.

Most private businesses are small- and medium-size, family-owned firms driven largely by the profit motive. While there is relatively little government intervention in the conduct of business, there is also comparatively little private spending on research and development. Local production thrives on its flexibility or its ability to retool and produce for new and expanding markets at low costs. The present dilemma is whether this system of production can continue to sustain Taiwan's export-led economic growth. Because of increasing world competition in labor-intensive exports, new government policy stresses the need to move toward technology-intensive production and exports. Private-sector response to this government call has resulted in strong growth in domestic fixed capital expenditures in the past two years. Newly opened technology parks in various parts of the island have attracted significant investments. However, some manufacturers have opted to move their low-end production offshore. Strong profit orientation rather than strong government guidance is now orchestrating Taiwan's economic future.

THE ECONOMY

Economic Background

A hardworking, homogeneous population, directed by an appropriate mix of government programs and policies, has been Taiwan's major economic resource. An early and extensive program of land/rural reforms provided strong economic incentives to increase agricultural production and to service the rising demands of the growing urban sector. Alongside rural reform came the early protection of infant industries that allowed nondurable consumer goods industries (such as textiles, plastics, and electronics) to develop without direct government involvement. These industries, which first saturated the domestic market, later became the backbone of Taiwan's export promotion drive.

Taiwan's more recent economic prosperity has been due largely to its consistent and determined policy of export-led growth despite growing diplomatic isolation. Although this outward-looking orientation has made the domestic economy more susceptible to the many unpredictable swings in the international market, trade has been extremely favorable for Taiwan. Because of the smallness of the local market, domestic exports have been the economy's mainstay and Taiwan's engine for growth. The island economy is the world's 13th-largest trading nation.

Taiwan's export-led industrialization strategy has proved to be a remarkable success. Only a generation and a half ago, Taiwan was an underdeveloped, agrarian economy, dependent on U.S. foreign aid for its sustenance, but with a small, albeit growing, manufacturing base. Today, Taiwan is not reliant on agriculture for growth. There has been a drastic turnaround in the nation's economic structure. Export-oriented industrial output contributes about 47 percent of gross domestic product (GDP), while agriculture accounts for a mere 4.8 percent. Moreover, Taiwan's dependence on the United States has been radically transformed from one of unilateral aid dependence to that of bilateral trade reliance.

But along with its remarkable success, Taiwan's trade orientation has brought serious problems. There are protectionist threats from Taiwan's major trading partners, particularly the United States, because of the economy's huge, albeit narrowing, merchandise trade surplus. The United States has frequently threatened to invoke its trade retaliatory provisions under Section 301 of the new U.S. Trade Act, which links import quotas and/or tariffs according to a foreign government's own import controls and export subsidies against American-made goods. The United States has been more successful in forcing the NT dollar to appreciate relative to the U.S. dollar. In the past year, the NT dollar rose only 1.3 percent against the U.S. unit, but this was after appreciating about 40 percent in 1986 and 1987. This currency revaluation has helped narrow the bilateral U.S.-Taiwan trade gap still heavily favoring the island economy. In 1988, Taiwan had an estimated US$10.4 billion trade surplus with the United States, a 35 percent drop from the $16 billion surplus in 1987.

Another unwanted consequence of Taiwan's trade performance has been Taiwan's amassing of massive foreign exchange reserves. Fortunately, this has slowed in the past year. However, foreign reserves remain high. While high reserves are a sign of a healthy economy, it puts strong pressure on the local currency and on the money supply and domestic prices to rise. The inflationary effects of money supply growth remain temporarily dampened because of cheaper imports and the government's continuous mopping up of excess liquidity. In all, despite the unwanted side effects of its export-led growth policy, Taiwan is not likely to detract from its trade orientation in the near future.

The country enjoys a very high and rapidly improving standard of living. Per capita GDP is now nearly US$6,000, up significantly from $1,562 only a decade ago. With higher living standards have come adverse externalities. Rapid industrialization has brought extreme pollution in the industrial centers. Concerns about the environment are now a growing national issue in Taiwan. And labor shortages threaten the continued expansion of the island's thriving economy.

Politics

Following the demise of President Chiang Ching-kuo in mid-January 1988, Lee Teng-hui was sworn in as the new president of Taiwan. Lee, a native Taiwanese, is expected to serve out the remainder of President Chiang's six-year presidential term, with the National Assembly electing a new president in 1990.

After being named permanent KMT Party chairman during the 13th KMT Party Congress in July 1988, President Lee fortified his control over the ruling party while affirming continued, but cautious, political and economic reforms. Twelve new members were named to the 31-member policy decision-making body, the Central Standing Committee. Nearly 120 new members were elected to the 180-member Central Committee, a prestigious body with little policy-making power. Most of the new KMT leaders are relatively younger members carefully selected by President Lee to appease the old guard while consolidating his own power. The present cabinet is a careful balance between reformers and conservatives and is expected to continue the political and economic reforms initiated under President Chiang.

Taiwan has embarked on considerable political and economic reforms in the past two and a half years. Under Chiang, the government lifted the emergency measures (or martial law) in force since 1949 to protect national security, granted permission to establish new political parties in the island, and allowed residents to visit their relatives in the mainland. Under Lee, the government has allowed indirect trade with and investments in China via third countries and opened the door for Taiwanese participation in nongovernment, international conferences that are scholarly, cultural, or sports-oriented and are held on the mainland. These are welcome signs of growing political moderation and of increasing participatory democracy in Taiwan.

Yet, in the longer term, Taiwan's relationship with the mainland will have to be more directly addressed. The opening of the nation's Legislative Yuan and National Assembly to more democratic elections is on President Lee's agenda, although the pace of this democratization remains cautious. Because of its claim as the only legitimate government of all China, it is hard to reform the present system of political representation where officials elected by their constituencies in the mainland in 1949 still make up the majority of the nation's 322-member legislative body. These representatives will continue to serve in this legislative body until their death or until new elections in the mainland can occur. Only about a fourth of the seats in the Legislative Yuan are allotted to Taiwanese members. But as legislative members from the mainland age, a restructuring of the existing political system is inevitable. With the ascent of native Taiwanese to positions of power (including President Lee), Taiwan's strong emotional ties to the mainland are disrupting the clamors for independence that have also increased in the past year. In all, without forgoing its long-standing claim as the rightful government of China, fundamental changes in the political structure, largely favoring a more representative political system, are likely and should be accomplished in the next five years.

In the meantime, the KMT is slowly adopting more pluralistic politics by welcoming more native Taiwanese into its fold and by fostering a more liberal attitude toward the opposition. Fundamental changes in the party's traditional approaches to political problems have been unavoidable because of the growing restiveness of the middle class, who have more readily taken to the streets, and to a more assertive local press to seek redress of grievances. The ruling KMT's continued political dominance in the long run will depend on its success in incorporating Taiwanese interests within its structure.

Recent Economic Activity

Although Taiwan's economy did not expand at a double-digit rate, 1988 was another exceptional growth year for Taiwan. Real GDP rose a remarkable 7.2 percent. Exports, which account for about 50 percent of GDP, were still the principal reason for the strong performance of this demand-driven economy. Exports grew 13 percent, while imports rose 44 percent. The economy showed a US$10.9 billion merchandise trade surplus for the year. This overall performance is in contrast to that of the previous year when real GDP soared 12.4 percent, exports and imports rose 35 percent and 46 percent, respectively, and the trade balance surplus was a record US$20.2 billion.

While Taiwan's exports are still dominated by traditional labor-intensive goods, such as textiles and footwear, small-scale electronics, and so on, there has been a considerable decline in the share of these exports in the economy's total exports. Significant inroads have been made in the exports of machinery, plastics, chemicals, and metal manufactures. Yet world competition remains stiff even at this higher level of export goods, particularly from other newly industrialized countries in Asia and Latin America. Government authorities have long recognized the need to reorient productive capacity from traditional labor-using industries to more upscale manufactures if Taiwan is to remain competitive in the world market. However, despite the launching of a new high-technology strategy five years ago, this next level of transformation of the economic structure has only recently taken root, forced by a tightening labor market. Only since 1988 has there been a resurgence in domestic capital expenditures aimed largely at modernizing existing plant and equipment. More expenditures on research and development are still needed, something that can be accomplished only with more government help.

Rising wages and concerns about the environment are slowly transforming the economic structure of the island economy. The relocation of Taiwan's environmentally hazardous industries to neighboring countries, as is already the case with a number of its labor-intensive factories (e.g., footwear manufacturing firms in China), is likely to happen on a larger scale in the long run. Very low unemployment rates and high wages have already forced firms to invest in more labor-saving technology or else to relocate overseas, particularly within the familiar grounds of the Pacific Rim, where labor and land are cheaper. The unemployment rate presently stands at an extremely low 1.41 percent, and wage growth last year (measured in US$) averaged a strong 18.2 percent. However, a more vocal labor movement is also emerging as industrial workers are becoming more aware of their rights under the Labor Standards Law and as strikes are no longer banned with the lifting of martial law.

Because of the relative stability of the NT dollar during most of the year, there has been a steady outflow of foreign funds that had earlier speculated on the appreciation of the NT dollar. An estimated US$8 to 10 billion of these foreign funds have been driven out of the economy since February 1988. This, along with a narrowing trade surplus, has slowed Taiwan's accumulation of foreign exchange reserves. Foreign currency reserves stand at about US$74 billion, while official gold holdings, buoyed by purchases of nearly US$4.55 billion for the first 10 months of 1988, are presently valued at US$5.3 billion. Taiwan's total foreign reserves, while hardly changed from the US$79.45 billion reported as of the end of 1987, are still large. It is equivalent to over 17 months of imports of goods and services when a three-month reserve ratio is usually considered adequate.

Excess liquidity continues to fuel the stock market. It is also responsible for soaring real property prices. In all, the outflow of domestic investment funds has remained hesitant, despite gradual liberalization of the financial system favoring investments overseas. While inflation has picked up from last year, it remains negligible as the strengthening NT dollar and the lowering of many tariffs has made imports cheaper.

Despite uncertainties posed by the appreciation of the NT dollar, the strong protectionist sentiments within the United States, and the September–October 1988 tailspin in local stock market prices, overall business confidence in the economy remains strong. Growth is expected to be lower in the coming years, although still relatively high in comparison to other industrial nations. Real GDP is expected to grow 6.7 percent in 1989 and average between 5 and 6 percent annually until 1994.

Monetary Policy

In 1987, the government replaced its foreign exchange controls, which had been in place for nearly 40 years. The new Foreign Exchange Control Regulations allow individuals and private corporations to hold foreign exchange and buy foreign securities. These rules are aimed at curbing the growth of both the foreign reserves and the money supply, since previously, all foreign exchange earnings in Taiwan had to be converted to domestic currency with the Central Bank of China (CBC).

Unfortunately, the early outflow of foreign exchange that followed the lifting of the exchange controls has been reduced to a trickle. The expected sudden outflow of investment funds from Taiwan has not materialized for a number of reasons. First, the exchange rate was not effectively stabilized before the lifting of the exchange controls. Many local investors held back in anticipation of further revaluations of the local dollar relative to the U.S. dollar. Instead, speculative money from overseas flowed into the economy, further exacerbating the growth of foreign exchange reserves and putting more pressure on the NT dollar to appreciate.

Second, domestic investors still remain constrained by the number of financial firms that can offer investments in foreign stocks and bonds. Moreover, few local investment companies can provide the conservative investment opportunities, particularly in U.S. real estate and other tangible foreign assets, preferred by cautious domestic investors. At present, five appointed local banks can invest abroad. However, none presently offers investment opportunities for the small investor in foreign stock and futures markets and in mutual funds. Four major local securities and trust companies also are allowed to issue certificates whose proceeds are invested in foreign stocks, bonds, and other securities. Yet the total amount they can manage is limited to US$160 million, a drop in the bucket compared to the US$75 billion reserves the economy presently maintains.

Third, an unclear regulatory environment governs the channeling of financial investment overseas. While foreign banks and brokerages want more access to local investors, there remains a huge gray area of murky regulations and licensing requirements in which these firms risk working. At present, foreign banks and financial firms pursue a wide spectrum of activities. A few actively pursue business and risk confrontation with official regulators, but others are content with providing information to the public and maintaining a presence in Taiwan. Finally, even if clearer financial reforms were instituted soon, these may not prompt a strong outflow of funds in the near term. With continued uncertainty in the international stock exchanges, there are few attractive international alternatives. With the appreciating NT dollar, local investments appear more favorable.

The strong growth in the country's exports has caused the Central Bank of China to amass record reserves and to allow the domestic money supply to grow at disturbingly rapid rates. For 1988, M1 money supply grew 24.51 percent despite the government's continuous mopping of excess liquidity by selling treasury bills, government bonds, and certificates of deposit. Domestic banks have also absorbed some of the economy's excess liquidity. Bank deposits have now about reached their limits, as average private propensity to save has remained close to an extremely high 27 percent. Not surprisingly, domestic interest rates remain at very low levels. The underutilization of capital only shows how the absence of effective and efficient financial intermediaries in Taiwan has lagged behind the island's productive capacity growth and industrial development.

The NT dollar presently exchanges at NT$26.2/US$1, up considerably from the NT$35.50/US$1 exchange rate at the beginning of 1987. Because of this appreciation, a peculiar problem has arisen with the nation's huge reserves. As most of Taiwan's reserves are U.S. dollar denominated, the CBC has often reported huge losses on its reserve holdings. For instance, from September 1985 to June 1987 when the local currency appreciated very rapidly relative to the U.S. dollar, the CBC reported over US$12 billion in paper losses. Other state-owned banks have been similarly hit. As the local currency continues to appreciate, these losses will continue until the CBC and the state-owned banks diversify their foreign currency portfolios.

More immediate concerns brought about by the appreciating NT dollar are (1) the effect it has on the country's trade surplus given that exports are made more expensive and imports cheaper and (2) whether local companies can continue to withstand the effects of this revaluation given the accompanying decline in price competitiveness of Taiwanese products. However, while these are valid concerns, they are not likely to reverse Taiwan's overall trade performance given Taiwan's remarkable export promotion record. At best, the appreciating NT dollar should slow considerably the growth of exports and encourage faster import growth in the years ahead. The economy, however, will continue to maintain a healthy merchandise trade surplus of between US$6 and $9 billion in each of the next five years.

Inflation

Consumer inflation averaged a very low 1.1 percent in 1988, despite strong domestic money supply growth and higher disposable incomes. This was largely because of lower import prices because of the appreciation of the NT dollar and the lowering of tariffs on many consumer imports. In 1989, consumer prices are expected to rise by between 3 and 5 percent. Delayed effects of money supply growth and higher disposable incomes were largely responsible for this inflation rate. However, cheaper imports, with the revaluation of the NT dollar and because of lower import tariffs, will continue to dampen inflationary pressures brought about by the high domestic liquidity.

Government Finance

Despite significant cuts in many import tariffs in recent years and increased foreign competition in the government's former tobacco and wine monopoly, public revenue was larger than public expenditures in 1987 and 1988. This is a remarkable turnaround from budgetary deficits in four of the six previous years. However, government deficits have never been too large, amounting to less than 1 percent of GDP in each of these deficit years. Government spending has contributed little, if any, to domestic inflation.

In a continuing bid to make better use of the economy's excess foreign reserves and to help narrow the nation's trade surplus with the United States, the government continues to push the completion of key infrastructure projects by 1990 with preferential U.S. imports. These projects include the modernization of Taiwan's telecommunications industry; the third phase expansion of the China Steel Corporation; the completion of important power projects, including a fourth nuclear power plant, a thermal power plant in Taichung, and a pump storage project in Sun-Moon Lake; the construction of a rapid mass transport system for Taipei; the construction of an underground railroad project in downtown Taipei; the continuation of flood control projects in the Taipei area; and the building of a second freeway in northern Taiwan. These government expenditures, totaling about US$23.5 billion, are also intended to help generate domestic demand, an important secondary stimulus to economic growth. Unfortunately, a number of these key projects have temporarily stalled because of government difficulties in purchasing private lands necessary for the completion of the infrastructure projects.

Foreign Trade

The economy's remarkable export resurgence, which started in late 1985, continues to fuel Taiwan's economic growth. Led by electronics and machinery and textiles, the country's exports rose 13 percent in

1988. This is despite the sharp appreciation of the NT dollar relative to the U.S. dollar in 1987 and persistent protectionist threats from the United States, Taiwan's major trading partner. Last year's strong export performance was accomplished largely on account of Taiwanese ability to capitalize on changing competitive positions in world markets arising from realignments of major international currencies. By taking advantage of the previous rise in value of the Japanese yen and major European currencies relative to the U.S. dollar, Taiwan has been able to prolong its export boom. In 1988, exports to Asia and to Western Europe increased approximately 31.6 percent and 25.5 percent, respectively. Not coincidentally, exports to the United States dropped. In 1988, exports to the United States dropped 1 percent compared to growth of 28.6 percent in the year previous. This pattern of export expansion cum diversification should continue in the near term as Taiwan decreases its trade reliance on the U.S. market by expanding in other untapped yet lucrative markets.

Taiwan's imports jumped 44 percent in 1988 because of a stronger NT dollar, reductions in many import tariffs, and continuing promotions by government to "buy American." This helped narrow Taiwan's trade gap with the United States. In 1988, Taiwan's merchandise trade surplus with the United States amounted to a US$10.4 billion, a 35 percent drop from that of a year earlier. Although imports continue to rise faster then exports, the economy enjoyed a healthy US$10.9 billion trade surplus last year. Further expected revaluations in the NT dollar relative to the U.S. unit and anticipated drops in economic activity in the industrial economies should hurt Taiwan's near-term export growth performance. Exports to the United States will slow, while Taiwan will continue to diversify its export markets. Already, the Taiwanese are considering rejoining the GATT. Moreover, because of Taiwan's relatively high level of technology and because of its skilled and relatively cheaper labor, the Japanese are finding Taiwan a cheap and convenient source of components for goods manufactured in Japan. Taiwan is also searching for new markets in previously unexplored regions like the Caribbean, Latin America, and the Middle East.

Along the lines of a more creative and open foreign policy, gradual expansion in socialist markets, particularly China, should also help Taiwan move away from its strong reliance on the U.S. market. Indirect trade with China is Taiwan's fastest-growing trade area. The China trade totaled US$2 to 2.5 billion in 1988, up from US$1.52 billion in 1987. Increasing the European market, Taiwan's third-largest trading partner, has also become a priority particularly in light of the upcoming formation of a single European Community (EC) market in 1992. To soften the likely drop in exports to the EC after 1992, local manufacturers are considering directly establishing factories in Europe. However, with this diversification of Taiwan's export markets only just begun, the island economy should remain vulnerable to conditions in the United States in 1990 and 1991. Because the United States has insisted on quick solutions to its global trade deficit problem, revaluations of the NT dollar rather than discriminatory protectionist legislation will be principally responsible for the slowdown in Taiwanese export growth in the near term.

In the longer term, Taiwan's export-led growth will also have to come from diversifying the product composition of its exports. High value-added items, such as electronics, machinery, and petrochemicals, should replace labor-intensive industries such as textiles and footwear. Diversification not only of markets but also of export products (toward more upscale manufactures) will be necessary for Taiwan's continued prosperity.

Because of the appreciating NT dollar and more liberalized import measures arising from the need to narrow the wide trade gap with the economy's trading partners, Taiwanese imports should increase faster than exports from 1990 to 1994. Imports from the United States will increase, particularly of consumer goods (because of more liberalized import measures) and capital goods (because of increased domestic investment expenditures). In the meantime, Japan will continue to be an important source of capital goods and intermediate components needed for Taiwan's exports.

Taiwan has always had deficits on the service account of its balance of payments. This is expected to change in the medium term with the liberalized foreign exchange rules now in effect. Taiwanese investments overseas are expected to increase as facilities (domestic and foreign) for channeling savings to overseas investments increase and improve.

Although Taiwan is considering rejoining the IMF, it is not a member of either the World Bank or the IMF. As such, it does not regularly report figures on its outstanding debt. Whenever it does report debt figures, Taiwan does not break down its debt according to components, so it remains difficult to monitor Taiwan's total indebtedness. Nevertheless, Taiwan has hardly any debt when viewed against its ability to pay. Most of the debt can be considered as short-term obligations arising from foreign speculation on the NT dollar. The WEFA Group estimates Taiwan's total 1988 foreign debt at roughly US$18 billion, US$12.6 billion of which is short term. Long-term debt service payments amount to a very low 3.3 percent of the total value of exports of goods and services.

Energy

Imported oil remains Taiwan's main energy source. Since the first oil crisis in 1972 and until 1983, oil imports increased because of the rapid expansion of the transportation sector and the petrochemical and metal products industries. Since 1983, however, these imports have fallen from 20 million kiloliter oil equivalent in 1984 to 18.8 million KL oil equivalent in 1986, despite the fall in crude oil prices worldwide. This happened because of the diversification of Taiwan's energy sources and because of general energy conservation efforts following the two drastic oil price hikes in the past.

At present, coal accounts for a hefty 21 percent of total energy consumption, nuclear power for 16.1 percent, and hydroelectric power for 4.4 percent. Just 10 years ago, coal accounted for only 10.9 percent of total energy consumption, nuclear power for 0.1 percent, and hydroelectric power for 4.0 percent. The nation's conversion to alternative energy sources other than crude oil has been a significant accomplishment. While the nation still depends significantly on imported oil, the nation's huge foreign exchange reserves constitute an additional backstop to any serious energy shortage that may arise from another oil shock.

PROSPECTS AND CONCLUSIONS

Political stability is likely to continue despite the nation's adjustment to a younger, Taiwan-born leadership and an increasingly noisy, but fragmented, opposition. Economic policies of the past are not likely to change in the near term. The government will continue to provide incentives and broad guidelines rather than dictate directives and regulations. Moreover, political liberalization and moderation, which was begun by President Chiang, should continue, providing a welcome atmosphere for sustained economic prosperity.

In the long term, Taiwan also needs to define its international political status. This has severely lagged behind the island economy's economic accomplishments. Although exports will continue to provide a strong impetus to growth, a more balanced economy will become evident in the long term as domestic expenditures continue to pick up. Inward-looking growth alternatives will focus on spending on infrastructure and cleaning up the environment. The opening of the economy will also see the development of the services sector, which has lagged behind industrial growth. Demand for services should pick up with rising real disposable incomes.

CHAPTER 18

A GROWING MARKET FOR U.S. COMPANIES

Fredrick F. Chien

INTRODUCTION

During the past 30 some years, the Republic of China on Taiwan, under a planned free economic system, has achieved an average annual economic growth rate of 9 percent along with a relatively equal distribution of income, becoming a model for other developing countries. With per capita GNP reaching US$6,333 in 1988, technology-intensive industries have replaced labor-intensive industries and capital-intensive industries as the mainstay of the industrial structure.

As the pace of economic liberalization quickens, the domestic market is opening to investors from abroad and the investment climate is improving substantially. However, the nation is also encountering a number of problems, such as continued NT dollar appreciation, excess liquidity, labor disputes, environmental pollution, and consumer litigation. All of these issues present opportunities for and challenges to the future development of the economy.

Concerning opportunities for U.S. companies, Taiwan's domestic demand for general consumer goods, heavy construction equipment, high-tech products, and pollution-control equipment is growing rapidly. National income is rising steadily and public infrastructure is expanding and improving. Now that a turning point has been reached in industrial upgrading, people on the island are paying much more attention to environmental protection. U.S. companies should take advantage of the opportunities made possible by these developments and by the substantial appreciation of the NT dollar to promote the export of the above-mentioned products to Taiwan.

THE TAIWAN ECONOMY IN TRANSITION

Economic Liberalization Moves Full Speed Ahead

In the face of new global economic conditions, the R.O.C. government in 1984 embarked on a program of economic liberalization with a view of eliminating outmoded administrative controls and regulations and giving fuller play to the market and price mechanisms, thus ensuring the optimal allocation and rational distribution of productive resources. These deregulatory steps have resulted in the dismantling of numerous restrictions such as the control of interest rates; a ban on the import of gold, wine, and cigarettes; state control of gas stations; tariff and nontariff barriers; import quotas; controls on the movement of capital; foreign exchange controls; and a ban on the issuing of licenses to new security firms.

As for the future prospects of development, the government has set timetables for various liberalization measures. The average real tariff (i.e., tariff revenue relative to total value of imports) rate will be cut to 3.5 percent by 1992, the same as in developed countries. In addition, the government will give foreign investors better access to the service sector. For example, the domestic container transportation and securities brokerage industries will be open to investment by foreigners. This deregulatory timetable has been set in hopes of achieving a better balance of trade and easing trade friction, accelerating industrial restructuring, putting an end to protectionist practices, encouraging market competition, and enhancing economic efficiency.

Adjustment under a Strong NT Dollar

In September 1985, the G-5 countries agreed on the directions national policies and exchange rates should take to facilitate growth and external adjustment. The major industrial countries committed themselves to supporting a gradual and substantial depreciation of the dollar to improve the U.S. deficit and to taking other measures to achieve better balance in global growth. As one of the major surplus countries, Taiwan has also played an important role in this currency realignment. The NT dollar appreciated 44 percent against the U.S. dollar from September 1985 to December 1988.

Trade statistics have already registered the effect of the NT dollar appreciation. R.O.C. exports priced in U.S. dollars increased a mere 13 percent in 1988 from the previous year while imports rose a steep 42 percent, resulting in a 41.3 percent annual decline in the trade surplus. Meanwhile, the contributions of the various sectors of the economy toward economic growth changed significantly. On the production side, industrial output increased 4.6 percent in 1988, while services, relatively invulnerable to export fluctuations, registered a 9.5 percent annual growth—an indication of the increasingly dominant role the service sector plays in economic growth. With respect to the demand side, because of currency appreciation, export expansion no longer accounted for the major part of economic growth. Net foreign demand for 1988 made a negative contribution to economic growth. At present, with private consumption and gross capital formation expanding rapidly, the growth of the R.O.C. economy has come to depend largely on the growth of domestic demand.

The Challenges and Opportunities of Abundant Savings

In the early years of the postwar period, Taiwan suffered from a low savings rate and a shortage of foreign reserves. Today, 40 years later, the situation is reversed: savings substantially exceeds domestic investment, and large, successive trade surpluses have led to a massive accumulation of foreign reserves.

While abundant savings help pave the way for further growth of the economy, the structural trade surplus and the mountainous foreign reserves have led to friction with trading partners, expectations of further currency appreciation, overly rapid money growth, and a potential threat to price stability. Faced with these problems, the country must accelerate the pace of its economic liberalization. The rapid increase in domestic demand and the readjustment of the industrial structure expected to accompany a faster rate of liberalization will provide opportunities to foreign concerns to increase their investment in and expand their exports to Taiwan.

A Reexamination of Rapid Growth

Labor Becomes More Assertive
One of the most important factors accounting for the outstanding performance of the Taiwan economy over the past 40 years is harmonious relations between labor and management. Workers in Taiwan enjoy a level of prosperity never experienced in Chinese history. However, with improved living conditions and a higher level of education, they now expect better working conditions. The emergence of political partisanship along occupational lines has made the resolution of labor-management disputes all the more difficult.

A Labor Standards Law is being implemented with the aim of protecting the welfare of laborers and guiding the management of enterprises. The Council of Labor Affairs, established in August 1987 to meet the needs of a changing work force, will be upgraded to the Ministry of

Labor Affairs under the Executive Yuan (the Cabinet). This new ministry will take the initiative in rebuilding a sound labor-management relationship so as to secure labor rights and pave the way for further social and economic development.

Growing Concern about the Environment

With incomes, living standards, and the level of education rising, concern has shifted from accumulating material wealth to providing a better quality of life and protecting the natural environment. Motivated by these concerns, environmental interest groups have sprung up virtually everywhere.

Fully committed to achieving a cleaner environment, the government has issued Guidelines for Current Environmental Protection Policy, which are to serve as a blueprint for both public and private efforts to upgrade environmental quality. The guidelines emphasize giving higher priority to environmental protection than to economic growth, making pollutors pay the cost of pollution abatement, paying compensation for pollution damage, increasing public investment in environmental protection, and encouraging energy-saving and pollution-preventing forms of investment and consumption.

The Growth of Consumer Consciousness

With a fast-growing economy, improved living conditions, and the development of mass communications, the people of Taiwan have shed the conservatism of the past and taken a much keener interest in public affairs. In the early 1980s, they began to speak out in defense of their interests, one of the foremost of which is the protection of consumer rights.

Schools now offer courses in consumer education, helping to spread knowledge about issues of importance to consumers. Consumer protection centers, set up by local governments and private organizations, offer services to consumers and participate in international consumer activities. Meanwhile, public representatives have taken up the cause of consumer protection, and government officials are emphasizing consumer welfare when drafting and implementing laws and regulations. A Commodity Labeling Law is already in effect, and both a Fair Trade Law and a Consumer Protection Law are being deliberated in the Legislative Yuan.

OPPORTUNITIES AVAILABLE TO U.S. FIRMS

Increased Demand for Imported Goods as a Result of Increasing Income and Enhanced Living Standards

Rapid growth of the economy has brought about a steady increase in the income of the people of Taiwan. GNP per capita reached US$6,333 in 1988, higher than even in some developed countries. Higher living standards, the government's economic liberalization policy, successive rounds of tariff cuts, and the accumulation of some US$75 billion in foreign exchange reserves have contributed to a burgeoning demand for imported consumer goods. This combination of conditions provides a golden opportunity for U.S. industries to increase export sales to Taiwan.

Demand for Imported Machinery and Equipment Grows as Public Investment Increases

Taiwan has spared no effort in expanding public investment—to meet the needs of long-term economic development, to satisfy the demand for continuing improvement in the quality of life, to effectively employ the huge amount of foreign exchange accumulated as a result of large trade surpluses, and to alleviate the almost unrestrained appreciation of the NT dollar over the past few years. Of the larger-scale public investments made since 1985, the 14 Major Construction Projects are the most noteworthy.

These projects encompass steel production, power generation, petrochemical production, energy development, telecommunications, irrigation, medicare facilities, tourism, and environmental protection. Total investment in the projects will rise to NT$700 billion by 1992, the year that most of them are expected to be completed. Meanwhile, the government is considering the feasibility of an additional some 20 large-scale projects, which may be approved and completed within the next few years. Total investment in public construction projects, including the 14, stood at NT$250 billion as of 1987 and is expected to grow at an increasingly rapid pace in the years to come. A significant portion of that growth will be accounted for by the purchase of certain equipment and materials from foreign countries. That means another outstanding opportunity for export-conscious U.S. firms.

Industrial Restructuring Creates Demand for High Tech

Dramatic changes have been occurring in the industrial structure of Taiwan. While the service sector is growing more rapidly than industry as a whole, within manufacturing, electronics has displaced textiles as the leading sales generator. Structural change of this type is expected to accelerate in the years ahead.

In the future, high-tech industries are certain to dominate the industrial mainstream, stimulating additional demand for high-tech products. This process will be catalyzed by the universal application of high-tech knowledge and an economic liberalization policy favoring the development of high technology. For example, while imports of household electronic products have grown at an average annual rate of more than 50 percent during the late 1980s, imports of high-tech-intensive consumer durables—color television sets, refrigerators, and sedans—have more than doubled annually. In addition, computers, facsimile machines, and microwave ovens are expected to be used far more extensively. Taiwan's "information-age" society is now ready for the development of specialized service industries that, in turn, will generate snowballing demand for all types of high-tech equipment, especially that relating to information processing and value-added networks.

Given industry's need for improved product quality, demand will grow rapidly for high-tech equipment, parts, and components, especially those that are of exceptionally high quality or that perform vital functions. Domestic firms with an interest in developing high technology will doubtless wish to strengthen technical cooperation with their foreign counterparts. With the United States serving as a leading source of technology, American firms will be among the major beneficiaries.

Growing Emphasis on Environmental Quality Creates an Expanding Market for Environmental Protection

Determined to achieve higher environmental quality, the government has enacted stricter pollution-control standards and has cracked down on factories that fail to meet them. Meanwhile, in a joint effort with private concerns, the government has stepped up investment in pollution control and prevention and has warned polluters to install the proper pollution-control equipment.

To satisfy the demand for environmental improvement, the government will promote development of a private environmental protection industry, with advanced environmental protection technology to be imported from the industrial countries. At the top of the shopping list will be such items as city refuse incinerators, drainage engineering, sanitary surveys, automatic operation equipment, equipment for the processing of industrial wastes, and facilities for the inspection of vehicle exhaust emissions.

Overseas Economic Cooperation and Development Fund Enhances U.S. Firms' Opportunities to Expand Exports to Developing Countries

To strengthen international economic cooperation, promote economic development, and discharge its obligations as a member of the international economic community, Taiwan in April 1988 inaugurated the International Economic Cooperation and Development Fund. The fund, whose initial operating capital has been set at NT$30 billion (equivalent to US$1.06 billion), will help promote economic development in developing countries and strengthen investment and trade ties with them through direct and indirect investment, loans, and technical assistance programs. By helping to stimulate economic activity in developing countries, the fund will provide opportunities to American firms to step up exports to the Third World.

CONCLUSION

Help from other countries, particularly in the form of U.S. aid in the 1950s and the 1960s, played an important role in Taiwan's economic success by laying a foundation for rapid economic growth. However, Taiwan would never have achieved the remarkable economic progress it has without the hard work and commitment of its people.

Taiwan today is the 13th-largest trading economy worldwide. With increasing affluence and equitable income distribution, its people will enjoy as even higher standard of living as domestic markets are opened wider to foreign imports under the economic liberalization program. Infrastructural investment, such as the 14 Major Projects, and investment in technical skills and other forms of human capital have made its work force so productive and so prosperous that many can now afford to buy luxury consumer goods and other products characterized by high income elasticity of demand—something that would have been almost unimaginable a few years ago.

In the manufacturing sector, investment is growing rapidly, not only in fixed assets and equipment needed to enhance productivity but also in intangible assets such as technical know-how, proprietary rights, patent rights, and copyrights—acquisition of which is vital to the success of Taiwan's drive to become a fully developed economy before the close of this century. Given the traditionally close ties between Taiwan and the United States and the steady upgrading of their trade and economic relationship over the past three decades, there is absolutely no reason to doubt that U.S. companies will play an important part in filling those needs.

Still, as the Taiwan experience demonstrates, the existence of opportunities is but one side of the equation of international trade. If success is to be achieved, those opportunities must be grasped and fully exploited. I sincerely hope U.S. industries will intensify their efforts to regain international competeness and take full advantage of the large and lucrative markets that await them in Taiwan, so trade between Taiwan and the United States will grow on a more even footing and their trading relationship will develop in a mutually advantageous manner.

APPENDIX

Contact Institutions

Offices of the Republic of China in Taiwan

Ministry of Economic Affairs:

Industrial Development and Investment Center
10F, 7 Roosevelt Rd., Sec. 1
Taipei
(02)394-7213
(Telex)10634 INVEST

Investment Commission
7F, 73 Ku-Ling Street
Taipei
(02)396-3697

Board of Foreign Trade
1 Hu-Ko Street
Taipei
(02)351-0271
(02)321-0567
(Telex)11434 BOFT
(Fax)886-2-3513603

China External Trade Development Council
4-7F, 333 Keelung Road, Sec. 1
Taipei
(02)738-2345
(Telex)21676 CETRA
(Fax)886-2-7576653

Offices of the Republic of China in the United States

Washington, D.C.
Economic Division, CCNAA
4301 Connecticut Ave., N.W., Suite 420
Washington, D.C. 20008
(202)686-6400
(Telex)440292 SINOECO
(Fax)202-3636294

New York
Investment and Trade Office, CCNAA
8th Fl., 126 E. 56th St.
New York, NY 10022
(212)752-2340
(Telex)752089 CITO UINY

CETRA, Inc.
41 Madison Ave., 14th Fl.
New York, NY 10010
(212)532-7055
(Telex)426299 CETRA NY
(Fax)212-2134189

Chicago
Commercial Division, CCNAA
Office in Chicago
8th Fl., 20 North Clark St.
Chicago, IL 60602
(312)332-2535
(Telex)282168 ROCTRADE
(Fax)312-3320847

Far East Trade Service, Inc.
Branch Office in Chicago
Suite 272, The Merchandise Mart
Chicago, IL 60654
(312)321-9338
(Telex)253726 FAREAST TRCGO
(Fax)312-3211635

Houston
Commercial Division, CCNAA
Office in Houston
1360 Post Oak Blvd., Suite 2150
Houston, TX 77056
(713)9619794
    9619785
(Fax)713-9619809

Los Angeles
Commercial Division, CCNAA
Office in Los Angeles
3660 Wilshire Blvd., Suite 918
Los Angeles, CA 90010
(213)380-3644
(Telex)910-3214021 ROC TRADE LSA
(Fax)213-3803407

San Francisco
Far East Trade Service, Inc.
Branch Office in San Francisco
Suite 603, 555 Montgomery St.
San Francisco, CA 94111-2564
(415)788-4304-5
(Telex)4974157 FETS SF
(Fax)415-7880468

CHAPTER 19

LEGAL ASPECTS OF DOING BUSINESS WITH TAIWAN

David C. Cheng
David J. W. Liu

PROTECTION OF INTELLECTUAL PROPERTIES
Patent Law
Trademark Law
Copyright Law
INFRASTRUCTURE FACILITIES

A Chinese proverb goes like this: When one enters someone else's territory, he shall follow the customs prevailing in that territory. The same is true when a corporation or individual does business with a foreign entity: He or she must know the basic laws and regulations that are relevant to the activity and the gist of how the systems operate. For foreigners to do business in Taiwan, they should understand that the legal system in Taiwan is that of a civil system, which means everything goes by "the book."

This is significant in the following aspects: First, clearly spelled out in "the book" are rules to follow with no exception or discretion available. Therefore, one must perform exhaustive analysis of the book to find all the relevant provisions to a case. Second, the book is limited in scope or might be unclear as to its application to a particular situation, which leaves much room for discretionary rulings or findings by the governmental agencies. Legal loopholes also exist. However, a prudent lawyer would not advise the use of legal loopholes without a thorough study of all the possible consequences.

This chapter will familiarize foreign investors or traders with the relevant statutes in force. As corporate life is usually perpetual, it is therefore recommended that professional advice is indispensable.

A detailed treatment of all the relevant statutes is not possible here, but copies of regulations mentioned can be obtained from the nearest R.O.C. trading office. Also, analytical assistance can be provided by any law firm in Taiwan.

Some important statutes or regulations are:

1. Statute for Investment by Foreign Nationals.
2. Statute for Encouragement of Investment.
3. Statute for Technical Cooperation.
4. Categories and Criteria of Productive Enterprises Eligible for Encouragement.
5. Criteria for Encouragement of Establishment or Expansion of Industrial and Mining Enterprises.

6. Categories and Criteria for Special Encouragement of Important Productive Enterprises.
7. Applicable Scope of the Strategic Industry.
8. Rules Governing the Screening of Applications for Exemption from Income Tax on Royalty Payments and Technical Service Fees Collected by Foreign Profit-Seeking Enterprise. (This is applicable to patent licensing, trademark licensing, technical assistance for plant construction, and technical know-how licensing exclusively for use by productive enterprises specified in the Applicable Scope of the Strategic Industry.)
9. Regulations Governing the Administration of Venture Capital Investment Enterprise.
10. Rules Governing the Guidance and Control of Export and Import Firms and Factories.
11. Criteria for Investment in Large-Scale Trading Companies by Overseas Chinese and Foreign Nationals.
12. Regulations Governing Securities Investment by Overseas Chinese and Foreign Investors and Procedures for Remittance.
13. Rules for Administration of Securities Investment Trust Fund Enterprises.
14. Guidelines for Screening and Approval of Establishment of Branches and Liaison Representatives Offices by Foreign Banks.
15. Statute Governing International Banking Business (applicable to offshore banking operations).

Other trades or businesses that are generally a subject of foreign investment include leasing companies, sales and distribution, purchasing operations, engineering service firms, and, more recently, the insurance industry. However, the government has promulgated what is known as the Negative List for Investment by Overseas Chinese and Foreign Nationals. A total of 392 industries fall under the following categories:

1. Agriculture, forestry, fishing, animal husbandry, and hunting (34 industries).
2. Mining and quarrying (16 industries).
3. Manufacturing (176 industries).
4. Electricity, gas, and water (4 industries).
5. Construction (6 industries).
6. Commerce (50 industries).
7. Transport, storage, and communications (31 industries).

8. Financing, insurance, real estate, and business services (42 industries).
9. Public administration social and personal services (33 industries).

In contrast, the government's policy is to encourage technology-intensive industries for the years to come.

The following sections will cover a general discussion of the legal system of the R.O.C.; government initiatives to attract trade and investment; import and export regulations; protection of intellectual property rights: patent, trademark, and copyrights; and a brief description of the infrastructure.

AN INTRODUCTION TO THE LEGAL SYSTEM OF THE R.O.C.

The administration of the R.O.C. legal system is the responsibility of the Judicial Yuan.

The court system is divided into three levels and has jurisdiction over all civil and criminal matters. The district court is the court of general jurisdiction and usually functions as the trial court or court of first instance. In addition, each district court has notary judges. All documents needing to be notarized must be submitted to the district court notary judge. No private citizens act as notaries public in the R.O.C. Each municipal government has a district court that is presided over by a chief judge. The high court, at the provincial or special area level only, is an appellate court. The Supreme Court is the court of last resort and the final level of appeal.

THE MINISTRY OF JUSTICE

The Ministry of Justice is a division under the Executive Yuan. This ministry is responsible for judicial training and for the assignment of judges and procurators. It also has a national law enforcement function carried out by the Ministry of Justice Bureau of Investigations. This is often considered to be the counterpart of the FBI in the United States.

THE SYSTEM OF LAWS

The supreme law of the land is the constitutional law and the regulations related to it. For criminal matters, there is the Criminal Code and the Code of Criminal Procedure. For civil matters, there is the Civil Code and the Code of Civil Procedure. The final source of statutory law is contained in the various administrative laws and regulations.

Commercial, criminal, and civil law follow principles similar to those in Europe and the United States, but there are differences in formalities and enforcement. Taiwan's legal structure is closest to that of the German civil court system. It was imported to China by students educated there at the end of the Ching dynasty. Thus, because it did not evolve naturally, it may seem unnatural to the Chinese who live under it now.

German law was chosen as the model instead of U.S. codes because its rigorous outline is clearer than the precedents U.S. law incorporates. But American preeminence in world trade since the end of World War II has made a strong U.S. contribution to commercial law in Taiwan.

The main thing a foreign person in Taiwan must remember is that unfamiliarity with the law, mainly its formalities, is a dangerous condition and he or she can become ensnared in difficulties or serious trouble if affairs are not handled properly. As always, ignorance of the law is no excuse. Foreigners may get the mistaken notion that they are working with a legal system that is backwards or prejudiced against them. But the law in Taiwan is rational. The visitor or investor here should not assume his or her experience at home applies in Taiwan.

Taiwan's courts recognize, when appropriate, the opinions and judgments of foreign courts without requiring litigation in court in Taiwan. This is true particularly when the foreign decision does not conflict with R.O.C. statutes, tradition or moral imperatives, or national policy. Recognition of the legal authority of each side's decisions must also be reciprocal. For example, it is common to successfully petition Taiwan courts to honor the decisions of foreign courts in property settlements and in securing payment of debts owed to parties abroad.

Foreigners can make an initial step in familiarizing themselves with law in Taiwan by purchasing an English-language translation of the Chinese law code. However, the translation was done 40 years ago and has never been amended.

Most foreign persons requiring legal services decide upon an attorney based on the recommendation of friends and business associates. In addition, the Bar Association offers a list of lawyers, the American Chamber of Commerce recommends AmCham members, the American Institute in Taiwan publishes a directory of U.S. firms and a list of other law offices, and while advertising is prohibited, some lawyers are listed in the privately published Yellow Pages available at hotel book stands and bookstores.

While it is not necessary to retain the services of an attorney who is experienced in Chinese law and also familiar with the law in certain foreign countries, there may be some value in retaining such services so a client can clarify the technical differences between law in Taiwan and that at home. A competent legal guide can boost the confidence of a foreign businessperson by explaining the legal system in Taiwan.

Foreign visitors may mistakenly believe they can get things done more satisfactorily by skirting the law. Their associates in Taiwan may encourage them to be dependent on them to do this. Foreign businesspeople may hear that they can selectively choose those aspects of the code they will disobey while following certain "time-honored" practices of the culture. They may curry favor with well-placed persons or those who claim special knowledge on shortcuts. Foreigners may be led to believe they can circumvent legal requirements or relegate them to the background.

One well-known example is the practice of using *gwansyi*, or personal relationships. These vary from family connections to old-boy networks to the most obscure connection if one side thinks he or she can stir up feelings of obligation. One thing must be remembered: if a case is correct with respect to the law, *gwansyi* is not important. While *gwansyi* has a strong position in Chinese custom, reliance on it in legal matters carries the seeds of disappointment and disaster, and maybe the loss of a friendship. The law is the law.

Another piece of the foreigner's baggage is the idea that bribes get things done. While this approach may apply among other circles of society, the great majority of officials in Taiwan's government are conscientious and responsible and shun this ancient practice. However, this area is another one in which a visitor's associates in Taiwan may try to impress him or her with their ability to solve problems with a well-placed *hungbao* or "red envelope."

Taiwan's legal system is rational and sound, and if a litigant's claims are accurate and stated properly, he or she will get justice. Persons who stress the need for *gwansyi* or suggest bribes most likely are trying to improve their own positions, not yours. The law prevails.

In some situations, foreigners may walk blindly into legal trouble and find themselves, for example, prevented from leaving the country by a court injunction although no charges have been proved. They don't like the idea of having to retain an attorney to fight what may appear to be whimsical injunctions. It is very important to Taiwan, and to the business prospects of persons from abroad, that they realize such cases do not represent discrimination against foreigners. They are a necessary aspect of legal procedure that makes full investigation of certain cases possible.

Problems may arise from other quarters, for example, matters related to recent changes in the patent, copyright, and trademark laws. Again, difficulties often arise because of ignorance. Also, foreigners may falsely believe a R.O.C. citizen will not suffer for infractions of these laws and so ask a Taiwan associate to do things they would never dream of doing themselves, or ask in another country.

Taiwan's reputation as a center for pirating has largely derived from the ability of technicians to produce for demand. Infractions of the intellectual property laws often come when R.O.C. manufacturers take orders for goods from foreign buyers who are well aware that what they are asking the Taiwan source to copy is a patented or copyrighted item.

R.O.C. manufacturers' participation in this deceit partly reflects their dependence on foreign buyers to come to them with designs and samples. This excessive dependence is also the reason there is now a stronger push than ever to get Taiwan manufacturers to start producing quality items under their own trademarks and to find their own marketing niches. While foreign buyers may justify illicit proposals by saying the civil penalties the suppliers may suffer are mild, their suppliers may come under severe criminal charges.

THE CRIMINAL CODE

The Criminal Code, its rules, and those laws relevant to the maintaining of good order are much the same as found in European countries, particularly German law, rather than U.S. law. Specific guarantees protect the rights of accused persons. Innocence is presumed, and the same constitutional guarantees exist as in most other developed legal systems.

The new National Security Law was legislated only in 1987, after 38 years of martial law. It will take time for the provisions and spirit of the new order to become institutionalized in the thinking of the people and those who must enforce and administer it.

Under martial law, some offenses the European and American legal systems would not consider serious were viewed as very serious in the R.O.C., especially those disturbing public peace, order, and social tranquility. However, intrusions into the everyday lives of the citizenry were minimal.

The Deadly Weapons Control Law promulgated June 27, 1983, puts weapons control under a separate statute, and offenders are tried in the regular court system. Any type of violation of the laws regarding the possession and use of prohibited drugs is viewed with great concern. Mere use or possession is punishable by up to seven years' imprisonment, and a conviction for trafficking in drugs can result in the death penalty. The limited drug abuse relative to Western standards and the low incidence of violent crime provides an investor with one of the safest environments in the world in which to live and conduct business.

THE CIVIL CODE

The Civil Code and its procedures cover many of the primary matters pertaining to relations among people. Many topics relating to the regulation of business are contained in separate specific enactments. A major departure from Western systems is the deemphasis on precedent in civil matters.

The Civil Code points out that civil matters should be regulated according to the applicable provisions of law. If no law specifically applies, the case should be decided "according to custom." If there is no applicable custom, the "general principles of law" can include precedent, but such previous decisions will not dictate a decision in a civil matter if there is an applicable statute or custom. This deemphasis on precedent may prove disturbing to a foreigner accustomed to its use.

Rather than relying on the court system or the application of statutory law or customs, a substantial number of civil disputes within the R.O.C. are settled through private negotiation. According to the Civil Law, the court may suggest negotiation in good faith before the matter comes to a judicial test. Many civil disputes are settled through such court-negotiated agreements.

GOVERNMENT INITIATIVES TO ATTRACT TRADE AND INVESTMENT

Various government offices and commissions are dedicated to assisting prospective investors and their legal counsel to ensure that every option is considered and every advantage and incentive is understood.

The Industrial Development and Investment Center

Established by the Ministry of Economic Affairs in 1959, the Industrial Development and Investment Center (IDIC) provides the primary link between the investor and the government agencies. It provides information about current investment opportunities, incentives, and regulations. The IDIC has four divisions:

1. The Investment Promotion Division provides consultation and other preliminary contacts.

2. The Coordination Division studies and makes recommendations on the simplification of investment procedures. It arranges meetings between investors and knowledgeable government officials to discuss difficulties encountered by investors. This division also helps investors locate plant sites and purchase land.

3. The Investment Research Division is responsible for the exploration and identification of investment opportunities.

4. The Information Division edits and publishes informational brochures and reference materials related to making investments in Taiwan, including statutory reference material in English.

The Joint Industrial Investment Service Center

The Joint Industrial Investment Service Center (JIISC) was set up by the Ministry of Economic Affairs (MOEA) in 1982 to provide one-stop service to overseas Chinese and foreign investors. It streamlines all administrative steps from making application for investment permission to establishing factories.

JIISC is also supported with staff from the following with the intent to put all investment-related services under one roof:

1. The Bureau of Entry & Exit Control of the Ministry of the Interior.

2. The Overseas Chinese Affairs Commission.
3. The Taiwan Power Company.
4. The Bank of Communications.
5. The Export-Import Bank of China.
6. The Telecommunications Supervision Department of the Taiwan Garrison Administration, General Headquarters.
7. The Police Department.
8. The Taiwan Telecommunications Administration.
9. The Hsinchu Science-Based Industrial Park.
10. The Export Processing Zone Administration of MOEA.
11. Other investment-related government agencies.

The Investment Commission under the MOEA

The Ministry of Economic Affairs established the Investment Commission (IC) to serve as the initiation point of the government investment screening and evaluation apparatus. Any foreign national intending to make an investment under the provisions of the Statute for Investment by Foreign Nationals must submit an investment application, together with the plans, a milestone or progression chart, and all other relevant data to the IC for approval.

The commission is made up of ranking officials from all the government ministries having an interest in such investments. If other applications are required to fulfill statutory or administrative prerequisites, these may also be filed through the commission. The IC may be authorized by any government authority to act on such applications in place of the actual office to which it is addressed. The IC is required by law to render a decision within two months from the time all the application procedures have been completed. The IC seeks ways to adjust the mandated requirements to meet the changing investment climate.

For instance, until August 1983, an inward remittance to finance an approved investment plan was required to be made within six months from the date of approval, and under unusual circumstances a six-month extension could be granted. However, economic conditions from 1981 to 1983 made this requirement a deterrent to investment plans. Therefore, the commission announced in August 1983 that the period within which the remittance had to be made had been extended from six months to three years.

In addition to the above office, several other governmental and quasigovernmental entities assist in various phases of trade and investment planning:

1. The China External Trade Development Council (CETRA, formerly CETDC) sponsors exhibitions of products of foreign design and promotes activities to open foreign markets for domestic products and domestic production. The Taipei World Trade Center (TWTC) houses the exhibits of over 2,000 leading import/export suppliers in a new seven-story complex. The trade center boasts fully computerized services, the latest in communications, and a multilingual staff, while providing excellent opportunities for market expansion and new product investment.

2. CETRA has established a foreign trade administration information system. The computerized operational systems included in this network are:

- A manufacturing and commercial management information system.
- A system for authorizing the processing of exports.
- A system to monitor mainland China's foreign trade movements.
- A system to monitor and keep record of international trade and properties.

The council also operates foreign trade information libraries in Taipei, Taichung, and Kaohsiung. These are open to Taiwan companies with permission from the Ministry of Economic Affairs.

3. The R.O.C.-U.S.A. Economic Council and U.S.A.-R.O.C. Economic Council sponsor a continuing series of trade and investment conferences that promote group discussions, hold seminars, and exchange visits in order to address problems and improve bilateral trade.

IMPORT/EXPORT REGULATIONS

Classification of Imports

Imports are classified into three categories: prohibited, controlled, and permissible.

Prohibited Imports. The import of narcotics and those items enumerated in the Customs Law is prohibited.

Controlled Imports. Goods on the controlled list include military supplies, national defense and communication equipment, ships, poisonous chemicals, antiques, jewelry, and some items that can be supplied locally. Alcoholic beverages, cigars, and cigarettes are open to only particularly approved countries.

In most cases, imports of these controlled goods are handled by government trading agencies subject to government regulations or allocation. However, productive enterprises and end-users who need to import them for their own use are still allowed to apply to the Board of Foreign Trade (BOFT) of the MOEA for approval on a case-by-case basis.

Permissible Imports. Goods not covered under the prohibited and controlled lists are placed on the permissible list and may be imported by registered traders. However, for commodities whose import permits are granted to government agencies, end-users, or private productive enterprises, no import applications from traders will be accepted, even if the commodities are on the permissible list.

Import Licensing

All permissible imports require import licenses issued by the BOFT. Applications may be made through authorized foreign exchange banks. At present, over 6,000 imported items have been entrusted to authorized foreign exchange banks for licenses for import that are normally valid for six months and entitle the importer to the necessary foreign exchange.

For political, diplomatic, or economic reasons, import is restricted on certain commodities from designated procurement areas. In recent years, the government has adopted a more liberal import policy and lifted restrictions on many commodities.

Government Procurement

The Central Trust of China (CTC) and the Taiwan Supply Bureau are two government trading agencies handling the import of products for government organizations and public enterprises.

Every government organization and public enterprise must file a detailed listing of its desired annual imports for screening and approval to the BOFT's Foreign Trade Screening Committee by the beginning of each fiscal year, July 1.

Priority for any given item will be given to Taiwan-made products if they meet specifications and requirements. However, if an import item is approved and an equivalent or appropriate substitute is not available in the domestic market, the foreign-made item will be purchased. Government trading agencies, upon receipt of a letter of authorization by government organizations and public enterprises, may undertake procurement abroad, usually through open tenders from the designated procurement areas.

Scheduled procurements are usually announced in local newspapers and on bulletin boards. Notices are also issued abroad through the branch offices of the above trading agencies. Bids may be tendered directly by the foreign bidder or through his Taiwan agent with power of attorney. The second option is much better; foreign exporters who appoint a local agent or have other capable representatives in Taiwan can identify opportunities at an early stage. This is an important advantage for successful marketing in this highly competitive sector of the local market.

Methods of Settlement

Under present practices, methods of settlement for imports may be classified as follows:

- Payment is made in foreign currency by letter of credit.
- Settlement will be made in foreign currency by the importer at the time of receipt of goods, or the shipping documents, or at maturity where the contract with the supplier is for payment on a document-against-payment (D/P) basis.

Classification of Exports

Exports are also classified into three categories: prohibited, controlled, and permissible.

Prohibited Exports.   Any item that is itself illegal or the possession of which is prohibited by law cannot be exported.

Controlled Exports. The export of goods on the controlled list can be applied for directly to the BOFT. Approval is based on the considerations that those items do not hurt the people's livelihood or economic development and that for strategic goods there should be no possibility of transshipment to the China mainland.

Since 1979, government policy has been to allow trade with a number of socialist countries, most of them in Eastern Europe: Czechoslovakia, the Democratic Republic of Germany, Hungary, Poland, and Yugoslavia. Since 1988, the R.O.C. government has debated whether to also lift barriers against direct trade with the Soviet Union, North Korea, Vietnam, and Laos.

Once the application is approved, the applicant should approach an authorized bank for an export license pursuant to the usual procedures.

Permissible Exports. Export licenses are issued automatically for permissible goods by authorized foreign exchange banks.

Export Licensing

All exports are subject to export licensing. However, unsolicited samples, gifts, advertising materials, personal effects, and parcel post on the permissible list not exceeding US$500 in value do not require licensing but must be declared to Customs.

In applying for an export permit on permissible goods, the exporter must submit an export application with relevant supporting documents (such as a letter of credit or a contract) directly to an authorized foreign exchange bank.

The export license is valid for 30 days. If the exporter fails to effect shipment within the valid date, the original license will be nullified.

Methods of Settlement

Payment for exports can be made in accordance with one of the following methods:

1. Letter of credit.
2. Advance payment by telegraphic transfer, demand draft, or mail transfer.
3. Documents against acceptance not exceeding 180 days after shipment.

4. Documents against payment.
5. Consignment in value not exceeding US$100,000 to the same destination.
6. Medium- and long-term deferred payments.

Payment for live animals, fresh vegetables and fruits, canned mushrooms, and asparagus is not permitted on a collection basis.

For exports on consignment or on a deferred payment basis, the exporter must first file an application for an export permit with the BOFT and, within one month of approval, apply to an authorized foreign exchange bank for an export license.

PROTECTION OF INTELLECTUAL PROPERTIES

Patent Law

The Patent Law provides three categories for the issuance of patents:

1. New inventions.
2. New utility models.
3. New designs.

Differentiation between the three is difficult but very important. The most clearly defined is a new design patent. This is the creation of the external appearance of an object, giving it a particular image that is of value. A design must be new with respect to its shape, pattern, or color. The new design must be a novel, original creation and arouse a sense of beauty. Unlike a new invention or new utility model though, it need not produce any technical or mechanical effects.

The difference between a new invention and new utility model, which requires both internal technical and mechanical accomplishments, is not so clear. The Administrative Court, discussing the differences in a 1981 decision, stated that a patentable invention uses a measure completely new in theory. Such a measure should never have been used before to solve the same problem.

A patentable new utility model differs from a patentable new invention in that, although the measure used in a new utility model may be a conventional technique that is not novel in theory, it is still considered to have met the requirements for a patentable new utility model if its spatial configuration is novel and can produce a certain effect or improve the efficacy of the article.

Distinguishing between new inventions, new utility models, and new designs is necessary in applying for a patent. The distinction is also important because of differing punishments for infringement of rights and term length of the patent. A new invention patent has a 15-year term, a new utility model patent's term is 10 years, and a new design patent runs only 5 years.

The most important reason for distinguishing between the three is for application purposes. If a new utility model is incorrectly identified as a new invention or new design, the Patent Office will reject the patent and the patentee must begin the process again. However, the filing date of the original application will remain the operative filing date as long as the application is filed within 30 days of receipt of the Patent Office's decision. The same is true when a new design is incorrectly identified as a new utility model. While the ultimate decision regarding which category the particular patent falls into is made by the National Bureau of Standards Patent Office, familiarity with the characteristics of each is helpful.

The criteria for each are as follows:

1. New inventions: novel and have industrial value.
2. New utility models: novel and practicable with respect to form, construction, or fitting.
3. New design: novel, aesthetically pleasing, and applicable to an object.

The law also provides for unpatentable items:

1. Foods, beverages, and habit-forming articles, except the manufacturing processes thereof.
2. New varieties of plants and animals as well as microorganisms, except the breeding processes for new varieties of plants and new varieties of microorganisms.
3. Diagnostic, therapeutic, or surgical methods for diseases of human or animal body.
4. Scientific principles or mathematical methods.
5. Rules or methods for playing games or sports.
6. Other methods for schemes that can be carried out only by means of human reasoning and memory.
7. The discovery of new uses of products, except for those of chemicals and medicines.

8. Inventions detrimental to public order, good customs, or health, or inventions the use of which would be contrary to the law.

Under existing laws, a foreign corporation that has not been recognized by the R.O.C. government is not considered a juristic person. Therefore, it is not a legal entity eligible to enjoy legal rights. Violation of the Patent Law is a criminal offense and prosecution can be instituted only upon complaint. A nonjuristic person does not have the right to either file a complaint, which would lead to public prosecution, or to initiate private prosecution. The amendment to the Patent Law will provide a foreign corporation that is a nonjuristic person with the capacity to file a complaint leading to a public criminal prosecution. This will enhance a patent holder's ability to secure enforcement and will increase the viability of the Patent Law.

Opposition or Cancellation Suits
The Patent Law currently provides for the suspension of all criminal and civil suits pending the issuance of an irrevocable decision on any opposition or cancellation suits against the applicable patent. This has led many infringers to institute opposition or cancellation actions against the patents they are accused of infringing. Until the lengthy opposition or cancellation action and its appeals are concluded, the infringement actions are stayed.

Maximum Penalty for Infringement
The current Patent Law has increased the maximum penalty for counterfeiting patented inventions to five years' imprisonment and/or a 50,000 yuan (NT$150,000) fine. The maximum penalty for imitating patented inventions will increase to five years' imprisonment and/or a 30,000 yuan (NT$90,000) fine. The proposed increase in the maximum punishment, the Ministry of Economic Affairs hopes, will be a strong deterrent and make infringement very unattractive.

Trademark Law

Several categories of identifying marks exist, including trademarks, service marks, and certification marks. R.O.C. Trademark Law provides for registration of two of these: trademarks and service marks.

A trademark distinguishes the products of one company from those of another. A trademark may consist of a word or words, a phrase, a person's name, a symbol, a picture, or any combination of these identifications. Trademarks must appear on the product. A service mark identifies the source of a service rather than the source of a product.

Taiwan accords protection to three kinds of marks: principal marks, associated marks, and defensive marks.

Principal Mark.   This is the mark first registered or filed. If two or more marks are simultaneously filed, one of them must be designated as the principal mark.

Associated Mark.   If a principal mark is registered, and an applicant wishes to register other similar marks for the same goods or for goods in the same class, the similar marks must be designated as associated marks.

Defensive Mark.   This is issued when the same applicant wishes to register the same design for commodities or services of different classes but of the same or similar nature. When an application for mark registration is submitted, the class of goods on which it will be used must be designated.

Registration Required for Protection
Unlike some countries that award protection to the first user of a trademark, Taiwan awards protection to the first registrant of a mark. The registrant acquires priority based on the filing date of the registration application. If two or more applications for identical or similar marks for use on the same goods or class of goods are filed on the same date, the determination will be made by drawing of lots. Not all marks, however, are eligible for registration.

Before it is eligible for registration, a mark must be markedly distinctive in its design. The design, with designated colors, shall be based on a word, drawing, symbol, or combination thereof and may include the name of the mark within the design. Words used in a mark shall include the pronunciation and shall be expressed in Chinese with Mandarin pronunciation. The Chinese pronunciation may be supplemented by words or letters in a foreign language. Foreign marks are not bound by these restrictions. The marks, however, may not be identical or similar to the national flag, the national emblem, the national seal, military flags, military insignia, official seals, or medals of the Republic of China, or the national flag of any other nation; or the image or the name of the late Dr. Sun Yat-Sen, or of a chief of state; or the Red Cross International sign, or the name, emblem, or badge of famous international organizations; or the Chinese "Standard Quality" mark, or any local or foreign mark of a certification nature; or a famous mark of another person used on the same goods in the same class; and so on.

Rights Acquired by Registration

The owner of a mark obtains, as of the date of registration, the right of exclusive use of the mark. The owner acquires the right to place the mark on goods, packages, or containers for sale in domestic or foreign markets. The registrant may also use the mark in television or print advertisements or as participation in an exhibition for the promotion of goods. If the mark consists of some foreign language, placing that portion on goods for export shall also constitute use. However, this right is limited to the registered design (not variations on its theme), and the use is limited to the same goods or goods in the same class as designated and registered.

The term of exclusive use is 10 years from the date of registration. The right is renewable for an unlimited number of 10-year terms. The application for extension must be made within six months before the expiration of the existing term. The original registration certificate and design of the trademark must accompany the application. Because the terms for associated and defensive marks are calculated from the date of registration of the principal mark, all related marks must be renewed at the same time. In addition to being renewable, the exclusive rights are also assignable, licensable, and inheritable.

Assigning, Licensing, and Inheritance of a Registered Mark

Assignment.   Although the Trademark Law provides for the assigning of registered marks, some limitations are imposed:

- A registered mark may not be assigned unless accompanied by assignment of the business.
- Associated and defensive marks may not be assigned.
- An assignment must be recorded with the Trademark Office within one year, and until the assignment is recorded, it is not enforceable against third parties.

- Before the rights are valid against third parties, the assignee must apply for a name substitution on the trademark registration application. The assignee's name replaces the original applicant's name.

Licensing. Licensing of registered marks is restricted for the same reason: preservation of the credibility of the mark. Licensing will be permitted only in two circumstances. The license amounts to an assignment and meets all of the requirements of an assignment. In other words, the business is also assigned, or the licensor of the mark directly supervises and controls the manufacture of the goods, thus maintaining a standard of quality of the goods bearing the mark. In addition, the goods produced under a license must indicate they are manufactured by a licensor.

Before any licensing agreement can take effect, it must be approved by the National Bureau of Standards and the Investment Commission of the Ministry of Economic Affairs. This approval is obtained by submitting an application, the licensing agreement, registration certificate of the applicable mark, and other relevant documentary evidence.

Licensing of marks, like licensing of patents, is governed additionally by the Statute for Investment by Foreign Nationals and the Statute for Technical Cooperation. In practice, a foreign national acting as licensor will have trouble obtaining approval. However, if the licensor is Taiwanese, and the licensee is a foreign national, or if both the licensor and licensee are R.O.C. nationals, the licensing approval will be much less difficult to obtain.

Penalty for Infringement of the Trademark Law

The owner of a registered mark has the exclusive right to use the mark. The owner may request an infringer to remove the infringement and pay for any damages suffered by it. In addition, if the owner knows of an incipient infringement, he or she may obtain an injunction to prevent it.

Contravention of the Trademark Law is a criminal offense. Penalties of up to five years' imprisonment and NT$150,000 fine are provided for various violations.

In addition, an individual who uses, with the intent to defraud another, a design identical or similar to a famous trademark of another country that is not registered in Taiwan on the same goods or class of goods shall be imprisoned for not more than three years, and/or fined 30,000 yuan (NT$90,000). Use of this punishment is restricted to marks owned by foreign nationals whose countries have concluded treaties or agreements with Taiwan providing reciprocal protection. The provision may also be invoked in cases where a reciprocity agreement has been concluded between civic bodies or organizations with prior approval of the Ministry of Economic Affairs.

Copyright Law

Scope of Copyright Protection
Protection is provided upon completion for the following categories of intellectual work:

1. Literary works and their translations.
2. Oral works and their translations.
3. Compilations.
4. Artistic, pictorial, photographic, and musical works.
5. Motion pictures.
6. Sound recording and videotapes.
7. Computer programs.
8. Maps.
9. Scientific, technical, or engineering design drawings.
10. Lectures, musical performances, stage presentations.
11. Choreography.
12. Other intellectual works.

A recent addition to the law expanded the methods of reproduction and transmission to include exhibition, visual display, broadcasting, oral public presentation, and performance. With these additions, the scope of Taiwan's copyright protection is comparable to international standards.

Completion of Registration Required for Protection
Automatic protection upon completion is accorded only to R.O.C. nationals. In addition, the burden of proof of completion date, and with it the right to protection, rests with the author. Registration can be used as prima facie evidence of the right to protection. Therefore R.O.C. nationals, as well as foreign nationals, should seek registration of intellectual works they desire to protect.

Copyright Holder Rights
The owner of a copyright has the exclusive right to publicly recite, broadcast, perform, exhibit, reproduce, compile, translate, lease, or

adapt the work. While an intellectual work cannot be the subject of compulsory execution, persons other than the copyright owner of a commercial audiovisual work may request approval to make a separate audiovisual recording two years or more after the first publication. The request must be in writing and specify the method of recording and amount of compensation. If the copyright owner does not come to an agreement within one month, the Copyright Office shall decide the amount of compensation and the request will be granted. In addition to this two-year limitation, the length of the copyright term varies according to the type of intellectual work involved.

A copyright may be held by co-owners, is assignable, inheritable, and may be the subject of a pledge. In order to be valid against third parties, the assignment, pledge, or inheritance must be registered with the Copyright Office. Although the author and the copyright holder need not be the same individual, the copyright holder may not publish the intellectual work in the name of anyone other than the author.

Duration of Copyright

The term of a copyright is calculated from the date of completion or, if the completion date is unknown, from the date of first publication. The copyright of an intellectual work is vested in the author for life unless otherwise prescribed by the law. A compilation, motion picture, sound recording, videotape, photograph, or computer program all have copyright terms of 30 years.

Remedies Available to Copyright Holders

A number of remedies are furnished to copyright holders. The Copyright Law provides for an injunction to prevent an incipient infringement as well as the right to file civil suit and receive damages for an infringement. A co-owner of a copyright may initiate civil proceedings without first obtaining the permission of the other co-owners. A copyright owner who is a foreign juristic person that has not been recognized by Taiwan also has the right to file a civil suit for compensation.

Compensation for the copyright holder for infringement will be calculated by the profit attained by the infringer and loss suffered by the copyright holder. The damages are to be not less than 500 times the retail price and if a retail price is absent, damages will be set by the court.

Infringers are jointly liable for damages, and they may be required to bear the cost of publishing in the newspaper the final judgment. A nonrecognized foreign juristic person may, like another copyright holder, file a private complaint as well as a complaint to initiate public prosecution.

When a complaint is filed with the competent governmental or public authority, the infringing work will be seized and the case transferred to the prosecutor's office for investigation. This is the first step in initiating a public criminal proceeding, which cannot be initiated without the filing of such complaint.

Violation of the Copyright Law is a criminal offense and is punishable by imprisonment.

INFRASTRUCTURE FACILITIES

Back in the 1960s and 70s, when Taiwan was carefully planning for its economic growth that is now considered the miracle of the 80s, the government of Taiwan realized how important the infrastructure is to economic growth. Consequently, huge amounts of capital were invested in the improvements of highways, railroads, harbors, airports, and telecommunications. Such investment and improvement is still continuing with the pace of economic and industrial growth.

Taiwan has five international seaports, Keelung in the north, Kaoshiung in the south, Taichung in the west, and Huslien and Suao in the east. They are all equipped with modern facilities and are sufficiently modernized to accommodate all needs. The Kaoshiung Harbor, ranked fourth in the world's seaports, has become one of the most important container transshipment centers in Asia.

The island has two international airports, one in Kaoshiung and the Chiang Kai-Shek International Airport in Taoyuan, about 40 kilometers southwest of Taipei. The Chiang Kai-Shek is equipped to handle 42 landings and takeoffs per hour. There are also smaller airports that provide passenger and cargo services linking all the major cities on the island and the offshore islands.

Highways and railroads lead to practically every door. Domestic and international telecommunications facilities are well developed and are more than sufficient to accommodate all business needs. Public utility services are available, with water and electricity supply in every corner of the island. Furthermore, the postal service of Taiwan has been remarkable for its speed and efficiency. All rates for transportation and utilities are either comparatively low or reasonably priced. By and large, the infrastructure of Taiwan is well prepared to meet any challenges of further modernization or continued economic growth.

CHAPTER 20

OPERATING A BUSINESS IN TAIWAN

Victor Young

FORMS OF INVESTMENT
    Technical Cooperation
    Representative Office
    Commercial Agency and Distributorship
    Branch Office
COMMERCIAL AND INDUSTRIAL SPACE
LABOR AND HUMAN RESOURCES

Establishing a foreign operation in Taiwan should be the result of normal and prudent business planning. Economic conditions and opportunities in Taiwan at the time and prospectively must be considered. Historically, business in Taiwan fell into broad categories of trading, labor-intensive manufacturing, and heavy industry. This will change.

As part of its continuing economic development, these traditional sectors are changing and should give way to new sectors that focus on high technology, value-added processes, financial services, professional services, and broader consumer-oriented businesses. Operating a business in Taiwan today is done in a mixture of specific regulations as well as flexibility and freedom.

The business activities coupled with tax considerations (discussed in a separate chapter), government-sponsored programs, and incentives should generally dictate the method and the form of doing business in Taiwan.

A Taiwan business may be organized in the form of a single proprietorship, a partnership, or a company (a corporation). Any person, whether Chinese or a foreign national, may engage in business as a member of a partnership or as a stockholder in a company. Only Chinese may be sole proprietors.

There are two types of partnerships in Taiwan: a general partnership and a partnership with "dormant" partners (similar to a limited partnership).

A general partnership is comprised of two or more persons who contribute capital to the business and manage it jointly. A partnership with dormant partners is one where the business is managed exclusively by the active partner(s), with the dormant partner(s) contributing capital to the business and sharing in its profits. The dormant partners do not participate in the management of the partnership and are liable only for the amount of their original capital contribution. The active partners are jointly and severally liable for all of the partnership obligations.

Partnerships are considered *profit-seeking enterprises* for R.O.C. income tax purposes. With the exception of professional partnerships (accountants, lawyers, doctors, and architects), partnerships are required to file income tax returns and pay income taxes at corporate rates on the profits they earn. In addition, each partner is required, as an individual, to declare after-tax profits from partnerships on a personal income tax return.

The corporate form of doing business in Taiwan, generally referred to as a *company,* is defined under R.O.C. Company Law as an entity organized for the purpose of making profits. There are four categories of companies:

1. Unlimited company.
2. Limited company.
3. Unlimited company with limited liability shareholders.
4. A company limited by shares.

All of these are separate legal entities distinct from its shareholders, directors, and officers. These companies are like corporations, with management centralized in the board of directors. They have the typical corporate characteristics including the power to enter into contracts, to hold property in their names, the ability to sue and to be sued, and continuity of life. The differences among the various types of companies lay principally in the extent to which the shareholders are liable for obligations of the company.

An *unlimited company* is comprised of two or more shareholders. The shareholders are jointly and severally liable for all of the company's obligations. This form is similar to a general partnership, and it is not a popular form of incorporation. The only difference from a general partnership is that the entity is subject to corporate income tax.

The *unlimited company with limited liability shareholders* is comprised of one or more shareholders with unlimited liability and one or more with limited liability. The liability of the limited liability shareholders is restricted to their capital contributions. It is similar to a limited partnership.

A *limited company* is comprised of not fewer than 5 shareholders but not more than 21. The liability of each shareholder is limited to his or her capital contribution. This is similar to a closed corporation.

A *company limited by shares* is the most popular corporate form of doing business. It is comprised of seven or more shareholders with capital divided into the number of shares. The liability of each shareholder is limited to the amount of shares held by each.

The *limited company* and the *company limited by shares* are the most similar to corporations outside of Taiwan and are the most important commercial and industrial forms of doing business in the Republic of China.

A *limited company*, in general, requires a minimum capital contribution of NT$500,000. Over 50 percent of capital must be owned by R.O.C. nationals, and 50 percent of the shareholders must be R.O.C. nationals. The chairman of the board of directors must also be a domiciled R.O.C. national.

A *company limited by shares,* in general, requires a minimum capital contribution of NT$1,000,000. At least seven of the shareholders must be registered with the authorities during the first year following formation of the company. At least 50 percent of shareholders must also be R.O.C. nationals, however, more than 50 percent of the shares may be owned by foreign nationals. The chairman of the board of directors and one of the supervisors must be elected from among R.O.C. national shareholders. The company limited by shares is required to issue common stock equal to par value. Preferred shares may be issued only if specifically stated in the articles of incorporation. Payment for shares issued may be paid in cash or in kind. Reduction of capital for a limited company is not allowed.

FORMS OF INVESTMENT

A foreign business or investor wishing to do business in Taiwan may use a variety of business forms. The policy framework and the environment in the country offers flexibility in structuring the business form that satisfies each investor need. Generally, the primary entry forms available to an investor are:

- Technical cooperation (i.e., licensing).
- Representative office or liaison office.
- Commercial agency and distributorship.
- Branch office.
- Local company as a joint venture with local partners.
- Local company wholly owned by foreign investors.

Most foreign businesses usually are established as a local company limited by shares or a branch office. Under certain circumstances, a branch office can be structured to engage in manufacturing or production. In most cases, Foreign Investment Commission-approved (FIA) companies can be wholly owned by a foreign investor.

Technical Cooperation

A foreign investor who is not intimately familiar with the environment in Taiwan or is undecided on direct investment may find a technical licensing program an easy and fast way to enter the Taiwan market. A foreign investor owning a valuable technology may license it to a local person or company to generate royalty income rather than engaging directly in manufacturing and sales activity in Taiwan. Even if an investor sets up an FIA company, he or she may still license technology and realize royalty income or technical service fees.

Typically, a technical cooperation approval (TCA) will have to be obtained from the Foreign Investment Commission to license know-how, trademarks, or patents. Ordinarily, royalty income to a foreign licensor who has received a TCA is subject to 20 percent income tax withholding. A foreign licensor may, however, apply for an exemption from withholding on licensing of R.O.C.-registered patents or certain know-how that is deemed to be of strategic importance.

Alternatively, a foreign licensor may structure an agreement without a TCA, but he or she should take into account all considerations and seek professional assistance.

Representative Office

If a company is engaged in procurement or similar activities in Taiwan in support of its business operations outside of the country, it can avoid the additional cost of setting up a local company or a branch by formally establishing a *representative office*. A representative office is not allowed to engage in profit-making enterprises. Therefore, it cannot act as a principal in buying or selling transactions. As somewhat implicit in its name, it may only coordinate local business affairs on behalf of an overseas principal. It must be careful not to engage in activity characterized as those of a business agency, branch office, or permanent office and company.

A representative office does not require Foreign Investment Commission approval; however, it must be registered with the Commercial Division of the Ministry of Economic Affairs (MOEA). It should be registered with the tax office of the district within which the office is to be located.

The foreign company should prepare a letter of appointment with the assistance of local legal counsel to establish the scope of the representative office's activities. A number of documents and forms need to be filed with the authorities as part of the registration process.

A liaison office can be set up by a foreign company that purchases goods from Taiwan and may, with the approval of the tax authorities, handle procurement-related matters such as locating prospective suppliers, inspecting merchandise, and following up on shipping schedules.

Commercial Agency and Distributorship

Foreign companies wishing to sell products in Taiwan may wish to appoint a local company as their agent or distributor. Because a foreign company will not be incorporated in Taiwan, the legal relationship with the local distributor is governed by provisions of the R.O.C. Civil Code. No formal approvals are required to enter into such a commercial relationship.

Branch Office

Many foreign companies choose to operate in Taiwan through the establishment of a branch office. This is a simple form of doing business because it is not a company incorporated in Taiwan, but merely an extension of the foreign company's head office. The foreign branch office can be established through application to the Ministry of Economic Affairs for recognition of the foreign parent company. No foreign company may do business or establish a branch office without prior recognition by the MOEA. Once recognized, the foreign company is submitting itself to jurisdiction of the courts and governmental agencies up to total paid-in capital of the foreign company.

A branch office constitutes a permanent business establishment under R.O.C. tax laws and, therefore, will be subject to taxes as if it were a local company.

A branch office need not comply with many requirements pertaining to R.O.C. corporations such as requirements for shareholders, directors, and supervisors. It requires only a litigious representative and a branch manager and must meet minimum capital requirements. The branch managers and representatives must be domiciled R.O.C. nationals or resident aliens.

As part of an application for branch office status, the head office of a foreign company must provide certain information, such as the amount of paid-in capital by the head office, a list of directors, and a description of the business and its location. In addition, an operating fund for the exclusive use of the branch office must be maintained in Taiwan. Again, the head office liability for the operations in Taiwan is not limited to the branch office's operating capital.

After recognition status has been obtained, the company still must obtain various licenses from a number of local authorities depending on the official location of the branch office, its activities, and the amount of operating capital.

The decision to set up a business in Taiwan must be made with consideration for current economic and commercial factors relative to a particular company, its business activities, or products. In addition to consulting with professionals, such as lawyers, accountants, and consultants, a foreign investor can also enlist the assistance of the Industrial Development and Investment Center (IDIC) of the MOEA.

The IDIC has the specific mandate to encourage foreign investment in Taiwan. It not only provides initial and followup assistance to foreign investors, including coordination with other governmental agencies on investment applications, but it can also assist in making appointments and arrangements for meetings with R.O.C. companies and individuals seeking foreign partners.

In addition, most countries have trade or foreign service offices in Taiwan to assist businesspeople in investing or establishing operations in the country. All of these organizations can be instrumental in identifying R.O.C. requirements, studying the legal, accounting, finance, banking, and tax considerations, and obtaining permits.

The regulatory framework for investment in Taiwan has been instrumental in R.O.C. business economic development. This includes initiatives and incentives geared toward opening Taiwan to foreign investment, including tax incentives and liberalization of foreign exchange controls. The following basic statutes should be considered when deciding to invest in Taiwan: Statute for Investment by Foreign Nationals, Statute for Investment by Overseas Chinese, Statute for Administration of Foreign Exchange, Statute for Technical Cooperation, and Statute for Encouragement of Investment.

Foreign investment in Taiwan may take the form of cash or materials, machinery, equipment, know-how, R.O.C.-registered patents or earnings, and capital gains from other investments in Taiwan. Cash investment can either be structured as straight equity investment or as equity plus debt by a foreign investor.

COMMERCIAL AND INDUSTRIAL SPACE

A company setting up operations in Taiwan has the option of leasing or buying space. However, land or facility purchases are restricted to FIA companies and domestic companies, and then only for those sites or buildings used in the direct operation of a business.

The decision of where to locate an operation is based on a number of factors unique to each business. There are no restrictions as to location of commercial or retail sites. For industrial sites, the four locations of operation are: Hsinchu Science-Based Industrial Park, export production zones (EPZs), government industrial parks, or private property.

In the Hsinchu Science Park and the EPZ, land is for lease only. Investors can purchase the existing factory building from the governmental agencies or from the current owners. Alternatively, investors can build new factories in the Science Park or in the EPZs.

Government industrial parks are available throughout Taiwan and usually are privately managed, although some parks are managed by governmental agencies. Generally, land can be purchased by an approved foreign-invested company. However, in most cases, sites have already been sold. Land and the improvements can be leased or purchased by contacting the present owners.

Private property and facilities are located throughout Taiwan and can be bought or leased by FIA companies. Foreign companies are not allowed to deal in housing developments other than by entering the construction market.

There is no standard practice for property lease contracts in Taiwan. Some contracts range from very simple to extremely detailed documents. Generally, these contracts will cover tenant responsibilities, landlord responsibilities, duration of lease, definition of lease premises, rental amounts, payments, deposits, termination, renewal, management of public space, maintenance, repairs, default, parking, and jurisdiction and governing laws. A title search should be undertaken for leases of industrial property.

The local unit of measure for real estate is the Chinese *ping*. One *ping* is equal to 36 square feet or 3.3 square meters. Rental space is calculated on the basis of total area including usable and unusable space, as well as common areas. Most companies' leases can range from one to five years with an option to extend the lease for the same amount of time. Consideration should be given to the real estate market, in general, in determining the best interests of landlord versus tenant for the terms of a lease.

Payment terms for leases will also vary, usually in multiples of monthly rent, which must be made as advance payment. It is not unusual for a landlord to request an entire year's rent in advance. Often, the landlord may request that a tenant supply a series of postdated checks, one for each month, to avoid the inconvenience of monthly collections. Normally, the rent is adjusted annually either by a set percentage or in accordance with the Consumer Price Index.

In 1989, real estate values increased rapidly in Taiwan, particularly in the Taipei area. In 1989, rental rates were:

- NT$1,500 to NT$4,000 per ping per month for office space.
- NT$4,000 to NT$25,000 per ping per month for retail stores.
- NT$700 to NT$1,000 per ping per month for factory buildings.

As in most other countries, the task of searching for and negotiating commercial and industrial sites can be difficult. It is easy to retain the services of a professional firm or real estate agent experienced in the field when seeking office or factory space.

LABOR AND HUMAN RESOURCES

One of the primary factors behind the rapid development of Taiwan has been an adequate and efficient labor force as well as an increasing pool of white-collar personnel.

Because of an emphasis on education, Taiwan has an abundance of talent in engineering, finance, and computer science and is particularly strong in export-related businesses such as banking, shipping, and manufacturing. However, there are weaknesses in areas such as consumer retailing, marketing, and some of the professions.

At one time, skilled and unskilled labor was relatively inexpensive. However, with economic development has come a change in the business environment in Taiwan. Shortages in labor have driven up the costs of manufacturing and producing in Taiwan. The shortage of labor in both blue- and white-collar sectors represents a significant challenge to Taiwan in the 1990s. Manufacturing, heavy industries, and construction have been hit hard by the simple shortages created by accelerated growth in the late 1980s. Compounding the problem is the emergence of a young, but very vocal, militant labor movement that is driving up the labor cost in virtually all manufacturing and production sectors.

After a long history of amicable labor-management relations, Taiwan is caught in a dilemma of how to control increasing labor costs without hurting the overall economy. Most of the manufacturing sector and a growing list of consumer and service business sectors are subject to the Labor Standards Law passed in 1984.

Work hours for laborers are usually eight hours per day, six days a week. Overtime is permitted with the prior consent of the labor union or workers and the approval of local labor authorities. The maximum overtime for male workers is 3 hours a day and 46 hours per month; for female workers it is 2 hours a day and 24 hours per month. Work hours for female and minor-age workers are more restricted.

Employees are also entitled to annual leaves ranging from 7 to 30 days after they have worked for more than a year.

An employee in Taiwan may voluntarily retire at age 55 after 15 years of service or at any time after 25 years of service. Retirement pay is calculated generally on the basis of 2 months' average wages for each of the first 15 years of service and 1 month's average wages for each year thereafter, up to a maximum of 45 months' average wages.

Under the Labor Standards Law, an employer must establish a

retirement fund. In addition, an employer is required to appropriate funds regularly for an employee welfare fund.

All employees in Taiwan are mandatorily covered by labor insurance for maternity, injury, sickness, disability, old age, death, and occupational hazards. The employer must fund 80 percent of the premium for occupational hazards. The recruitment of employees is fairly basic. There are only a few employment agencies in Taiwan, although there are a number of executive recruiting firms (usually management consulting firms). Most hiring is done through placements of advertisements and public postings.

CHAPTER 21

FINANCIAL AND TAX CONSIDERATIONS

Norris L. H. Chang
Makoto Taketomi

The articles on trade financing and protection, banking and local financing, and exchange fluctuations and controls are based on information available as of November 1988.

TRADE FINANCING AND PROTECTION

Export Financing

Export advance loans are available to finance exports. Although the amount that can be borrowed depends on the creditworthiness of the borrower, where a letter of credit (L/C) is issued, loans will generally be made up to 85 percent of the amount of the L/C or the amount of the contracted business, with a maximum period of six months. As of November 1988, the applicable interest rate was 5.5 percent p.a. When exports are transacted on a documents against payment (D/P) or documents against acceptance (D/A) basis, 70 percent to 80 percent of the value of the contracted business can generally be borrowed. It is also possible to receive financing during the period when export proceeds are being collected. In general, local banks will require the guarantee of the officers of the borrowing enterprise.

Many foreign-capital-related enterprises receive financing from local branches of foreign banks because it is possible to obtain export advance loans denominated in U.S. dollars there. The period is ordinarily up to six months and the interest rate is SIBOR (Singapore Interbank Offered Rate) or LIBOR (London Interbank Offered Rate) plus 1 to 2 percent p.a.

Medium- to long-term export financing is available from the Export-Import Bank of China. Taiwanese manufacturers of machinery, plants, and other capital goods for export are eligible for financing from the Export-Import Bank to provide deferred payment financing to their customers.

Also, for exports to the United States, one U.S. bank provides factoring finance, but because this is more expensive than bank loans, it is not used often.

Import Financing

Import usance financing is usually provided by issuing an L/C, carrying financial arrangements, on a U.S. dollar basis with a maximum period of 180 days and an interest rate 1 to 2 percent p.a. over the bank's cost of funds.

In general, the issuance of an import L/C requires a deposit of 10 percent or more. Finance for this deposit is also available. The Export-Import bank of China grants large-scale credits for imports of plant, equipment, and raw materials necessary for domestic industries.

Export Insurance

The Export-Import Bank of China handles three types of export insurance.

Comprehensive D/P and D/A insurance covers short-term export sales and ordinarily covers a maximum of 90 percent of the amount of the exchange bill up to 180 days. The insurance premium differs according to the period, conditions in the importing party's country, and other circumstances. The exporter is protected from nonpayment by the importer, bankruptcy, and other credit risks as well as from requisition or confiscation in the importer's country, and from war, revolutions, and similar contingencies. For bank negotiations of D/P D/A basis export bills, this insurance is ordinarily a condition.

In addition, medium- and long-term export insurance is available that covers exports of capital goods and services rendered abroad. There is also comprehensive export finance insurance that covers nonpayment of export loans made by commercial banks.

BANKING AND LOCAL FINANCING

An outline of financial institutions in Taiwan by the type and the services follows.

Financial Institutions

The Central Bank of China.

Domestic banks.

Specialized banks.

Investment and trust companies.

Foreign banks.

Credit cooperative associations.

Credit departments of farmers' associations.

Credit departments of fishermen's associations.

The postal savings system.

Life insurance companies.

Property and casualty insurance companies.

Bills finance companies.

Securities finance company.

Domestic banks hold the largest share among the various financial institutions mentioned above.

The Central Bank of China

The Central Bank of China issues bank notes, is the bank for other banks, and is the government's bank. It carries out financial policies through setting the official discount rate, conducting operations in open markets, handling reserve deposit requirements, and so on. Also, The Central Bank of China supervises and directs financial institutions such as commercial banks.

Domestic Banks

As of September 1988, there were 16 domestic banks with a total of 650 offices.

Bank of Taiwan (65).

City Bank of Taipei (27).

Bank of Communications (13).

The Farmers Bank of China (34).

The Central Trust of China (4).

Land Bank of Taiwan (58).

The Cooperative Bank of Taiwan (90).

The First Commercial Bank (107).

Hua-nan Commercial Bank (90).

Chang-hua Commercial Bank (106).

The Export-Import Bank of China (1).

City Bank of Kaohsiung (4).

The International Commercial Bank of China (23).	Shanghai Commercial and Savings Bank (7).
Overseas Chinese Commercial Banking Corporation (11).	United World Chinese Commercial Bank (10).

Of the above banks, the first 12 are government, prefecture, or city operated and the last 4 are privately operated. To increase efficiency, privatizing publicly operated banks is being considered. Nearly all domestic banks have their head offices in Taipei and a network of branches throughout the country. Most of the domestic banks are commercial banks. Their main businesses are taking various types of deposits and providing short-term loans. Although credit is principally extended by short-term loans, through rollovers of short-term loans, a good deal of essentially long-term financing is being provided. Some domestic banks have been designated specialized banks that provide financing for specific industries. These are the Bank of Communications (development financing), the Farmers Bank of China (agriculture financing), the Land Bank of Taiwan (agriculture financing), and the Export-Import Bank of China (export and import financing).

The largest part of commercial financing comes from the Bank of Taiwan, The International Commercial Bank of China, and the three largest commercial banks—The First Commercial Bank, Chang-hua Commercial Bank, and Hua-nan Commercial Bank.

Local Branches of Foreign Banks

Thirty-two foreign banks had branch offices in Taipei as of September 1988. Of these, three also had branches in Kaohsiung. In addition, several foreign banks have representative offices. Although the foreign banks engage in ordinary commercial banking activities such as deposits and loans, in order to protect local financial institutions, they are subject to various restrictions on the number of offices and other matters. The total value of deposits received is also restricted. Therefore, foreign banks tend to concentrate on foreign-trade-related business.

Although the share of foreign banks among all financial institutions is small, they are strong in foreign-trade-related transactions and, as it is relatively easy for them to provide foreign-currency loans, many foreign enterprises deal with both foreign banks and local commercial banks. Foreign banks in Taiwan are:

Dai-ichi Kangyo Bank.

Citibank N.A.*

Bank of America.*

Bangkok Bank.

American Express International Banking Corporation.*

Metropolitan Bank and Trust Company.

Chase Manhattan Bank, N.A.*

Irving Trust Bank.*

First Interstate Bank.*

Chemical Bank.*

Toronto-Dominion Bank.

International Bank of Singapore.

Westpac Banking Corporation.

First National Bank of Boston.*

Rainier National Bank.*

Grindlays Bank Ltd.

Deutsche Bank.

Societe Generale.

Banque Paribas.

Hollandsche Bank-Unie N.V.

Lloyds Bank International Limited.

Bankers Trust Company.*

Manufacturers Hanover Trust Company.*

Development Bank of Singapore.

Royal Bank of Canada.

Amsterdam-Rotterdam Bank N.V.

Hong Kong & Shanghai Banking Corporation.

Credit Lyonaise.

Banque Nationale de Paris.

Standard Chartered Bank.

Security Pacific Bank.*

Banque Indosuez.

---

*U.S. banks.

Other Institutions

Specialized Banks.   In addition to the various types of specialized banks described above, eight medium business banks located throughout Taiwan provide medium- and long-term credit to small- and medium-sized enterprises.

Investment and Trust Companies.   Presently, eight investment and trust companies are engaged in management and operation of various types of trust funds, providing medium- to long-term loans to productive industries, making direct and indirect investments, providing guarantees, and supplying other services.

Insurance Companies.   There are 8 life insurance companies and 14 property and casualty insurance companies. In Taiwan's high-growth economy, their business has developed rapidly, and they serve as an important source of funds for the financial and capital markets.

Bills Finance Companies.   The three bills finance companies' activities include acceptance of short-term securities, buying and selling in the secondary market, and acting as intermediary for government bonds.

Securities Finance Company.   There is only one such company. Its activities include providing funds for settlement of stock exchange transactions to securities companies and lending of stocks.

Financial Markets

In Taiwan, the call market for transactions in short-term funds between banks was set up in April 1980. In addition, a money market open to a large range of participants has developed rapidly in recent years. This market handles treasury bills (TBs), commercial paper (CP), banker's acceptances (BAs), and negotiable certificates of deposit (CDs). The maturities of instruments handled in the money market is less than one year, but the interest rates change according to the supply and demand of funds.

A unique underground market is pointed out to exist in Taiwan. Although it appears that a large amount of funds is actually being handled there, detailed data are unavailable.

In June 1984, an offshore financial market was initiated in Taiwan. At present, however, it is not being used very actively in comparison with those in Hong Kong and Singapore.

Maximum and Minimum Interest Rates

In recent years, credit conditions have been very relaxed. Under these conditions, the liberalization of interest rates was carried out in February 1986. Before that, the Central Bank of China set bank interest rates at the same time as it set the official discount rate. The Bankers Association now sets the maximum interest rate for deposits and the maximum and minimum interest rates for loans based on the consideration of the central bank's discount rate. After review by the Central Bank of China, each bank publishes its own deposit and loan interest rates within the range established by the Bankers Association. For large deposits (more than NT$1 million), it is possible for the customer to negotiate the interest rate with the bank. Banks consider the credit standing of the client, the amount and period of the loan, collateral, and other factors to determine loan interest rates within the maximum and minimum rates. Principal interest rates are shown in Table 21–1.

Raising Funds

If a foreign enterprise is interested in raising funds from outside, it can deal with local commercial banks, foreign banks, medium business banks, investment and trust companies, and other financial institutions. Depending on the type and size of the borrower, the amount of funds, and other conditions, the greater part of domestic borrowings by foreign enterprises comes from local commercial banks, foreign banks, and the money market through these institutions.

In dealing with local commercial banks, there are no special restrictions on foreign enterprises. In ordinary times, transactions are made on a commercial basis.

TABLE 21–1
Principal Interest Rates

Type	Annual Interest Rates (%)	Note
Deposits		
Passbook	2.00	Max.
Passbook savings	3.75	Max.
Time and time savings	6.25	Max. within 1 year
	6.75	Max. over 1 year
Checking	—	—
Loan		
Short-term	9.00 and 5.00	Max. and min. within 1 year
Medium- and long-term	9.75 and 5.50	Max. and min. over 1 year
Official Discount Rate		
Rediscount	4.50	
Accommodation against secured loan	5.50	
Temporary accommodation	9.00	

Note: As of September 1988.

Source: The Central Bank of China.

There are various restrictions on foreign banks with regard to financing on a Taiwan dollar basis, so this area is mainly for local commercial banks. Among them, the funds of the top five banks mentioned above account for the largest share. For both local commercial banks and foreign banks, there are limits on loans to a single company.

Raising Short-Term Funds

Unsecured bank loans are generally made on the basis of a promissory note. The guarantees of about two officers of the company will be required. Secured loans are made on a documentary basis. Both movable items, such as machinery and equipment, and immovable items, such as land and buildings, are accepted as collateral. However, evaluation standards are strict (about 50 percent to 60 percent of the market value) and the procedures are rather complicated, so in many cases a guarantee from the bank of the parent company, a standby letter of credit, or the guarantee of the parent company are required instead.

In Taiwan, postdated checks are in circulation rather than promissory notes and exchange bills, and there are many cases of loans on promissory notes, supported by postdated checks as a form of security. However, in recent times, the issuance of domestic L/Cs and the discounting of documentary bills based on these L/Cs have gradually become widespread.

Although overdrafts are not common, enterprises with a good credit standing might be able to negotiate this with a bank. However, a large line of credit will probably not be granted.

The maximum and minimum limits for loan interest rates have been described previously. Each bank announces its minimum interest rates for loans. Major commercial banks quoted a prime rate of 6.75 to 7.25 percent p.a. as of November 1988.

For borrowing from local commercial banks, differences in applicable rates occur depending upon the supply and demand for funds; the credit standing of the borrower; the type, amount, and period of the loan; security; and other conditions. However, it was possible for the borrowers of good credit standing to negotiate for a lending rate below the prime rate.

For reference sake, the level of interest rates on call loans in the money market was 4.56 percent p.a. at the end of 1987, 5 percent plus in the first half of 1988, and 4.19 percent p.a. at the end of September 1988.

Commercial paper (CP) has only a brief history in Taiwan but has rapidly come into use. In principle, CP must first be guaranteed by a bank dealing with the issuing company, then transferred to a short-term finance company for underwriting and sales. The interest rate for three-month CDs at the end of September 1988 was 5.05 percent p.a.

Banker's acceptances (BAs) have come into use in recent years as a means of raising short-term funds. BAs must be based on a commercial transaction, thus differing from commercial paper. Also, BA issuance is relatively inexpensive and simple. The three-month BA interest rate was 4.56 percent p.a. as of the end of September 1988.

In addition, in Taiwan, intercompany borrowing, especially between members of the same group, is common. Among large companies, there are cases where the employees' deposits play a fairly important role as a source of raising operational funds. For small- to medium-size companies, funding from the underground market still exists.

No domestic factoring services are available in Taiwan.

Raising Medium- to Long-Term Funds
Although short-term funds are the nucleus of all funding, medium- to long-term funds are also available from commercial banks in Taiwan.

The Bank of Communications, the Land Bank of Taiwan, and the investment and trust companies are all specialists in handling medium- to long-term financing. As of November 1988, the prime rate for medium- to long-term loans of the Bank of Communications and the specialized banks, including the Land Bank of Taiwan, ranges from 7.25 percent p.a. to 8.00 percent p.a. Ordinarily, because equipment or real estate is required as collateral and because the procedures are complex, it appears foreign companies are not active borrowers of long-term funds. However, for specified fields of industry and for pollution control facilities, preferential measures regarding interest rates, loan periods, and other terms are available if various conditions are met. Issuance of bonds is not very common.

Although many leasing companies have been established, the size of the lease market remains rather small.

Borrowings from Abroad
With borrowings from abroad, it is necessary to obtain prior approval from the Central Bank of China. In ordinary cases, with the exception of short-term funds of less than six months, approval is granted on a case-by-case basis; these funds are restricted to payments for imported foreign machinery and equipment and other items. Changing imported foreign funds into Taiwan dollars is prohibited.

Deposit Transactions

Taiwan Dollar Deposits

Foreign companies, regardless of their form of entry provided they make their deposits in their own name (as registered in Taiwan), are able to make resident deposits; also, foreigners working in Taiwan can make resident deposits, and no restrictions on deposit transactions with banks are exercised.

The maximum limit for deposit interest rates has been described previously. In accordance with this limit, each bank publishes its rates by type of deposit and by maturity. As of November 1988, the annual rates posted by three leading commercial banks (The First Commercial Bank, Hua-nan Commercial Bank, and Chang-hua Commercial Bank) were as follows: passbook deposits yield 1.75 percent; one-month time deposits, 4.0 percent; three-month deposits, 4.50 percent; six-month deposits, 5.00 percent; nine-month deposits, 5.25 percent; one-year deposits, 5.25 percent; and two- and three-year deposits, 5.5 percent.

Taiwan dollar deposits by nonresidents are not permitted.

Foreign Currency Deposits

In Taiwan, it is possible to make foreign currency deposits in designated foreign currencies, such as U.S. dollars and pounds sterling. However, only savings and time deposits are available. It is possible to deposit into and withdraw from these accounts the proceeds of foreign funds received, foreign-currency loans, foreign exchange bills, and foreign currency cash (for U.S. dollars only). But where exchange into Taiwan dollars is involved, partial restrictions exist.

Equity Financing

Stock Exchange

Taiwan has only one stock exchange, in Taipei. The fundamental law on stock transactions is the Securities Transactions Law, and the government agency administering it is the Securities and Exchange Commission, which is under the jurisdiction of the Ministry of Finance.

Enterprises in Taiwan do not readily disclose financial data and composition of assets; there have been relatively few cases where funds have been raised by listing stocks on the stock exchange or through the public subscription of company bonds. Thus, equity financing has not been very active. Financing of industries has been mainly carried out through the commercial banks. A characteristic of securities markets in Taiwan is said to be the insufficiency of information regarding corporate activities and performance. However, transaction volume is extremely large when the number of listed stocks and the current market value are taken into consideration.

As of the end of 1987, the number of listed stocks on the stock exchange was 141, with a par value of NT$287.3 billion and a total current market value of NT$1,386 billion. Transaction volume in 1987 was NT$2,669 billion. In the first half of 1988, an enormous cash flow into the stock exchange resulted in a tremendous boom in stock prices.

Policies have been adopted to promote growth in the stock exchange. These have included the requirement for all incorporated companies with paid-in capital exceeding NT$200 million to publicly trade their stocks. This does not apply to foreign capital enterprises unless the company wishes to do so and makes an application to list its shares. Also, an incentive has been given for listed enterprises in the form of a 15 percent reduction in the corporate income tax.

EXCHANGE FLUCTUATIONS AND CONTROLS

Foreign Exchange

The currency in Taiwan is the New Taiwan (NT) dollar. The foreign exchange market shifted to a floating rate system in February 1979. The spot exchange rate of the Taiwan dollar is decided and announced by the five main foreign exchange banks (Bank of Taiwan, International Commercial Bank of China, First Commercial Bank, Chan-hua Commercial Bank, and Hua-nan Commercial Bank), which fix the central rate for the day's spot U.S. dollar transactions based upon the weighted average of the previous day's interbank spot U.S. dollar transactions.

The Taiwan dollar had not moved much against the U.S. dollar in the past several years, fluctuating within the NT$38 to about NT$40 level. However, from the latter half of 1986—reflecting the increase in its trade surplus and the huge jump in its foreign currency reserves—the currency started to appreciate rapidly. At the end of 1985, one U.S. dollar was equivalent to NT$39.85 but at the end of 1986, the rate was $1 equals NT$35.50 and appreciated further to $1 equals NT$28.55 by the end of 1987. In the first half of 1988, the dollar stabilized in the NT$28.50 to about 29.00 range, and at the end of September 1988, it was NT$28.93.

The spread of the U.S. dollar quoted by foreign exchange banks was NT$0.05 plus/minus against the central rate, but, where a single transaction exceeds $30,000, each customer can negotiate with the bank within the range of NT$0.20, plus/minus of the central rate. Futures transactions were suspended as of the end of September 1988.

Foreign-Exchange-Transaction Designated Currencies

The following 14 official exchange rates are announced daily: U.S. dollar, Australian dollar, Hong Kong dollar, Singapore dollar, pound sterling, Canadian dollar, French franc, Belgian franc, deutsche mark, Swiss franc, Dutch guilder, Austrian schilling, South African rand, and Swedish krona. Currency transactions are overwhelmingly in U.S. dollars.

Also, the Japanese yen is quoted by the five main foreign exchange dealing banks and transactions are undertaken. The Bank of Taiwan deals in other currencies to a limited extent.

Foreign Exchange Regulations

Foreign exchange control in Taiwan is based on the Foreign Exchange Control Regulations. The government office with jurisdiction over exchange regulations is the Ministry of Finance, and the regulations are administered by the central bank. Banks must first be approved by the central bank to handle foreign exchange transactions. Such banks are called appointed banks. Foreign currency was highly controlled until July 1987 when a substantial liberalization was carried out. Although foreign exchange restrictions regarding payments in foreign currency were abolished to a large extent, to prevent the uncontrolled inflow of foreign exchange, restrictions were reimposed and became stricter. The following outlines the situation as of November 1988.

Foreign Exchange Received
Proceeds from exports and services rendered can be received without restriction. However, it is necessary to submit a notice of receipt of foreign currency to the central bank.

In addition to the above, foreign currency of US$50,000 or less per year may be received by simply submitting the notice of receipt of foreign currency to the central bank.

With regard to foreign exchange received in addition to the above, a permit must be obtained in advance from the central bank.

Foreigners with resident certificates may receive salaries from overseas—deemed as labor expenses—with no restrictions.

Foreign currency received by nonresidents is limited to US$5,000 per time.

Foreign Exchange Payments

Foreign currency remittances for foreign trade transactions as well as work and services rendered are not restricted. However, it is necessary to submit the notice of payment in foreign currency to the central bank.

Foreign currency remittances by enterprises and individuals that total less than $5 million annually—and with each remittance being less than $1 million—are unrestricted. But for remittance over US$1 million, a 10-day period of nonperformance is required. If the central bank does not suspend handling of the transaction within this period, it is deemed that approval has been granted.

With regard to cases other than the above, it is necessary to obtain the prior approval of the central bank. However, with regard to overseas remittances by foreign-capital-related corporations, the following separate provisions are still in force.

Overseas Remittances by Foreign-Capital-Related Corporations

With regard to overseas remittances of investment principal, profits, dividends, interest, and capital gains on the principal, regulations require a report to the central bank. However, as previously mentioned, because of the liberalization in foreign exchange controls, it is most likely only a question of time before these restrictions will be abolished.

- Investment principal and profits: One year after the commencement of an approved investment business, an application for remittance of the total amount is possible.
- Dividends and profits: With regard to approved investments, there are no special restrictions.
- Principal and interest on loans: For approved loans, there are no restrictions.
- Royalties and fees: If based upon an approved contract, there are no special restrictions.

TAIWANESE TAX STRUCTURE

The tax framework of Taiwan is fairly simple compared to other developed countries. Each tax falls under the jurisdiction of a specific tax law, such as the income tax law, rather than a single all encompassing tax code. The Ministry of Finance enforces tax laws through its Department of Taxation and Customs Division. The National Tax Bureau and various local tax jurisdictions are responsible for collection and administration. The taxes can be summarized under the following categories:

National Taxes	Provincial Taxes	Local/City Taxes
Income taxes	Business tax (VAT)	House tax
Estate and gift tax	License use tax	Amusement tax
Customs duties	Stamp tax	Deed tax
Commodity tax	Harbor dues	Land value tax
Securities transaction tax		Land value incremental tax
Mining lot tax		

Income Tax

The income tax can be divided into profit-seeking enterprise income tax and consolidated personal income tax.

Profit-Seeking Enterprise Income Tax

In Taiwan, all domestic business enterprises are subject to profit-seeking enterprise income tax on all income generated from "sources within and outside of the R.O.C." For R.O.C. companies, this generally means income from all sources regardless of repatriation to Taiwan. Foreign companies in Taiwan that are profit-seeking enterprises are subject to income tax only on their R.O.C. source income.

The R.O.C. Income Tax Law focuses on the business and not the form of doing business; it applies to sole proprietorships, partnerships, corporations, and joint ventures alike. All profit-seeking enterprises incorporated under the R.O.C. Company Law including subsidiaries of foreign companies are considered domestic. The income tax return must be filed within three months after the close of the taxable year unless an extension to file has been granted. The tax rates are progressive, ranging from 15 percent to 25 percent. Capital gains are treated as ordinary income and included in the taxable income. Gains on sales of land are not included in the taxable income. Gains on securities transactions of listed companies, however, are subject to income tax effective January 1, 1989.

Most branch offices, agencies of foreign companies operating in Taiwan, are considered domestic profit-seeking enterprises and are subject to income tax on income generated in Taiwan. A liaison office or a representative office established by a foreign company's home office to provide assistance on business transactions is not considered doing business in Taiwan and, therefore, not subject to income tax.

Consolidated Personal Income Tax
Individual income tax is imposed only on Taiwan source income. Regardless of nationality or length of stay, an individual with Taiwan source income is subject to individual income tax at progressive rates from 6 percent to 50 percent.

Foreign nationals are subject to different tax rates depending upon whether they are residents for tax purposes. Foreign nationals will be considered residents for tax purposes if they stay in Taiwan for 183 days or more in a calendar year, which will be accumulated and computed based on the dates stamped on the passport.

For an individual who stays in Taiwan not more than 90 days within a taxable year, the income tax payable for the income derived from sources in Taiwan shall be withheld (20 percent withholding tax) and paid at the respective sources; the taxpayer need not file an income tax return. The income tax shall be exempted for income derived from employer(s) outside Taiwan.

An individual who stays in Taiwan more than 90 days but less than 183 days within the same taxable year is subject to withholding tax at 20 percent on Taiwan source income paid in Taiwan.

Other Significant Taxes

Value-Added Tax
The value-added tax (VAT) is a general sales tax charged as a percentage of the selling price of goods or services rendered within the territory of Taiwan. The VAT is presently assessed at 5 percent of the invoice value.

Commodity Tax
Commodity tax is a one-stage sales tax imposed on domestically produced finished goods or imported finished goods. The current rates range from 2 percent to 80 percent.

Custom Duties

Custom duties are assessed on imported goods at rates set forth in the tariff schedule.

Investment Incentives

The existing Statute for Encouragement of Investment was enacted to encourage investment and expedite economic development. The statute, effective until 1990, provides for major tax reduction preferences to both local and foreign investors and has achieved its purposes to a large degree. The Ministry of Finance is contemplating a new statute for those rules extensively applied, incorporating them into other existing laws or regulations.

The following are the more significant features of the statute:

- Five-year or four-year tax holiday or accelerated depreciation method.
- Reduction of the profit-seeking enterprise tax from 25 percent to 20 percent for various government-encouraged industries.
- Investment tax credit ranging from 5 percent to 20 percent of capital investment exceeding NT$600,000 on automation equipment or pollution-protection equipment of that year.
- Tax credits for research and development expense of a productive enterprise at 20 percent of the difference between current year and the highest of the previous five years' R&D expense.
- Duty-free importation of machinery and equipment for certain qualified productive enterprises approved by the government.

Recent Tax Developments

The recent years have been a turning point in the R.O.C. economy. In order to meet the changing demands of its maturing economy, the R.O.C. government is striving toward liberalization and internationalization. The government is expected to make major revisions to the existing tax system when the Statute for Encouragement of Investment expires at the end of 1990.

In July 1987, a Tax Reform Commission was established with a goal to revamp the tax system in order to meet the needs of a rapidly changing economy. It is our understanding that the future tax changes will focus on the following significant areas:

- The Statute for Encouragement of Investment may be extended beyond 1990, or the rules of this statute may be incorporated into other existing tax laws or regulations.
- The scope of current tax exemptions and tax holidays will be diminished to focus mainly on providing greater tax incentives to capital-intensive, technology-intensive, and service industry investment projects.
- Overall reduction in tax rate, specifically profit-seeking enterprise income tax and consolidated personal income tax.
- More detailed regulations on international taxation, especially geared toward minimizing international tax evasion.

TAX PLANNING

Choosing a Business Form

Before January 1987, a foreign branch could not apply for many of the tax incentives applicable to a foreign subsidiary in Taiwan. This resulted in most of the foreign manufacturing enterprises and joint ventures choosing the form of Taiwan subsidiaries. Since January 1987, the Statute for Encouragement of Investment has been revised to encompass branch offices of foreign companies.

Although it is advantageous to set up a subsidiary in Taiwan, it may create tax disadvantages in the home country (e.g., double taxation). With the current statute revision, it may be better from a tax planning standpoint to establish a Taiwan branch. Foreign subsidiaries already established in Taiwan may apply for a change in status to a branch.

If a company is engaging in procurement and similar activities in Taiwan in support of business operations outside Taiwan, then it can establish a representative office. Because a representative office is not a taxable entity, it is not allowed to engage in profit-seeking activities, but it may coordinate local business affairs on behalf of an overseas principal.

Alternative Method of Tax Calculation

Any international profit-seeking enterprise engaged in international transport, construction contracting, providing technical services, or machinery and equipment leasing in Taiwan may elect the deemed-profit method of tax computation. It may apply to the Ministry of Finance to adopt 10 percent (for international transport business) or 15 percent (for the others) of its total local revenue as its taxable income.

The R.O.C. loss carry-forward rule (i.e., three years carry-forward only) does not apply to an enterprise using this deemed-profit method.

For a qualified enterprise (stated above), it may consider the deemed-profit method using the following criteria:

- If estimated taxable income is higher than the deemed-profit percent (i.e., 10 percent or 15 percent stated above).
- If a stable business trend is projected, not resulting in net taxable loss in one year and income in the following year (since using deemed-profit method does not allow for loss carry-forward).

Expatriate Tax Planning Considerations

For an individual who stays in Taiwan not more than 90 days within a taxable year, the income shall be exempted for income derived from employer(s) outside Taiwan. Therefore, the individual should arrange for compensation to be paid overseas.

With proper tax planning, an expatriate's R.O.C. taxes may be greatly minimized. The following significant compensation items (non-taxable to the expatriate) should be directly paid or reimbursed by the employer and not included as a lump-sum allowance:

- Employer-provided housing.
- Cost of furniture.
- Moving expenses.
- Traveling expenses.
- Home leave expenses.
- Tax equalization expenses.

If not properly segregated from the expatriate's gross compensation, the above items will be taxable to the expatriate.

INTERPRETING TAIWANESE
FINANCIAL STATEMENTS
Credibility Improved

Taiwanese enterprises traditionally focused on tax reporting for their financial statements. This has contributed to an overall lack of awareness of financial management concepts. Financial institutions placed more importance on collateralized loans than on loans based on the actual financial performance of businesses. These circumstances led to instances of falsified financial statements for the purpose of evading taxes or obtaining loans.

In recent years, the quality and credibility of Taiwanese financial statements have greatly improved because of the following changes:

• Business enterprises gradually understand the importance of establishing an effective financial management and reporting system.
• The MOF has made tremendous efforts to improve the professional standards of CPAs in Taiwan. The SEC under the MOF scrutinizes the required interim and final financial reporting of listed companies and publicly traded companies in Taiwan. Furthermore, there has been tight enforcement of timely public disclosure of these SEC-regulated companies' financial information.
• Major financial institutions have changed their lending policies and guidelines. Companies with more than NT$30 million in bank loans are required to furnish audited financial statements (annually) to the banks. Accordingly, the banks are approving loan applications on the basis of audited financial statements certified by qualified CPAs (especially the internationally accredited CPA firms).
• The professional quality and standards of CPAs are being continuously upgraded. This is supplemented by the active role of the R.O.C. Accounting Research and Development Foundation, which has issued more than 30 technical pronouncements within the last four years.

Key Review Points

In interpreting and reviewing Taiwanese financial statements, the following key points must be noted:

• Because of insufficient working capital, a company may be using short-term funds for long-term capital investment because short-term loans are easier to obtain. This increases the credit risk of repayment.
• Related-party transactions must be scrutinized because of the large number of family-run enterprises in Taiwan. Except for SEC companies, most family-operated local companies do not comply with the necessary related-party financial statement disclosures.
• For family-operated companies in Taiwan, it is common to provide mutual guarantees for business purposes, including bank loans, taxes,

and purchase commitments. These related-party guarantees may not be fully disclosed for non-SEC companies in Taiwan.

• Because of variances in financial and tax reporting, major book-tax differences for local enterprises may exist. Care must be taken in reviewing both the financial reports and the income tax returns with the related tax assessments. Situations may arise where there is a net loss per books but a substantial taxable income, thus resulting in a current tax liability.

• According the R.O.C. Tax Law, accumulated net taxable income after taxes, in excess of government-allowed amounts (e.g., for manufacturing company equivalent to its registered capital), is required to be distributed on a timely basis. A violation of this regulation is subject to government enforcement, i.e., imputed dividends. Because of the variance in financial and tax reporting mentioned above, care must be taken to identify this potential exposure.

• According to R.O.C. Company Law, companies must comply with the minimum registered capital requirement. However, it is not unusual to find that non-SEC companies' shareholders may have withdrawn the funds for personal use and reflected it as an intercompany business transaction on the books.

PART 5

CHINA

AN UPDATE ON THE BUSINESS ENVIRONMENT IN CHINA AFTER JUNE 4, 1989

Foreign investors' assessment of China's business environment before June 4, 1989, was positive: China's stable government and continuous economic reform policy, which are the two most important and basic conditions for foreign investors to make their decisions.

The Tiananmen Square military crackdown on June 4, 1989, shocked the entire world. In the aftermath of the crackdown, the United States government, joined by other leading countries in the world, announced economic sanctions and travel restrictions for U.S. citizens to China. The World Bank and other international lending agencies postponed loan projects committed prior to June 4 and suspended new projects.

Therefore, both overall economic growth and expansion of Chinese trade are now likely to be less buoyant than envisioned in the commentary in the following chapters. In fact, a modest retrenchment has already begun, resulting in a serious shortage of funds, a downturn in industrial production, and a decline in foreign trade. Sources of foreign exchange have been substantially reduced due to drastic decreases in tourist revenues and foreign borrowings. At the same time, inflation is still at a double-digit level. This situation will probably last for another year to year-and-a-half or until foreign investors and tourists are reassured of the existence of a stable and orderly government.

However, the dramatic changes in East Germany and other Eastern European countries in recent months followed by the Soviet-American summit meeting in Malta will affect and probably improve U.S.-China relations as evidenced by the visit to Beijing made by Brent Scowcroft, the U.S. National Security Advisor, as an emissary of President Bush to inform Chinese leaders of discussions between the U.S.-Soviet leaders and to convey President Bush's message of continuing normal and good relationship with China.

It is reasonable to conclude that after a period of retrenchment China's business environment will improve based on the following:

- International lending agencies are beginning to resume their loan projects.
- Tourist business is starting to pick up.
- Confidence shown by some multinational companies, already operating in China by not pulling out after June 4.
- The U.S. government's current decision to confirm the importance of a harmonious relationship with China.

CHAPTER 22

THE PEOPLE'S REPUBLIC OF CHINA: A NEW WORLD OF BUSINESS OPPORTUNITIES?

Zhang Shou

RAPID GROWTH IN FOREIGN TRADE AND AN
INCREASINGLY IMPORTANT MARKETPLACE
MARKED PROGRESS IN UTILIZATION OF FDI
AND A BETTER INVESTMENT CLIMATE
    Provision of Protection by the Legislation in Force
    Promotion of Capital Inflow by Offering Preferential
        Treatment in Taxation, Foreign Exchange, and Other
        Financial Aspects
    Efforts to Create an Attractive Business Climate for
        Foreign Investment
    Reform of Management System to Increase Efficiency
PROPER UTILIZATION OF FOREIGN LOANS AND
CHINA'S INCREASED ENTRY INTO THE
INTERNATIONAL CAPITAL MARKETS

My deep appreciation goes to Professor Li Guangan and Mr. Wu Yongke for their kind assistance in writing this chapter.

The world today is an open one. With the advance of science and technology and socialized mass production, the scope of interrelations of production and cooperation grows ever wider and economic interactions in the global context ever closer as well. No country owns all the resources and technologies required for its domestic development. Likewise, a country that is isolated and closed cannot expect advancement all on its own. Complementarity is shared among all nations by way of economic cooperation and technical exchange for joint development.

The open policy is an imperative necessity for China's modernization scheme. China's historic closed-door practices are a major reason the nation's economy and social development has been backward and stagnated. Because its natural resources per capita is not high, China will have to import some materials. In addition, China, being a developing country with poor foundation and shortage of funds, needs to attract foreign capital to make up for its own deficiencies. China also needs to raise the present level of science and technology as well as business management to gradually narrow the gaps with developed countries. The open policy China now pursues is a long-term principle that conforms to the law of economic development.

Promotion of foreign trade, foreign direct investment (FDI), and foreign loans constitute the principal part of China's open policy, which at the same time presents to other nations, developed countries in particular, a new world with business opportunities.

RAPID GROWTH IN FOREIGN TRADE AND AN INCREASINGLY IMPORTANT MARKETPLACE IN WORLD TRADE

China is endowed with vast territory and rich natural resources. It also enjoys abundant labor forces and traditional production technologies. A generally complete economic structure with solid foundations has taken shape. Along with its economy and external relations, China's foreign trade has also experienced rapid growth, and the country has developed into one of the major markets in the world trade community.

Thanks to the success of the reforms and open policy, China since 1979 has made significant achievements in its foreign trade and direct investment. The customs office reports the total volume of import and export of China stood at US$82.7 billion in 1987, four times more than 1979 (US$20.64 billion) and an average annual increase of 16.7 percent, much higher than the world average (5.6 percent) for the corresponding period.

China's capacity to expand its export for foreign exchange earnings will determine, to a great extent, how far its open policy can go and will affect the scale and schedule of domestic economic advancement. Export promotion will be especially necessary to improve the ability of hard currency generation. In 1987, the export volume of China reached US$39.5 billion, an increase of over four times compared to 1978 (US$9.75 billion). Two shifts in the export composition are currently being practiced—from primary products to manufactures, and from manufactured goods of rough machining to fine-processed manufactures. The share of primary products exported fell from 53.5 percent in 1978 to 33.6 percent in 1987, while the manufactures rose from 46.5 percent in 1978 to 66.4 percent in 1987. At a time when the price of primary goods is dropping in the world trade, the two shifts have played an important role in improving China's export and foreign exchange earnings. In addition, the market composition of China's export has also become more diversified and reasonable.

As with its export, China's import has evolved from a unitary type into over 10 diversified forms, including such arrangements as compensation trade, leasing, processing of foreign-supplied materials, and assembly of customer-provided components, thus expanding international cooperation. The composition of imports has also changed. The share of manufactured imports increased from 73.1 percent in 1978 to 84 percent in 1987, and the primary goods imported decreased from 26.9 percent to 16 percent, respectively. The changes indicate China has put foreign advanced technology and key equipment on the top of its import list. The annual average growth rate of imports for the period is 16.5 percent, slightly lower than that of exports. The level of import has supported the readjustment and further development of the national economy. By the analysis of the China Model connected to Project Link, every increase of 1 percent in China's export from 1980 to 1986 has raised the national income by 0.156 percent,while every 1 percent up in import helped increase the national income by 0.167 percent.

Because of the sustained growth in foreign trade and changes in the composition of commodities, the share of China's total world trade volume has increased greatly. In 1978, China ranked 32nd in the world, but in 1988 it ranked 14th with a record US$100 billion. The gap in trade level with leading countries is being narrowed, and China has become an increasingly major market in international trade.

TABLE 22–1
China's Foreign Trade by Countries and Regions, 1986

Economic Groupings	Total Trade Volume with Percentage Share	(US$100 million)	
		Export	Import
Developing countries and regions	80.68 (13.42%)	51.21 (18.95%)	29.47 (8.91%)
Developed countries	326.42 (54.31%)	104.31 (38.6%)	222.11 (67.14%)
Centrally planned economies	*67.17 (11.2%)	29.09 (10.77%)	38.08 (11.51%)
Hong Kong and Macao	118.59 (19.73%)	78.53 (29.0%)	40.06 (12.11%)
Others	8.11 (1.34%)	7.0 (2.57%)	1.11 (0.34%)
Total	600.97	270.14	330.83

China now has trade relations with diverse countries and regions. In 1986, China's export to Hong Kong and Macao, Japan, the United States, Europe, and Canada amounted to US$18.284 billion, more than 67 percent of the total. At present, China has trade relations with 175 countries and regions (see Table 22–1).

It is predicted that China will continue to focus its trade primarily on developed countries and regions while keeping and expanding its ties with the Soviet Union, Eastern Europe, and the third world.

MARKED PROGRESS IN UTILIZATION OF FDI AND A BETTER INVESTMENT CLIMATE

China still faces such challenges as shortage of capital and low level of technology and management. Modernization requires an active and efficient use of foreign funds and technologies to make up for China's own shortfall. The Chinese government has been encouraging foreign companies, enterprises (including those registered in Hong Kong and Macao), and other economic entities or individuals (hereinafter referred to as foreign investors) to set up Sino-foreign equity joint ventures, cooperative enterprises, and wholly foreign-owned ventures (foreign-invested enterprises) within China.

The Chinese government has endeavored to create a more favorable climate for foreign investors in the following aspects.

Provision of Protection by the Legislation in Force

The current constitution of China stipulates clearly that the state shall permit private economy to exist and to develop within the scope set by law because the private economy is a supplement to the socialist economy of public ownership. The state protects the legitimate rights and interests of private economy and also provides guidance, supervision, and administration of private economy. The fundamental law states the Chinese government is committed to protecting the legitimate rights and interests of private economy including foreign-invested enterprises. To this end, various laws and regulations on specific issues have been promulgated to ensure its implementation. Since 1979, more than 200 laws and implementing regulation on foreign investment in China have been in place to guarantee foreign investors the status, rights, liabilities, and responsibilities in legal form. The foreign investors are also guaranteed by the law to manage the enterprises by international practices, with autonomy over production plan, fund-raising, procurement, product sales, employment, and dismissal of labor. Among the laws are Joint Venture Law of the People's Republic of China, China-Foreign Cooperative Enterprise Law, and Law of Wholly Foreign-Owned Enterprises of PRC.

Promotion of Capital Inflow by Offering Preferential Treatment: In Taxation, Foreign Exchange, and Other Financial Aspects

In October 1986, the State Council of the People's Republic of China promulgated Provisions for the Encouragement of Foreign Investment, or the 22 Articles, followed by a dozen regulations for implementation. These provisions are formulated to create a better investment climate, facilitate the inflow of capital and advanced technologies, improve product quality, and promote export for more foreign exchange earnings.

In the 22 Articles, the state grants special preferences to two types of foreign-invested enterprises: (1) production enterprises whose products are mainly for export and have a foreign exchange surplus after deducting from their total annual foreign exchange revenues the annual foreign exchange expenditures that occur in production and operation and have the foreign exchange needed for the repatriation of the profits earned by foreign investors (referred to as export enterprises), and

(2) production enterprises possessing foreign-supplied advanced technologies that are engaged in developing new products and upgrading products for export to increase foreign exchange generated by exports or for import substitution (referred to as technologically advanced enterprises).

The state grants the following preferential treatment in taxation and fees to these two types of enterprises.

1. They are exempt from payment to the state of all subsidies to staff and workers, except for the payment of or allocation of funds for labor insurance, welfare costs, and housing subsidies for Chinese staff and workers in accordance with the provisions of the state.

2. Priority shall be given to those enterprises in obtaining water, electricity, and transport services, and communication facilities needed for their production and operation. Fees shall be computed and charged in accordance with the standards for local state enterprises.

3. When foreign investors in those enterprises remit abroad profits distributed to them, the amount remitted shall be exempt from income tax.

4. After the expiration of the period for the reduction or exemption of enterprise income tax in accordance with the provision of the state, export enterprises whose value of export in that year amounts to 70 percent or more of the total product value of their products for that year may pay enterprise income tax at one half the rate of the present tax.

The export enterprise in the special economic zones and in the economic and technological development zones and other export enterprises that already pay enterprise tax at a rate of 15 percent and that comply with the foregoing conditions shall pay enterprise income tax at a rate of 10 percent.

5. The technologically advanced enterprises may extend for three years the payment of enterprise income tax at a rate reduced by one half after the expiration of the period of reduction or exemption of enterprise income tax in accordance with the provisions of the state.

6. Export products of foreign-invested enterprises, except crude oil, finished oil, and other products subject to special state provisions, shall be exempt from the consolidated industrial and commercial tax.

7. After application to and approval from the tax authorities, foreign investors who reinvest the profits distributed to them by their enterprises in order to establish or expand export enterprises of technologically advanced enterprises for a period of operation of not less than five years shall be refunded the total amount of enterprise income tax already paid on the reinvested portion. If the investment is withdrawn before the period of operation reaches five years, the amount of enterprise income tax refunded shall be repaid.

The Chinese government also provides that after examination by the Bank of China, these two types of enterprises shall be given priority in receiving loans for short-term revolving funds needed for production and distribution, as well as for other needed credit.

Special foreign exchange policies are also worked out to help foreign-invested enterprises with their foreign exchange balance:

1. A foreign exchange market allows foreign-invested enterprises, under the supervision of the foreign exchange authority, to trade their foreign exchange surpluses among each other.
2. Domestic users are encouraged to purchase import substitution products from the enterprises at international prices, and payment could be made in foreign exchange and partly in local currency.
3. The enterprises that enjoy the preferential treatment are encouraged to sell their products abroad through the marketing channel of the foreign investors to achieve a comprehensive compensation.
4. Foreign investors are encouraged to reinvest their share of renminbi (Chinese currency) earnings into enterprises that may generate or increase foreign exchange income, and they shall enjoy the same preferential treatment for foreign exchange investment.

With the additional promotional measures, the foreign exchange balance is expected to improve.

Efforts to Create an Attractive Business Climate for Foreign Investment

An open coastal strip has evolved since 1979. To start with, China opened the provinces of Guangdong and Fujian and set up four special economic zones (SEZs). Then 14 coastal port cities, including Shanghai, Tianjin, and Dalian, were declared opened one after another. In 1986, the coastal area was further expanded to the Pearl River Delta, the Yangtze River Delta, and the triangular area in southern Fujian Province. In 1988, China opened another 100 counties and cities. A coastal open strip with a population of 150 million has developed. The strip is rich in relatively cheap and efficient labor resources, high in science and technology, and also enjoys good transport and other infrastructure facilities. The open provinces and cities within the strip enjoy preferential treatment in foreign trade and investment. All these are favorable to foreign entrepreneurs who want to invest and do business in China.

The open coastal cities and regions, particularly the provinces of Guangdong and Fujian, are playing a pilot role and have also made marked achievements in attracting foreign investment. Table 22–2 illustrates their 1987 performance.

The market system in the four special economic zones is being established and perfected. At present, markets for labor, capital, capital goods, and foreign exchange have been initiated, while markets for technology, information, and real estate are taking shape. An environment has been created in which enterprises can operate and develop on their own and compete. In the late 1980s, special efforts were made to speed up the energy, transport, and telecommunications industries within the SEZs, resulting in expansion of domestic and international direct-dial telephone lines and improved infrastructure, making the SEZs all the more attractive to foreign investors. In 1987, the total industrial output of the four SEZs (Shenzhen, Shantou, Xiamen, and Zhuhal) amounted to 10.5 billion RMB yuan and the export volume neared US$2 billion. As much as US$2.16 billion of foreign investment was actually used in the 4,000-odd foreign-invested ventures in operation. As a result, an export-oriented economic structure has come into being.

To offer a better environment for investment to match economic development, China has stressed an advanced international telecommunication system. As of the end of 1987, China had more than 2,300 international long-distance telephone lines, 17 times more than in 1978, and over 900 telegraph lines, nearly four times 1978. China has direct international lines with 49 countries and regions and has international telecommunication services with all countries and regions. China has expanded its international direct-dial telephone business to over 150 countries and regions instead of the original 22. In China, more than 50,000 users have international direct dialing. In addition to the international telephone, telex, public telegraphy, facsimile, television, and broadcasting information services, long-distance direct dialing, public speed facsimile, customer facsimile, data communications, and information indexing hae been opened in recent years. Diversified telecommunication services available in China have made the business environment increasingly attractive.

TABLE 22-2
Foreign Investment and Percentage Shares by Selected Cities and Provinces (US$100 million)

Rank	Contracts		Contracted Value		Amounts Actually Used	
1	Guangdong	6,634 (59%)	Guangdong	97.5 (51.3%)	Guangdong	32.8 (48.2%)
2	Fujian	1,152 (10.2%)	Shanghai	20.6 (10.9%)	Beijing	6.0 (8.9%)
3	Shanghai	477 (4.2%)	Beijing	18.3 (9.6%)	Shanghai	5.9 (8.7%)
4	Liaoning	372 (3.3%)	Shanxi	11.0 (5.8%)	Tianjin	2.8 (4.1%)
5	Beijing	362 (3.2%)	Fujian	8.8 (4.7%)	Fujian	2.6 (3.9%)
6	Tianjin	277 (2.5%)	Liaoning	6.2 (3.3%)	Liaoning	2.1 (3.2%)

Reform of Management System to Increase Efficiency

Foreign-invested projects are managed at two levels in China: central and local (province, municipalities, and autonomous regions). The limits of authorization are defined by total investment value. Projects valued below the set approval ceiling are classified as below-ceiling projects, while those above the limit are called above-ceiling ones. Any production projects below ceiling that also match the investment priority of the state are free from national balance in construction and operation or in foreign exchange and do not involve product export quota or license control. But they are subject to examination and approval of the local government or related ministries/departments under the State Council. The above-ceiling production projects are subject to approval by such designated central governing bodies as the State Planning Commission (SPC), the Ministry of Foreign Economic Relations and Trade (MOFERT), and the State Administration of Industry and Commerce (SAIC).

At present, 16 provinces and cities (Beijing, Shanghai, Tianjin, Guangdong, Fujian, Hainan, Liaoning, Habei, Shandong, Jiangsu, Zhejiang, Guangxi, Shenzhen, Zhuhai, Shantou, and Xiamen) are authorized to approve foreign-invested projects valued above US$30 million. Other inland provinces and cities and those departments in charge under the State Council are now empowered to approve foreign-invested projects valued at no more than US$10 million. Nonproduction projects, whatever their value, are examined and approved by local authorities unless otherwise noted by the central government.

The procedure for establishing foreign-invested projects is explained in detail in the Regulations for the Implementation of the Law of the People's Republic of China on Chinese-Foreign Joint Ventures (see Chapter 4). Table 22–3 illustrates the approval authorities at different stages of the procedure.

To spur greater inflow of capital, the Chinese government has tried to simplify the formalities to increase efficiency. One example is the establishment of a foreign investment service center in Tianjin where authorized representatives involving project evaluation and approval all work in the same building and under the direct leadership of the municipal government. Another example is in Shanghai, which has created a foreign investment committee headed by the mayor to provide all-in-one service to make the approval procedure as simple as possible. Foreign

TABLE 22–3
Approval Authority for Foreign-Invested Project

Project Procedure	Authority for Above-Ceiling Projects	Authority for Below-Ceiling Projects
1. Project proposal	State Planning Commission	Local planning (economic) commissions or governments
2. Feasibility study report	State Planning Commission	Local planning (economic) commissions or other designated departments
3. Joint venture agreement, contracts, and articles of association	Ministry of Foreign Economic Relation & Trade	Local commissions for foreign economic relations and trade
4. Registration and issuance of business license	State Administration of Industry and Commerce	Local administrative bureaus for industry and commerce

business people are generally pleased with the improved efficiency so far.

As a result of the promotional measures elaborated above, foreign investment in China has witnessed marked progress. Table 22–4 shows the performance of foreign direct investment (FDI) between 1979 and the end of 1987.

TABLE 22–4
Foreign Direct Investment in China (1979–1987)

Forms	Number of Projects	Contracted Value (US$100 million)	Value Used (US$100 million)
Equity joint ventures	4,630	67.37	33.00
Cooperatives	5,194	108.51	32.22
Wholly foreign-owned ventures	184	10.09	1.52
Offshore oil projects	44	28.68	22.36
Total	10,052	214.65	89.10

The inflow of capital in China increased in 1988. The total contracted value stood at about US$12.5 billion, of which FDI was $4.5 billion. In the early years when China started to absorb FDI, foreign capital was focused on nonproduction projects, resulting in an irrational structure of investment. However, starting in the second half of 1984, FDI in China experienced a distinct change in direction.

Joint ventures with relatively large investment, advanced technology, and high-grade products have been set up; for example, the nuclear power station in Guangdong Province, the Pingsuo open-pit coal mine in Shanxi Province, Shanghai Yaohua-Pilkington Glass Co. Ltd., Shanghai Volkswagen Automobile Co. Ltd., and Tianjin Otsuka Pharmaceutical Co. Ltd. If hotels and other services are excluded, there are more than 500 production projects valued at over US$5 million each and also some 70 projects each with an investment exceeding US$10 million. As of the end of 1987, the composition of FDI in terms of funds actually used was: hotels and other services, US$3.8 billion; energy (including offshore oil exploration), US$2.91 billion; textile and light industry, $140 million; electronic and machinery, $510 million; raw material industry, $340 million; and agriculture, animal husbandry, and fishery, $170 million. The sources of capital actually used (by percentage shares) are Hong Kong and Macao (57.3 percent), the United States (14.5 percent), Japan (13.6 percent), the United Kingdom (2.5 percent), France (1.7 percent), and Australia (1.1 percent).

The structure of investment was greatly improved in 1988. As of November 1988, 85 percent of the 480 contracts for foreign-invested ventures were production projects. Export-oriented and technologically advanced enterprises made up the majority of the total.

FDI has played a positive part in promoting China's economy in the following areas:

1. It has helped make up some of the shortage of funds needed for domestic construction. The share of foreign funds actually used in the total capital investment of state-owned enterprises is gradually increasing.

2. It has promoted export and foreign exchange balance. For the over 5,000 foreign-funded ventures already in operation, there has been increased export and foreign exchange earnings. Most or even all of the ventures in Tianjin, Dalian, Beijing, and Shanghai have managed to balance their foreign exchange receipts and disbursement, and some are running with good returns.

3. Advanced technologies and business management skills were injected into the ventures. A batch of equity joint ventures with advanced technology were set up to fill in the gap in certain industries with such products as the program-controlled telephone exchangers, plate glass by floating production, and optical fiber cables.

4. It has increased employment opportunities and improved labor force quality.

Likewise, FDI has benefited foreign investors. Of the 5,000 ventures in operation, 85 percent are running well with good returns. A 1988 survey jointly conducted by an American consulting company and Chinese institutions revealed that 22 percent of the 70 Sino-U.S. equity joint ventures had greatly exceeded the expected targets, 72 percent met or went beyond the goal, and only 6 percent failed to meet the target. In 1988, the Chinese newspaper *Economic Daily* singled out the top 10 Sino-foreign joint ventures, and 3 of the most prominent were Sino-U.S. ventures—Beijing Jeep Co. Ltd., Shanghai Foxboro Co. Ltd., and China Huipu Co. Ltd.

However, foreign investors sometimes still encountered problems when operating in China, such as difficulties in obtaining loans in local currency to cover the costs for startup and operation; low efficiency of labor forces from some regions; an imperfect legal system; and conflicts arising in the transition from the existing economic system to the new. China is making every effort to bring its economy into order, create a better environment for economic development, and deepen the reforms. With these efforts, the investment climate in China will be enhanced.

PROPER UTILIZATION OF FOREIGN LOANS AND CHINA'S INCREASED ENTRY INTO THE INTERNATIONAL CAPITAL MARKETS

Foreign funds are also available through foreign loans, including loans from international financial institutions. In using loans, China needs to consider its ability to service the debt and the ability of a matched domestic financial and material supply. It also needs to orient the inflow of loans into a reasonable direction for high efficiency. To cover its own shortfall and invigorate the economy, China must use foreign loans in a proper and efficient manner. Between 1979 and 1987, China used more than US$26.55 billion. In 1986, more than US$7 billion of foreign loans came from commercial banks, which China has nearly paid back. At the end of 1986, outstanding debt totaled $12.286 billion, 62 percent of which was long-term preferential loans from foreign governments or international financial institutions. In 1988, the contracted amount of foreign loans stood at approximately $7 billion.

China has a unified policy for the use of foreign loans and well-defined responsibility. The State Planning Commission (SPC), the Ministry of Foreign Economic Relations and Trade (MOFERT), the Ministry of Finance (MOF), and the People's Bank of China (PBC) are responsible for working out the medium- and long-term plan as well as the annual plan in terms of the scale and priority of the foreign loans. The plans are submitted to the State Council for final approval.

Loans above the set ceiling are subject to approval from the SPC and other departments concerned. For loans below the ceiling, the approval authorities are the departments in charge under the State Council, provinces, autonomous regions and municipalities directly under the central government, and those cities specially listed in the national economic plan. Those governing bodies, after approving the projects, shall also report to the SPC, MOFERT, MOF, and PBC. The competent authorities, defined by sources, nature, and application of the loans, are empowered to do business with foreign institutions and to manage the loans.

MOFERT works with government loans; the MOF is responsible for World Bank loans; and the PBC for IMF and Asian Development Bank (ADB) loans. The Ministry of Agriculture, Animal Husbandry, and Fishery is in charge of the International Agricultural Development Fund. The Bank of China (BOC) handles energy loans from Japan Export and Import Bank. For commercial loans and bond issuance, the approved authorities are the BOC, Bank of Communications, China International Trust and Investment Corp. (CITIC), China Investment Bank, as well as one or two BOC-authorized financial institutions in every locality of Guangdong, Fujian, Shanghai, Tianjin, and Dalian. Other financial institutions authorized by the BOC to borrow money abroad are subject to approval from the People's Bank of China on an item-by-item basis. China National Technical Import and Export Corp. under MOFERT is entrusted with international bidding in using foreign loans.

A strict responsibility system is being adopted in China in using foreign loans. Any ministry or local government that borrows money on its own is liable for its repayment. Foreign loans that are borrowed in the name of the central government will be repaid by the competent authorities or localities, or out of the project, unless examined and approved by the SPC, MOF, and finally by the State Council. The liability of repayment is already clearly defined when approving the project proposal. Guided by the national general guidelines, policies, and plans to use foreign loans, the State Administration of Foreign Exchange Control is empowered to manage the national foreign debt issues, supervise the foreign exchange and debt, set up and perfect a national monitory and statistical system on foreign debt, and also to release official data on foreign debts.

China mainly uses foreign loans for development projects, such as fixed asset investment, especially in infrastructure, energy, transport, and raw material industries. Projects for export promotion are also weighed heavily. The development projects build potential for future economic growth, while the export promotion projects help with the future debt payment.

Chinese economists generally believe three major indicators identify whether the scale of foreign loans for a country is reasonable: (1) debt service ratio (DSR), that is, the ratio of principal and interest due against the foreign exchange earnings of the same year; it is appropriate to keep DSR at no higher than 15 to 20 percent; (2) it is proper that outstanding foreign debt is kept not more than the export earnings of the same year; (3) the ratio of foreign loans to the fixed asset investment of the year. The ratio is advised to be maintained at about 10 percent.

As for the composition of loans, the share of short-term debt in the total debt is recommended to be kept at about 25 percent. And it is inadvisable to have too high a percentage share for commercial loans. By following these criteria, the scale of foreign loans in China is reasonable, and China has a relatively high creditability.

Foreign loans have played a positive role in helping readjust and promote the national economy in the following ways.

1. It helped ease the pressure on the "bottleneck" sectors of the economy. The input of funds has resulted in an expanded capacity in energy and transport industries.

2. Advanced technologies from abroad have served to renovate and upgrade outdated equipment and technologies in a group of Chinese enterprises; some of the production techniques in China have now approached or even reached the world level.

3. It has improved the level of project management. For example, the methodology of economic appraisal for World Bank projects is now widely used in project management in China with positive results.

However, problems in using foreign loans still remain. For instance, China needs to strengthen its coordination and supervision at the macro level. The current irrational composition of loans with too high a share of short-term and commercial loans may make the debt-service burden heavier. Narrow selection of foreign currencies may also conceal possible future risks arising from the fluctuations of foreign exchange rates. The portion of foreign loans used for export promotion is generally small, which is not good for generating hard currency earnings to service the debt.

Other promising business opportunities for foreign investors may also involve introduction of technology, Chinese overseas investment, contracting engineering, labor contracts, banking business overseas, tourism, and other economic and technical cooperations.

China is now at the second stage of its strategic plan for economic development, namely, to redouble the GNP and ensure a good life for its people when this century ends. One important device to help meet this target is to open China wider to the outside world and expand its cooperation with the rest of the world.

In the years ahead, China will promote export-oriented industries with competitive products that yield quick returns. The two shifts in export composition are to be quickened. Efforts will be made to generate more nontrade earnings. The foreign trade system is now under further reform to meet the trade target.

China will continue to attract FDI and create more foreign-invested ventures. The open regions are to be expanded steadily, and foreign capital will be channeled centrally into renovating the existing enterprises. By China's sectoral policy, infrastructure and basic industries are to be further developed and the creation of technologically advanced or export enterprises encouraged.

China will keep using government loans and loans from international financial institutions with moderate scale, reasonable composition, and quick returns. The scale of debt and the direction of capital inflow need to be supervised and controlled to improve China's balance of payment. Moderate borrowing, proper use of loans, and ability to repay will surely promote confidence and better cooperation between China and the rest of the world.

CHAPTER 23

CHINESE MARKETS
AND PRODUCTS

Henry X. H. Sun

INTRODUCTION

The People's Republic of China is the most populous country in the world. According to recent government data, China had a population of 1.1 billion in 1988. China is also the third-largest country in land area (after the Soviet Union and Canada). It has a total land territory of 9.6 million square kilometers. However, only 10 percent of its territory can be cultivated.

China also has the largest hydroelectric potential and the largest coal reserves in the world. Its major economic resources include iron, petroleum, mercury, tin, tungsten, antimony, manganese, molybdenum, vanadium, magnetite, aluminum, lead, zinc, and uranium. China is also a major agricultural producer; about 45 percent of its population is engaged in agricultural production. The main agricultural products in China are rice, wheat, other grains, and cotton. China's biggest industrial products are iron, steel, coal, machinery, textiles, garments, petroleum, and chemicals.

According to data from the State Statistical Bureau,* the total industry output value in China rose 16.5 percent in 1987, to 1,378 billion yuan RMB, about US$372 billion; heavy industry increased 16 percent, to 722 billion yuan RMB; and light industry increased 16.8 percent, to 656 billion yuan RMB. In 1987, the output of leading heavy industrial products included 56.1 million tons of steel, 43.9 million tons of steel products, 180 million tons of cement, 9.62 million tons of sulphuric acid, 2.73 million tons of soda ash, 17.1 million tons of chemical fertilizer, 472,000 automobiles, 40,000 tractors, 146,000 pieces of machinery and tools, electricity-generating equipment for 9.2 million kilowatts, 909 locomotives, and 1.92 million tons of civilian ships. Major light industrial products reached 40.91 million bicycles, 19.38 million television sets, 18.63 million tape recorders, 2.39 million cameras, 9.92 million washing machines, 3.98 million refrigerators, 4.3 million tons of yarn, 16.7 billion meters of cloth, 260 million meters of woolen textiles, 10.1 million tons of paper and paper products, and 5.11 million tons of sugar. These data indicate China's consumer market is much bigger than its current domestic supply capacity. Thus, there is always a market for imported consumer products.

Since 1979, China has made significant strides in foreign trade, thanks to the implementation of economic reforms and the opening to the outside world. According to China's Ministry of Foreign Economic Relations and Trade, the total volume of import and export in China in 1987 amounted to US$82.7 billion, three times more than 1978. This shows an average annual increase of 16.7 percent, much higher than the 5.6 percent growth rate of world trade in the same period.

China's total export volume reached US$39.6 billion in 1987, four times higher than in 1978. Traditionally, China's leading exports are textiles, agricultural products, and crude oil. However, two changes occurred in 1987; China moved from exporting mainly primary products and raw materials to manufactured goods and from mainly manufactured

---

* All data used in this chapter were from two sources: *The Statistics Annual Book of China 1988* and the *Almanac of China's Foreign Economic Relations and Trade 1987.*

goods and rough machinery to fine processed manufactured products. Primary products dropped from 53.5 percent of exports in 1978 to 33.6 percent in 1987, while the portion of industrial products increased from 46.5 percent in 1978 to 66.4 percent in 1987.

Traditional leading imports are iron, steel, raw material, and machinery. In the past decade, the structure of imported products has also changed. The proportion of manufactured goods increased from 73.1 percent of imports in 1978 to 84 percent in 1987, while that of primary products decreased from 26.9 percent in 1978 to 16 percent in 1987. These changes indicate China has switched its import priority to advanced technologies and essential key equipments. The average annual import growth in the corresponding period is 16.5 percent, slightly lower than that of export. The above necessary imports have induced readjustment and development of China's domestic economy.

Since 1978, the pattern of China's foreign trade has also shifted from a mainly unitary type into more than 10 forms of operation, including compensation trade, technology transfer, leasing, licensing, processing with customer-supplied materials, and assembling of supply components. This flexibility in trading practice expanded the scope of foreign exchanges and international cooperation in economy and technology.

China has also opened its door to foreign direct investments. The forms of foreign direct investments may be classified into three categories: equity joint ventures, contractual joint ventures, and wholly owned foreign ventures. Most of these ventures are in industrial areas, such as manufacturing, mining, energy, and transportation, and a few are in the service sectors. From 1979 to June 1988, the Chinese government approved more than 12,000 investment projects from foreign businesspeople and enterprises in Hong Kong and Macao; the contracted investment volume reached US$23.5 billion, and the actual investment amounted to nearly $10 billion, with more than 5,000 enterprises already established.

China has a solid foundation in modern international economic exchanges and investment. The major material attraction to foreign businesspeople is the abundant labor source at a very low price. Similarly, land and natural resources are very inexpensive compared with the international market. In addition, the Chinese government is encouraging foreign direct investment with various incentives and adopting different policies and regulations for the promotion of China's foreign trade. In the following sections, we will discuss the Chinese market and products with regard to foreign trade patterns and foreign direct investment in China.

CHINA'S FOREIGN TRADE PATTERNS

China exercises strict control over exports and imports in an effort to conserve foreign exchange, adjust domestic supplies of key commodities, comply with bilateral agreements limiting trade (as in textiles), and protect infant industries. The goals of China's policy are to maximize and diversify exports and, in the short run, to limit imports to essential goods, technologies, and raw materials that China cannot produce by itself. China employs a variety of tools to accomplish these goals, including import and export licensing, tariffs, foreign exchange allocation, import substitution regulations to meet its foreign trade goals, and export subsidies to correct the antiexport bias of China's domestic price structure. It is important for foreign companies to understand China's foreign trade pattern or structures.

China's Export Pattern

After establishment of the People's Republic of China in 1949, primary products dominated about 80 percent of China exports and industrial finished products only about 20 percent. China was then an agriculture and raw material exporting country with a very low level of industrialization. Since 1978, foreign trade patterns have developed rapidly in China with the restoration and development of the national economy and especially with the implementation of the open-door policy. In 1986, China's export value reached US$27.1 billion, in contrast to US$6.9 billion in 1976, an average annual growth rate of 14.7 percent. During this period, primary products and finished manufactured goods each accounted for about 50 percent of exports.

In the meantime, there was a great change in the exports of primary products. The proportion of exports in cereals, edible oil, and foodstuffs was reduced from 24.2 percent in 1966 to 14.5 percent in 1983 and in raw materials from 15.2 percent to 9.5 percent, while the proportion of minerals and fuel increased remarkably. China started to export petroleum in 1971, and by 1976, the export of crude oil and refined products reached US$842 million, 12.7 percent of the total volume of China's export. In 1983, petroleum products jumped to 21 percent of total Chinese exports. Of finished manufactured goods, the share of machinery and electronic products increased from 3.5 percent in 1976 to 14.9 percent in 1983. However, China's exports are still dominated by labor-intensive and resource-intensive products that have relatively little technological sophistication and generally little value added.

Based on historical data and development trends, China's export patterns in the near future may be predicted as follows: Primary products rated 54.2 percent of the total export in 1985 will drop to 44.7 percent in 1990. In this category, foodstuffs will increase from 15.6 percent in 1985 to 18.4 percent in 1990. Raw materials will drop from 9.2 percent in 1985 to 7.9 percent in 1990. Fuels, including oil and coal, will drop from 28.3 percent in 1985 to 18.4 percent in 1990. Finished products will increase from 45.8 percent in 1985 to 55.3 percent in 1990. In this category, chemical products will increase from 2.3 percent to 3.2 percent, machinery and equipment will increase from 3.6 percent to 10.5 percent, and textiles and other light industrial products will increase slightly from 31.9 percent to 32.4 percent.

The above data indicate the portion of primary products in China's export patterns will continue to decline. Labor-intensive and resource-intensive products will also decline from 85 percent in 1985 to 75 percent in 1990. If Chinese machinery and electronic equipment continues to reach international standards, China could expand its export of machinery and electronic equipment to about US$4 billion, approximately 10 percent of total export volume in 1990. Because oil prices in the next five years are likely to remain well below the 1985 level, the portion of oil and petroleum product export will decline significantly. But agricultural and sideline products will retain an important place in China's export. However, China's limited arable land per capita will prevent any major expansion of the export of agricultural products, and the Chinese government will shift from exporting general agricultural products to fish breeding, poultry raising, animal husbandry, and the processing of sideline products.

China's Import Pattern

Although China is a low-income country, the structure of its import is different from other developing countries. Not only does China export primary products, but it also imports industrial raw materials, minerals, and other primary products in large quantities. Industrial raw materials constitute a large proportion of China's total import. Historically, this category has comprised 40 to 60 percent of China's imports. This import pattern is similar to that of the developing countries. Two reasons account for this kind of import pattern: (1) although China has a large territory with rich resources, the endowment per capital is quite limited, and (2) the industrialization process in the 1950s emphasized heavy industry, which demands large-scale resources.

China's imports also concentrated on a few stable commodities. Even in recent years, these stable commodities have consistently accounted for about 60 percent of China's total imports. These stable commodities are steel, nonferrous metals, fertilizer, iron, chemical fibers, wool, timber, rubber, pulp, paper, hides, industrial chemicals, wheat, and sugar.

The major problem with China's import patterns is that the proportion of technologies and equipment as a means of production is relatively small, whereas the proportion of consumer products and raw materials is high. Even within the machinery, equipment, and production means, the composition is not rational. The Chinese government recognizes this problem and is trying to make the following changes:

1. Reduce the import of complete sets of equipment and increase the import of key equipment.
2. Increase the import of software technology and reduce the import of hardware.
3. Increase the import of advanced specialized technologies and reduce the import of general basic technologies.
4. Increase the import of production means and decrease importation of consumer goods.

China's seventh five-year plan reflects these four major points of change in China's import patterns. With this plan, it is predicted that China's import pattern will be changed as follows: Import of production means will increase from 82.8 percent in 1985 to 85 percent in 1990. In this category, machinery and equipment, including the import of technologies, will increase from 31.9 percent in 1985 to 39 percent in 1990. The import of raw and semifinished materials will decrease from 50.9 percent in 1985 to 46 percent in 1990. China's import of consumer products will decline from 17.2 percent in 1985 to 15 percent in 1990.

In this section, we discussed the general patterns of China's foreign trade and its major changes. Official statistics show China has been increasing its export of technology-intensive and manufactured products and its import of advanced technologies, key equipment, and materials needed in production of exports. It has also been decreasing its export of primary products and import of consumer products. This information reveals what products China is likely to import in the near future and what are good exports to buy from China in the near future. This can provide a basic guideline for selecting markets and seeking resources in China.

PRIORITIES OF FOREIGN DIRECT INVESTMENT
IN CHINA

China is a relative newcomer to the international market of foreign direct investment. It was only on July 8, 1979, that the Law of the People's Republic of China on Chinese Foreign Joint Ventures was promulgated. The Chinese government subsequently adopted laws, regulations, and policies aimed at encouraging foreign investment. As mentioned earlier, from 1979 to June 1988, the Chinese government approved more than 12,000 projects with direct foreign investment. The total contracted investment value reached US$23.5 billion and the actual investment amounted to nearly US$10 billion. The following pages provide information on the incentives, structure, and future trends of foreign direct investment in China.

Incentives of Foreign Direct Investment in China

Since 1979, foreign direct investment has played a positive role in China's economic development. The following major benefits have been recognized by the Chinese government:

1. The shortage of funds needed for domestic economic development has been made up to some extent by foreign direct investment. The share of active foreign investment in total capital of state-owned enterprises has gradually increased.

2. Foreign direct investment plays an important role in the promotion of China's export. With over 5,000 foreign-invested enterprises already in operation, there has been an enormous increase in export and foreign exchange earnings. Foreign direct investment in coastal cities and some other major cities, such as Shanghai, Beijing, and Tinjiang, generally maintained the balance of foreign exchange among the enterprises themselves.

3. Through foreign direct investment, advanced technologies and managerial skills have been introduced in China. China has established or is setting up many technology-advanced joint ventures that are playing a pilot role in industrial development and scientific research. Some products from foreign-invested factories have filled in the gaps in related industrial fields in China.

4. Foreign direct investment has been providing and increasing employment opportunities in China and improving the quality of the Chinese labor forces.

In view of the importance of foreign direct investment in the national economy, China has established investment incentives, which have been broadening since the late 1970s. The special economic zones, 14 coastal cities, the inland cities, and the provinces all promote investment with unique packages of tax exemption, reduction, and other type of incentives. The type of incentives available to a foreign investor depends on the type of investment: whether it is an equity joint venture, contractual joint venture, or wholly owned foreign venture; whether it is service or manufacturing-oriented; whether it involves advanced technologies; and whether it is export-oriented. These incentives include significant reductions in national and local income taxes, import and export duties and land fees, and priority arrangement in obtaining basic infrastructure services.

On October 11, 1986, the China State Council promulgated the Provision for Encouragement of Foreign Investment. The purposes of this provision are to improve the investment environment in China, better absorb foreign direct investment in advanced technologies, raise product quality, and expand Chinese exports. It also contains a series of preferential terms for foreign direct investment that is export-oriented and technology-advanced.

Structure of Foreign Direct Investment in China

According to statistics from China's Ministry of Foreign Economic Relations and Trade, by the end of 1986, foreign direct investments totaled US$19.99 billion and involved 8,189 signed agreements. In 1985, total foreign direct investments in China amounted to US$16.66 billion of which 29.7 percent were in real estate and public-service sectors, 29.4 percent in industrial sectors, 12.4 percent in geological prospecting, 6.1 percent in service and catering, 2.4 percent in construction industry, 2.2 percent in transportation, post, and telecommunication sectors, 2 percent in agriculture and fishery, 0.6 percent in finance and insurance services, 0.6 percent in culture, education, and public-health sectors, 0.1 percent in science and technology research, and 14.5 percent in other areas. The largest portion of foreign direct investment was made in the fast returning sectors, such as hotels, real estate, and manufacturing, whereas long-term investments in scientific research take a very small portion.

In China, 20.5 percent of the total foreign direct investments were made in the form of equity joint ventures, 49.3 percent in the form of contractual joint ventures, and 3.1 percent in the form of wholly owned foreign ventures; the rest are in various economic forms of cooperation. Contractual joint ventures, or cooperative ventures, are the most common form of foreign investment in China because they have the least investment risk. They are usually set up with foreign technology and equipment and with Chinese labor, land, and other sources. The wholly owned foreign ventures have the largest investment risk.

The major portion of foreign direct investments in China came from the following countries and areas: Hong Kong/Macao, about 63.8 percent; the United States, 13.1 percent; Japan, 9.8 percent; Britain, 2.3 percent; France, 1.6 percent; Singapore, 1.2 percent; and West Germany, 1 percent. These foreign direct investments were mainly scattered in the following cities and government departments: Guangdong province, 37.7 percent; central government ministries, 19.5 percent; Shanghai city, 11.2 percent; Fujian province, 5.9 percent; Beijing city, 4.7 percent; Shanxi province, 3.8 percent; Liaoning province, 2.8 percent; and Shandong province, 2 percent. Hong Kong and Macao companies are close to Guangdong province where several special economic zones are located, so they have the largest portion of foreign direct investment in China.

New Trends in Foreign Direct Investment in China

Today, the Chinese economic system is a combination of central economic planning and free market mechanism. Central government economic plans still control the major aspects of China's national economy, but the free market plays a more and more important role in China's economic development under the guidance of state planning. In Chinese central planning, the most important and basic plan is the five-year plan set up by the State Council of China and the People's Congress. In the five-year plan, the new development trend of China's national economy is clearly stated, and its specific index should be a good indicator of the trends of foreign direct investment and international exchange. The seventh five-year plan of China (see the appendix) emphasizes that from 1986 to 1990, China will give priority to development projects in such areas as energy, transportation, communication, raw and semifinished materials, and especially to projects for power generation, port facilities, petroleum industry, and to the technology transformation of the machine building and the electronic industries. Also, China will give priority to projects that will increase China's ability to earn or conserve foreign exchange through exporting or import replacement. This will create conditions for China to strengthen its debt servicing ability and encourage further foreign investments. In this context, projects involving advanced technology and the managerial skills that produce new products, equipment, and materials and increase exports and import substitution will be the trends of foreign direct investment in China. This will certainly raise China's productivity and narrow the development gaps between China and the West. Scarcity of foreign exchange will remain a serious constraint on China's economic development for a long time; China will continue to increase its exports to earn enough foreign exchange for its imports, and it will increase the scope of foreign capital utilization and international economic and technical cooperation.

The five-year plan reveals the Chinese government will curtail foreign direct investment in the following areas: (1) advanced technology that other Chinese enterprises have already imported and created excess production capacity or that cannot produce products to export, (2) projects that neither export their product nor absorb advanced technologies and management expertise, (3) projects whose products are subject to state export quotas, such as cotton, woolens, and linen fabrics. Foreign direct investments will be forbidden in the following areas: projects that are not allowed to be set up internationally because they are harmful to state sovereignty and security or because they contaminate the environment, and projects that simply import assembly lines and foreign parts and components solely for Chinese domestic markets.

CONCLUSION

The Chinese market has a potential of 1.1 billion consumers with fast-growing purchasing power. With the implementation of economic reform and an open-door policy, the Chinese government has been encouraging foreign trade and investment since 1978. China has promulgated laws, regulations, and policies and given incentives to promote the international exchanges and foreign direct investment in China.

In the near future, China will increase the export of technology-intensive and manufactured products and decrease the exports of primary products; increase the import of advanced technology and key equipment and decrease the import of consumer products. According to the seventh five-year plan, China's priorities are foreign direct investment in export-oriented and technologically advanced projects, especially in the development of energy, transportation, communications, and raw materials. Foreign direct investment in these projects, whether equity joint venture, contractual joint venture, or foreign wholly owned venture, will be given incentives including exemption or significant reduction in national and local income tax, import and export duties and land fees, and priority in obtaining infrastructure services.

APPENDIX

THE SEVENTH FIVE-YEAR PLAN OF THE PEOPLE'S REPUBLIC OF CHINA FOR NATIONAL ECONOMIC AND SOCIAL DEVELOPMENT (EXCERPTS)*

VI. Foreign Economic Relations, Trade and Technological Exchange

Chapter 33 Import and Export

Section 1. Scale and Structure of Import and Export.   In the five-year period, the total volume of import and export will grow at an average annual rate of 7 percent, reaching US$83 billion by 1990. Export will grow at a rate of 8.1 percent and import at a rate of 6.1 percent.

Export: We shall continue to increase exports of petroleum, coal, nonferrous metals, grain, cotton, etc. In addition, we shall gradually increase the proportion of manufactured goods in the total volume of export.

Import: Priority in import will be given to software, advanced technologies, and key equipment, as well as to certain essential means of production that are badly needed and in short supply on the domestic market.

Section 2. Policies and Measures for Increasing Foreign Exchange Earnings Through Export.   We shall establish an integrated system for the production of export commodities and enhance our capacity to earn foreign exchange through export. In organizing production, in supplying funds, raw and semifinished materials, fuel, power and packing materials, in assisting technological transformation and in providing transport services, we shall always give priority

---

* Adopted at the Fourth Session of the Sixth National People's Congress on April 12, 1986.
Source: *Almanac of China's Foreign Economic Relation and Trade 1987.*

to export commodities. We shall encourage initiative in the production of export commodities by applying economic levers. The quality of export commodities must be improved, so as to make them more competitive in the world. We shall conduct investigation and research of international markets and improve sales promotion and services. We must expand trade ties with all other countries and regions and make active efforts to open up new markets. We must faithfully implement contracts and deliver commodities on time, so as to maintain a good reputation in the world market.

Section 3. Management of Import and Export.   To promote foreign trade we shall continue to reform the system by which it is managed. For some time to come, our most important task will be to strengthen and improve the macroeconomic control and management system, and to reasonably regulate import and export by increased use of such economic levers as exchange rates, customs duties, taxation and export credits, to be supplemented with administrative means when necessary. As the macroeconomic management system gradually improves, we shall delegate more decision-making power to government departments and local authorities and, in particular, to enterprises engaging in export in order to encourage them to expand foreign trade.

Chapter 34 Use of Foreign Capital and Introduction of Technology

Section 1. Use of Foreign Capital.   In using foreign capital, we shall give first priority to construction projects in such areas as energy, transport, communications, and raw and semifinished materials, and especially to projects for power generation, port facilities, and the petroleum industry, and also to the technological transformation of the machine-building and electronics industries. We shall give second priority to projects that will increase our ability to earn foreign exchange through export and to produce substitutes for imports.

To use foreign capital effectively, we shall diversify the areas in which it is used, further improve the laws and regulations concerning foreign affairs, and improve our investment environment. Macro-control over the use of foreign capital will be improved so as to increase economic results and social benefits.

Section 2. Introduction of Foreign Technology and Expertise.   In introducing foreign technology, we shall give priority to the transformation of existing enterprises. First we shall import technology and equipment that will help increase our capacity to export and to produce substitutes for imports.

We shall enhance our cooperation with foreign engineers and technicians and invite foreign experts to China to advise and consult with us.

Chapter 35 Special Economic Zones, Coastal Cities, and Other Areas Opening to the Outside World

Under the guidance of the state plan, these cities and areas should systematically carry out construction and development with emphasis on key projects. We shall continue to apply special policies and flexible measures in Guangdong and Fujian provinces.

In the special economic zones of Shenzhen, Zhuhai, Shantou, and Xiamen, we shall make greater efforts to improve the existing infrastructure and develop supporting industries for projects that use foreign capital. We shall concentrate on completing construction in those areas where development has already begun, gradually building an export-oriented economy that is based on industry and advanced technology and earns foreign exchange through export.

The 14 open coastal cities and Hainan Island should, in the light of their own conditions and characteristics, exploit their advantages to introduce investment from abroad and establish lateral ties at home. In this way they will systematically expand economic and trade relations with other countries and technological exchanges with them. In planning new areas for economic and technological development, the open coastal cities should adhere to the principle of expanding gradually and only in accordance with their capacity, so that each new undertaking will be successful and profitable.

In the open areas such as the Changjiang River and Zhujiang River deltas and the triangular area in southern Fujian province, we shall gradually build an economic structure in which agriculture serves processing industry and processing industry serves trade. In these areas we shall do a good job in technological transformation and the introduction of advanced technologies to expand export and earn more foreign exchange.

Chapter 36 Contracted Projects in Foreign Countries, Sending Labor Abroad, and International Aid

In carrying out projects abroad and supplying labor to foreign countries, we shall continue to abide by contracts, ensure quality, seek small profits and act in good faith, so that the work in this field will expand. We shall strive to improve our management of these projects and to open up new areas of business.

By acting on the principles of equality and mutual benefit, stress on practical results, diversity of forms and common progress, we shall continue to do our work well in offering or receiving aid.

Chapter 37 Tourism

To increase foreign exchange earnings and promote friendly contacts between people of different countries, we must expand our tourist industry. We plan to receive 5 million tourists from abroad in 1990.

Under unified state planning, we shall mobilize all quarters to develop the places of interest to tourists. We shall speed up the training of people engaged in the tourist industry and expand production and sale of tourist commodities.

Chapter 38 Foreign Exchange Receipts and Payments

We must try to increase foreign exchange earnings and economize on their use, maintaining a basic balance and keeping necessary reserves. We shall tighten centralized control over foreign exchange and foreign loans, rationally readjust the spending of foreign exchange and vigorously enforce discipline in this regard.

CHAPTER 24

THE CHINESE
BUSINESS ENVIRONMENT

Jamie P. Horsley
Sue-Jean Lee

THE REGULATORY ENVIRONMENT FOR TRADE
AND INVESTMENT
THE LEGAL SYSTEM
INITIATIVES TO ATTRACT BUSINESS
SELLING TO CHINA: DISTRIBUTING PRODUCTS
AND SERVICES
BUYING FROM CHINA: SOURCING PRODUCTS
MORE COMPLEX FORMS OF DOING BUSINESS
PROTECTION OF INTELLECTUAL PROPERTY
COMMUNICATIONS AND TRANSPORTATION
U.S.-CHINA BILATERAL AGREEMENTS/RELATIONS
CHINA'S CHANGING ENVIRONMENT

During the decade since the adoption in late 1978 of the open policy by the People's Republic of China, China has undertaken far-reaching economic, social, and legal reforms designed to raise the standard of living of its people, invigorate the economy, and integrate China into the international community. Yet China remains an underdeveloped, poor country, struggling to overcome an inadequate infrastructure and industrial base and to reconcile the apparent benefits of introducing market mechanisms with political ideology and the centrist mentality of the ruling Communist Party. China is not an easy place in which to do business and invest.

THE REGULATORY ENVIRONMENT FOR TRADE AND INVESTMENT

China's foreign trade and investment activities are overseen and regulated by central and local government authorities. At the central level, the executive branch of government is the State Council, which is made up of the premier, vice premiers, and state councilors. Reporting to the State Council are eight state commissions, including planning, science and technology, education, and others; four major state administrations; more than 30 national ministries overseeing industry, trade, finance, and government affairs; three ministry-level industrial corporations; and China's central bank, the People's Bank of China.[1] In the provinces and cities, most of these entities have offices or bureaus that fulfill similar functions at the local level, participating in and approving foreign economic activity that falls within the authority of the provincial/municipal government.

A few key entities in this government structure that foreign businesspeople need to be aware of when trading with or investing in China, are explained below.

State Planning Commission (SPC)

The SPC is responsible for establishing China's five-year economic plans, which set national goals for the production of goods and services. Projects that fall within these five-year plans often have to be approved by the SPC. Since its merger with the State Economic Commission in 1988, the SPC is also overseeing implementation of these plans. Local planning commissions are responsible for the economic plans of their localities with the national plan as a guide.

Ministry of Foreign Economic Relations and Trade (MOFERT)

MOFERT is the central ministry responsible for all matters relating to the planning and control of foreign trade, investment, and economic cooperation. Established in 1982, MOFERT was formed by merging the former Import and Export Commission, the Ministry of Foreign Trade, the Ministry of Economic Relations with Foreign Countries, and the Foreign Investment Commission. MOFERT's 20 operations bureaus

---

[1] "China's Government Structure," *China Market Intelligence,* April 1988.

implement state economic policies, including the establishment of quotas, issuance of import/export licenses, approval of joint ventures and other forms of foreign investment, and the drafting and review of treaties, laws, and regulations. Under MOFERT are 16 national-level foreign trade corporations with local branches around the country that maintain much control over the trading of products within their areas of responsibility. In addition, MOFERT has established six research and information centers to support its operations.

Local Commissions of Foreign Economic Relations and Trade (COFERTs)
Replicated at the provincial and city levels of government are local commissions of foreign economic relations and trade that function in much the same way as MOFERT does on the central level, with regard to overseeing foreign trade and investment activities. Decentralization of decision-making authority and foreign trade reform of recent years have resulted in an increased importance and greater involvement of local COFERTs in project approvals and regulation of trade activity.

Export-Import Corporations
Foreign trade transactions in China are handled almost exclusively by export-import corporations, also called foreign trade corporations (FTCs), that act as trade agents for factories or end-users. Traditionally, the national-level FTCs under MOFERT, through central and local branch offices, had monopolistic control over the trading of products in their industries. With the implementation of trade reforms introduced over the last decade, the authority to carry out trade transactions has been expanded to industrial ministries, which in some cases have set up their own export-import corporations, and to provincial/municipal localities, where hundreds of new trading corporations have been established to compete for foreign trade business. In addition, China has ministry-level corporations that control the production and marketing of products in three key industries: nonferrous metals, petrochemicals, and shipbuilding.

Industrial Ministries
China's economy is overseen by industrial ministries that supervise the development and administration of industrial sectors. Organized with vertical lines of authority from the central offices in Beijing to the local bureaus in provinces and major cities, each ministry is responsible for its

industry's macroeconomic policy strategies, implementation of state and local plans, allocation of funds for development, approval of projects, and the seeking of foreign economic cooperation. Industrial ministries have traditionally held so much control over their product areas that any business transaction involving products from more than one ministry is virtually impossible to consummate without the agreement and cooperation of all the responsible ministerial authorities.

People's Bank of China (PBOC)
The People's Bank of China functions as China's central bank, responsible for the management of financial business throughout the country, formulation of macroeconomic policies, management of credit funds, and maintaining the stability of China's currency, the renminbi (RMB). As such, the PBOC issues currency and adjusts the country's money supply, manages interest rates and exchange rates of the RMB, prepares credit plans, controls the state's reserve funds, regulates financial markets, and participates in international financial activities on behalf of the government. The PBOC also acts in a leadership capacity supervising and coordinating the business activities of China's specialized banks and financial institutions.

Bank of China (BOC)
The Bank of China is a specialized state bank that deals in foreign exchange business, organizes foreign exchange funds, settles international accounts of foreign trade and nontrade transactions, handles deposits and loans to and from international banks and other international remittances, and buys and sells foreign exchange and gold on the international markets. With the authorization of the State Council, the BOC can also issue foreign currency bonds and securities for the state. The BOC has close to 300 overseas branches, most of them in the Hong Kong/ Macao region and others in Singapore, the United Kingdom, Luxembourg, and the United States. BOC has also established correspondent relationships with over 3,300 banks in 150 countries and regions.

State Administration of Exchange Control (SAEC)
Incorporated into the People's Bank of China in 1982, the SAEC and its local branches are responsible for the country's control of foreign exchange. The SAEC manages foreign exchange funds and foreign loans, formulates RMB exchange rate policy, adjusts and publishes official exchange rates, supervises the implementation of state plans for foreign

exchange revenue and expenditure, and administers foreign exchange income and expenditure of all enterprises, organizations, and individuals within China. The SAEC also has authority for approving banks and financial institutions that can conduct foreign exchange business.

State Taxation Bureau and Local Tax Authorities

The State Taxation Bureau, a division within the Ministry of Finance, is responsible for managing state tax revenues, formulating tax laws and tax control systems, and supervising the financial affairs of collective enterprises in urban and rural areas. In addition, the State Taxation Bureau has the power to interpret China's tax laws informally. The bureau and local tax authorities issue rulings relating to the various forms of Chinese-foreign economic cooperation in the form of notices and replies and handle tax issues relating to these enterprises.

THE LEGAL SYSTEM

One common misconception among foreigners is that China lacks a legal system. To the contrary, China now boasts a quite comprehensive system of laws, including a civil code, a civil procedure law, foreign investment laws, business registration rules, a detailed tax system, environmental protection regulations, product liability, customs laws, and so forth. National legislation, which must not conflict with China's 1982 constitution, is supplemented by a growing body of local law. Moreover, China has designated certain areas as "special economic zones" (Shenzhen, Shantou, and Zhuhai in Guangdong province, Xiamen in Fujian province and all of the recently created province of Hainan Island), "economic and technological development zones" or "open coastal economic zones," and "open coastal cities" in which more preferential policies and laws than those generally applicable are implemented. In light of the complexity of the system, the foreign businessperson would be well advised to seek professional guidance when undertaking business activities in China.

Such professional advice can increasingly be obtained locally within China. Chinese law and accounting firms, as well as a variety of consulting companies, have proliferated in China. In addition, many of the major international law firms, accounting firms, banks, and consulting companies now have offices in Hong Kong and China dedicated to assisting foreign businesspeople in China.

INITIATIVES TO ATTRACT BUSINESS

Through the adoption of much-needed laws to regulate economic activity and investment and the entrance into a variety of bilateral and international treaties on such matters as investment protection, the avoidance of double taxation, and judicial assistance, China has taken a variety of initiatives to attract foreign investment. After a particularly steep downturn in foreign investment in 1986, China promulgated the Provisions on the Encouragement of Foreign Investment, more commonly known as the "22 Articles," to reiterate such principles as the right of autonomy of foreign investment enterprises in matters such as hiring and management as well as to introduce new forms of preferential tax, land use, customs, and other treatment for foreign investment enterprises that are export-oriented or that will introduce advanced technology to China.

SELLING TO CHINA: DISTRIBUTING PRODUCTS AND SERVICES

At first glance, China may appear to some companies as a large market of a billion-plus consumers, ripe for developing demand for their products or services. However, as many companies have learned during the first decade of China's open policy, not all foreign products and services have found easy access into the market. With China's planned economy, imports generally are determined according to development needs set by the government, and enterprises are allocated foreign exchange for purchasing goods that comply with those needs. Measures used by the government to maintain control over imports include import licenses, quotas, tariffs, and quality inspection requirements, as well as allocation of foreign exchange for imports. These measures are used to stem excessive inflow of nonproductive imports, such as consumer or luxury goods, that could drain the country's limited foreign exchange reserves. Such a drain occurred in 1984–85, when spending by local officials got out of hand after decentralization of decision-making authority was introduced. Import licenses, in particular, are used for preventing large-scale duplication of importing the same kind of equipment and technology by competing enterprises all over the country.

One important factor behind these controls is that China's need for importing foreign goods, equipment, and technology is dependent on China's need to export more products. Given China's often-stated reluctance to incur trade deficits or foreign debt, how much China can buy from foreign countries will depend on how much China can sell abroad to earn the foreign exchange for imports.

In general, the kinds of products appropriate for that market include products that are (1) needed by China for targeted modernization goals but not available, or available in short supply, domestically; (2) made with advanced technology; and (3) export-enhancing. This is not to say that all others do not have a chance, but, companies should assess their potential in China in terms of how well their products, services, or technologies meet China's stated plans and needs.

For the newcomer to the market, selling to China is best facilitated through experienced local distributors, agents, or trading companies. As mentioned earlier, there are a number of Chinese enterprises, as well as companies located in Hong Kong, other Asian countries, and the United States, that can offer these services.

BUYING FROM CHINA: SOURCING PRODUCTS

Before reforms in the trading system in the early 1980s, buying from China was relatively less complicated than it is today. The national trading corporations under what was then the Ministry of Foreign Trade had a monopoly on trade transactions, each having responsibility in noncompeting industries, so foreign companies at least knew which entity to go to when sourcing products in a particular industry sector. With decentralization reforms in the trading structure, the number of enterprises that can now handle foreign trade transactions has increased to more than a thousand.

On the central level, some industrial ministries have set up their own import-export companies to represent factories under their supervision, and there are also three ministry-level state corporations that oversee the nonferrous metals, petrochemicals, and shipbuilding sectors. On the local level, many new trading corporations have sprung up to compete for trade-related services, and enterprises have been given more freedom to deal directly with foreign buyers or to select their trade agents.

While decentralization has created more flexibility and options with which foreign buyers could source goods, it has also resulted in a host of new difficulties, such as confusion over which Chinese companies have direct access to the factories, which have the authority to engage in trade, and which are reliable contract partners. Newcomers to the market should be aware of the fluid situation and seek the assistance of well-informed and experienced trade agents.

Just as with imports, the Chinese government also controls the country's key export products and commodities in order to monitor quality and quantities exported and the enterprises exporting them and to maintain relative stability and uniformity of export prices. These objectives are achieved through the use of export licenses, tariffs, and quotas. In 1988, MOFERT instituted a three-tier exports classification system that groups export products and commodities into three categories. Products in the first and second tiers are subject to tighter state control either because they are in short supply domestically or because export competition among local exporters has created excessive variances in export prices.[2] Both groups include a broad range of goods from agricultural and food products to textile goods and natural resources such as crude oil and minerals and metals. First-tier products remain under tight central control of the FTCs, while second-tier products are subject to monopolistic controls of provincial trade authorities. Export items are added to these categories as the need for controlling them arises. The third-tier category includes all other products that can be traded relatively freely by any authorized foreign trade corporation. Foreign buyers should inquire about updated listings periodically in order to determine which enterprises or organizations to work with and whether export licenses are required for the goods.

MORE COMPLEX FORMS OF DOING BUSINESS

A foreign company seeking to do business in China beyond the simple trading transaction can adopt an increasing number of methods, including setting up a representative office,[3] leasing, licensing, compensation trade, processing and assembly, service centers, equity or cooperative joint ventures, and the establishment of wholly foreign-owned enterprises in China. Some of these methods are described below.

Compensation Trade.   Given the inconvertibility of the RMB, the Chinese like to use compensation trade, where the foreign side sells

---

[2] *China Market Intelligence,* December 1988, p. 2.

[3] Procedures for setting up a representative office are included in the next chapter, "Practical Business Considerations in Modern China."

equipment or technology to the Chinese party, which uses the same to produce a commodity that can be given or sold at a discount back to the foreign side. Compensation trade, in addition to conserving precious foreign exchange, also involves deferred payment, and thus is a form of financing. A variation of compensation trade is countertrade, in which a commodity not produced using the financed items is utilized to pay back the foreign seller. No laws directly govern this form of doing business, and the foreign party is exempted from Chinese tax on the product payback and on the imputed interest component thereof.

Processing and Assembly. Processing and assembly (P&A) is a form of compensation trade in which the foreign party supplies raw materials, parts, components, equipment, and/or packaging materials for processing or assembly by the Chinese party. The Chinese party is paid a processing fee, and the foreign party takes back the end product. Items imported to be used in the P&A process are generally exempted from having to obtain an import license and from customs duty and import taxes, so long as the finished goods are all exported out of China. If a portion of the goods is sold on the Chinese market, duties and taxes will be levied retroactively on the portion not exported.

P&A is governed by national legislation that requires government approval by MOFERT or its designee of all P&A contracts and filing of such contracts for the record with MOFERT, as well as with the local customs authority. Given the growing importance of P&A, many localities have also passed their own regulations. In general, the Chinese party undertaking P&A must be a Chinese legal person specifically authorized to engage in P&A, or else it must entrust a foreign trade corporation to sign the P&A contract jointly with it and the foreign party.

Licensing of Technology. The import of foreign technology by Chinese entities is governed by national legislation. In general, Chinese law requires that technology licenses should not last longer than 10 years, at the end of which term the Chinese licensee owns the technology free and clear and has no further obligation to pay royalties or, except in the case of technology still covered by a valid Chinese patent, to preserve confidentiality. Foreign licensors must warrant that they own the technology and that it can accomplish objectives specified in the license contract. In return, Chinese licensees must pay royalties and maintain confidentiality during the term of the license.

Foreign licensors may not, without special approval, impose various restrictions on the Chinese licensee, including tie-in clauses, limitation of export markets, unequal conditions for the exchange of improvements of the technology, and the like. MOFERT's Technology Import Bureau or the local COFERT must approve all technology import contracts before they can come in force. Such contracts are to be submitted for approval within 30 days after signature. The approval authority may question any of the contractual terms on legal or business grounds. The contract must be approved or rejected within 60 days of its receipt and, if the approval authority fails to comment within that time, the contract will be deemed to have been approved.

Equity Joint Ventures. Chinese-foreign equity joint ventures (EJVs) are Chinese limited liability companies formed in accordance with China's 1979 Law on Chinese-Foreign Equity Joint Ventures (the EJV Law). Pursuant to the EJV Law, the investors in an EJV must sign a joint venture contract, which is somewhat akin to a shareholders' agreement, and formulate articles of association for the resulting company. The liabilities of the investors in EJVs are limited to the amount of equity they agree to invest, as set forth in the joint venture contract.

Under the EJV Law, the foreign investor must contribute at least 25 percent of the EJV's registered capital, or equity. As a matter of law, there is no maximum percentage limitation (below 100 percent) on the amount of equity that a foreign investor can own, but in practice most recent EJVs have been owned 50-50 by the Chinese and foreign sides. The investors in an EJV are issued investment certificates rather than shares, and their profit split is determined strictly in accordance with the percentage of their equity contribution.

Under the EJV Law, foreign investors can contribute as equity cash (almost always foreign exchange), intellectual property, machinery, equipment, and other tangible assets, but not the value of services; the Chinese side can contribute the same, plus the right to use the site on which the EJV will be located.[4] If the Chinese side contributes the right to use a site, under applicable financial regulations it is supposed to also

---

[4] Although the Chinese government, on behalf of the people, continues to own all land in China, the right to use land can, pursuant to a 1988 amendment to the Chinese Constitution, now be granted (usually for a fixed period), assigned, bequeathed, and sold. Foreigners can now also obtain land-use rights in China, and it is possible that the EJV Law will be amended to reflect their new ability also to contribute sites to an EJV.

pay the rental, referred to as the "site use fee," for the site during the term of the EJV. The two parties are to assess and agree on the value of the respective contributions, except that the value of the right to use the site is to be determined in accordance with local government standards.

EJVs are operated under the supervision of a board of directors, pursuant to their articles of association. Under current law, the Chinese side must appoint the chairman of the board, and the foreign side is entitled to appoint a vice chairman. The parties may determine between themselves who is to appoint the management, which runs the day-to-day operations of the EJV and is answerable to the board of directors.

EJVs must have a fixed term, which is normally more than 10 years but less than 30, although periods exceeding 30 and even 50 years may be approved. At the end of the joint venture term, the EJV Law contemplates a liquidation, which MOFERT insists must be based on the net book value of the assets of the EJV, and a final distribution to the parties of the net remaining assets, again based strictly on the equity percentages of the parties. Buyout clauses that call for any party that wishes to continue the business of the EJV on its own to purchase the interest of the other party, at a price that takes account of going concern value, have been approved by some local COFERTs but are disliked by MOFERT.

The joint venture contract, the EJV articles of association, and a feasibility study on the EJV prepared jointly by the parties must be submitted to MOFERT or the local COFERT for approval. After approval, the EJV is registered with the local administrative bureau for industry and commerce and is issued a business license.

In addition to the EJV Law and its implementing regulations, a plethora of special rules on taxation, labor, registration, land use, debt-equity ratios, the timing of contributions, accounting and lending, as well as a host of domestic legislation applicable to all Chinese entities, governs the operation of EJVs.

Cooperative Joint Ventures.   Cooperative joint ventures (CVs) are sometimes referred to as contractual joint ventures. Like EJVs, they involve the investment by Chinese and foreign parties of cash, tangible property, technology and other industrial property rights, and site use rights, as well as, generally, joint management of the project. CVs also require approval of MOFERT, or the local COFERT, and registration locally. However, CVs differ from EJVs in several important respects.

First, a CV can be organized either as a limited liability company with a board of directors, like an EJV, or as a partnership in which each investor retains its separate legal identity and bears unlimited liability for its share of the obligations of the CV. The parties to a partnership-type CV normally appoint a joint management committee to oversee the CV operations. Under either form, there is no requirement in the 1988 Law on Cooperative Joint Ventures (the CV Law) that the Chinese side must appoint the chairman of the board or head of the management committee. The parties are free to decide how the CV is to be run and may even entrust sole management of the CV entirely to the foreign party or to a third party.

The parties to CVs are free to determine their respective obligations and share of profits in any manner they please, rather than based on equity percentages. Thus, except for purposes of meeting certain debt-equity ratios that are applicable to EJVs and CVs alike, they do not have to value their contributions. Reportedly, in addition to the types of investment allowable under the EJV Law, services and labor may be contributed to a CV.

At the end of the CV term, the parties may agree that all of the assets of the CV will be turned over to the Chinese side. In such a case, the CV Law permits the foreign investor, with the approval of the financial and tax authorities, to recover its investment out of pretax profits, before termination of the CV, provided it is willing to reinvest the funds should the CV be unable to discharge its liabilities upon termination.

Although CVs still outnumber EJVs and other forms of investment in China, the legal regime governing CVs is still very sketchy and, increasingly, foreign investors are utilizing the EJV vehicle. Nonetheless, in view of the great flexibility in terms of profit split, possible early recovery of investment and management control that the CV affords, CVs remain an attractive possibility for many foreign investors.

Wholly Foreign-Owned Enterprises.   Wholly foreign-owned enterprises (WFOEs) are Chinese legal persons established in China, pursuant to the 1986 Law of the People's Republic of China on Wholly Foreign-Owned Enterprises (the WFOE Law), that are 100 percent owned by foreign entities or individuals. They are treated for some purposes, such as taxation, like a foreign enterprise and for others like a domestic Chinese enterprise. Thus, for example, if a WFOE signs a contract with another Chinese enterprise, the contract is governed by the domestic contract legislation, rather than the Law on Economic Contracts with Foreign Interests. While WFOEs were initially viewed with caution and relatively few have been approved to date, the Chinese government is looking with more favor on them because they introduce foreign capital, equipment, and technology; employ Chinese labor; and contribute to China's modernization program, without requiring the expenditure of much or any Chinese capital.

Pursuant to the WFOE Law, WFOEs must normally "utilize advanced technology and equipment or export all or a major portion" of their products. WFOEs must, like EJVs and CVs, be approved by MOFERT or, more recently, the local COFERT, depending on the size of investment. A registration application must be accompanied by draft articles of association of the WFOE (and often a feasibility study prepared by the foreign investor). Such applications are handled by the offices in charge of foreign investment under the local people's government or through the auspices of local trust and investment or other consulting companies.

The WFOE Law promises noninterference in the management and operation of WFOEs. However, WFOEs must have a Chinese "department in charge" that supervises them, and, because they are operating in a planned economy, WFOEs unavoidably must have good relations with the various Chinese government agencies. Having a Chinese "sponsor" entity to help smooth the way is also advisable.

PROTECTION OF INTELLECTUAL PROPERTY

Trademarks.   Trademarks of foreign companies can be registered with the Trademark Office of the State Administration for Industry and Commerce, through the auspices of a designated trademark agent, under the 1983 Chinese Trademark Law and its 1988 Implementing Regulations. Trademark registration is on a first-to-file basis. Registration gives the trademark owner the exclusive right to use, assign, and license its mark in China for up to 10 years, after which the registration is renewable for additional 10-year periods. Trademark licenses must also be registered with the Trademark Office. Service marks are not registrable in China. However, China has joined the Paris Convention for the Protection of Industrial Property Rights, under which China has an obligation to protect the service marks of persons from signatory countries.

Patents.   China promulgated its long-awaited Patent Law in 1984, and it went into effect April 1, 1985. Exclusive patent rights can be granted to Chinese and foreign entities and individuals for novel inventions, utility models, and industrial designs. Applications are to be filed with the State Patent Office through a designated patent agent in the case of foreigners.

The Patent Law provides for deferred examination, opposition proceedings, assignment and licensing of patent rights, recognition of priority of foreign patents in certain circumstances, and enforcement of patent rights in the event of infringement. Patentees must practice their patents in China through manufacture of patented products or processes or by granting licenses to others to do so.

Inventions are granted a 15-year patent, and design and utility model patents are for five years, with possible three-year extensions. Patents will not be granted for (1) scientific activities, (2) the rules and processes of mental activities, (3) methods of diagnosing and treating diseases, (4) foodstuffs, beverages, and flavorings, (5) pharmaceuticals and substances derived from chemical processes, (6) breeds and varieties of animals and plants, and (7) substances derived from nuclear conversion processes. However, process patents may be granted for foodstuffs, beverages, and flavorings and pharmaceuticals and substances derived from chemical processes. China is revising its Patent Law.

Copyrights. China has not yet promulgated a Copyright Law, although it has established a State Copyright Office to draft such a law. In the meantime, Chinese law may afford limited protection to foreign authors who choose to publish their works first in China, under China's General Principles of Civil Law. However, it is difficult to protect computer software, which is not covered by the Patent Law, under existing Chinese law.

COMMUNICATIONS AND TRANSPORTATION

As China moves toward modernization, one of the major challenges the country faces is development of an adequate communications and transportation infrastructure that can keep up with the current rapid pace of industrial and economic growth. After more than 20 years of isolationism and self-reliance, China's open policy revealed how far China had fallen behind the West technologically, particularly in the transport and communications sectors.

Development of the country's air transport system was virtually at a standstill before the modernization program began in the late 1970s. Increased business with foreign countries has resulted in a trade volume that has outgrown the handling capability and capacity of existing port facilities. Much of the equipment and technology still in use in China's railways dates back to before World War II, and the current network of roads and highways is grossly inadequate to provide a viable transport alternative to the overburdened rail system.

China's telecommunications system leaves much to be desired. Domestic and international telephone lines have been in existence primarily for official or business purposes. Services are distributed unevenly among major cities and industrial centers (three to five telephones per 100 people in large cities) and available only on a limited basis in rural areas (national average of one telephone per 130 people).

However, China has made much progress in these sectors during the last 10 years. They have been targeted for priority development in the state's five-year economic plans. With the help of World Bank and Japanese Overseas Economic Cooperation Fund (OECF) loans, China has purchased foreign equipment and technology that have increased rail capacity by 30 percent from 1981 to 1985 and improved port operations, with targeted expansion to include 120 deep-water berths and 80 smaller berths by 1990. In addition, foreign technical assistance and Chinese-foreign jointly funded projects have begun the construction of 10 major highways, with another 6 planned for the eighth five-year plan period (1991–95).

Major reform of China's air transport system in 1985, including breaking up the monopoly control of the Civil Aviation Administration of China (CAAC) into six regional carriers, has facilitated expansion and modernization of the entire air transport system. This includes purchasing and leasing new aircraft from abroad, building additional airfields, and improving airport facilities, such as upgrading air traffic control equipment and systems. In telecommunications, China planned to expand the number of telephones from 6.3 million sets in 1985 to 10 million sets by 1990 and to modernize existing equipment to include the use of digital communications, optical fiber transmission, and computer-controlled telephone exchanges. From the perspective of gains already made, as of 1988, direct-dial long-distance service is available in more than 300 cities.

Having leaped into a modernization program that spans the broad economic spectrum of infrastructure improvements from science and technology advances to industrial renovation and expansion, China has many competing development goals for the country's limited resources and foreign funds. Transportation and communications, however, will continue to remain high on the priority development list, as China recognizes the level of growth in industry and domestic and foreign trade will depend on these two sectors.

U.S.-CHINA BILATERAL AGREEMENTS/RELATIONS

Since the normalization of relations between the United States and China in 1979, both countries have signed more than 20 bilateral agreements that range from consular communiques, to cultural and science and technology protocols, to treaties governing trade, tax, and maritime agreements. These agreements have contributed to expansion of economic cooperation and trade over the last 10 years. With bilateral trade exceeding $14 billion in 1988, the United States maintained its position as China's third-largest trading partner, behind Hong Kong/Macao and Japan. And, as of 1988, the United States was China's second-largest source of foreign investment, after Hong Kong/Macao.

A list of major U.S.-Chinese bilateral agreements affecting business transactions and operations in China follows:[5]

- Agreement on Trade Exhibitions, May 10, 1979.
- Agreement Concerning the Settlement of Claims, May 11, 1979.
- Agreement on Trade Relations, July 7, 1979.
- Agreement Relating to Trade in Cotton, Wool, and Man-made Fiber Textiles and Textile Products, September 17, 1980. Lapsed December 31, 1982; new agreement reached August 19, 1983.
- Agreement on Maritime Transport, September 17, 1980. Lapsed December, 1983; new agreement reached December 15, 1988.
- Agreement on Grain Trade, October 22, 1980.
- Agreement on Investment Insurance, October, 1980. (Administered by the U.S. Overseas Private Investment Corporation.)
- Agreement with Respect to Mutual Exemption from Taxation of Transportation Income of Shipping and Air Transport Enterprises, March 5, 1982.
- Quarantine and Health Requirements for Cattle Exported from the United States to the People's Republic of China, June 1, 1983.
- Quarantine and Health Requirements for Swine Exported from the United States to the People's Republic of China, June 1, 1983.
- Agreement for the Avoidance of Double Taxation and the Prevention of Tax Evasion with Respect to Taxes on Income, March 21, 1984.

---

[5] The U.S.-China Business Council files.

Negotiations on a bilateral investment treaty that would provide basic reciprocal guarantees and protection for the business activities of investors began as early as 1982, but stalled in 1986 because of differences in four areas: expropriation, dispute settlement, transfer of capital and funds, and treatment by host country. While discussions between the Office of the U.S. Trade Representative and the Chinese have continued on an informal basis, as of early 1989, there were no indications the two sides are nearing solutions to the differences. To date, the lack of a bilateral investment treaty has not deterred U.S. investment interests in China. However, companies should consult with the U.S. Department of Commerce for updates on the progress of the investment treaty negotiations, as well as for information on other bilateral agreements.

In the wake of China's harsh crackdown on the pro-democracy movement and the massacre in June 1989, the United States Congress has imposed economic sanctions against China. Companies should consult with the United States Department of State on the continued effect and applicability of these sanctions.

CHINA'S CHANGING ENVIRONMENT

While the business environment in China is far from ideal and the economic picture is clouded by uncertainty as China copes with a demanding yet restraining growth and modernization process, there is still cause for optimism. The difficulties of doing business in China are very real and may persist for some time, but it is important to note that the Chinese government is also aware of them. In a country dominated by a Communist Party sensitive to questions of national independence and economic sovereignty, China's commitment to the open policy and foreign participation in its economic development is still remarkable.

As China moves cautiously forward with economic reforms, there will be swings in policy decisions and in decentralization and recentralization of controls, often creating confusion not only for foreign businesspeople but for Chinese officials and enterprise managers as well. Companies with long-term objectives for the China market and a willingness to make the commitment to China have come to expect the ebbs and flows of the changing environment and must be determined to stay with and develop their business opportunities. The China market is not right for every company, and it poses a challenge for most that pursue it. Newcomers should approach the market with careful preparation and understanding of China's business environment.

CHAPTER 25

PRACTICAL BUSINESS CONSIDERATIONS IN MODERN CHINA

May C. Huang
Steven Lu
Emily Ou

SETTING UP A REPRESENTATIVE OFFICE

Since late 1980, foreign companies have been permitted to establish permanent offices in China under the auspices of a resident representative office (rep office).

The rep office functions as a liaison and marketing vehicle for the foreign company. It serves as a display window within China, promoting a company's products or services to a consumer market that is largely immobile in terms of international travel. A rep office in a key location can also serve as a vital listening post to gather project information or bidding documents, assess the domestic market conditions, and monitor new laws and regulations that may influence a company's overall plans for China.

A rep office provides the foreign company and the selected resident representatives a few privileges not available to the common visitor or others without a formal presence. These privileges include:

- Importing a large shipment of personal belongings duty-free.[1]
- Granting of a multiple entry and exit visa valid up to six months for the representative and any accompanying family members.[2]
- Importing of motor vehicles for either office or personal use duty-free (but all local vehicle registration fees and related taxes will be applicable).
- Hiring of Chinese nationals (including secretaries, office assistants, bookkeepers, drivers, nannies, and so on) through the local Foreign Enterprise Service Company (FESCO).
- Signing of long-term leases for both residential and office accommodation.
- Identifying one's establishment by installing nameplates and showing the rep office's contact address on business cards.[3]

---

[1] In practice, this could be spread out over a six-month period and unlimited shipments from the date of first arrival in China as long as all intended imports are listed and approved by the customs office immediately upon first entry.

[2] To be applied for following the issuance of the Resident Representative Certificate by the local State Administration for Industry and Commerce. Extensions are automatic within the effective period of one's representative certificate, which is one year in duration.

[3] Under present regulations, foreign law firms are excepted. This could be conveniently remedied by registering under another name in China (e.g., ABC International Consultants) that does not offer any suggestion to the provision of legal advice.

The activities and registration procedures of a rap office are guided by a set of regulations that include:

- Interim Regulations of the P.R.C. Concerning the Control of Resident Offices of Foreign Enterprises (October 30, 1980).
- Notice of the General Administration for Industry and Commerce of the P.R.C. Concerning Registration of Resident Offices of Foreign Enterprises (December 8, 1980).
- Procedures of the People's Bank of China for the Establishment of Representative Offices in China by Overseas Chinese and Foreign Financial Institutions (February 1, 1983).
- Procedures of the State Administration for Industry and Commerce of the P.R.C. for the Registration and Administration of Resident Offices of Foreign Enterprises (March 5, 1983).

One should also check for any attendant regulations for rep offices promulgated at the local or municipality level.

For banking and insurance institutions, with the exception of the four foreign-chartered banks based in Shanghai, all foreign financial companies are limited to a marketing role. The regulations stipulate foreign banking offices must be nonprofit-oriented. For insurance requirements, within China, the People's Insurance Company of China has the monopoly on all insurance activities.

Sectors that have favored the rep office arrangement include freight forwarding, engineering firms, traders, computer companies, lawyers, banks, and accountants and management consultants.

The rep office registration process involves applying to the relevant government organization overseeing the business scope of the foreign company and, following formal approval by the host organization, applying for registration with the local branch of the State Administration of Industry and Commerce (SAIC). Article 4 of the registration regulations (1980) details the designation of relevant host organizations:

- Exporters and importers, manufacturers, or shipping agents apply through the Ministry of Foreign Economic Relations and Trade (MOFERT).
- Financial or insurance companies fall under the People's Bank of China.
- Maritime transport is to contact the Ministry of Communications.
- Air transport needs to approach the Civil Aviation Administration of China (CAAC).

- All others are under the appropriate industry's governing ministry, bureau, or commission.

The initial application to the host organization must be accompanied by evidence of the company's incorporation, information regarding the background and responsibilities of the representative, and a bank statement showing capitalization and credit from the appointed financial institution of the head office. Rep offices of foreign financial or insurance companies need to supply additional information such as an audited financial report, a copy of its charter, and the structure of its board of directors.

Once the application is approved, a certificate of approval will be issued. The foreign company will then have 30 days to register with the local SAIC, followed by opening an account at a domestic bank, and registering with the local tax authority. The representative can then apply for a resident permit, entry/exist visa, and register with the tax authority for payment of individual income tax in China.

The entire application process averages between two and six months. The approval certificate from the host organization is good for three years, while the registration certificate lasts for one year. Moreover, any changes in business activities, personnel, or office location need to be reported and adjusted by the SAIC and recorded on the registration certificate.

The rep office is liable to both the consolidated tax (ICCT) and/or the profits tax (FEIT). The representative and foreign office personnel will be subject to the individual income tax (IIT).

For the ICCT, a rep office that renders agency services including liaison, negotiation, middleman; conducts market surveys; collects commercial information; and provides consultancy services on behalf of head office or clients will be taxed on the commissions, rebates, handling charges, and other fees earned. This income has to be declared for calculation of the ICCT regardless of whether the proceeds are received by the rep office in China or the head office. Any subsidiary income earned that is not under the preceding description needs to be reported to the appropriate tax bureau and assessed. Even where a rep office earns no income, an NIL return has to be filed quarterly with the local tax bureau.

Where a rep office performs negotiations and preparatory and supplementary activities, including liaison, and collects commercial information for its head office (excluding related companies) for engaging in trading of goods (excluding agency services), the net income represented by the difference between selling and purchase cost will be exempt from tax provided a sales contract is entered into directly between the head office and the Chinese buyer. The purchase contract entered into with the goods producer concerned and the related invoices must be furnished to the taxation bureau for approval of the exemption.

The term *head office* includes associated companies of the same corporate group under the certain conditions resulting in similar tax-exempt status.

There are three assessment bases for the ICCT and FEIT: actual, deemed, or expense grossing up. An established rep office has to apply for one of these methods at the tax bureau for its tax calculations.

Under the actual basis, full information on all revenue and expenses substantiating the commission income needs to be produced. A full bookkeeping function needs to be developed and followed by the rep office. For rep offices that cannot provide the tax bureau full and correct documentation in support of its income, the tax bureau will, based on the transacted business turnover, determine the income chargeable to ICCT. The deemed commission rate is generally 3 percent.

In cases where appropriate documentation to separate between trading self-owned goods and provision of agency services by the rep office cannot be produced, the tax bureau will estimate the gross income by referring to the rep office's level of expenses. ICCT is then payable on the estimated income.

The Foreign Enterprise Income Tax (FEIT) is basically a profits tax assessed at year-end. For rep offices that have established accounting procedures in accordance with international accounting standards and maintained proper books of accounts with adequate supporting evidence to enable the appointed local auditor to ascertain income, expenses, and the resultant profits or loss, the FEIT is levied on the actual results so calculated. Where profit or loss cannot be accurately assessed, the FEIT is levied on either a deemed profit of 10 percent of gross income or by the expense grossed-up method.

In the interest of promoting foreign trade in the new China, various preferential tax treatments are provided to the rep office.

- Any rep office appointed by the Chinese to act as agent in marketing products abroad will be exempt from the tax on the commission income.
- The maximum rate for the ICCI is limited to 5 percent, plus a 10 percent local surtax, for a total effective rate of 5.05 percent.

- Rep offices established in the Guangzhou municipality will be exempt from the local income tax where annual taxable income is under RMB 250,000. For taxable income between RMB 250,000 and RMB 1 million, the rep office enjoys a 70 percent reduction in local income tax. Municipal governments may extend additional preferential tax treatments: companies should consult the local tax authorities where the rep office is to be established and determine the specific regulations.
- Rep offices located within the special economic zones are regarded as foreign enterprise. Therefore, they will be subject to a preferential income tax at 15 percent.
- If the rep office can show evidence of vouchers, appointment letters, or other relevant documents substantiating that part of its agency service has been provided outside of China, upon examination by the tax bureau, only 50 percent of the income shall be considered as China-derived income and subject to Chinese taxation.

LOCATION AND FACILITY

Despite China's open door policy and coastal cities' development, the strategic locations for rep offices have largely gravitated to three sites: Beijing, Shanghai, and Guangzhou. Each of the three locations presents a different market orientation for the foreign company. These three sites have probably the best-developed infrastructure and support services in China to attract and sustain the many needs of the representatives and their families.

The strategic questions to be addressed in making a locational choice are:

- Who is my target audience in China? Will it be the state government organs that control the five-year plans? Or will it be the local factories, manufacturers, and Sino-foreign joint ventures?
- Which site offers the most leverage to cover outlying regions?
- Which area is most likely to garner economic growth over the medium term?

The cost factor in setting up a rep office in China is not a decisive issue in location choice once the decision to enter China is made. All locations mentioned are expensive to any foreign investor, and there is little margin of difference among the sites mentioned. For example, a recent international survey revealed Beijing ranks with Tokyo, New York, and Zurich in the annual cost of office and residential space in U.S. dollars. At present, many foreign companies hope prices will decline following the Asian Games in Beijing in 1990 when modern facilities become available.

Beijing, the capital city, offers any company wishing to build *guanxi*, or old friend status, the best possible situation because it is populated by the most senior officials in China's huge government bureaucracy. On a more practical note, the presence of the headquarters for the ministries, commissions, and import and export corporations provides convenience in gathering timely information ranging from project announcements to new laws and regulations.

The municipality of Shanghai is the industrial and financial nerve center of China. The current municipal government is eagerly attracting foreign ventures to upgrade its obsolete stock of industrial machinery, to improve product quality to compete globally, and to learn Western management and operation techniques. In addition, international lending agencies and individual government programs, such as the U.S. Trade Development Program, are assisting in some large infrastructure development projects. On top of all this is a building boom reminiscent of Beijing in the mid-1980s. The city is also in the center of the greater Shanghai economic zone, allowing any foreign company to cover the neighboring provinces of Jiangsu, Zheijiang, Anhui, Jiangxi, and Fujian.

Guangzhou heads the march toward winning foreign trade and investment ever since it received a special economic zone designation with its near-autonomous reign over its own economic destiny. Thanks also to the close familial ties with its laissez-faire neighbor Hong Kong, Guangzhou is well on its way to becoming a hinterland of Hong Kong as Hong Kong reverts back to Chinese control in 1997. The proximity to Hong Kong and Macao alone, for those who have experienced long train rides or flight delays in China, warrants serious consideration of Guangzhou in establishing trade ties with China.

CHINESE FACILITIES: THE SHANGHAI CASE

Commercial building development has taken a backseat to four- and five-star hotels because tourism ranks higher in priority in raising much-needed foreign exchange. Shanghai has two new commercial high rises and several others are to be completed in 1990.

At the first joint venture commercial building, Union Building, rentals run US$1 per square meter per day and it is fully leased. The Rui Jin Building is a Japanese turnkey project with modern facilities. The daily rental ranges from US$1.2 to $1.4 per square meter. The buildings supply water, but electricity and parking are charged separately.

New projects such as the ultramodern Portman Center and a local project, the Consulate Mansion Building, are to open by 1990 and should add much-welcomed competition and supply to the market. Office space shortage has forced newly organized rep offices to set up in local or joint venture hotel rooms. The rental cost is slightly higher as the hoteliers realize most companies are biding time until new commercial projects are completed.

Residential accommodation is still expensive, although an abundant supply of housing for expatriates is on the horizon. Most centrally located local and joint venture hotels do good business renting suites on a long-term lease to expatriates. The average rental in hotels would be about US$3,000 to $4,500 per month depending on the number of rooms occupied. Full service is provided, but cooking facilities are usually not available.

Families who want to cook at home can now choose from a few joint venture villas and deluxe apartments. These new offerings usually include clubhouse facilities such as swimming pool, tennis courts, squash courts, and even food and beverage outlets. Monthly rentals for one bedroom start at US$2,500 and range up to a proposed US$6,000 (mid-1989 rates) for a three-bedroom suite in the Portman Center.

Transportation in and out of Shanghai is relatively adequate. There are daily flights to Hong Kong and Japan. Weekly schedules including direct service are available to North America, Singapore, and European destinations. Domestic flights offer good connections, but regularity and punctuality are far from guaranteed. As China's busiest port, ocean freight is a mainstay for the city's economy and international links. The Shanghai port capacity has been exceeded in recent years with the rapid industrialization process, and World Bank-financed expansion is planned.

Ground transport is adequate; Shanghai has three main train routes to interior cities. The biggest problem is inner-city travel. Most rep offices import a vehicle for the business (and maybe personal use) since the car can enter China duty-free. Local taxis are hard to find, with a ratio of roughly one cab per 1,000 population. Although some taxi fleets have been forced to provide meters recently, the many "private" cab-drivers continue their poaching on the unsuspecting foreign traveler by asking for exaggerated fares, refusing to provide official receipts, or adding other passengers.

As a cosmopolitan city, Shanghai's food supply poses no problem for the expatriate. A variety of pricey imported food as well as a good selection of local fresh supplies are available at a number of retail outlets and markets. Food and beverage outlets in hotels and Hong Kong-China joint venture restaurants are abundant, but Western food is still restricted to the joint venture hotels.

Rep offices will find it difficult to hire local staff conversant in the main language used daily at the office, e.g., English, German, or Japanese. The P.R.C. national can only be hired through the local Foreign Enterprise Service Company (FESCO). The rate the foreign company pays to FESCO has to be in hard currency, while FESCO pays the employee in local currency and at about half the rate it actually receives from the companies. Therefore, a rep office should be prepared to offer meal allowances or overtime pay in hard currency to overcome a job applicant's morale problem.

Telecommunication is improving, particularly for overseas calls. International direct dialing, telex, and telefax lines are all available. Local calls still represent an often time-consuming ordeal because the phone utility is changing its switching systems and increasing capacity at the same time. The charges are higher than one is accustomed to in the West because telecommunication is still considered a luxury in China.

Educational facilities for families with young children could pose a major concern. Children under four can enter an international nursery currently run by the British Consulate, but it runs only a half day for three days a week. The Shanghai American School offers grades one through six with frequent vacations because it honors both major Western and Chinese holidays. The quality of teaching staff is usually satisfactory, but because most are spouses of expatriates on two- to three-year assignments, the turnover rate is high. Local Chinese schools now accept expatriate children. Although the fee is much lower than the aforementioned, the Chinese schools do ask for hard currency payments.

Medical facilities are grossly lacking in Shanghai. Expatriates are restricted to treatment at two locations: the foreigner's clinic at the Hua Dong Hospital and the Shanghai-American Medical Center at the Number One People's Hospital. Hospitals in China do not serve food or have air-conditioned rooms. One possible remedy is to use local hospitals in absolute emergencies and travel to either Hong Kong or Japan for other medical needs. Some expatriates have an open ticket to Hong Kong for just that purpose. A new medical outfit called S.O.S. now offers emergency flights on customized planes from China, usually to Hong Kong.

To serve banking needs, the office accounts could easily and best be handled by the People's Bank of China since the office's expenses will be in hard currency in China and large transactions in foreign exchange are usually required monthly. Many expatriates leave their pay offshore (usually Hong Kong) with an international bank with branches in the home country. Monthly personal expenses, including local income taxes, are met by transferring into China a small amount monthly to an account at a Chinese bank or into one of the four foreign banks with full branch operations in Shanghai. (The four foreign banks are not permitted to offer interest on the net balance in personal savings accounts; only Chinese banks in Chinese territory can do so.)

Finally, recreational facilities need improvement. The zoo and the one amusement park are generally overcrowded for a relaxing visit, particularly with young children. Greenery is a rarity in this industrial city with its 13 million population. There is hardly any sight-seeing beyond four to five tourist spots. The most favored recreational activity for Shanghai-based expatriates is short trips to Suzhou or the scenic Hangzhou or to climb on a plane to Hong Kong or Thailand. Few places in the world have such a dense population as Shanghai, and companies should be generous with their rest and recreation expense offerings to a resident representative in order to enhance morale, personal health, and loyalty.

CHINESE LABOR AND PERSONNEL

Most foreign investment enterprises (FIEs) have experienced labor and personnel problems, but this issue is not as critical as issues such as foreign exchange, power shortages, productivity, and so on. Also, the situation is undoubtedly improving.

Autonomy

Unlike the representative offices of foreign firms, FIEs have autonomy in the employment and dismissal of their Chinese staff. Recruiting can also be conducted outside the areas where enterprises are located.

FIEs may select one of the following recruitment approaches. Some joint ventures leave recruitment to the Chinese partners or the local labor bureaus through a collective contract. The drawback to this is that foreign investors are frequently supplied with unnecessary staff or staff whose loyalty is divided between the staff supplier and the foreign enterprise.

In most cases, foreign investors prefer a direct employment relationship with their Chinese personnel. To play an active role in recruitment, foreign investors may go through newspaper advertisements, universities, or research institutes. Many employers believe hiring new college graduates avoids bad work habits inherited from previous work experience. However, training new graduates can be very time consuming and costly.

Foreign investors are usually discouraged from recruiting directly on campus without coordination with the local labor bureau. They are encouraged to provide the local labor bureau with detailed qualifications of the job openings and let the bureau locate the candidates for the investors to interview.

Employment Contract

Before 1986, most FIEs were required to sign collective contracts with either the local labor bureau or the labor union in the enterprise. It is now permissible, or mandatory in some cities, for FIEs to sign individual employment contracts with their Chinese employees. However, some local labor bureaus or labor unions are not comfortable with the new system and continue to press for collective contracts to maintain their control over the workers.

Recruitment Issues

Transfer of Candidates from Other Units
Suitable employment candidates have usually been attached to Chinese units, and few units are willing to release qualified personnel. They either reject the transfer or request compensation for the release, which in one reported case was RMB 10,000.

To improve the investment climate, the Ministry of Labor and the Ministry of Personnel require Chinese units to actively support the transfer of their staff solicited by FIEs. In practice, such requirement appears very difficult to enforce, especially when candidates are located in other cities or provinces.

Housing
Although FIEs offer higher salaries, many Chinese are uncertain about giving up a secure "iron rice bowl" with housing, which FIEs have difficulty providing. So far, only a few FIEs have been willing to construct housing for their employees.

Qualified Middle-Level Managers
Some joint ventures have reportedly complained about the insufficiency of qualified middle-level managers. To fill this gap, FIEs often have to transfer expatriates to China, which can be very costly. Some joint ventures have yielded to political pressure in selecting managers, but it is costly to train them in managerial skills.

Dismissal Problems

Theoretically, FIEs may dismiss workers according to the terms of employment without the approval of the labor bureau. The enterprises, however, are required to notify various units, including the enterprise's labor union, which usually will not accept this decision easily.

FIEs are generally required to provide severance pay. The local labor bureau or union often presses the enterprise to follow the practice.

IMMIGRATION: EXPATRIATES' WORK VISAS

Foreigners working for FIEs and living in China must apply for a multiple entry visa (categorized as "Z" work visa), which can be renewed annually. Foreigners working for representative offices of foreign firms can obtain only a six-month "Z" visa. Citizens of Hong Kong, Macao, or Taiwan must apply for a "compatriot certificate," which allows them to stay in China without a visa.

Foreigners who expect to stay in China for more than one year and holders of compatriot certificates for more than three months must apply to the local public security bureau for a residence permit. Applicants, other than those holding compatriot certificates, are required to submit a physical examination certificate showing they do not carry AIDS or other diseases.

COMPENSATION

Chinese Nationals

Nonmanagerial Staff
While representative offices of foreign firms have to go through certain government agencies to hire and pay their Chinese staff, most FIEs are free to hire on their own, determine wage levels of their Chinese staff, and pay them directly.

Wage structure and scales vary from one locality to another and from one enterprise to another. The wage structure of an FIE generally consists of a basic wage, bonus, and subsidies.

Basic Wage.   According to the 1986 Labor Autonomy Provisions, wages paid by all FIEs must not be lower than 120 percent of the average wage paid for similar work in state-run enterprises. A maximum of 150 percent was provided before 1986 and has now been eliminated to allow FIEs to pay wages as high as they prefer to motivate their staff. However, some cities still observe the ceiling of 150 percent. Chinese authorities have not set a definition of average wage. Different localities have different interpretations. While some cities consider average wage as the basic wage, others refer to it as take-home pay, which includes the basic wage, bonus, and subsidies. As an example, the average take-home pay for a Chinese employee in FIEs in Beijing and Tianjin is between RMB 250 and 300 (approximately US$68 to $81).

Bonus.   An FIE may determine its own bonus system and establish a fund for bonus and welfare using part of pretax profits. To control the budget, most FIEs set a percentage of basic wage as the bonus ceiling. Within this ceiling, bonuses are awarded based on the performance of the whole enterprise and the individual employee. Moreover, an additional bonus is given at the end of the calendar year.

Subsidies.   Subsidy payments are considered by most foreign investors as the most confusing element of compensation to Chinese staff. Some subsidies are paid directly to employees for rent, meals, haircuts, transportation, or one-child bonus. Others are paid to the local government or the Chinese partner for medical insurance, pension fund (20 percent of total wages of Chinese employees in most cases), education, housing, general labor insurance and welfare, labor union fee (2 percent of total Chinese employee wages, including basic wage, bonuses, and subsidies), and other costs.

The components of subsidy payments vary from one enterprise to another. It is advisable to negotiate a fixed subsidy amount, instead of paying subsidies based on a certain percentage of basic wage, in which case subsidy payments will inflate along with the basic wage.

According to the 1986 "22 Articles" issued by the State Council, FIEs that qualify as export-oriented or technologically advanced are exempted from paying subsidies other than those for housing, labor insurance, and welfare costs.

Managerial Staff

By law, senior management positions in a Sino-foreign joint venture should be allocated among Chinese and foreigners. For instance, the chairman of the board of directors must be Chinese, while the general manager can be from the foreign side.

Many joint ventures have had trouble determining wage levels for Chinese management personnel. The Chinese often insist on being paid at the same level as foreign managers on the "equal pay for equal work" principle. Most foreign investors resist this because the pay scales for foreign managers are usually based on the living standard in their home country. Also, foreign managers are generally more experienced than their Chinese counterparts. In addition, firms usually pay a premium to compensate them for working abroad. Besides, most of the salary paid to a Chinese manager does not go to the manager, but to the Chinese partner of the joint venture or some government unit. The only way to solve this problem is through negotiation because no regulations or guidelines are available on this issue.

Expatriates

Because China is considered a hardship area, companies usually provide special compensation packages to attract and retain high-caliber employees for China assignments. The elements of compensation packages for expatriates in China vary by company. The following are common features:

Base Salary

The base salary paid to expatriates is usually determined according to the same structure used in the home country.

Foreign Service Premium/Hardship Allowance

On top of the base salary, most companies pay their expatriates extra premium for working abroad or hardship allowance for working in areas like China, or both. This payment is usually a tax-protected financial incentive and is calculated as a percentage of the base salary.

Factors considered in determining the premium include language and cultural differences, separation from family and friends, living and working conditions, differences in health and sanitation standards, and political climate. The average foreign service premium is about 15 percent of the base salary, but the hardship allowance ranges from 10 to 65 percent.

Housing Allowance

Many expatriates in China stay in hotels. Joint venture apartments are now becoming available, but the average rental costs are substantially higher than those in other international cities, such as Hong Kong or New York. For instance, a furnished apartment unit with approximately 150 square meters at the Beijing Lido Holiday Inn costs US$6,000 per month for rental, US$360 per month for the management fee, plus utility charges. A furnished townhouse of about 140 square meters in Guang Ming Apartment costs more than US$10,000 per month for rental.

Most companies pay the difference between the cost of an employee's hypothetical home country housing and Chinese housing. In practice, employers pay for all housing costs in China and then deduct a hypothetical housing deduction from the employee's paycheck. Factors considered in determining the hypothetical housing deduction include salary level, size of family, and the cost of housing in the home base before transferring to China.

Other Living Allowance

The living allowance is designed to equate the cost of commodities and services (such as meals, transportation, laundry, telephone, and so on) in the overseas location with those in the home country. The amount of this allowance varies according to salary level, marital status, and number of dependents residing abroad with the employee.

While most foreign companies pay their expatriates in China a living allowance on a per diem basis, a few allow their expatriates an expense account.

Home Leave
Companies usually pay transportation costs to their expatriates and accompanying family members for one or two home leaves per year. A few companies even pay for the hotel expenses incurred.

Rest and Relaxation (R & R)
Since Western-style recreations are lacking in China, most expatriates are granted two or three R & R trips a year, each of which may last for one week. Companies pay either the expenses for airfare and actual accommodations or a per diem.

The location designated as the R & R point varies from one company to another. Some pay for R & R only to Hong Kong, some allow other Asian destinations, and others allow Europe or Hawaii. Some companies pay a per diem without designating any location.

Others
In addition to the above, companies often pay for moving, annual medical checkups, education of dependents, tax return preparation, and family emergency leave.

In most cases, foreign companies provide their expatriates in China with a tax equalization program. This program protects expatriates from paying more or less income tax on the base salary than would have been paid if the expatriate had remained in the home country. In practice, a hypothetical tax deduction will be withheld from the employee's paycheck. Meanwhile, the employer will be responsible for the employee's income tax in China. The tax equilization program brings foreign companies extra financial burdens. Companies should be aware that Chinese tax authorities have adopted a gross-up method to treat the tax reimbursement as part of income.

IDENTIFYING AND WORKING WITH APPROPRIATE BUSINESS PARTNERS AND GOVERNMENT ORGANIZATIONS

After identifying the objective for doing business in China, it is essential to do extensive research on:

- The supply of raw materials, whether they are locally available or have to be imported.

- Which Chinese government organization has the authority to control these raw materials.
- Which officials will be approving such a project.

The above information is necessary for making initial contacts and establishing relationships to help identify the right business partner.

There are many ways of making contacts, but the easiest way of identifying the right partner is to consult people who are knowledgeable about and up to date with China's organizational structure—such as the U.S.-China Business Council, the National Committee on U.S.-China Relations, and professional firms with representative offices in China.

Having the right business partner almost guarantees the success of a China venture. But in evaluating a potential partner, it is important to find out the relationship of the partner to the approving authorities and whether this project is within the framework of the overall China development plan. If the answer to either of these questions is unclear or negative, then the foreign investor must be prepared to face difficulties and uncertainties later.

Because of China's inadequate telecommunication facilities and bureaucratic internal procedures, Western businesspeople are often puzzled about not receiving acknowledgment of their telexes or other messages. Therefore, it is important to know exactly which officers are responsible for the project on the Chinese side. These may not necessarily be the highest ranking officials, making it all the more important to identify them as contacts. Conversely, the foreign businessperson should also appoint a person on the home country side of the project as the single direct contact. This communication link can cut down on lost time in the communication process. It may be worthwhile to consider involving an expatriate or local representative of a Western professional firm to provide such facilitating services.

NEGOTIATING WITH THE CHINESE

Much has been written and said about how difficult, time-consuming, and frustrating negotiations with the Chinese can be. However, sufficient, effective homework and the right partner can reduce or eliminate many of the difficulties.

A good negotiating team should have at least three levels of company representatives: a vice president or higher rank officer who can make a decision on the spot, a technical person, and a China expert. It is important to have these people involved on a continuous basis because Chinese are more at ease talking to "old friends" than "new faces."

The China expert should have a good knowledge of Chinese culture as well as the necessary Chinese language skills. Most Chinese business organizations have interpreters who are fluent in English. But during business negotiations, which usually involve large groups of Chinese representing all the units and departments involved with the project, it is often impossible for the Chinese interpreters to absorb all the key issues and translate them accurately for all participants. Furthermore, many Chinese interpreters learned English from textbooks and may have trouble with Western idioms and business terms. By having a Chinese expert at negotiation sessions, the foreign businessperson is assured a better, more complete understanding of the discussions, possibly avoiding future misunderstandings.

Most Western businesspeople run on tight schedules, but sufficient time must be allowed for negotiating with the Chinese. It is not customary for the Chinese to discuss sensitive issues on the first day. That meeting is reserved for getting acquainted, evaluating the other party, and discussing general terms. However, during breaks and at social functions, the Chinese expert on the foreign team can usually find out informally the key issues to be addressed. As a general rule, the Chinese will host a dinner or luncheon on the first day, and the foreign party is expected to host a similar party for the group at the end of the negotiations. Most negotiations average five days, depending on the complexity of the project.

A good understanding of the Chinese culture can make negotiations go more smoothly. Some of the important issues are probably better dealt with during private discussions, where an understanding between parties can sometimes be reached. This can prevent some lengthy discussions and perhaps arguments at the negotiating table later.

Sometimes the head of the Chinese negotiating team may seem to be an extremely tough customer, creating difficulties about issues that seem trivial or even irrelevant to the foreign investor. But it is important to realize that he is merely trying to do his job as he sees it. If the proposed project is already on China's approved project list, he will eventually come around in resolving these issues.

In summary, if the foreign investor is well prepared; if the project is financially feasible, both to the foreigner and to the Chinese; if good contacts have been made; and if the foreign businessperson deals with the right Chinese expert and the right Chinese partner from the start, negotiating with the Chinese will not be too difficult and could turn out to be both a pleasant and interesting experience.

CHAPTER 26

FINANCIAL AND TAX CONSIDERATIONS

Marsha A. Cohan
Raymond V. Haley
Marina Wong

COMMON FORMS OF DOING BUSINESS IN CHINA
    Representative Offices
    Compensation Trade and Manufacturing of Products with
        Supplied Materials
    Consignment Sales and Service Centers
    Contracted Projects
CONCLUSION
INTERPRETING CHINA'S FINANCIAL STATEMENTS

COMMERCIAL BANK SERVICES FOR TRADE AND INVESTMENT IN CHINA

INTRODUCTION

As trade and investment relationships between China and Western countries grow, many companies, both large and small, find themselves involved with this market in new and significant ways. Regardless of the type of business being conducted, financing inevitably plays a key role. It is increasingly rare to find a Chinese buyer not interested in some form of credit, particularly in light of the current domestic credit squeeze in China. Knowing how to arrange the required finance can often mean the difference between success and failure in business negotiations in China.

TRADE FINANCE

China has gradually introduced competition into its domestic banking system in an effort to improve efficiency and customer service. For many years after the Communists took power in 1949, only the Shanghai branches of the Hongkong and Shanghai Banking Corporation (HSBC) and three other foreign banks were allowed to remain open. However, in 1985, HSBC opened a branch in Shenzhen, and since then, a growing number of international banks have opened branches in China's special economic zones. These foreign bank branches are permitted to engage in letter of credit transactions denominated in freely convertible foreign currencies (the Chinese currency renminbi is not freely convertible).

Foreign bank branches in China may also maintain foreign currency deposit accounts and make foreign currency loans that are exempt from the normal 10 percent withholding tax on interest charged to offshore borrowings. In addition, China has reactivated a number of domestic banks, such as the Bank of Communications, that compete both with the Bank of China for domestic business and with domestic and foreign banks for foreign currency business. The result is greater competition and wider choice when selecting a bank to work with in China.

Exports to China

Domestic enterprises in China are required to use the Bank of China or one of the other domestic banks when opening a letter of credit (L/C) in favor of a foreign supplier. Typically, the L/C states payment will be made at the opening bank's counters, and exporters should stipulate that the L/C specify payment by telegraphic transfer to minimize delays. The Bank of China is not a member of the International Chamber of Commerce's Uniform Customs and Practice for Documentary Credits ICC no. 400, but the bank does tend to follow its guidelines. Exporters to China should enquire whether their bank will negotiate bills drawn under Bank of China L/Cs or if the documents will be handled on a collection basis. The latter often means the exporter must wait longer to receive payment. Bank of China does not encourage foreign banks to add their confirmation to its L/C, so confirmations are usually done on a "silent" basis. Foreign bank branches in China are permitted to open L/Cs on behalf of foreign-invested enterprises (FIEs) (joint ventures and wholly foreign-owned enterprises) and may provide import loan facilities to FIEs. The volume of this business relative to that of imports by domestic enterprises is small but growing.

Imports from China

In the past, foreign companies dealt mostly with large Chinese foreign trade corporations directly under the Ministry of Foreign Economic Relations and Trade (MOFERT) and several ministries related to particular industries, but today the number of entities authorized to trade with foreigners has multiplied. Therefore, it is more important than ever for foreign investors to know whom they are dealing with and verify their capacity to engage in the trade under negotiation.

Because the letter of credit is expected to mirror the terms of the underlying purchase contract entered into with a Chinese exporter, it is worthwhile to note the following points:

- All documents required for negotiations of the letter of credit should be done in English.
- If the purchase terms are Cost, Insurance, and Freight (CIF) or Cost and Insurance (C&I), the letter of credit terms should call for an insurance policy covering Ocean Marine Cargo Clauses All Risks (including Warehouse to Warehouse Clauses) and War Risks Clauses of the People's Insurance Company.
- Supplementary risks such as strikes, riots, and civil commotion and rejection risks may also be covered.
- All letter of credit charges incurred in China are for the account of the opener, but if the underlying contract allows, charges may be for the account of the beneficiary.
- Negotiation of a letter of credit may be restricted to a foreign bank branch in China if the opener wishes. Many Chinese exporters routinely negotiate their documents at foreign bank branches in China to take advantage of the high-quality service being offered.
- Documents certified by a Chamber of Commerce or Consular Office should *not* be called for because these are not provided in China.
- Shipping documents issued by China Travel Service (HK) Ltd. or other branches of China International Travel Service (CTS) are considered in China as Marine Bills of Lading although CTS is not a shipping company. If CTS bills of lading are not acceptable, this must be specified in the letter of credit.

It is advisable to work with a bank familiar with Chinese business practices in order to avoid unnecessary headaches. International banks that have branch operations in China are particularly useful because the letter of credit will usually be advised and negotiated by the in-country branch of the bank concerned.

FINANCING FOREIGN INVESTMENTS IN CHINA

Risk Analysis

Foreign investment in China, whether it is in the form of joint venture or a wholly foreign-owned enterprise, typically involves arranging foreign and domestic loans to finance a portion of the investment. Generally these investments are viewed by bankers as startups, even if the Chinese partner is contributing an existing plant, because foreign investors face a number of risks they may not encounter in their home countries. Foreign and domestic bankers analyze projects in basically similar ways with a view to determining if the project's cash flow is sufficient to pay principal and interest on debt. The project's feasibility study and joint venture contract are important documents used in determining the viability of individual projects.

In addition to normal credit analysis, some elements that represent risks of particular significance in China's business environment are listed below.

Foreign Exchange

Chinese regulations encourage each project to be self-sufficient in terms of foreign exchange because China's own foreign exchange reserves are small relative to total potential demand. While China's "22 Articles" provide that import substitution projects receive foreign exchange, in reality it is very difficult for the domestic sales of an FIE to be denominated in hard currency. Therefore, it is key to come up with a workable plan to generate foreign exchange for required imports, foreign currency debt service, expatriate management remuneration, and dividends. Chinese authorities normally prefer FIEs to export a portion of their production to cover hard currency requirements, even when domestic demand outstrips local supplies. Foreign investors and their local partners are increasingly adept at finding inventive solutions to this chronic problem.

Supply Risk

Both domestic enterprises and FIEs face supply risk, which can take many forms. Because of high economic growth and inflation many commodities are in short supply or are available only at prices much above the world market price. Also, many inputs required in technologically intensive products, such as airplanes, automobiles, and computers, cannot be sourced locally because of quality specifications. Delivery of raw materials can be delayed because of China's inadequate transportation system, and enterprises are often forced to overstock inventories to guard against shortages.

Infrastructure

When one sees the modern hotels and office buildings springing up all over Beijing, it is easy to forget China is still a very poor country where basic services cannot be taken for granted. Foreign investors should know that land is scarce and the transfer of land use rights is complicated. The country is investing heavily to upgrade transportation and telecommunication services but standards vary widely. Power and water supplies are especially critical. An estimated 25 percent of industrial capacity is idle because of insufficient electrical power, and drought is a recurring problem.

The above factors tend to increase the completion risk of projects in the development stage and the operating risk faced when they go into production. Hence, banks tend to treat feasibility studies with caution when assessing the viability of projects for which a loan is being considered. This accentuates the importance of other factors, such as the strength and experience of the partners in the project, their financial resources, and their commitment to supply the management and training required for the project. Predicting future competition is vital because it is not unusual for China to go from shortage to surplus, as the growing hotel glut in several cities demonstrates. Perhaps most important is the partners' relationship (*guanxi*) with key Chinese authorities, because getting things done in China's huge bureaucracy is often a daunting task.

Security

China's commercial law related to mortgages and security interest in personal property is still in its experimental stage. For the most part, both domestic and foreign banks prefer to have straightforward guarantees to cover their loans. Domestic banks in China demand increasingly stringent security requirements for RMB loans to FIEs because their tight liquidity is exacerbated in part by delinquent loans to money-losing domestic enterprises. In many joint venture agreements, the Chinese partner is responsible for arranging the RMB loans required, but ability to carry out this assignment should be closely watched in the current environment.

The question of what is an acceptable Chinese guarantee for a foreign currency loan has long been a central issue to foreign bankers in China. It is rare now to see the Bank of China, CITIC, or the handful of other first-tier financial institutions issue a guarantee for a joint venture loan. Foreign commercial banks play a key role in projects where an internationally well-known borrower or guarantor is not present. In such cases, the State Administration of Foreign Exchange Control (SAFEC), a department of the People's Bank of China (PBOC), China's central bank, performs a particularly important function as China's watchdog on foreign borrowings. SAFEC periodically publishes a list of institutions that are approved to borrow or guarantee foreign loans, and other borrowers and guarantors must be approved by SAFEC on a case-by-case basis. All foreign loans in China must be registered with SAFEC within 10 days of signing the loan agreement. SAFEC approval of a loan does *not* signify that it is backed by the full faith and credit of the government (i.e., sovereign risk), but because SAFEC is responsible for monitoring and supervising foreign borrowings, its approval gives foreign bankers some additional comfort. SAFEC approval is not, however, meant to be a substitute for a bank's own credit analysis of a given borrower or guarantor.

PROJECT FINANCE

High-Priority Projects

When bidding on major infrastructure projects such as power plants and steel mills, foreign suppliers are typically requested to provide financing for all or part of the project. This usually involves arranging export credit and soft loans if available, and commercial bank loans cover any remaining amounts needed.

When formulating supporting finance proposals, there are numerous ways to optimize the attractiveness of the offer. As an example, when multiple sourcing is possible, a supplier should see which source can bring the best financing terms for its portion of the contract. Tax-advantaged leasing, as in the case of aircraft, is another option. Soft loans are frequently sought by Chinese buyers in major projects, and these loans are done on a government-to-government basis with MOFERT usually representing China. In the United States, Eximbank has a small amount of funds in its so-called war chest, but these funds are available only in certain cases where competing financing violates OECD guidelines. Others, including several European countries, Canada, and Japan, offer China substantial soft loans on much easier terms in order to support exports.

To determine whether export credit or soft loans are available, the first step is to ascertain the project's sponsorship. Government export credit agencies usually will accept only Bank of China or first-tier Chinese financial institutions, which will be involved only if the project is a high priority of the state. To qualify for a soft loan, the project must be approved by both MOFERT and the export credit authority of the donor country. Hence, it is necessary for a supplier and the supplier's banker to liaise with the proposed borrower/guarantor, the relevant planning commission, MOFERT, and the export credit agency to determine if subsidized export credit and/or soft loans are available for a particular project.

The balance of financing required for high-priority projects can often be obtained through syndicated commercial bank credits, which are usually priced at a margin over the London Interbank Offered Rate (LIBOR). Such syndications are frequently arranged in Hong Kong, which is where international banks manage their China business. The proceeds of LIBOR-based loans are sometimes swapped into fixed-rate obligations by taking advantage of the capital markets capabilities available in Hong Kong.

Local Projects

Many other worthy projects are approved at the municipal or provincial level and must rely upon their own resources to obtain the required foreign credits. Because they do not receive allocations of funds from the central government, they tend to be more flexible in their approach to attracting export credit and commercial bank loans. Similar to financing an FIE, it is important to analyze the proposed borrower/guarantor and ascertain whether it is approved by SAFEC for the transaction under consideration. Foreign commercial banks can sometimes facilitate export credits, such as in the case of an Eximbank intermediary loan. In this instance, the commercial bank accepts the Chinese risk, and the ultimate Chinese borrower receives the benefit not only of Eximbank's consensus rate financing but also of the lower exposure fee applicable to the risk category of the foreign bank. Commercial loans for local projects are also available and, as in the case of financing FIEs, if the loan is made by a foreign bank branch located in China, there is no withholding tax on interest.

FOREIGN EXCHANGE ADJUSTMENT CENTERS

In order to provide enterprises in China an incentive to export and a mechanism for them to buy and sell foreign exchange, a number of foreign exchange adjustment centers (FEACs) have been established under the People's Bank of China in various cities. While the FEACs are still in a developmental stage, the volume of business is growing dramatically. For example, in 1987, the Shenzhen FEAC recorded US$100 million in transaction value, and in the first six months of 1988, trading volume increased to US$800 million.

The key feature is a floating, negotiated exchange rate that permits enterprises to sell hard currency earned from exports at a rate much higher than the official rate. In some centers, FIEs are permitted to trade with domestic enterprises, and this practice is expected to spread eventually to all FEACs. At the Shanghai FEAC, open floor bid and offer quotes are available, and several foreign banks such as HSBC are licensed commercial brokers that act on behalf of FIEs and domestic enterprises. While not a panacea for all of the problems faced by investors in China, the FEACs are undoubtedly helping many FIEs resolve the problem of balancing foreign exchange.

CONCLUSION

Finance remains a key consideration when evaluating trade and investment opportunities in China. There are many potential sources for financing projects in China, and it is advisable to determine which ones are available at an early stage. Because China regularly issues new regulations governing trade and investment activities, it is important to work with banks that have the expertise and resources to help in a unique and potentially very rewarding market.

GOVERNMENT SOURCES OF FINANCIAL ASSISTANCE FOR PROJECTS IN CHINA

Companies doing business with China may find difficulty in obtaining financing from traditional sources of funds because of the unusual risks inherent in their activities. Such companies may find help from various U.S. government agencies that offer financial assistance to U.S. investors and exporters of U.S. goods and services. The following summarizes the major financing programs available for business with China.

FEASIBILITY STUDIES: TRADE AND DEVELOPMENT PROGRAM

The U.S. Trade and Development Program (TDP) provides financial assistance for feasibility studies and other planning services for major public-sector projects in developing countries. In fiscal year 1988, TDP spent over $5 million (approximately 20 percent of TDP's budget) in China.

No-Interest Loans to U.S. Investors

U.S. companies planning to expand their operations into China may apply for TDP no-interest loans to fund feasibility studies. To be eligible, a company must intend to make an equity investment in a project the Chinese government considers to be a priority and that has significant potential for the export of U.S. goods and services. A company selected to receive a no-interest loan will be reimbursed for up to 50 percent of its feasibility study's cost (typically between $50,000 and $150,000). Regardless of whether the company proceeds with the investment, it must sign a four-year, noninterest-bearing promissory note in favor of TDP for the amount reimbursed by TDP.

Grants to Chinese Entities for U.S. Services

TDP also provides grants for feasibility studies for projects selected by MOFERT that have significant U.S. export components and for training programs relating to such projects. Grant awards are made to Chinese entities, which then select U.S. contractors, usually through a competitive bidding process, to perform the feasibility study or provide the training program. Announcements of projects for which feasibility studies are sought appear in *The Commerce Business Daily*. Under this program, U.S. companies cannot apply directly to TDP for feasibility study grants, but TDP will consider awarding training grants to U.S. as well as Chinese entities.

Further Information

Further information on TDP programs in China may be obtained from the Office of the Director, TDP, Room 309, SA-16, Washington, D.C. 20523, telephone (703) 875-4357.

INVESTMENT: OVERSEAS PRIVATE INVESTMENT CORPORATION

The Overseas Private Investment Corporation (OPIC) promotes private investment in developing countries through the insurance of investments of U.S. businesses against certain political risks[1] and the financing of projects involving significant U.S. participation. OPIC programs have been available to U.S. investors in China since 1980 pursuant to an agreement between the governments of the United States and China.

OPIC provides financial assistance on a "project finance" basis, requiring that the project be commercially viable and possess the ability to repay the financing. The Chinese government considers this form of finance attractive because no sovereign guaranty or cash outlay by it is required. OPIC provides direct loans or loan guaranties for up to 50 percent of the financing of a new project and up to 75 percent of the financing of a project expansion.

As security for its financing, OPIC generally obtains a first security interest on the fixed assets and real property of the project company, together with any other appropriate collateral. Because China still lacks established mechanisms through which security interests can be perfected and enforced, OPIC will consider accepting other forms of security for loans made to projects there, such as guaranties from creditworthy institutions. OPIC also requires the project sponsors to enter into completion agreements that provide that the sponsors will provide additional funds if necessary to complete the project.

Direct Loans

Direct loans are available only to U.S. businesses with annual sales of less than $120 million. Direct loans typically range in amount from $250,000 to $6 million and have a term of between 5 and 12 years, depending on the ability of the project to repay. Interest rates are based on the commercial rates available at the time the loan commitment is made. OPIC does not make concessional loans.

Guaranties

All U.S. companies, regardless of size, are eligible to apply for OPIC's guaranties, which are issued in amounts of up to $50 million and mature in 5 and 12 years, depending on the ability of the project to repay. OPIC determines the terms of the guaranteed loan other than the interest rate and, if requested by the borrower, will assist in finding a lender willing to provide the funds. Interest rates are determined by the lender subject to OPIC's approval and may be fixed or floating. Because OPIC's guaranties are backed by the full faith and credit of the United States, interest rates on OPIC-guaranteed financings are approximately the same as those obtained by other U.S. government agencies. Lenders eligible to receive OPIC guaranties are U.S. financial institutions that are more than 50 percent beneficially owned by U.S. citizens, corporations, or partnerships (U.S. persons), and foreign financial institutions that are at least 95 percent owned by U.S. persons.

Fees

OPIC charges a commitment fee of 0.67 percent per annum on the undisbursed portion of each loan or guaranteed loan and a one-time facility fee in the amount of 1 percent per annum on the full amount of the loan or guaranty commitment. On guaranteed loans, OPIC also charges a guaranty fee of approximately 2 percent per annum on the outstanding principal amount of the loan.

Eligible Projects

OPIC financing is available only to commercially viable projects sponsored by people with a proven track record in the business of the project or a similar business. Projects may be in a variety of sectors, including manufacturing, energy, mining, agriculture, fishing, forestry, and processing. Service industries may be eligible for OPIC financing if they provide significant developmental benefits to the host country. OPIC policies and congressional requirements prohibit OPIC from financing military projects, gambling casinos, alcohol production, and projects deemed to hurt U.S. employment or the U.S. economy. Also, OPIC generally does not finance infrastructure projects.[2]

Projects must involve significant U.S. equity and management participation and must be at least 51 percent privately owned. Exceptions may be made for projects that are less than 51 percent privately owned if they are privately managed and if there is other significant U.S. involvement. Wholly government-owned projects are not eligible for OPIC financing.

Applications and Further Information

Applications for OPIC financing should include a description of the project, information, including financial information, regarding the sponsors of the project, and a copy of the business plan for the project. They should be sent to the Business Development Group, OPIC, 1615 M Street, N.W., Washington, D.C. 20527. General inquiries may be addressed to the Finance Department at the same address. Telephone inquiries may be made to the Business Development Group, (202) 457-7037, or to OPIC's general information hotline, (202) 800-6742.

EXPORTS: EXPORT-IMPORT BANK

The Export-Import Bank of the United States (Eximbank) helps exporters of U.S. goods and services compete with other exporters that receive export credit subsidies from foreign governments. Eximbank's programs include a finance program, through which Eximbank makes and guarantees loans to U.S. exporters, banks, and foreign buyers, and an insurance program administered by Eximbank's agent, the Foreign Credit Insurance Corporation (FCIA).[3] All of Eximbank's programs are available for China under an agreement signed in 1981 by Eximbank and the Bank of China.

Working Capital Guaranty Program

Eximbank guarantees export-related working capital loans made by commercial lenders to creditworthy small- and medium-size businesses. The loans may be used for the purchase of inventory or raw materials, manufacturing, marketing, or other export-related activities. The guaranty covers up to 90 percent of the principal amount of the loan and a portion of the interest.[4] The term of the guaranty is usually up to 12 months. Eximbank requires that the exporter secure the loan with inventory, accounts receivable, or other sufficient collateral so the outstanding balance of the loan does not exceed 90 percent of the value of the collateral. Fees for working capital guaranties include an upfront facility fee of 0.5 percent and a quarterly usage fee of 0.25 percent of the average outstanding balance of the guaranty, due within the 15 days following the end of each calendar quarter.

Export Credits

Eximbank offers direct loans, loans to intermediaries, and guaranties for financing the purchase of U.S. capital equipment and services. Eximbank provides medium-term financing (up to $10 million with one- to seven-year terms[5]), typically used for smaller sales of capital equipment, services, and spare parts, and it offers long-term financing (over $10 million with 7- to 10-year terms), generally used for turnkey projects or sales of major capital goods such as industrial equipment, electric power plants, locomotives, and commercial aircraft. It does not provide credits for sales of agricultural products,[6] commodities, raw materials, or other goods and services that require short-term financing and can be supported by FCIA insurance.

Eximbank will finance up to 100 percent of the U.S. content of a U.S. export item containing foreign-made components incorporated into the export item in the United States, provided the amount financed or guaranteed does not exceed 85 percent of the total contract price of the item and the total U.S. content is not less than 50 percent of the contract price. Eximbank requires that the foreign buyer make a minimum cash payment of 15 percent of the contract price.

All Eximbank financing for exports to China must be the direct obligation of or guaranteed by the Bank of China (BOC) or another Chinese entity acceptable to Eximbank. For long-term financing, it is likely that the BOC will be required to serve as obligor or guarantor. Chinese purchasers interested in long-term financing should contact the Second Credit Department of the BOC Head Office in Beijing.

Direct Loans

Eximbank extends fixed interest rate loans to foreign buyers of eligible U.S. exports. The interest rate charged is the minimum rate permitted under the Organization for Economic Cooperation and Development (OECD) Arrangement on Official Export Credits. In November 1989, the OECD rate applicable to loans to China was 8.3 percent. The OECD rate is subject to change semiannually on January 15 and July 15.

Direct loans are extended only upon evidence that foreign governments are providing export credit subsidies to competitors of U.S. exporters, except in the case of loans for the purchase of the exports of small U.S. businesses where the loan amount is no more than $2.5 million and the loan term is no more than seven years. Fees charged for direct loans are a commitment fee of 0.5 percent per annum on the undisbursed balance of the loan and an exposure fee payable by the exporter on each disbursement. The amount of the exposure fee varies with the repayment term and the type of risk involved. The exposure fee may be included in the export price and financed.

Intermediary Loans

Eximbank extends loans to intermediaries that make loans to buyers of eligible U.S. exports that face officially subsidized foreign competition. Any intermediary lender is eligible to apply.

Financial institutions unrelated to the exporter may borrow from Eximbank for medium-term loans at the OECD rate less 0.5 percent to 1.5 percent, depending on the loan value. For long-term loans and for medium-term loans made to parties other than such financial institutions, Eximbank charges the OECD minimum rate. Intermediaries must lend at the minimum OECD fixed rate but may charge fees.

Eximbank charges an exposure fee for intermediary loans. Where an intermediary loan is combined with an Eximbank guaranty, a commitment fee of 0.5 percent per annum is charged on the undisbursed balance of the loan, and an exposure fee is charged for the guaranty. This exposure fee covers the intermediary loan as well.

Guaranties

Eximbank guarantees the repayment of loans from U.S. or foreign private-sector lenders to creditworthy foreign buyers of U.S. exports. Eximbank guaranteed loans may be made in U.S. dollars or other convertible currencies acceptable to Eximbank. The guaranteed loans bear market interest rates, which may be either fixed or floating.

An Eximbank guaranty carries the full faith and credit of the U.S. government and is unconditional and freely transferable. It covers 100 percent of the principal and a portion of the interest[7] on the guaranteed loan. However, on medium-term loans, the exporter or lender must give a counterguaranty to Eximbank in the amount of 2 percent of the commercial risk, unless a sovereign borrower or guarantor is a party to the transaction. Since Eximbank considers the BOC to be "sovereign," no counterguaranty is required when the BOC is a party to a transaction. Fees charged for guaranties are a commitment fee of 0.125 percent per annum on the undisbursed balance of the guaranteed loan and an exposure fee that is payable by the exporter upon each loan disbursement. The exposure fee may be included in the export price and financed.

Others

Eximbank offers additional specialized programs, including guaranties for political risk only; the Engineering Multiplier Program, which provides financing for exports of preconstruction architectural or engineering services; and guaranties of payments on certain cross border leases.

Preliminary Commitments

Eximbank will extend to the BOC or any Chinese buyer or to a U.S. exporter or bank a preliminary commitment setting the terms and conditions of financial assistance it is willing to offer for a particular transaction. Preliminary commitments generally expire after 180 days but may be renewed at Eximbank's discretion. Once a buyer decides to buy American and before expiration of a preliminary commitment, the prospective borrower or obligor must apply to convert the preliminary commitment to a final commitment for a loan or guaranty.

Applications and Further Information

Applications for Eximbank financing may be obtained from Eximbank, 811 Vermont Avenue, N.W., Washington, D.C. 20571. Upon submission of completed applications to Eximbank, a $100 processing fee is charged. General inquiries may be addressed to the Asia division at the above address or by telephone to (202) 566-8885. There is also a business advisory hotline: 1-800-424-5201.

CHINA'S TAX SYSTEM—AN OVERVIEW

The People's Republic of China, which has a complex domestic tax structure, did not have a systematic way of taxing foreign business until 1980 when the following two major tax laws applicable to foreign business activities were introduced: the Individual Income Tax Law (IITL) and the Joint Venture Income Tax Law (JVITL). In the following year, the Foreign Enterprise Income Tax Law (FEITL) was promulgated.

In addition, China has designed a variety of tax regimes to attract foreign investment into special economic zones, economic and technical development zones, and numerous other coastal cities.

This section outlines the tax structure generally applicable to foreign business and describes some common forms of doing business in China and their tax implications.

THE INDIVIDUAL INCOME TAX

Scope of Charge

Individuals are taxed under the IITL according to their residence status.

Residents for Less Than One Year

An individual not residing in China or an individual residing in China for less than one year is subject to taxation on income gained within China. However, an individual who resides in China for less than 90 days cumulatively in a calendar year is exempt from taxation on the salaries and wages paid by an employer outside China for services performed within China.

Residents for One Year or More

Under the IITL, an individual is taxable on income gained within or outside China if he or she resides in China for one year or more. However, if the individual resides in China for not more than five years, the income gained outside China will be taxable in China only if it is remitted to China. In 1983, China amended its policy concerning non-China-source income. An individual whose residency in China for one year or more or for more than five years is due merely to his or her employment and he or she does not intend to reside permanently in China will not be taxed on income gained outside China.

Income chargeable with individual income tax includes wages, salaries, service fees, royalties, interest, dividends, bonuses, property rentals, and other income determined to be taxable by the Ministry of Finance.

Tax Rates and Allowable Deductions

Wages and salaries are taxed monthly at the following progressive rates and there is a monthly deduction of RMB 800.

Range of Monthly Income (RMB)	Tax Rate (%)
Under 800	Exempted
800–1,500	5
1,501–3,000	10
3,001–6,000	20
6,001–9,000	30
9,001–12,000	40
Above 12,000	45

Since August 1, 1987, the amount of individual income tax on wages and salaries was reduced by 50 percent.

Income from compensation for personal services, royalties, interest, dividends, bonus, and lease of property and other kinds of income are taxed at a flat rate of 20 percent. For income from compensation for personal services, royalties, and property rental, a deduction of RMB 800 is allowed for expenses if the amount in a single payment is less than RMB 4,000; for single payments in excess of RMB 4,000, a deduction of 20 percent is allowed.

THE CONSOLIDATED INDUSTRIAL AND COMMERCIAL TAX

Scope of Charge

The Consolidated Industrial and Commercial Tax (CICT) is applicable to all entities and individuals engaged in the production of industrial goods, purchase of agricultural products, importation of foreign goods, retail trades, transport and communication, and the service industries. It is computed on the basis of the income from the sale of commodities, payment for the purchase of goods, and income from the service industries.

Tax Exemption

Exemption from CICT is granted to Chinese-foreign joint ventures, cooperative operations, and wholly foreign-owned enterprises for all export products except crude oil, refined oil, and those products otherwise specified by the Ministry of Finance. Raw materials, components, and packaging materials imported for the manufacturing of export products are exempted from custom duties and CICT. Exemption or reduction of CICT is also available on machinery, equipment, and building materials imported to China by companies with foreign investment under some conditions.

Tax Items and Rates

The table of CICT rates lists over 100 industrial and agricultural products. Another table of rates covers retail trade, transport and communication, and service industry. Rates range from 1.5 percent for cotton gray cloth to 66 percent for grade A cigarettes. Any industrial product not listed specifically in the table is taxed at 5 percent.

Tax rates for service and retail trades range from 3 percent to 7 percent. Transport and communication is subject to a rate of 2.5 percent.

THE JOINT VENTURE INCOME TAX

Scope of Charge

The Joint Venture Income Tax Law (JVITL) is applicable only to equity joint ventures with Chinese and foreign investment organized as limited liability companies under the Joint Venture Law. These equity joint ventures are taxed on the net income derived from production, business, and other sources, either within or outside China. The law does not contain the capital gains concept. Income or loss on the sale of a fixed asset is accounted for in the same manner as revenue income or loss.

Tax Rates

The income tax rate is 30 percent flat. In addition, a local income tax is levied at the rate of 10 percent on the amount of income tax payable, bringing the total tax rate to 33 percent. An income tax of 10 percent is normally levied on the amount of profit remitted abroad by the foreign investors, though exemption from this tax has been granted to certain favored joint ventures under the State Council regulations to encourage foreign investments promulgated in October 1986.

Payment of Tax

Joint venture income tax is levied on an annual basis, payable in quarterly estimated installments. Provisional payments are due within 15 days after the end of each quarter. A final settlement must be made within five months after the end of each year.

Tax Exemptions

A newly established joint venture scheduled to operate for 10 years or more may be exempted from income tax in the first two profit-making years after recovering previous losses carried forward and allowed a 50 percent reduction for the following three years. Further periods of tax reduction have been made available to export enterprises and technologically advanced enterprises under the regulations promulgated in October 1986 to encourage foreign investments.

A participant in a joint venture that reinvests its share of profit in China for a period of not less than five years may obtain a refund of 40 percent of the income tax paid on the amount reinvested. If the reinvestment is in export enterprises or technologically advanced enterprises, all the tax paid can be refunded.

THE FOREIGN ENTERPRISE INCOME TAX

Scope of Charge

The Foreign Enterprise Income Tax Law (FEITL) covers foreign companies, enterprises, and other economic organizations, with or without establishments in China, that operate independently or in cooperation with P.R.C. enterprises, as long as there is no equity participation by China. Such nonequity projects as contractual joint ventures or cooperative ventures, including joint oil development projects, are covered by this law.

Taxable income is the net income in a taxable year for foreign companies having establishments in China. For those foreign companies without establishments, income tax shall be levied on certain categories of China-source income such as interest, dividends, rentals, and royalties on a withholding basis.

Tax Rates

Foreign enterprises with establishments in China are taxed at progressive rates that range from 20 percent on the portion of annual income up to RMB 250,000 to 40 percent on income over RMB 1 million. In addition, a 10 percent local surtax is levied on the taxable income, bringing the effective tax rates from 30 percent to 50 percent.

For foreign enterprises without establishments in China, a withholding tax of 20 percent will be levied and withheld from each gross payment of the above-mentioned income.

Payment of Tax

This tax is levied on an annual basis and paid in four quarterly estimated installments. Provisional payments are due within 15 days after the end of each quarter. A final settlement shall be made within five months after the end of a year.

The 20 percent flat tax withheld for interest, royalties, dividends, rentals, and other payments to a foreign enterprise must be paid by the withholding unit to a local tax office within five days of each withholding.

Tax Exemptions

Unlike equity joint ventures, foreign companies enjoy an exemption for the first profit-making year and a reduction for the following two years only if they are engaged in low-profit operations. The minimum operation period of 10 years also applies.

For foreign companies without establishments in China, the income tax or interest from loans, advances, and deferred payments obtained under credit contracts or trade contracts signed between 1983 and 1990 with Chinese concerns may be paid during the effective period of the contract at a reduced rate of 10 percent. Leasing fees obtained by foreign leasing companies by way of the lease sale method between 1983 and 1990 may also be taxed at a reduced rate of 10 percent. Interest on loans from foreign banks to China and certain P.R.C. organizations at preferential rates is exempted from income tax. Fees arising from the transfer of proprietary technology will under certain conditions be taxed at a preferential rate of 10 percent. Installation, technical assistance, and instruction fees were exempt from income tax before 1990 so long as no proprietary technology was transferred.

Merger of the Corporate Tax Laws

A draft law called P.R.C. Enterprise with Foreign Investment Income Tax Law intended to unify the tax liabilities of all enterprises with foreign investment, i.e., equity joint ventures, cooperative joint ventures, and wholly foreign-owned ventures, is being discussed in China.

The draft law lists two proposed tax rates, 25 percent for central tax and 5 percent for local tax or, alternatively, 30 percent central tax and 3 percent local tax. Foreign enterprises currently paying tax at 50 percent would therefore enjoy a tax reduction under the unified tax law of at least 17 percent. Losses under the draft law may be carried forward indefinitely instead of for five years under existing tax laws.

In special economic zones and in economic and technical development zones, the rate of national income tax is proposed at 15 percent, the same as the existing rate. A new rate of 20 percent is proposed in coastal open economic zones.

The draft law has also included a clause on related companies' transactions, which is absent in the two existing income tax laws. In January 1988, China promulgated the Tax Regulation Concerning Related Companies Transactions in the Shenzhen Special Economic Zone, which applies to equity joint ventures, cooperative ventures, and wholly foreign-owned companies. The draft aims to extend this concept to the rest of China.

STAMP TAX

China recently reintroduced the stamp tax. Both the Provisional Regulations and the Implementing Rules on Stamp Duty came into effect on October 1, 1988. Individuals and enterprises executing any of the following documents are required to pay the new tax:

1. Contracts for the sale of goods, processing work, construction work, property leasing, carriage of goods, storage and safekeeping, loans, property insurance, and technology.
2. Documents transferring property rights.
3. Business account books.
4. Registration certificates concerning rights and licences.
5. Any other documents, determined as dutiable by the Ministry of Finance.

Tax rates range from 0.003 percent for property insurance contracts to 0.1 percent for contracts for leasing of property. Taxpayers must compute the tax and purchase and affix the stamps on their own. Stamps are to be affixed at the time the document is executed or obtained. If a documentation is executed by two or more parties and each party retains a copy, each party must individually affix the full amount of tax stamps to the copy it has retained. However, duplicates or manuscript copies of documents on which stamp duty has already been paid are exempted.

The Implementation Rules provide that all Sino-foreign equity joint ventures, cooperative joint ventures, wholly foreign-owned enterprises, and other foreign companies that pay the consolidated industrial and commercial tax in China may deduct the actual amounts paid in stamp duty from such consolidated industrial and commercial tax payments.

COMMON FORMS OF DOING BUSINESS IN CHINA

Apart from equity joint ventures, cooperative joint ventures, and wholly foreign-owned companies, other common forms of doing business in China include representative offices, consignment sales and service centers, compensation trade, and contracted projects.

Representative Offices

The registration regulations concerning representative offices promulgated in December 1980 disallow these offices to conduct any profit-making activities, and the tax authorities generally did not require representative offices to file tax returns. However, because some offices were engaging in actual business, the Ministry of Finance in May 1985 promulgated the Interim Regulations Concerning Imposition of Industrial and Commercial Consolidated Tax and Income Tax on Permanent Representative Offices of Foreign Enterprises. Income generated by representative offices taxable under the said regulations is subject to the FEITL at the normal progressive rates applied to the net income. Consolidated Industrial and Commercial Tax at 5.05 percent is also payable on the gross taxable income. When the profit or loss of a representative office cannot be accurately ascertained, a deemed profit at 10 percent of gross income will be assessed by the tax authorities on which the income tax is levied.

Three categories of income are included in the regulations as taxable, and the regulations also provide for two nontaxable cases.

The taxability of a representative office depends largely on the nature of activities carried out by the representative office and its head office. Tax planning may therefore be possible by registering the right corporate vehicle in China.

Compensation Trade and Manufacturing of Products with Supplied Materials

Compensation trade is a form of trade and credit whereby China obtains foreign capital and foreign advanced technology or equipment, and payment or repayment is effected in stages by delivery of finished products, mostly produced by or with the equipment and technology so introduced.

Generally, foreign businesspeople supplying production equipment or technology under the compensation trade arrangement are not required to pay any tax in China unless the foreign businessperson receives a royalty or license fee from the Chinese party.

Under an agreement for manufacturing or assembling of products with supplied materials or parts, the foreign party supplies all or part of the raw materials and component parts and the Chinese party manufactures or assembles products in accordance with the foreign party's requirements. The foreign party usually also supplies the equipment and technology, and the prices payable for such supplies are offset against the processing fee payable to the Chinese enterprise.

This type of arrangement is not subject to any tax in China, unless the raw materials and component parts so imported and the finished products so produced are sold within China.

Consignment Sales and Service Centers

Foreign enterprises are finding it increasingly necessary to establish service centers to meet their obligations to provide service and maintenance to their Chinese customers, following increased sales and marketing activities in China. Normally a Chinese enterprise will be contracted to establish a service center to perform the maintenance services, with the foreign enterprise supplying spare parts and technical support. It is important for the arrangement to be structured such that the service center will not be regarded as a dependent agent of the foreign enterprise.

In addition, the selling price of the spare parts to the P.R.C. customer must be determined by the Chinese party and the foreign party is not involved in the management of the service center; otherwise, the foreign enterprise may be subject to both the foreign enterprise income tax and consolidated industrial and commercial tax.

Contracted Projects

A foreign company engaged in construction, installation, assembly, or other service projects in China is deemed to have an establishment in China by virtue of the project site and is therefore taxable under the FEITL on its China-source income. The FEITL does not set a minimum period within which a contracted project can be completed without creating an establishment for tax purposes. However, for companies involved in relatively short projects and those that cannot substantiate the costs and expenses, a deemed profit basis will be applied. The deemed profit rate set by the Chinese is currently 10 percent of the gross receipts from a project, and the FEITL progressive tax rates are applied in arriving at the income tax payable.

The Provisional Regulations of the Ministry of Finance Regarding the Levy of the Industrial and Commercial Tax and Enterprise Income Tax on Foreign Businesses Contracting for Project Work and Providing Labor Services promulgated on July 5, 1983, provide for two exemption cases before December 31, 1990. The first concerns the provision of ancillary installation, construction, training or related services pursuant to a contract for the sale of equipment to a Chinese entity. The second relates to the provision of technical instruction, consultation, and other technical services by a foreign company to a Chinese enterprise for the reform of their existing technology.

CONCLUSION

The tax structure for foreign business in China is relatively simple compared to the complex systems that operate in highly industrialized countries. It is also generally conventional. The establishment of such structure by China within a relatively short time is admirable. However, because the tax laws have not been seasoned by practice and considering the variety of forms of foreign investment permitted in China, ambiguities and inadequacy are inevitable. Chinese officials are now trying to resolve these problems.

Further developments in the tax structure for foreign business will depend on China's commitment to foreign investment and the changes occurring on its domestic tax front. It is the intention of Chinese tax authorities to ultimately unify the two different tax systems that exist currently for enterprises with and without foreign investment.

INTERPRETING CHINA'S FINANCIAL STATEMENTS

In a socialist planned economy, accounting systems are part of the regulatory means to monitor the economic activities of all state enterprises to ensure a high level of conformity within established economic plans of the state. Uniform accounting systems and regulations are prescribed for all entities nationwide. These are essentially fund management-oriented. The emphasis is on the recording of how specific funds allocated have been used according to the designated purpose.

However, the accounting systems and regulations referred to above do not apply to enterprises with foreign investment, such as equity joint ventures, cooperative joint ventures, and wholly foreign-owned enterprises. As in many other fields, separate legislation has been enacted for foreign-invested enterprises. Thus, to the investors or other users of accounts, such as creditors or management, a basic understanding of the accounting regulations affecting these foreign-invested enterprises is essential to facilitate a proper interpretation of the accounting statements so compiled.

Currently, only one piece of accounting legislation addresses equity joint ventures specifically, namely, the Accounting Regulations of the People's Republic of China for Joint Ventures using Chinese and Foreign Investment together with its detailed implementation rules. In addition, uniform charts of accounts and accounting systems have been specifically prescribed for industrial equity joint ventures. These are contained in a booklet titled "Chart of Accounts and Accounting Statements for Industrial Joint Ventures using Chinese and Foreign Investment." All these were promulgated by the Ministry of Finance in 1985. Although these are specifically addressed at equity joint ventures, in the absence of any other specific accounting laws, they are applied to all foreign-invested enterprises. Other than the accounting law, the Joint Venture Income Tax Law and the Foreign Enterprise Income Tax Law also contain provisions affecting accounting issues. These must also be taken into account where appropriate.

In essence, the accounting concepts and principles underlying the above regulations are, in many respects, the same as internationally accepted accounting principles. These include:

- Compilation of accounts on historical cost convention.
- Accrual basis/matching of income and expenses.
- Consistency.
- Going concern.

The major difference lies in the nonconformity to the accounting prudence concept, which requires that provision is made for all known losses whether such amount is known with certainty or is a best estimate in the light of the information available. This fundamental difference has led to differences in accounting treatment for certain items. As an awareness of these differences is considered useful to arrive at a more meaningful appraisal of the results and financial position as reflected by the income statement and balance sheet, the major differences are highlighted below:

Receivables—no provision for doubtful debts is permitted in the accounts of foreign-invested enterprises.

Inventory valuation—inventory must be stated at cost; the international practice of valuing inventory at the lower of cost and net realizable value is not applicable to foreign-invested enterprises; furthermore, no provision for slow-moving, obsolete, or damaged inventories is permitted.

Investment—this must always be stated at cost and no provision for permanent diminution in value is permitted.

Tangible fixed assets—this also must always be stated at cost and no revaluation whatsoever is permitted.

Foreign currency translation—only realized exchange differences are recognized; year-end monetary assets and liabilities denominated in foreign currencies are not to be translated at closing rate, that is, no recognition is made of unrealized exchange differences.

Perhaps the most crucial of the differences highlighted above is that relating to the treatment of assets and liabilities denominated in foreign currencies. By the very nature of their constitution and activities, foreign-invested enterprises are normally engaged in many foreign exchange transactions, such as importing raw materials and exporting finished goods. As a result, their accounts may contain a significant foreign currency element, such as loans, payables, receivables, or foreign currency bank balances. Devaluation of renminbi against other foreign currencies in the last few years has left many foreign-invested enterprises, especially those partly financed by long-term foreign currency loans, in a significant unrealized exchange loss position that is not apparent from the face of the accounts.

Chinese authorities have begun to recognize the problem associated with this accounting issue and have promulgated the Supplemental Provisions on Accounting for Foreign Currency Transactions by Joint Ventures, which took effect December 31, 1987. These provisions have partly redressed this issue by permitting the use of closing rate to revalue foreign currency assets and liabilities subject to the agreement of the local Finance and Tax Bureau to reflect the proper exchange risk exposure. However, this has addressed the issue only from the angle of the fluctuations in official exchange rate. Introduction of the foreign exchange adjustment centers (swap centers) has given rise to another, maybe more realistic rate reflecting the market value of renminbi. To what extent should such swap center rates be used in evaluating the net worth of the foreign investor's investment? In the appraisal of the accounts, this is but one of the questions posed to assess the extent to which the investor's capital may be steadily eroded in monetary terms.

This section has set out a brief outline of the accounting regulatory framework applicable to foreign-invested enterprises in China. Generally, the accounting principles adopted are similar to internationally accepted accounting principles except for the prudence concept. Differences in accounting treatment arising from this are identified and discussed. These are to be borne in mind in applying the normal analytical techniques on the accounts to assess the economic performance and asset worth of an enterprise. To arouse an awareness in these differences is not intended to provide any answer but to provoke more inquiries on the face value of some accounts items as a basis for the conduct of a more meaningful appraisal of the accounts.

ENDNOTES

[1] In China, OPIC provides insurance against loss or damage to an investor's physical assets caused by political violence (including war, revolution, insurrection, and civil strife) and against expropriation. Insurance against currency inconvertibility is not available in China. Further information on OPIC's insur-

ance program may be obtained from OPIC, 1615 M Street, N.W., Washington, D.C. 20527, telephone (202) 457-7059, telex 440 227 OPIC UI.

[2] Infrastructure projects in China may be eligible for financing from the World Bank or the Asian Development Bank.

[3] FCIA policies cover the political and commercial risks of nonpayment on short-term (up to 180 days) and medium-term (181 days to five years) export receivables. For more information on FCIA, contact Eximbank or FCIA at 40 Rector Street, 11th Floor, New York, N.Y. 10006, telephone (212) 306-5000.

[4] Interest will be covered up to an amount equal to 1 percent plus the U.S. Treasury rate for loans of a comparable term.

[5] The following applies to medium-term financing:

Contract Value	Maximum Term
Up to $50,000	2 years
$50,001–$100,000	3 years
$100,001–$200,000	4 years
$200,001–$10,000,000	5–7 years

[6] Financial assistance is available from the Export Enhancement Program of the U.S. Department of Agriculture to exporters to China of U.S. agricultural commodities. Interested exporters should contact the Commodity Credit Corporation, 14th Street & Independence Avenue, S.W., Washington, DC 20250-1000, telephone (202) 382-9150 or 382-9240.

[7] The portion of the interest covered on a fixed-rate, U.S. dollar loan is the lesser of the Treasury rate for a comparable term in effect at the time of loan pricing (the Treasury Rate) plus 0.5 percent and the rate on the promissory note of the borrower to the guaranteed lender (the Note Rate) minus 0.5 percent. On a floating rate loan, Eximbank covers the lesser of a rate based on a preselected basis (the prime rate minus 2 percent, LIBOR minus 0.25 percent, or the Treasury Rate plus 0.5 percent) and the Note Rate minus 0.5 percent.

INDEX

Omnibus Trade and Competiveness Act, 39, 78

OPIC
advantages over private insurers, 34
distribution of assisted projects, 36
equity financing, 36
finance programs available to Far Eastern countries, 36
financing portfolio of, 36
insurance volume of, 34
nonfinancing incentives, 37
Pacific Engineers and Constructors Ltd. (PECC) and, 35
percentage of portfolio allocated to Far East, 36
program constraints, 34–35
provision of political risk insurance, 33
P.T. Gunung Salak geothermal project and, 36
retention amount of, 35
self-sustaining nature of, 36
suggested consolidation with other agencies, 52
types of coverage, 33

Overseas Private Investment Corporation; see OPIC

P

Pacific Engineers and Construction Ltd. (PECC), 35
Paris Universal Copyright Convention, 46
Patent Cooperation Treaty of 1970, 46
Patents; see also China, intellectual property rights; Japan, intellectual property rights; Korea, intellectual property rights; and Taiwan, intellectual property rights
advantages of PCT over Paris Convention, 73
coordinating foreign and U.S. patents, procedures for, 73
export license, importance of, 74
life of U.S. patents versus foreign patents, 73
Patent Cooperation Treaty (PCT), 73
priority patent rights, 72
time frame and, 72
People's Republic of China; see China
"Postindustrial era," 6
"Postindustrial" philosophy, 6–7
Prime Minister Nakasone, 181
Prime Minister Takeshita, 182
Private export insurance, 34
Project identification document (PID), 37
Project Paper (PP), 37

Q–R

Racketeer Influenced and Corrupt Organizations Act (RICO), 64
"Report on Consumer Trends in China", 19
Republic of China; see Taiwan
Republic of Korea; see Korea
Robinson-Patman Act, 64
ROC; see Taiwan
ROK; see Korea

S

Sago shosha, 5
San Miguel Corporation, 38
Sears World Trade, 52
Securities Transactions Law, 225
Service industries, 7
Sherman Act, 69–70
Singapore
aggressive policies of, 51
copyright agreement with United States, 47
TDP funding to Singapore Polytechnic, 41
Sovereign immunity, 65–66
Foreign Sovereign Immunity Act (FSIA) and, 65
Stockholm Convention for the Protection of Industrial Property, 46

T

Taiwan, 423–504
banking and local financing, 486–93
deposit transactions, 494
equity financing, 494–95
financial institutions, 486–90
financial markets, 490
interest rates, 490
raising funds, 491–93
business climate, background information, 441, 447–48, 474
Central Bank of China, 487
Civil Code, 458
commercial and industrial space, 480–81
court system, 454
Criminal Code, 457–58
economy, 427–39, 441–44
appreciation of N.T. dollar, 442–43
background, 427–29
and consumer consciousness, 444
and energy, 438
and environment, 444
and foreign trade, 435–38